Running the World

Running the
WORLD

The Inside Story of the
National Security Council
and the
Architects of American Power

David J. Rothkopf

PublicAffairs · NEW YORK

Copyright © 2005 by David J. Rothkopf.
Published in the United States by PublicAffairs™, a member of the Perseus Books Group.
All rights reserved.
Printed in the United States of America.

BOOK DESIGN AND COMPOSITION BY JENNY DOSSIN. TEXT SET IN ADOBE MINION.

Library of Congress Cataloging-in-Publication Data
Rothkopf, David J. (David Jochanan), 1955–
Running the World : the inside story of the National Security Council and the architects
    of American Power / by David J. Rothkopf
p. cm.
Includes bibliographical references.
ISBN 1–58648–248–3
1. National Security Council (U.S.) I. Title.
UA23.15.R68 2005
355'.033073—dc22   2005041907

FIRST EDITION
10 9 8 7 6 5 4 3 2 1

For Adrean, Joanna and Laura,
the committee in charge of running *my* world

Contents

Good government obtains when those who are near are made happy and those who are far off are attracted.

—Confucius

I must fairly say, I dread our own power and our own ambition; I dread our being too much dreaded . . . it is ridiculous to say we are not men, and that, as men, we shall never wish to aggrandize ourselves in some way or other . . . we may say that we shall not abuse this astonishing and hitherto unheard of power. But every other nation will think we shall abuse it. It is impossible but that, sooner or later, this state of things must produce a combination against us which may end in our ruin.

—Edmund Burke

Introduction

WE WERE IN a maharajah's garden in Jodhpur. It was a warm January afternoon. Great purple flowers hung over the walls of the garden and filled the air with their fragrance.

My father and I had come a long way across India during the preceding three weeks, laughing and arguing, eating prodigious amounts of delicious but, in one instance, rather toxic food, and hoping against hope that our driver's almost impossible luck would hold. He was a slight young man who was undistinguished by anything other than a single long red fingernail and an astonishing lack of aptitude for his chosen profession. We sped in our small beige Ambassador car at mind-numbing speeds down narrow Indian highways that were marked more often by wrecks and wayward cattle than by signs. Every destination was therefore enthusiastically welcomed with one or more Kingfisher beers, a few silent prayers of thanks, and then the kind of animated discussions that come only with survivor's rush, alcohol, or both.

By the time we got to Jodhpur, several of those discussions blended together to form a kind of intellectual leitmotif for this father-son bonding trip. The central issue: whether men could make a difference in shaping the course of history or whether we were all essentially surfers, riding the tides of our times, acting like we were in charge because we were on top but all the while aware that we could be swept under by any of a countless number of forces beyond our control.

There are a number of reasons why this topic came to dominate our trip. One was that I was relatively young, thirty-three, and my father was sixty-three. I was full of hubris and hope that a chance would come around for me to influence history, to make a mark. My father, an exceptionally accomplished scientist and teacher, had been chastened somewhat by experiences that seemed elemental rather than driven by human choice. He had escaped the Nazis in late 1939 and four years later returned to Europe as a lieutenant in the U.S. field artillery. There he combed through the wreckage of a battered continent, looking for signs of the almost three dozen relatives who had died in the concentration camps. Back in the United States, he conducted scientific research on how we learn, and over the years the course of his research was buffeted by the fads and fashions of the times and the changing funding priorities of the military or of Bell Laboratories, where he worked.

Our India trip also took place during a period of considerable change globally. It was January 1989, the beginning of the end of the Cold War. The first stirrings and demonstrations of Czechoslovakia's velvet revolution had begun. The Berlin Wall would fall only eleven months later. The Soviet Union was tottering.

Although around us were the trappings of the Raj, we were in an India that was warming to globalization. Two decades earlier, my father had been part of a project to put a television satellite above Gujarat in an effort to bring new channels of education to the impoverished students of that province. By 1989, investment bankers had begun to root around, agitating for reforms that would come over the ensuing decade and help India position itself as a player to be reckoned with in the information age.

Our rambling, trans-India debate was thus in character and in step with the times. And so we jousted, with heat, vindaloo, mysterious ingredients, and East Coast Jewish intellectual dinner battle intensity bringing beads of sweat to our foreheads: Was Gorbachev driving Russian reform or were the exigencies of ruling a faltering empire driving Gorbachev to reform? Were the charming playwright Vaclav Havel or the rough-around-the-edges shipyard worker Lech Walesa people who could actually mobilize a nation or redirect destiny, or were they selected by circumstance—active, visible, contributing—but far less important than greater forces that were harder to put a face on? What about Napoleon, I would ask, or Newton, or Einstein? Wasn't Napoleon simply a reaction to the French Revolution, just another vainglorious Frenchman seeking to reclaim the crown of Charlemagne? Wasn't Leibniz inventing the calculus at the same time as Newton? Did Einstein's wife write his papers? And wasn't he himself just a symptom of a global cultural movement toward relativism made possible by increased technological capabilities that allowed us to measure things more precisely, see greater distances, see smaller objects, tie theories of the unseen to evidence of what really was?

I fought with a kind of existential intensity on these issues, feeling that if human beings couldn't really affect history, then we were doomed not only to effective passivity but also to knowledge of our own helplessness, which was even worse.

To this day, I'm not really sure where my father stands on this question, whether he was just baiting me or whether he was really convinced that we're merely passengers who can perhaps choose the fish or the meat main course but otherwise have to sit back, relax, and enjoy the flight.

My own feeling that you can make a difference ultimately brought me to Washington, a city full of people who share this belief (or delusion) despite all its history and pathologies, which inevitably confound the efforts of the best intentioned. The question has arisen again and again: In this day and age, can any one individual or any small group of individuals alter the course of history, shape great outcomes, or make a difference?

If any one individual could claim to have decisive impact it ought to be the president of the United States. History has given the United States awesome power and resources, and the U.S. Constitution has given the president an enormous array of rights, privileges, and responsibilities when it comes to wielding that power or drawing on those resources. In a number of areas, of course, the president's power is constrained by congressional or judiciary checks and balances. But in one area in particular, the management of U.S. foreign policy, the president's power has always been great, and it has grown over time.

During the Cold War, the power of the United States to act internationally was constrained by the countervailing interests and strengths of the Soviet Union. We could act, but we always had to anticipate and compensate for a reaction from our large adversary. With the demise of the Soviet Union—a historical trend that was unfolding unbeknownst to my father and me as we sat in that maharajah's garden—the global power of the United States and its leaders grew to unprecedented heights.

Indeed, in the new global environment, not only was the power of the U.S. leadership unprecedented, it was also unanticipated. In a system in which the legitimacy of the leaders derives from the consent of the governed, American leaders were effectively making decisions affecting the lives and fortunes of tens and hundreds of millions, of billions, who did not choose them, did not understand what they were doing or how they were doing it, did not, in many cases, even know who they were. We were the de facto leaders of the global community, crowned by history and circumstances but lacking the confirmation of any global referendum on the matter.

Here in the United States, the president and the small group around him who helped make foreign policy decisions had a unique status in the U.S.

government. Even though our national security apparatus had been devised after the Second World War to help ensure that power was not too concentrated around the president and that it was wielded via a transparent, measured process, even though the Constitution gave Congress the powers to ratify treaties and to declare war, even though the War Powers Act attempted to constrain the president's ability to undertake hostile actions without congressional approval, even though Congress had budget-approval power and attempted to increase its role in almost every aspect of federal operations—despite all this, the national security advisor and his or her staff remain among the most influential entities in the federal bureaucracy that are not subject to direct congressional oversight. They were part of the Office of the President. The president's decisions with regard to their policies and actions were considered privileged, part of the authority granted him by the Constitution.

This group also operated, even in the midst of the information age, beyond the understanding of many Americans. The world of the National Security Council is a shadowy one, shrouded in mystery and mystique, the inner sanctum of the most powerful ruler the world has ever known. It is home to some of the president's most influential partners and collaborators, yet perhaps fewer books have been written about it than any other of the major components of the U.S. government. National security advisors have rivaled secretaries of state and defense in influence for decades, and yet few have been profiled or examined.

Indeed, the term National Security Council itself can be misleading. To some, it is the body created by statute in 1947 to manage U.S. national security policy; this advisory body consists of the president, the vice president, the secretary of state, and the secretary of defense, with the chairman of the Joint Chiefs of Staff and the director of central intelligence as observers. To others, it is the larger group of agency heads sometimes called to NSC meetings. To still others, it is the staff of the NSC—once a tiny support team, now a force unto itself—the organization by which the various views and capabilities of the U.S. government are reconciled, harmonized, and, ideally, knit together to create effective action. To the most knowledgeable, the National Security Council is all these things and it is also the de facto NSC, which is the group of officials and friends of the president, those close to him from family, politics, or other walks of life who are his decision-making collaborators and the implementers of decisions that are made.

This little-understood group is perhaps in the best position of any group of a few human beings anywhere to influence history, to shape our times and our future. The ever-shifting "committee" is the most powerful the world has known—and yet, paradoxically, to most it is unknown, and even to those who know of it, it is misunderstood. Many of those who participate in it, including notably many presidents, don't fully understand its importance or know how to make the best use of it, and this failing has had disastrous consequences both domestically and internationally.

I had written about the NSC as a journalist even before my trip with my father to India. Four years later, I found myself invited to Washington to join the Clinton administration and began to have the chance to view it more closely. Indeed, I began to participate in its actions, not as a member of its inner circles, but as someone active at the edges of those circles.

Initially I came to Washington to serve as Deputy Under Secretary of Commerce for International Trade Policy Development—a mouthful, to be sure. As a result of having such a wonderful title, I quickly learned that the longer your title in Washington, the less important you were likely to be.

My first full day on the job, I settled into the very large chair at my very large desk in my very large office in the very large and dusty Commerce Department and waited for the action to come to me. Nothing happened. I looked around the huge office—its drab wood paneling and the two flags that hung limply behind my desk—and I knew that I had really arrived. Still, for a little while nothing happened. Flies buzzed. The lights on the phone did not blink on. And then, a staffer appeared at the door and asked to speak with me.

I beckoned him in and said, "How can I help you?"

"I have a matter that needs your attention, Secretary Rothkopf," he said. Or at least I recall he said that. As a deputy under secretary I was technically entitled to be addressed as Secretary Rothkopf by staffers but seldom was unless they were really trying to butter me up or we were in some public setting in which they felt it made them look more important. So maybe I just hope he said that. Or maybe I was just hallucinating. But, in any event, he went on: "We have some documents you need to sign."

I inquired as to what matter of global significance I would now be asked to weigh in on, feeling certain that in just moments I could call my father to tell him that, indeed, I was one of those who would be moving history around, at least in small increments.

"It is a trade sanction issue, Sir," he said, which sounded good, important, worthy of a big office with flags in it.

"Really?" I intoned because in such situations one intones rather than merely reply. "Give me the background . . ." I said this because it seemed businesslike and because it could be very helpful, since I had absolutely zero experience with trade sanction issues of any type.

And so he laid out what was to be the first great action of my career at the periphery of the center of the most important government in the history of the world. It was, if I recall correctly, a matter pertaining to tiger penises. Yes, penises. Of tigers. Some country was illegally exporting tiger penises. Apparently there is an active market for big-cat genitalia in Asia, where men consider it an aphrodisiac and women no doubt consider it further proof that men are ridiculous.

My first official act as a government official was to sign a memo opining on why the United States needed to impose sanctions against trafficking in the reproductive organs of large animals.

And I learned an important lesson. Government may seem rather institutional and imposing on the outside (and it appears even more gray, institutional, and boring inside the Commerce Department), but on the inside it can be absurd. Not always, of course. Sometimes it is a place where great people struggle to do great things. That happens far more often than you would imagine.

But quickly I learned one of the most important lessons of Washington, namely, that the men and women who occupy important offices are not, as I once thought, all Olympian figures who have it all figured out, who have worldviews and philosophies and who reference Hobbes and Locke in their minds as they calculate how to best serve the greater good. Very often they are just people like you or me (or even worse).

This message was driven home to me shortly after the tiger penis sanctions episode when I was told to attend what my memory tells me was my first meeting of one of the joint deputies committees of the National Security Council and the National Economic Council. The deputies committees are where various deputy secretaries and under secretaries gather to help put together policy formulations and suggestions for their "principals," the cabinet secretaries they serve. The group of principals then uses this material as the basis of its advice for the president. Often the deputies would bring their own deputies to these lesser but nonetheless important gatherings (I was a deputy to a deputy, which is the bureaucratic equivalent of a double negative).

I will admit that every time I went to one of these meetings during the three years that I was in the government, and every one of the many times I have gone to the White House in the years since, I have been thrilled to be there. You have a sense of history and the grandeur of the place and that doesn't fade, even in the face of the intrigues, absurdities, and frustrations of working within those halls.

The first meeting I attended of the deputies committee was, I think, co-chaired by Deputy National Security Advisor Sandy Berger, who would later serve as national security advisor, and by Bo Cutter, who was Bob Rubin's international deputy at the National Economic Council. Present were a variety of senior officials, including, if I recall correctly, Under Secretary of the Treasury (later Treasury Secretary) Larry Summers, Assistant Treasury Secretary (and later Under Secretary) Jeffrey Shafer, Under Secretary of State Joan Spero, Assistant Secretary of State Daniel Tarullo, Deputy U.S. Trade Representative (later U.S. Trade Representative) Ambassador Charlene Barshefsky, and a group of other support players and people whom I have no doubt forgotten.

It was a hot day for autumn, and the room in the Old Executive Office Building was disappointingly dusty and institutional. There was just a beat-up conference table, some file cabinets around the walls, dirty windows with venetian blinds, and, in one corner, an overflowing wastebasket. I cannot remember the subject.

What is remarkable about the meeting and what is relevant to our discussion here is precisely how unremarkable it was. As I looked around the table, I was struck by the fact that while this was a distinguished and intelligent group of people I would come to know as very able public servants, they all looked like people I had gone to high school with. They joked and teased each other like people I went to high school with. They bickered like people I went to high school with. One of them had his shirttails untucked and remnants of what looked like a pretty unappetizing lunch cascading down his shirt, tie, and jacket front. One stared at the ceiling for the whole meeting, mumbling to himself, and later tried to launch an empty soda can into the overstuffed wastebasket from across the room— unsuccessfully, I might add. He did it without any regard for the discussion then going on. I was a bit taken aback, I'll admit it.

They yawned, they said absolutely inane things, and they talked without moving the issue forward. They made a fairly compelling case for the view my father had argued: If these were people at the pinnacle of power, almost certainly we were all being swept along by events outside human control. In short, they were fairly ordinary people.

Now this may not be a startling revelation to everyone, but it was an eye-opener for someone who had grown up as a kid participating in dinner table discussions in which we referred to Henry Kissinger as a kind of epic character, the way other families might have referred to Babe Ruth or Hank Aaron.

Over the years, in meetings of significantly greater consequence, while I got to understand the enormous strengths of many of my colleagues in the government and came to know others of exceptional capabilities who had served in other governments, the lesson of this meeting never left me. The people in these high offices were not a breed apart. They were human, prone to foible, sometimes grew tired, sometimes grew tiresome, sometimes were capable of inspired and inspiring acts, and always were changed by their interactions by their other, very human colleagues.

After I left the government, I joined Kissinger Associates, the consulting firm founded by former Secretary of State Kissinger, as a managing director. I actually had the office next to Henry. After that I started a company with another former national security advisor, Tony Lake. In working with them and getting to know many of their peers, I also came to see more closely that even those who have made a lasting impression on history are full of quirks and idiosyncrasies and a panoply of flaws and even endearing traits.

And so the question of how human beings influence history became even more interesting to me because the human beings in question became more human. I have had the opportunity, for over a decade, to view the small clusters of people who comprise this "most powerful committee in the history of the world" especially closely, and to consider how personality and process, structure, and historical context interact.

That is the context for this book. Its goal is to contribute to a better understanding of the nature of the group of American policymakers who are charged with deciding how the world's greatest nation makes its way in the world at a time when the actions of that group have come under great scrutiny. With some luck it will help bridge the gap between understanding the great import of what is going on and how matters of such import are and can be handled by fairly ordinary people.

Over the past year, I have interviewed over 130 individuals who have played prominent roles in the interagency process that shapes U.S. international policy. Among them are many cabinet secretaries, almost all living national security advisors and their deputies, National Security Council members, policy-level officials from many agencies, and foreign officials who have interacted with them. In recalling excerpts from those interviews, it is my hope thus to collaborate with the members of "the committee" as it evolved during the Cold War to help tell the story of the group, its failures, its strengths, and its development. The primary focus of this story is the post–Cold War period in the life of the National Security Council. What happened earlier is explored to the extent that it affects or informs where we are today.

This account is therefore not a moment-by-moment retelling of the story of the National Security Council. Rather it is an impressionistic, collaborative portrait of the leaders of the modern world engaged in the politics, court intrigue, and drama of any Shakespeare play. But I hope it is more than that. It also aspires to give a sense of the story of "the committee" and of some of its most interesting and important members and their beliefs, ambitions, conflicts, and downfalls. It is also, however, about more abstract but still important subjects: how power ebbs and flows, how processes evolve and influence outcomes, and how such an organization comes to view itself, its role, its rights, and its responsibilities. In short, it is a story of American leaders grappling with American leadership.

In a way, this story is a small, narrowly focused attempt at answering the question my father and I debated as we made our way across Rajastan. If any human beings are in a position to actually drive history, it is the members of this committee who find themselves in charge of the realities of leading the world. This is a look at them with an eye toward their influence and the factors that have influenced them. Almost certainly it will not resolve the debate between me and my father. But hopefully it will shed a little light on one dimension of it and do so in a way that is beneficial to both policymakers and average citizens who are interested in the nature of power in the modern world.

DAVID ROTHKOPF

Bethesda, Maryland
Spring, 2005

Running the World

1

The Committee in Charge of Running the World

Gentlemen, you can't fight in here—this is the war room.
—Dr. Strangelove

FOR A COUNTRY that is the world's greatest democracy—and one that regularly pats itself on the back for this distinction, hawking its native political theories as avidly as it does its soap and its pop stars—it is remarkable how deficient and decaying our political system is. A particularly insidious element of this deficiency is the ignorance of the electorate about their government.

It used to be, in the bygone days of American education, that the teaching of civics was a given and that every child was expected to have a basic understanding of the workings of our government before he or she was sent out into the world. Unfortunately, that is no longer the case, and it is but one symptom of a pernicious epidemic of civic ignorance.

What this means is that just as the world's most powerful democracy reaches a pinnacle of unchallenged supremacy unmatched in the history of the planet, those who are charged with the fundamental decisions for that democracy—many of which have profound international conclusions—are singularly ill-prepared to thoughtfully consider or even understand those decisions or their implications. In a country in which entire television channels are devoted to the sale of cubic zirconium products but there is not one single hour of mainstream programming devoted to news from the rest of the world, it should not be surprising that even as American troops were waging the first battles of the war against terror in Afghanistan, a National Geographic Society and Roper

Organization survey found that 83 percent of Americans aged eighteen to twenty-four could not find that country on a map. In the same study, more Americans in that age group knew that the island on which a popular reality show took place was in the Pacific than could find Israel on a map. Almost a third of those surveyed estimated that the U.S. population was over a billion people, roughly three times the actual number. Of course, there was some good news in the study. Even though fewer than half the American respondents could find France, the United Kingdom, or Japan on a world map, this is not necessarily a sign of xenophobia— about half could not find New York State on a map of the United States either.[1]

When you consider what any foreign policy specialist answers when asked what should guide U.S. actions overseas ("the national interest"), and then recognize that only events the public is actually aware of can be addressed in a political debate on that national interest, this sweeping ignorance of the rest of the world becomes a profound constraint on America's ability to fulfill its responsibilities to itself or to the rest of the world. Who determines the national interests of a disinterested nation? The many can't, so it is left to the few.

Yet today, most Americans don't even participate in the basic business of democracy, much less make an effort to understand the workings of the machinery that turns the will of the people into action.

Jay Leno and Howard Stern have their audiences in stitches with the idiotic answers of ordinary Americans who don't know how many senators there are or how many amendments comprise the Bill of Rights. But they wouldn't dare ask people what the National Security Council is, because they probably couldn't find two members of their staff who knew or could agree. In my own informal polling of a couple of dozen folks I met in the street in Bethesda, Maryland, and in downtown Washington, D.C., I got six answers that could roughly be considered correct. More people thought it was a super-secret government spy agency (probably confusing it with the National Security Agency, a big employer in nearby Fort Meade, Maryland), but mostly what I got were mumbles and wild guesses. Several people thought it had something to do with the stock market. Four thought it was the real name for the Department of Homeland Security.

But the fact is that even those in the know are often confused by what they mean when they refer to the NSC. The entity described and created under Title I of the National Security Act of 1947, which was signed into law by President Harry S. Truman on July 26, 1947, was defined thus:

Sec. 101 (a) There is hereby established a council to be known as the National Security Council (hereinafter in this section referred to as the "Council").

The President of the United States shall preside over the meetings of the Council: Provided, That in his absence he may designate a member of the Council to preside in his place.

The function of the Council shall be to advise the President with respect to the integration of domestic, foreign, and military policies relating to the national security so as to enable the military services and the other departments and agencies of the Government to cooperate more effectively in matters involving the national security.

The Council shall be composed of—

1. the President;
2. the Vice President;
3. the Secretary of State;
4. the Secretary of Defense;
5. (the original designee is no longer a member);
6. (the original designee is no longer a member); and
7. The Secretaries and Under Secretaries of other executive departments and of the military departments, when appointed by the President by and with the advice and consent of the Senate, to serve at his pleasure.[2]

The National Security Act of 1947 went further in its definition of the council. Not only did it include the above positions—the act also created one of those positions, the secretary of defense—it also created the Joint Chiefs of Staff and the Central Intelligence Agency. The leaders of both groups, the chairman of the Joint Chiefs and the director of the CIA, were to serve as advisors to the council.

However, to think that this strict legal definition of the council is what most people in Washington mean when they speak of the NSC would be making an error. First, even the formal meetings of the National Security Council are usually (per item 7 of the act above) attended by other cabinet and sometimes sub-cabinet members at the "pleasure" of the president. While this sounds like an antiquated bit of legal writing style, it actually cuts to the core of the NSC's identity. It was created to serve the president, and each individual president has tremendous latitude to shape both the institution of the NSC and the formal and informal mechanisms of his or her White House national security apparatus that augment or even compete with it. In this respect, the NSC is built differently than other parts of the U.S. government, in which the Constitution provided for institutional structures to be more important than the influence of any one person. This one is all about the influence of one person—in fact, its shape is constantly changing as a result of a series of transactions between the president and its members in which he or she offers or withdraws access, trust, influence, and power. Statutes and history are far less important than these transactions, which continuously remake this powerful entity—in each of its several forms, including those that most closely resemble the body created by the National Security Act of 1947 and those that are only loosely based on or related to it.

Of the several shapes taken by the "committee," formal meetings of the NSC are among the rarest (and in some administrations, they have been exceedingly rare). Consequently, the activities associated with the council are ongoing and extremely influential via a set of apparatuses that grew up in the wake of the 1947 act but were utterly unanticipated by its authors. These include meetings of the sitting members of the council (cabinet members and sometimes without the vice president), who have over time come to be known as the "principals committee" of the NSC. They also include the meetings of sub-cabinet members designed to prepare policy choices for the principals, who have, since the first Bush administration, been known as the "deputies committee." In the modern operations of the White House, there might be multiple such meetings—on widely divergent subjects—taking place every day. Furthermore, as we shall see, one of the ways new administrations shape their identity is by redefining, early on, the committee structures that determine how the cabinet and other government agencies interact with each other, prepare papers for the president, and create and implement policy. This process is one of Byzantine complexity and produces mind-numbing strings of acronyms and appellations, most of which are designed both to differentiate the current administration from its predecessors and to lock in the bureaucratic pecking order in a way that favors those influencing the drafting of the documents. Such efforts, almost always the first or among the first presidential directives of a new administration, offer instant and deep insights into the likely dynamics of the new team, the outlook of the president, and the soap operas that are likely to ensue.

Beyond even all these meetings, which participants will refer to as NSC meetings even though they are not the formal meetings of the council per se, are the activities of the NSC staff. This staff was initially envisioned as a tiny advisory team, a few professionals, most perhaps military men, who could help support the president in administering the national security side of the government. Over time—and this is much of the story of the NSC—this group has inexorably gained power. Today it is a formidable government force, with more personnel than some cabinet-level agencies, and vastly more powerful than any of the vastly larger major bureaucracies.

Initially, the manager of this team was thought of as a kind of second-tier (or lower) job. The 1947 act states in paragraph c of the section quoted earlier:

> The Council shall have a staff to be headed by a civilian executive secretary who shall be appointed by the president.[3]

This executive secretary post, however, has been superseded by a more senior position that not only was unanticipated in the act but also is not actually defined in any legislation.[4] That person is known today as the assistant to the president for national security affairs or, less formally, the national security advisor. The national security advisor has now achieved cabinet-level status—although he or she does not have to face Senate confirmation, unlike cabinet appointees—and is seen as a peer and sometimes as a "first among equals" on the principals committee of the NSC, chairing those meetings and being the president's go-to person on day-to-day national security issues. This position was first made well known by Henry Kissinger and subsequently has been occupied by a succession of exceptionally important individuals, including Brent Scowcroft, Zbigniew Brzezinski, Colin Powell, Anthony Lake, Sandy Berger, and Condoleezza Rice. Others in this group include the tragicomic team Robert McFarlane and John Poindexter, who were among the six national security advisors who served during the Reagan years, and the early pioneers of the post, including Robert Cutler, Gordon Gray, and McGeorge Bundy.

Supporting the president's national security advisor is the National Security Council staff, which has grown to as many 200 members, ranging from very senior policymakers with the clout of cabinet secretaries (one, Richard Clarke, achieved principal-level status during the Clinton years as he led that administration's counterterrorism experts) to much more junior analysts and support staff. Very often it is this staff that drafts the papers, the speeches, and the letters for the president to sign, that coordinates with other agencies, and that meets with foreign ambassadors, congressional staff, lobbyists, "friends of the president," and special interest groups. It is this staff that people most frequently refer to as the NSC in Washington.

And none of this refers to the even more influential and more difficult to pin down "informal" or "ad hoc" national security mechanisms in the White House, the inner circles around the president, many with no formal standing other than the favor of the commander-in-chief, who are often the last and most influential to speak to him before he makes a decision or delivers a speech. This group, which includes First Ladies and other first family members, school friends, girlfriends, occupants of the Lincoln Bedroom, journalists, and others, is constantly shifting, hard to pinpoint, and often of vital importance.

Does all this lead to confusion? Absolutely, even at the innermost core of the organization. For example, when Zbigniew Brzezinski hired a former student to his staff to handle congressional relations, she—one of the first women to serve in this very old-school, male-dominated world—balked, worrying that she would not be doing the kind of policy work that had drawn her, like Brzezinski, an immigrant born in Eastern Europe, into foreign affairs. He responded that she should not get so hung up on her job description that she talk herself out of a job. She was, after all, "on the NSC." And that was something. So Madeleine Albright stayed, reporting to personnel who inquired what she would be doing. She told them, as Brzezinski had, that she would be "on the NSC."[5] Of course, they argued that wasn't possible as she, a young staffer, was not actually president, vice president, secretary of state, secretary of defense, or any of the cabinet members President Jimmy Carter had named to his NSC. After some back and forth, it became clear that she meant the NSC staff, and she settled into a job that would help launch a career that ultimately included a seat for her on the statutorily defined National Security Council when she became America's sixty-fourth secretary of state in 1997.

Stardust in Our Eyes

IF MISCONCEPTIONS about the nature of the several National Security Councils—the statutory one, the standing committees of the council, the council staff, and the informal ad hoc council—are easy to come by among Washington insiders, the problem is compounded for average Americans, who get their information about the world's most important committee through several very coarse, distorting media filters.

In some respects, our ignorance about issues of foreign policy is trumped by our ignorance of the ways we make foreign policy or the people who conduct our foreign policy. It should go without saying that such a flaw makes it even harder for the body politic to effectively judge those policies, their authors, and their stewards. This issue becomes more conspicuous at a time when American decisions on whether or not to act internationally have an impact on not only everything from jobs to security on any main street of any community in America, but also on the lives of hundreds of millions and sometimes billions of people around the world.

We are the Goliath of our age. But unlike the biblical Goliath, the debilitating blow to the head that we have suffered is a self-inflicted wound.

Ignorance of the real issues, the real processes, and the real actors is compounded by the surfeit of pseudo-knowledge surrounding the issues and institutions governing our decisions with regard to the most important issues of our day. Some of this is created by the hard-to-authenticate rumors, conspiracy theories, distortions, and misunderstandings of the Internet and its world of blogs, special interest Web sites, and the like. Some of it is created by the perverse processes of modern television programming, in which a caller in a double-wide in Tulsa, Oklahoma, is given network airtime to speculate on the location of Osama bin Laden—as if his opinion on the subject was informed by special insight or mattered in any other way. And, of course, much if not most of it comes from what happens when we get stardust in our eyes, when most of our knowledge of vital entities like the NSC or any of the manifestations of the committee in charge of running the world comes from the entertainment media. At the peak of its success, the 2000 season premiere of NBC's *The West Wing* attracted an audience of 38 million people—millions more than the total number of viewers attracted by the three major broadcast networks' news offerings (which probably devoted less coverage to international issues than did *The West Wing*). Hence we should probably not be surprised that whatever "knowledge" people do have of the critical inner workings of the U.S. government almost certainly come more from these fictional sources than from other, more reliable sources.

The result are a few stereotypes, a good number of conspiracy theories, and a lot of images of serious men (and a few manlike women) around massive oaken tables in darkened, key-lit rooms passionately pounding on tables, launching air strikes, and occasionally looking up to view the state of the world on high-tech monitors displaying astonishing amounts of detail about distant locations full of evil foreigners. The first movies to contribute to this image include classics like 1964's *Seven Days in May* and Stanley Kubrick's *Dr. Strangelove*. In both, the military schemes and attempts to control the civilian government like puppets. In *Seven Days in May*, despite attempts at verisimilitude that included dressing Kirk Dou-

glas in his costume uniform and surreptitiously filming him walking into
the Pentagon (where filming was forbidden), the lasting images are of
shadow, of war-mongering, power-hungry military leaders, and of conspiracy.[6]

Dr. Strangelove is probably the closest thing there is to a national security classic. It, too, was born amid the nuclear hysteria of the early sixties
in the year of Lyndon Johnson's famous "Daisy" campaign advertisement
showing a little girl picking flowers, oblivious to an ominous countdown
to Armageddon taking place. While the movie is set in a Hollywood version of the Pentagon's War Room, the imagery of blustering, medal-laden
generals and demented civilian policy advisors has endured for decades.
It's hard for people of a certain generation to forget that dark, smoky
room with the gigantic round table and board of illuminated maps—
"He'll see the board!" This movie also gave us the immortal line, "Gentlemen, you can't fight in here—this is the war room," which drips with irony
for the average viewer and all the more so for people who understand the
kind of internecine warfare that is endemic to the upper tiers of the U.S.
foreign policymaking process.

Some of those who offer us popular glimpses into this inner sanctum
are somewhat better schooled in the realities of the place. Nonetheless, the
former staffers who write novels about the White House tend to be the
ones who love the drama that infuses life there. In fact, the opening pas-
sages of Richard Clarke's *Against All Enemies* and even the *9/11 Commission Report* make you feel like you are reading a novel, because the issues
described are so exceptionally dramatic in nature. Another former NSC
staffer who tried his hand at depicting the life he led—well, at least a
cleaned up version of it—is that famed "hyperthyroid marine," Lieutenant
Colonel Oliver North.

In his 2002 potboiler *Mission Compromised*, North recounts the exciting adventures of his hero, a marine officer named Peter Newman, who
happens to be newly in charge of the NSC's "Special Project Offices." This
thinly veiled defense of North's role in one of the NSC's darkest hours
includes the following fairly accurate description of the workaday NSC:

> Notwithstanding rumors Newman had heard to the contrary about this
> White House administration, the National Security Council's administra-
> tive and security office in the Old Executive Office Building was a hub
> of efficiency. The people who worked in the third-floor office of this gray
> stone building next door to the White House were older. He surmised
> that these were professionals, not political appointees. Unlike others he

had seen that morning in the West Wing, the men were wearing coats and ties instead of jeans, and the women had on dresses and skirts. He noted, as any U.S. Marine would, that the men in this office had what he considered to be decent haircuts, and here, at least, it was the *women* who wore ponytails and earrings.

A woman who introduced herself as Carol Dayton, and identified herself as the NSC's administrative and security officer, handed Newman a checklist of offices to visit, forms to fill out, and documents to sign. In less than two hours, the Marine major had taken care of all the obligatory paperwork, been photographed for the treasured blue White House pass, had his retinas scanned, had his fingers printed, had signed reams of nondisclosure agreements for classified security "compartments" he had never known existed, been issued access codes for the White House Situation Room cipher locks, and been taken on a quick, cursory tour of the old structure so he wouldn't get lost on his way to work.[7]

In addition to providing this general overview of the NSC offices, North also provides a general description of the Situation Room.

The National Security Advisor was in his shirtsleeves, his suit coat draped over one of the twenty or so chairs in the room where presidents had been meeting with their most trusted advisors since Dwight David Eisenhower. It was, Newman observed, a very small room for so many big decisions.

As they moved into the wood-paneled conference room, Harrod closed the door behind them . . . Newman sat, taking a seat across the smooth, polished mahogany table from Harrod—unaware that the Director of Central Intelligence usually occupied the chair that he had chosen during meetings of the National Security Council.[8]

And he also describes his old office, which was later occupied by counterterrorism czar Richard Clarke and, during the first term of the George W. Bush administration, was the office of Deputy National Security Advisor for Communications, Jim Wilkinson.

There was a large mahogany desk in the southeast corner beside a window that also overlooked the memorial to the first president. Beside the desk was a built-in counter that, judging by the wires running like spaghetti from fixtures in the wall, once held banks of computer terminals and phones. Against the interior wall was a large circular table with six chairs around it. . . . "When all the systems are hooked up, this is the best office in the NSC besides my office," said Harrod, gesturing. "It must have driven the striped-pants peons from State, DOD, and Langley nuts to have this prime piece of real estate occupied by a Marine lieutenant colonel."[9]

And in presenting the description that way, it is absolutely clear that it delighted the marine lieutenant colonel to drive the "striped-pants peons" nuts.

But despite the penchant for depicting the scenes that take place in the world of the national security team at the helm of the U.S. government in dark, shadowy images, these fictional depictions, even the best informed of them, shed precious little light on the real dynamics of power within the NSC or their significance. The NSC instead provides a useful setting, a hub of power that draws the storyteller precisely because it is not well understood and thus offers considerable license to authors.

In fact, much of what is important in the workings of this most powerful of all the world's committees is to be found in the details that exist beyond the view of the general public: in the importance of personal relationships; in the important role that informal meetings, even accidental ones, play in influencing outcomes; in the constraints and the limitations of process; in the political and bureaucratic subtexts that outlive presidencies.

Hence many of the better stories of this world go untold. Some are secret. Some are just invisible. For every Henry Kissinger who becomes an icon recognizable the world over, sometimes even seen in television commercials, there are countless other stories and characters of equal dramatic promise that have yet to be discovered by a public whose interest in this place is limited to times of crisis or depictions that place movie stars in the roles of real-life heroes and villains.

The story of the committee in charge of running the world is the same kind of tale that has entertained people since the beginnings of storytelling: the court drama. In fact, in *Our Own Worst Enemy*, published in 1984 and written by I.M. Destler, Leslie Gelb, and a man who less than a decade later would be national security advisor, Anthony Lake, there is a description of two classes of actors around the president, "barons" and "courtiers." A baron by their definition was a "senior official in charge of an important domain within the presidential realm."[10] The authors go on to say, "Like kings in the Middle Ages, Presidents have 'courtiers' in the White House who gain influence by responding to both their personal needs and their political priorities. And these courtiers come inevitably into contact with the barons."[11] With all such rivalries come intrigues, competition, historical animosities, and human follies that undo well-made plans.

Consequently, the modern history of the NSC has a Shakespearean feel to it. Born after the biggest war the world has known and put into place by an accidental ruler who rose to great challenges, the NSC evolved under the reign of a wily and deceptively brilliant great general whose crucial, quiet decisions set the stage for the world order for decades to come. He was succeeded by a young prince who came to office thanks to the dirty dealings of his manipulative courtier of a father and who then surrounded himself with an inner circle that included his own brother and the elites of the land. This young king was murdered and another accidental president was brought into office, one whose own great ambitions were brought down thanks to the entanglements bequeathed to him posthumously by his predecessor.

The leader that followed, our modern King Richard, came to the throne after a brutal career-long struggle to do so. At his side was a brilliant advisor who gained so much power that he began to be seen as a rival to his benefactor. Before the rivalry could reach its inevitable conflict, the king was brought down in the greatest scandal the country had ever known.

What followed was a national struggle for its own identity in which the image of the good nation was so deeply tainted by scandal and the ugly side of war that the country and its leaders were to spend a decade and a half grappling with their own limitations and identity in the world. One of these, himself an actor, undertook that healing but was himself almost undone by assassins and scandal. In the end, he was saved by the collapse of the "evil empire" that was the greatest enemy of the state.

His successor also helped create another Shakespearean chapter in the story when he won a great victory on the world stage but then stopped before deposing his enemy and thereafter lost office. This unfinished business hung in the air, haunting the White House even through the tenure of another president, who brought a remarkable mix of triumph and personal flaws, achievement and low comic scandal to the office, until the earlier president's son took office and sought to expunge the ghosts of his father's incomplete agenda by using a national calamity as a pretext to go again to war and to finally defeat his father's enemy.

Throughout these absolutely Elizabethan goings-on, of course, the business of the court was a rich tapestry woven by a remarkable cast of characters that also would have made Shakespeare proud: James Forrestal, the creator of the modern national security system who would die by his own hand; Robert McNamara, the brilliant secretary of defense whose fate

evokes that of Prometheus as he is forced for decades to suffer the gnaw-
ing of his conscience at his innards; Henry Kissinger, who recognized that
in modern courts, great diplomats must master the media even as they
orchestrate relations with enemies and allies alike; and fierce internecine
battles between Kissinger and Melvin Laird or James Schlesinger, between
Zbigniew Brzezinski and Cyrus Vance, between George Shultz and Caspar
Weinberger, or perhaps worst of all, within the administration of George
W. Bush between Colin Powell and Donald Rumsfeld. There is the comic
ineptitude of Iran-Contra's delivery cakes to ayatollahs and secret missions with Ollie North leading to the attempted suicide of yet another
national security principal, Robert McFarlane, and convictions for him
and many of his colleagues. There are affairs and romances and quashed
ambitions and all the stuff hinted at but only superficially revealed in novels or television programs. Heck, there's even a little sex appeal as
Kissinger dates starlets and offers his teutonic rumble about power being
the ultimate aphrodisiac. More recently the country singer Steve Earle
croons:

> *Oh Condi, Condi beggin' on my knees*
> *Open up your heart and let me in wontcha please*
> *Got no money but everybody knows*
> *I love you Condi and I'll never let you go*
> *Sweet and dandy pretty as can be*
> *You be the flower and I'll be the bumble bee*
> *Oh she loves me oops she loves me not*
> *People say you're cold but I think you're hot*[12]

Two Degrees of Henry Kissinger

LOVE SONGS TO national security advisors notwithstanding—
and thankfully there is only one such song—the impulse in
popular literature and media to focus on the human drama, the personal
relationships that drive and shape policy decisions, is not so unhealthy,
even for the serious student. Indeed, of the few serious policy tomes written about the national security apparatus of the United States, there is
vastly too much focus on policy and process and too little on people, their
work culture, their philosophies, the psychology of the interaction, and
the psychology of their times.

From the more than 130 interviewees for this book who have lived and breathed inside the U.S. foreign policy apparatus during the last sixty years, it's apparent that there are five main factors that shape how this apparatus works. Listed in descending order of importance, they are:

Personality and the "sociology" of an administration. This factor begins with and emanates from the president. But it is strongly influenced by the community of decision makers with which he surrounds himself, notably the "inner circle," those closest to him.

Domestic political context. To wield power, you have to have it first. Consequently, for the all the pronouncements about foreign policy specialists being "above" politics and how politics should be kept out of foreign policymaking, it never happens and it would be naive to expect it. Every key decision in the history of the White House foreign policy apparatus has been shaped in important ways by domestic political considerations. Consequently, understanding those politics and how the U.S. political environment has changed (almost entirely for the worse) is critical to understanding how this process will and can work.

International context. The United States does not act in a vacuum, and despite our unchallenged supremacy among nations in terms of military and economic capabilities at this moment in time, we are not invulnerable, nor are we possessed of unlimited power. In fact, we are simply the leading member of a community. Understanding the dynamics within that community also proves to be essential to understanding U.S. options, actions, and consequences.

Ideology and/or governing philosophy. Although an element of personality and of politics, the ideologies of key players and their political factions and the underlying governing philosophies of individuals, groups, and their eras are important because sometimes they constrain or inform behavior in subtle and powerful ways. Even the most casual observer can see that ideology creates policy handcuffs, that leaders who act on the faith that their worldview is right invite history to offer the nuances they will not or cannot see, and that "purely pragmatic" government actions stripped of underlying philosophy can be as dangerous as those driven by any particular dogma.

Structure and process. It is easy to disdain the wonkish work of those who focus on the structure and process of our policy apparatus, but the reality is that decisions about who is on what committee, what committee makes what decision, who recommends, who implements, how they do it, and what is required to start or stop an action can have a profound impact on events.

In the course of this book, one objective will be to use the observations of many of the participants in the "court drama" that we will be observing to illustrate and explore these five factors. But to return to the issue of "who" these players are is not only worthwhile because their relationships and beliefs are key drivers behind the actions we are most interested in, but also because in the end it is important to remember that this is not the story of an institution; it is the story of people.

You can find thousands of Web sites today with theories about who those people are and how they are linked. Some of these theories are harmlessly stupid. Some are the old-school, rather banal conspiracy theories of those who fear high-level organizations like the Council on Foreign Relations (I'm a member, I confess) or the Trilateral Commission. Some are more insidious, like the current popular misconception that somehow there is a group of monolithic, lockstep "neocons" driving Bush administration policy (there is not). Yet when one does examine the nature of the people who are members of the inner circles of U.S. international policymaking with an interest in uncovering facts rather than developing theories, some interesting patterns emerge.

These people do have a lot in common—an extraordinary amount—because the world of America's foreign policy elite, from which the members of this group are drawn, is a very exclusive one. Indeed, like many of the courts of Europe, there is a kind of aristocracy of American foreign policymaking that is more permanent and enduring than any of the rulers who come and go.

Some members of this group "inherit" their place in it. Senator Prescott Bush passes on his seat at the table to his son George H.W. Bush, who in turn passes it on to his son George W. Bush, who may next pass it on to his brother, Florida Governor Jeb Bush. The similar tale of Ambassador Joseph Kennedy, President John F. Kennedy, Senator Robert Kennedy, Senator Edward Kennedy, Representative Joseph Kennedy, Representative Patrick Kennedy, and Lt. Governor Kathleen Kennedy has also been frequently cited. But within the world of the national security elite, similar ties exist. One of the fathers of the modern NSC, the first defense secretary, James Forrestal, did not live to see his son Michael Forrestal serve on the NSC in the 1960s. Secretary of State John Foster Dulles served at the same time as his brother Allen Dulles ran the CIA.

One of the first "official" national security advisors, McGeorge Bundy, worked alongside his brother William, who served at the State Department and had an earlier career at the CIA. Bundy's deputy and successor Walter Rostow also served at the same time alongside his brother Eugene Rostow. Another senior Clinton political advisor, Harold Ickes, was the son of the Franklin Roosevelt cabinet secretary of the same name. Former under secretary of defense and career ambassador Frank Wisner Jr. is the son of Frank Wisner Sr., a former senior CIA official who was reputedly involved in the overthrow of the Arbenz regime in Guatemala in 1954 and the Mossadeq regime in Iran in 1953. Democratic presidential candidate John Kerry's father was a career foreign service officer. Senator John McCain's father was a commander-in-chief of the U.S. Pacific Fleet, Admiral John McCain.

But there are other clusters of senior foreign policy officials that are perhaps even more telling about the nature of this elite who rise to be the principal advisors to the president of the United States. For example, they begin their careers in many of the same places. Much has been made of the fact that President George W. Bush and his 2004 challenger John Kerry were two years apart at Yale and that both were members of the Skull and Bones secret society and that Bill Clinton also went to Yale (law school), as did his wife and as did 2000 vice presidential candidate Senator Joseph Lieberman. Vice President Dick Cheney also went there but dropped out. Bush also went to graduate school at Harvard (business school), the same university that was attended by 2000 Democratic nominee Al Gore.

But a look at the roots of the foreign policy elites reveals similar concentrations of leaders attending the same schools. The father of "containment," George Kennan, attended Princeton, as did Secretary of State George Shultz. At Princeton, future secretaries of defense Frank Carlucci and Donald Rumsfeld were roommates and wrestling teammates. Also in Carlucci's class of 1952 was future secretary of state James Baker. Wisner also attended Princeton, as did future under secretary of defense Walter Slocombe, who was helping the Bush administration rebuild the Iraqi army in Baghdad while another Princeton grad, Robert Mueller, was handling the home front while running the FBI. Carter administration Deputy National Security Advisor David Aaron, who later served in multiple capacities in the Clinton administration, was at Princeton at the same time as Wisner and Slocombe. Richard Perle got his master's degree there a few years later. Shortly thereafter, future national security advisor Anthony Lake studied there and, for a while, roomed with future UN ambassador Richard Holbrooke. Senior National Security Council staffers such as David Gompert, Franklin Miller, and Ambassador Karl "Rick" Inderfurth also attended Princeton at roughly the same time in the mid-1970s.

Naturally, there are a few other schools that have also bred large concentrations of leaders. Madeleine Albright studied at Columbia with future national security advisor Zbigniew Brzezinski as her dissertation advisor. Future CIA director George Tenet also studied there. Brzezinski taught at Harvard at the same time as Kissinger, and much has been made of their budding academic rivalry at the time. They both studied with William Yandell Elliot there, as did future policy planning official and author of *The Clash of Civilizations* Samuel Huntington. Among others who got some of their early taste not only of the international issues they would one day cope with but also of the people they would spend their careers working alongside were future defense secretary James Schlesinger, future State Department official and head of the Council on Foreign Relations Leslie Gelb, Kissinger student and future Republican Party foreign policy fixture Peter Rodman, Sandy Berger, Anthony Lake, future treasury secretary Robert Rubin, Berger's future deputy national security advisor Jim Steinberg, Douglas Feith, future NSC senior director and Ambassador Stephen Sestanovich and *The End of History* author Francis Fukuyama. Faculty members include current Harvard president and recent treasury secretary Lawrence Summers; former and current NSC staffers Morton Halperin, Robert Blackwill, Lawrence Lynn, Robert Pastor, and Jessica Stern; and many others. The list goes on and on.

Not surprisingly, once out of school certain career choices increased the likelihood that an individual would remain influential within this community. Names from the career military obviously top this list, including, of course, President General Dwight Eisenhower, President Lieutenant Jimmy Carter, Secretary of State General Colin Powell, former Secretary of State General Alexander Haig, two-time National Security Advisor General Brent Scowcroft, former National Security Advisor Admiral John Poindexter, former National Security Advisor Lieutenant Colonel Robert McFarlane, former presidential staff secretary General Andrew Goodpaster, former National Security Advisor General Robert Cutler, former Deputy National Security Advisor and former Director of the National Security Agency General William Odom, former Deputy National Security Advisor Admiral Jonathan Howe, and, of course, countless members of the Joint Chiefs of Staff, their chairmen, vice chairmen, commanders-in-chief (CINCs), North Atlantic Treaty Organization (NATO) Supreme Allied Commanders, military aides, and others of significance.

Career foreign service officers also surface regularly, including influential names from the "permanent" policy community of their eras like former Under Secretary of State Ambassador Thomas Pickering and current Ambassador to Baghdad and former UN Ambassador John Negroponte.

In addition to beginning from a remarkably concentrated list of elite academic institutions and often choosing similar career paths, common experiences typically forged key clusters of officials into groups that have survived the many changes in Washington and remained at the center of policymaking. Some such groups were created by people who served together in challenging but career-making environments, such as in the Vietnam War or the Gulf War.

Other such groups were formed in each administration as it confirmed another class of senior foreign policy specialists by appointing them to key positions, recruiting rising candidates to assist them, and then passing them on—either through the party-agnostic career path or to one of the two big competing "teams" of the foreign policy community, the Republican or Democratic foreign policy establishments. Within these communities, there is remarkable continuity, with significant crossover among key players among all administrations, and particularly among those of like party affiliation.

Among all such groups, perhaps the most remarkably influential is the group of people who served with or were directly influenced by Henry Kissinger. Kissinger, whose endurance as a national figure is remarkable on many levels, may actually have left his greatest legacy in the degree to which he influenced the attitudes, outlooks, methods, and beliefs of those who worked with him. His influence was especially great because he served both as national security advisor and as secretary of state, and he is the only individual to serve as a national security principal for eight consecutive years (two presidential terms) during the past several decades (although, as of this writing, Condoleezza Rice and Donald Rumsfeld are in a position to equal this accomplishment). The result is that even today, almost thirty years after he left office, we are still being led by those he led or those very close to them.

To illustrate the point, play the game Two Degrees of Henry Kissinger with all the national security advisors who followed him. The objective is simple: identify those who worked for him as aides, on his staff, or directly with him in some capacity (noting his special influence during his time in government, during which he was undoubtedly the "first among equals" on foreign policy), or those who worked directly for such a person. Every single national security advisor since Kissinger is, in fact, within two degrees of Kissinger:

- General Brent Scowcroft: 1 degree—was Kissinger's deputy national security advisor

- Zbigniew Brzezinski: 1 degree—was on the faculty at Harvard with

Kissinger, served with him on the President's Foreign Intelligence Advisory Board (PFIAB)

- Richard Allen: 1 degree—worked with Kissinger on the Nixon administration transition and then on Nixon's NSC staff

- Judge William Clark: 2 degrees—worked for former Kissinger aide Alexander Haig at the State Department

- Robert McFarlane: 1 degree—worked with Kissinger on NSC

- Admiral John Poindexter: 2 degrees—was McFarlane's deputy

- Frank Carlucci: 1 degree—worked with Kissinger during the Nixon administration

- General Colin Powell: 2 degrees—was Carlucci's deputy

- Scowcroft again: 1 degree—as above

- Anthony Lake: 1 degree—was a Kissinger aide

- Samuel Berger: 2 degrees—was Lake's deputy

- Condoleezza Rice: 2 degrees—was on Scowcroft's NSC staff

- Stephen Hadley: 1 degree—worked with Kissinger on NSC

Furthermore, in other senior positions, you find that U.S. foreign policy has been dominated by those within one or two degrees of Kissinger for the past three decades, particularly those in top leadership positions since the end of Cold War.

In the first Bush administration, the president had been the CIA director when Kissinger was secretary of state in the Ford administration. Scowcroft, as noted above, was Kissinger's deputy. Cheney was White House chief of staff during the Ford administration. Baker had not worked directly with Kissinger, but clearly was surrounded with people who had. In the second Bush administration, we again have Cheney. We have Rumsfeld, who was secretary of defense while Kissinger was secretary of state during the Ford administration and who had worked with

Kissinger during the Nixon administration when he was ambassador to NATO. Powell and Rice, as noted above, had second-degree linkages to Kissinger. Both of Clinton's national security advisors are noted above. Furthermore, numerous senior Clinton advisors, such as Holbrooke and Slocombe, had first-degree linkages, while others, such as Albright, had second-degree linkages.

The linkage games underscore just how small the pool is from which the NSC is drawn. It could be played with other important central figures, perhaps, but few who combine both the web of linkages and the intellectual influence of Kissinger. Still, any such exercise would emphasize that within the small, one-company town of Washington, D.C., the foreign policy community feels even small, even inbred. All the insiders, all the members of this committee over time know the others well and recognize that they will no doubt deal with one another for their entire lives. Among them are old animosities, extremely complex relationships, friendships that have withstood the test of time, loyalties, knowledge, old school ties, and other deep linkages.

Truly, the committee in charge of running the world, the White House leadership of the American foreign policy establishment, is a world within a world and a world unto itself. Of course, that's ironic, given that this comparatively insular group is meant to be our interlocutor with the world and our interpreter of it. But before you begin planning your own conspiracy theory Web site, ask yourself: Would you really want it any other way? Would you really want such important decisions made by people with less experience, who didn't know one another, who had not seen the cycles of recent history unfold?

The only way to begin to answer that question is to consider this group's record, its strengths, and its shortcomings—to somehow begin to shine a light on the activities that flicker in and out of our field of vision, receding between crises, distorted by media misperceptions and dramatic license, obscured by ignorance and apathy on the part of the American electorate and by the inscrutability of the system to the rest of the world.

2

Washington's Choice

To administer justice to, and receive it from every great power with whom they are connected will, I hope, be always found the most prominent feature in the administration of this country.

—George Washington

The responsibility of great states is to serve and not to dominate the world.

—Harry S. Truman

AS THE Second World War drew to a close, the United States was in a position that had never before been seen in the history of the modern world. A great nation, with the power and resources to extend its influence to every corner of the globe, it was without rival. Virtually every other great power or would-be great power of the day—England, France, Germany, Italy, Japan, Russia—had been devastated by the war of the preceding six years. Fifty percent of all world trade passed through the United States. We not only had led an alliance that defeated our enemies, but also had played the dominant role in achieving our victories—and our victories had not just been resounding, they had been complete. We had demanded unconditional surrender from foes that had previously been thought to be at the pinnacle of global power. What is more, isolated by two oceans from the wrack and ruin of industrialized total warfare, we emerged relatively unscathed.

As a consequence of its unequaled power, unequaled reputation, and unmatched resources, the United States had a profound choice to make.

Would it use its unprecedented power to build an empire, as earlier great powers had? Or would it choose a different path, one more consistent with its arguments that it was liberating enslaved countries, that it was attempting to spread the principle of self-determination and the American ideals of international conduct that had evolved from Washington's Farewell Address through Wilson and Roosevelt? And what role would it play in the global community whose destiny it would shape? Engaged and active? Or would it simply return to within its shores and once again avoid the "entangling alliances" that Thomas Jefferson warned against in his inaugural address? It was a choice of such moment that its ramifications still resonate throughout the world today.

General George Washington: One Individual's Choice

BY 1783 General George Washington's stature was unequaled within the fledgling nation he had battled to bring into existence. He achieved one of history's great military victories while leading a small, underprovisioned army against the British Empire, then the greatest military force in the world. He had done so with dignity and while earning the utmost respect from his men. The reality, indistinguishable between the Washington of myth and the Washington of fact, is that Washington could very likely have had any role he sought in the life of the new country.

Yet, Washington chose a remarkable path. He traveled to Annapolis and resigned the first commission ever given out by the government of this new country. And he made his way along the forty-odd miles of road that separated the country's legislature on the banks of the Chesapeake to his home at Mount Vernon on the banks of the Potomac River.

Throughout history, victors in war had sought power in exchange for their labors. Cromwell and Marlborough were but two relatively recent examples from British history that had illustrated this point. But Washington, like the often-cited example of the Roman farmer-soldier Cincinnatus, chose to return to his fields and his family.

Of course, he knew what he was doing. On the one hand, by retiring and urging his soldiers to return to their prewar roles, he was underscoring his commitment to the preeminence of civil authority. On the other, he knew that he was cementing a reputation that mattered to him greatly. Even King George III, perhaps with some self-interest, said that if Washington went through with his plans to retire, "he will be the greatest man in the world."[1] The famous painter John Trumbull wrote that this master of strategic retreat's final retreat from public life "excites the astonishment and admiration of this part of the world. 'Tis a conduct so novel, so unconceivable to people, who, far from giving up powers they possess are willing to convulse the empire to acquire more."[2]

Thus, Washington solidified his reputation for being a great man not with a spectacular accomplishment but by a simple choice, to give up personal gain for a greater good that he valued more.

When called to return and ultimately to assume the presidency, which Washington did with predictable modesty, resistance, and graceful acquiescence to the public will, he was obligated, through his actions, to establish the parameters, tone, and precedents for a presidency where none existed before.

The presidency was an idea that some viewed with suspicion because of the potential for a strong president to play a despotic role. Indeed, when it was proposed at the Constitutional Convention that the role be filled by a single person, there was palpable unease in the room. But despite admonitions to the contrary, a strong presidency was embraced as a direct consequence of the fact that many expected the former commanding general to fulfill the role. In other words, without the existence of a man like Washington, the job of president as we currently conceive it very well might not exist. Even dyed-in-the-wool republicans like Jefferson believed that with Washington in the office, it might well amount to an appointment for life, with the president playing a role much like that of a king. John Adams, in some respects the ur-revolutionary, himself began to refer in speeches and writings to the idea of the country becoming some kind of a republican monarchy. This was partially and paradoxically a tribute to America's great leader of the day.

And so, in this environment, Washington stepped into the uncharted waters of the presidency and acquitted himself with the same grace and desire to place the institutions of government above any individual that had marked his departure from military service six years earlier. He acted with dignity and reserve, bringing to the role necessary formality. But he also eschewed any suggestions of monarchy, taking pains to ensure that people knew he had no desire to pass the role on to his children and that he intended to retire at the end of his term, and expressing relief when the House of Representatives proffered on him the fairly simple title of "Mr. President" rather than some of the more resplendent options that had been bruited about.

Notably—and this example is worth remembering when we consider the case of some of his more recent successors in the presidency—Washington tolerated and actually embraced a wide range of views in his cabinet, a division that began with the fierce struggle between Jefferson, his secretary of state, and Hamilton, his secretary of the treasury. While this rivalry was symbolic of the party split between Jefferson's Republicans and Hamilton's Federalists, and of the divide between pro-French elements (led by Jefferson) and pro-British elements (led by Hamilton), a more imperially inclined leader might have demanded adherence to his views above all others. Rather, the general listened to his advisors and their strong disagreements; weighed them, often taking much more time to do so than they would have liked; and then made solid decisions that he expected to be enforced. He did not tolerate backbiting and division. He sought a range of views within his councils but demanded that the government speak with a single voice. Indeed, the esteem in which he was held grew as his role as an honest broker, a conciliator, and a true leader in his new job became clearer. The result was that to virtually all contemporary and subsequent historians there is a single view: the character of this man became the glue that held a new administration together and the foundation on which a stable republic was built. Again, had he chosen self-aggrandizement, personal reward, and placing himself above the law when Congress disagreed with him, as he easily could have and as many if not most might have done, the outcome would have been very different. Instead Washington carefully, repeatedly, and very publicly invested his hard-earned political capital back into the government he had helped found, into its laws and its institutions.

He ensured that the Constitution was interpreted properly and made a number of momentous choices along the way. He could have chosen to make his vice president a kind of prime minister, but did not, thinking that such a move, not inconsistent with the wording of the Constitution, undercut its intent. He established traditions for seeking the advice and consent of the Senate and constraining the role of the House on international matters. He also did not tolerate it when, on one visit to the Senate to address such matters, the senators' queries and comments went far beyond what he felt was appropriate, infringing on his role as chief executive, or, as he often put it, chief magistrate. He invented the concept of cabinet that essentially remains in place today. He also understood the need to communicate what he was doing and went across the country to do so.

Then, after this record of remarkable achievement in which he secured the stability and viability of the new government, he once again demonstrated the maxim that a great exit reveals more about a great actor than a great entrance. After an abortive attempt to leave office after one term was thwarted by the fragility of the government in 1792, four years later, he retired once again to Mount Vernon. The tradition set a precedent that was violated only once in the history of the country—by Roosevelt in the midst of a global crisis that he felt warranted his staying on—and that was then enshrined in the Constitution by the Twenty-second Amendment more than a century and a half after Washington left office. Of course, it was more than a tradition; it was the clearest and most powerful statement that anyone could make that, no matter how great the power of the presidency might become, the power resides with the office and not with the man in it, and that the people who elect our leaders are the ultimate power and the leaders themselves only their servants.

Had not the greatest man in the country, the one who could have taken any path, the one to whom virtually no one would stand up, chosen the course he did, it is substantially less likely that the republic would be here today or that democracy would have taken root and spread so successfully worldwide. Thus, Washington's great choice was not simply the choice not to be king; it was a string of decisions, including the choices to peacefully leave the offices of commander of the army and later of president, the choice to place himself beneath the law and at the will of the people, and above all, the choice to serve rather than dominate. The subordination of his own personal fortunes to the greater good of the society he sought to build sent a message that the American Revolution was not, like so many others, simply an excuse to enable one group to wrest power away from another but truly was a watershed, the birth of a new system founded on philosophies that had grown out of frustration with centuries of abuse by aristocracies and others for whom the objectives of government and the self-interests of the governors were inextricably interwoven.

The Choices Confronting Washington's Political Heirs

REVERBERATIONS AND echoes of Washington's choice have been visited on the city that now bears his name many times over the past two centuries, but perhaps never with consequences for so many as during the two peaks in America's global power: our victory at the conclusion of the Second World War and our victory in the Cold War sixty years later. At both times, America's position in the world was analogous to Washington's position in America at the end of the Revolution. We were the unassailable, unchallenged leader among all nations. Indeed, in the wake of the Cold War victory, Secretary of State Madeleine Albright chose to characterize the United States as the "indispensable nation," a term that echoed the title of James Thomas Flexner's four-volume biography of Washington, *The Indispensable Man*.

Washington wrote the words that appear at the beginning of this chapter in a letter early during his presidency. But in his Farewell Address he added that his vision of America's future on the international stage was "for a free, enlightened, and, at no distant period, a great Nation, to give mankind the too novel example of a People always guided by exalted justice and benevolence. . . . Can it be that Providence has not connected the permanent felicity of a nation with its virtue?"[3]

These comments suggest that Washington envisioned a day in which a larger, more powerful United States, finally immune to becoming a pawn in the games played between the old powers of Europe, would entertain a foreign policy in which justice rather than narrow self-interest was seen as the driver of our international actions. Indeed, he echoed on one particular front the current policy ambitions of Democrats and Republicans alike to be seen as an example of the success of republican government and thus to become its greatest advocate in the world. As Patrick Garrity wrote in *The National Interest* in the fall of 1996, as we were grappling with the confusing new realities of the post–Cold War era, while "Washington's general remedy for keeping America on an even keel was to stress the proper role of interest in foreign policy . . . 'no nation is to be trusted farther than it is bound by its interest; and no prudent statesman or politician will venture to depart from it.'"[4] Garrity goes on to say that in his Farewell Address Washington "argued that America's pursuit of its legitimate national interests in the world—especially when it came to questions of war or peace—ought to be 'guided by our justice.'"[5]

Garrity also notes that

Washington did not act according to the modern dichotomy between "realism" and "idealism" in the formulation of foreign policy. He agreed with both Hamilton (the supposed realist) that nations act solely out of their own interest; and with Jefferson (the supposed idealist) that there is but one standard of morality for men and for nations. . . . And even though he dearly hoped that America would soon develop its own, distinct national character (which would help liberate it from the entice-

ments of both the French and the English and the divisions they sought
to foster), he added the admonition that we required "a decent respect for
the opinions of mankind."[6]

In the wake of the Second World War, our role was much like that of
Washington at the time of the Constitutional Convention of 1787. If there
was to be a chance for peace and stability, we had to play an active role not
only in winning the war but also in establishing the peace through creating a
global civil society. We had to set aside the compelling lure of attending only
to domestic issues and recognize that if we did not apply our talents,
resources, and particular view of "our justice" to the establishment, funding,
management, and cultivation of that greater community, we would very
likely face the kinds of problems we had in the 1930s. We had to make the
same choice that Washington did, to harness our power for the greater
good—and even then, we had to do as he did and resist the temptations to
create a global community that was too self-serving, to rig the system too
much (and the fact that some would argue we rigged it plenty while others
would argue we didn't go far enough suggests that we did manage to strike
some sort of balance, if not a happy one). We had the military, political, and
economic power to dominate, and instead we chose to invest in rebuilding
even our enemies and then engaging them and others through a global civic
architecture that surpassed anything ever before seen on the planet.

In the remarkable period of institutional creativity that followed the
Second World War, not only did we create global institutions such as the
United Nations, the World Bank, the International Monetary Fund, the
International Labor Organization, the seeds of the World Trade Organiza-
tion, and international courts of justice plus great military alliances like
NATO and the administrative structures that implemented the Marshall
Plan and oversaw the rebuilding of Europe (which led indirectly to the
establishment of what became the European Community) and Japan, we
also created a number of important domestic institutions to help manage
our role in this new global community.

Among these were the institutions created as part of the National Security Act of 1947, which included the National Security Council, the Central Intelligence Agency, the Department of Defense, the Joint Chiefs of
Staff, and the Department of the Air Force. As we shall see, many factors
played into the creation of these agencies and departments, but their overall goal was to ensure the security of the United States and to preserve our
interests internationally through the effective management of the resources
available to the U.S. government. Of particular importance was learning

from the experiences of the Second World War to ensure that we could balance our political and diplomatic interests and capabilities with our military and intelligence interests and capabilities. This was essential because another new feature of the postwar era was the specter of the Cold War and the likelihood that we would be engaged in a new kind of global competition, one that would forever end the notion that America existed apart from the world and could retreat to its own shores and turn off "foreign entanglements" like they were programs on that other postwar development of considerable importance to our story: the television.

Of these new institutions, over the almost six decades since they were created, the National Security Council has come to be the hub of all U.S. international engagement, the place where formal policies are adopted, agencies offer alternative choices to the president, and the president decides on the world's most powerful nation's course of action with (or without) regard to the rest of the planet. It became both the policy creation mechanism and the policy implementation mechanism that helped harness and coordinate the actions of an increasingly complex government in an increasingly complex world.

Consequently, and ironically, after the ups and downs of the Cold War and a long, torturous period of American self-doubt that reached its nadir in the days of Vietnam and Watergate, it was this product of America's greatest moment of institutional creativity—of its highest embodiment of the principles and ideals underlying "Washington's Choice"—that played a central role in revisiting that choice with the birth of a new era on September 11, 2001. It also led to the present-day leaders of the United States reaching a stunningly different set of conclusions about what to do with American power and prestige.

Indeed, in the years since the end of the Cold War in 1991, the National Security Council and the policy arms of the government that connect to it have been the hub of an ongoing debate concerning what America should do now that we once again attained the heights of power last seen in 1945 and the years immediately after the Second World War. This time, we were the only superpower remaining standing, dominant militarily and economically. What is more, we were the dominant power of a new age, one in which new technologies of telecommunications and transportation made it possible for us to project force or the power of our ideas to any corner of the world at a moment's notice. While our relative power may not have been as great as it was in 1945, our reach was certainly far greater.

Once again, the challenge for the United States was what to do with that power to best advance our national interests. It was a debate that would take the better part of a decade to coalesce into a clear set of ideas. During the Clinton years, it seemed as though the direction would be more Trumanesque, more oriented toward the further development of an international community in which we would play a leading role. But after the stunning attacks of the first year of the new century, there was a sudden change in the tone of that debate and in the driving philosophies shaping America's choices.

This time, frustrated with the inability and unwillingness of the sixty-year-old institutions of the international community to respond to our requests for support in avenging the September 11 attacks, our leaders chose a different course. Rather than investing our power and prestige into civil institutions of the global community in which we found ourselves playing the decisive leadership role, they chose to go it alone, to use our power and resources to advance our interests as they defined them. And rather than showing a "decent respect for the opinions of mankind," we set aside past notions of "our justice" and consequently rejected the path that had distinguished the country and its leaders at our birth and at the previous moment of our greatest triumph. The words from Truman's first address as president to a joint session of Congress—that the "responsibility of great states is to serve and not to dominate the world"—were drowned out by concepts like preemption and unilateralism, ideas that were more founded in raw power than they were on the philosophies of America's founders. Advancing democracy may have been our ultimate objective, but we certainly did not choose to achieve it via the strengthening of the global laws or institutions we had once established for just such a purpose. Even if one result of our effort proves to be a net positive in the context of one region, such as the Middle East—and as of this writing the jury is still out on that point—achieving it by placing ourselves above and beyond the influence of global institutions or the rule of law will only serve to seriously damage the international order that we have sought to build since the end of World War II.

Understanding what role human behaviors and the character of individuals play in determining the character of a nation like the United States—how the choices of our leaders become the pivotal choices of our eras for global society—is one of the principal objectives of this book. When we examine the evolution of the national security apparatus of the U.S. government from 1947 to the present, we discover that no other factor is more central to determining whether we succeed or fail in preserving or advancing our national interests and ideals than the character of the people we put in the positions to lead us.

Many aspects of character are no longer emphasized as they were in Washington's day. It has often been said that the miracle of the American Revolution was the coincidental appearance of so many remarkable minds at a single time and at a single place in history. As a class they are distinguished from today's leaders in that they actually believed that philosophy was a discipline they should study and contemplate. They were not only the heirs of Locke, Hobbes, Rousseau, and Burke, but they also knew who these thinkers were. They discussed their writings and they debated the prevailing views of enlightenment Europe.

Today such debates are considered the province of smoky French television programs and irredeemable academics. In place of philosophy, which involves developing a system of belief based on questioning and reasoning, many of our modern leaders have embraced ideology, which is based on having a system of beliefs essentially stripped of the questions. Indeed, doubt and introspection are frowned on as offering the appearance of indecision. It is likely that the deliberate, slow reasoning of Washington, which many of his subordinates regarded as rather painful to watch, would be seen as weakness today. Certainly, painstaking debates on the philosophy of our government and the responsibility of that government to those people it rules over would simply not be tolerated. Yet, we live at a time of such change in the global community that many fundamental philosophical ideas, such as the social contract or the relationship between individuals in one country and the governments of another country whose daily actions have an impact on their lives, ought to be the subject of open debate. Absent that debate, the characters of all our leaders and our groups of leaders are diminished and unnecessarily constrained. And absent having philosophy as a driver of decisions, a greater role is given to expediency, politics, personal relationships, bureaucratic imperatives, and other factors, which, although important in a practical sense, are less likely to elevate outcomes or align them with ideas of justice or long-term national interests.

Virtually every administration in the past sixty years has had a moment in which circumstances have taken the measure of its character, a turning point at which the true nature of the president and his closest advisers is revealed. In these crucibles of crisis or slower pressure cookers of unfolding events, we repeatedly watch veneers crumble and even careerlong characteristics fall away and we discover the core nature of the key actors. For some administrations, like that of Harry Truman, there were a number of such moments—beginning with his succeeding Roosevelt, his deciding whether to use the atomic bomb, his deciding whether to acknowledge the new state of Israel, and his embarking on the Korean War and the Cold War. For Eisenhower, it was almost certainly fending off the pressures to bring the Cold War to a head. For Kennedy, it was his two Cuban crises. For Johnson and Nixon it was Vietnam—and Nixon, of course, also had another test of his own devising. Ford's was to heal the nation. Carter's took place in Afghanistan and neighboring Iran. For Reagan, character was revealed in how he managed his confrontation with the "Evil Empire" and how he was very nearly undone by his inattention to the details of his own administration. For the first Bush, it was the Gulf War and managing the world as the Cold War wound down. For Clinton, it was searching for a post–Cold War paradigm and a crisis of personal behavior. For the second Bush, it was responding to the September 11 attacks and waging the war on terrorism.

These crises not only revealed the character of our leaders—and certainly, in each of these cases, the character of the president's team was almost as important to determining the outcome as was the character of the leader himself—but they also helped shape public perceptions worldwide of the character and reputation of America.

As in Washington's day, it is a circle. Events call out for great men. Great men rise up and then, as Heraclitus prophesied, "character determines fate."

With George Washington, the United States and the world were lucky. The modern era has been bounded by tests against the standard he set. America's moment of greatest glory came when, in the era of the "greatest generation," we rose to that challenge and emulated him. Today, our futures hang in the balance because we have not followed the path set by our first leader 200 years ago. Where we go from here will be determined by whether we understand the contrast between our actions in these two great moments in recent history and their implications for the world of the future.

3

Greatness Thrust Upon Them

We have learned that we cannot live alone, at peace: that our own well-being is dependent on the well-being of other nations, far away. We have learned that we must live as men, and not as ostriches nor as dogs in the manger. We have learned to be citizens of the world, members of the human community.

—Franklin Delano Roosevelt

AFTER A LIFETIME observing history in the making as a television news anchor, Tom Brokaw conjured up what will be a lasting legacy of his own with his phrase "the greatest generation." It resonated perfectly with the nation's sense of those men and women who saw us through the most brutal conflict the world had ever known and, in so doing, both defeated evil incarnate and, at the same time, acted with what seemed great nobility and commitment to the global greater good. These people were also our fathers and mothers, grandfathers and grandmothers, and it elevates us all to think that we actually come from greatness.

Not surprisingly, the underlying truth of America's role in the Second World War is not fully depicted in heartfelt hagiographies like Brokaw's or in the burnished images of our memories or in *The Longest Day*. It doesn't diminish the greatness of what was achieved to acknowledge these underlying truths either. Human beings are flawed. Our triumphs are all that much greater because they are not only victories over our enemies but also over ourselves.

Just as understanding the horrific nature of Nazism is not possible unless we accept the reality that all Germans were not monsters but that they were in fact ordinary people like us—who enabled monstrous behavior, supported it, and sometimes committed it—many of America's most magnificent actions during and immediately after the Second World War and the leadership of a few exceptional individuals is best understood in the context of the flaws, mistakes, and very dark decisions that also were part of the story of Washington at war.

The largest of these flawed acts—ignoring the evidence of the Holocaust and turning their backs on the Jews and other victims of the Nazis or opting for brutal onslaughts against civilian targets such as the firebombing of Dresden—and the most controversial actions of the government—such as the nuclear attacks on Japan to end the war—overshadow some of the lesser known or discussed problems that were obvious to observers. But these lesser problems reveal much about both the character of the individuals involved and what was working and not working in our government as we closed that chapter in our history. Consequently, they loomed large in the minds of those who were contemplating the next stages of America's growth and its role in the world.

Two important problems could be considered central on many levels: one concerned dysfunction at the center of our government, and the other had to do with U.S. public attitudes and opinions.

Franklin Roosevelt is among our most mythologized presidents today. He is seen as a political and diplomatic colossus who overcame his personal handicaps to rescue the country from depression and then save America and the world from the darkest, most remorseless enemies we have ever faced. During his presidency, he was quite successful at what today would be called "spinning" the press and shaping his image, and he did so in a way that perfectly suited the prejudices of the times—hiding his disability and managing to be seen both as a champion of the common man and as a member of the ruling class all at once. This last bit of political legerdemain is of special importance in American political history; it was first accomplished by Washington, Adams, and Jefferson, and more recently, by John F. Kennedy and George W. Bush.

Yet Roosevelt was no master administrator of the American government, nor was he a leader who embodied terribly democratic impulses when it came to decision making. Instead, he preferred to keep information to himself, to operate secretively, to work primarily with a very small group of advisors, and, quite often, to cement his hold on the reins of power and confuse his enemies by offering contradictory, confusing views and directives. Unfortunately, this tended to confuse his colleagues in the U.S. government as well.

In the words of Arthur Schlesinger, as quoted by Robert Dallek in his excellent biography of Roosevelt, *Franklin D. Roosevelt and American For-*

eign Policy, 1932–1945, Roosevelt "deliberately organized—or disorganized—his system of command to insure that important decisions were passed on to the top. His favorite technique was to keep grants of authority incomplete, jurisdictions uncertain, charters overlapping. The result of this competitive theory of administration was often confusion and exasperation on the operating level; but no other method could reliably insure that in a large bureaucracy filled with ambitious men eager for power the decisions, and the power to make them, would remain with the President."[1]

The president's closest advisors were well aware of his approach. Secretary of War Henry Stimson, seventy-four at the time of the Japanese attack on Pearl Harbor and a senior statesman among Roosevelt's senior statesmen, had little patience for it. Stimson wrote in his diary "about Roosevelt's 'indecision' over Germany: 'Never has anything I witnessed over the last four years shown such instance of the bad effect of our chaotic administration and its utter failure to treat matters in a well organized way.'"[2] He lambasted Roosevelt's "looseness" in running his government and his eagerness to "sign any paper" that one advisor presented him "without waiting for the criticism and counsel of the others."[3] Roosevelt even boasted of this "technique" of managing government to another cabinet member, Henry Morgenthau: "I am a juggler, and I never let my right hand know what my left one does."[4]

Other members of the administration shared these concerns, some more acutely than others. Foremost on this list was Harry Truman, who must be seen as one of the most egregious victims of the Roosevelt treatment at the time of his ascension to the presidency on April 12, 1945. Truman entered the nation's highest office utterly unprepared for it by his 1944 running mate. The two had met formally only twice between January 1945, when Truman took the oath of office as vice president, and Roosevelt's death in April. Truman was not briefed on the details of the atomic bomb, the Yalta summit, or the secret agreements Roosevelt had reached with other world leaders before assuming office.

Along with the new president, others in the government had seen the consequences of Roosevelt's management style and determined that something needed to be done so that should the U.S. ever again face similar crises, the system of government would ensure a better process, capturing the views of more of the best minds available before decisions were to be made. Leading this group was Secretary of the Navy James Forrestal, an intense and exceptionally capable bureaucrat who had fought his war in the trenches separating the army, the navy, the State Department, the White House, and our allies.

Coming out of the war, the weaknesses of Roosevelt's approach to managing the team he had administering U.S. foreign policy were not, of course, the only things on the minds of Truman and his colleagues in the government. There was the rebuilding of a planet devastated by conflict, the potential threat posed by the Soviet Union, and, taking precedence above both of these, the question of what America's role in the postwar world would be. America was, historically, a nation that had taken Washington and Jefferson's admonitions to avoid "entangling alliances" to heart. In July 1941, with Europe at war, only 17 percent of the American people felt we should have become involved in it. Without the attack on Pearl Harbor, we would almost certainly have let the cancer of war spread farther without action.

In the wake of the First World War, American isolationism crushed Wilson's dreams of a functioning League of Nations and, in part, contributed to the conditions that allowed the rise of Hitler's Germany, Mussolini's Italy, and Emperor Hirohito's Japan. By 1945, after four bloody years of brutal conflict abroad, the same voices were heard again calling for a withdrawal to our shores, to domestic issues, and away from the dangerously foreign.

Republican Senator Robert Taft, one of the most influential members of the Senate and a member of one of America's most important political dynasties, denounced the Marshall Plan in March 1948 as "European TVA," comparing it to the Depression-era make-work initiatives of the Tennessee Valley Authority—poison to Republicans, as it was a Roosevelt signature program.[5] Another Republican leader, Representative Charles Halleck, responded to the watershed ideas of the Truman Doctrine by asserting, "The people don't like it."[6] Other such comments in support of keeping America out of the world's business and the world out of America's business were as commonplace then as they are today.

In short, in light of the management style and priorities of the recently departed but nonetheless iconic wartime president, his predilection against process and openness in domestic and international dealings, and the nation's predisposition against internationalism, the explosion of internationalist institutional creativity that followed the Second World War was by no means a foregone conclusion. Rather, that creative explosion was driven by the fortunate coincidence of a group of remarkable men in positions of power in the United States when we needed them the most, a coincidence that itself harkens back to a similar one at the founding of the republic.

Those men—Harry Truman, George Marshall, Dean Acheson, George Kennan, Clark Clifford, James Forrestal, W. Averell Harriman, Arthur Vandenburg and a secondary cast that included Dwight Eisenhower, John

McCloy, Robert Lovett, Charles Bohlen, and Ferdinand Eberstadt among others—laid the foundations for the institutions that today bind the world community and ensure the United States a permanent and unrivaled place within that community.

The sweep and scope of that transformation was stunning. Within a decade of the Pearl Harbor attack, the United States had led the Allies to victory in the Second World War; signed the United Nations Charter with nearly unanimous approval from the Senate; implemented the Marshall Plan; fulfilled the promise of the Truman Doctrine with substantial peacetime aid to Greece, Turkey, Western Europe, and Japan; and committed itself to the North Atlantic Alliance, the North Atlantic Treaty Organization, the Military Defense Assistance Program, the creation of the International Monetary Fund, the World Bank, the International Labor Organization, the foundations of what was to become the World Trade Organization, the Far Eastern programs of the Economic Cooperation Administration, the Mutual Security Program, and the Point IV Program. In addition, to manage what it saw as its permanent role in executing those programs, it transformed its national security apparatus, modernizing its military and creating the Department of Defense, the modern Joint Chiefs of Staff, the U.S. Air Force, and two potentially powerful new agencies to focus exclusively on ensuring successful management of our world affairs: the Central Intelligence Agency and the National Security Council.

It was one of the few occasions when what came out of a transformation was as stunning as the transformation itself. And there is plenty of reason to believe that much of it might not have happened if Roosevelt had lived to complete his fourth term as president.

· · ·

Man has learned long ago that it is impossible to live unto himself. This same basic principle applies today to nations. We were not isolated during the war. We dare not become isolated in peace.

All will conclude that in order to have good neighbors, we must also be good neighbors. That applies in every field of human endeavor.

—Harry S. Truman at the San Francisco UN conference[7]

EVEN BEFORE the institutional structures that we recognize today were in place, a group of men found themselves the de facto members of a "committee in charge of running the world" with

America's assumption of world leadership at the end of the Second World War. And, not surprisingly, this first ad hoc grouping of leaders shares many characteristics with those who were to follow. First, many of them were drawn from privileged backgrounds, from the eastern establishment or the military elite. Second, many had been working with one another in some capacity for quite some time. Third, institutional and historical rivalries and personal ambitions divided the group. Fourth, proximity to the president was vitally important to success in the group (Clark Clifford, a junior officer at the end of the war, developed more influence with Truman on some issues—such as recognition for the new Jewish state in the Middle East—than men like General George Marshall, who was, in the eyes of much of the nation, a kind of demigod). Fifth, ad hoc groupings based on common interest almost always trumped institutional groupings that were dictated by law or custom. Relationships based on comfort brought about by the alignment of interests and demonstrable loyalty drove the committee much as they drive its successors to this day.

To understand how the group worked, it is essential to spend a little time among the key players.

Such discussions must begin with Harry Truman. He entered office as if ascending, like a drab, bespectacled, droopy-suited version of Botticelli's Venus, from what his vice-presidential predecessor John Nance Garner had characterized as a "bucket of warm spit," the vice presidency itself.[8] He was stunned to become president. David McCullough recounts vividly the famous anecdote of Truman's stupefied silence after learning of Roosevelt's demise. When he was finally able to talk he turned to Eleanor Roosevelt and asked whether there was anything he could do for her. She responded, "Is there anything we can do for *you*? For you are the one who is in trouble now."[9] However she, like most of the nation, underestimated the man.

Within days Truman had begun to convince the senior staff around him, the men who would be his collaborators in the invention of the modern world, that there was much more to Harry Truman than the wry Missouri senator and former haberdasher portrayed in the dismissive newspaper stories of the day. He immediately ordered a written report summarizing the diplomatic problems in Europe. Within less than a week Averell Harriman, Charles Bohlen, and their State Department colleague Joseph Grew were briefing Truman on the growing Soviet threat, and they found him an exceptional student. He was an avid reader of history, and his knowledge manifested itself in briefings and had to be recognized even by those on his team who were initially skeptical. Dean Acheson recounted a briefing during one particularly hot day in August 1945 when Truman "awed" him with a virtuoso display of strategic knowledge of the issues of the eastern Mediterranean during a discussion of aid for Greece and Turkey. Acheson commented, "When he finished, none of us doubted he understood fully the implications of our recommendations."[10]

However, Truman also won the respect of doubters because he quickly established a management style that was strikingly different from that of his predecessor. He delegated authority and often followed the recommendations of his trusted advisors. He knew his stuff—but he also knew what he did not know. He was more disciplined and had a greater appreciation for process than his predecessor. As an old Senate hand, he knew how to translate policy ideas into political action, and this won him even more adherents. Finally, of course, he was tenacious. Even as those in the top echelons of the U.S. government came to understand his strengths, the American people, weary of war, seeking a change, missing the glamour of Roosevelt and the adrenaline-driven urgency of his era, suddenly cooled to the president. Many of his achievements, such as the signing and implementation of the National Security Act of 1947, took place when he was hitting historic lows in public acceptance and undertaking initiatives that were often politically unpopular while at the same time rebuilding his political base well enough to win election again in 1948.

Perhaps most important, Truman truly believed that America had a set of global responsibilities and that, as he said in his first address to Congress, on April 16, 1945, just days after assuming office and with the nation (and, no doubt, the occupant of its highest office) still in shock, the "responsibility of a great state is to serve and not to dominate the world."[11] It was a credo that he not only believed fervently—he believed it early. Although he did not play a direct role in drafting the Senate resolution for the creation of the UN in 1943, he was, according to McCullough, the "acknowledged guiding spirit."[12] Although still just a senator, he recognized that "the United States could not possibly avoid the assumption of world leadership [after the Second World War]."[13] That same year, he revealed the roots of this conviction in the experience of watching, after returning from his time as an artillery officer during the First World War, as efforts to win that peace failed: "History has bestowed on us," he said, "a solemn responsibility. . . . We failed before to give a genuine peace—we dare not fail this time. We must not repeat the blunders of the past."[14]

As career diplomat Dennis Ross, Mideast negotiator for Presidents George H.W. Bush and Bill Clinton, would tell me, "Every administration has its own sociology—its own culture. And it always emanates from the president."[15] Truman's appreciation for history, his tenacity, his career within and respect for institutions of government, and his innate character of openness and honesty drove the interactions of the constellation of policymakers around him. To some, like General George Marshall, he showed great deference and patience, even when pushed to the limits by the soldier-statesman's hauteur. Yet he stood his ground with such men and even stood them down, as he did with General Douglas MacArthur when he recalled him from the Pacific. To some, like Acheson and Harriman, he forged the best relationship possible between "a simple fellow" from Missouri and products of the eastern elites. And with some, with his true intimates, those closest to him in the White House, such as Clark Clifford, he played cards, took vacations, and had the relaxed, candid exchanges that are so essential to virtually all effective leaders. In short, he had the ability of the practiced politician to adapt to his audiences, to actually hear them and be made better by them, but always to advance his personal agenda.

How he worked with the team around him is well illustrated by his effectiveness at managing the processes around the development of the Truman Doctrine and the Marshall Plan in which others, such as Acheson, were given a clear lead and the chance to play a formative role in the development of the initiatives—but in all cases where the end result was a policy that was consistent with and advanced Truman's core beliefs.

Two related policy processes that unfolded during Truman's first term had implications for decades to come. The first concerned the greatest emerging threat the United States faced in the postwar environment, the Soviet Union. This single threat led to the creation of the central organizing principle around which all U.S. foreign policy was shaped for almost half a century. That was followed by the domestic-institution-building process that led to the National Security Act of 1947 and the creation of an apparatus designed to manage the foreign policy created largely in response to the perceived growing threat from the Soviets. A future implication of these actions was that this system—designed largely around addressing one concern—would undergo a significant identity crisis once that concern disappeared.

In an American government that can hardly keep one thought in its head at any one time, it is remarkable to think of the welter of activity within the Truman administration in those first couple of years after the war. Consider that it was in a span of four months that Truman delivered his doctrine, Marshall unveiled "his" plan, and the National Security Act of 1947, which laid the groundwork for the modern national security mechanisms of the U.S. government, was signed into law. In something like 120 days, the United States took the foreign policy stance that would define its role in the world through almost the end of the century.

Clark Clifford, in his memoir of the period, cites British historian Arnold Toynbee's observation that "it was not the discovery of atomic energy, but the solicitude of the world's most privileged people for its less privileged as vested in Truman's Point IV and the Marshall Plan . . . that will be remembered as the signal achievement of our age."[16] It's a noble sentiment, and certainly, on some level, it is true. But there is more to it than that. Clifford's own comment that these policies helped "the President and the United States, in the period from 1945 and 1950, [save] the free world" hints at that additional element.[17]

Truman's words, as he stepped up to the rostrum before a joint session of the House of Representatives and the Senate at lunchtime on March 12, 1947, give a sense of what he had in mind:

> At the present moment in world history nearly every nation must choose between alternative ways of life. The choice is too often not a free one . . .
>
> I believe that it must be the policy of the United States to support free peoples who are resisting attempted subjugation by armed minorities or by outside pressures.
>
> I believe that we must assist free peoples to work out their own destinies in their own way.
>
> I believe that our help should be primarily through economic and financial aid which is essential to economic stability and orderly political processes.[18]

Or consider the words spoken before the graduates at Harvard's Tercentenary Theater beneath sunny skies by the former general, now secretary of state, George Marshall, who stood before them in his plain gray sack suit, white shirt, and blue necktie:

> The truth of the matter is that Europe's requirements for the next three or four years of foreign food and other essential products—principally from America—are so much greater than her present ability to pay that she must have substantial additional help or face economic, social, and political deterioration of a very grave character. It is logical that the United States should do whatever it is able to assist in return of normal economic health in the world, without which there can be no political stability or assured peace. Our policy is directed not against any country or doctrine, but against

hunger, poverty, desperation and chaos. Its purpose should be the revival of a working economy in the world so as to permit the emergence of political and social conditions in which free institutions can exist.[19]

Like all such speeches, these are well-crafted blends of the underlying truth and the impression the speakers sought to give. In both, there is a real theme of altruism and defense of important ideals. But both are also absolutely clear in their language, the first's pledge to assist "free" peoples against "outside pressures" and the second's transparent lie that "our policy is not directed against any country or doctrine." The battle lines for the Cold War were being laid in the way we oversaw the rebuilding of the world after the war that had just ended.

America's commitment to playing a leading role in the world was driven by the lessons of the failures to "win the peace" that followed the First World War. This was an entire generation for whom those failures were still fresh in the imagination. And, just as the failures of Vietnam would haunt advisors to the president into the twenty-first century, and indeed become a centerpiece of the 2004 presidential election, these failures to come up with a viable postwar order in the 1920s were crucial to determining policy in the late 1940s. One element of the lessons of those failures was the need for an institutional structure for the global community and an investment of political capital into the structure by the powers that mattered. But another lesson was recognizing that from the rubble and frustration of wars grows the next generation of enemies. This in turn led to a desire to rebuild Germany and Japan in ways that provided opportunities for growth within the new international system rather than incentives to ignore, deceive, or work around that system.

This idea is a central one to understanding many of the issues of the twenty-first century, from the phenomenon of terrorism to that of political unrest in failed states or the inability of new institutions within countries to gain traction. In all these situations, the critical analysis that needs to be made concerns a national or regional stability threshold. The stability threshold in any political system, from your local community to the emerging global system, turns on whether the majority of key players within that system—those with the power to make the system work or to disrupt it—believe that working within the system is more likely to produce a better future for themselves, their families, or the units of society they represent than working outside of the system. Even if there are some stragglers or those who resist the system, if the majority are thus invested in it, it will work, and it will resist attempts to upset it—provided the system also has effective mechanisms for dealing with such attempts and for avoiding the pitfalls of "tyranny of the majority." Awareness of this "stability threshold" is important, whether one is evaluating the progress of national development or building larger institutional structures worldwide.

It was clear in 1945 that there was disagreement around the world about the nature of the system that would be in the best interests of most people. A fundamental ideological divide about the organizing principles of society split the nations of the "free world" and the totalitarian states of the communist world. To some informed and perceptive members of the policy community around President Truman—and to Truman himself as he came to know Stalin and the Soviets—it was clear that the international system could not reach the desired stability threshold, because the Soviets saw it as in their interests to have it organized around a different set of ideas and ideals, ranging from their ideological views on the distribution of wealth and the various threats capitalism posed to the Soviet Union and its ruling class, to their much longer-standing views about empire and Russia's role in the world.

Professionally, Truman and the small cluster of advisors around him were steeled by the war and the urgency of purpose that war brings. The historical developments of their lifetimes, which included the two world wars, shaped their approach to problem solving, interaction, and the advice they gave the new president. Particularly for those who saw the rise of the Soviet Union up close, such as U.S. Ambassador Averell Harriman and his deputy, George Kennan, the application of these life lessons to the Soviets' apparent desire to play fast and loose with their commitments to the postwar order made at the Yalta summit and before resulted in an ever-grimmer set of conclusions.

As noted earlier, within days of assuming office, Truman had received a briefing on the Soviet Union from his top diplomats, including Harriman, Dean Acheson, future vice president Nelson Rockefeller, State Department liaison to the White House Charles Bohlen, and Under Secretary of State Joseph Grew. For Truman, it was critical now to remedy the information blackout that Roosevelt's neglect and secretiveness had imposed on him. Harriman was one of several Soviet hands in the government who had come to be increasingly concerned about the direction that country was taking. Another, William Bullitt, a former ambassador to Moscow, had recently written a series of articles in *Life* magazine that described the dark realities of Soviet power. According to one account of the meeting, Harriman spoke about Soviet expansionism, global ambitions, and the "barbarian invasion" that threatened Europe. Truman was intent, and he asked many questions. He wondered how to interact with senior Soviet officials and noted, perhaps somewhat optimistically, and perhaps naively, "The Russians need us more than we need them."[20]

The meeting was a watershed in U.S. policy. While Harriman repeatedly stressed that he was "not pessimistic" and that he hoped to find a workable solution with the Soviets, he also sounded the first alarms for Truman. When Truman met a few weeks later with Stalin's foreign minister, Vyacheslav Molotov, his tone was dramatically tougher than Roosevelt's had been at Yalta during his last meeting with the Soviets. Some speculated that Roosevelt, too, had been losing patience with Moscow, but none believed that he would have been as direct and tough as Truman was with Molotov in confronting him over the Soviets' apparent inclination to disregard promises they made at Yalta and to take steps to undermine an independent Poland in favor of one that was more in a Soviet orbit.[21] Indeed, Molotov complained that he had never been spoken to as Truman was speaking to him, to which the new president replied curtly that the best way to avoid the situation was for the Soviets to live up to their promises in the future.

This interaction, triggered by the April 19 briefing and another on the 23rd, contributed to Truman's own hardening attitude toward the Soviets. But the president's attitude was being formed in a harried atmosphere, and, working with a very small staff in the White House and having regular contact with perhaps a dozen or two senior State Department, War Department, and senior military officers, he would hear repeatedly from the same members of this small group; their own views were reinforced so often that it would have been hard to know where unvarnished fact left off and analysis began.

Note, however, that even in the simpler, smaller-government days of Truman, the size of the group the president regularly came into contact with was much the same as it is today; given the demands of the president's schedule, it would be difficult for him to have regular contact with more people than that. Consequently, in White House after White House, we see a group of perhaps a half dozen to at most a dozen or so who constitute the inner circle of advisors and decision makers. This group, which after all is much like the small group around Roosevelt that caused such consternation among members of his administration, remains the most important component of any administration's national security process, because it is called for not by an act of Congress but by human nature. Trust and rapport are, in the day-to-day operations of any government, much more important than the formal mechanisms of governing.

One of Truman's "wise men," one of the great pillars of the American establishment, John J. McCloy, was then serving in the War Department. Just a few days after the Russia briefings, he sent a memo to Truman detailing what he had recently witnessed during a tour of Europe. "There is complete economic, social and political collapse going on in central Europe," he wrote, "the extent of which is unparalleled in history unless one goes back to the collapse of the Roman empire."[22] In a follow-up meeting with the president, McCloy offered his conclusions about what this state of affairs augured. The tragedy of European conditions were "likely to be followed by political revolution and communist infiltration."[23] This sentiment was underscored in a July 1946 joint memo from McCloy and his boss, Secretary of War Stimson, contending that the destruction of German industry could produce an "infection which might well destroy all hope we have of encouraging democratic thinking and practices in Europe."[24] This in turn—and not the undistilled altruism usually credited for the subsequent policies—led the two to support a plan to support and revitalize Europe economically, the first time such a plan was introduced into policy discussions involving the president. It is noteworthy today that this recommendation regarding rebuilding, this seed of the Marshall Plan, came out of the War Department and not out of the State Department. Then as now, sixty years and many similar situations later, no agency of the U.S. government is really devoted to postconflict economic reconstruction, even though there is probably no single, repeating area of U.S. activity of greater importance in our recent history, nor one in which our performance has been so consistently underwhelming, with the exception of the Marshall Plan. In the wake of the debacle in Iraq, it may be said that the provenance of this proposal also undercuts the idea, made popular during the Rumsfeld era, that the Defense Department is utterly incompetent to take the lead in conceiving such efforts to win the peace.

Warnings such as those from McCloy and Stimson would have rung false without the "cooperation" of the Soviets. On a bitterly cold night in early February 1946, while standing on the stage of Moscow's fabled Bolshoi Theater at an election rally, Stalin threw down the gauntlet as never before. He asserted that the differences between communist ideals and capitalist corruption would lead to another major world war in the 1950s, a war he predicted would come with America in a depression following its postwar bubble. A month later, on March 2, the Soviets ignored yet another of their promises by failing to withdraw from Iran on schedule. Because Iran had never been part of the Soviet or Russian empires before, this was further evidence of expansionism and a desire to continually test the limits of U.S. and Western acceptance of Soviet ambitions.

It was in this atmosphere that George Kennan, one of the most skeptical members of America's foreign policy inner circle when it came to the
Soviet Union, dispatched his famous "long telegram." Although Kennan
was stationed in Moscow throughout this period, he had a great deal of
influence because of his incisive mind and the great respect he engendered
in his colleagues. His 8,000-word analysis of Soviet intentions and their
implications for the United States concluded that the Soviets were largely
driven by their own insecurities and that a Western alliance was required
to prevent Soviet expansion. Although this was not the first time Kennan
had offered such a view, this time, he felt, he had struck the "bell at which I
aimed—squarely and set it vibrating."[25] The analysis, reaching a White
House charged with mounting concerns about the Soviet intentions, had
a galvanizing effect on postwar U.S. foreign policy.

Among those most struck by Kennan's telegram was Secretary of the
Navy James Forrestal. He made the document required reading for his
senior staff and for the top officers in the navy. Later, as we shall see, it was
his sense of the potential threat posed by the Soviets and of the need to
improve the ability of the United States to wage a total war against them—
given the shortcomings he had seen in Roosevelt's management of the
conflict during the Second World War—that led Forrestal to become one
of the principal forces behind the National Security Act of 1947, the NSC,
and the modern U.S. national security apparatus.

Others were equally influenced by Kennan's views. Acheson later said,
"The year 1946 was for the most part a year of learning that minds in the
Kremlin worked very much as George F. Kennan had predicted they
would."[26] In the midst of this steady drumbeat of news and analysis about
the Soviets and their worrisome intentions, another report appeared, this
one prepared by Clark Clifford, the lanky, affable, deceptively shrewd lawyer
from Missouri who had worked his hometown connections into a job as
naval aide to the president and later as his counselor. Clifford would become a trusted advisor to four Democratic presidents (Truman, Kennedy,
Johnson, and Carter) and, through the way he served Truman, would set
some precedents for the role that would ultimately be played by the national
security advisor.

Like many such future policy memos produced for modern presidents,
the Clifford-Elsey report "American Relations with the Soviet Union" was
not the view of just one man or two, but an interagency survey of views,
incorporating perspectives from top officials in the State Department, the
War Department, and the military services.[27] In fact, it was the first interagency foreign policy review of U.S.-Soviet relations and, as such, set many

important precedents. It argued that forming an integrated policy and a coherent strategy to resist Soviet expansionism was a matter of national security. It also singled out the "crossroads of Europe"—Turkey, Greece, and related issues—as being particularly volatile and important in the near term (facts that would later be reflected in the focus of the Truman Doctrine).[28] The report's final recommendations were these:

> In conclusion, as long as the Soviet Union adheres to its present policy, the United States should maintain military forces powerful enough to restrain the Soviet Union and to confine Soviet influence to its present area. All nations not now within the Soviet sphere should be given generous economic assistance and political support in their opposition to Soviet penetration. Economic aid may also be given to the Soviet Union [as well as] private trade with the U.S.S.R. . . . Even though Soviet leaders profess to believe that the conflict between Capitalism and Communism is irreconcilable and must eventually be resolved by the triumph of the latter, it is our hope that they will change their minds and work out with us a fair and equitable settlement when they realize that we are too strong to be beaten and too determined to be frightened.[29]

Truman responded to the Clifford-Elsey report by demanding all copies that had been made of the document and immediately locking them away for fear that their release would "blow the roof off the Kremlin" (which was to be, ironically, the implicit objective of all U.S. foreign policy for more than forty years to follow).[30] Although the Clifford-Elsey report is a good deal less famous than Kennan's telegram for several reasons,[31] the study seems to have had a greater impact on Truman than some of the other briefings and documents he received because it underscored, illustrated, and detailed a consensus among his top foreign policy advisors—including Forrestal, Acheson, and Kennan—that the Soviet threat needed to be contained and that containing it proactively needed to be the centerpiece of U.S. foreign policy from then on. The Clifford-Elsey report also shows the power of proximity—how members of the president's personal staff regularly have influence disproportionate to their protocol rank in Washington.

Within weeks the theory was tested as the Soviets demanded a joint Soviet-Turkish defense system for the strategically located Dardanelle Straits. This latest example of Soviet expansionism and designs on Turkey triggered a joint effort among Truman aides, including Acheson and Forrestal, to send a swift and clear message to the Soviets that their moves would not be tolerated. They wrote a memo stating that "Turkey must be preserved if we do not wish to see other bulwarks in Western Europe and the Far East crumbling at a fast rate."[32] A day later, on August 15, they briefed the president. Acheson, formerly one of the least hawkish members of the team, argued that the "only thing that will deter the Russians will be the conviction that the U.S. is prepared, if necessary to meet aggression with force of arms."[33] Truman agreed, saying, "We might as well find out . . . whether the Russians are bent on world conquest."[34] A tough message was sent to Moscow. Almost immediately, the president got a reply. The Soviets capitulated and agreed to shelve the issue. The new U.S. Cold War foreign policy was being put into action.

In the late spring of 1947, Secretary of State Marshall traveled to Moscow to a foreign ministers' meeting. The meeting left him frustrated by the lack of progress he was able to make with the Soviets. Stalin treated him indifferently and was unresponsive to his efforts to break the stalemate between the two sides. Marshall returned to the United States convinced that chaos in Europe was working to the advantage of the Soviet Union and that something had to be done to stabilize the situation. Shortly after his return, on April 29, he summoned George Kennan and told him to begin working on a plan to help restore Europe's economy. He noted that this was not a plan to "combat communism," which presaged the disingenuous nature of similar affirmations in the speech he would later give announcing the plan. Almost the entire inner circle of Truman's foreign policy team worked on shaping the plan, including Forrestal, Clifford, Acheson, Kennan, and, of course, Marshall.

With a different group, at a different time, under a different president, some other outcome might have been possible. Had they not witnessed the aftermath of halfway measures in the wake of the First World War, the plan might have been narrower. Had they not come through a resounding victory and been so confident, the plan might not have been so sweeping or generous. Had they not seen the Soviets as such a threat, it might not have been imbued with such urgency. Had they not been so committed to America's ongoing engagement in the world, it might not have been produced at all. In short, their collective experiences and the close nature of their collaboration—not to mention the remarkable nature of the group involved—produced a watershed program that was part of a string of postwar policy initiatives that laid the groundwork for policy and process for much of what was to follow. Marshall's military training and expectations and what he felt a staff could provide led him to create the policy planning shop at the State Department. Similar military views on what a staff could achieve were held by Marshall's contemporary Eisenhower when he was president and would shape the first effective use of the NSC.

.   .   .

Truman and his men were the first group in history to make international policy for a legitimate global superpower. Wilson's and Roosevelt's teams had to establish America's preeminence. The Axis leadership aspired to such a role. But Truman's group had it whether they wanted it or not. And not only were they essentially improvising a global system as they went along, they were working without precedent.

Coordination between the Department of State and the Department of War as well as among the separate and still powerful branches of the military had been a real challenge during the Second World War. At the same time, enabling the president to effectively use all the tools in his geopolitical toolbox and giving him the benefit of the collective and often divergent views of the departments responsible for those tools was seen to be increasingly essential.

As with many of the lessons of the Second World War, there were illustrations from the First World War of ineffective responses to the same problems. It is probably fair to say that it actually took two world wars to convince the American people that active international engagement was their destiny—one war was simply not enough to break 150-year-old prejudices.

Coordination among agencies at the time of the First World War consisted of little more than letter writing among cabinet secretaries. Of course, the government was much smaller then, and virtually the entire group of top policymakers could be gathered in a single room. Government being what it is, they seldom were. Precursor coordinating groups, such as the Joint Board of the Army and the Navy, which coordinated activities between then-separate departments, and the Joint State and Navy Neutrality Board, which was formed to help provide advice on issues of diplomacy and international law, were initially specialized groups with fairly narrow missions.

Men of vision and a sense of what was possible did offer alternatives. One of them was the young, handsome, ambitious, well-bred assistant secretary of the navy, a cousin of a former president himself. On May 1, 1919, Franklin Roosevelt wrote to the secretary of state:

It is a fundamental principle that the foreign policy of our government is in the hands of the State Department. It is also an accepted fact that the foreign policy of a government depends for its acceptance by other nations upon the naval and military force that is behind it. . . . Hence, it is submitted for the framing of our policies, it is necessary for the State Department to know how much they will cost to maintain by force in order to assign them their relative importance. Conversely, it is necessary for the Navy Department to know what policies it may be called upon to uphold by force in order to formulate plans and building programs.[35]

Having thus laid out his premise, Roosevelt submitted his proposal for a permanent policy coordination mechanism that included a carefully prepared chart (essential for all good government reorganization schemes even today) showing lines of communication and respective duties for the army, the navy, and the State Department. It was a big plan that had at its center a Joint Plan Making Body.

Roosevelt was no doubt disappointed when he received no response from the secretary of state. However, as it turns out, the grand and visionary plan ended up a victim of the malfunctioning bureaucracy it was designed to help repair. Through what at least one historian characterizes as a "mistake," but which seems a little convenient to be just a mistake, the proposal was accidentally delivered not to the secretary of state but to the State Department's Division of Latin American Affairs, where it sat, unopened, through not only Wilson's tenure in office but also through Harding's, Hoover's, and even Roosevelt's.[36]

A similar proposal surfaced in 1921, twenty years to the day before the attack on Pearl Harbor, this one authored by both the secretary of the navy and the secretary of war. Again, indicating the relative independence of the various agencies and State's status as the senior agency, this one too went down in flames, dispatched into Secretary of State Charles Evans Hughes's outbox with a notation that "this appears to me to be in substance a suggestion that at least provisionally matters of foreign policy be submitted to the Joint Board. I question the advisability of this."[37] In other words, turf wins again.

As war loomed in the late 1930s, and with Roosevelt now president, Secretary of State Cordell Hull sought to open communications among agencies by creating a Standing Liaison Committee that would have representatives appointed to it from State, the Navy Department, and the War Department. State's representative was an under secretary. The chief of naval operations and the army chief of staff were their services' representatives. This group, the first U.S. government entity designed to facilitate foreign policy consultation, then fell victim to one of the first laws of Washington: "Where you stand depends on where you sit."

Whereas the young Franklin Roosevelt, as assistant secretary of the navy, saw a personal advantage to greater interagency coordination—a chance to broaden his own scope of interests and to advance the interests of the Department of the Navy—President Franklin Roosevelt was, as noted earlier, much less interested in interagency coordination when it only interfered with his prerogatives as commander-in-chief. As a result, during the war he consulted directly with service chiefs and with the small group of his closest advisors, such as Harry Hopkins and Averell Harriman, and with key Allied leaders, such as Churchill and Stalin. The State Department became of secondary importance to him, and the Standing Liaison Committee faded away in the middle of the war.

Two years later, when the focus of U.S. government efforts included complex surrender negotiations and the shifting of attention to postwar needs and diplomacy, Roosevelt acknowledged this new situation with the creation of the State-War-Navy-Coordinating Committee, an assistant secretary-level group. As a midlevel organization, the committee had to clear its decisions with the Joint Chiefs of Staff and then seek the approval of the secretary of state and then the president. Consequently, its direct influence was limited, but it did play an important role in shaping postwar policies and became the direct antecedent to the National Security Council.

The shape of the reforms that led to the NSC was influenced not only by circumstances but also by the dispositions of three central actors. One was Truman. In his memoirs, he wrote, "One of the strongest convictions which I brought to the office of President was that the antiquated defense setup of the United States had to be reorganized quickly as a step toward insuring our future safety and preserving peace."[38] Before becoming the nation's chief executive, Truman had worked actively for defense reform; he had even gone so far as to publish a magazine article in late 1944 advocating the consolidation of the army and navy on the grounds that two separate and uncoordinated military departments would inevitably be inefficient. This outlook, which makes sense even today, was fought vigorously by those with vested interests in one or the other service.

During the war and immediately afterward, Truman would say that the United States was "damn lucky" to have won the Second World War, given its weak military organization. On more than one occasion he remarked to Clifford that "if the Army and the Navy had fought our enemies as hard as they fought each other, the war would have ended much earlier."[39] Similarly, Robert Kimmitt, who was on the National Security Councils of

Presidents Ford, Carter, and Reagan, noted, referring to the National Security Act of 1947, "I think what the Act said was that we're growing up as a country, and we have to recognize a worldwide responsibility. While the results of World War II were successful, the way we went about getting there was not a model for how we would act in the future. You needed to begin to recognize these varying strands of national security decision making, and you had to bring them together in a way that gave responsibility for each of the areas to the appropriate department or agency. But the Act recognized, I think really presciently, the cross-cutting nature of what we do today."[40]

As is only fitting, the most significant effort to produce coordination and greater efficiency among major U.S. government agencies during the past sixty years itself was born of a bureaucratic rivalry, advanced through another, and created new ones. When it was deemed that the interagency tensions between State and the defense establishment and the tensions within the defense establishment were tolerable no longer, Truman requested plans for postwar reorganization. The War Department produced one such plan that called for a unified military department under a single, powerful civilian secretary. Given the size of the army, this was not surprising. Their assumption was that such unification would suit their purposes.

James Forrestal had come to a similar conclusion. Forrestal was a master bureaucrat who had made an art form of working the Navy Department's historical ties to Capitol Hill. He recognized that unless he dug in his heels and worked his patrons in Congress, the traditional independence of the department would be at risk. He asked Ferdinand Eberstadt, his close friend and collaborator throughout decades of government service, to devise an alternative plan. Eberstadt, a former chairman of the Army-Navy Munitions Board and vice-chairman of the War Productions Board, responded three months later with a 250-page comprehensive solution to the reorganization challenges facing the U.S. national security establishment.

In his transmittal letter to his friend Forrestal, Eberstadt establishes his core premise: "The military services are but a part of the national machinery of peace or war. An effective national security policy calls for active, intimate and continuous relationships not alone between the military services themselves but also between the military services and many other departments and agencies of Government."[41]

The plan itself called for many components of what later became the National Security Act of 1947 and the amendments refining it in 1949.

Eberstadt's approach, which was embraced by Forrestal, called for a looser network of coordinating committees and bodies than the more hierarchic plan offered by the Army-dominated War Department. Consistent with the experience that Eberstadt had in dealing with the business world in his procurement and production capacities during the war, it was a more corporate model, and one that resisted concentration of authority in a Defense Department that Forrestal could not control. Instead, it focused on the creation of three agencies: the National Security Council (NSC), the Central Intelligence Agency (CIA), and the National Security Resources Board (NSRB). The NSRB would balance the nation's supply of resources with its military demands, while the CIA would provide the vital upward flow of information to the top officials. At the center of the scheme was the NSC, which was to be a "permanent vehicle for maintaining the active, close and continuous contact between the departments and agencies of our government responsible, respectively, for our foreign and military policies and their implementation . . . charged with the duty (1) of formulating and coordinating over-all policies in the political and military fields, (2) of assessing and appraising our foreign objectives, commitments and risks, and (3) of keeping these in balance with military power, in being and potential. It would be a policy-forming and advisory, not an executive body."[42]

Forrestal worked diligently to bring key supporters into his camp. Among his most important early wins in this effort was with Clark Clifford, who as special counsel at the White House had come to recognize the need for some policy coordination group that would help address defense and foreign policy issues. Clifford, like Eberstadt, Forrestal, and many others who had survived the past several decades, had come to believe that the distinctions between peace and war had disappeared, leaving America in a world of perpetual crisis for which we would need to prepare. Clifford also saw that he was filling such a role on an ad hoc basis and that it would help address some of the infighting and rivalries with which he was regularly confronted.

Throughout the fall of 1945, with the war over and postwar planning now dominating the attention of America's leadership, Forrestal worked his idea behind the scenes. Meanwhile, in October, Truman received a report from the Joint Chiefs of Staff on army and navy restructuring that included the views of a number of his top generals and admirals. This report was significant in that it represented the beginning of negotiations among the services as to the shape of the postwar national security establishment. Although Truman had been committed for some time to ending "piecemeal legislation and separate planning in the services," as he wrote in his memoirs, an October 1945 navy report on postwar security had convinced him that a "national defense program involved not just reorganization of the armed forces but actual coordination of the entire military, economic and political aspects of security and defense."[43]

On December 19, 1945, Truman delivered a message to Congress requesting a series of defense reforms. The message itself called for a single department of national defense run by a cabinet secretary; three coordinated military branches, each headed by an assistant secretary; a chief of staff for the military, which would rotate among the three branches and would have genuine command authority and an advisory body to the president and the secretary, consisting of the chief of staff and the commanders of the three branches.

Throughout the yearlong process that led to the Hill negotiations and during them, Forrestal was a Rock of Gibraltar. Immoveable. Truman had even once called him in to the Oval Office to broker a deal between his vision and that of War Secretary Robert Patterson, but to no avail. Truman soon came to feel, in Clifford's words, that he was left "with a choice between concessions to the Navy or no bill at all."[44]

For those in the navy and those who were or are admirers of his vision, Forrestal's strength seems admirable. But, as is so often the case, there was more to it than that. In fact, Forrestal may be the best illustration of the dictum that while all people have weaknesses, the most successful are those who can turn their greatest weaknesses into their greatest strengths. Forrestal was tough and resolute. But he was beginning to show signs that deep inside he was actually wound far too tightly. His staff reported a number of strange incidents in Forrestal's behavior during this period. Once, he commanded that his plane turn around in midflight because he could not decide whether or not to give a speech he had been planning to deliver at his destination. Sometimes he would become so consumed by his activities—even just reading a book—that it was impossible to rouse his interest away. Shepherding through his vision of the new U.S. national security structure was Forrestal's finest hour in many respects, and yet it was also the beginning of the end for him. He was starting to show signs of the mental illness that would lead to his suicide just a couple of years hence.

Clifford wrote many years later:

Looking back on his mental breakdown and death, one can surmise that his extremely emotional behavior, his obduracy, and his intensity were all early signs of the illness that would end his life. But at the time this was not apparent to me or anyone else. Later, I recalled little occurrences that I had dismissed as quirks, but appeared ominous in retrospect. When he and I played golf, for example, Forrestal did not engage in the casual conversation that makes golf such an enjoyable and relaxing pastime. Instead, he would practically run from shot to shot, pausing only for a moment to line up the next effort. On a tennis court, where he was a scrappy competitor, he also rarely spoke. When he learned of the poker games [with the President] on the [yacht] Williamsburg, he asked me to invite him into the game; I did, but because he was unable to relax like the others around the green table, the President never let him become a regular.[45]

Clifford describes a more certain symptom of Forrestal's illness: "After he died, I remembered only one glimpse into the bottomless darkness of his internal crisis. Sitting directly behind him during a Cabinet meeting near the end of 1948, I noticed that he had scratched raw a spot on the top of the back of his head with his fingernail. As the meeting progressed, he continued to scratch until it was the size of a half-dollar. I watched in silent horror as blood slowly oozed from the spot."[46]

Clifford's efforts to broker an accord between Forrestal and Patterson finally did produce an agreement in January 1947. On the sixteenth, Patterson and Forrestal sent the president a letter describing the reforms they could agree on. The Patterson-Forrestal agreement called for separate, independent service departments, each headed by its own cabinet secretary, who had direct access to the president. Patterson and the army's hope for a strong secretary of defense gave way to a much weaker secretary of national defense with almost no staff and no real authority, and who sat atop a small bureau called the National Military Establishment. The proposal also did not include Clifford's stated preference for a powerful head of the Joint Chiefs of Staff. It did, however, call for the creation of the National Security Council.

During the ensuing months, the debate about the reforms continued. General Marshall worried about the power—which he considered "almost unlimited"—that was being granted to the new central intelligence entity.[47] He also saw that it would overlap with the State Department's National Intelligence Agency. Finally, he suggested that the new arrangement might "dissipate the constitutional responsibility of the President" and would water down the role of the secretary of state.[48] He was against the NSC, the CIA, and the resources board. Ultimately Marshall was placated by language underscoring the advisory role of the NSC. Further refinements slightly increased the power of the secretary of national defense, particularly over influencing budget issues.

In the end, the bill, very much resembling the Forrestal and Eberstadt plan even though most of the leaders who had only recently defeated Nazism and the Empire of Japan were arrayed against it, passed. Truman, who had wanted even more reform, rationalized the progress they had made by saying: "We can't always start out with a complete and finished organization; you must remember that since 1798 there has been a Navy Department and since the beginning of the Republic there has been a War Department. . . . It is hard to work on a bureaucracy like that."[49] Forrestal was less magnanimous about the drawn-out negotiations around the Act, asserting days before the final signing of the bill that there had never been a real army-navy understanding and expressing pessimism about the accord, saying that "there were very few occasions that I could recall where the language of the mortgage had made the bonds good."[50] Almost sixty years later, however, George W. Bush's first national security advisor, Condoleezza Rice, would remark, "I think that they came up with a magnificent set of ad hoc solutions to a lot of bad problems. In retrospect it looks like an absolutely brilliant set of institutions that in fact turned out to be brilliant and lasted the test of time."[51]

After the signing of the National Security Act of 1947, Truman had, as most great men do, a bit of luck as far as his ambitions for the implementation of the reforms were concerned—although he hardly knew it at first. He asked Secretary of War Patterson to become the first secretary of national defense. Patterson refused. Truman then asked Forrestal to take the job, Forrestal accepted it, and was sworn in on September 17, 1947. Within a year, he too became a sterling example of the "Where you stand depends on where you sit" maxim. The new entity—the one he had eviscerated in a year of negotiations—was, after all, too weak. The new secretary needed real power. Truman finally had the advocate he needed to complete the reforms he had originally sought. Clifford would later write that Forrestal's conversion was "brave and enormously costly for him, alienating many of his closest friends in the Navy, and it added enormously to the strain under which he was working."[52]

Together Forrestal and Clifford proposed eleven new points of legislation, including the creation of a real Department of Defense with more authority, a deputy secretary of defense, and the reforms to the Joint Chiefs that they wanted, as well as reducing the statutory membership in the NSC to just four members and relocating the NSC to the Executive Office of the President. Delighted with the progress that had been made in the direction of the changes he wanted, Truman submitted the proposals to Congress, which passed them into law as the Reorganization Bill of 1949.

The National Security Act of 1947 did not create the position of national security advisor. That was to come a few years later in the Eisenhower administration. Instead, it created the position of executive director of the National Security Council. This job, which was envisioned as a low-key, staff secretarial job, initially went to Rear Admiral Sidney Souers. Souers, who, like Truman, had been a member of the military reserves and had a background in the private sector (Truman was a haberdasher; Souers ran a Piggly Wiggly, and later headed an early incarnation of the CIA), had a number of advantages. He was a poker-playing friend of the president and was therefore both trusted and unthreatening to his boss, who did harbor concerns that the NSC, if mismanaged, could encroach on his authority as president. The members of his staff were assigned from the armed services and generally performed a liaison role. The budget of the new entity was $200,000.

After attending the council's first meeting on September 26, 1947, Truman participated only sporadically in council discussions. Of the almost sixty meetings held before the onset of the Korean War, he attended only eleven. When the president was absent, the secretary of state chaired the meetings until the vice president was added to the council in the 1949 reforms; thereafter the vice president assumed the chair's role in the absence of the president. Truman chose this arm's-length approach because he wanted to ensure that no one thought he was captive to the council's decisions. The council would deliberate and then advise him. He would then determine whether or not to heed its advice.

During these first years, the council was gaining its sea legs. Prior to the 1949 reforms, the NSC was seen as unwieldy and its role was ill defined. The executive director, still the only statutorily named role on the council staff even though it is now a secondary position, was a support function, although a respected one. Clark Clifford continued to perform as a quasi national security advisor by retaining his role as the aide closest to the president in the White House with a national security and foreign policy brief. Later, when Averell Harriman became an assistant to the president, he played a similar role and Truman later made him a member of the council—the first time such an advisor was also actually on the group. Both of these men were trailblazers, establishing precedents for a certain type of policy leadership and advisory service to the president at the center of an evolving national security establishment. Historians have debated who was the first "true" national security advisor. It doesn't matter. Between them, they shaped the institution in its early days and helped it achieve legitimacy.

Truman initially called for meetings every two weeks, but after a while meetings became more sporadic. Truman resisted efforts early on to turn the group into an analog for the kind of cabinet government practiced in Britain, in which the decisions of the group took precedence over the decisions of an individual. Truman also asserted that Congress did not necessarily even have the authority to demand the president take any group's advice. Nonetheless, because he thought the policy coordination function was so important, he nurtured the group along, and it produced a significant number of papers. Reflective of the threat that gave birth to the NSC, the very first such paper, NSC-1/1, approved covert action in Italy to undercut efforts by the Italian Communist Party to take control in that country. Subsequent papers addressed further approvals for covert action, specific policy positions on evolving issues from Berlin to Asia, and overall policy regarding the U.S. use of nuclear weapons.

Early meetings were attended only by statutory members of the NSC, but gradually others joined them, and soon the meetings became, in the eyes of some participants, such as Forrestal, too big and unwieldy. Attendance lists were adjusted. Because many issues concerned budgeting and economic strength was seen as a key underpinning of national power, Truman required that his secretary of the treasury also start to attend.

In late 1949, Souers sought to return home to St. Louis to handle some personal matters. In a history of the NSC from its origins through to the last years of the Cold War, *Keepers of the Keys*, John Prados quotes Souers's memo to Truman advising him as to what qualities to look for in his successor, the next executive director of the NSC, as good advice for any president: "He should be a non-political confidant of the President—a trusted member of the President's immediate official family," but he "should not be identified with the immediate staff of personal advisers. He must be objective and willing to subordinate his personal views on policy to his task of coordinating the views of all responsible officials. . . . His job is not to sell the President an idea with which he is in sympathy but rather to insure that the views of all interested departments and agencies are reflected." He also noted that the executive director "must be willing to forgo publicity and personal aggrandizement."[53]

While there is much to recommend these views, as the job has evolved over the years, the quiet, neutral, facilitator role of the top man at the NSC would give way something quite different from what Souers could have expected. Truman obviously gave Souers's views a great deal of thought and respected them to such an extent that even as he promoted Souers's assistant, James Lay, into the executive director post, he asked Souers to stay on as a consultant, which he did.

Early in the life of the NSC, much as during its origins, the difficulties of balancing the conflicting interests of different cabinet departments headed by men with large egos and differing agendas became clear. Neither Dean Acheson, as secretary of state, nor Louis Johnson, who replaced Forrestal after the first secretary of defense committed suicide by jumping from his window at the Bethesda Naval Hospital, was always in harmony with the views of one another or with the procedures advanced by the NSC. Johnson, for example, believed that defense budgets needed to be contained, a view few of his successors would hold to. Acheson felt defense spending was critical to American strength and worked with Under Secretary Paul Nitze to produce aggressive spending plans to underwrite the military, new weapons such as the hydrogen bomb, and new programs to undercut communism worldwide. But in addition to spending on nuclear programs, the debate around this policy paper produced its own explosions—notably from Johnson, who balked at the State Department's efforts to use the NSC process to create a "consensus" view at odds with his own. He blew up, asserting that he would not be cornered into giving advice to the president that he did not hold with.

Truman's early concerns about the role of the NSC faded, however, as the organization faced its first major test with the onset of the Korean War in 1950. At that time, Truman immediately recognized the value of having the NSC serve as the mechanism for war planning and related foreign policy management, and he convened weekly meetings of the group, every Thursday. Thereafter, Truman missed only seven of the seventy-one NSC meetings held between the beginning of the war and the end of his term in office.

Given the importance the NSC was about to take in the war planning process, Truman initiated another series of reforms. Attendance at the meetings was limited to the named members, the treasury secretary, the chairman of the Joint Chiefs, the Director of Central Intelligence (DCI), and his assistants Harriman and Souers. Truman also refined the staff structure at the NSC, replacing the previous structure with individuals from the key agencies represented by the principals noted above. These would be the senior staff, and they in turn would be supported by staff assistants. This revitalized staff structure was particularly important in both tying together the activities of the several agencies and in providing the policy, drafting, and coordinating roles dictated by the leadership.

Other additions came later. One of special significance among them was the creation of the Psychological Strategy Board (PSB), which consisted of under secretary–level representatives from State, Defense, and CIA. The objective was to develop and manage the implementation of psychological warfare strategies that were seen to be central to victory in the Cold War.

For all these changes and despite the growing importance of the NSC, it lacked the staffing, the history, or the standing in the eyes of the principal makers of U.S. national security policy—notably the president of the United States—to be much more than an adjunct to other traditional means of policy creation and coordination. The president still relied more on personal staff members such as Harriman and Clifford, he still relied on conversations with old friends from the Senate, and his cabinet still sought the traditional independent status that their predecessors had enjoyed for centuries. Consequently, as the end of the second term of the president who created the NSC drew to a close, it was by no means certain that the institution would take hold or grow in power.

For Truman's three immediate successors, however, the precedents of his era and those first commitments to a permanent international leadership role for the United States, a policy of containment against the Soviet Union, and the institutions that such policies would require, would remain the critical foundations on which they themselves would build— or improvise—their approaches to wielding the ever-growing power of the free world's great superpower.

4

Gulliver Embarks: Leaders, Leadership, and the Difference Between the Two

If you wish to avoid foreign collisions, you had better avoid the ocean.
—Henry Clay

There are no wise few. Every aristocracy that has ever existed has behaved, in all essential points, exactly like a small mob.
—G.K. Chesterton, *Heretics*

Providence never intended to make the Management of publick Affairs a Mystery, to be comprehended only by a few Persons of sublime Genius, of which there seldom are three born in an Age.
—Jonathan Swift, *Gulliver's Travels*

LEMUEL GULLIVER had sailed for many years before his ship went aground northwest of Van Diemen's Land. But after his ship came apart on a great rock, he soon awoke to find himself bound to the earth by many small ropes and even his long hair. Around him were many small people, the citizens of Lilliput, and in that moment he discovered the strange sensation of being a giant, greater than all those around him, and at the same time being at the mercy of those who appeared to be much smaller than him.

Gulliver learns a great deal from this experience—and from his other experiences sailing to the remote corners of the globe, finding trouble, and escaping from it. And even though he is a fictional character whose author lived 350 years ago, much of what is reported in *Gulliver's Travels* has a ring of truth about it, as though it were written about the very subject of this book.

The "few Persons of sublime Genius" could have been a reference to the community of foreign policymakers who have long treated their discipline as a blend of science and art so exalted that no one could comprehend it who was not a member of their world, their clubs, and their old boy network. Certainly, almost any American today would find some truth in the observation that "whoever could make two ears of corn or two blades of grass to grow upon a spot of ground where only one grew before, would deserve better of mankind, and do more essential service to his country than the whole race of politicians put together."[1]

There are many tiny threads, some invisible, all surprisingly strong, that bind modern Gullivers. As the United States embarked on its new role as the world's most powerful nation in the days after the Second World War, it could hardly imagine that within a few years, for all its power, it would be constrained in ways that precluded victory in two small corners of Asia, or hamstrung in the United Nations that it created, or that the flip side of containment was being bogged down worldwide in small struggles that sapped our strength, tested our will, and made us wonder about the future of American power. In the same way, as the three presidents who presided over the new world that Truman had helped usher into being discovered, being the "leader of the free world" did not exactly mean that they possessed unlimited power. Even at home, they found that everything from political realities to their own foibles to the groupthink and intrigues among their advisors would frustrate them just as did the tiny restraints on the comparatively giant Gulliver.

.   .   .

There are few greater illustrations of the power of these constraints and the requisite ability of strong leaders to recognize such constraints and work within them than in the circumstances surrounding the presidency of Dwight David Eisenhower, one of the most often underestimated of our modern leaders. Eisenhower came into power with a set of attributes and circumstances that were auspicious at the very least and would seem to have been potentially awesome in terms of the power and latitude that they portended.

When Eisenhower ran for the presidency in 1952, America was still seen as the nation that saved the world and certainly as the planet's greatest power despite the rhetoric and saber-rattling of the Soviet leadership. Within America itself, there could hardly have been a more popular individual than Eisenhower, who had led 5 million Allied troops to victory in Europe and later also served as army chief of staff, the president of Columbia University, and then the first Supreme Allied Commander in Europe, the head of NATO's military forces. He brought with him decades of command and policy experience, a record of historic successes, and a Kansas-bred, all-American charm and warm image that was hard to beat in the America of the 1950s.

With such credentials and in such an environment, one might imagine that Eisenhower could have become the modern-day equivalent of Washington, the essential American, a man whose personal choices drove the nation that led the world. But in the modern America of political parties, of established checks and balances, of a deep belief that the system was greater than any individual, that was not the case. Eisenhower was wooed by both parties because of his appeal, much like Colin Powell in more recent times. The career-long independence required of military leaders makes them appealing to large groups in both parties (although the bases are always skeptical of the unaffiliated). But Eisenhower rebuffed Truman's entreaties (among others) that he become a Democrat (and in so doing alienated Truman to such a degree that the transition between the two was among the chilliest in memory, with nothing but a few pleasantries spoken in the car on the way to Eisenhower's swearing in).

Instead Eisenhower chose the Republican Party, in large part because he felt that Truman and his administration had been too "soft" in addressing the communist threat. This issue of relative toughness in fighting the perceived communist enemy was as central to the campaign of 1952 as the issue of relative toughness in fighting terrorism was in 2004. And, as in 2004, the Republican Party contained a range of views, from those of the conservative right, who felt that communism needed to be confronted and rolled back, to those of the more centrist or liberal Republican bent, who felt that the problem required a combination of strength and diplomatic adroitness—that it could be managed.

Anthony Lake, a keen student and noted teacher of U.S. national security policy and processes who served as national security advisor during Clinton's first term, observed about the 1952 election:

> It followed a lot of patterns we see today. Eisenhower was being pressured from the right in his own party, by people like Ohio Senator William Taft

and others, to take a very tough stance versus the communists and Truman's "softness" on communism. This boxed him in when he became president. This base was then pressuring him to take a tough stand early for "liberation" and to show that he would take a demonstrably different approach than did Truman, Acheson, Kennan, and their policy of containment.[2]

Lake went on to note that this phenomenon of being pressured by the political base of each party locks the candidates of the respective parties into patterns they have found it hard to break. Republicans, perceived by many during the postwar era as coming from a party that is tougher and more confrontational internationally, end up offering tougher rhetoric during campaigns and therefore are seen as more hard-line—which actually has positioned them to broaden their base by seeking peace or avoiding confrontation. Democrats, on the other hand, who are often seen as coming from a party that has been more historically antiwar, find themselves having to be more aggressive to broaden their base.

In short, patterns of American politics and the nature of our political system today impose a set of constraints that begin to work on our candidates before they are even elected to office. Eisenhower's constraints, though fewer than perhaps experienced by a lesser man or one who was less popular or one who did not, as he did, win election by a wide margin, were nonetheless reflected in the political calculus of Republican Party leaders of the day. As Richard Nixon writes in his memoirs, "Eisenhower wanted his campaign to be waged as a crusade against the corruption of the Truman Administration and against its foreign policy, which he felt had played into the Communists' hands in both Europe and Asia."[3] However, some in the party felt that Eisenhower's stance was not sufficiently hawkish toward communism, which led to the choice of Nixon as a running mate. Nixon notes that Eisenhower was viewed "as the candidate of the Republican party's Eastern liberal establishment,"[4] whereas Nixon was not only from the West but also, as a congressman, having led the pursuit of accused communist spy Alger Hiss, was seen as a strong anticommunist and one who could engage in tough political attacks while the general's reputation remained untarnished.

Nixon did as expected on the campaign trail, accusing Truman and especially Secretary of State Acheson of having lost China, much of Korea, and Eastern Europe to the communists. He tarred Democratic candidate Adlai Stevenson with the same brush, accusing him of having been a "graduate of Acheson's 'Cowardly College of Communist Containment'" and drew a clear distinction between the parties when he said that he would rather have a "khaki-clad President than one clothed in State Department pinks."[5]

While Nixon's language seems almost comically overstated, it was not inconsistent with the rhetoric of the times, which was heated to a boil by the red-baiting of men like Nixon and Senator Joseph McCarthy. Consequently, by the time he took office, Eisenhower faced a major challenge: how to develop a foreign policy that would actually work and not invite unneeded peril while still placating these strident voices within his party, on Capitol Hill, and even within his own administration.

.   .   .

The first steps for Eisenhower were to build an operating system for his government and a team to run it that worked for him. Unlike Truman, who came to the job ill-prepared for its managerial demands and who succeeded largely by virtue of the strength of his character and convictions, and unlike the calculated but debilitating disorganization of Roosevelt, and indeed, perhaps unlike any other president of the twentieth century to that point, Eisenhower came to the office with an extraordinary amount of organizational leadership experience and was thoroughly steeped in foreign policy and national security issues.

After decades of running army organizations, whether in the Philippines or as the head of policy planning at the outset of the Second World War or shortly thereafter as the Supreme Allied Commander in Europe, Eisenhower knew how to run a staff and make it work to his liking. Indeed, during the campaign he had even made an issue of the way Truman's White House staff, including the new National Security Council, was mismanaged. For this he had invited a Boston banker who had also been a brigadier general and military staff officer named Robert (Bobby) Cutler to draft two speeches attacking Truman and to make some recommendations about changes that might be needed to improve the structure. Once Ike was elected, one of his first orders of business was to adopt one of Cutler's ideas and create the new position of Special Assistant to the President for National Security Affairs, to which he appointed Cutler. Even before his inauguration Eisenhower introduced Cutler to his team as a central player and a man of cabinet stature.[6] This was a far cry from the concept of NSC leadership that had first evolved, but it was certainly what was needed, and the fact that the position survives to this day despite countless efforts to reinvent the NSC—and that it has only grown in power—is testimony to Eisenhower's judgment in perceiving the need for this position. Cutler's first task as the first official national security advisor was to prepare a detailed analysis of the NSC operation and make recommendations about its reform.

Cutler, an extremely intelligent, self-effacing man with an excellent sense of humor, began by talking to a number of those closest to the operations of the previous entity, including Eberstadt, Marshall, and Lovett, and with staff who had stayed on, including NSC Executive Director James Lay. Although this review showed Cutler that his critique of the Truman NSC had been too harsh, it also enabled him to propose a series of sweeping changes to restructure the NSC to provide the kind of organized, dependable, systematic staff support that Eisenhower demanded. "He knew how to use his staff," notes General William Odom, a former National Security Agency director. "And very few people understand what staff is and how to use it."[7]

Eisenhower had thought these issues through and had strong opinions about them. "Organization cannot make a genius out of an incompetent," he wrote in his memoirs, nor could it "make the decisions which are required to trigger necessary actions."[8] Disorganization, however, he felt, could "scarcely fail to result in inefficiency and can easily lead to disaster."[9]

At the heart of the Eisenhower organization was the Planning Board, a committee consisting of assistant secretary–level representatives from NSC agencies and chaired by Cutler. The purpose of the group was to gather the policy views of each of the key cabinet departments on critical issues. Then the "board subjected those positions to what Cutler called an 'acid bath,' sharply delineating them and identifying and specifying points of disagreement. The board was strictly instructed not to water down disagreements or cover them up. Instead 'policy splits' were to be spelled out (often in parallel columns) so that they might be debated by the NSC and resolved by the President."[10] Some future NSCs would take a different approach—seeking to build consensus on a view advising the president—but the Eisenhower-Cutler approach required significantly more courage from participating bureaucrats. It is always easier to hide within a consensus and a process that demands one. When the process demands your best thinking, even if it is at odds with everyone else, the policymaker is more exposed but the president has the benefit of real choices.

Another component of Eisenhower's system was clear instructions to his team that they were to act as presidential advisors rather than as representatives of their individual agencies. Naturally, in Washington, this was not always possible given institutional pressures. Eisenhower soon recognized that it was even less possible in larger meetings, where multiple agency representatives might be present, and he came, as all presidents ultimately do, to strongly discourage larger gatherings in favor of a larger number of smaller ones.

The Planning Board usually met twice a week. Its job was to push ideas up the "policy hill" to the principals of the NSC, laying out matters clearly enough that all knew exactly where the best minds at each agency stood, where the divisions were, and what the questions the president needed to resolve were. The NSC itself, atop this "hill," met every Thursday morning, usually around 10:00 a.m. Eisenhower was typically present and active in these meetings; in fact, he attended almost 90 percent of the 366 sessions held during his presidency. When he was not present, Vice President Nixon or the secretary of state chaired the sessions. This was a much more regularized process than during the Truman period and, indeed, much more regular than the process would be again for decades, if ever. Former Defense Secretary James Schlesinger notes that Eisenhower "had NSC meetings, as I recall, once a week, maybe once every other week, but they met all the time. And if you turned on the radio you would hear that 'the president today again met with the National Security Council'; there was no mention of what they discussed, but he met regularly with them. And I think that what you have is . . . a reflection of the personalities of the president and that over the years, since the 1950s in particular, American society has become more and more informal and . . . that formal procedures are regarded increasingly as an encumbrance."[11]

But if there is one maxim that is repeated in virtually every text written on the subject of providing national security decision support for the president, it is that the system must be organized to suit the personality, needs, and style of the president—and this system suited Eisenhower to a tee. (He did not take a similar interest in the day-to-day management of domestic affairs, which he left more to White House Chief of Staff Sherman Adams and Secretary of the Treasury George Humphrey, with Adams earning the sobriquet "deputy president" in this regard.)

Once the policy was determined by the president in an NSC meeting, it was passed on to the other important new committee created in the Eisenhower system: the Operations Coordinating Board (OCB). This committee was created to ensure the implementation of policies, and as such it formed the downhill slope of the "policy hill." It was chaired by the under secretary of state and included deputy or under secretary–level representatives from other agencies. It reported back to the NSC on the progress that was being made in implementing policies and on decisions taken to implement them. Cutler was actively involved in both of these creations and ensured that they worked in a disciplined way within the portions of the policy apparatus assigned to them, but he personally chaired the policymaking side of the operation rather than the implementation side.

In addition to this system, Eisenhower sought to bring together an inner circle that reflected his personal views and could work with him. Not surprisingly, many of these individuals were former military officers with whom he had worked during his army years. In one famous incident, frustrated by the inability of his team in the early days to follow through on assignments they had been given, he announced, "I do not intend to be my own Sergeant Major."[12] Several days later a similar problem arose, and he repeated the assertion. He then assigned Brigadier General Paul "Pete" Carroll to the staff secretary role he had grown used to when commanding troops. Sadly, Carroll died young, just a year or so later, and he was replaced by another officer who had served with Eisenhower at NATO, Colonel (soon to be General) Andrew Goodpaster. Goodpaster became his principal aide covering foreign policy and national security matters and occupied the office next to the president's. He played the role of fixer, envoy, and confidant and managed to do so without inflaming potential rivalries with other members of the team. Of course, as Goodpaster noted to me, Eisenhower would not have tolerated signs of such rivalries and, as he does in so many areas, Goodpaster gives credit for the smooth operations of the team to his boss.[13]

The White House congressional liaison office was headed by General Wilton Persons, and Eisenhower's old chief of staff General Walter Bedell Smith was CIA director. Seldom had there been, even in wartime, more military brass in and around the pinnacle of U.S. power. Yet Eisenhower is also known for having carefully framed the potential threat of the growing power of the U.S. "military-industrial" complex. This kind of balance was typical of Eisenhower, who sought even to balance his close personal staff, his military colleagues, and his other cabinet staff with regular use of outside advisors and consultants, including from heads of organizations as diverse as Standard Oil and the Steel Workers, Monsanto Chemical, and several universities.

Once his well-conceived group of advisors and advisory structure was in place, augmented by powerful cabinet secretaries like Secretary of State John Foster Dulles, to whom Eisenhower regularly turned and whom he gave considerable lead to when it came to articulating and serving as the spokesperson for U.S. foreign policy, Eisenhower could turn his attention to the great issues of his day. Naturally, high on the list was addressing his promise to "go to Korea" and to find an acceptable end to that surprisingly costly and intractable contest. But also looming at the top of his list was what to do more broadly about the threat of communism and what stance to adopt. Should he—must he—respond to the aggressive demands from within his own party to take steps to "roll back" communism? Or was there another path that would not repeat what he saw as Truman's mistakes and yet would not produce some of the explosive and potentially devastating consequences of a rollback approach gone wrong?

To handle this issue, Eisenhower once again used a carefully crafted process and a carefully selected group of individuals whom he knew he could count on to achieve the outcome he wanted. This effort, known as the Solarium Project because the participants met in the solarium of the White House, produced a foreign policy outcome that rivals Kennan's "long telegram" or his "X" article for its importance to the formation of U.S. policy in the second half of the twentieth century. It also underscores the influence of ad hoc processes when they are personal initiatives of the president.

Goodpaster, one of the participants, described the situation and the approach: "You had the death of Stalin early in 1953. And there were a lot of ideas back then about what should be done. People around the president, high up in the government, wanted to capitalize on it. A lot of people brought a lot of agendas to this issue and tried to push them on the president. He didn't respond too well to that kind of pressure, and he did not want to get swept up in a political wave."[14]

Goodpaster continued: "The military, the chiefs, had had this idea of a "date of maximum danger"—which was a notion Eisenhower did not accept when he was at NATO or then as president. He said, Look, the danger exists. It's going to increase in some ways. It's going to decrease in some ways. And we will just have to deal with that."[15] But special interest groups in the party and the military were unrelenting on this point because they felt it would bring matters to a head with the communists. Eisenhower, according to Goodpaster, who was one of his closest aides throughout this process, began to handle the situation by consulting with Dulles at State, Cutler on the NSC, and key White House staff.[16]

One way Eisenhower sought to counter communism was by "projecting America's story abroad," as Goodpaster put it.[17] This involved a restructuring and reemphasis in the whole psychological warfare process. Truman's Psychological Strategy Board had been folded into the Operations Coordinating Board because the Eisenhower team, seeking a coherent view of all policy options and choices, thought that to separate psychological tools from others at our disposal was a mistake. But the Eisenhower team still believed in the power of psychological warfare because they had seen it work during the Second World War and because it was especially well suited to the demands of the Cold War.

In May 1953 White House solarium, Eisenhower sought to define the core, fully integrated policy toward the principal threat we faced: communism. "Eisenhower came up with the idea of identifying three alternative main lines of basic policy. One would be containment. The second would be drawing a line with the threat of full-scale retaliation if that line were breached. And third was a rollback, the idea which had figured prominently in the campaign. Eisenhower's idea was to set up a small group of very carefully selected people."[18] Headed by Cutler, Dulles, and Walter Smith, the NSC-led task force included George Kennan, Dean Rusk, General James Doolittle, and Admiral Leslie Stevens, who in 1951 had given a lecture to the National War College about the need to compose a "national strategy" that had impressed Eisenhower.[19]

Goodpaster observed it all from his office next to the president. Today he sits amid books and papers at the Eisenhower Institute and rattles off the details of these sessions like they were yesterday. Around him are articles he is working on, books by friends and old colleagues, and a few mementos, including a small bust of himself, one of the many awards he has won over a long and distinguished career. Now one of the eldest of Washington's foreign policy elder statesman, he is a permanent member of the inner circle whose opinion to this day carries considerable weight.

"Eisenhower put each of these men in charge of a group of seven or eight people, each charged with making the very best case they could for that particular line of policy. I was still serving with NATO in Europe at the time and he brought me back to participate in the 'rollback' group. And he told me later, he said, 'Well, I wanted to be sure that I had one man that I could at least hope had some common sense participating in the rollback study.'" This last comment was a sign not just of how the general bonded with his staff—he once commented that he'd be a happy man if his son grew up to be like Goodpaster—but it also offered an insight into Eisenhower's views of the more extreme advocates of rollback within his party and the administration.[20]

We met very secretly during the summer of 1953 on the National War College grounds, they being out of session during that summer; a hot summer, I might say. And we worked for about five weeks to generate the best case we could; each for his respective line of policy. At the end, we met in the White House in the library on the ground floor. Eisenhower had the heads of the cabinet departments, their number twos, number threes, and the chiefs were there. Each group made its presentation of about forty-five minutes. And at the end of it, Eisenhower himself jumped up and said, 'Now I'd like to summarize and comment on what we've heard,' . . . and he spoke without a note for about forty-five minutes.[21]

And as George Kennan said to me, he showed his intellectual ascendancy over every man in the room. And I said on occasion, George, that includes you and me. And George would say, Yes, because Eisenhower understood the military side of it as well as the foreign policy side. And he understood the foreign policy side as well as the military side. And out of that, he drew a conclusion as to what should be the central line of policy, which was essentially containment, with, as Eisenhower said, drawing language from the rollback group, "keeping the hope of freedom alive."[22]

Eisenhower was caricatured as a kind of "president in a gray flannel suit," a corporate president who liked memos and papers and process more than substance. In retrospect, however, it is clear that this is terribly unfair. What Eisenhower did with the Solarium Project was to make all those who had strong views feel that they were being heard. James Schlesinger describes the Solarium exercise "as moving from the rhetoric of the campaign, and not particularly Ike's rhetoric but the Republican rhetoric in general down to what today is referred to sometimes derisively as a realistic foreign policy. So they jettisoned the notion that we were going to destroy the Soviet Union and that we were going to roll back its gains."[23] Eisenhower felt the political constraints on him and, rather than struggling against them, he worked within them, producing an outcome that in the end was authored by all factions and thus was hard for any to go against.

The issue in play was the most consequential of the second half of the twentieth century, not just for the United States, but for the entire planet. Had Eisenhower played politics and acted in a way that pandered to the rhetoric of the anticommunist extremists in his party, it could have precipitated a confrontation with our nuclear adversary, resulting at the very least in a bloody war and at the most extreme, a nuclear catastrophe that would have altered life on this planet irrevocably.

The Solarium Project therefore was not just the work of a good executive or a master bureaucrat or even a canny politician; it was a magisterial illustration of an effective president in action, perhaps one of the signal events of the past sixty years of the American presidency. Naturally, there were many other actions and decisions in and around Eisenhower's presidency at the time that reinforced this view, and it would be unfair not to note that what he was building on were Truman policies that he himself had criticized. But imagine a lesser man in the job—which is not so difficult, given his coronary artery disease, his heart attack, his stroke, and his young, inexperienced, comparatively more hawkish vice president. (And indeed, that young vice president benefited later during his own presidency from the tutelage of the often underestimated but nonetheless estimable general, even though, as Schlesinger notes, he "observed [the process] from somewhat afar.")[24]

As Goodpaster notes, after this process, the "notion of a rollback with either military action or the threat of military action sank without a trace at that time. And instead we shifted our focus to keeping the hope of freedom alive and doing whatever the CIA could do to assist groups that would be resistant to subjugation or domination by the Soviets."[25]

Goodpaster softens a bit and then says introspectively, "I have often felt and said, I don't think we told Eisenhower a thing that he had not thought of in advance. And I think he knew precisely where he wanted us to come out, and he wanted to have this group of people hear it all—in the term that we came to use—'each in the presence of all,' and have it very thoroughly aired. And then he asked that we stay and work all of this into a basic national security policy paper. We'd been away from our homes and really working very hard for about five weeks and we resisted that and got him to turn it over to the NSC Planning Board under Bobby Cutler. And they generated what was called the Basic National Security Policy Paper that was really the guideline for the Eisenhower administration."[26]

Goodpaster emphasizes when he reflects on these days that Eisenhower was under a lot of pressure also from former colleagues in the military, the Joint Chiefs especially, who felt that he would be responsive to their admonishment that the United States seek a "showdown" with the Soviet Union. "Eisenhower said," he recalls, "that the last thing in the world I would ever do is push them to a showdown; we've got to work our way through this. So he'd given a lot of thought to the nuclear issue—he had been working on it since 1945, I had worked it with him at NATO—and his awareness of where the invention of the fusion weapon [the hydrogen bomb] could lead in terms of devastation was deeply on his mind. And that's how he came up with his so-called Atoms for Peace Initiative. I've forgotten how many drafts of that he told me he had worked through, it's something like twenty. So, he brought the government into line with his views through clear thinking, a strong commitment, and a lot of hard work."[27]

This activist involvement in initiatives that were important to him not only belies the caricatures of Eisenhower as disconnected, it also illustrates an important element of his interpretation of the role of president as "conductor." He orchestrated his advisors and the leaders around him into a chorus supporting his views. Naturally, he was not always successful, but he was certainly better than he was given credit for at the time. Part of his success is due to his ability simply to play the part. He was a good actor. One story that illustrates this point is told by James Schlesinger, who, as a young man, was teaching at the Naval War College in Newport, Rhode Island, one summer. Eisenhower stayed in a house on the grounds as a kind of vacation getaway and would occasionally be seen by the faculty, who watched him with avid interest. He would take a small launch from his house to a waiting car at another location on the oceanfront grounds of the college and then be driven off to meetings. One day, during the height of the desegregation battles around the time of *Brown v. Board of Education,* the launch was seen coming across and Schlesinger and others gathered to catch a glimpse of the president. He got out of the boat and into his car, where he was briefed—presumably on the situation in Little Rock—by a staff aide. Eisenhower was then seen to turn beet red and grab the aide by the lapels and scream at him. He was clearly furious, according to Schlesinger, but when the president realized he was being observed, he instantly changed his entire demeanor—his complexion returned to normal and he resumed his famous avuncular smile, waved, and drove off.

There are many similar reports about Eisenhower's temper and his willingness to use it in close quarters. Many close to him, including Nixon and the general's wartime chief of staff General Walter Bedell Smith, commented on the stresses of taking the heat so that their boss could appear to be the happy grandfather that the public loved. In Nixon's memoirs, he quotes Smith as reminiscing about his years with Eisenhower late one night, growing somewhat emotional and saying with tears welling up in his eyes, "I was just Ike's prat boy. Ike always had to have a prat boy, someone who'd do the dirty work for him. He always had to have someone else who could do the firing, or the reprimanding, or give any orders which he knew people would find unpleasant to carry out. Ike always has to be the nice guy."[28] Similarly, Schlesinger recalls that "in public, he let Dulles go out and take the heat on all sorts of things like massive retaliation while Eisenhower just smiled and was the good guy."[29]

Eisenhower knew how to work his inner circle. Some would gather for drinks with the president late each day in his office—Adams, Persons, Cutler, his second-term national security advisor Gordon Gray, John Foster Dulles, some of his colleagues from the military, and the outside advisors that he invited to join as informal consultants to his inner circle. Some played golf with him. They cultivated easy access and he grew to know them well enough that he could read them as he needed to. In meetings, he would systematically go through the group seeking their views, ensuring that they felt they had his respect and were being consulted. Often he would begin with John Foster Dulles on foreign policy issues and then would turn to Dulles's brother Allen, who ran the CIA after Bedell Smith, to give an intelligence briefing. If financial issues were involved— and Eisenhower prided himself on recognizing the importance of good fiscal management, actually requiring that all NSC policy papers have analysis of any and all financial implications appended to them—he might turn to George Humphrey of Treasury. Then he would step in and, as Goodpaster described, take over the meeting and discuss the issue, play devil's advocate where he had to, challenge ideas, drill down to the bedrock questions underlying the issue.

Goodpaster comments, "He wanted to be sure that everybody was there who had a real hand and responsibility in the area. We had a couple of ground rules. No nonconcurrence through silence. People were obliged to speak up. And the problem would be aired 'by each in the presence of all.' And if we got the decision right then as we left, then that's what we were going to do."[30]

> There were a couple of lapses early in the administration. Once, a man from the Defense Department came out of a meeting and stated in a public setting that "this is what was decided but I didn't agree with it." The man quickly came to understand that his future was very short. There was a clear understanding that we weren't going to do that and that provided a discipline of decision making. Ike would do the same with Congress too. The cabinet secretaries would give a brief and then Eisenhower would say this is where I think we should go but I want to know where you stand. And at that point the recognized leader from the Congress, [Georgia Senator] Dick Russell, for instance, would say, Mr. President, that's a decision for you to make. And Eisenhower would say, Yes, I'm prepared to make it, but I need to know whether you're really going to stand with me. There would be some squirming around but he really held to it. And he said—not to them but to us—on occasion, I saw them walk out on Harry Truman, and by God they're not going to do that to me.[31]

While Allen Dulles and CIA senior staff such as Bedell Smith were actively involved in policy discussions, it is also clear that Eisenhower did not want intelligence to be dominated by policymakers. They were to serve, as provided for in the National Security Act of 1947, as advisors, just as the military were. The 5412 Committee, an executive body also known as the "Special Group", established by NSC-5412/2 in December 1955 to review and approve covert action programs initiated by the CIA, handled intelligence operations and other such issues. Concerns such as reconnaissance missions and the U-2 flights that caused such consternation late in Eisenhower's tenure were handled by people like Goodpaster at arm's length from the president. The national security advisor—Cutler or his successors (Gray during the Gary Powers U-2 crisis)—would report to the president on decisions of the group, but he was careful to keep the processes separate. Schlesinger observes:

Ike, of course, was superb at this particular business. If you look at the structure of intelligence, and by structure I include all of the assets of the photo satellites, U-2s, and so forth, all of that came right out of Ike's head. It is still the way we do business today. The offshore reconnaissance of the Soviet Union, he took all of this seriously. The portrait of Eisenhower that you get from liberal historians or from the liberal press is about this simpleton who wandered around golf courses. It is just a total misapprehension of how he handled his office. But what he cared about, which was relations with the Soviet Union in particular, and staying out of Southeast Asia, for example, he was totally in charge.[32]

Eisenhower was an experienced consumer of intelligence. Indeed, Goodpaster notes that he would have had very little patience for some of the discussions that were taking place during 2004 about intelligence reform because they were predicated on a faulty notion: that the intelligence process was perfectible. Eisenhower knew what bad intelligence good intelligence teams could produce.[33] The intelligence operation that helped him win the Second World War is also the one that told him a few days before Christmas during the winter of 1944 that "there was activity around Maastricht but we're not sure what it is" (in Goodpaster's words).[34] What they missed was the massing of the German army before their final great offensive, the one that produced the Battle of the Bulge.

Eisenhower used experience, toughness, and guile to achieve a number of major policy victories and his ultimate goal of ensuring that the world was peaceful and stable on his watch. But, of course, he did not always achieve what he sought to do. A telling and resonant example lies in the growing set of problems the administration faced in Indochina. Early in 1954, Eisenhower sent 200 U.S. military mechanics to Indochina to support French operations in that country in their fight with communist insurgents led by Ho Chi Minh. However, the French continued to suffer setbacks, and within the NSC the debate turned to what to do. Admiral Arthur Radford, chairman of the Joint Chiefs, proposed a plan called Operation Vulture, in which the United States would use three tactical nuclear weapons to send a strong signal to the insurgents that once the United States got involved, the conflict would not go their way and that they should retreat. Eisenhower and Dulles did not embrace this approach, feeling that it would be warranted only in the face of blatant Chinese intervention in the conflict. However, Eisenhower also felt that it was likely that the situation would deteriorate further, and in March of that year he seemed to be warming to the idea of more U.S. involvement, warning congressional leaders that he might have to undertake such steps on very short notice if the tide at the battle of Dien Bien Phu turned much worse.

As reports from the battle came in suggesting that the situation was growing graver for the French each day, NSC deliberations addressed the importance of getting other allies involved. Nixon urged Eisenhower on, arguing that he had great strength with the Congress and should he lead, they would follow. But Eisenhower was unsure because, despite his strength and the options available to the United States, he was worried about the message that our acting alone would send, and he felt that support from the Congress and from abroad was equally shaky. Nixon wrote in his diary, "The President had backed down considerably from the strong position he had taken on Indochina in the latter part of the previous week. He seemed resigned to doing nothing at all unless we could get the allies and the country to go along,"[35] and he was skeptical about whether that was possible.

Nonetheless, that spring, Dulles went to Europe to try to get the British and the French to join in a concerted opposition to the communists throughout the region. Radford met with Churchill, who put him off by noting that if the British were unwilling to fight to save India it was highly unlikely that they would be willing to fight to save a corner of Asia with which they had few if any historical ties.

The Ho Chi Minh–led forces, however, scored new victories, and by the NSC meeting on April 29, matters were very grave. Nixon wrote: "The President was extremely serious and seemed to be greatly concerned about what was the right course to take. After the reports were made, Harold Stassen said that he thought that decision should be to send ground troops if necessary to save Indochina and to do it on a unilateral basis if that was the only way it could be done."[36] His diary entry concludes with a paragraph that could just as easily have been written about President George W. Bush's deliberations about Iraq. It reflects a classic dilemma for American leaders as they discover that great power alone is not enough to enable them to act as they might want to elsewhere in the world: "The President himself said that he could not visualize a ground troop operation in Indochina that would be supported by the people of the United States and which would not in the long run put our defense too far out of balance. He also raised the point that we simply could not go in unilaterally because that was in violation of our whole principle of collective defense against communism in all places in the world."[37]

In this respect, Eisenhower was very much a product of the times, a strong believer in the need for functioning international institutions and alliances to act as our first line of defense—well ahead of the option of the United States acting alone. As it happened, by early May, Dien Bien Phu had been overrun by the Vietminh, and the French were out of Indochina soon afterward. The open wound festered, however, and the debate about how to treat it would preoccupy the next three presidents of the United States.

During Eisenhower's second term in office he had to contend not only with a decline in his health—which underscored the value of the strong NSC system he had put in place—but also with a series of troubling developments that caused Americans to wonder aloud whether we had entered a period of decline relative to our great adversary. In 1957, the Soviets beat the U.S. into space with Sputnik. Tensions with the communists in Asia flared repeatedly. By the time the Soviets blocked the progress of a small U.S. convoy on its way to Berlin, the pressure to take strong action was great, and the military offered options for sending in up to 20,000 troops should the Soviets block the main Berlin access route again.

Eisenhower took charge again, but instead of working entirely within the NSC process, he relied on a series of smaller meetings with advisors in the Oval Office and a process managed by his national security advisor at the time, Gordon Gray. Gray had succeeded not only Cutler, who did two stints as national security advisor broken up by a short term by Dillon Anderson, but also the temporary service of William H. Jackson. Gray was the son of a tobacco millionaire and a very smooth, courtly gentleman who lacked Cutler's directness but who was also highly experienced in national security matters, handling issues as diverse as the security clearance of physicist J. Robert Oppenheimer and the direction of the Office of Defense Mobilization.

During his tenure, Gray actually expanded the role established by Cutler, both through his own skills and because the president was less healthy and needed a close national security advisor who could take up the slack. During the Berlin crisis, for example, Gray managed the process of collecting interagency views on how to handle the problem. The State Department and the Pentagon dragged their feet and submitted their papers only shortly before the NSC session at which they were to be considered. This annoyed Gray, who suggested to the president that he might actually play more of an enforcer role with the agencies, ensuring that they fully met the president's needs. He also sought and received clearance to oversee the creation of contingency plans for the U.S. government in the case of different outcomes in Berlin and like situations. The president granted his requests to broaden his role and authority, and the result was that by 1960, some thirteen years after the creation of the NSC, the role of the national security advisor had finally assumed much of the authority and scope of responsibility of its equivalent today. Gray brought the position a long way forward—even making it somewhat more visible than it had been under Cutler, who thought the job required a "passion for anonymity."[38]

The Berlin crisis itself also produced the move away from formal NSC sessions in times of crisis that would mark most presidencies. Although it took Eisenhower longer to make this move, given his love for process, in the end, he found that large formal meetings that involved rows of back-benchers from various agencies were not conducive to the kind of frank, open discussions with every person serving the president rather than his own agency. At the same time, he sought support from his NSC staff to provide the papers and options discussed in the meetings that would later be cited as the precedent for the growing influence of the staff itself as a player in the policy creation process. In terms of tactics, the Berlin problem was solved through the methodical, unflappable approach to working these kinds of issues that Eisenhower had embraced early as a consequence of the Solarium Project. Behind-the-scenes negotiations, also involving the British, produced a willingness on the part of the Russians to consider a summit to discuss the issue.

Ultimately, the shooting down of a U-2 reconnaissance plane during the election year of 1960 would sour the Russians on the summit idea and produce a heated campaign debate on the effectiveness and toughness of the Eisenhower administration. The young Democratic candidate, John F. Kennedy, like Eisenhower before him, made an issue of the way the president had used his National Security Council, which was seen as an ineffective "paper mill." A critical congressional review of the NSC by another influential Democratic senator, Henry "Scoop" Jackson, of Washington, fed the Kennedy criticisms and the public view that something was wrong in the Eisenhower White House. Ironically, Kennedy even managed during the campaign to take a stand to the right of his opponent, Vice President Nixon, on issues such as toughness with the communists in Southeast Asia and Cuba—largely because Nixon felt politically constrained from showing his real hawkish views, as they might alienate the center in a hotly contested race. Later, this strange switch of roles would box Kennedy into certain hawkish stands that would cause him and the world great unease and even embarrassment.

5

Bound in Lilliput

I guess the way you learn to do things is to do them imperfectly.
—McGeorge Bundy

PRIOR TO THE 1960 campaign, Kennedy had taken positions on Fidel Castro and communism in the Western hemisphere that put him, in true senatorial fashion, in several places on the issue. On the one hand, he had accused the Eisenhower administration of mishandling Castro's takeover in Cuba by claiming, in the book *The Strategy of Peace*, that if they had offered the "fiery young rebel a warmer welcome in his hour of triumph, especially on his trip to this country," perhaps the young, baseball-loving new leader of the island nation might not have "gone over" to the communist side.[1] The implication of this remark, later the object of much criticism, was that somehow Castro was not driven by any internal aspect of his character, but rather that he existed only relative to the United States and that our reaction to him made him who he was. This is a fascinating example of the national narcissism that recurs throughout our recent history.

Earlier Kennedy had said, "There is little question that should any Latin country be driven by repression into the arms of the Communists, our attitude on non-intervention would change overnight. . . . We know—or surely ought to know—that Latin America is certainly as essential to our security as Southeast Asia."[2] This analysis, which later proved to be false or at least open to debate, suggested that perhaps the warm embrace he had thought would have "turned" Castro was not the approach most in line with the interests of the American people.

Both statements, however, have to be seen more in their political context than from the point of view of objective analysis. Kennedy was positioning himself to run for president when the upheavals in Cuba were an issue dominating the headlines; many Americans were worried about the impact of having a communist satellite state ninety miles off the coast of Florida, or "eight minutes by jet," as Kennedy put it. He was trying to stake out a position that was differentiated from that of the Eisenhower administration and to weaken them and their likely candidate, Vice President Nixon.

Afraid of being attacked for his youth and inexperience, Kennedy felt it was important to establish his bona fides when it came to the Cold War. The result was that as the campaign heated up, Kennedy moved farther and farther to the right on the issue—so far to the right, in fact, that his stance produced a set of circumstances that might have been comic were they not, in the end, so painful.

The Eisenhower administration had been closely monitoring events in Cuba since Castro's takeover in January 1959. In the circles closest to the president, in the 5412 Committee that handled intelligence issues, and in the CIA—and egged on by staunch anticommunists such as the vice president—plans had been put into motion to depose Castro. Such efforts, successful earlier in the decade in places such as Guatemala and Iran, were seen as an essential part of Cold War strategy then and did not fall into disrepute until the 1970s.

These operations were, of course, secret. Consequently, Nixon found himself in the absurd position of working during his day job on plans to depose Castro and then in his campaign work trying to fend off attacks claiming that not enough was being done and that the Eisenhower administration had been ineffective or even "soft" in its response to the emerging communist threat in Cuba—but without being able to cite the secret work being done behind the scenes.

Kennedy stepped into, as it turns out, one of the classic traps of the U.S. political system.[3] He was trapped by ambition, party, and circumstance into a position that would ultimately trigger the greatest political division in postwar American history and would lead to a profound national introspection and questioning of our credentials and capabilities as a superpower and "leader of the free world."

The ambition that motivated Kennedy was clear. He was willing to run a tough, aggressive, and ruthless campaign designed to seize every advantage possible. The election was going to be close, and he would need to fight for every vote (or at least those that could not be bought, as some have alleged).[4]

As for the role party played in cornering Kennedy into the position of having to err in the direction of confrontation and ultimately entanglement with the communists, one element had to do with running in the wake of two unsuccessful campaigns by Adlai Stevenson, the erudite Illinois politician who would later play a role in Kennedy's own dramas as his UN ambassador and who was an advisor to Kennedy during the race. Stevenson was not seen as tough enough, and during the 1950s the Republican Party had become the party of America's greatest war hero. In fact, it was during the Eisenhower administration that the Republicans came to be seen as the party that was willing to engage more resolutely in the overseas battle against communism, whereas earlier they had been perceived as a voice for American isolation. Kennedy felt he could not win in the current environment if the Democrats presented themselves as anything but steel-willed.

Circumstances, of course, played an enormous role in this trap. Eisenhower's administration had been very effective in keeping the peace, strengthening alliances, and sending a consistently tough message to our adversaries. In retrospect, that seems clear. But, at the time, after the postwar euphoria had ebbed and as we had increasingly become aware of our limitations, the constraints on our allies, and the power of our main adversary, doubt crept in about the certainty of American domination in this new era.

Kennedy exploited the national uncertainty. In late October 1960, Kennedy denigrated the administration (and in particular Vice President Nixon, known for his confrontation with Nikita Khrushchev in a model kitchen in Moscow—the famous "kitchen debate") by saying, "If you can't stand up to Castro, how can you be expected to stand up to Khrushchev?"[5] Nixon, squirming because he could not detail the steps that were secretly being planned within the councils of the president, could hardly contain himself, and in mid-October he implied that steps had been taken to help fight Castro. The very next day, Kennedy, apparently fearing an "October surprise" invasion of Cuba, gave a speech in which he stated, "We must attempt to strengthen the . . . democratic anti-Castro forces, in exile and in Cuba itself, who offer eventual hope of overthrowing Castro. Thus far, these fighters for freedom have had virtually no support from our government."[6] In so doing, he evoked the political corollary to the old admonition "Be careful of what you wish for"— although in politics it is a little worse: "Be careful of what you call for—as you may actually have to end up doing it." General William Odom, head of the National Security Agency under Reagan and Zbigniew Brzezinski's military aide, recounts:

I once asked Goodpaster if Eisenhower had still been in office in the spring of 1961, would we still have had the Bay of Pigs. He said, "Interesting you bring that up . . ." [CIA Deputy Director for Plans] Richard Bissell initiated the planning, I guess in '59, and the idea, according to Goodpaster, was to create a Cuban military unit that could, after Fidel had been overthrown, enter Cuba and become the core of a post-Fidel Cuban army. The objective for the plan was not to overthrow Fidel. Eisenhower approved this limited concept only for the contingency that Castro's regime collapsed or was overthrown by Cubans in Cuba. The CIA-created force was not to invade Cuba. No invasion, no provocations. Eisenhower was briefed on it in the summer of '60. General Goodpaster, as Eisenhower's staff secretary, took the notes at the meeting with Bissell and his assistants. After they met, Goodpaster turned to Ike and said, "Mr. President, if you don't watch it, that plan will take legs of its own." Eisenhower snapped back, "Not while I am president!" Goodpaster responded, "Yes, Mr. President. That's the problem. You won't be president much longer."[7]

Within days the likely significance of Eisenhower's hand leaving the tiller of state became clear as the heat of the political campaign began to influence the debate between his young would-be successors. Nixon labeled Kennedy's call for arming rebels "probably the most dangerously irresponsible recommendation that [Kennedy] had made during the course of the campaign."[8] This was a moment of magnificent hypocrisy in American politics: Nixon allegedly felt that Kennedy's recommendation was irresponsible because Kennedy was calling for something that he knew, if it was actually being implemented, would necessarily remain secret—and in fact he had been briefed on the plans. In private, within the Oval Office and in other senior White House gatherings, it was Nixon who had been the one advocating arming the anti-Castro Cubans. As Trumbull Higgins writes in *The Perfect Failure: Kennedy, Eisenhower, and the CIA at the Bay of Pigs*, "One wonders what Nixon had in mind when he said that Kennedy's policy (and his own in secret) would violate five American treaties, 'would lose all our friends in Latin America . . . [and] would be an open invitation to Mr. Khrushchev to come . . . into Latin America.'"[9] In fact, as Higgins points out, Nixon was actually pushing for an invasion of Cuba from Guatemala before the election to help his own candidacy. This spiral of hypocrisy produced one bizarre certainty: The only group in America that saw the alignment between Nixon's hidden beliefs and Kennedy's politically calibrated beliefs were the leaders in the CIA who drew encouragement for their plans from both sides.

Consequently, CIA Director Allen Dulles and Deputy Director for Plans Richard Bissell proceeded with their planning for an invasion of Cuba manned in large part by anti-Castro Cubans. In doing so, they continued a trend in their agency to move from being objective analysts of intelligence to being advocates for particular policies. It was not at all what had been intended by the National Security Act of 1947, and it would ultimately burden the CIA for many years to come, after it produced too many mistakes—of which the one cooking in late 1960 would go down in history as perhaps the biggest of all. The planning process continued in meetings held through the last days of the Eisenhower administration.

When Kennedy came into office, one of the first things he set about doing was dismantling the Eisenhower NSC apparatus. He had attacked it during the campaign in yet another politically motivated critique that ended up haunting him. Now it was time for a change. As in all such cases, the change began with the people with whom the president surrounded himself. At the center of this group was new national security advisor, McGeorge Bundy.

It's galling (for a Columbia graduate) to realize that once again the pivotal moment in this historical choice seems to have come at a Harvard graduation ceremony. Bundy, then dean of Harvard's Arts and Sciences Faculty, was sitting on the platform and found himself next to Harvard overseer and graduate, John F. Kennedy. They began to speak, and Kennedy asked Bundy if he would interested in helping out with the campaign. Bundy agreed and, from that casual beginning, was soon an important national security advisor to the president.

Bundy had descended from two of America's most patrician families, the Lowells and the Bundys of Boston; had attended the best schools; and did well while majoring in mathematics. Later he did his service in the Second World War, and then did some work on the Marshall Plan. Bundy became dean of the Harvard Faculty of Arts and Sciences when he was only thirty-four.

To add to the striking homogeneity of the Kennedy national security team, Walt Rostow was named Bundy's deputy. Though of Jewish origin, Rostow was also from the Cambridge academic community, having served as an advisor to Kennedy's campaign while still in his faculty role at the Massachusetts Institute of Technology. Together, the two men began to work at Kennedy's side, initially following through on promises to streamline the White House national security apparatus. Bundy cut the staff from 71 to 48 and refocused it around regional issues. In an important innovation, he gave individual members of the team responsibility for specific portfolios, a development that would later lead to charges that the Kennedy team had replaced the White House "paper mill" with their own mini–State Department. Eisenhower's innovation, the Operations Coordinating Board, was shut down a month after the Kennedy team arrived.[10] This was certainly more than just a campaign promise being fulfilled. It hinted at Kennedy's natural allergy to formal staff processes and his affinity for informal, tightly knit advisory groups. This temperament would both get him into trouble and, later, help produce one of the most efficient high-level decision-making mechanisms the U.S. government has ever seen, at a moment when one was urgently needed.

The explanation for the structural changes was articulated in a letter written months later to Senator Henry Jackson in response to his inquiry into NSC operations. In the letter, Bundy quotes his predecessor, General Bobby Cutler, who had said that "the Council is a vehicle for a President to use in accordance with its suitability to his plans for conducting his great office. . . . A particular virtue of the National Security Act is its flexibility. . . . Each President may use the Council as most suitable at a given time."[11] He goes on to explain that the president was more comfortable in smaller meetings with his secretary of state (Dean Rusk) and his secretary of defense (Robert McNamara) and that this drove the way they organized themselves. After noting the abolition of the Operations Coordinating Board, he emphasizes that "the President has made it very clear that he does not want a large separate organization between him and his Secretary of State." Finally, he concludes that the third major change made by the Kennedy team was that they have "deliberately rubbed out the distinction between planning and operations" that existed in the Eisenhower years.[12]

Eisenhower, of course, saw this as a mistake and said as much on several occasions. Goodpaster, in a reference to the process and the role played by Kennedy aide and preeminent American presidential historian Richard Neustadt, said, "Dick, bless his soul, had a major hand in scrapping the so-called paper mill of the Eisenhower time but later on, after the Bay of Pigs, Eisenhower pointed out the mistake to Kennedy and said he had blinded himself and was simply not receiving the kind of support a president needed and deserved."[13] Odom sees it in less delicate terms: "Look at what Mac Bundy did when Kennedy became president. He decimated the NSC staff, all that bureaucracy that Kennedy had criticized Ike for having in his NSC staff. Bundy reduced it in size from several scores of staff aides to about eleven. Soon after the Bay of Pigs, he apparently realized that he was in trouble, that his staff was too small to provide the president with the kind of support that he needed."[14] Blurring the distinction between policy and operations played a big role in the problems that resulted. Policy and operations are best kept separate for the same reason that the military advises on policy but does not make it. They are too invested in their own success or failure, as they must be.

This certainly proved to be the case with the Bay of Pigs operation. Immediately upon entering office, Kennedy, Bundy, and their team saw themselves being caught between different schools of thought on what type of Cuban operation was likely to work. On February 18, 1961, McGeorge Bundy illustrated this when he placed two position papers, one by Richard Bissell, the CIA deputy director for plans, and one by Thomas Mann, assistant secretary of state for inter-American affairs, on President Kennedy's desk along with a cover memo that he himself wrote:

> Here, in sharp form, are the issues on Cuba. Bissell and Mann are the real antagonists at the staff level. Since I think you lean to Mann's view, I have put Bissell on top.
>
> The one hope I see is in an early—even if thin—recognition of a rival regime. I think if a Government-in-Exile can be surfaced promptly we could and should follow Mann's suggestion of working toward its recognition fairly soon. (We could also put in a full trade embargo against Castro, and you could sorrowfully read him out of the liberal family in a strong and factual speech about his outrages.) Then, conceivably, we could hold back Bissell's battalion for about three months and even build it up somewhat. And when it did go in, the color of civil war would be quite a lot stronger.[15]

The fact that four months earlier presidential candidate Kennedy had been briefed on the operations and, although surprised at the scope of the plans, had then gone out and called for similarly strong action as though such planning was not taking place did not seem to weigh in Bundy's assumptions about his boss's position. Either that or Kennedy was not fully clear either internally or in terms of his communications on this issue with his staff about how boxed in he had become. In any case, the analysis provided by the CIA suggested that their plan was sound enough to allay any concerns the president might have about following through on his campaign promises. The plan included the following elements:

• Continuous massive air power would be used against Cuban troops.
• Uprisings against Castro should occur within weeks of the landing.

- Should these uprisings not occur or should they fail, the United States would intervene militarily and overtly in response to the appeals of a provisional government established on a relatively large beachhead that would include the small city of Trinidad.
- After probing from Kennedy, the CIA added a third alternative, an "easy escape hatch": "At worst, the invaders should be able to fight their way to the Escambray [mountains] and go into guerrilla action."[16]

Kennedy was not satisfied with the plan, however. It is one thing to call for action as a candidate and quite another to be responsible for it as a president. He had pressed for a less visible and more deniable alternative: "Could not such a force be landed carefully and quietly and make its first major military efforts from the mountains—then taking shape as a Cuban force within Cuba, *not as an invasion force sent by the Yankees?*"[17] He was in the trap, writhing around looking for a comfortable position within it.

Now Kennedy had the Bissell and Mann papers in front of him and was forced to choose. Bissell had written:

A Landing in Force: The Joint Chiefs of Staff have evaluated the military aspects of the plan for a landing by the Cuban opposition. They have concluded that "this plan has a fair chance of ultimate success" (that is of detonating a major and ultimately successful revolt against Castro) and that, if ultimate success is not achieved there is every likelihood that the landing can be the means of establishing in favorable terrain a powerful guerrilla force which could be sustained almost indefinitely. The latter outcome would not be (and need not appear as) a serious defeat. It would be the means of exerting continuing pressure on the regime and would be a continuing demonstration of inability of the regime to establish order. It could create an opportunity for an OAS [Organization of American States] intervention to impose a cease-fire and hold elections.[18]

Mann's conclusion, for all intents and purposes, was the opposite:

My conclusions regarding this proposal are as follows:
(1) The military evaluation of this proposal is that "ultimate success will depend upon political factors, i.e., a sizeable popular uprising or substantial follow-on forces." It is unlikely that a popular uprising would promptly take place in Cuba of a scale and kind which would make it impossible for the Castro regime to oppose the brigade with superior numbers of well armed troops.[19]

While Bissell, along with most of the other advisors involved, concentrated on phase one (the invasion and holding of the beachhead), Mann alone concentrated on phase two (how to deal with the fallout and the situation in Cuba) and concluded that the plan would not work.[20] Like many other State Department officials before and since, however, he had failed to analyze the political situation on the ground in the country that mattered the most to this plan: the United States. Here the political dialectic that Anthony Lake cited came into play, forcing Kennedy into a bind. As his brother Robert later said, "If he hadn't gone ahead with it, everybody would have said it showed that he had no courage. . . . Eisenhower's people trained these people, it was Eisenhower's plan; Eisenhower's people all said it would succeed—and we turned it down."[21] Bundy later also pointed out that "the Republicans would have said that 'We were all set to beat Castro, and this chicken, this antsypantsy bunch of liberals'" had gone belly up at the last minute.[22]

Three other factors were on Kennedy's mind: the "disposal problem," that is, if the trained exiles were not sent into Cuba they might go to the United States or other Latin American countries and cause trouble;[23] the Soviet reaction in other parts of the world, such as Laos and Berlin; and the fact that an overt invasion would cost the United States its moral high ground.

In response to the president's request for a less risky plan, the bidding process among the various stakeholders continued. The CIA offered its views. State fretted about them. The military expressed its reservations. The president balanced these views and saw them through the filter of his much more informal consultative process, which is to say a process that did not give him the full benefit of dispassionate, rigorous analysis in which the assumptions and assertions of key players and agencies were sufficiently challenged and potential consequences debated by all the others. By March 1961, the CIA presented a less spectacular phase one plan: the Zapata plan, a landing on the less overt Bay of Pigs at night that could more plausibly be a solo operation by Cuban exiles.

Still, a fundamental misconception remained. For Kennedy, phase two of the operation meant Cuban guerrilla warfare, but for the CIA it meant U.S. armed intervention. The CIA was counting on the president's having the political will to back up its plan with further force if necessary. It was a total miscalculation. Higgins sums it up: "As Kennedy was reluctantly becoming aware, the political sine qua non of the invasion—no overt American support—would remain to the end incompatible with its military sine qua non—large scale and open American backing."[24]

The climactic meeting occurred from 6:00 to 8:18 p.m. on April 4, 1961, at the State Department in a small conference room beside Rusk's office.[25] Senator William Fulbright and presidential advisor Arthur Schlesinger denounced the operation: it would ruin the U.S. image. McNamara favored it. Rusk supported the operation but emphasized the diplomatic cost to the United States. Nitze argued against Fulbright's position but never aired his own concerns. Adolf Berle, a Kennedy advisor on Latin America, wanted a low-key operation, as did Kennedy, who finally asked for a show of hands. Among those who supported the operation was Mann: "As everybody present expressed support, I did the same. I did this because I did not wish to leave the impression that I would not support whatever the President decided to do."[26]

The result was what Higgins called the "perfect failure."[27] On April 18 Bundy told Kennedy that the situation was "not good." That evening Admiral Arleigh Burke, chief of naval operations, asked Kennedy for the air support:

Kennedy: [I don't] want the United States involved in this.
Burke: Hell, Mr. President, but we are involved.

. . .

B: Can I not send in an air strike?
K: No.
B: Can we send a few planes?
K: No, because they could be identified as United States.
B: Can we paint out their numbers or any of this?
K: No.
B: Can we get something in there?
K: No.
B: . . . If you'll let me have two destroyers, we'll give gunfire support and
  we can hold that beachhead with two ships for ever.
K: No.
B: One destroyer, Mr. President?
K: No.[28]

That night the president cried.[29] As well he might have. The operation had been doomed on every level. It was ill conceived. Those who had conceived it had been in the position not only of advocating it, but also of providing the intelligence to support their assertions. There had been no systematic process for vetting the assertions involved. The president and his men were inexperienced in dealing with such crises. The plan had been made by a predecessor and they feared they would be blamed for bungling it. The president had politically called for such a plan, urged it, but personally did not have the will to carry it through—and suspected that the American people did not either. (After the fact, while meeting with Eisenhower in a kind of postmortem session on this, Kennedy heard his predecessor explain that he did not think that the American people would support the loss of American life to liberate Cuba either.)[30]

In the wake of the failure in the Bay of Pigs, Kennedy realized that he was hostage to the information and analysis that was provided to him by cabinet agencies. He depended on State and Defense to relay cables giving information about developments and on the CIA to give their interpretation of the intelligence they were gathering. Furthermore, Kennedy had ignored Goodpaster's advice that the president's daily intelligence briefing should come from a disinterested party. It did not. Early in the administration, Bundy had taken over the responsibility for the president's morning briefing as well.

At another level, the administration suffered because, unlike Eisenhower's team, which was heavily populated with military brass, Kennedy's team was essentially civilian (although many had served in the military during the Second World War) and had no in-house "decoder" for the information and analysis sent in from the military. Kennedy believed in the power of brilliant minds. But brilliant minds without experience were not enough. A balance was needed. The search for this balance has been reflected in the history of the national security advisor position. By far the two groups with the greatest representation in the ranks of national security advisors are academics (Bundy, Rostow, Kissinger, Brzezinski, Allen, Lake, and Rice) and military men (Souers, Cutler, Goodpaster, Scowcroft, McFarlane, Poindexter, and Powell). The system seems to work best when there is a balance among the NSC leadership (Scowcroft from the military and Gates from the CIA, Berger from the political side and Donald Kerrick from the military side, Kissinger from the foreign policy side and Scowcroft from the military side).

Consequently, in the wake of the Bay of Pigs failure, Kennedy undertook or accelerated certain changes. First, he and Bundy moved forward with the idea of establishing a modern message "nerve center" in the White House so they could receive cable traffic and other information in real time. This center would be part of an effort to reduce the dependence of the president and his closest advisors on the "experts" from elsewhere in the government. The CIA had failed to apprise the president of the operational development of their plan or of the consequences of changes in that plan. For example, Walt Rostow said later, "When CIA changed the site, the impact of the shift didn't filter up to the President. Earlier the planners told Kennedy that if the invasion failed, the exiles would escape into the mountains north of Trinidad and undertake guerrilla operations against Castro. Later, as defeat of the invasion force seemed imminent, we expected the survivors to flee to the hills. They did not because of the swamps surrounding the bay. Had Kennedy known the details of the landing site change, he might have made different decisions."[31]

The new nerve center, which became known as the Situation Room, was located in what had been Franklin Roosevelt's map room during the Second World War. It consisted of a small conference area, a projection storage room connected to the conference room, and space for support staff. The center would give the president immediate access to news from around the world when it happened. Once it was in place, instructions were given to ensure that the flow of information was maintained around the clock. To this day, the operation remains true to this original purpose, although naturally it is significantly more sophisticated technologically.

From this harsh lesson Kennedy recognized that he did in fact need more operational coordination and that he needed it to be led by people he could trust. He also wanted those people, such as Bundy and Rostow, close at hand, so, in a move that would have ramifications for every cabinet department and the entire operating structure of the U.S. government, Kennedy moved his national security advisor, his deputy, and the executive secretary of the NSC into a small suite of offices on the ground floor of the West Wing of the White House adjacent to the Situation Room. Later Henry Kissinger would comment to me that in Washington, the most important thing was "proximity, proximity, and proximity"— that the fact that his office (at the time moved upstairs into the fine, large corner office that has been occupied by national security advisors ever since) was just down the hall from the president, a few steps from the Oval Office, made all the difference in the world in terms of his relative influence compared with other cabinet secretaries. When Kissinger became secretary of state, one reason he kept the national security advisor's office and title was that he knew the power that comes from being easily and constantly accessible to the president.

Bundy gained greater responsibility for managing interagency policy development processes, and he and Rostow split duties according to topic areas in which they had special competencies. In so doing, they took another large step toward establishing the modern national security advisor and deputies positions.

The degree to which this team learned from their early mistakes is illustrated well by the way they handled the subsequent crisis associated with the discovery of Russian missiles in Cuba in October 1962. Although Kennedy had not warmed to the idea of formal NSC meetings (he held only ten in 1962), he did recognize that some formal structure was necessary to manage critical issues or crises. When, on October 14, a U-2 spy plane took reconnaissance photos of what appeared to be Soviet missile emplacements under construction in Cuba, it triggered an instant reaction from an administration that was now much better equipped to handle a challenge.

Among the first things Kennedy did, in order to get the kind of thoughtful and reliable interagency advice he felt he would need in standing up to the Russians, was to convene a secret new White House group called the Executive Committee, or ExComm. The ExComm was the NSC created in Kennedy's eyes. It was a smaller group, consisting of the advisors he most wanted to hear from, and it became a kind of permanent, floating mechanism that worked throughout the missile crisis, convening either in the White House cabinet room or, when the president was not involved, in the offices of the State Department. During the two weeks of the crisis, the group met thirty-seven times. When the president didn't chair it, his brother Bobby often did. Included were key players such as McNamara, Rusk, and Bundy and others such as General Maxwell Taylor, who had been brought in as a special military advisor to Kennedy (that filter or "decoder" he really needed on military issues) and who had risen quickly to chairman of the Joint Chiefs of Staff. Interestingly, although the idea was for a compact group, the ExComm was highly flexible and had over seventy people cleared for participation in its discussions. Despite the group's size, however, there was not a single leak from the group during the crisis, given the universal sense of the gravity of the issues being discussed.

The ExComm first met on October 16, 1962, at 11:50 a.m. in the White House cabinet room.[32] Kennedy secretly hit the switch under the conference table, activating the tape recording system he had installed—setting another precedent, one that would cause serious problems for one of his successors. Studying the missile images from Cuba, he asked:

Kennedy: It's ready to be fired?
Graybeal (CIA photoanalyst): No, sir.
K: How long have . . . we can't tell that, can we, how long before they fire?
G: No, sir.
. . .

McNamara: It seems extremely unlikely that they are now ready to fire, or may be ready to fire within a matter of hours, or even a day or two.

...

Rusk: Mr. President, this is a ... there is an overwhelmingly serious problem. It's one that we, I think all of us, had not really believed the Soviets could carry this far.[33]

During the course of the discussion the participants laid out a series of options. According to Arthur Schlesinger's account of the session, with attack options among the most favored, Robert Kennedy passed a note to his brother: "I now know how Tojo felt when he was planning Pearl Harbor."[34]

At the second ExComm meeting, that evening at 6:30 p.m., the choices were refined and the debate continued. The participants heard a report that the missiles could be "fully operational within two weeks," although one might be ready much sooner.[35] The choice, according to McNamara, who remained coolly analytical throughout, impressing other members of the team with his incisive intellect, was now between the political and the military. One option would be for the United States to negotiate with Khrushchev, although this would "likely lead to no satisfactory result."[36] Alternatively, they could take a hybrid approach combining blockade and the threat of attack, explained McNamara. (When Bundy asked who they would attack, McNamara replied, "The Soviet Union.")[37] Yet another choice was a massive invasion that would likely involve well over 100,000 men and was almost certain to trigger a Soviet military response elsewhere in the world.

By the following day, the ExComm was dividing into factions. Dean Acheson and the chiefs were arguing for an invasion, saying that other choices would make the United States look weak. State's George Ball made the case for a diplomatic resolution, thinking it more desirable because he simply did not believe that the Russians understood fully the position they were putting the United States into with the missile gambit. McNamara backed the blockade because he felt the other options would either be ineffective or way too dangerous.[38]

Within a day the positions shifted because new intelligence showed missiles in Cuba that were capable of reaching virtually anywhere in the United States (intermediate-range missiles in addition to the medium-range missiles first identified).[39]

McNamara: We consider nothing short of a full invasion as practical military action, and this only on the assumption that we're operating against a force that does not possess operational nuclear weapons.

Kennedy: Why do you change . . . why has this information changed the recommendation?[40]

McNamara was concerned that with so many targets, the result of the strike option would either be inadequate or tantamount to invasion anyway—and a tripwire for Soviet reaction elsewhere.

RFK: What do we do when . . . he moves into Berlin?

Bundy: [Joking] If we could trade off Berlin, and not have it our fault . . .

McNamara: Well, when we're talking about taking Berlin what do we mean exactly? Do they take it with Soviet troops?

JFK: That's what I would see, anyway.

McNamara: I think there's a real possibility of that. We have U.S. troops there. What do they do?

Taylor: They fight.

McNamara: They fight. I think that's perfectly clear.

JFK: And they get overrun.

McNamara: Yes, they get overrun, exactly.

RFK: Then what do we do?

Taylor: Go to general war, assuming we have time for it.

JFK: You mean nuclear exchange?

Taylor: Guess you have to.

. . .

JFK: Now the question really is what action we take which lessens the chances of a nuclear exchange, which obviously is the final failure. And at the same time maintain some degree of solidarity with our allies. Now, to get a blockade on Cuba, would we have to declare war on Cuba?[41]

At this point the ghosts of Pearl Harbor once again reentered the room (we are all products of our generations). While Bundy argued that a first strike had strategic advantages, he made the wry analogy with December 7, 1941, when he said that "Sunday has historic disadvantages."[42] This in turn brought Bobby Kennedy back to his similar concerns and he began to argue for blockade.

Shortly thereafter the meeting broke up and the president went swimming as a way to clear his head. Afterward he met with Dean Acheson, by now the most senior of the country's senior statesmen, who dismissed the analogy with the Japanese surprise attack and indicated that he was leaning toward surgical strikes. Later the president and Soviet Ambassador Andrei Gromyko had their famous confrontation in which Kennedy told the Russian that the United States would not tolerate Soviet offensive weapons in Cuba and Gromyko acknowledged nothing, unaware that photos of the missile sites were sitting in the desk in front of him.

Near midnight on October 18 Kennedy sat down alone in the Oval Office and turned on the tape recorder and spoke. The result is the four and a half minute "JFK monologue" in which he recollects how "during the course of the day, opinions had obviously switched from the advantages of a first strike on the missile sites and on Cuban aviation to a blockade."[43]

In the final instance, as is always the case in such matters, the decision was made by Kennedy alone. However, as the transcripts show, Kennedy was in fact much more balanced in his views than many analysts from either the traditional or revisionist sides have given him credit for. He made the decision with an acute awareness of the international linkages, recognizing that any action by the United States in Cuba would reverberate in Berlin and Southeast Asia. Unlike in some of the more recent crises, options were not prematurely narrowed; the scant information coming from the Soviets, the intelligence community, and his advisors was evenly weighed, and decisions made in this forum were then implemented through the formal NSC structure. In one of the best managed crises of the period, the informal Kennedy NSC system worked essentially as planned.

Scholars of presidential decision making, such as William Newmann, have summarized the tendency of the NSC to move toward a restricted decision-making group in what they call the "evolutionary model."[44] All presidents begin with a similar set of intra-agency NSC and NSC staff–based processes, although it should be noted that until very recently, all presidents felt that an important part of defining the identity of their administration was throwing out their predecessor's processes, structures, and even nomenclature. This clearly cost Kennedy and would actually harm every ensuing administration until the practice was stopped in the late 1980s and early 1990s as bipartisan agreement around a working model evolved in the transitions from Carlucci to Powell to Scowcroft and then to Anthony Lake.

The president's brother was, from the outset, his most important advisor. Even though Bobby Kennedy was nominally the attorney general, he played a central role in national security matters. That this was nepotism at work did not escape many. But perhaps in those days, it was also not such a big departure. Bobby's role was unprecedented in the freedom he had to intervene where he saw fit and the closeness he had to the president. Perhaps there is no equivalent in terms of that closeness since Woodrow Wilson's wife Edith was said to run the government after his stroke—and there is no equivalent for an individual to have so much power so disproportionate with his appointed office until perhaps Dick Cheney in the second Bush presidency. (Although some cabinet secretaries did play a kind of oversized role as we will see in the cases of Henry Kissinger, James Baker, and arguably, Robert Rubin.)

·   ·   ·

John Kennedy's death and the sudden ascendancy of Lyndon Johnson produced few immediate changes in the structure of the group around the president who were expected to advise on national security issues. Continuity was critical. Sending a message to the American people that the institutions of government were functioning and that the team they had elected was still in power was of primary importance. That is why, in many respects, the Johnson era must be seen as an extension of the Kennedy era. Bundy continued as national security advisor, and when he departed to become head of the Ford Foundation, his deputy Walt Rostow stepped up in his place. Even Bobby Kennedy remained in his position as attorney general despite the bitter animosity that separated him from the new president.

What would divide them further, beyond ambition and their own bitter history together, was another legacy from John Kennedy, Vietnam. As President Kennedy was contemplating running for reelection in 1963, he and his advisors had come to the conclusion that an increased U.S. involvement in Vietnam was becoming an inevitability. The great foreign policy lesson of their generation was "no more Munichs." Appeasement of an enemy could only produce disaster. And once again, the tough anti-communist rhetoric Kennedy had used in 1960 would edge him into a position that neither he nor any of his advisors could fully grasp, and which would torture many of them and the country for decades after the death of the young president.

When Kennedy took office there were fewer than 700 U.S. military advisors in Vietnam. The United States had seen Ho Chi Minh's insurgency as a threat for years, but the focus of our policy had been to provide low-key assistance to the government of President Ngo Dinh Diem in Saigon. The military advisors were the most visible but still little-noted core of a group with financial, diplomatic, and covert assistance to back them up. That assistance was not sufficient to shore up Diem's fragile government—there had been a coup attempt by members of Diem's own military two months before Kennedy's inauguration—and there were calls for Kennedy and his team to increase support from their first days in office.

These calls were initially met with cautious moves described in an early Kennedy NSC action memo (NSAM-52), which increased the commitment of advisors to over 1,000 and expanded the aid available to Diem and the Army of the Republic of Vietnam (ARVN). Next, the president dispatched the deputy national security advisor Walt Rostow and General Maxwell Taylor to Vietnam on a fact-finding mission. While their assessments of the deteriorating situation on the ground may have been correct, their assessments regarding the consequences of what they considered to be appropriate U.S. responses were stunningly wrong. Taylor estimated that the United States would need to deploy no more than 8,000 troops to Vietnam to assure the position of our allies in the South and stated flatly: "The risks of backing into a major Asian war by way of (South Vietnam) are present but are not impressive."[45] In retrospect, of course, it is easy to wonder just what impressive risks might have been. Despite the confidence-shaking communist advances of the late 1950s and the American stumble on that Cuban beachhead described earlier, Taylor and his colleagues were still in the throes of what can only be described as America's postwar hubris—and their miscalculations ultimately would trigger the sequence of events that would puncture that hubris for decades to come. (Though, hubris, as it turns out, is one of the most resilient organs of the human psyche and, like the tails of certain lizards, it grows back comparatively rapidly.)

The output from the Taylor-Rostow mission contemplated expanding collaboration with the government in the South and expanding U.S. operations in the region from covert intrusions into neighboring states or the North to bombing missions. The president's key advisors, Rusk, McNamara, and Bundy, largely embraced the mission's findings. Here began one of the most pernicious illnesses afflicting the policy process: groupthink. Although there were divisions within the group, momentum toward consensus started to build, and the collective agreement of the principles created more momentum, and so on. Kennedy's brilliant young technocrats were especially vulnerable to the persuasive power of their own elegant logic. It made it hard to admit the possibility, let alone the desirability, of alternatives. Instead their youthful arrogance reinforced itself.

One dissenting voice was a member of the president's foreign policy inner circle, the number two man in the State Department, Under Secretary of State George Ball. Ball spoke out as early as November 4, 1961, the day after Taylor and Rostow returned, decrying their findings and warning that Vietnam could turn out to be worse than Korea. He added that our intervention in Vietnam was not, as we had and would continue to argue, to repel a communist invasion, as had been the case in Korea. Rather, we were getting ourselves involved in what was essentially a domestic dispute for Vietnam, a homegrown revolutionary situation.

Later, after the Taylor-Rostow report recommendations were passed on to the president with the advice that he embrace many of them, Ball expressed his concerns directly to the president. It is to the credit of Dean Rusk that he had an accommodation with his deputy that encouraged him to take his own independent stand in meetings with the president, thus assuring that the president got the benefit of the best thinking of his team, rather than a watered-down version, diluted by bureaucratic loyalties. The president dismissed his concerns, saying "George, you're just crazier than hell. That isn't going to happen."[46]

Ball, as quoted in Prados, subsequently commented to his chief of staff, "We're heading hell bent into a mess and there's not a Goddamn thing I can do about it. Either everybody is crazy or I am."[47] Within a year, there were over 11,000 American troops in Vietnam.

Still, the situation on the ground did not improve, and political rancor flamed further against the Diem administration when Diem's brother's wife, Madame Nhu, referred to the immolation death of a protesting monk as a "barbecue." Diem's response, although overtly critical of his sister-in-law, was ultimately to authorize a series of raids on Buddhist pagodas in August 1963. Within two months, Diem was deposed in a coup and murdered. The coup, conducted by Vietnamese generals, had been okayed in advance by the Kennedy administration, who realized that their allies were doing more harm than good to the now-collective cause.

Within three weeks, Kennedy was dead, but the wheels set in motion in Vietnam continued to turn. Johnson monitored activity in the country through the same set of eyes, ears, and minds that were available to Kennedy. There were a few additions to the group, including longtime Johnson loyalist Bill Moyers, who served very much as the new president's chief of staff and who had a special brief for international issues. Of course, Johnson worked the group differently. He was a product of the Senate, a man who like to use his bigger-than-life qualities to cajole, persuade, seduce, or intimidate people one-on-one, whether in person or over the phone. As James Schlesinger, a cabinet secretary in the Nixon, Ford, and Carter administrations who was working as a defense analyst at the time, relates:

There is a story when Johnson became president that tells you a great deal about him. I will presume it is true. On his second or third trip on Air Force One, the Air Force steward comes into the private cabin where the president sits, is very deferential with the new president of the United States. And Johnson, who loved abusing power, just sitting there, asks, "Well, son, what are you doing?" "Sir, can I get you something to drink or to eat?" Johnson looks at him and he says, "Yes, of course. I would like to have a Dr. Pepper." The steward looks somewhat alarmed, goes racing off. You hear all of this rattling going on in the galley and about fifteen minutes later the steward reappears and says, "Sir, I am dreadfully sorry but we do not seem to have any Dr. Pepper on board Air Force One." Johnson looks at him and he says, "You don't have any damn Dr. Peppers? What the hell is the matter with the Air Force? I am going to talk to the Secretary of the Air Force about this. What is your name, son?" And the poor steward is beginning to go to pieces.

"Get me the phone," he said. He gets the White House operator. "Get me Sam Pepper down in Waco, Texas, or whatever the name was, the fellow that was head of Dr. Pepper. Sam, I am sitting here on Air Force One and I am telling you I just asked for a Dr. Pepper and these damn people in the Air Force couldn't produce one. Let me tell you this, Sam. From this day forward, the Air Force is going to have Dr. Peppers available." After a while the conversation ceases. . . . Well, the Air Force is the United States Air Force. Needless to say, from that day forward Air Force One was stocked with Dr. Pepper, and from that day forward Lyndon Johnson never again asked for a Dr. Pepper. He had gone through this entire act just to torture this poor steward. That was Johnson's problem and, as you say, kind of the personality of a president.[48]

Johnson liked informality, a trait he carried to extremes by continuing discussions with key aides while he was in the bathroom—or, in one instance with Moyers, while he was actually having an enema. The most important difference between him and Kennedy managing his team, though, had to do with his introduction of a habit he had developed in the Senate, which was to host Tuesday lunches for his core team. According to Harold Saunders, NSC old hand and former assistant secretary for Near Eastern and South Asian affairs:

Lyndon Johnson wanted an NSC system that would force the bureaucratic elements out there, before recommendations came to the White House, to sort out their differences. I picture him as saying to Bob McNamara and Dean Rusk, Look, you guys are smart. I know your departments have differences. But I'd like you two guys to sit down and you figure out and recommend to me what you would do if you were in my shoes. And then come on over to lunch on Tuesday and we'll sit down and each of you can say why you disagreed. And so, we'll take it apart there, but I want the bureaucracies' energies going into making up something that we can realistically do, not exacerbating the fights among them.[49]

The lunches—private, small, attended only by those Johnson really wanted to work with—in effect largely supplanted the NSC process although, of course, it continued to operate and support the president and play its formal role.

These Tuesday sessions regularly included McNamara, who had become a *primus inter pares* in the cabinet. In the words of his successor, Clark Clifford, "In my years in Washington, only a handful of people below the presidential level have dominated the scene: George Marshall, Dean Acheson and Henry Kissinger all come to mind. But no one ever held the capital in greater sway than Robert S. McNamara did from 1961 until the end of 1967."[50] He had transformed his department in ways that Forrestal could only have dreamed of. The former president of the Ford Motor Company had taken important steps toward modernizing the way U.S. public officials worked and thought, bringing his systems analyst perspective to issues along with awesome intelligence, sangfroid, and energy. His actions not only elevated him but marked the coming of age of a Defense Department that was just under fourteen years old when he took office—and that in turn added to his stature, transforming the balance of power within an NSC structure that was originally created to help ensure that the fledgling department could hold its own with the State Department, the bureaucratic *grand dame*. Vietnam would be McNamara's undoing, the place where doing the best he could at his job ultimately came into conflict with what he saw as doing the best he could as a person. But throughout the period, until he could endure the pressure no longer, he was the leader of the inner circle. Indeed, his leadership is what gave him, in the eyes of the public, the disproportionate share of the blame for the fiasco that was to become Vietnam.

Influential in this dynamic was the fact that dealing with military leaders never came as easily to Johnson as it had to Eisenhower. Military men such as General Goodpaster, who served during the Johnson years in a senior capacity in Vietnam, naturally saw that as a weakness. Goodpaster commented on how uncomfortable he was with the way Johnson would snap at the brass—his own service chiefs—and that he would never invite them to the Tuesday lunches that were where the real war planning was taking place.

McNamara drove the groupthink, both in the Tuesday lunches and via his frequent, often extraordinary conversations with the president (many of which are now available in transcript form). His counterpart at the top of the pyramid in the government was Secretary of State Rusk, an always thoughtful yet forceful and sometimes hawkish southerner whom Johnson also came to rely on. Indeed, for Johnson, dealing one-on-one with these two men was far preferable to big staff meetings, and later in his term he would actually cede power from the NSC back to State, through the institution of the Senior Interdepartmental Group (SIG), chaired by the under secretary of state.

However, in the era of Lyndon Johnson, larger than any institutional reforms, larger than the collective power and personalities and his team, larger than even the personality of his predecessor or his own great ambitions for himself and his country, would loom Vietnam. How it was dealt with was illustrated well by the events that triggered the ultimate escalation of the conflict to levels that even Kennedy, who had commented to those around him that he anticipated escalation in his second term, wouldn't have imagined.

In 1964, not only were the generals who had overthrown Diem themselves overthrown, but by summer's end there were seven governments of South Vietnam. American military strength had doubled again from the end of 1962 and had reached over 22,000 troops. A series of war games in Washington, simulations conducted by the military but involving senior officials from the NSC and the administration's foreign policy leadership, produced some very disconcerting results: it would, it turned out, be rather hard to win in Vietnam. Nonetheless, there was no will to back down. Indeed, the president and his core advisors were looking for a way to mobilize public support for more aggressive efforts in Indochina. "And Johnson simply misunderstood the war for that reason," notes Schlesinger. "The notion that Ho Chi Minh could be bought off with little things like the Mekong Valley Authority was quite plausible, if you are dealing with, say, the senator from Missouri. It is not very plausible if you are dealing with a man who, despite the Uncle Ho aspects, is a committed communist and a committed nationalist."[51]

Shortly after 4:00 a.m. on August 2, 1964, cables arriving at the Pentagon's National Military Communications Center from the Saigon station provided the trigger they were seeking: The destroyer *USS Maddox* reported being approached by North Vietnamese attack boats and responding. Just over seven hours later Johnson met with Secretary Rusk, Under Secretary of State Ball, Deputy Defense Secretary Cyrus Vance, and General Earle Wheeler. They were uncertain who authorized the attack on the *Maddox*, and so they decided to send a protest to Hanoi and expand the patrols in which the *Maddox* was engaged.

General Maxwell Taylor, writing from the embassy in Saigon, protested that this response would be too timid and likely to embolden the North. Consequently, Johnson made a stronger statement, but within two days another attack was reported on the *Maddox*. The reaction to the alleged attack was heightened in the context of intelligence warnings of hostile activities had been received earlier. Later, the veracity of the attack reports, which were initially alleged to consist of between nine and twenty-six torpedoes fired at the *Maddox* and another destroyer, the *C. Turner Joy*, came into question.

Nevertheless, McNamara, after briefly meeting with Vance to convince himself that at least something had occurred, told an NSC meeting at midday:

> North Vietnamese PT boats have attacked the DeSoto Patrol consisting of two U.S. destroyers, the *Maddox* and the *C. Turner Joy*, approximately 65 miles off North Vietnam in the Gulf of Tonkin. Presently we believe 9 or 10 torpedoes were fired at the Patrol. Two of the PT boats were reportedly sunk and three to six were fired on. So far, we have no casualties. Nearby U.S. aircraft carriers are providing continuous air cover.[52]

He went on to advise a retaliatory air strike. After the NSC meeting, Rusk, McNamara, CIA director John McCone, Bundy, and Vance joined Johnson for one of their lunches. From what is available in the record, it is evident that the decision was made to launch a strike on five coastal bases plus an oil depot.

That evening, at an NSC meeting, McNamara continued to stress that attacks had occurred:

> The President: Do they want a war by attacking our ships in the middle of the Gulf of Tonkin?
>
> CIA Director McCone: No. The North Vietnamese are reacting defensively to our attacks on their off-shore islands. They are responding out of pride and on the basis of defense considerations. The attack is a signal to us that the North Vietnamese have the will and determination to continue the war. They are raising the ante.

The President: Are we going to react to their shooting at our ships over 40 miles from their shores? If yes, we should do more than merely return the fire of the attacking ships. If this is so, then the question involves no more than the number of North Vietnamese targets to be attacked.

Secretary McNamara: Our intelligence officers report that a Chinese Communist air regiment is moving to North Vietnam.

USIA Director Carl Rowan: Do we know for a fact that the North Vietnamese provocation took place? Can we nail down exactly what happened? We must be prepared to be accused of fabricating the incident.

Secretary McNamara: We will know definitely in the morning. As of now, only highly classified information nails down the incident. This information we cannot use and must rely on other reports we will be receiving. [The information refers to the National Security Agency (NSA) intercept warning. It was later found to refer to the August 2 attack but was misinterpreted by the analyst at the time.][53]

Half an hour later Johnson, Rusk, and Wheeler met with congressional leaders and proposed the Tonkin Gulf Resolution to authorize retaliation for the attack. Congressional leaders then actively supported the resolution, which gave Johnson wide-ranging authority to escalate the war. The resolution itself had been drafted many weeks before the incident.

On the face of it, the main decision-making error that the few participating in the response to these developments made was the weight given to separate and not necessarily reliable intelligence flows. The fact that the NSA had intercepted a North Vietnamese communication, apparently warning that an attack was imminent, served to bias the remainder of the information gathered, both on the *Maddox* and in the Situation Room. The information about the second attack was, as it turned out, suspect. However, given that Johnson's team was looking for an incident to put the already drafted resolution before Congress when one seemed to have occurred, a reasonable effort to nail down the facts as might have been done in other circumstances likely seemed counterproductive. In short, groupthink can become powerful enough to drive leaders to twist events and intelligence to support conclusions they have already reached. In this case, that is apparently what happened—consequently making this both a prime example of the intelligence–analysis–policy development synapses misfiring and a precedent for several notorious similar instances that would come in the decades to follow.

Despite the expanded latitude Johnson gained from the resolution, he was loath to use it until he had won election in his own right, which he did handily in November 1964. Within two weeks of his inauguration, in response to a North Vietnamese attack on American installations in Vietnam's central highlands, Johnson authorized the first major bombing attacks against the enemy. The bombing operation, which had been contemplated and discussed in different forms since the Taylor-Rostow mission, was code-named Rolling Thunder.

It is worth noting that the prosecution of war in Vietnam had not yet drawn widespread protests in the United States. In the wake of Rolling Thunder, sixty percent of the public supported Johnson.[54] Eighty-three percent of surveyed Americans said that they supported the bombing, and almost the same proportion said they supported the objective of "keeping the communists from taking over all of Southeast Asia."[55] This provided powerful support for the group who felt that we would inevitably win through applied strength since our power was inexhaustible and unassailable relative to our tiny enemy.

In these circumstances, the courage that George Ball continued to show in voicing his criticisms within the president's formal and informal councils was remarkable—as was Rusk's willingness to continue to bring the naysayer with him to the meetings. Ball was supported by almost no one at the highest levels of the administration and by only a very small group of others, including a few State Department Asia hands (who had actually studied the situation and produced a gloomy analysis of what would be possible for us to achieve in Vietnam), plus a couple respected gray-heads, John Kenneth Galbraith and Senate Majority Leader Mike Mansfield. However, he was soon joined in his opposition to expanding our efforts in Vietnam by an unlikely ally, Clark Clifford, the former Truman aide who had grown even more respected in Washington thanks to stints as an advisor to President Kennedy and then to Johnson. Clifford started to echo Ball's arguments in behind-the-scenes communications with the president. In a May 17, 1965, letter written in response to the review of a letter from the CIA director regarding expanding our operations in Vietnam, Clifford wrote:

> I believe our ground forces in South Vietnam should be kept at a minimum, consistent with the protection of our installations and property in that country. My concern is that a substantial build up of U.S. ground troops would be construed by the Communists and by the world as a determination on our part on the ground.
>
> This could be a quagmire. It could turn into an open ended commitment on our part that would take more and more ground troops without a realistic hope of ultimate victory.

I do not think the situation is comparable to Korea. The political posture of the parties involved and the physical conditions including terrain
are entirely different.[56]

Just over two months later, Clifford was called on to participate in
another meeting of the president's most senior advisors concerning Vietnam. He was a civilian at the time, but his commentary on the situation in
the room on that July day in 1965 speaks volumes about how America
wandered so far into the swamp that Vietnam became:

> These men had been deeply influenced by the lessons of the Cuban Mis-
> sile Crisis, especially the value of "flexible response" and "controlled esca-
> lation." Their success in handling a nuclear showdown with Moscow had
> created a feeling that no nation as small and backward as North Vietnam
> could stand up to the power of the U.S. These men were not arrogant in
> the sense that Senator Fulbright and others later accused them of being,
> but they possessed a misplaced belief that American power could not be
> successfully challenged, no matter what the circumstances, anywhere in
> the world.[57]

And so we discover yet another of the cords that bind down the American Gulliver, this one perhaps more subtle than the domestic political
pressures and traps into which presidents regularly fall or the inability to
mobilize allies to support our international endeavors. This one is the collective blindness caused by groupthink, the collective misperceptions
caused by the joint misinterpretation of common experiences, the breakdown of the advisory process when policymakers become too closely
involved with a cause and advice becomes advocacy. Perhaps it took hold
in the dark days after the Bay of Pigs and during the Cuban Missile Crisis
when the men of the ExComm were forged by necessity into a cohesive
unit; perhaps it was exacerbated by the trauma of the assassination; and
almost certainly it was made worse by the deepening bunker mentality
associated with the entanglement in Southeast Asia. In any event, groupthink worked its distorting effects on the national security deliberations of
the United States at the same time as other constraints took their toll,
including the one that would soon bedevil Johnson and his advisors,
which is the lack of political will among the American people to actually
use the power we have at our disposal.

So it would be with these men and Vietnam, although the upshot of the
meeting attended by Clifford would ultimately be the approval of General

William Westmoreland's request to increase U.S. troop strength in Vietnam by more than 100,000 men in 1965 and more again in 1966.

The voice of George Ball in that meeting almost certainly echoed in the ears of the attendees for the rest of their lives. Clifford recounts the scene:

> When I entered, George Ball was speaking. "We can't win," he said, his deep voice dominating the Cabinet Room. "The war will be long and protracted, with heavy casualties. The most we can hope for is a messy conclusion. We must measure this long-term price against the short-term loss that will result from a withdrawal.
>
> Producing a chart that correlated public opinion with American casualties in Korea, Ball predicted that the American public would not support a long and inconclusive war. World opinion would also turn against us. Ball said he knew that withdrawal was difficult for a President. "But almost every great captain in history at some time in his career has had to make a tactical withdrawal when conditions were unfavorable." He compared the situation to that of a cancer patient on chemotherapy: we might keep the patient alive longer, but he would be fatally weakened in the long run.
>
> Looking straight at Ball, the President said—not harshly, but with deep concern, bordering on anguish, I thought—"Wouldn't all these countries—Korea, Thailand, Western Europe—say Uncle Sam is a paper tiger? Would we lose credibility by breaking the word of three Presidents if we give up as you propose? It would seem to me to be an irreparable blow, but I gather that you don't think so."
>
> "If we were actively helping a country with a stable, viable government, it would be a vastly different story," Ball replied.
>
> One by one, the other senior members of the Administration lined up against Ball. McGeorge Bundy argued in his usual crisp style that Ball's views constituted a "radical switch in policy, without any evidence it should be done." Ball's arguments, he asserted, went "in the face of all that we have said and done."
>
> "It will not be quick," he added, "No single action will bring victory but I think it is essential to make clear that we are not going to be thrown out."
>
> Ball interrupted: "My problem is not that we will get thrown out, but that we will get bogged down and won't be able to win."[58]

In retrospect, the subsequent comments of the more senior members of the group ring hollow. Rusk dismissed the risk of casualties and said,

"Vietnam must be an example for the entire Free World."[59] Henry Cabot Lodge, an elder Republican statesman who had been Richard Nixon's running mate in 1960 and who had just agreed to become ambassador to Vietnam, said, "There is a greater threat of World War III if we don't go in than if we go in. I cannot be as pessimistic as George Ball about the situation in Vietnam."[60] McNamara said, "Our national honor is at stake."[61] In this, he was certainly correct.

Clifford continued to argue against the escalation in private. He did not persuade the president. Within two years, the results of U.S. efforts in Vietnam had been so disappointing that McNamara resigned. Clifford, supposedly a hawk, had been chosen to replace him. Many cited Clifford's eventual public statements that the war could not be won as a sign that he, too, had turned and had thus alienated his president, who felt betrayed. But Clifford had been among the first to forcefully oppose the war in his counsel to Johnson. Johnson had knowingly selected a voice of dissent against the war to lead the Department of Defense. Undoubtedly this reflected his recognition that the war was unwinnable and his own unflagging hope that he might somehow find a way to restore his bonds with the American people and his place in history in the job he had coveted for so long.

American foreign policy failed in Vietnam because the country's leaders, and most of all the administration's inner circle of policy analysts, could not listen to clear warnings, could not heed clear analyses, did not believe there was anything that the United States could not achieve if it put its mind to it—they did not, in short, recognize that even the most powerful nation in the history of the world has limits. They also illustrated a vital point that would haunt generations of their successors. The greatest of all limitations on power is not political, diplomatic, or circumstantial—it is failed power. Implied power is great: the superpowers were most super with regard to the wars they did not fight. But power that fails the test of application will be long doubted. With the great failure in Vietnam, America ushered in an era of self-doubt that would bring new forms of limitations and at times paralysis.

In one of his memos about Vietnam to Johnson, George Ball dryly quoted Ralph Waldo Emerson, and, in so doing, implied that he too knew it was already too late.

Things are in the saddle and ride mankind.

6

America in Decline, the NSC Ascendant

Ours is a society of nuclear giants and ethical infants.
—General Omar Bradley

A ROUND MY FAMILY dinner table, in Summit, New Jersey, in the early 1970s, there were differing views on Henry Kissinger, all of them loud. For my grandmother, hearing his name was enough for her to reach for her blood pressure medication or a scotch on the rocks. My mother, the voice of McGovern liberalism at the table, largely agreed with her mother on this one, but she had a kind of admiration for his star quality and intellect that mitigated her impulse to condemn him purely for his association with Richard Nixon.

My father, frankly, reminded me a little of Kissinger. Both had accents (though Kissinger's is much thicker, which some suspect is due as much to a shrewd marketing instinct as to a fondness for guttural consonants). Both were refugees from Europe. Both had escaped the Nazis. Both had gone back to Europe in the U.S. Army. And my father was the more politically centrist, pragmatic member of the household analytical community. My mother managed the family as Adlai Stevenson would have. My father offered occasional doses of realpolitik when they were required.

Consequently, Kissinger always loomed large for me. He was powerful. He was always the smartest man in the room. He was sometimes seen with a starlet. Truly, if anyone during my high school years strode the world stage, it was Henry. He also had a sense of humor and made witty comments—for example, about power being the ultimate aphrodisiac and academic infighting being so fierce because the stakes were so low—who could resist smart, funny, and powerful?

That Kissinger should become post–Cold War foreign policy's first "crossover" superstar—transcending academia, leaping the beltway in a single bound and achieving bona fide celebrity status in addition to winning an extraordinary standing among government leaders worldwide, is remarkable. An immigrant, a man whose accent has survived long after those of some who came to this country after him had faded, a man who writes in sometimes dense academic prose, an individual who can be remote and witheringly acid at times, he has enjoyed the kind of career trajectory that both defied and then defined stereotypes. As a consequence, today he is still seen as one of the most influential, and perhaps the most influential, American foreign policy figure of the entire era in which the United States has been a global leader. Everything about him is seen in the context of his remarkable reputation, through a lens of unprecedented media coverage, adulation, and denigration. It is hard to see the man because he is so obscured by his image, which he himself played a very significant role in creating.

Kissinger had been an important foreign policy figure long before he became national security advisor to Richard Nixon. He had come to national prominence with a treatise on nuclear strategy written for the Council on Foreign Relations in the mid-1950s. He was a noted member of the Harvard faculty. He had been an advisor to the governments of Eisenhower, Kennedy, and Johnson. In each case, he was admired for his brilliance and, in the end, his relations with the governments in question ended frustratingly for at least some of those involved. He had been approached to work with Kennedy and for a while was an advisor to the president. But he refused to give up his role as a public speaker, to toe the party line in speeches, and thus alienated Kennedy loyalists. For a while he had maintained a lesser consulting arrangement, but he ruffled feathers by pushing to keep his secret papers in his office at Harvard. During the Johnson administration he undertook an initiative to help pass word through some people he knew to the North Vietnamese that the United States sought a negotiating channel. While this seemed helpful on its face, Johnson administration insiders felt that Kissinger later worked through his contacts and with Anna Chennault, widow of World War II Flying Tigers leader Claire Chennault, to convince the North Vietnamese to put off progress on the negotiations because they would do better if Nixon won the election. It is alleged that this back channel was also misconstrued by Nixon during the campaign into his famous "secret plan" to win the Vietnam War.

Thus, when Nixon approached the famous, German-born national security specialist during his campaign, Kissinger was already a very well-known figure in the foreign policy community. He had been most closely linked with Nelson Rockefeller and the Rockefeller family, who were his patrons, but he had also very carefully built up a global network of connections and media relationships that would prove essential to him in his work in the Nixon administration and again later, as he cultivated his other business interests and the burnishing of his legacy. But for all the speeches and the television appearances, for all the years of study, for all the relationship building, clearly Henry Kissinger's life was transformed when he signed on to the Nixon team and began on the path to become Richard Nixon's national security advisor and later his secretary of state.

This dramatic transformation lay not simply in Kissinger's having landed important jobs working close to the president but rather in how closely the two worked together: Nixon and Kissinger cannot fully be seen as separate characters. They were to a large extent two parts of a whole, complementing each other, augmenting each other, often infuriating each other, and in the end creating together the smallest, most powerful, most brilliant, and sometimes—thanks largely to the paranoid and "strange" Richard Nixon—most dysfunctional inner circle of all those that shaped and implemented the international policies of the world's most powerful nation. Together they created the modern NSC and were arguably the most influential U.S. foreign policy figures of the late twentieth century.

.   .   .

America in 1968 was a nation in flames. Robert Kennedy and Martin Luther King had been murdered. Cities rioted. Vietnam festered. The fact that we sent Apollo 8 around the moon that Christmas was an ironic grace note underscoring what our dreams of America were and how starkly they contrasted with our reality.

For the generation of men who had lived through the great triumph of the Second World War it was baffling. Surely in twenty years we had grown richer, our technology more advanced, our country more experienced internationally. Yet, we were pinned down in a tiny nation in Southeast Asia, prisoner to a committed enemy, to the will of our ally on the ground to support our initiatives (or not), and to our own promises and expectations.

The 1968 election thus became a referendum on what kind of America we wanted. In one of those twists of U.S. politics that would have been bizarre were it not so very common, the more hawkish of the candidates, Richard Nixon, who had recently said that not to fight in Vietnam was to invite World War III, was marketing himself as the peace candidate, and President Johnson, who was so committed to establishing a "Great Society" here in America, was accused of tearing deeply into the fabric of that society with his policies—ones he had largely inherited from his predecessor. Like many American political campaigns, therefore, it was a cynical affair, with Democratic nominee Hubert Humphrey forced to defend policies he did not much like, and Richard Nixon promising a plan for peace he did not really have. As is almost always the case in such contests, the America people voted for change in the face of discomfort and they voted for the hope of peace that Republican "competence" in foreign affairs might bring. They wanted to feel good, to recapture some of that sense of promise that had ushered in the postwar era. Instead, the 1970s were to bring greater divisions and introduce ghosts that would haunt America, American politics, and American foreign policy into the next century.

It would seem that Richard Nixon was the classic rider of the tides of history. He rode out of the Second World War into politics. He rode the red scare and his time on the House Un-American Activities Committee onto his party's presidential ticket. He rode Eisenhower's leadership to at least a share of a record of accomplishment (although Eisenhower had famously undercut Nixon when asked by a reporter to think of a significant contribution Nixon had made to the administration, responding, "Well, if you give me a week I might be able to think of one.")[1] Now, atop a wave of dissatisfaction with policies he had once advocated, he rode out of exile, back into power, into the office he had long dreamed of.

But Nixon was to offer a twist. Truman and Eisenhower had been masters of their times. Kennedy and Johnson had been victims of their times. But Nixon would be brought down by his own hand, undone by his own character. He would change and define his times as few had done. Beside him for many of his greatest triumphs and some of his darker defeats would be Henry A. Kissinger, his partner. In the years after they left office, Kissinger would regularly make the case, implicitly or explicitly, that he played the central role in leading Nixon to their successes and that he periodically stepped in to save Nixon from himself. But many who were there and had a close-up view of the closest and most unusual high-level partnership in American history, would say that in fact Nixon was the defining force in the relationship—for good and for ill. With the answer somewhere in between, it is perhaps best to look at them as two parts of a whole.

They were a fascinating pair. In a way, they complemented each other perfectly. Kissinger was the charming and worldly Mr. Outside who provided the grace and intellectual-establishment respectability that Nixon lacked, disdained, and aspired to. Kissinger was an international citizen, Nixon very much a classic American. Kissinger had a worldview and a facility for adjusting it to meet the times, Nixon had pragmatism and a strategic vision that provided the foundations for their policies. Kissinger would, of course, say that he was not political like Nixon—but in fact he was just as political as Nixon, just as calculating, just as relentlessly ambitious; they were two versions of Sammy Glick, one a Quaker from California, the other Jewish from Germany. And like Sammy Glick, the hero of the classic American striver novel *What Makes Sammy Run?*, these self-made men were driven as much by their need for approval and their neuroses as by their strengths—living proof of the aphorism that great men succeed because of their neuroses whereas lesser men are kept from succeeding by theirs.

Kissinger could be too smooth, almost unctuous. Nixon was too coarse, too stiff. His flair for expletives, now famous as deletions from the transcripts that marked his downfall, was apparent to all who knew him even briefly. During his first and only meeting with his NSC team, his one effort to bond with them, this man who was one of the great politicians of his age showed his remarkable knack for blurting out the impolitic when he stressed the importance of the NSC team because of the contempt he had for those "impossible fags" over in the State Department.[2]

As in all great dramas, what makes the story of this smallest of all inner circles so important—and indeed, what makes the stories of each of these inner circles fascinating—is the degree to which it reflects the zeitgeist and even the psychological state of the nation. Looking back at the Nixon era, we are left with memories of Watergate and Vietnam, of distrust of those in power, and of questioning our leadership we had done at no time before or since in American history. It is not just the story of the use or the abuse of power but also of the torment of the characters involved. That is why it has lent itself to art as few other periods, with operas by Robert Wilson and films by Oliver Stone lifting the drama to classic levels, echoing Shakespeare.

Why was that? I think it was largely because the torment of Richard Nixon and of Nixon and Kissinger as a team and of the nation all stemmed from similar circumstances. Nixon, Kissinger, and America in the late 1960s and early 1970s lived with the fresh memory of the era of American greatness that produced victories in Europe and Japan and presided over the rebuilding of large tracts of the planet. They aspired to similar heights and then, having scaled them, discovered that the view was not what they thought it might be. They discovered Gulliver bound to the beach in Lilliput. They lived in an era in which people theorized openly on American decline. Kissinger himself has been accused of being a kind of declinist, a European at heart who always saw America as a kind of *arriviste* giant. They would come to epitomize the torment of a nation coming to grips with its own limitations—much like the struggle of men of a certain age coming to realize that for all their achievements, life was not going to be as they had dreamed it, that the things that had raised them up had also planted the seeds of their demise.

A few years before Nixon came to power, the strain of recognition of America's unexpected place in the world was reflected in Thomas Pynchon's masterpiece *V*, in which he wrote,

> "Why America is sitting on its ass," brooded Johnny, "is the same reason our ship is sitting on its ass. Crosscurrents, seismic movements, unknown things in the night. But you can't help thinking it's somebody's fault."[3]

People wanted someone or a group to blame for their frustration that things were not exactly working out as planned for America. The Left blamed the Right. The Right blamed the Left. Civilians blamed the military. The military cursed their lack of support from civilians. And in the center were Nixon and Kissinger coping with all that while attempting to lead the world.

.   .   .

After the 1968 election, the Nixon transition team hunkered down at the Hotel Pierre in New York. The Pierre is an elegant fixture on the southeast corner of Central Park, a more "old money" Fifth Avenue society matron than its near neighbor on Central Park South, the better-known Plaza. Back in the 1960s, the optics of a Republican president-elect operating out of an upper-crust setting in the toniest neighborhood of Manhattan rather than in Washington or in more humble hometown digs did not bother anyone. The constant media scrutiny of the trivial and the elevation to metaphor of everything that passes before a television camera had not yet become the norm. The semiotics of politics were much simpler. The biggest difference between then and today was what wasn't news, wasn't visible, wasn't fair game. Back rooms were still in the back, still out of sight. They were still filled with men who drank and smoked and cursed and pulled strings while they worked into the night and knew they could do it all without being discovered. They were pals with reporters and a wink and a nod went a long way.

Nixon and Kissinger had been thrown together when Nixon's campaign foreign policy aide, a young conservative named Richard Allen who would later become Ronald Reagan's first national security advisor, recognized that he was too conservative and perhaps too young to assume the advisor's role. Kissinger was not only prominent but also closely associated with the Rockefeller wing of the Republican Party, the moderate wing of the party back when it had a moderate wing. According to Isaacson, "Allen . . . helped bring Kissinger into the Nixon camp."[4]

Nixon asked Kissinger to put together a plan for how his White House national security apparatus would work and how the interagency process around it would work. Early in this process, Nixon, a veteran of the Eisenhower system, sought the assistance of Andrew Goodpaster, then a general serving as the deputy commander of U.S. forces in Vietnam. Nixon pulled political strings to get Goodpaster back from Vietnam, with the help of President Johnson, who respected Goodpaster and had used him as his liaison with Eisenhower throughout his term.

Goodpaster was happy to cooperate and certainly found the Pierre considerably more comfortable than his posting in Saigon. He had been uncomfortable with Johnson, having felt him unsuited for the job of president. He thought that Johnson had been strong on domestic issues, that he "understood their methods and goals and how to work the system," but that he had never grown comfortable with doing the same with the military.[5] So when Nixon and Kissinger called, Goodpaster came in and collaborated on the development of an approach with which he, like his new principals, was more comfortable. "We worked," he recalls, "to set up a system that would draw from Eisenhower but which would not narrow down options to a single line of policy. Nixon always wanted to have several lines of policy evaluated."[6]

At the center was, as Kissinger NSC staffer Harold Saunders put it, "Richard Nixon, lonely in his study, with his long yellow pad, making up his pro and con columns. For him, he knew from the beginning that if the bureaucracy put all its energy into coming to one recommendation, he'd never have any decision to make; he'd never have any choices. So the mantra was to bring to the president all reasonable options. And that's probably the way that it worked during the best NSC years, say, from 1969 to 1971."[7]

James Schlesinger, who started in the Nixon administration handling defense and intelligence issues in the Office of Management and Budget and would later become secretary of defense, CIA director, and then the nation's first energy secretary, says Nixon learned "what I will call the façade from Eisenhower. He knew that Ike was in charge and he, Dick Nixon, wanted to be in charge in the same way. He had less patience with the staff system, so the NSC process was really more of a kind of an education for Nixon. And in turn, he used the set of procedures that he and Henry developed to push over his ideas rather than to listen to anyone else's. And Henry, well, he did all the preparation of the memorandum that would go on top of the NSSM [National Security Study Memorandum], and my guess is that the memorandum was never shown to anyone else other than Nixon. And so Nixon used Henry as a way to make and then deliver decisions with Henry taking a good deal of the guff from the bureaucracy for decisions that Nixon himself has made."[8]

Goodpaster recalls that setting up an interagency system that did not have the State Department in charge of too many critical committees was a priority for Nixon. The rationale was that if State was in charge it would simply lead to conflicts with the Department of Defense and "they wouldn't accomplish very much," according to Goodpaster. He continued:

> So this was an issue that turned out to be really a gut issue for them in the setting up of Nixon's apparatus. I recommended strongly and Henry agreed that the interdepartmental groups should be chaired by someone from the White House. The State Department tried to fight this, and my good friend Under Secretary Alexis Johnson came to work on me but it was unavailing. Then they went to work on Henry. That was unavailing. And finally they got [William] Rogers—who was going to be secretary of state—to go see Nixon, and Nixon stood fast and said, no, the chairing would be done—in other words the agenda would be set—by somebody from the White House.[9]

"So," Goodpaster noted, the die was cast,

> and that offered the power to Henry and Henry availed himself of it. And of course, with Nixon, you didn't have a man with the tendency toward openness that Eisenhower had. He was very convoluted and did a lot of thinking by himself or just through talking with Henry. And some would say it was distorted, but I would actually give pretty high marks to the way Henry and President Nixon conducted that. . . . There's no doubt that there was more of a grasp of foreign and security affairs during that time

than we had had before, which just adds to the tragedy of the mess Nixon got himself into."[10]

Kissinger recalls:

I had no fix on the subject of who should chair the interagency groups. But Andy Goodpaster and even more strongly Eisenhower were passionately opposed to the State Department chairing an interdepartmental group. They said the Pentagon would never go along with that and that it would lead to constant sabotaging and that the State Department will end up sitting on everything that they don't agree with. I called Eisenhower twice and I think Nixon and I went out to see him once on this. It was only part of the process, but Andy talked to Nixon and there was absolutely no doubt in Nixon's mind that he didn't want the State Department in on this because, as I said, I was actually agnostic on this issue. But this is how the structure was arrived at.[11]

The details of the structure were hammered out in an eighteen-page paper prepared for Kissinger by Morton Halperin, one of the brightest of the rising stars in the national security establishment, a top arms control specialist in McNamara's Defense Department and a man whose calm, professorial manner must have been a comforting reminder of academia to his long-standing friend Kissinger. The paper was critical of certain key aspects of the Johnson-era NSC process, including the weight the president gave the Tuesday lunches and how their informality often resulted in unclear communications and follow-through. This is a bit of an irony, of course, given that while every administration ends up stepping away from the formal NSC process and finds a comfort zone with some smaller, less formal process, none would make the group smaller or less formal than the double-act fashioned by Nixon and Kissinger. The paper also suggested that Johnson-era policy work done in the NSC was inadequately substantiated or explored in the policy papers produced by the group.

The structure recommended in Halperin's paper ultimately evolved into one that included eight major interagency policy groups.[12] There were also interdepartmental groups with regional focuses. Of these groups, which generally involved representation at the level of deputy secretaries or under secretaries of those agencies and advisory groups that played a statutory role as members or advisors to the NSC (State, Defense, Joint Chiefs, and CIA) plus key economic officials when appropriate (Treasury, Council of Economic Advisors, and Office of Management and

Budget), most ended up being chaired by the president's national security advisor. Groups that were not chaired by Kissinger often ended up having to direct their papers to those that were. The system would produce two types of papers, once again adopting new acronyms to put a fresh stamp on the fusty world of the bureaucracy (and to confuse future generations). Interagency committees would produce National Security Study Memoranda (NSSMs) that would offer agency views on the most important issues of the time and force the agencies to think ahead and anticipate the challenges they would face. Papers outlining policy decisions would be called, straightforwardly enough, National Security Decision Memoranda (NSDMs). In addition, the NSC would produce a variety of other memoranda and reviews of policy, which grew in importance as the NSC was increasingly seen as the engine driving U.S. foreign and national security policy.

In the argot of the strategic nuclear policy of the day, Halperin's paper—much like those offered before and especially after it by national security advisors—was the equivalent of a devastating bureaucratic first strike. It concentrated unprecedented power in the hands of the national security advisor and his team at the NSC and, when adopted by the president, ensured that the White House would drive national security policy throughout the Nixon years. Furthermore, Kissinger would enlarge that team much more aggressively than any of his predecessors. Although he started with only twelve professionals on his staff, within a couple of years there were eighty professionals working for the NSC. Like many such plans, Halperin's used myriad committees to mask the Nixon-directed shift of power to the White House, creating the illusion of a commitment to the interagency process. And also like many such plans, it diffused power through a system so complex that it should have been apparent that it would not work precisely as structured. Government systems tend to work well in inverse proportion to their complexity or size; the more complex the system, the less likely it is to have great results.

Shortly after Christmas, Kissinger submitted the plan to the president-elect, who quickly approved it—prior to the first meeting of Nixon's proposed group of NSC principals. The fact that they arrived to find the structure of their operations in place and that Nixon had made the decision alone, based on the advice of Kissinger, was "uncomfortable" for many of them and, in the words of someone who was close to the meeting, "probably infuriated" a number of them.[13] Although the cabinet had yet to be approved by the Senate or the president inaugurated, the operating style of the Nixon White House was already established.

The NSSM process was an important one for the Nixon White House, and, despite typical grumbling from the agencies for which it created more work, it produced something very unusual among White House staffs and interagency leadership groups of any period: forethought. Indeed, even today, senior policymakers look back on the Kissinger era as a halcyon time for planning ahead and anticipating change. Kissinger himself would speak with great pride of preparing contingency plans for different challenges— particularly with regard to confrontations with the Soviet Union—in which his team would put together notebooks that even included the cables to be sent in the event of certain triggering actions. In today's world in which virtually everything is reactive to the relentless demands of the twenty-four-hour news cycle, it looks particularly appealing. "In many situations which developed," said Kissinger, "we weren't surprised. We were prepared and had thought our options through in advance."[14]

Kissinger maintains that despite the accumulation of power within his office from the beginning, the interagency meetings were "very important to my approach."[15] Of course, Secretary of State William Rogers and Defense Secretary Melvin Laird resisted being pulled into a system in which they were secondary to Kissinger, although their struggles proved to be futile. The reasons were manifold. First, Kissinger notes, was the "peculiarity of Nixon. He didn't like to see too many people."[16]

Then there was Kissinger's rule of proximity. "The security advisor is down the hall from the president. The cabinet members are ten minutes away by car. You wouldn't think that it would make any conceivable difference, because it takes you ten minutes to set up an appointment with the president if you are in the building. But the proximity of the security advisor just makes it easier to call him in."[17]

Kissinger identified the uniquely supportive role of the national security advisor to the president in person: "The president sees the security advisor as being at his disposal, representing his interests, whereas the secretary of state is seen as representing the bureaucracy. . . . After all, the State Department has 180 clients. So they have a lot of things to get done each day which have a necessary priority for them. So the operation of the State Department, for example, is basically answering cables. It is very hard when you are secretary of state to say, the hell with this, now let's talk about long-range problems and work back from that. It's very hard for them. So what the State Department can do is offer proposals for the next meeting. It doesn't tell you where to go in the long term. That's what we tried to do. And the security advisor also ends up dealing with and knowing the problems that are of greatest interest to the president—which inevitably has to include all or many or most of the major policy issues."[18] Kissinger concludes his reflection by noting that until the State Department gets organized to do conceptual thinking, the leading role he claimed for the national security advisor will remain in place.[19]

Among those who look back on the period as a high point for the policy formation process itself are many of the young men who were Kissinger or administration staffers and continued to serve in government in increasingly influential roles afterward. Although their views are not universally positive on every aspect of Nixon-era policy, the degree to which there is unanimity about the quality of the process and of Kissinger's genius for keeping the big picture in mind (and for having thought that big picture through) is remarkable.

One junior civil servant working in the Pentagon on arms control issues at the time was Richard Clarke, later to become famous for challenging the Bush administration for failing to take action to protect the United States against terrorism before and after the September 11, 2001, attacks. Clarke notes that "Kissinger put an awful lot of emphasis on this process of open debate, options, analysis of outcomes, analysis of assumptions. And it was really a high art that resulted in the writing of a good policy paper."[20]

> The good policy paper laid out the issue and then provided a lot of good detailed background and technical background and political background and then it stated assumptions and stated goals so that if people quibbled about those assumptions or goals you could have a debate. But at least you knew where the rest of the paper was coming from—it was coming from a certain set of assumptions. There was always a good intelligence tab or appendix that provided all the data that the intelligence community knew. And then there were options, and under each of the options there was either a pro-con list or a list of evaluative criteria to evaluate each of the options on the same set of criteria: how would the allies react, how would the Congress react, would the Russians agree to it, how would it get us to our goals, and how close would it get us to our goals. And it was all very transparent. You could see the flow of thought.[21]

"Henry started out," continues Clarke, "with this model in which there were two documents. There was the review document or study document [NSSM] and then subsequently there was the decision document [NSDM]. And Henry maintained a discipline about that that subsequent administrations didn't."[22]

Jonathan Howe, a military aide to Kissinger who later went on to become an admiral and deputy national security advisor under the first Bush administration, echoes this praise for the Kissinger process. He notes, "One thing that I thought was missing in many other administrations, although everybody tries to achieve it, is the kind of very thoughtful strategic planning we did then. In other words, an effort to look out to the long term, conceptually, at what you are trying to accomplish, not in terms of the next six months or the crisis at the moment, not just in a four-year term, but what do we need to do over the next ten, fifteen, or twenty years and how do we get there. And this resulted in Kissinger's ability, in my view, even when we were in the midst of a frantic crisis—which was very consuming—to be able to sit back and try to figure out what we are trying to do with this, how are we going to come out, and what should we be doing about it rather than moment-to-moment management of the crisis which everybody was involved in."[23]

That description fits with what Kissinger calls his basic administrative philosophy, which was not to do the things that somebody else can do. "I spent a major portion of my time on medium- and long-range issues and wrote many of my memos to the president on these subjects. For example, take the Mideast. I had said that we had as a strategic objective to drive the Russians out of the Middle East. People laughed when I said it in 1969. But our strategy was to block everything that the Soviets backed in the Middle East. This was a systematic policy. So when the [October 1973] war broke out, I did not have to ask what the strategy should be. It was instead a question of implementing something we had already thought through."[24]

Schlesinger also admired the output of the process—and given the tension that later played a significant role in his relationship with Kissinger, such praise is not necessarily a given. He remembers that much of the "best work" was done in the early series of NSSMs that set policy for the administration (165 NSSMs were completed during Nixon's first term). "For example," Schlesinger notes, "one was based on Nixon's conviction that he could exploit the differences between China and Russia and set up triangular policies. And the memo that was produced examined both the political dimensions and assumptions by which we maintained our defense establishment and the nature of the defense establishment and the commitments we should be making. In fact, these early pivotal memoranda were Nixon's variation of the Solarium exercise."[25]

Kissinger issued seven strategic policy prescriptions within a day of the president's assumption of office. The first of these, NSSM-1, dealt with Vietnam. It was prepared by a team that included Daniel Ellsberg, then at

Rand (who would later leak what became known as the Pentagon Papers). This memorandum included a series of questions for the agencies to answer about Vietnam and our future there. The responses to these questions took up over 1,000 pages and were boiled down to a document half that size by Ellsberg. The "summary" was then used as the basis for an options paper, which in turn was used to frame the administration's first NSC meeting discussion of the subject. As Kissinger intended, it included all the options available to the United States except of one, "extrication," or simply and swiftly pulling out, which was deemed anathema and inflammatory to the military.

Another of this batch, NSSM-3, ordered the State and Defense Departments and the CIA to evaluate "our military posture and the balance of power."[26] Kissinger intended the study to be a sweeping reexamination of U.S. strategic and military policy, with particular interest in reconsidering the doctrine of assured destruction. Kissinger had long been a critic of this policy, which, in theory, would deter a Soviet nuclear attack by "maintaining at all times a clear and unmistakable degree of damage upon any aggressor or combination of aggressors even after absorbing a surprise first strike."[27] He questioned the appropriateness of doctrines based on massive retaliatory attacks, arguing that strategies of limited war would be more useful in an era of mutual vulnerability and calling assured destruction the "most inhuman strategy for conducting a war. . . . It was all very well to threaten mutual suicide for purposes of deterrence, particularly in case of a direct threat to national survival. But no president could make such a threat credible except by conducting a diplomacy that suggested a high irrationality—and that in turn was precluded by our political system."[28]

No issue, not even Vietnam, was considered to be of greater concern to the foreign policy community, and indeed, it was in certain respects a kind of existential question for the entire planet. The "order" of the Cold War era derived from a policy that was not only difficult to justify in the context of the U.S. political system but also that was virtually impossible to justify from the standpoint of any morality or ethical perspective regardless of its culture of origin. Kissinger had made his name in this area, and NSSM-3 represented not only an important initiative to adjust policies that were central to American foreign policy. It also offers important insights into the tensions this debate triggered among agencies of the U.S. national security community.

Philip Odeen, a defense specialist on the NSC from 1971 to 1973, noted that NSSM-3 "was useful within the Pentagon. It forced discussions about issues that a lot of people in the services, and the [Joint Chiefs of Staff] in particular, did not want to address. They didn't even want to think about them."[29]

Kissinger, however, had an ally in Ivan Selin, the acting assistant secretary of defense for systems analysis, who had worked in the Pentagon's Office of System Analysis (OSA) during the last two years of the Johnson administration. Like Kissinger, Selin had questioned the feasibility of both counterforce targeting and assured destruction but had received little support from his superiors in McNamara's Pentagon to evaluate existing strategies or explore alternatives.[30] Nonetheless, in the final months of the Johnson administration, the OSA drafted a proposal for revising U.S. nuclear strategy. With Kissinger's support for a comprehensive review of U.S. nuclear doctrine, Selin's aide Laurence Lynn, who had moved over to the NSC from the Defense Department, headed the NSSM-3 project and drew on his work with Selin in the OSA as he composed the report.[31]

NSSM-3 was completed in May 1969. One of its primary conclusions was that strategic superiority was not a viable long-term policy option. The memorandum noted that "up to now, the main criterion for evaluating U.S. strategic forces has been their ability to deter the Soviet Union from all-out aggressive attacks on the United States."[32] But the authors of NSSM-3 rejected the idea that a nuclear war might be characterized as a series of "spasm reactions," instead speculating that such a conflict "may develop as a series of steps in an escalating crisis in which both sides want to avoid attacking cities, neither side can afford unilaterally to stop the exchange, and the situation is dominated by uncertainty."[33] Consequently, in situations where the Soviet Union considered itself likely to be attacked by U.S. nuclear weapons, it might launch a preventive counterforce attack "using a portion of its strategic forces to strike U.S. forces in order to improve its relative military position."[34]

NSSM-3 cautioned that these hypothetical scenarios "have no precedent in Soviet military doctrine or tradition," making it "highly unlikely that such a situation would develop."[35] Even so, a U.S. capability for early "war termination, avoiding attacks on cities and selective response capabilities might provide ways of limiting damage if deterrence fails."[36] Overall, the interagency report questioned the continued utility of assured destruction as a component of U.S. strategic policy.[37]

While the study met Kissinger's goal of highlighting shortcomings in existing U.S. nuclear strategy, NSSM-3 did not provide him with alternative approaches. In June 1969, President Nixon, who shared his security advisor's discomfort with the suicide-or-surrender options laid out for him, agreed with Kissinger that further response options were needed and authorized "the Pentagon to devise strategies to meet contingencies other than all-out nuclear challenge."[38] However, the military bureaucracy still proved to balk easily. As Kissinger recalled:

> Our military establishment resists intrusion into strategic doctrine even when it comes from a White House seeking to be helpful. When I entered office, former Defense Secretary Robert McNamara told me that he had tried for seven years to give the President more options. He had finally given up, he said, in the face of bureaucratic opposition and decided to improvise. I was determined to do better; I succeeded only partially. Civilian defense planners were reluctant because more options would require some new forces, complicating budgetary decisions. The service chiefs were reluctant because they prefer to negotiate their force levels by bargaining with each other, rather than submitting them to the tender mercies of civilian analysts who, experience has taught, are more likely to emasculate than to strengthen them.[39]

Despite the request from the White House for a follow-up review of NSSM-3, which was conducted under the auspices of the NSC, Kissinger had difficulty "gaining access to military targeting activities to see exactly what targeting options did in fact exist. He found that the effort to implement Nixon's executive order ran up against the extreme reluctance of the military establishment to consider an alternative strategy."[40] In fact, the Joint Chiefs of Staff responded only after concerted White House pressure, a campaign of persuasion that was furthered by a major foreign policy address to Congress in February 1970, in which President Nixon rhetorically asked,

> Should a President, in the event of a nuclear attack, be left with the single option of ordering the mass destruction of enemy civilians, in the face of the certainty that it would be followed by the mass slaughter of Americans? Should the concept of assured destruction be narrowly defined and should it be the only measure of our ability to deter the variety of threats we may face?[41]

The speech, written largely by Lynn, was meant to publicly convey to the American public and the Soviet leadership that in a changed strategic environment, the United States could no longer place its confidence in assured destruction to deter possible Soviet aggression. However, Nixon's high-profile remarks, particularly the rhetorical queries that were added by Kissinger, were directed at a second audience "to signal unequivocally to the bureaucracy that the executive branch was most serious about devising more selective, limited options to be introduced into U.S. war plans."[42]

By February 1970, the White House and the Joint Chiefs had come to an agreement for exploring the basis of a new strategic policy, termed strategic sufficiency, which would provide the president with greater flexibility and expanded capability to target U.S. nuclear forces. According to Kissinger, the Joint Chiefs decided to play a cooperative role in reexamining U.S. war plans because "they understood that the doctrine of 'assured destruction' would inevitably lead to political decisions halting or neglecting the improvement of our strategic forces and in time reducing them."[43]

Meanwhile, the far-reaching study also called for a comprehensive reassessment of the American military posture and the implications for foreign policy of various strategies and budgets. For instance, a 1970 NSC report entitled "The Nixon Doctrine for Asia: Some Hard Issues" cited some of the implications from the study, noting that the "NSSM 3 projected cutback in our ready divisions after Vietnam is a fundamental manifestation of the Nixon doctrine for Asia. It was based on a realistic downgrading of likely threats, the feeling that five or six divisions couldn't stop Chinese hordes anyway, the aversion to another Asian ground war, and the need for defense budget savings. We have recognized in effect that for Asia we have been spending a great deal of money for forces that we suspect are insufficient against a threat which we do not believe will materialize."[44]

After the completion of NSSM-3, the NSC was directed to look at "less than all-out attacks."[45] As their exploration of options other than assured destruction continued, the State Department began to raise objections. Some officials in Foggy Bottom were uneasy that the development of plausible limited nuclear options would increase the likelihood that such weapons would be employed, while others expressed concerns that the multiplicity of strategic options would increase demands from the military for more weapons systems. And with Strategic Arms Limitation Talks (SALT), due to begin in April 1970, arms control proponents feared that the development of limited nuclear options would interfere with efforts to reduce superpower weapon stockpiles.[46]

The investigation was put briefly on hold during SALT (which ended inconclusively in August 1970), and more comprehensive studies followed as the NSC launched a "Strategic Objectives" review in early 1971. The Pentagon initiated a separate inquiry not long afterward.[47] In 1972,

Kissinger raised the profile of the studies, creating a new interagency group, the Defense Program Review Committee, chaired by the national security advisor, to develop more nuclear options in order to enhance deterrence and limit the consequences of a nuclear exchange.[48] Kissinger later ordered NSSM-169, a full interagency review to examine a series of limited-war options involving small-scale nuclear strikes and demonstration shots of nuclear weapons, together with problems associated with the loss of the U.S. counterforce option as a result of the destruction of the Minuteman force from Soviet attack.[49]

By the fall of 1973, a group headed by Odeen at the NSC prepared a Nuclear Weapons Employment Plan (NUWEP), which provided detailed targeting guidance to the Joint Chiefs of Staff and became the basis of NSDM-242, "Policy for Planning the Employment of Nuclear Weapons." NSDM-242 stated that the United States needed a "more flexible nuclear posture" that "does not preclude U.S. use of nuclear weapons in response to conventional aggression."[50] In the event of conflict, the goal was "to seek early war termination on terms acceptable to the U.S. and its allies at the lowest level of conflict feasible."[51]

At first, little happened after NSDM-242 was completed as David Aaron, an arms control specialist on Kissinger's NSC (who would later be deputy national security advisor under Carter) "feared the political consequences of [the] memorandum could be dangerous," since he and several fellow staffers believed it contained language that supported those in the Pentagon who favored a more provocative counterforce first-strike policy.[52] However, while Aaron tried to "study it into oblivion," Pentagon support for the decision memorandum was growing, particularly after the appointment of James Schlesinger as secretary of defense.[53]

Schlesinger, who shared Kissinger's skepticism about assured destruction, decided to utilize his powerful post to put NSDM-242 into practice.[54] At a January 1974 lunchtime press conference Schlesinger announced, without informing Kissinger (much to the national security advisor/secretary of state's displeasure, not surprisingly), that he was implementing a "change in targeting strategy" in order to develop alternatives to "initiating a suicidal strike against the cities of the other side," replacing assured destruction with a doctrine consisting of a "set of selective options against different sets of targets" on a much more limited and flexible scale."[55] After Secretary Schlesinger's public announcement, President Nixon signed NSDM-242 the following week. As we will see in subsequent chapters, this shift in policy, beginning with NSSM-3, was carried forward in the Carter administration by Secretary of Defense Harold Brown and, despite harsh rhetoric to the contrary, began a process of reevaluating America's nuclear stance that led to the major reductions in nuclear weapons of the Reagan era and thereafter.

Clearly, not all of the work of the NSC resulted in the kind of long-term ramifications of this particular paper. However, it is a useful illustration of the strength and nature of the behind-the-scenes policy formation process of the Nixon-Kissinger era.

As national security advisor, Kissinger assembled a team that was quite extraordinary. One of his executive assistants, Lawrence Eagleburger, later became secretary of state for the first President Bush. Another of his assistants, Anthony Lake, later became national security advisor to President Clinton. Another assistant, the one who remained at his side longest during this tumultuous time, Winston Lord, later became ambassador to China, assistant secretary of state for East Asia, and head of the Council on Foreign Relations. Kissinger's first military assistant, Colonel Alexander Haig, was a four-star general and White House chief of staff by the end of the Nixon administration and secretary of state in the Reagan administration. One of his military aides, Major George Joulwan, became the Supreme Allied Commander in Europe. One of his military aides, General Brent Scowcroft, later became Kissinger's deputy as national security advisor and subsequently became the only man to serve as national security advisor to two presidents. One of his closest aides and a key speechwriter, Peter Rodman, went on to hold senior posts in several Republican administrations, including a post in the Rumsfeld Defense Department in the second Bush administration. John Negroponte, who supported Vietnam peace negotiations, became U.S. Ambassador to the United Nations and later ambassador to Baghdad. Another young staffer, Richard Holbrooke, also later became Ambassador to the United Nations and played the central role in negotiating the Dayton Peace Accords that ended the conflict in Bosnia. John Lehman of the staff became secretary of the navy. Walt Slocombe became under secretary of defense in the Clinton administration. Lynn Davis became under secretary of state in the Clinton administration. Fred Bergsten, who led the international economics team, became assistant secretary for international affairs of the treasury. His successor, Bob Hormats, became assistant secretary of state and deputy U.S. trade representative. Another military aide, Colonel Robert McFarlane, was by the Reagan years one of Kissinger's successors as national security advisor.

"I think it was unique," says Winston Lord. "I don't think we'll ever see those conditions again. In principle, the system was not so great—in some respects lousy, even—but it produced some good foreign policy because

Nixon and Kissinger were so damn good . . . and the NSC staff . . . well, excuse the immodesty because I was part of it, but it was an extraordinary staff. If you look at everybody on that staff that has gone on since to be secretaries of state, NSC advisors, ambassadors, it just goes on forever."

The Nixon administration was unique for several reasons. Number one, Nixon had tremendous capacity, experience, desire to run foreign policy. So you had a president who wanted to control it, who distrusted the bureaucracy, particularly the State Department, figuring they were a bunch of either thoughtless bureaucrats or left-wing Democrats or both. But also, even if they weren't, he wanted to control it. Secondly, you had Henry, of course, not exactly resisting the situation. Thirdly, you had Nixon purposely choosing a loyal but hardly aggressive Secretary of State. And fourthly, you had issues at that particular time in history which lent themselves to tightly controlled, secretive negotiations. And I was involved in all three of those as Henry's special assistant: the opening to China, the Vietnam negotiations, and the discussions concerning détente with the Russians."

You can argue whether these had to be secretive to that degree, but the point is, all three of those were distinguished by dealing with totalitarian communists. You could deal with a few leaders; you didn't have to deal with the parliaments, public opinion, and so on. And they involved delicate negotiations, which couldn't really be done by a big committee. These talks involved politically risky moves by both sides. Thus, you could make the case for secrecy in each case. So the combination of the issues that were the most urgent, the personality and the expertise of the president, the abilities of the NSC advisor and his staff, and the nature of the Secretary of State combined to create a system that has never been the same before or since in terms of the total dominance by the White House. I mean not only did we run policy, in most cases, at least on those issues I mentioned, the secretary of state and the State Department and the Defense Department didn't even know what the policy was.[56]

Mort Abramowitz, one of America's top diplomats for the past three decades, notes:

Henry and Nixon conspired to do virtually everything. They tried to keep Laird and Rogers out. Rogers was easy to keep out. Laird was harder because he had forces in the Pentagon. But between Henry being sort of a

genius and having a powerful staff and having Nixon want to keep everyone else out—conspiring to keep State even out of things like letter writing—the result was unparalleled dominance. In fact, the period is a little
analogous to what happened during the second Bush administration,
except instead of it being a dominant national security advisor in partnership with the president, it's the vice president.[57]

Nixon's personal staff, his longtime aides such as Chief of Staff H.R.
(Bob) Haldeman and domestic policy advisor John Ehrlichman, were wary
of the power that Kissinger was acquiring, but they also saw him as an
important facilitator for Nixon's interests and a buffer that could protect
the president in the event that there were policy problems. They never
became close with Kissinger, nor he with them. The relationship was fairly
formal and remained somewhat at arm's length. Kissinger dealt directly
with Nixon, yet for all their collaboration, the two of them never became
terribly close either. In fact, Kissinger would come to be known among his
staff for mocking the president behind his back, noting when he was drunk
or ranting or going off to extremes. Although the president's closest staff
knew of this and consequently never fully trusted Kissinger, they also recognized that he would know when to ignore the president's more extreme
directives or, alternatively, when to try to redirect or contain them.

In short, over time, the group came to function together in a way that
helped it deal effectively with a volatile world. The Soviet Union and the
Cold War were the defining factors in virtually all U.S. foreign policy at
that time. They were the elephants, or, more appropriately, the bears in the
room in every discussion. Consequently, they were permanent constraints, and every U.S. foreign policy decision made in the postwar
period before the early 1990s had to be weighed in terms of potential
Soviet response. In effect, they were a built-in check on the United States
as a superpower, much as we were a built-in check on them. This kind of
balance of power produced both tension and stability. When it disappeared with the collapse of the Soviet Union, the opportunity opened up
for the United States to act more freely and, to some degree, less thoughtfully and less cautiously, because the counterbalances to our power were
less clear.

Nixon and Kissinger faced three distinct, major foreign policy tests in
addition to the continuous one constituted by the Soviet Union: in China,
in Vietnam, and over the war in the Middle East. Each would reveal both
their penchant for secrecy and a flair for the dramatic. In each is evident
the enormous concentration of power in the hands of one or two men.

Each shows a broader geopolitical vision, a sense that no matter the size or importance of the initiative, it was a piece in a larger strategy and its connections to other issues of import were being taken into consideration. Taken together, they provide both a picture of the great aspirations of the actors, for themselves and for their country's role in the world, and evidence of the limitations on that country.

.   .   .

Changes in American policy toward China were high on Nixon's agenda. He had broached the subject of an opening to mainland China in a *Foreign Affairs* piece in 1967, writing of "pulling China back into the world community . . . in the long run."[58] However, he had a shorter-term goal of rapprochement with the Chinese Communist Party (CCP) leadership as part of a strategy to resolve the Vietnam conflict while creating additional leverage in the superpower struggle with the Soviet Union.[59] As Nixon would say in private meetings, "With a country as big as China is, with that population, with that strategic location, it's far better to talk to the Chinese than to fight them."[60] And, of course, as has often been noted, the opening to China was something that only someone with Nixon's ironclad anticommunist credentials could even contemplate. Kennedy considered it, but concluded it would be political suicide. This is an aspect of the obligation to work against type in American politics. If Kennedy, a Democrat, were to appear soft on China, he would immediately be tarred for playing into stereotypes of Democrats as not being tough enough. Since Nixon was in some respects viewed as an extremist on defense issues, against communism, and the like, there were concerns that he would make the world more dangerous with his confrontational views; for him to make a statesmanlike gesture actually softened his image in a positive way. Hence the pronouncement "Only a Nixon could go to China."

Nixon made vague allusions in his first presidential press conference about "looking forward" to an upcoming, previously scheduled Warsaw ambassadorial meeting with CCP representatives (which was later canceled), although he also qualified his remarks, noting, "I see no immediate prospect of any change in our policy," and reiterated themes of hopes for long-term changes in relations with China in subsequent statements.[61] Other subtle and more tangible intimations of ending decades of hostility with "Red China" could be found in the reference to China as the "People's Republic of China" in NSC foreign reports.[62] Additionally, the administration lifted a series of minor travel and trade restrictions.[63]

But Nixon had a more comprehensive overhaul of China policy in mind and planned to carry out this revolution from within the White House. John Holdridge, an Asia specialist on the NSC staff, recalled a meeting between the president and his NSC team in November 1969 in which the "whole NSC senior staff trooped into the cabinet room and sitting in the center was the president and on his right was Henry A. Kissinger. And the president went on to say—and in no uncertain terms—that policy was going to be the privilege, the area of concern of the National Security Council. . . . So that set the stage for what we were doing. We were running foreign policy."[64] The selection of William Rogers as secretary of state reflected the striking change in the institutional balance of power. Herbert Levin, a staff member for East Asian affairs on the NSC, echoing earlier comments we have seen, noted, "Nixon knew what he was doing when he appointed Rogers, because he intended to do these things himself."[65]

To facilitate the compartmentalization of China policy, Nixon brought Kissinger "along as part of that whole apparatus to try to see what he could do," according to Holdridge, although the Harvard professor was not an expert on Chinese affairs.[66] The new president sent a memo to his national security advisor in February 1969, asking, "How do we establish relations with China?" Kissinger responded several days later with NSSM-14, "U.S. China Policy."[67] The study, the focus of an NSC Senior Review Group meeting chaired by Kissinger in May, reviewed U.S. relations with both mainland China and Taiwan and formed the basis of a broader reevaluation of its policy of isolation toward the country.[68] The national security advisor also ordered the NSC staff to prepare, without State Department input, a series of policy papers on China. As Levin recalled:

People on the outer fringes of the preparation, like myself, drove exercises in the pre–word processor days to find out everything that was on the government's books about China, what there was in law, what there was in the Federal Register, what there was in letters to chairmen of congressional committees, what there was in communications with other governments. We developed these encyclopedic books. Amazingly, it didn't leak that we were doing all this. Many of my colleagues in the State Department and the CIA believed that this was Henry simply having everyone else spin their wheels, wasting their time so they wouldn't get too curious about anything that might really be happening. In fact, their work was the mortar and the bricks of what happened when the grand policy designs actually took form. They heavily influenced policymaking by the information and analysis they provided, though they had little opportunity for formal policy advocacy.[69]

The NSC staff penned several more NSSMs on China policy in early 1970, including one on the tricky issue of China's admission into the United Nations that the president expressly wanted done "without any notice to people who might leak."[70]

While Kissinger gets and deserves much of the credit for what was accomplished with China, close observers argue that Nixon was the driving force behind the policy and that Kissinger had to be nudged along. Says James Schlesinger, "Back in the middle 1960s, Nixon had already conceived of this approach to China. He was much more enthusiastic about it than Henry was, certainly at the outset. Henry was much more of, initially, the skeptical college professor. China was primarily Nixon's own policy."[71]

Nixon writes in his memoirs that this concealment was necessary for his China initiative because "with advance warning, conservative opposition might mobilize in Congress and scuttle the entire effort."[72] Levin echoes this point, stating, "One of things that I think drove President Nixon and Henry Kissinger was the need to split the domestic conservative opposition."[73] Winston Lord, Kissinger's special assistant, cites a broader array of actors who would have to be left out of the loop for the China gambit to succeed:

> You were dealing with very sensitive issues where the President and Kissinger didn't want a lot of people in on it and a lot of leaks, and so on. And it's a lot easier to deal with these issues running it out of the White House, and the NSC staff, and back channels, and secrecy, and cutting out the State Department, than it would be dealing with NATO, Europe, or even the Middle East and some of the others.[74]

Thus, the focus on keeping the number of actors involved in Nixon's China initiative strictly limited was part of the administration's controversial strategy to establish relations with the CCP leadership, and the NSC represented a nexus of that White House–controlled effort. Lord added, "Prior to the China trip there were some in the State Department who worried that we would upset our relations with Russia, which in their eyes were more important. Which is ridiculous. It helped our relations with Russia. That was one of the main reasons to deal with China—to improve our relations with Moscow."[75]

This last point underscores how individual steps in the opening to

China were viewed in a comprehensive global context, as a result of the foreign policy worldviews, the intellectual engagement, and the profound understanding of the dynamics of international relations brought by Nixon and Kissinger.

The State Department, in Nixon's critical words, hadn't had a "new idea in the last twenty-five years,"[76] and Kissinger went to extensive efforts to keep Secretary Rogers, Assistant Secretary of State for East Asian and Pacific Affairs Marshall Green, and the rest of their department isolated from the China policymaking process. Kissinger relates numerous cases of a "tug-of-war" in which a reluctant, unadventurous State Department was overruled by the more forward-thinking White House.[77] The pattern of restricting State Department involvement continued after Kissinger and Nixon had visited China: Kissinger related an anecdote about how Lord, at the time a special assistant to Kissinger, the designated note-taker for the president's 1972 meeting with Mao Tse-tung, had been cropped from the official photo to soothe feelings with an aggrieved State Department because none of the department's officials were permitted to attend the meeting.[78] Lord himself adds, however, "I think it is fair to say, though, that in the end, State wasn't opposed to the China initiative. They simply were sensitive to the risks because they were so worried about the Soviet Union."[79]

While State Department officials continued to be targeted by Nixon and Kissinger, NSC officials who had moved over from State were playing an important role in setting the administration's new China policy, thus underscoring yet again the fact that in Washington, changing location often means changing positions.[80] As W. Richard Smyser, a senior NSC staffer, noted:

> Some of the key NSC players were Foreign Service officers, who were theoretically supposed to be loyal to the secretary of state. . . . One of the interesting phenomena of American bureaucratic functioning is how persons who were career Foreign Service officers would take the coloration of the White House when they were on the NSC and manifest the loyalty they had sworn to observe to the president and to the U.S. government as a whole, not necessarily institutionally to the State Department.[81]

Meanwhile, the Defense Department, the CIA, and the vice president, along with the State Department, were out of the loop on the China initiative.

Nixon describes how Vice President Spiro Agnew, who had expressed reservations in a 1971 NSC meeting about the trade and visa concessions made by the administration, "inadvertently careened into this diplomatic China shop" when he made intemperate remarks about the Chinese leadership's "ping pong" diplomacy.[82] And, according to Richard Solomon, a senior NSC staff member, the exclusion of the CIA meant:

> The one price that Henry paid in terms of the China opening, in terms of his dealings with the intelligence community, was that the compartmentalization of the policy process meant that he couldn't even turn to the CIA for support in learning about senior Chinese leaders that Winston and others ran into in Pakistan on the first trips. . . . Finally, I developed a covert "off-line" arrangement with CIA analysts to draw on the intelligence community's expertise and grasp of history—despite Henry's efforts to compartmentalize the process. . . . Well, Henry didn't want any of this information out of the NSC system, but I had a relationship where I could at least test some of my own ideas about what was going on with these intelligence analysts who did have access to history and a database that otherwise was not being brought into the system.[83]

Thus, as Solomon states, "by the time I showed up on Kissinger's NSC [in 1971], China policy was a one-man show. It was all run out of the White House."[84] That is, of course, a bit of an exaggeration. It was a two-man show.

Nixon and Kissinger put together a series of back channels to establish contact with China, usually without the knowledge of the State Department and other key foreign policy actors in the administration. The president began by asking French President Charles de Gaulle in March 1969 to inform the Chinese of his desire for a new American approach to relations, which was then conveyed by the French ambassador to Beijing. Additional lines of diplomatic contact were routed through Pakistan and Romania to expand the dialogue with the Chinese—elements of a strategy that were not fully revealed to NSC principals—and discussions and signals continued to be sent between the two sides in 1970 and early 1971.[85] While this back-and-forth diplomatic process was unfolding, Kissinger prepared for the hoped-for negotiations by commissioning a series of interagency studies on China policy.

After this lengthy period of back-channel communications, largely via Romania and Pakistan, the Chinese leadership agreed in April 1971 to receive, secretly, a high-ranking administration official. Upon hearing the news from Kissinger at a state dinner at the White House, the two men privately toasted the event with brandy in the Lincoln Sitting Room. Nixon and Kissinger went through a list of potential envoys to send to Beijing. Secretary of State Rogers was not seriously considered, as the national security advisor reportedly "rolled his eyes upwards" in response to the president's suggestion.[86] Nixon ultimately selected Kissinger, who speculated that he was chosen by the president because he "understood our policy best." "Another factor was undoubtedly that of all the potential emissaries I was the most subject to his control. I was on the White House staff; I had no means of publicizing my activities except through the White House press office."[87]

This mission is often cited as marking the "operationalization" of the national security advisor and the NSC—a dangerous line to have crossed in light of mistakes made with later NSC "operations" such as Iran-Contra. But previous national security advisors, such as Rostow, had taken such trips, as had de facto national security advisors, such as Harriman. In the end, hewing to the notion that the principal advisor to the president on critical international issues should sit in his or her office minding papers would be a ridiculous waste of a vital asset. Naturally, there are those with an institutional horse in this race, such as State Department types, who would be more than willing to handle top-secret sensitive assignments for the president themselves. However, because few are political appointees or have the trust or proximity to the president that the national security advisor does, this is highly unlikely happen. Kissinger's trip and his subsequent efforts as an emissary in terms of Middle East shuttle diplomacy, the Vietnam negotiations, or in exchanges surrounding the issue of détente with the Soviet Union were all important contributions that could best be carried out on the president's behalf by his national security advisor.

A great deal of energy went into preserving the secrecy of Kissinger's mission to China.[88] The U.S. ambassador to Pakistan was personally informed by Kissinger of the true purpose of his "information trip" to South and Southeast Asia, but neither the embassy staff in Islamabad nor the secretary of state were told.[89] Agnew and Defense Secretary Melvin Laird also had to be talked out of planned visits to Taiwan without being told the real reason why these trips would be unwelcome.[90]

The secret portion of the trip began in Pakistan, where a faked illness permitted Kissinger, along with NSC Asia specialists Lord, Holdridge, and Smyser, to slip away on a Pakistani plane to Beijing.[91] The NSC had already been drawn into efforts to deny information to the State Department on Kissinger's initiatives on Vietnam and arms control, when, as Lord put it, "You'd have to prepare a meeting of senior officials, or even a trip. State might not even know about the initiative. But if they knew about it, then they would get a sanitized MEMCON, as opposed to the real MEMCON."[92] The scale of deception grew to a comical degree with Polo I, as Lord described the subterfuge that he helped organize as they traveled to Asia:

> The classic example was the trip to China. We were on this small plane, purportedly going to India, Pakistan, Vietnam, and Thailand. We had briefing books, and I had to maintain three sets of briefing books, on the same small airplane, that we were passing around. One set for those who were going into China, namely Smyser, Lord, Holdridge, and Kissinger. Another set were for those knowing that people were going into China, but were part of the cover team staying back in Pakistan, namely Hal Saunders and one or two others. And then the third briefing book was for those who didn't even know there was going to be a China leg. And I swear to God, we'd get them all updated and I'd put my head on a pillow, and Kissinger would then wake up and look at it and want it redone again, and I've got to do all three all over again. It's one thing to redo a memo, but to redo three versions! But that was the classic sick case. . . . You not only had to be careful. You can't have people looking over your shoulder. You'd got to hand out the right book to the right person.[93]

Winston Lord enjoyed a historic moment when he became the first American official in China in twenty years after he went to the front of the airplane when it crossed the border. Kissinger, who was sitting in the back of the plane at the time, "never forgave [Lord] for that; [he] elbowed me aside and got off the plane first" in Beijing.[94] Lord has turned the delivery of that funny little story into something of a high art, a set piece in the tale of a great American diplomatic breakthrough—but his use of the story also reveals something of the light touch, the emphasis on humor and charm that so often is overlooked as a powerful asset that Kissinger and his team utilized in their missions and activities. Indeed, Kissinger's dry delivery and impish humor, which contrasted with his self-made image as the man with the most gravitas on the planet, is undoubtedly not only cherished by his friends and family but also a technique he used to send a message to individuals with whom he was dealing, to say, in effect, We have a personal connection, we are close, beyond formality. As diplomatic tools go, it was every bit as powerful as his formidable intellect—and perhaps more.

With the absence of direct communications facilities between China and the United States, and given the extreme degree of confidentiality of the visit, Kissinger had no contact with the White House while he was in Beijing. Nixon and Kissinger agreed that when he slipped back to Pakistan, he would use the code word "Eureka" if his mission had been successful; accordingly, he sent a one-word cable, conveyed by Al Haig, to the president.[95]

Kissinger returned to China with President Nixon in February 1972, accompanied by Rogers, Lord, and Holdridge, and at the conclusion of the high-level trip the two countries jointly issued the Shanghai Communiqué. Nixon's national security advisor had begun to draft the Shanghai Communiqué with Chou En-lai the previous October, when he met in Beijing with the Chinese prime minister to lay the groundwork for Nixon's upcoming visit.[96] Kissinger continued to hammer out the details during the February 1972 summit, usually in late-night sessions with the Chinese vice foreign minister and generally without State Department participation. As Lord describes it:

> We went over in October of '71 with a draft of the Shanghai Communiqué essentially done within the NSC, but picking up some ideas from State. It was a typical diplomatic draft with two sides agreeing and getting together on issues. Chou En-lai totally rejected it after checking in with Mao. He said, "This is crazy. We haven't talked to each other for 25 years. It's dishonest. It will make our allies suspicious, and it won't make any sense to our publics. So let each side state its own positions, and then we can state where our views converge." We drafted the whole damned thing overnight. They stated their positions on ideology and on specific issues, and we stated ours. I won't go into detail, but essentially it was done without State at all.[97]

That exclusion proved to be problematic when Secretary Rogers made a last-minute objection, after State Department officials—having finally seen the communiqué—pointed out that Taiwan was not specifically mentioned among U.S. defense treaty partners in Asia in the document.

Concerns about the reaction of congressional conservatives and the bad publicity stemming from State Department leaks resulted in a rare acknowledgment of State Department misgivings, and the Shanghai Communiqué returned to the negotiating table. In the end, both American and Chinese negotiators deleted all references to U.S. treaty partners, sidestepping the sensitive Taiwan issue, and thus securing a sea change in relations between the two countries.[98]

The China initiative was a watershed on several levels. It amounted to a breakthrough in relations between the world's most powerful nation and its most populous. It also changed the global balance of power equation in a fundamental way, as Nixon and Kissinger had intended. Although China was still struggling to get its sea legs as an international power, its size and power made it a useful counterbalance in discussions between the United States and the Soviet Union and in terms of regional issues. The mission was also seen as validation of "Nixon the Statesman" and is cited by many on his team as an important factor in his 1972 landslide reelection.

For Kissinger, however, the mission was an even bigger breakthrough personally (a fact that did not go unnoticed by the somewhat jealous, always paranoid Nixon.)

Richard Holbrooke, who would later play an important role in the Carter administration's efforts to normalize relations with China, observes, "Kissinger created the concept of the modern national security advisor. He was the first one who truly went operational. From Kissinger on, all of them have had some operational responsibilities."

> Kissinger therefore changed everything. But the real issue is, should a national security advisor travel on his or her own? The fact that Henry first did so in secret suggests they were concerned about it themselves at first. Henry will tell you with some pride that his name was not in the [newspapers] for the first two years [of Nixon's presidency], but the truth is, it wasn't in the papers because Nixon didn't want it there. But Nixon and his men couldn't control Henry's image after China. After the secret China trip, which was as dramatic a piece of theater as we will ever see in foreign policy—because it was, in fact, conducted in secret and only revealed after it was all over and successful—that's what made it so dramatic.

"From then on, Kissinger was a superstar and the NSC job was forever transformed," remembers Holbrooke from his offices high above Central Park in New York, considering a role that he himself might one day play. "Even twenty years later, I remember going to visit Tony Lake right after he got the job. He was already beginning to assume a far more activist role than he said he wanted to see in a national security advisor back when he was at State [as head of Policy Planning for Carter]. Given his earlier relationship with Kissinger, I teased Tony, saying 'I think there's some kind of vapors in the paint here that Kissinger left and it infects almost every occupant there.'"[99]

.   .   .

Of course the penchant for secrecy that was manifested in the China dealings, while justifiable in terms of the mission and the times, has to be seen as a symptom of something more when taken in the context of the history of the Nixon administration. Part of it was the lingering culture of secrecy that had endured since the Second World War and masked our covert actions from Guatemala to the Bay of Pigs, from the fall of Diem to our blundering assassination schemes for Fidel Castro. But part of it was also the Nixon administration's culture of distrust. Nixon, suspicious by nature, a prober into conspiracies by profession, a victim of back-channel attacks throughout his career, and an insider well aware of what the other guy might do, infused every element of his team's operations with his own paranoia.

Even harsh Nixon critics must acknowledge that he knew whereof he spoke when it came to conspiracies and plots to undo him. Indeed, one of his finest hours had come on the evening of his election defeat in 1960, when, knowing that Chicago Mayor Richard Daley had ordered Cook County, Illinois, polls kept open until he knew how many votes Kennedy would need to beat Nixon—and thus seeing all the telltale signs of the fix that historians have subsequently concluded was in, Nixon decided not to contest the election. This was both a grace note and an acknowledgment by Nixon that he knew how the game was played.

Unfortunately for him, the rules of the game changed on his watch. Jack Kennedy could fiddle the election results in 1960 and then be virtually canonized by the American public, but that was not to be the case for Nixon. In June 1972, the arrests at the Watergate complex in downtown Washington set in motion a chain of events that would reveal the very old-school way Nixon was playing the game, the corruption and disregard for the law inherent in that approach, and the depths of the obsession with secrecy in the White House. After all, the "plumbers unit" in the White House (which was co-headed by former Kissinger staffer David Young, who subsequently moved to England to escape the glare of the Watergate scandal and founded an international affairs commentary publisher called Oxford Analytica) was established to eliminate leaks in the Nixon White House. Ironically, in the end, its existence led to the greatest laying bare of backstairs White House operations in history and permanently contributed to greater transparency in the White House and virtually all of its operations.

Although Kissinger was not touched by Watergate, it affected him to the extent that it compromised the president, his partner in foreign policy, consequently placing more of a burden on Kissinger not only to handle things on his own but also to provide "good news" for the beleaguered administration. That said, his office, his NSC, was infected by the same kind of paranoia that gripped the rest of the administration. Kissinger, too, feared that leaks could be his undoing, and he went to great lengths both to keep his activities secret and to clamp down on and identify violators.

Secrecy may have enabled Nixon and Kissinger to obtain better results in negotiations with the Vietnamese, the Soviets, the Chinese, and within the Middle East. In retrospect, it is hard to say the same for some of the secret deals that were struck with the Russians to facilitate the SALT agreements and détente, the secret wars in Southeast Asia, the secret initiatives to destabilize regimes such as that of Chile's Socialist President Salvador Allende, or, during the Ford years, the secret wink and nod given to Indonesia's President Suharto before his bloody onslaught against East Timor, which left hundreds of thousands dead.

To be fair, we are decades removed from the context of the times, from the standard operating procedures of the day, and from the degree to which the Soviet Union was genuinely thought to be a pernicious threat that could infect any corner of the globe with deadly consequences. But perhaps the single greatest factor that led to the degree of secrecy that marked the activities of Nixon and Kissinger and their team—which included keeping major portions of their own administration in the dark—was the growing divisions at home over Vietnam.

To be sure, there were major protests and even riots in the streets in 1967 and 1968 over the war. But Vietnam was a tear that kept growing, particularly when Nixon's "secret plan" for peace never materialized. Nixon had won office with the promise of a "secret" undertaking. You get what you bargain for in American politics—and the message he got was important too: "secrecy" sells. (Lord comments on the "secret peace plan" that helped Nixon win office: "The closest thing he had to a secret plan to end the war in 1968 was using the Russians to lean on Hanoi as well as the Chinese. One of the reasons for the opening to China was to isolate Hanoi, have Russia (whom we approached via détente largely for this reason) and China both lean on Hanoi.")[100]

Once in office, Nixon had to deliver on the "plan." Political priority number one was ending the war and the unprecedented division it was causing in American society. Never had an international issue split the country so profoundly. Unfortunately, Nixon quickly discovered what George Ball had warned of: that Vietnam had become a quagmire in which there were no desirable options. As Kissinger wrote, the "guerrilla wins if he does not lose; the conventional army loses if it does not win."[101]

Thus, a tie was a win for the North Vietnamese and a stalemate was a tie. In this calculus, dragging the war on was in their interests, and their people were already living under such harsh conditions that the prolongation of the war was unlikely to lead to a change in political will in Hanoi. Indeed, a war between a democracy and a totalitarian state is hardly a fair fight, because the discomfort of the people has vastly greater consequences in the former. Consequently, campus protests in America were much more dangerous to Nixon than hundreds of thousands of U.S. troops and carpet bombing were to Ho Chi Minh.

Early in the administration, Nixon and Kissinger initiated a committee called the Vietnam Special Studies Group to help coordinate planning for the war. This group was to help manage the crisis on the ground while other efforts by Nixon and Kissinger to end the war got under way. Nixon went to Europe in March 1969 to talk to the allies (an obligatory first trip for a president in those days) and to run down feelers through France and Russia to move forward with talks with the North, an effort Kissinger had been working on since the late Johnson administration. The trip did not produce any breakthroughs, and when Nixon returned he found that fighting had intensified in Vietnam. Nixon felt that toughness with the Vietnamese was the only way to bring them to the table—you only make peace in such circumstances when war is proven to be a less desirable option. However, Defense Secretary Melvin Laird, a former congressman and a highly respected, thoughtful, moderate voice who would be the toughest of all of Kissinger's cabinet colleagues for him to best in bureaucratic infighting, was strongly opposed to directly bombing the North as a way of punishing them for the escalation of the conflict.

The next best option in the minds of the Joint Chiefs and U.S. commanders on the ground was to bomb North Vietnamese assets in Cambodia. In an NSC meeting on March 16, 1969, Nixon ordered the start of bombing in Cambodia. Because the administration thought the bombing would be controversial and seen as an expansion of the war that Nixon had been elected to bring to an end, it was kept secret.

Within a few weeks, another prong of the Nixon-Kissinger strategy was put in place when the administration began yet another secret initiative, this one to reduce American casualties by shifting more of the combat burden to the South Vietnamese. This approach, called Vietnamization, had also been pursued during the Johnson administration. The sticking point was that the South Vietnamese were not terribly enthusiastic about the idea, and their leaders sought to maintain as much U.S. support as possible.

On its face, the initial Nixon-Kissinger approach—an effort to advance diplomatic talks with the North, strengthen public resolve with tough action on the ground, and use back channels to shift the burden to the South and thus reduce the U.S. casualties that were triggering the bad headlines and political unrest in the United States—made a lot of sense. It was a policy that represented the consensus views of the entire Nixon national security team, even if many of them had been forced to fight rearguard actions to defend their views. However, all three components of the plan initially depended on secrecy.

And that was not to be. Six weeks after the bombing in Cambodia started, the *New York Times* ran a front page story revealing what was going on. Nixon was apoplectic. The administration's efforts would be undone if such leaks continued—in his eyes, they were a threat to our national security. Kissinger immediately contacted the FBI for assistance in tracking down the leakers. He spoke to FBI Director J. Edgar Hoover multiple times in a single day to ensure that sufficient efforts were being made to identify the source for the story. Suspicion initially focused on Mort Halperin, among others, because he was seen as a liberal voice on the NSC staff. Within four months, Halperin had gone from rising star to leak suspect, and Kissinger did not hesitate to use whatever tools he had to against his friend—largely because of his sense that national security warranted it. Their efforts in Vietnam would come to nothing if they could not be conducted as planned, and further setbacks in Vietnam would be dangerous for the United States on many levels.

Kissinger soon edged Halperin out of his position of responsibility in the NSC by suggesting to him that he would remove himself from suspicion if he were no longer in a position to see sensitive materials. Halperin, who realistically had no choice but to accept the approach or resign, was then essentially forced to leave the NSC because he could no longer see classified information. (Such privileges are always important, but especially so in an administration in which virtually every major initiative was secret.)

Although this was an unsettling incident and a preview of things to come, the plan with regard to Vietnam continued to unfold. Nixon had already let Soviet Ambassador Anatoly Dobrynin know that he sought "avenues other than the existing negotiating framework,"[102] a reference to the talks begun at the end of the Johnson administration in a last-ditch attempt to turn the tide of public opinion and both win the election for Hubert Humphrey and reform the public perception of Lyndon Johnson. Those talks, bogged down by discussions about secondary issues such as

the shape of the negotiating table and perhaps undercut by Nixon-cam-
paign–related back-channel messages to the Vietnamese, had been mud-
dling forward, but Nixon and Kissinger felt that more direct high-level
communications were needed.

Kissinger initiated contact with two senior Vietnamese emissaries,
Xuan Thay and Mai Van Bo, through an old friend, Jean Sainteny, a former
French colonial official in Hanoi. (Sainteny's wife had been a student of
Kissinger's.) Naturally, the mission was secret, with Kissinger supposedly
doing some sightseeing in Paris but slipping away to meet with the Viet-
namese in Sainteny's apartment.[103]

While Kissinger set an ambitious goal for reaching a settlement with the
North Vietnamese, progress was slower than desired. And although
changes in strategy associated with Vietnamization—for example, the
reduction of high-risk missions, such as large-scale sweeps—actually cut
U.S. combat fatalities almost in half from the first part of 1969 to the second, the drawing out of the conflict was thought to be undercutting the
administration's political credibility. Among the various approaches Nixon
and Kissinger considered seriously was one that involved significant escalation of the war in the North. This approach, to show that the United States
was willing to go as far as it took to achieve a desirable outcome, even
included discussion of the U.S. use of tactical nuclear weapons, echoing
discussions among Eisenhower's team (of which Nixon had been a part)
during the Korea conflict. The fact that we had such an extensive nuclear
arsenal meant that the option of using it would inevitably come up. It
almost certainly worked to our advantage in terms of how we were perceived by our enemies. However, that was as far as it could go. Actually
using nuclear weapons was very unlikely, as much because of the political
consequences at home and among our allies as because of potential tactical
or strategic advantages vis-à-vis our enemies.

Nixon felt, however, that we needed to be seen as ready to use all our
resources, ready to press the button, in order to achieve maximum leverage. "I call it the Madman Theory, Bob," his chief of staff, Bob Haldeman,
quoted him as saying. "I want the North Vietnamese to believe I've
reached the point where I might do anything to stop the war."[104]

The next major manifestation of that toughness came as negotiations
were dragging along unsatisfactorily in early 1970. Kissinger was facing
one of the unscripted consequences of secrecy. As his aide Lord put it, "We
were more generous in our offers to Hanoi than the New York Times edito-
rials [that] were beating up on us for not being generous. So that's the
price you pay for secrecy."[105]

Early that year, Cambodia's Prince Norodom Sihanouk was ousted and that country went "into play" among the region's various forces. A Cambodian general, Lon Nol, took up the baton of the country's leadership and was drawn into an alliance with the South Vietnamese when, after consultation with South Vietnam's Vice President Ky, South Vietnamese forces supported Cambodian objectives with attacks against the North Vietnamese. This suited the objectives of the South, which was seeking to win greater U.S. support again and now had an "expansion" of the North Vietnamese threat to point to.

Within the NSC, staffers began to see this as the slipperiest slope in the region—the growing conflict had the potential to actually drive the North Vietnamese further into Cambodia and potentially into positions of greater strength or influence. Among those on the staff who sounded such warnings were Anthony Lake, then thirty years old and already seasoned by time as a diplomat in Vietnam, as well as William Watts and Larry Lynn.

As the fighting between the South and the North grew more intense, the United States continued to provide support in arms and weapons to Lon Nol and the South, while General Creighton Abrams and other members of the U.S. military leadership urged authority to do even more. NSC meetings and discussions within the Washington Special Action Group (another of the committees in the NSC's convoluted hierarchy of interlocking committees) took place in an effort to "forge a consensus" that never actually came. Nixon was pressing for greater action in support of Lon Nol, and Kissinger was searching for solutions to help the president achieve his goal. Kissinger had initially hoped that South Vietnamese action alone would be sufficient to solve the problem—provided the Army of the Republic of Vietnam (ARVN) had sufficient U.S. support. But some in the U.S. military leadership were coming to the conclusion that support from (U.S.) Military Assistance Command Vietnam was required. At the same time, Secretaries Rogers and Laird were expected to do as they did, which was to oppose further escalation of the war. In the NSC, all views were advocated, with Kissinger and General Westmoreland arguing for the "middle path" of ARVN attacks, Vice President Agnew supporting General Abrams's combined-attack option, and Laird and Rogers arguing against the combined operation. Nixon was frustrated. This was not the outcome he had wanted. He began to work the system outside of committees, as was his wont. He spoke to Kissinger throughout the day on April 23, pushing toward action. Meanwhile, hints in the press of a U.S. inclination to invade Cambodia produced more anxiety and desire for secrecy at the top. Kissinger worked the system on behalf of his boss and soon convened a "military briefing" that did not include Laird or Rogers. CIA director Richard Helms also attended. At the meeting Joint Chiefs of Staff chairman Admiral Thomas Moorer, with whom Kissinger had a strong working relationship, and the CIA boss both supported an expanded operation into Cambodia.

Meanwhile, in the NSC, staffers who were opposed to expanded operations began an effort to head them off. Indeed, the NSC of this era was, in a very real sense, a reflection of the American public, with several important staffers—including some who were originally very close to Kissinger—beginning to be deeply troubled by the administration's actions in Southeast Asia. Lake, Morris, and Lord led the way with a paper that they hoped would reveal the dangers of the plan of action that seemed to be the one Nixon was leaning toward. Later that day, along with staffer Larry Lynn the three met with Kissinger, who accused them of being "his bleeding hearts club"—in other words, of being typical of the "soft" liberal views of the antiwar crowd. They argued that the information about Cambodia was sketchy, that consequences of an invasion were not fully thought out, that it could lead to an expansion of the war elsewhere in the region, and that it would be devastatingly costly from a domestic political perspective.

Over the following weekend, Nixon mused on the issue at Camp David while hanging out there with his pal Bebe Rebozo. Thus, at this critical juncture in America's Vietnam history, the inner circle of the U.S. government expanded to include one of the president's drinking buddies, a not entirely reputable businessman from Florida. Kissinger flew up to Camp David and back, and the discussions continued after Nixon's return to Washington. At one point, aboard the presidential yacht, they also included the attorney general, Nixon political crony John Mitchell.

Kissinger tried to pour oil on the roiling waters of his staff, but to no avail. John Prados recounts that Kissinger met with William Watts over the weekend and tried to reassure him. Watts then said, "When I came to work for you, my sense of loyalty was first to the American people, secondly to you, and finally to Richard Nixon. I'm against this operation on every count and I'm resigning."

"Your views represent the cowardice of the Eastern Establishment!" Kissinger roared back.

Watts stalked off into the Situation Room, where he told Win Lord what had happened.

Not long after, Al Haig entered looking for Watts, angry. Kissinger was in his office, enraged, reportedly throwing papers around. "What the hell did you say to Henry?" Haig asked. "He's furious."

Watts announced he was leaving the NSC staff whereupon Haig began to argue too. Watts had no interest in Haig's objections. Then Haig put on his best parade ground voice and thundered, "You've just had an order from your Commander-in-Chief and you can't refuse!"

"Fuck you, Al," Watts shot back. "I just have and I resign."[106]

On April 26, an NSC meeting was held with the supposed intention of making a decision on the issue of Cambodia. In reality, Nixon had made up his mind and Kissinger had come around to his view. They orchestrated the meeting to get the go-ahead with the invasion and approved the decision memo that day. Laird and Rogers protested—not in that meeting, but in a private meeting with the president afterward, to no avail. Preparations were to be made for a speech that could reveal the attack (after the fact). Haig gave the job to Morris and Lake. They also resigned before the invasion was publicly announced.

Later Kissinger would make light of the incident, noting that Lake actually resigned several times before leaving his office, playing it up to the press. But the issue was far more divisive, complex, and dark than that. Within a short time after the resignations, FBI wiretaps were placed on these staffers' phones. Recriminations and even lawsuits followed. Ultimately, Lake received an apology from Kissinger for statements he had made at the time of the break. The letter of apology hung in his study for years.[107]

The Cambodia invasion produced the greatest divisions and debates of the war. Within four days of the president's speech announcing the invasion, campus protests produced the infamous images of Kent State, where four students were killed by national guardsmen. Over 800 universities closed or were shut down by strikes. Nixon and his staff went further and further into a kind of siege mentality that undoubtedly contributed to decisions taken in the run-up to Watergate and beyond.

When Kissinger reflects on Vietnam, he notes that during the early days of the administration, the "State Department took a powder on Vietnam. No one wanted to touch it. So I was allowed to give the briefings on it initially and that shaped the opinion of the administration thereafter."[108] But by May 1970, there was no doubt about how foreign policy was being made in the Nixon administration. Nixon drove, Kissinger navigated, and the others had the choice to make comments from the back seat or get out of the car.

.   .   .

Kissinger, working with a staff that numbered more than 100 in late 1970 and would grow to over 150 during his tenure, handled other issues during the first term that drew his attention away from Vietnam. Notable among these were the arms control talks with the Soviets that were designed to reduce tensions between the two nations, the idea of "détente." Within the logic of reduced tensions and a better ability to strike a balance among the various interests of the world's great powers, the approach made considerable policy sense. But it, too, alienated many and left scars among some, particularly in the military.

General William Odom, later the military aide to Zbigniew Brzezinski during the Carter administration and the head of the National Security Agency during the Reagan administration, states, "I turned down a job on [Kissinger's] NSC during my last months serving in the American embassy in Moscow in 1974. There I had witnessed a great deal about Kissinger's implementation of the détente policy. Much of it was a sellout to the Soviets. I simply could not imagine trying to work as a staff aide to facilitate such a policy. As an officer, of course, I would have accepted a directed assignment to the NSC staff, but since I was given a choice, the assumption being that I would jump at the chance, I refused. Ambassador Walter Stoessel, who passed on to me Kissinger's offer, was astonished, at first refusing to believe me."[109]

The peace deal that would ultimately win Kissinger and Le Duc Tho the Nobel Peace Prize was signed in Paris on January 27, 1973, after slow troop withdrawals and retaliatory bombing missions that reassured the South that the United States had not abandoned them.

Of course, the war did not end for two more years, and Kissinger never went to pick up his prize. It was too controversial, and the continuing volatility in Vietnam led him to believe that going to pick up the award when peace was not actually at hand would produce a storm of controversy. The Nixon administration at that time in 1973 could ill afford the controversy. Watergate was starting to dominate the headlines and with it, half of the partnership at the center of U.S. foreign policy would be forced to retreat to manage his defense and ruminate about his darkening fate.

Meanwhile, after Nixon's reelection, the inevitable changes that occur in an administration that has been in office for four years took place—exacerbated, of course, by the turmoil that Watergate was beginning to generate. Although some contemplated Kissinger's departure because he was becoming so high-profile in his own right that he was overshadowing the president, he was also popular and seen as competent, and the wounded administration could ill afford to lose him. Indeed, the fact that Kissinger understood this power was displayed in his frequent tactical resignations—threats designed to move the president's views toward his own or away from some perceived calamity. "They were a tool he used," said one former staffer, "like a weapon in his arsenal to manage the president and the bureaucracy. They needed him more than he needed them—or so they thought. He played it like a virtuoso."[110]

To Kissinger's benefit, his loyal aide Al Haig had also become a Nixon favorite and by May 1973 had risen to become chief of staff at the White House. He was seen as rock solid and competent—a striking contrast with his reputation during his years as secretary of state in the Reagan administration, by which time he had come to be seen as something of an unguided, ego-powered missile. But Haig played a central role in ensuring that Kissinger finally achieved the ultimate victory in his battles with William Rogers. Haig helped engineer Rogers's resignation (although Rogers would not be edged out by the chief of staff and forced the president to ask for his resignation) and the appointment of Kissinger as secretary of state on August 22, 1973. Kissinger brought along many of his top NSC aides, including Winston Lord, Helmut Sonnenfeldt, and Lawrence Eagleburger, while keeping Assistant Secretary Joseph Sisco as the department's top Middle East official. Although Kissinger formally retained the title of national security advisor, his deputy, Brent Scowcroft, ran the day-to-day operations of the NSC, assisted by Peter Rodman.[111]

This completed the ascent of Henry Kissinger to a position of power in the U.S. government unrivaled by any non-president in American history. He was, as far as international affairs was concerned, the prime minister, the driving force behind U.S. policy, its chief architect, its chief spokesperson, its chief engineer, and its chief driver. Nixon could no longer address himself to critical issues and, consequently, when crisis came in the fall of 1973, it was Kissinger who was all alone in the inner circle.

Less than seven weeks after Kissinger's swearing in, at 6:15 a.m. on October 6, 1973, Sisco woke the new secretary of state in his suite at the Waldorf Towers in New York with news about the outbreak of hostilities in the Middle East. One hundred thousand Egyptian troops and 1,000 tanks attacked Israeli forces on the east bank of the Suez Canal while 35,000 Syrian troops and 800 tanks broke through Israeli positions on the Golan Heights.[112] Once again, Washington was surprised by the turn of events in the Middle East, although State Department intelligence analysts, interpreting Egyptian military maneuvers and belligerent statements uttered that spring by President Anwar Sadat, had predicted on May 31 that the chances were "better than even" of a regional war. Kissinger had responded that summer by ordering the drafting of a new contingency plan in the event of a renewal of Arab-Israeli hostilities, but little urgency had been attached to the task, which was never completed.[113]

Scowcroft convened the first of two meetings of the Washington Special Action Group (WSAG—the group Kissinger had established as a crisis management and response mechanism) on October 6, where the participants—including Defense Secretary Schlesinger, Joint Chiefs of Staff chairman Admiral Thomas Moorer, Deputy Secretary of State Kenneth Rush, CIA Director William Colby, Deputy Assistant Secretary of State Alfred Atherton, and Deputy Assistant Secretary of Defense for International Security Affairs James Noyes—were presented with incorrect information from the CIA that the military preparations taking place did not indicate that a full-scale war was about to break out. The misconception was later corrected, but when Kissinger arrived in the White House Situation Room that evening to chair the next WSAG meeting, "one cabinet member was calmly reading the comic strips in the local newspaper. Other WSAG participants were bantering lightly about the crisis," according to William Quandt, the NSC's Middle East specialist.[114]

Once Kissinger arrived, serious discussions about the U.S. response began. The group's consensus was that Israel would prevail within a matter of days. For the next several days, Kissinger tried to advance a cease-fire *status quo ante* to the warring parties while limited arms deliveries were made to Israel.[115] In a meeting that day with Chinese Ambassador Huang Chen, Kissinger openly laid out his strategy:

> Our strategic objective is to prevent the Soviet Union from getting a dominant position in the Middle East. That is our basic objective. Israel is a secondary, emotional problem having to do with domestic politics here. Our objective is always, when the Soviet Union appears, to demonstrate that whoever gets help from the Soviet Union cannot achieve his objective, whatever it is. . . . The second principal objective we have in the current crisis is not to create a situation in which a country uses international disputes to attack and then ask for a cease-fire after it has gained some territory. So we advocate now a return to the *status quo ante* before the fighting started. . . . So we want to say now that we are for a return to the cease-fire line, so we can say it later when Israel has broken through into Syria.[116]

In line with this objective, Kissinger put together an elaborate form of linkage. To Soviet Ambassador Anatoly Dobrynin, he promised that he would push for most favored nation (MFN) trade status for the Soviet Union if they showed restraint in the Middle East. To Israeli Ambassador Simcha Dinitz, he promised that he would resupply the Israeli military if Jewish leaders would withdraw their support from Senator Henry Jackson's effort to attach an amendment linking Soviet policy on Jewish emigration to the granting of MFN status.[117]

However, the premises behind Kissinger's policy did not acknowledge the situation on the battlefield, and by October 9 Israeli Prime Minister Golda Meir told Ambassador Dinitz to phone Kissinger at night, which he did twice, to inform the secretary of state of their increasingly dire situation. The depth of Israeli concerns was even more vividly captured by the Israeli government's decision to place their Jericho nuclear weapon delivery systems on alert.[118]

A number of policy options were considered in the emergency WSAG meeting that took place after Kissinger's hourlong discussion with the Israeli ambassador, with Kissinger pushing for a secret resupply of Israel that included planes, ammunition, and the eventual replacement of all Israeli military equipment losses once the fighting had ceased. Defense Secretary Schlesinger objected to Kissinger's plan, saying that it would enrage the Arabs when they discovered the resupply effort, but Nixon, who met privately with the Kissinger after the meeting, backed his secretary of state.[119]

By the next day, October 10, the Soviets had begun a limited resupply effort of their Syrian ally, sending them ammunition and fuel but doing little else, in accordance with the MFN deal they had with Kissinger. Over the next two days, Schlesinger reversed his opposition to Kissinger's resupply plan but decided to use U.S. military transporters rather than a private charter arrangement that had been proposed by Kissinger but was later seen as impractical.[120] On October 12, at the urging of Nixon (who had been convinced by Haig, who had in turn been convinced by Schlesinger), Kissinger organized the supply of F-4 fighters and substantial munitions via U.S. military transporters, which began on October 13, a week after the fighting began.[121]

Notably, as Kissinger was directing all this activity, President Nixon remained preoccupied with the growing Watergate scandal.[122] Political bombshells, including the resignation of Vice President Spiro Agnew and the "Saturday Night Massacre," took place at the same time as the latest Arab-Israeli conflict, and no NSC meetings were held during the October War.[123] In fact, Kissinger did not want Nixon flying back from Florida, where he was dealing with the fallout stemming from Agnew's corruption charges, telling Haig, "I would urge you to keep any Walter Mitty tendencies under control."[124] Consequently, Nixon, as Quandt writes, had little involvement in the day-to-day policy details as the crisis unfolded, largely ceding control to his secretary of state/national security advisor, who relished the expanded autonomy.[125]

By October 19, the tide had turned decisively in Israel's favor in the war, and Kissinger, waiting for an opportune moment to get the warring parties to end the hostilities, received a personal invitation from Soviet leader Leonid Brezhnev to come to Moscow "in an urgent manner" to negotiate an immediate cease-fire.[126] Kissinger flew to Moscow on October 21, intending to agree to a solution that would save Egypt's Third Army, which was being surrounded by Israeli forces, while stalling for time to allow Israel to consolidate its territorial gains. Ironically, his task was complicated by President Nixon's pronouncement to Brezhnev—made without consulting Kissinger—granting "full authority" to his secretary of state to craft an agreement. Kissinger had intended to draw out the negotiating process by referring proposals back to Washington.[127]

More worrisome, as Kissinger discovered once he arrived in Moscow, Nixon provided formal instructions for what he was to offer in his talks with Brezhnev, directing the secretary of state not only to seek a cease-fire but to ask the Soviets to work with the United States to fashion a comprehensive regional peace plan. Kissinger's master plan entailed cutting the Soviets out of the diplomatic loop and having the United States serve as the indispensable middleman for both the Arabs and the Israelis. Consequently, he ignored the president's instructions and limited his agenda the following morning with the Soviet leader to finding an agreement to implement an immediate cease-fire.[128]

To Kissinger's "amazement," the Soviets had agreed, within four hours, to his plan for a simple cease-fire, to support the implementation of UN Security Council Resolution 242 calling for "withdrawal of Israeli armed forces from territories occupied," and support for direct Arab-Israeli negotiations to resolve other outstanding problems. The speed of the agreement upset Kissinger's plans to buy time on the battlefield for his Israeli allies, and he tried to slow the pace of discussions by inventing a story that he had left some relevant papers back at his guesthouse, which he could not submit until later that day. His ruse was undone by his assistant, Peter Rodman, who missed Kissinger's signals and proudly presented the documents to the Soviet foreign minister.[129]

One day later, Kissinger flew directly from Moscow to Israel, without much advance warning, to meet the prime minister as her forces were tightening the noose around Egypt's Third Army. She reluctantly accepted the cease-fire on October 22, and Kissinger triumphantly returned to Washington. However, by the time Kissinger arrived back in the United States, fighting had resumed and the Soviets were charging that Israeli forces had violated the agreement, possibly with American backing. To express his displeasure, Brezhnev sent a note directly to Kissinger, "a highly unusual procedure that indicated his awareness that Kissinger, rather than Nixon, was now running the show."[130]

As Egypt's situation became increasingly desperate, President Sadat called for the introduction of U.S. and Soviet troops to the Egyptian side of the cease-fire line, a move that Kissinger opposed, concerned about the pretext of expanded Soviet diplomatic and military involvement in the region. In between talks with Ambassador Dobrynin, Kissinger received a call from the president, who wanted to talk not about the renewed crisis in the Middle East but rather to engage in an emotional discussion about his clouded political future.[131] When Kissinger returned to his tense discussions with the Soviet ambassador, he reiterated his opposition to the presence of Soviet troops in the region. Several hours later, at 9:30 p.m. (4:30 a.m. Moscow time), Dobrynin relayed a "very urgent" message from Brezhnev that the Soviets were prepared to unilaterally deploy peacekeepers to the region to enforce the cease-fire if the fighting continued.[132]

Kissinger relayed the message to Nixon and convened an ad hoc session of the NSC one hour later, attended by Secretary Schlesinger, CIA director Colby, Joint Chiefs chairman Moorer, Haig, and Scowcroft but without the president.[133] In the time between Brezhnev's message and the upcoming meeting, Kissinger conferred with Haig, who recommended that the president not be woken up to attend the discussion.[134] The two officials also decided to hold the meeting in the White House, rather than the State Department, as originally planned, with Kissinger chairing the session as the president's assistant rather than as secretary of state, in order "to preserve at least the fiction of presidential control."[135] Around midnight, the participants decided to send a signal to Brezhnev and the Politburo leadership to desist from sending troops by placing U.S. nuclear forces on DEFCON III, the highest level of peacetime alert. President Nixon learned about the decision the following morning.[136]

A message came from the Soviets the next morning backing away from the previous threat and accepting an American suggestion that nonmilitary observers rather than soldiers be sent in.[137] Kissinger held a WSAG meeting on the morning of October 25 in which he requested a contingency plan for sending U.S. forces to the Middle East, but the cease-fire held and the U.S. alert was lifted the following day.[138]

During this crisis and others that followed, the degree to which one unelected man, Kissinger, dominated decision making is unprecedented. Whether one thinks it was too much or not, it cannot be denied that Kissinger rose to the challenge. His priority seems to have been primarily to thwart the Soviet Union, both in the eyes of public opinion and strategically in the Middle East. He managed to accomplish this under the extreme time constraints established by the crisis both in the Middle East and at home. While efficiency at the time seems to have required it, Kissinger nevertheless made all the decisions, including moving U.S. troops into nuclear alert—setting what was later seen as a dangerous precedent.

It is not surprising, therefore, that when Gerald Ford became president after Nixon's resignation in August 1974, he was wary of Kissinger's authority. Nonetheless, he felt compelled to keep in place the system he inherited in order to ensure the continuity he felt was necessary to heal America's wounds. Ford, a career congressman who became vice president after Spiro Agnew resigned in disgrace, was by no means the clumsy, clueless man many, including Chevy Chase on *Saturday Night Live*, have portrayed him to be. According to Kissinger, he was an extremely effective president and "perhaps the most underrated in recent American history."[139] Kissinger, who possesses a degree of intellectual snobbery, regularly commented about the quality of Ford's mind. That Ford is an able thinker should not be a complete surprise, given that he graduated from Yale Law School and had a stellar and effective career in the House of Representatives.

During Ford's first year as president, the system worked as it had before, with Kissinger dominating the apparatus of the government like a modern Colossus of Rhodes, one foot in the State Department and one in his NSC office at the White House. He used one job to facilitate his objectives with regard to the other and was effectively impossible to check, even though he did have opponents such as the new defense secretary, Schlesinger, who had known Kissinger at Harvard, was every bit his intellectual equal, and was not afraid to challenge him. Indeed, Schlesinger was willing to challenge anyone, which subsequently led to his falling from favor with Ford, who would replace him a year later with Donald Rumsfeld, a young, rising star of the Republican Party and the one bureaucrat who really got the best of Kissinger in a couple of battles later in the administration.

Ambassador James Dobbins, a career diplomat who later became a specialist in failed states, from Bosnia to Haiti to Afghanistan, for the Clinton and George W. Bush administrations, recalls, "The Ford administration was very professional. I actually worked for Kissinger when he was both national security advisor and secretary of state. I was working for his counselor, Hal Sonnenfeldt. And when we actually did our memos, we had White House and State stationery and we would do our memos on one or the other, depending on how we wanted to route it and whether we wanted to avoid anyone else in the State Department."[140]

Ultimately, Ford got his footing as president and began to notice problems in the operation of the administration. He had doubts about Schlesinger's loyalty and was also under pressure regarding CIA operations, as Watergate and Vietnam misadventures that had involved (or had been perceived to involve) agency personnel gave rise to new public distrust of the agency. Ford's right-hand man, to whom he gave the title of "coordinator" rather than chief of staff, was Rumsfeld, and Rumsfeld had been having run-ins with Kissinger since assuming the role, particularly over trying to keep the president front and center before the press. Rumsfeld resented having to do this and was one of the instigators of an effort to actually underscore to the press differences between Ford and Kissinger so that Ford could be seen as his own man.

On November 2, 1975, the consequences of the growing tensions were announced to the public. Schlesinger was out, to be replaced by master bureaucratic maneuverer and new youngest secretary of defense in history, Donald Rumsfeld. William Colby, the quiet, professorial, exceptionally intelligent career intelligence officer who had risen to become director of the CIA, was fired and replaced by another rising Republican star, George H.W. Bush, who reportedly accepted the post in exchange for agreement not to compete against Ford for the Republican presidential nomination. Rumsfeld was replaced by his young protégé from Wyoming, Dick Cheney. And Henry Kissinger gave up one of his titles, that of national security advisor, in which role he was replaced by his deputy, General Brent Scowcroft. Each of the rising players in this mix was ultimately to go on to play a profound role in the future history of American foreign policy—although virtually none of their most significant work would take place during the remainder of the "caretaker" Ford administration.

Comments Dobbins, "It was a considerable diminution of Kissinger's power when he gave up the national security advisor job. He still had a lot left and is probably the leading figure in the modern history of American foreign policy. But it was still a diminution of power, and it was interesting to see that play itself out. Kissinger would expect Scowcroft to defer to him, and Scowcroft would very pleasantly say, you know, Henry, I don't think that's going to work."[141]

Jonathan Howe recalls, "Brent was and is a very modest and open guy. A kind of ideal, low-key professional director of the NSC staff and advisor to the president. But remember that during that time frame there was a lot of congressional pressure behind the Kissinger job split, saying that one person should not be both secretary of state and national security advisor, and so when Brent took over it was incumbent on him to ensure that there had been a real split, that he was his own man. He and Kissinger were still close and good collaborators, but Brent knew the boss was President Ford."[142]

Ford himself says:

I had good relationships with both Henry and Brent, and I used them as they should have been used under the law that was passed in 1947. I depended upon a good relationship with Henry as secretary of state, and he was a first-class one. But I, at the same time, used Brent and his new responsibilities as the head of the NSC according to the law there as well.

Strictly, I used Henry for the primary purpose of executing and formulating foreign policy for my administration. At the same time, Brent, as head of the NSC, would make comments and observations and consult with me directly on policy and the choices we faced. However, I would also say that Henry was the primary promoter of foreign policy decisions and he made certain that I was the final determining person in making a judgment. I was president. Commander-in-chief. Henry made recommendations. And if I wanted additional background, I would turn to Brent.[143]

Commenting on the notion that somehow Kissinger's role substantially diminished when he became secretary of state alone, Winston Lord, who ran the policy planning shop for Kissinger when he was at State, said, "It's all bullshit. I mean, Henry ran foreign policy when he had one hat, when he had two hats, and when he had one hat again. And Brent was loyal and good with Henry but he was not a balance against Henry. I mean Henry fully ran foreign policy until the end of the Ford administration. Of course, it did make sense to make the change on some level. After all, when he wore two hats, he could send himself a memo and then approve it, which was ridiculous. Even Henry in a candid moment would tell you it was kind of a weird system."[144]

Robert Gates, who worked on the Scowcroft NSC under Ford and later was deputy national security advisor for the first President Bush, noted that even after the change, the "real decisions were going to be made, in the first instance, by Henry Kissinger sitting down with the president, deciding what was going to be done, and what everybody else really thought didn't matter very much. I mean, the truth is neither Kissinger [nor his successor Brzezinski] were trusted very much by the other principals."[145]

Scowcroft himself notes that the core difference between the Nixon period and the Kissinger period was the president himself. During Nixon:

> It was a very tightly controlled NSC. Kissinger and Nixon knew what they wanted to do—often it was Nixon pushing the idea in the first instance—and after they agreed, it was just a matter of shepherding the flock to do what they wanted to do. . . . Ford was not an expert in foreign policy. He was an expert on budgets but not foreign policy. And so he wanted to step back and ask, "What is this world about? What are my options?" And then Kissinger would present some options—A, B, C, D. Ford would then turn to me and ask, "Are there any other options?"[146]

In Scowcroft's comments and philosophy the contrast with Kissinger could not be clearer. Kissinger was the auteur of his own foreign policy. Scowcroft was the great collaborator. Yet, interestingly, in the contrast lies an important lesson about the NSC and how it operates. These two men—one flamboyant, brilliant, egotistical, and creative and the other dry, extremely but not flashily intelligent, and bureaucratically skilled but trusted by his colleagues—represent perhaps the two most successful national security advisors in history. They were and are friends and later were colleagues at Kissinger's consultancy, Kissinger Associates. They are stunningly different and yet, as we shall see when we examine Scowcroft's more important tenure as national security advisor during the first Bush administration, they achieved great things and provided great service with totally different styles and approaches.

Yet the one thing that links them in their successes is their partners. Richard Nixon and George H.W. Bush were probably the two presidents since Eisenhower who were best equipped to manage U.S. foreign policy. They drove their policy in partnership with their national security advisor (and in Bush's case, in a real three-way collaboration involving Secretary of State James Baker). It is often said that a good process does not guarantee a good outcome but a bad process guarantees a bad outcome. Well, a corollary is that a good national security advisor or a good national security team, in the end, depends heavily on the character and capabilities of the president to succeed.

Still, despite the extraordinary backgrounds, qualities, and idiosyncracies that Nixon and Kissinger brought to their roles, the reality is that they were elevated, torn at, and immutably altered by the era that brought them to power. They inherited a nation bitterly divided over Vietnam, one torn by racial strife, one rattled and energized by the rise of a new generation, one witnessing the very fabric of society being rewoven before its eyes with the first stirrings of the information age: the moment the nation started viewing itself and the world through the pixelated filter of the television screen. Internationally, too, America's role was being debated in the context of a Cold War that seemed to pit two equal adversaries against one another with the ultimate outcome in doubt. They stepped to center stage and like other actors were transformed by the setting around them, but even more so by the views and roles their audience projected upon them. Thus, much of what they did quickly became symbolic, their actions assumed relevance beyond their intrinsic importance, and their struggles mirrored the struggles of generations and society at large. Because they were political figures, this fact in turn, changed them, limited them, and empowered them. It was a heightened era and as a consequence their legacies remain heightened in our consciousness three decades later.

Just as they can hardly be viewed apart from one another, so too, they cannot be viewed apart from their times. Such a view explains much of what otherwise would seem inexplicable in retrospect even when it does not excuse it.

7

A Superpower in Search of Itself

It is a new world that calls for a new American foreign policy—a policy based on constant decency in its values and on optimism in our historical vision.

—President Jimmy Carter, May 22, 1977
Address at University of Notre Dame

I'M NOT EASILY intimidated, but Zbigniew Brzezinski was exceptionally impressive the first time I met him, when I was a young aide to Brooklyn, New York, Congressman Stephen Solarz and Brzezinski was national security advisor. Solarz and I met with him in a conference room in the Old Executive Office Building before a briefing that Brzezinski had agreed to do for some of Solarz's constituents. The neatly dressed former professor, already seen as a dominant force in the Carter administration, was polite but extremely disciplined, exuding a kind of intellectual rigor seldom seen in Washington. He spoke with a moderate Polish accent despite having grown up in Canada after his father, a Polish diplomat, decided to remain in that country after the communist takeover in their homeland. At the time the decision was made to stay in North America, Brzezinski was seventeen. He attended McGill University, where he excelled academically, and then went on to graduate school at Harvard.

It was in the world at Harvard that he studied and later taught alongside Henry Kissinger, a man with whom he would be compared for the rest of his life because of their accents, their common academic and professional backgrounds, their roles as national security advisors, their brilliance, their ambition, and their intensity. The comparison is a bit facile, though, because they are very different on many, many levels. Kissinger has an easier charm and uses humor more frequently. Brzezinski's humor often seems to have more of an edge to it. Kissinger is more drawn to the social whirl, whereas Brzezinski is clearly the more devoted to his family of the two. Kissinger glitters. Brzezinski burns. Kissinger is a German Jew. Brzezinski is a Polish Catholic. Kissinger, like so many German Jews, is in a number of respects more German than Germans, more European than Europeans, and he spent much of his career focused on the great power relations among European states or mingling with European elites with whom he shaped many elements of his *weltanschauung*. Brzezinski's focus seems to have been more colored by his family's experience of losing their homeland to the Soviet Union, and he became a much more careful student of the USSR, Russia, and the communist world. While both are brilliant and accomplished academics and writers, Kissinger's forte is in understanding the complex interrelationships of global power; Brzezinski, no slouch in that regard to be sure, has distinguished himself throughout his career with a number of books that were remarkably prescient about the future, whether he was writing about the onset of the information age (which in the early 1970s he called the technotronic era) or the factors weakening the Soviet Union (which he cited years before it was popular in the mainstream to contemplate the decline or downfall of the Soviets) or anticipating the shape of the post–Cold War era in the 1990s and in this century.

In their views of foreign policy, there are several areas where differences between the two men are apparent—their views of the Soviets, of U.S. interests with regard to Israel, of the relative importance of values such as human rights in foreign policy, and of the appropriate use of secrecy. But in one area the difference between them is fundamental, and, since the two men abutted one another in the leading foreign policy advisory roles of their administrations, defines a watershed in the evolution of America's foreign policy and how we viewed our leadership role and our mission in the world.

Kissinger and Nixon's actions suggested that at least to some degree, they saw the world in terms of America's decline and the potential rise of the Soviet Union. They acted as though worried that the tides of history had turned against the United States. Brzezinski and, by extension, Carter saw the world in terms of the decline of the Soviet Union and the opportunity that created for the United States. Brzezinski characterizes the Kissinger view as being that of a "Spenglerian" declinist, a reference to Oswald Spengler, the German philosopher and mathematician who wrote *The Decline of the West*. Spengler postulated:

The last century [the nineteenth] was the winter of the West, the victory of materialism and scepticism, of socialism, parliamentarianism, and money. But in this century blood and instinct will regain their rights against the power of money and intellect. The era of individualism, liberalism and democracy, of humanitarianism and freedom, is nearing its end. The masses will accept with resignation the victory of the Caesars, the strong men, and will obey them.[1]

Spengler's theory was based on the idea that the modern era in the West was much like that of ancient Greece or Rome and that, like those civilizations, we would ultimately be undone by our less enlightened, more brutal instincts. Kissinger of course did not articulate or adopt quite such an apocalyptic view. Rather, his theories and his actions suggest that he and Nixon were uncertain of how long America could endure on top. Such doubts are not surprising when considered in the context of the upheaval of the 1960s and 1970s, the weakness of our allies, the range of troubles confronting us on the horizon, and reports that the Soviets would soon be capable of equaling our military technologically and in terms of destructive power.

In an article on the subject in *The National Interest* by Neil McInnes in 1997, Harvard's Stanley Hoffmann is quoted as saying, "Henry, in his melancholy, seems to walk with the spirit of Spengler at his side." McInnes continues:

Kissinger himself has said that he conducted policy "with a premonition of catastrophe." He has admitted to "a perverse fascination" with Spengler's historic pessimism, but says he rejected Spengler's notion of the inevitability of decay; indeed, he had said as much in his 1950 Harvard thesis. Nevertheless, critics have claimed to detect a fatalistic defeatism in his policies, something which flowed from a belief that American civilization had passed its high point, like so many before it and had to accommodate the rising forces represented by the USSR, "Sparta to our Athens." This became, briefly, a political issue in the 1970s, when retired Admiral Elmo Zumwalt said Kissinger had told him such things; Ronald Reagan declared that the Sparta/Athens=USSR/USA analogy was a lapse of faith that was making Kissinger too keen to cut a deal with Moscow. Kissinger said his views were being distorted and misrepresented, and from what we know of his sympathy with the Kantian idea of moral freedom we can believe him. But at least one of his biographers maintains there is a "kernel of truth" in the suggestion that the former Secretary of State was a case of Spenglerian pessimism.[2]

Many contemporary observers felt that Kissinger and Nixon were acknowledging decline through policies such as détente, in which they adopted a strategy that seemed to be intimating our weakness by suing for a balance with the Soviets, and the accompanying SALT negotiations seeking to balance our strategic capabilities. You don't sue for balance if you can easily afford or achieve superiority. At least, so goes the argument, and objectively it makes some sense.

Since the 1950s, Brzezinski had been devoting himself to the study of the Soviet Union and communist systems. Brzezinski, who speaks Russian, wrote about the innermost workings and evolving dysfunctions of the Soviet system. In a series of books and articles, Brzezinski pinpointed the weaknesses in the Soviet political and economic systems that could lead to the gradual breaking down of that system. He saw the cracks in the façade and anticipated the disintegration to come better than virtually any other foreign policy figure of comparable stature.

Brzezinski broke through the wall of groupthink that had immured the NSC until the mid-1970s. The argument that America was in decline, or at least the argument that America was at a potential disadvantage in the competition with the Soviet Union, was founded on the narrow focus on strategic arms and arms control issues that had priority during the height of the Cold War. This is the only way to explain how an adversary with a corrupt and failing political system and a corrupt and failing economic system representing a group of peoples held together by force rather than affinity could be assessed as our equal purely because of the number of nuclear warheads they had and their capacity to deliver them. Even historians like Paul Kennedy (*The Rise and Fall of Great Powers*) have decried the impulse among contemporary strategists—among whom he cites Kissinger—to "all too often have equated weapons-systems policy and military posture with 'Grand Strategy.'"[3] (Eisenhower implied a somewhat more balanced view when he spoke of a "grand equation" of American power, referring to the balance that must be struck between equally important domestic economic and domestic military power.)

Brzezinski—who, for all his similarities with Kissinger, brought a very different perspective to the job—would help design and construct a bridge to a different approach in collaboration with Jimmy Carter, the most unlikely foreign policy activist, after Harry Truman, ever to assume the presidency.

Carter, born in rural Georgia in 1924, was raised as a kind of golden boy of his time and place. He was a good student and a churchgoing Baptist, and he attended the U.S. Naval Academy and became a submariner working under the guidance of the idiosyncratic and brilliant Admiral Hyman Rickover, who transformed the U.S. Navy by creating the modern nuclear submarine service. After his career in the navy and time working on his family's peanut farm, Carter entered politics and rose to become governor of Georgia, becoming a symbol of the "new" South. He was enlightened, antisegregationist, and committed to the modernization of a state that still suffered the open wounds of the racial strife of the 1960s.

He was also deeply ambitious. Outwardly Carter seems a quiet, self-effacing man, a man of great faith. But he is also intensely self-confident and possessed of a very high belief in both the power of his own intelligence and his ability to achieve what he sets out to do. In these characteristics, he is like most men who ultimately become president—although you get the distinct impression that he, like Nixon, falls into the category of men who were fueled in their quest for the job by a desire to achieve the highest office in the land as opposed to other, also ambitious men, such as Ronald Reagan and Bill Clinton, who may have pursued the job also out of a compulsion to be liked by as large an audience as possible, or the Kennedys or the Bushes, who seem to have pursued the job largely because they felt they were supposed to.

Carter wrote about Brzezinski in his memoirs, "To me, Zbigniew Brzezinski was interesting. He would probe constantly for new ways to accomplish a goal, sometimes wanting to pursue a path that might be ill-advised—but always thinking. We had many arguments about history, politics, international events, and foreign policy—often disagreeing strongly and fundamentally—but we still got along well. Next to members of my family, Zbig would be my favorite seatmate on a long-distance trip; we might argue, but I would never be bored."[4] Brzezinski, in turn, has called Carter, "shrewd, rather deliberate yet fundamentally very decent and engaging." He admired his intelligence and yet was aware of his "occasionally surprising naivete," admired his "dedication to principle" but expressed concern about his "excessive tactical flexibility," admired his situation management skills but felt that they sometimes paid a price for his overstatements, appreciated his serenity but also noted the chills that came when their relationship endured "major shifts from genuine warmth to sudden distance."[5]

Brzezinski and Carter met when Brzezinski was serving, in addition to his teaching post at Columbia, as executive director of the North American branch of the Trilateral Commission. The commission brought together senior business, government, and academic representatives from Europe, the United States, and Japan to help address issues they faced as the leaders of the developed world as well as potential challenges from the developing world. Brzezinski had been introduced to this club of influentials when he came to the attention of David Rockefeller, chairman of Chase Manhattan Bank, after the publication of Brzezinski's book *Between Two Ages*, in which he highlighted many of the difficulties confronting the world's developed, communist, and less developed countries.

The Trilateral Commission is one of those clubs of establishment insiders that provoke in conspiracy theorists visions of men in gray suits gathering to run the world. The Council on Foreign Relations, the Bilderberg Conference, the Pugwash Conference, the Bohemian Grove, and the annual meeting of the World Economic Forum in Davos, Switzerland, are all such gatherings. As anyone who has ever participated in any of these events will tell you, at best they are excellent networking opportunities and forums for the exchange of interesting ideas—and they seldom offer much more than that. Indeed, it stands to reason that a good conspiracy would require a much smaller group of people operating much farther from the limelight. That said, in the 1970s, the Trilateral Commission was in its prime, and many who ended up playing important roles in the Carter administration were drawn from its ranks. The list includes Vice President Walter Mondale, Secretary of State Cyrus Vance, and Secretary of Defense Harold Brown—which means that with Brzezinski and Carter, every member of the inner circle of that administration's foreign policy apparatus had worked with the commission. Others who were important to the administration, such as Deputy Secretary of State Warren Christopher (later Bill Clinton's first secretary of state), Carter arms control chief Paul Warnke, State Department head of policy planning Tony Lake, Assistant Secretary of State for East Asian Affairs Richard Holbrooke, and director of the Political Military Bureau at State (and future head of the Council on Foreign Relations) Leslie Gelb, were also members of the Trilateral Commission or had worked with the group as authors. That's how conspiracy theories get started; the fact that over time various members of this group would be at each other's throats would no doubt be discounted by committed conspiracy theorists as a clever distraction.

Carter had been recommended to Brzezinski as a potential member of the group, a high-profile politician representing a new trend in American politics who was also known to be interested in broadening his horizons and deepening his knowledge about international issues. Brzezinski helped Carter join the group and was quickly impressed by him as a potential rising star. Just as it takes an almost pathological need for the job to enable someone to sustain the travails and to work the decades it might take to become president, it takes a similar level of ambition and regular application of that ambition to rise up the policy ladder. Merit alone does not bring advisors to the attention of potential patrons or potential presidents. Consequently, every single figure in this book has spent much of his or her career working the system—getting involved in networking groups, getting published, going to cocktail parties, developing connections, sending encouraging notes to those on the rise, offering to help.

In 1974, when Brzezinski learned that Carter was considering running for president, he dropped him a line offering his services. Carter accepted the offer and during the course of 1975, Brzezinski and Carter communicated periodically. Brzezinski offered memos and articles and ideas and suggestions, and Carter found them useful. Eventually, after Brzezinski had told his wife how struck he was with Carter's performance at a Trilateral meeting in Japan where he made the case for a balanced approach to achieving peace in the Middle East, Muska Brzezinski suggested that he play a more active role in Carter's campaign. "Put your money where your mouth is," she said. "If you like him and believe in him, don't wait for developments, come out and support him."[6] Brzezinski made a donation to Carter's campaign and started "more systematically" writing papers for Carter—even though at the time the Georgia governor barely showed up on the national political radar, with poll ratings down around 2 percent. Brzezinski, who was known well to all the candidates in the race and could no doubt have worked with most of them, had placed his bet on the longest shot in the race. Soon he was Carter's top foreign policy advisor, his resident "professor" on issues that were of much greater importance to Carter as a presidential candidate than they had ever been when he was dealing with local issues in the Peachtree State.

Carter's campaign was as much a watershed in American politics as the foreign policies he and Brzezinski and the other members of the administration promulgated would be. The nation was numb in the aftermath of both Watergate and Vietnam. While few in the street would consider or articulate questions about American decline as academics might, people knew in their gut that something was deeply wrong, that this was not the America they had been raised believing in, and that much of the blame lay inside Washington, inside the establishment—and in the Oval Office itself. Nixon was a discredited villain. Gerald Ford, who had pardoned Nixon, knew that he would have to run at a distance from the man who had appointed him to the vice presidency. Sensing the need for a new coalition, he dumped his own vice presidential candidate, Nelson Rockefeller, a Kissinger patron, and put Senator Robert Dole, of Kansas, on his ticket. Ford was a decent man and ran offering a return to traditional values and the best traditions of American politics.

Jimmy Carter was something altogether different. He spoke softly and simply of giving the American people a government as good as its people. He was an unknown, and he seemed very different from most professional politicians. He was a born-again Christian from the Deep South who taught Sunday school and actually seemed to believe in it. He was the anti-Nixon, perhaps honorable to a fault. He was straight out of the populist traditions of American politics, and yet he was something new—and he signaled something new.

In the postwar era, America was changing in dramatic ways quite apart from its role in the world. Rural black populations from the South were continuing to move into cities. Suburbs were sprouting around those cities as middle-class families, now with cars and good highways and transport systems, began to commute. And slowly, the population continued its historic shift away from the place where European settlement originated, in the Northeast, to the West and the South. The Sunbelt was beginning to be born.

American politics reflected this shift. Whereas in the past, presidents had been from the East or the Midwest, Johnson had been from Texas and Nixon from California. Yet both of these men were creatures of the Washington establishment, and now that establishment was under siege. So, a new trend, running against Washington insiders, began. Carter was the first outsider from this group and the first from the Deep South. Reagan, too, would run as an outsider, from the Far West. And although George H.W. Bush was about as eastern establishment as an American can be without being named Adams, he managed to run as a Texan who could relate better to outside-the-beltway America than the Massachusetts governor, Harvard-educated Michael Dukakis. Less sleight of hand was needed for Arkansas Governor Bill Clinton or, for that matter, George W. Bush, who seemed more Texan than Sam Houston despite his bloodlines or his Skull and Bones membership at Yale.

Another trend began with Carter that may have been somewhat more pernicious. Carter became the first candidate to openly and vigorously profess his faith as testimony to his character and his nature as a person. That in and of itself is certainly not a bad thing. But with his success in so doing, he opened up an era in which presidents and presidential candidates began to wear their religious affiliations on their sleeves and in which religious groups grew to have ever greater political significance. Given the historical consequences of such connections between religion and politics, the founding fathers had carefully sought to build a nation founded on a separation between church and state that has gradually begun to erode.

But given Nixon's transgressions, America needed a Sunday school teacher from far outside the orbit of Washington, D.C., and with Carter's surprising electoral success, they not only got him but also triggered a host of important trends that have carried through to the present day. Indeed, as we shall see, with Carter they also got a president would confront a host of issues that seem rather different from those of America's recent past and rather similar to those we face today.

One of the themes of Carter's campaign was to differentiate himself from Ford and Nixon, and one of the few things that these two very different men had in common was Henry Kissinger. On the campaign trail, Carter decried the Lone Ranger diplomacy of the previous administrations. He didn't beat around the bush on this point. "As far as foreign policy goes," he stated, "Mr. Kissinger has been the president of this country."[7] After the election, there was a concerted effort to ensure that the foreign policy formation process during the Carter years would contrast substantially with those that preceded it.

Carter made Brzezinski his national security lead during his transition and discussed a variety of different combinations of personalities and structures with him. In his memoirs, Brzezinski writes:

> I started off by saying that he ought to think of appointments within the context of three alternative types of foreign policy leadership: there was direct and dominant Presidential leadership, in which a strong President (like Nixon) is assisted by a dominant White House (Kissinger) overshadowing a weak Secretary of State; there was, secondly, the model of a predominant Secretary of State, as with Dulles under Eisenhower or Kissinger under Ford, with a relatively passive President and a nonobtrusive White House; and thirdly, there could be a more balanced "team" arrangement, combining a strong President (like Kennedy) with a relatively secure and strong Secretary of State (Rusk) with an equally confident and energetic White House (Bundy). I said that I assumed that Carter would strive for the third model. In the back of my mind I did have the feeling that although he might naturally gravitate toward the first model, in view of the Kissinger legacy he would find it awkward to admit it.[8]

"Moreover," Brzezinski adds, "at this stage, I did genuinely believe that the team approach would work."[9]

During the same conversation, Brzezinski explored with Carter the strengths and weaknesses of various secretary of state candidates, including George Ball, whom Brzezinski saw as a flawed candidate because of his tough stance with regard to Israel; Cyrus Vance, who Brzezinski noted "would fit well into my third model of a balanced leadership in the area of foreign affairs"; and Paul Warnke, whom he saw as a bit soft on the Soviet Union.[10] They also discussed various candidates for the national security advisor position, and Brzezinski noted a number of others, including Harold Brown, a former secretary of the air force and president of the California Institute of Technology.

Later, after the appointment of Vance as secretary of state, Carter and Brzezinski discussed what role Brzezinski might play, and Brzezinski proposed either deputy secretary of state to Vance or assistant to the president for national security, expressing a preference for the latter. One week after that, Carter called Brzezinski while he was at a party in New York City. According to Brzezinski, Carter's tone was light and it was clear he enjoyed toying with Brzezinski in a friendly way:

> "Zbig, I want you to do me a favor—I would like you to be my National Security Advisor."
>
> "That's no favor—that is an honor. And I hope and feel confident that you won't regret your decision," Brzezinski replied.
>
> "Actually, I knew as of some months ago that you were my choice but I had to go through these processes of selection. But I knew all along," Carter then noted.[11]

Among the challenges for Brzezinski and Carter, once the positions in the administration had been filled, was devising a structure for the national security and foreign policymaking apparatus. Again, neither the National Security Act of 1947 nor any other law actually determines how the various players will interact or what role they will play in the daily work of the administration. That is why it has been so important in each administration to immediately establish a working structure. (The importance of this step would be particularly well illustrated later, with the Reagan administration, which really never got around to it.)

Because of Carter's presumed preference for a more balanced, team-driven approach than that of the Kissinger years, Brzezinski collaborated on a plan with the man who had been designated to be his deputy, David Aaron, a former Kissinger NSC staffer who had been an advisor to the new vice president, Walter Mondale, when Mondale was in the Senate. The plan they proposed to Carter would have seven different committees, a majority of which would be chaired by cabinet secretaries, such as Vance at State; Brown at Defense; Michael Blumenthal, the incoming treasury secretary; or Admiral Stansfield Turner, the incoming CIA director. Only three of the committees would report to Brzezinski in this scheme: those pertaining to arms control, sensitive intelligence, and crisis management, matters that demanded the president's personal involvement or attention. (The three corresponded to those areas of greatest importance or "prestige" in the context of the Washington foreign policy community.) The proposed structure had the number of committees as under Nixon or Ford, but it was different in terms of who was to participate and chair the groups.

Carter rejected to the proposal when it was presented to him during a planning session on St. Simon Island, off the Georgia coast. "Too many committees," the president-elect said. "I want a simple, cleaner structure."[12] So, sitting in a cottage on St. Simon, Brzezinski and Carter worked out a different scheme, this one with only two committees. The Policy Review Committee (PRC) was to deal with foreign policy issues, defense policy issues, and international economic issues. It would be chaired by whichever cabinet secretary was closest to the issues being discussed (in practice, in all but a handful of instances, this turned out to be the secretary of state). Twice a year it would be chaired by the CIA director when intelligence budgets were being discussed. The second committee, the Special Coordination Committee (SCC), would deal with intelligence policy issues that had to do with covert and otherwise sensitive operations, arms control, and crisis management. This group would be chaired by Brzezinski. Whenever possible the meetings would be attended by the cabinet members themselves, not by subcabinet officials, as was the case with many of Kissinger's committees. To enhance the functioning of this structure, at Carter's first cabinet meeting he informed his team that he was elevating the national security advisor to cabinet status. It was a first and sent an unmistakable message.

The message was equally clear when Carter surprised the other members of the cabinet with the new structure during another meeting on St. Simon. Since it was a fait accompli, all they could do was accept it—or appear to. Brzezinski translated the structure into two presidential directives, which were submitted to Carter a few days before his inauguration. Aaron collaborated on these, as did Brzezinski's special assistant, Karl "Rick" Inderfurth, both of whom would, like so many of the Carter team, serve in senior capacities during the next Democratic administration, that of Bill Clinton, over a decade later.

The first of these memos completed the now predictable if vaguely absurd task of renaming presidential memoranda. What were once NSSMs became Presidential Review Memoranda (PRMs) and what were NSDMs became Presidential Directives (PD). The second PD outlined the new structure of committees and processes that would be implemented under Carter. These documents were signed on the eve of Carter's inauguration and were distributed to the cabinet immediately after the president was sworn in. Not surprisingly, there was some discomfort with the system. It was a bureaucratic first strike of the first order. The system essentially gave responsibility for the most important and sensitive issues to Brzezinski, and the vague definition of what constituted crisis management essentially ensured that if anything came up that was important, it could be claimed by the White House.

Vance was unhappy and asserted that he had not been consulted, even though the plan had been brought up at the island retreat. He and Brzezinski met to discuss the issues, and ultimately Vance came to accept the new approach. Over a quarter century later, Vance supporters from the State Department still smart from this first "Brzezinski" move and assert that with this step he did precisely what the president had said he was not going to do, and that is "become another Kissinger." Indeed, the divisions that began with this issue spread into one of the most bitter rivalries in executive branch history, and it ultimately resulted in Vance's resignation over differences about the appropriate response to the Iran hostage crisis that would dominate the last years of the Carter administration and reverberate for years.

The tension was not due simply to turf rivalries between the State Department and the White House and NSC staff but also to the tug-of-war over who would serve as the president's principal foreign policy spokesperson on key issues. The patrician Vance did not embrace the media spotlight in the way that a modern foreign policy leader must (since so much of diplomacy was already being conducted by the late 1970s via television), and as a result, Brzezinski says, he was forced to— and asked to—step up into this role. Vance "wasn't very good at selling the policy," says Brzezinski. "That's why I ended up on television even though the original intent was for me to be practically invisible. Then, when the Secretary of State complained about that and said that I'm propagandizing myself by being on television, the President told him quite explicitly, 'I told him to do it.' And that was true. I never appeared on television without an explicit request from the President."[13]

Vance protégés argue that this analysis ignores Brzezinski's own formidable drive to be the president's principal policy collaborator, but the reality is that, as ambitious as Brzezinski was and as direct and aggressive as he could be in his bureaucratic style, this structure could not have evolved without the support or direction of the president—who in fact embraced and largely shaped it. Indeed, although Jimmy Carter came into the office amid sniping that as governor of Georgia he was ill prepared for the foreign policy challenges he would face in the presidency (Bill Clinton and George W. Bush would face the same kind of criticism), it is clear from his early actions that international affairs was important to him and that he was going to take a very hands-on approach in that area. The evidence that he did is expressed best by the fact that 80 percent or more of his book *Keeping Faith: Memoirs of a President* is about international issues—they were in many respects his passion, his legacy, and his undoing. (Though skyrocketing inflation and a lousy economy sure didn't help.)

Although Carter dominated the team he gathered around him as he conducted the affairs of state, its members were not relegated to the kind of secondary roles on foreign policy that all but Kissinger had for most of the Nixon years. Indeed, although the rows between Vance and Brzezinski that were to break out over issues of policy and primacy were cited as a sign of dysfunction in the Carter administration, they are also clear testimony to the fact that both strong personalities were given prominent roles and that Carter valued them as much for their differences as for their individual contributions. But beyond the traditional roles for traditional players around the heart of the NSC, there were some new players in the mix in Carter's inner circle.

Perhaps foremost among these in historical significance was the inclusion of the vice president. Carter had picked Mondale, an experienced senator from Minnesota, to balance his campaign ticket both geographically and in Washington know-how. The two developed a good rapport, and Carter came to depend on Mondale as a trusted advisor. At the same time, Carter fashioned for the vice president an operational role that was unprecedented in U.S. history. The job that Vice President John Nance Garner had said was "not worth a bucket of warm spit" periodically had slight upgrades. Truman was left out in the cold and essentially ignored by Roosevelt; Nixon was invited to meetings and sent on some important missions by Eisenhower but still was the butt of jokes even from the president; Johnson, though given responsibility for NASA and used for his Senate connections, was essentially an outsider in the Kennedy administration; Agnew was a punch line even before he was forced to resign in disgrace; and Ford was essentially hired in case the president had to resign.

Even Rockefeller, a prominent former New York governor, was essentially an in-house consultant during the Ford administration.

Mondale, however, was a real partner to Carter. As Carter noted, "We agreed that he would truly be the second in command, involved in every aspect of governing. As a result, he received the same security briefings that I got (which was a departure from past practices), was automatically invited to participate in all my official meetings and helped to plan strategy for domestic programs, diplomacy and defense."[14] Mondale was a full member of the inner circle, and one of the ways this fact was unmistakably communicated in the language that Washington could understand was that the vice president's office was moved inside the West Wing of the White House for the first time. (His ceremonial and staff offices remained where they are today, in the Old Executive Office Building.) In addition, as noted earlier, Mondale's national security aide, David Aaron, became Brzezinski's number two at the NSC, and Mondale staffer Richard Moe was cited by Carter as an especially valuable aide.

"I feel that what we call the executivization of the vice president has been a very good thing in general," says Mondale, "and it has been sustained since Carter introduced it in 1977. But the key is the essential personal differences that exist in each case, the personal relationships between the president and vice president which are always more important than the black letter descriptions of the relationship."[15]

Mondale remarks that it was Carter's commitment to the idea from the start that made it happen, made it more than some of the promises of "partnership" other vice presidents have received and which then were ignored. "I really did have an open invitation to attend all meetings. Saturday discussions and on. If Deng Xiaoping comes to town, I'm there with Carter and that sort of thing. I also had any number of private discussions with him. It was understood that whenever I wanted access I would have it."[16] What at the time was a welcome upgrade for him, Mondale today recognizes has produced what he considers the "metastasizing" of the idea with the Cheney vice presidency.

Brzezinski observes, confirming the important role that Mondale played, "the Vice President would participate in informal meetings with the President. He would attend some of our more formal committee meetings. But he didn't have a staff of his own, nothing in foreign affairs. To some extent that was because I had pre-empted that. I made my deputy (David Aaron, a former Mondale staffer) his principal on foreign policy, and the result was that he did not need to have such a large foreign policy staff."[17]

Of course, like other presidents, Carter brought with him a group of close personal advisors and friends from his previous life, in his case from Georgia—a group that would have important roles in his inner circle, his NSC kitchen cabinet. These included Chief of Staff Hamilton Jordan, who grew to play an important role in foreign policy deliberations; press secretary Jody Foster; domestic policy advisor Stuart Eizenstat; Attorney General Griffin Bell; and Office of Management and Budget Director Bert Lance. Of Lance's subsequent resignation under pressure, Brzezinski writes, "I believe that the Carter Presidency and especially economic policy might have taken a different turn if Lance had not been forced out. His departure was a searing experience for Carter. . . . With the departure of Lance, Carter lost the one person in the White House who was genuinely his peer, and I certainly was only a partial substitute."[18]

But there was one other person in the inner circle during the Carter years who was certainly Carter's peer and who also had an unprecedented role: his wife, (Eleanor) Rosalynn Carter. In addition to carrying out ceremonial duties, the role a First Lady typically plays, Rosalynn Carter truly was the president's closest advisor. She sat in on and participated in substantive meetings, from discussions of personnel choices to political strategy to major foreign policy deliberations. In his description of the 1978 Camp David peace negotiations, Carter cites turning to Rosalynn several times, and he mentions calling her first after receiving good news and bad.[19] Brzezinski, too, in his memoirs, when writing about his relationship with key players, includes a section on his relationship with the First Lady. "Her influence on her husband was considerable," he writes, "and was exercised almost openly. Carter—at least to me—was not embarrassed to admit it."[20] He also comments that she was tough, quick to form opinions, and would offer comments on central issues of the day. "She had a knack for getting to the guts of a problem. When I briefed her on the crisis that had developed over the Soviet brigade in Cuba and commented that the President had ordered us to protest to Brezhnev, she cuttingly observed, 'But Brezhnev already has a cabinet full of our protests.'"[21] When Hillary Clinton arrived on the scene to play a major role in her husband's administration, the trail had been blazed by Rosalynn Carter. Similarly, Nancy Reagan's influence over her husband's decisions, which caused Reagan administration aides to curry favor with her, had a precedent in the Carter years; Brzezinski's savvy White House court skills were in full evidence in the way he cultivated that relationship.

Carter's team met informally more often than formally. Friday morning breakfast meetings were attended by Carter, Mondale, Vance, Brown, and Brzezinski, and later Jordan and occasionally others. As in past administrations it was in meetings like these that much of the real work— once imagined for formal NSC meetings, which were infrequent and usually done for history's sake, for major decisions—was done. Vance, Brown, and Brzezinski also had their own weekly lunch, and Carter and Mondale typically had a private lunch each week. So did Carter and his wife, each Thursday, to discuss management issues associated with the White House, their schedules, and any other issues that were important. Says Brzezinski, "Smaller groups obviously generate more discussion and give the President the opportunity to engage in a much more intimate view of the issues. You can't make policy through informal procedures, but you can crystallize directions and then supervise both the implementation and coordination via the formal process."[22]

Mondale's assessment was that "the president wanted a strong NSC":

> The fact that he picked Brzezinski and Vance, who he knew would be on the opposite sides of many things, was deliberate. He wanted to get the issues ventilated, and he thought that the way to do it was to have people that were strong willed with different views and then that would also leave him in charge of decision making. So he clearly wanted that.
>
> "The president was . . . a detail man. He wanted to be in charge of these decisions. He wanted to make them himself. He wanted to understand and be responsible for these things in a hands-on way, not as a distant business manager like Reagan would be. He was also one of those eighteen-hour-day guys. He was very bright and would consume all this stuff that came in. He had an intense personal grasp of details. This translated into what one senior White House staffer from the Carter years described as 'terminal micromanagement.' The president was voracious, which was good, but it also enabled him to become embroiled in everything to a painful level of detail. Sometimes it could be paralyzing."[23]

As for the informal gatherings, Mondale says, "The Friday breakfast was extremely valuable. It was initially intended to be some of the members of the NSC, but it was more informal. It was the President, Zbig, Vance, Brown, usually Jody and Ham were there. I was there. And sometimes we might have Jones, who was chairman of the Joint Chiefs, or Stan Turner, depending on the issues. But I found that breakfast really, really helpful because it was totally informal. It was just who the president wanted to see. It was one of those environments where you felt you could speak candidly. Maybe you shouldn't have. But you felt you could. And I think the president got an awful lot out of those meetings, too."[24] Other participants concurred that it was in these sessions and in some of the Saturday morning informal conversations with the president that some of the best collective thinking was done.

As in most administrations, Brzezinski and Carter kicked off their operation with a series of PRMs that dealt with what they determined would be front-burner issues or issues that would arise in the near term. These included memoranda looking at what U.S. policy should be concerning the Panama Canal and how to manage the handover to the government of Panama; one on SALT; one on the Middle East; one on South Africa and Rhodesia; one on Cyprus; one on mutual and balanced force reductions (MBFR); one on an upcoming economic summit and trilateral (U.S.-Europe-Japan) policies; one on North-South strategy; one on European policy; one on military force positions; one on intelligence community structure and mission; one on Korea; one on Philippine base negotiations; and one on nuclear proliferation.

As part of this policy framing process, Brzezinski and his team also drafted a list of ten goals that included strengthening trilateral relations, expanding political and economic relations with emerging powers, enhancing North-South relations by stimulating greater economic stability in the developing world, moving from strategic arms limitation talks to strategic arms reduction talks, normalizing U.S.-Chinese relations, obtaining a comprehensive Middle East settlement, promoting peaceful transformation in South Africa and rebuffing a Soviet-Cuban presence in southern Africa, restricting the level of global armaments, promoting human rights, and maintaining a strong defense. Given that Carter ended up serving only one term, the degree to which many of these goals were achieved or advanced is remarkable, although evaluations of his administration over the years have been lukewarm at best, with some of the crises Carter and his team faced overshadowing their considerable achievements.

Brzezinski's team at the NSC included a few holdovers from the Ford years, such as Bob Hormats, who handled international economics, and Roger Molander, who handled SALT issues. Brzezinski's military aide was Colonel William Odom (promoted to general while serving on the NSC staff), who had worked with Brzezinski at Columbia. Another former academic colleague, Samuel Huntington, came in to do what he had done while writing with Brzezinski earlier, that is, to assess the state of relations between the United States and the Soviet Union. Also in the group were regional specialists such as Robert Pastor, who joined the NSC fresh from defending his doctoral dissertation to handle Latin America; Robert

Hunter, who handled Western Europe; William Quandt, who handled the Middle East; and some, like thirty-one-year-old Jessica Tuchman, formerly of the staff of Congressman Morris Udall, who handled clusters of global issues, including human rights. Among Brzezinski's special assistants was Bob Gates, who would later be deputy national security advisor and then head of the CIA. His congressional liaison work was handled by a former young staffer of Senator Edmund Muskie's named Madeleine Albright. Brzezinski established another precedent by hiring a dedicated press staffer to the team, Jerrold Schecter, formerly of *Time* magazine. This worried some who saw it as a play for more exposure for Brzezinski, but it also provided important expertise when it came to handling foreign policy–related press issues. The practice was adopted again in later years by the Clinton administration and the second Bush administration; in the latter, the press lead for the NSC gained the title of deputy national security advisor. Overall, Brzezinski tried to trim the NSC staff from its large size under Kissinger, and he began with about twenty-five professionals on the team.

The presence of women in high-level roles was also something that was new, a sign of the times, although some of the old-school men in this community had a hard time adjusting to it. Jessica Tuchman, now Jessica Tuchman Mathews, head of the Carnegie Endowment for International Peace, noted that when she met at one point with Admiral Rickover, he actually said, "What's a nice girl like you doing in a place like this?" She also notes that James Schlesinger would regularly refer to her as "lassie" in meetings but that she was accustomed to that kind of behavior; one of her key Pentagon contacts, she said, a three-star general, "patronized me like crazy."[25] Indeed, it was only a few years earlier, in 1971, that women were first permitted to join the Council on Foreign Relations; Mathews's mother, the acclaimed historian Barbara Tuchman, was one of the very first female members.

Madeleine Albright had been working for Senator Muskie, of Maine, before her sudden call to the NSC:

I worked for Muskie until a particular Friday before moving over to the NSC/White House. Muskie was on the Law of the Sea Advisory Committee and, of course, Maine has a long coastline. So, on behalf of Muskie, I wrote a letter to President Carter saying how very important the Law of the Sea was but asked him to understand that we have all these fishermen in the state and we should not stop them from earning a living. We put the autopen signature on the letter and sent it over to the White House. A few days later I left my job and went to the NSC. Upon arrival, I found this bloody letter I sent the week before. So, I did what a staffer should do: I wrote back—to myself, so to speak—and I explained on behalf of the President that I was very sorry about the fishermen but the national interest was really much more important. We signed it "Jimmy Carter" and off it went. This was proof of the Washington adage "Where you sit is where you stand."[26]

Brzezinski's NSC staffers are, to this day, very loyal to their former boss, and use words like "stimulating," "exciting," "remarkable people," and "fun" to describe their experiences on his NSC staff. He, in turn, was very open with them, pledging from the beginning to brief them on his exchanges with the president, provided that they held them in confidence, and involving them in high-level activities, often those including the president, when possible. There was a feel of a university or think tank about the NSC in those days; it was even described by Richard Burt, of the *New York Times*, as a "floating seminar"—a sobriquet that would be applied later to a very similar group of people during the next Democratic administration, that of Bill Clinton. That was what Carter wanted and what Brzezinski was comfortable with, and the Carter NSC ran well internally. As for its interaction with other agencies or the hand dealt it by fate, that is another story.

The Panama Canal Treaty was an early triumph for Carter, especially considering how unpopular giving up the canal was. Carter and his team knew long before his inauguration that they would have to deal with what promised to be a tough issue. They recognized that negotiations with the Panamanians were necessary, that ultimately our control of the canal would have to be phased out, and that Panamanian sovereignty would have to be recognized. What is more, they knew that the year before, thirty-eight senators—more than the number needed to kill a treaty—supported a resolution opposing a new treaty. Those senators also enjoyed broad support among the American people, according to the polls.

Defense experts felt that militarily defending the canal would be extremely difficult for the United States, involving potentially a 100,000 troops to fend off an enemy bent on seizing control of the waterway. It would be easier to defend the canal, Defense Secretary Brown said, "by a cooperative effort with a friendly Panama [instead of an] American garrison amid hostile surroundings."[27] Also, given the administration's rhetoric and inclinations toward improving the U.S. image in the developing world, they wanted to be able to pursue the politically unpopular but correct approach of finding a way to give back control of Panama's most important asset while still protecting our strategic interests in the zone.

Carter's team calculated that action could be taken while the new president's popularity was high, and the president believed that he could make the case in a compelling enough fashion to turn public and legislative opinion. With the conclusions of PRM-1 shaping the administration's position, Carter's team engaged the Panamanians very early—Vance met with his counterpart, Aquilino Boyd, just days after the inauguration, and negotiators were meeting in Panama by Valentine's Day. Carter named former ambassador to the Organization of American States Sol Linowitz, a man who was revered among his colleagues in the legal and diplomatic communities for his grace, integrity, and wisdom, to be his representative on the negotiating team.

The negotiations turned on several key issues, described in two treaties. One covered joint operation of the canal for the remainder of the twentieth century, after which the Panamanians would assume full responsibility for the canal. The second guaranteed the neutrality of the canal and the right of the United States to defend its interests there. The negotiations were tricky, and they stalled around demands for huge U.S. payments to the Panamanians. Ultimately, it took the direct intercession of Carter via a letter to Panamanian President Omar Torrijos to resolve the issue, and by early August it was done. Although it had taken longer than the Carter team had hoped, they had achieved in eight months what had not been accomplished in fourteen years of negotiations before that point.

The difficult part was just beginning, however, since almost eight out of ten Americans were opposed to giving up the canal, and less than one in twelve supported the idea.[28] Hence, the battle shifted to persuading Congress and the American people of the merits of the deal. It is easy to understand why, given this environment, it made sense to have dedicated congressional liaison and press personnel associated with the NSC.

Carter wrote in his diary on August 9, 1977:

> Ford, Kissinger and Baker all gave me encouraging reports on their attitude concerning the Panama Canal treaty, and unless the public pressure is too heavy on them I think they can help me a great deal in the Senate. . . . This past Saturday we sent all the senators a telegram urging them not to speak out against the treaty until they know the details of the agreement. Apparently it worked with most of them—except a few nuts like Strom Thurmond and Jesse Helms.[29]

Opposition to the Canal Treaty became a priority for conservative groups led by Ronald Reagan, the former California governor who had made his first serious run for the presidency in 1976. Carter countered with a little political theater and through the fast work of his State and NSC teams, convened a meeting of leaders from around the hemisphere to observe the treaty's signing on September 7, 1977. The event went off well. Carter noted in his memoirs that Torrijos took him aside and began to weep as he expressed his nation's gratitude for the effort.[30]

Although the signing event increased public support for the treaties, the next several months were spent working the corridors on Capitol Hill, trying to win one Senate vote at a time to reach the total of sixty-seven needed for ratification of the treaty. During such an effort, Carter's foreign policy inner circle undertook a role that often comes to senior administration leaders. They became political operatives, working the Hill for votes.

By February 1978—a congressional election year—public support for the treaties finally went positive, with 45 percent favoring them and 42 percent opposed.[31] But then—and possibly because of this surge—a new wave of opposition was mounted by Senators Robert Dole, Helms, and others, who made charges ranging from accusing Torrijos's family of drug trafficking to suggesting bribery of high U.S. officials. Although all the charges ultimately proved untrue, it was Washington politics at its nastiest—and it can serve as a reminder to all present-day Americans that politics in the United States has been a dirty business, going back to the lies and lie-driven scandals that swirled around Alexander Hamilton, Thomas Jefferson, and other members of Washington's administration. Every generation says that it's worse than ever and yearns for the civility of yesteryear. There was no civil yesteryear. As one former high official in the Carter administration said to me, "the stakes are too high for these guys to play clean—especially when they can't win on the merits."[32]

In his recollections of the vote-counting, vote-gathering period, Carter recounts in his diary:

> I asked Cy to go to spend full time on the Hill, and also to ask Henry Kissinger to do the same thing. I then asked Harold Brown and the Joint Chiefs to join them there, and Fritz [Mondale] will be spending full time—all working personally with members of the Senate. . . . I had lunch with Senator Stennis to try to get his vote on the treaties, but failed. President Ford [who had been helping Carter] promised to use his influence with Heinz, Bellmon, Brooke and Schweiker. . . . Later on in the day Rosalynn called Mrs. Hatfield in Montana. She called Mrs. Zorinsky. . . . This has been one of the worst days—knowing that we were lost, then gaining a little hope.[33]

Vance's deputy, Warren Christopher, meanwhile was working on drafting amendments that would be acceptable to key supporters of the bill. That Kissinger was asked to play such an active role in mustering Republican support was indicative not only of his status as the Republican Party's senior statesman but also was a harbinger of similar undertakings in administrations to come. Kissinger embraced the opportunity to remain active—and it was indisputable that there was no figure in American life with more instant authority on foreign policy issues.

In short, all the stops were pulled out, and after twenty-two days of Senate debate, on the very last day, at the very last hour, after countless side deals and the considerable attention of the members of Carter's foreign policy inner circle, Senators DeConcini, Bellmon, Hatfield, and Cannon all decided to support the treaty, giving it sixty-eight votes. Carter wrote, "It will always be one of my proudest moments and one of the great achievements in the history of the United States Senate."[34] The statement about its place in the history of the Senate may be somewhat self-serving, but certainly for a new president, unschooled in foreign policy, entering office and going against public opinion to do what he saw as the right thing for the United States was certainly an act of great political courage, and the treaty's passage was a remarkable accomplishment. It would not have been possible if his NSC principals' team had not been so experienced and did not work so well together as a team in this case. It would also not have been possible without the support of Republicans Ford, Kissinger, and members of the previous administration, which anticipated the fissures between the centrist or moderate Republicans who made such bipartisan agreement possible and the conservatives led by the likes of Reagan and Helms, whose approach was polarization whatever the cost.

The difficulty of passing tough national security legislation in the more polarized, partisan Washington environment—its existence illustrated by the Panama case but the underlying tensions born of the Vietnam and Watergate rifts that had exacerbated the tensions and rivalries that have always divided the parties—has had other unintended consequences. Harold Brown, sitting recently in his office at the Center for International and Strategic Studies in Washington, said to me:

Let me mention something that came to me as I was trying to go to sleep a couple nights ago. You mentioned that I was the first scientist to have been Secretary of Defense. The interesting thing to me is the way the job has changed over time and how the people selected for it have changed.

Of the first eight secretaries of defense after the creation of the job with the National Security Act of 1947—that is, up through Bob McNamara—only one could be described as someone who was heavily involved in politics. That's Louis Johnson. You have Forrestal. You have Marshall. You have Lovett. Charlie Wilson. Neil McElroy. Gates. McNamara. Then, of the following thirteen, only four have not been politicians. Start with Clark Clifford—never elected to anything, but clearly a politician. Then Richardson. And then Jim Schlesinger—not. Rumsfeld—politician. Me—not. Weinberger had been in the California legislature. Carlucci was not. Then Cheney. Then Aspin. Then Bill Perry—not. Then Bill Cohen. Then Rumsfeld again. It's a major change.

"So the question," Brown suggests, "is why did this happen?"

Clearly, the important people, the presidents who made the appointments by and large were looking for people with political skills since 1969—not for people with managerial skills or technical skills. It all became more of a political issue—more important to be able to fight the political battles regarding budgets and legislation and so forth. And of course, since the end of the Cold War, it is more of a political issue because it is no longer even clear what national security is.[35]

Another early focus of the Carter administration bears out the difficulties of working in the modern political environment equally well, but in this case, the outcome for the Carter team was less satisfying. It concerned arms control.

Jimmy Carter, a former nuclear engineer, had expressed interest in eliminating nuclear weapons and soon after becoming president requested a study by the Pentagon on the possibility of reverting to a "minimum deterrence" capability limited to 200–250 nuclear delivery vehicles.[36] His defense secretary, Harold Brown, had expressed doubt in a March 1975 speech about counterforce strategies, stating that nuclear war–winning strategies were impractical. In contrast, Zbigniew Brzezinski embraced to some degree his predecessors' shift to a more flexible targeting strategy, writing in his memoirs:

In my judgment, an effective deterrence theory had to take fully into account not only the capabilities of the opponent whom we wished to deter—as well as war doctrine. Over the years, I had become increasingly concerned that our existing deterrence doctrine, based on the principle of mutually assured destruction, had been formulated largely in a setting of actual U.S. superiority in the early sixties. . . . But that asymmetry had gradually changed in the course of the preceding decade and a half. . . . Accordingly, I felt that the United States could no longer afford to disregard the Soviet doctrines guiding the possible use of the growing Soviet capability . . . [and] had to accommodate itself to this new reality and our defense doctrine and programs should be adjusted accordingly.[37]

The president-elect and his incoming national security team received briefings on the U.S. strategic nuclear war planes before entering office, and the NSC issued a series of PRMs that reviewed the U.S. defense posture soon after Carter's inauguration. A reappraisal of the Nixon-Ford position resulted from PRM-10, "Comprehensive Net Assessment and Military Force Posture Review," and a subsequent five-month interagency study supervised by Samuel Huntington, the NSC staffer responsible for national security planning.[38]

PRM-10 was completed in June 1977 and the massive project—which Brzezinski's military assistant William Odom said was meant to look at a net assessment in "all the major categories of power," not just military power—involved eleven task forces and 175 people located in agencies throughout the national security bureaucracy.[39] After the release of the interagency study, the Brzezinski-chaired, cabinet-level Special Coordination Committee held a series of meetings on the subject the following month.[40] After extended debate, which included the active voices of Secretaries Vance and Brown, President Carter issued a directive entitled "U.S. National Security" in August 1977 that reaffirmed the Nixon-Ford–era standard in the "absence of further guidance for structuring U.S. strategic posture."[41]

The report also declared that the "United States will maintain an overall balance of military power . . . at least as favorable as that that now exists" and that the United States would also maintain the capability of inflicting "unacceptable damage" on the Soviet Union in the event of a Soviet first strike. PD-18 further instructed the Pentagon to develop limited nuclear responses and maintain a reserve of strategic forces that would be used in the event of an extended nuclear war.[42]

Carter's national security advisor had intended that these reviews would "spur within the Defense Department a broader review of our strategic doctrine and also interest the President himself in this difficult and complicated issue."[43] But frustrated with the Pentagon's slow response, Brzezinski himself promoted efforts by the administration to craft a new nuclear doctrine and began by "strengthening" the NSC cluster dealing with military issues. Odom recalled that "for the next two years, based on the kind of analyses we had done in PRM-10, we had to work slowly to try to bring the realities to the eyes of the President, the eyes of the Secretary of Defense, Secretary of State and make them realize that we had to tackle some of those policies from very fundamentally different directions."[44]

Brzezinski adds, commenting on the dynamic behind this and other initiatives, "It wasn't the Defense Department running foreign policy, nor the State Department running foreign policy. It was the White House setting the pace and direction for both." He does then also observe, regarding the growing disparity in the influence between those departments that began during the Kennedy era and was already clearly manifest by the Carter years, "In the Department of State you have the glory of the office, to fly around in a big plane and to appear at international meetings. But you don't have the clout. The Secretary of Defense spends money while the Secretary of State begs for money. That's a big difference."[45]

Led by Odom, the defense staff cluster did, however, work closely and constructively with Defense Secretary Brown's staff in the Pentagon.[46] Meanwhile, Brown had shifted in his views on nuclear doctrine, testifying before Congress in 1979 that "it would be the height of folly to put the United States in a position in which uncontrolled escalation would be the only course we could follow."[47] Brzezinski observed that as a consequence of the NSC-Defense cooperation, the defense secretary "had become much more interested in greater flexibility and is clearly moving away from a rigid deterrence posture"—and at a May 1979 NSC meeting, Brown and Brzezinski agreed on the need for a new strategic targeting policy. In contrast to the hostility of the Pentagon when Kissinger launched NSSM-3, the Strategic Air Command was supportive of these efforts as well.[48]

Deputy Secretary of State Christopher, who also attended the meeting, had raised objections, and concerted State Department opposition slowed progress on the project. However, Brzezinski directed Odom in early 1980 to begin work on a new formal directive on nuclear weapons doctrine, and by May of that year, Brzezinski "was in a position to submit the document for Presidential approval."[49]

Despite Secretary Vance's continued skepticism, in July 1980 President Carter backed Brzezinski and Brown and signed a presidential directive, "Nuclear Weapons Employment Policy," which modified U.S. nuclear strategy by shifting and expanding targeting priorities from those mandated by Nixon (from 25,000 to 40,000 potential target installations).[50]

With this new directive, the key task of a U.S. nuclear strike shifted away from eliminating economic recovery targets and instead focused on destroying the political and military leadership of the Soviet state (including strategic military targets, leadership bunkers, and command, control, communications, and intelligence (C^3I) facilities).[51] The Carter administration also sought improvements in the survivability of U.S. command, control, and communications (C^3) infrastructure required for an extended nuclear conflict.[52]

According to Raymond Garthoff, despite their collaboration, Brzezinski and Brown had different interpretations of the impact of the new directive. Secretary Brown argued that the conclusions did not represent a new strategic doctrine, but rather a refinement of previous explanations of strategic policy, insisting that this countervailing strategy was not a first-strike strategy: "Nothing in the policy contemplates that nuclear war can be a deliberate instrument of achieving our national security goals. . . . But we cannot afford the risk that the Soviet leadership might entertain the illusion that nuclear war could be an option—or its threat a means of coercion—for them."[53] In contrast, Brzezinski placed less emphasis on deterrence and more on the war-fighting concepts in his interpretation of the presidential directive.[54]

Simultaneously the administration worked a parallel initiative through the NSC's Special Coordination Committee (SCC), one that pertained to the U.S.-Soviet SALT negotiations. Carter attended the first session of this new entity on February 3, 1977. He opened the discussion with general motivational remarks about the team and the system he had put into place, but before leaving he emphasized his desire to engage in a SALT process with the Soviets that produced deep cuts. Brzezinski was to play a key role in the SCC sessions, as John Prados recounts in *Keepers of the Keys*:

> Brzezinski deliberately tried to balance the hards and the softs by the order in which he called on them to speak. Zbig reserved the final say for Cy Vance, then summarized and reported the SCC deliberations to the President. Carter followed up directly at his breakfast with Vance, Mondale and Zbig. Harold Brown was only later admitted to the foreign policy breakfasts as were Hamilton Jordan, Jody Powell and special counsel Hedley Donovan.[55]

This led to a process that engaged the skills of the top specialists on the NSC team—individuals such as David Aaron, Roger Molander, and Victor Utgoff—in strategic arms limitation talks. Vance, Brown, and Arms Control and Disarmament Agency (ACDA) director Paul Warnke and their staffs also played an important role in developing a series of options that ranged from extremely comprehensive cuts to essentially working with the agreement reached by President Ford in Vladivostok during the talks of the preceding administration. Carter pushed the team for an aggressive approach, and at a principals-only meeting of the SCC that also included the president and the vice president, he approved the approach recommended by Brzezinski, which involved significant steps beyond Vladivostok, including, notably, a ban on intercontinental ballistic missile (ICBM) modernization.

Brzezinski shepherded the process closely and even went so far as having Bill Hyland, working for the NSC, oversee the delivery of the negotiating instructions to ensure that they did not get into the hands of the State Department until the instant of their departure. The national security advisor also managed the key decision-making meetings involved in the process in a way that he thought would preserve the equities of the military and not cut too deeply into arms stockpiles they felt were essential. He did this by, for example, ensuring that Brown joined him in meetings with the president, Mondale, and Vance. As it happened, Mondale, who had a reputation as something of a dove, was a "pleasant surprise" to his more moderate colleagues, and during the course of the administration he "regularly showed extremely sophisticated knowledge of military issues and a real commitment to protecting America's defense structure."[56]

The final set of proposals to be offered to the Soviets, as laid out in PD-7, which was approved on March 22 after a formal NSC session, did lead with the deeper cuts because of Carter's commitment to this approach. A slightly more moderate option was the fallback position.

Unfortunately, the administration then did what many administrations do during their first months in office; it made a "learning curve error." The Soviets had not been prepared for the depth of the U.S. proposal, and their sclerotic and somewhat paranoid leadership could neither respond to it swiftly nor fully trust the motives behind the approach. Vance's talks with Brezhnev went very badly, and he felt uneasy doing what his predecessor Kissinger surely would have done, which is improvising, thinking on his feet, and exploring avenues by which the discussions might be salvaged. Subsequently, in the press, Brzezinski took the line that the United States had made a good faith effort to make a constructive proposal and implied that the Russians were the ones who had dropped the ball. While this is true to some extent, it is also true that understanding one's negotiating partner is a key to success and the U.S. team showed very little sensitivity to the likely reactions of the Soviets at that time. One former NSC staffer speculated that this might not have been entirely an accident on the part of Brzezinski, who "should have known and perhaps even did know" that they might not react well to the more extreme proposal and "who had backed a more moderate set of cuts."[57] But others deny that this was a calculated attempt to "show the Soviets for what they were."[58]

The negotiations were rekindled and then went on for another nine months. Critical issues that became central included parameters for telemetry encryption, the Backfire bomber, and limits on the number of warheads allowable per long-range missile. The SCC managed the process, State and ACDA led the negotiations, and Brzezinski kept tabs on them through his new head of the Soviet team, Reginald Bartholomew, a rising young diplomat who would be a prominent figure in U.S. foreign policy circles for the next several decades. In the middle of the process Paul Warnke resigned, suffering from a real problem in Washington—the inability to make the kind of money he needed to support his family from his government job.[59] By late December 1978, the negotiations were down to short-strokes and via a series of long-distance communications between Vance overseas, Brzezinski and the SCC in the Situation Room in Washington, and Carter at home in Plains, Georgia, the basics of a final deal were hammered out—but not without complications. The long-distance communications and differing positions about where to come out on encryption-related issues caused a considerable hiccup in the negotiating process. Vance got it back on track, and in June 1979, Carter and Brezhnev signed the SALT II Treaty at a summit meeting in Vienna.

After that, the politics of Washington and Capitol Hill kicked back in, and the treaty became a hockey puck to be batted back and forth by the left and the right in the Senate. Once again the two-thirds majority required to ratify a treaty was needed. The problem was exacerbated when a controversy arose over the alleged presence of a brigade of 2,000–3,000 Russian troops in Cuba. Hawks saw this as further evidence of the malevolent intentions of the Soviet. Brzezinski fell more into this category within the administration. Given his well-founded distrust of the Soviets and his general sense that the United States could prevail by confronting them, whether it be in Cuba or the Horn of Africa or elsewhere in Africa, he urged a tough line against their expansion. He was, to a greater extent than many of his colleagues, more committed to containment than "balance." The initial problems with the brigade issue had more to do with communications strategy than with national security strategy. The administration downplayed the presence in Cuba and then Vance, essentially on his own, let a more serious assessment of the Soviet presence slip. Opponents in Congress jumped on it, and the administration's team handling the issue—which was the PRG since it had not really qualified as a "crisis" until the communications problems—did not produce real progress.

Brzezinski was frustrated with Vance's management of this set of events and wrote in one of his weekly memos to the president:

> You may not want to hear this, but I think that the increasingly pervasive perception here and abroad is that in U.S.-Soviet relations, the Soviets are increasingly assertive and the U.S. more acquiescent. State's handling of the Soviet brigade negotiations is a case in point. I recommend that in the future we will have to work for greater White House control.[60]

Carter responded in the margin (as he did in detail with most of the memos he got): "Good!"

Later Carter turned to the old reliable technique of convening a group of gray heads to offer sensible perspectives. He did this against the recommendation of Brzezinski—who no doubt saw it is an "x" factor in managing the process. Brzezinski has written since that one of the key judgments that needs to be made before outsiders are brought in to assist with issues is to figure out where they are likely to come out to ensure that they advance what you see as the administration's interests. This view reveals something about Brzezinski—but it is worth noting that others, such as Eisenhower during Solarium, took precisely the same view. Indeed, it is very common among successful managers of the bureaucratic process who understand the costs of being blindsided.

The wise men included Mac Bundy, Henry Kissinger, Brent Scowcroft, Bill Rogers, Dean Rusk, George Ball, John McCone, Linowitz, and the ubiquitous Clifford. Essentially, all but Kissinger said that they felt the brigade had been there all along and was not a big deal. Brzezinski commented archly later that "the group did meet and then widely circulated reports of the administration's alleged disarray."[61]

One of the by-products of the controversy, however, and of the political divisions in Washington was that the SALT II Treaty was never ratified. Its architects often note that it was followed as a guideline in any event, but it was also used by conservatives to suggest that the Carter team was too soft on the Soviets and on arms control. This is unfair on several levels. First, it is unfair because in case after case, key members of the administration led by Brzezinski sought a tough stand against the Soviets, in some cases a tougher stand than in previous administrations. For example, while exploring nuclear targeting options, Brzezinski, who understood the structure of Soviet society, felt it would be important to target the Russian nationalities who were at the head of the government in order to "decapitate" that government and take advantage of the weakness of a structure in which ethnic centrifugal forces would start to pull away in the event of a collapse or destruction of the center. In Africa and later with Afghanistan, in which the United States actually sought to make the Soviet invasion of that country the "Soviet Vietnam," in cutting the Soviets out of any role in Middle East peacemaking, and in strengthening relations further with China, Brzezinski offered views that were actually a harbinger of the even tougher U.S. stance seen during the Reagan years—the waning years of the Cold War. He and Huntington, in books like *Political Power: U.S.A./U.S.S.R.*, saw a weakening of the communist system on many levels, and he worked to take advantage of that. In addition to laying the groundwork for what Brzezinski later called "assertive détente" (an approach that was, of course, justified by actions such as the Soviet invasion of Afghanistan), among the other notable outcomes of this review process was a decision that called for the creation of military rapid response forces—the first stirrings of the "transformation processes" embraced by the military and touted as a breakthrough in strategy by Donald Rumsfeld twenty-five years later.

It is worth noting that the Carter years were extremely full on the international front, even by typical U.S. standards. Within a few weeks, the shah left Iran, Deng Xiaoping made his historic visit to Washington, Khomeini returned to Iran, and a peace mission was sent to the Middle East and followed by the signing of the Egypt-Israel peace treaty. At the same time, looming large in the background, was the energy crisis and the faltering economy.

In fact, one of the very greatest challenges to senior officials in the modern U.S. government is that they literally find themselves going from one crisis-driven meeting to another with very little time in between to absorb what is happening, place it in context, or strategize. For example, Carter writes in his memoirs that while the Panama negotiations with the Senate were taking place:

> It was remarkable how many different things I had to work on during these last few days: a very serious nationwide coal strike, energy legislation, my upcoming trip to Latin America and Africa, a burgeoning crisis between Israel and Egypt plus an Israeli invasion of Lebanon, the United Nations disarmament conference, the midwinter Governors Conference, final approval of our complete urban program, a forthcoming trip by

Brzezinski to China to work on normalization, war in the Horn of Africa, our proposals to prevent bankruptcy in New York City, negotiations with the British on air-transport agreements, a state visit by President Tito of Yugoslavia, final stages of the SALT negotiations, the Civil Service reform bill, the coming state visit of Prime Minister Takeo Fukuda of Japan, a decision about whether General Alexander Haig should stay on at NATO (where he had moved as Supreme Allied Commander), F-15 airplane sales to Saudi Arabia, a visit by Israeli Defense Minister Ezer Weizman and preparations for an early visit by Prime Minister Begin, and a major defense speech at Wake Forest the day after the treaty vote.[62]

While some would argue that this is an excellent rationale for delegating more than Carter typically did, virtually all of these issues would require the chief executive's attention for some time during this period, and virtually all were quite complex and demanding. The context created by this welter of activity within the White House and the NSC is hard to communicate in a book and hard for outsiders to imagine. But certainly it explains the eighteen-hour days, the high burnout rate, and the need for a sense of humor and good relations among colleagues. In this kind of tense environment, the slightest tear becomes a larger and larger rip, which, as we will soon see, is what took place with the growing tensions between State and the NSC, Brzezinski and Vance.

One of the early areas in which the split manifested itself had to do with the president's long-held desire to move toward normalization of relations with China. Of course, the seeds of discord were brewing from the days before the administration, when Carter and Brzezinski arrived at a national security operational structure that ensured the centrality of the NSC and marginalized State on key issues. Vance balked at this but accepted it either because of the arguments for it offered by Brzezinski and Carter or because he had no choice. Nonetheless, Richard Holbrooke, Tony Lake, and Peter Tarnoff, Vance's chief of staff, had tried to alert Secretary Vance that Brzezinski was trying to put the NSC at the center of the foreign policymaking process at the State Department's expense. When you speak to them about this period, they argue, as do many of Vance's supporters, that Vance just simply didn't play ball the way Brzezinski did, that he had too much character and dignity. Brzezinski staffers to this day say the Vance-Brzezinski split was overstated, that the system worked pretty well, and that Vance's role was diminished it was because of the bureaucratic inertia and lack of creativity of the State Department (a refrain heard from administration to administration).

The tension between these men—and from time to time between their staffs—may have stemmed from traditional State-NSC rivalries, differences between their character types (the patrician Vance and the hard-charging, "confrontational" Brzezinski), or differences in worldview over how to approach the Soviet Union, as is often suggested. Harold Brown commented:

> Brzezinski had, I think, a much more apocalyptic view of the world and especially a different attitude toward the Soviets. And he is also a more confrontational individual. He is not necessarily abrasive—but more willing to push things hard on a personal basis. That is not to say he used his position as the last person to talk to the president improperly. At least, in formal terms, my belief is that he always correctly reflected other people's views, gave his own, but didn't try to force a compromise.
>
> Nonetheless, I think his was a more confrontational personality. And he had a very fundamental difference with Vance in that he believed that concessions to the Russians merely encouraged them to press further, and he was willing to use almost any device or any other relationship with other countries to contain them. He saw relations with other countries in those terms.[63]
>
> That was the big difference on China. Clearly, Vance was willing to play down U.S. relations with China in order to get better relations with the Russians. Brzezinski's view was that we should use China as a weapon against the Soviets. And inevitably, I think we did to some degree, and I played a part in that. My own position was more in between. I felt that we should not avoid improving relations with China in order to make life easier in dealing with the Soviets. In any event, it was a very fundamental clash both in policies and in styles between those groups. And it really damaged the administration badly.[64]

During the Carter years China policy primarily revolved around the issue of the full normalization of relations with the People's Republic of China—and emerged soon after President Carter took office. Holbrooke, who would become assistant secretary of state for Asia, was asked by the president for his opinion about Brzezinski as national security advisor and raised concerns about his working relationship with Secretary of State Cyrus Vance, given the marked differences in their worldviews on the Soviet Union. Subsequently, Vance and Brzezinski articulated dissimilar opinions on the impact of China on the U.S. geopolitical competition with the Soviet Union, with Brzezinski hoping to utilize the "China card" in order to help curb the Soviets. In contrast, the secretary of state viewed an evolving U.S.-China security relationship as detrimental to the détente relationship and "pos[ing] substantial risks for our relations with Moscow and for our relations with Tokyo and other Asian allies."[65]

The first flash point occurred in the first weeks of the administration, in February 1977, after the Carter team learned of a secret agreement between the Chinese leadership and President Nixon to complete normalization during his second term. Holbrooke and Michel Oksenberg, the NSC director for China policy, were directed to recreate the record that had led to this pledge. Not only were they were successful in establishing the secret understandings reached by Nixon and Kissinger, but they also promised to maintain a cooperative working relationship; Holbrooke told Oksenberg in January, "I want to make one commitment with you—one promise. We will not keep secrets from each other. We will tell each other everything we know so that there is no rivalry between us."[66]

Another tangible sign of Holbrooke's interest in promoting interdepartmental dialogue was his establishment of the East Asian "informals," an interagency foreign policy coordinating mechanism that one participant described as particularly effective in managing elements of the government's Asia policies. The informals included the senior Asia staffers from the NSC, the deputy assistant secretary of defense for international security affairs–Pacific, and the deputy director for operations for the CIA, and met every Monday afternoon in the assistant secretary's office at the State Department.[67]

The comradeship expressed at the deputies level, however, was not matched among their bosses, and J. Stapleton Roy, who worked on the State Department China desk for the first few years of the Carter administration (and later served as ambassador to China from 1991 to 1995), observed that "there was a collegial approach on the policy, which then became heavily affected by personality differences between key practitioners," particularly the breakdown of the Brzezinski-Vance relationship.[68] The problems began when Brzezinski approved Oksenberg's recommendation to reaffirm the Nixon-Ford assurances and sent his memo directly to the president without consulting Vance. Vance was irate and "warned the national security advisor not to make policy recommendations to the president without clearing them first through the State Department." Vance disagreed with the decision to endorse the previous administration's normalization initiative and demanded that the Oksenberg memo be withdrawn and that all copies of the original memo be collected and shredded.[69]

The plans for normalization went forward, nonetheless. In June 1977, PRM/NSC-24 noted that "it was in America's interest to complete normalization," and Carter surprised Vance when he informed him that he would be traveling to China in August to discuss normalization with the Chinese Communist Party (CCP) leadership. The trip went badly, particularly when Deng Xiaoping accused Vance of backtracking on President Ford's positions on Taiwan.[70]

The visit ended on an even poorer note. On the eve of the secretary of state's departure from Beijing, a newspaper story was leaked in the United States claiming that the White House was pleased with the "flexibility" displayed by China in their talks with the Americans about normalization, a claim meant to embarrass Vance and provoke the CCP, which it did. State Department officials suspected that Brzezinski was behind the damaging leak.[71] According to Richard Solomon, an NSC staffer under Kissinger, the "[Chinese leadership] put [Vance] down because they wanted to stall the normalization talks, but they also wanted to increase their leverage on normalization issues, so they humiliated Vance by saying his positions were a setback and his trip to Beijing had been bad. In this way, they gave an opening to Brzezinski, who picked up the opportunity to supplant Vance as the primary interlocutor with the Chinese."[72]

While strolling back from lunch one day in November, Brzezinski asked Oksenberg if he could arrange for the national security advisor to be sent to China. The NSC staffer informed a Chinese diplomat over lunch of Brzezinski's interest. The personal lobbying bore fruit several days later at a farewell luncheon at the White House for a retiring Chinese diplomat, who publicly offered an invitation to the national security advisor before a surprised and chagrined Vance and Holbrooke.[73] Vance had strongly opposed a Brzezinski visit to China, seeing it as a return to the diplomacy of the Nixon-Kissinger era. The unexpected invitation further eroded relations between Holbrooke and Oksenberg, who falsely denied the assistant secretary's contention that he had been "playing games."[74]

After several months of "badgering" by Brzezinski (using the hour he had each morning to brief the president to press his case), President Carter decided to deploy his national security advisor instead.[75]

Having outmaneuvered Vance once again, Brzezinski was then accused of taking multiple opportunities to exclude or humiliate State Department staffers on his China mission, limiting the number of officials permitted to help plan the trip or their presence on his mission. Richard Holbrooke, the department's top Asia official, was not allowed to attend a key meeting with Deng in Beijing, nor was he permitted to read Brzezinski's talking points for the national security advisor's meetings with the Chinese leadership. Holbrooke later complained that he had been subjected "to the most humiliating treatment" by Brzezinski, and efforts to get himself added to the meeting with Deng failed, with Brzezinski reportedly telling a State Department aide, "Screw you. I'm not going to," in response to one last, desperate plea.[76] The only token acknowledgment of collaboration came when Brzezinski attributed a well-received banquet toast that he had given to "close collaboration with my State Department colleagues."[77]

Overall, Brzezinski had a much more pleasant meeting with the Chinese than Vance had. Brzezinski wrote that he confidently believed, "I was the top official in the Carter Administration in whom [the Chinese] had genuine confidence and had whose strategic perspectives to some extent they shared," and, perhaps as the CCP leadership had hoped, his hard-line views on the Soviet Union meshed well with their interpretations of their powerful neighbor.[78]

Brzezinski also addressed the sensitive issue of the U.S. military relationship with Taiwan, explaining to the Chinese leadership in deliberately unclear terms that "this consideration must be borne in mind when resolving the issue of normalization and when defining the full range of relations during the historically transitional period of our relationship with the people of Taiwan."[79] On the flight back from China, Brzezinski wanted to ensure that no one in the State Department saw his "memcon" transcript of his talks with Deng before he briefed the president, so Oksenberg was directed by his boss to deny Holbrooke access to the materials. Holbrooke lost his temper and "grabbed Oksenberg by the collar and accused him of violating the pledge they had made to each other at the outset of the administration" to cooperate.[80]

Despite the success of Brzezinski's meeting, issues relating to the U.S.-Taiwan relationship, particularly on the sore subject of arms deliveries, remained unresolved, and Carter held a meeting with his China staff in October to try to resolve them. As a result of the meeting—which did not include Vance, whom Brzezinski was able to exclude—Carter decided that he would try to complete normalization by the end of the year.[81] By November 1978, U.S. Ambassador Leonard Woodcock presented a proposal to establish full diplomatic relations on January 1, 1979, with the People's Republic of China, and the CCP responded in a mostly positive fashion in mid-December.

Brzezinski secretly met with a Chinese envoy at the White House—deploying Oksenberg to ensure that the State Department did not learn of the encounter—to inform the diplomat of the American counterproposal that Ambassador Woodcock would be presenting before Deng. Woodcock's report and transcript of the meeting, which seemingly settled the remaining issues on U.S. arms sales to Taiwan, was not distributed to Oksenberg or anyone from the State Department, on Brzezinski's orders.[82]

A few remaining details needed to be worked out, according to Brzezinski, but a deal on normalization could be announced in three days, ahead of a SALT deal with the Soviets that Secretary Vance was close to completing. Despite Brzezinski's order not to tell the State Department that an agreement on normalization was near completion, Oksenberg asked Roger Sullivan, a China specialist at State, to assist him, telling Sullivan to call in sick and come over to the Old Executive Office Building and to leave Holbrooke and the rest of the State Department in the dark. Warren Christopher, who was acting secretary of state while Vance was in Geneva, became suspicious that something was going on at the White House and finally was granted access by Brzezinski to Woodcock's account of his meeting.[83]

Christopher eventually convinced the national security advisor to permit Holbrooke, the State Department's top Asia expert, to read Woodcock's cable and the draft of the final American counterproposal.[84] Finally given the chance to view the document that evening, Holbrooke pointed out an ambiguity about the U.S. right to sell arms to Taiwan that would anger congressional supporters of the island nation. Holbrooke, with his customary flair for the dramatic, told Brzezinski that the proposal would generate a "congressional problem of monumental proportions."[85] But Brzezinski, typically, was unmoved by the rhetoric.

He dismissed those concerns and the American ambassador to China was told to inform Deng that President Carter would announce a normalization agreement in three days.[86] However, one day before the president's broadcast to the nation, the Chinese ambassador to the United States met with Brzezinski at the White House to discuss some postnormalization details, and toward the end of the meeting he mentioned the CCP leadership's satisfaction with the U.S. decision to fully end arms sales to Taiwan. Brzezinski responded that the administration had only agreed to a one-year moratorium, after which sales of defensive arms would resume. The Chinese diplomat disagreed with Brzezinski's understanding of the interpretation of "no new commitments," and the national security advisor realized that the normalization accord could be derailed just hours before President Carter's announcement.[87]

The problem facing the White House was analogous to what had occurred in 1972, when Kissinger shut the State Department out of the drafting of the Shanghai Communiqué, only to reopen the negotiations after Marshall Green, one of Holbrooke's predecessors, pointed out a flaw in the agreement. And similar to 1972, the national security advisor ordered last-minute negotiations; Brzezinski quickly cabled Ambassador Woodcock, instructing him to meet with Deng to ensure that they understood that the cutoff of arms sales to Taiwan was temporary. After a final, contentious meeting just hours before the president was going to speak about the agreement on national television, Deng resignedly gave his consent to the American position on arms sales to Taiwan.[88] As one Carter administration State Department official familiar with the normalization negotiations bitterly recalled, "Zbig may be proud of this little game but it served no purpose."[89] The personality clashes increased the likelihood that there would be a policy meltdown over Taiwan, but they should not conceal the real issue: that U.S. policy towards Taiwan and China since 1972 has been inherently Janus-like, attempting to appeal simultaneously to two political elites between whom often very little trust existed. Tension would flare up periodically, often unexpectedly—such as when in 2005 China passed a law that allowed the government to declare war on Taiwan at any time without further debate if Taiwan declared independence. Such saber-rattling emphasized that that the one-China policy, two-China dialogue was inherently unstable for the U.S. Furthermore, activist NSC directors working at odds with their colleagues at State just added to the overall sense of rockiness.

When Holbrooke recalls the maneuvering over normalization in 1979, he concludes:

> From Kissinger on, all of them had some operational responsibilities. Brzezinski, because of his long personal rivalry with Kissinger and the fact that he was Kissinger's immediate successor, was most determined to outdo Henry. Others, like Brent Scowcroft and Colin Powell, were more laid back. The national security advisor, as you know, has several functions-body person for the president, coordinator of foreign policy and national security between different agencies, and then the operational role. It is the operational role that is most complicated. Before Kissinger, under the only other two modern NSC people, Rostow and Bundy, it wasn't done. So Kissinger changed everything and Brzezinski reinforced it. It often undercuts the Secretary of State.[90]

Holbrooke's comments illustrate the tension that existed in the relationships between key players at the time. Insiders might comment that it is ironic since both Holbrooke and Brzezinski are seen as abrasive, self-interested competitors in the bureaucratic wars. But objective observers would also note that they are two of the most capable and talented foreign policy specialists the Democratic Party has had during the past several decades—arguably the two best in terms of all-around knowledge, skills, creativity, and intellect. The question arises: Is tension between such people inevitable to some degree? The reality is that we see it often—Kissinger vs. Rogers, Kissinger vs. Schlesinger, Kissinger vs. Rumsfeld, Vance vs. Brzezinski, later Shultz vs. Weinberger, Lake vs. Holbrooke, and Powell vs. Rumsfeld. While it can be minimized and is not constructive, it is also a by-product of having talented people with huge egos playing for huge stakes. The critical issue in each of these cases is whether the president was willing to tolerate it, or to engage to resolve it, or whether it served his purposes. Carter himself has challenged the State Department account of the events surrounding the normalization of relations with China.[91]

As had been evident in the Roosevelt administration, some leaders feel that conflicts between their advisors are not such a bad thing, that it shows they have strong, independent-minded advisors and it leaves the leader squarely in charge. Although the Brzezinski-Vance feud disturbed Carter, he accepted it and, indeed, understood from the beginning what he was getting. He notes that he was warned that Brzezinski was "aggressive and ambitious" and that he might not be "adequately deferential to a secretary of state," but he goes on to say, "Knowing Zbig, I realized that some of these assessments were accurate, but they were in accord with what I wanted: the final decisions on basic foreign policy would be made by me in the Oval Office and not in the State Department. I listened carefully to all the comments about [Zbig], considered the factors involved, and decided that I wanted him with me in the White House."[92]

He then goes on to refer to the State Department as a "sprawling Washington and worldwide bureaucracy" and says, "I rarely received innovative ideas from its staff members" whom he characterized as "mild and cautious."[93] He saw the inertia of the department as a "beneficial restraint on overly rapid actions" and that "in many ways Cy Vance (whom Carter characterizes as his closest friend in the Cabinet) mirrored the character of the organization he led."[94] However, in the case of the delicate normalization talks with China, Carter not only supported the subterfuge led by Brzezinski but said he directed it in order to protect the sensitive negotiations. Writing in 1999, he recalled that "I was leery of channeling my proposals through the State Department, because I did not feel that I had full support there. . . It was because of my orders to hold information closely so that our efforts would not be subverted."[95]

President Carter's reticence for utilizing the State Department was reinforced by concerns that Foggy Bottom leaked like a sieve, stating that "In the State Department, nothing is secret. There is a pipeline between the *Washington Post* and State Department."[96] Worried that if the normalization negotiations were made public, Carter feared that "the furor would abort what we were trying to accomplish"[97] and, more broadly, had tired of "disgruntled subordinates in the State Department... [who] had been a constant source of complaints to the news media regarding the national security adviser's having too much influence over foreign policy."[98] Carter knew what he was doing.

Still, the old scars remain. One very senior Clinton administration official told me that in a dispute with another very senior Clinton administration official, when it got tense, one of them made reference to the fact that one of them was a "Vance" person and the other a "Brzezinski" person—implying a divide that would remain for all time. Yet they too worked it out. And the China normalization effort ended a success, as had Panama and the negotiating process around SALT.

.   .   .

The biggest and most celebrated success of the Carter era, the one for which he is most remembered, centered on a thirteen-day marathon negotiating session in the Maryland woods at Camp David. The effort, the capstone of Carter's early commitment to achieving a breakthrough in the Arab-Israeli conflict, was one case in which the State Department and the NSC teams worked together in very close harmony. But it also illustrated the extraordinary degree to which Carter's diplomacy was conducted by Carter. Here, the fact that he was a hands-on manager made a significant difference for the better. He took the process very personally, was well prepared for it by his staff, and tackled the big problems in closing the epochs-old rift between Israel and Egypt personally.

His relationship with Anwar Sadat, the president of Egypt, is encapsulated well in the passage from his memoirs in which he writes, "On April 4, 1977, a shining light burst on the Middle East scene for me. I had my first meetings with President Anwar Sadat of Egypt, a man who would change history and whom I would come to admire more than any other leader."[99] The bond between the two was mutual, and it enabled Carter to keep Sadat in the negotiations at several key junctures when they were breaking down, often as a result of the tough stance of Israel's prime minister, former underground fighter Menachem Begin. Carter and Begin could not be described as close. Nonetheless, it was often personal diplomacy, including the kind of very direct conversations that could only take place between two leaders in private, that produced the breakthroughs and communicated the leverage needed to achieve the deal.

So much has been written about the Camp David process that it would be hard to shed much light on it here. However, in the context of the operations of the NSC and the high-level interagency process, it should be noted that unusually close collaboration existed between the two in the extensive preparations for Camp David peace talks. For instance, a secret planning group with Vice President Mondale, Vance, Brzezinski, Deputy National Security Advisor David Aaron, NSC Middle East specialist William Quandt, and several other State Department officials was formed in May to coordinate the administration's strategy. One author concluded that the "cooperation of State Department and NSC officials enabled Carter and Vance, as the principal negotiators, to be ahead of the Israelis and Egyptians on technical and negotiating issues and thus to keep the initiative."[100] Brzezinski and Quandt were present at the talks at Camp David, but the national security advisor expressly acknowledges that Vance had a pivotal role during the difficult negotiations.[101]

Former NSC Middle East specialist Hal Saunders notes:

> On the team that worked on the Middle East ... there was a group of people that had been virtually unchanged under three administrations. It was virtually the same people give or take a little bit here and there. The incredible competence of that team was critical to the success of the meeting.
>
> When Vance came in and succeeded Kissinger, he was so well versed that we never read a briefing memo for him on where things were. The only memo we started working on was what we wanted to do next. It was a cohesive professional team. My feeling has long been that it's the people who make this system work; it's not the structure itself.[102]

In this way foreign policy becomes a club in which there is a first tier of specialists, usually no more than a hundred, who are the U.S. resident experts for a generation on each area of policy. They get to know each other very well and often work together very well. When administrations change, when we are lucky, the groups who pass the baton in each area are so well connected to one another, know each other so well, that there is real continuity. The only problem is when, because of politics or ideology, people who are outliers or who have little experience are appointed—and then, no matter how smart these individuals are, they suffer from the learning curve problem. Having a mix of people, some civil servants, some from the "permanent expert community" and others from the outside, is optimal—but from time to time in our recent history we have gotten the mix wrong. Not at Camp David, however.

Meanwhile, as this rare episode of NSC–State Department harmony was coming to fruition at the Camp David summit, the unraveling of the shah's regime in Iran would shatter that interagency peace, and its consequences would embroil the Carter administration for the rest of its term. For a few individuals in the administration, the U.S. entanglement in Iran did not come as a surprise, as they had recognized the growing strategic importance of the region even before the problem broke. As military aide William Odom recalls:

> I remember when Samuel Huntington came into my office one day in the late spring in 1977, asking me where the United States was most likely to have a confrontation with the Soviet Union. I answered, "Iran." When he asked why I reached that conclusion, I said that it was largely a hunch. He agreed, but then elaborated a set of criteria for anticipating what he called "crisis confrontations" ("cri-cons" became his acronym for them). He had developed an impressively rigorous method for anticipating cri-cons. He had five or six criteria that drove you right to Iran as the most probable location. He really provided a first-class conceptualization of the problem. That is an example of the quality of planning that went into the PRM–10 Comprehensive Net Assessment under Huntington's direction. That was the kind of policy planning that [former Secretary of State George] Marshall had had in State, but only after he created the Policy Planning Staff and separated planning for current policy operations. After Marshall left State, I don't believe any later secretary of state ever restored this planning-operations split that Marshall and Eisenhower found imperative for managing U.S. strategy.[103]

The crisis that embroiled this staunch American ally was unexpected to most NSC and State Department officials who were responsible for policy in the region. As the shah's serious political difficulties belatedly came to the attention of most U.S. policymakers in late 1978, Brzezinski became increasingly troubled by the intelligence and analysis provided by the State Department. He primarily blames U.S. Ambassador to Iran William Sullivan (as does President Carter), secondarily fingering Vance, his deputy Warren Christopher, and the head of the Iran desk, Henry Precht, for the disjointed administration response.[104]

The rift within the administration began fairly early on in the crisis and led to the concurrent—and sometimes inconsistent—consideration of both diplomatic and military action against the new Khomeini regime.[105] President Carter was unable to decide whether to heed the counsel of Brzezinski, who wanted to encourage the shah to suppress the revolution (or, if the shah was unable to do so, encourage a military dictatorship that could), or that of Vance's more cautious State Department, which suggested that the administration reach out to opposition elements in order to smooth the inevitable transition to a new government.

In another policy battle, in order to address Brzezinski's unhappiness with the intelligence and analysis being provided by the State Department, the national security advisor established a private back-channel relationship with Iranian Ambassador Ardeshir Zahedi.[106] While Brzezinski downplays the Zahedi connection, Vance was angered by the national security advisor's end run around the State Department. The back channel, which Brzezinski denied existed, was then closed.[107] Brzezinski was also involved in other back channels that circumvented the State Department, as in November 1978, when he deployed a businessman and former CIA officer to Iran to provide an assessment of the situation in the country.[108]

Meanwhile, Brzezinski's expanded role on Iran, Michael Ledeen argues, further hampered the policymaking process. Ledeen writes that the national security advisor, having gained control of the administration's Iran policy in November 1978 as the situation worsened, subsequently provoked "a torrent of leaks to the press, mostly from angry State Department officials." Carter was angered by the continued leaks, which highlighted the divisions within the administration and made public the dire expectations that some officials had expressed about the shah's political future.[109]

Despite these machinations, a divided Washington watched as the shah fled the country in mid-January and the political vacuum was filled by Ayatollah Khomeini, who triumphantly returned from exile. The first post-shah regime included some moderate figures, and Brzezinski himself talked privately in Algiers with two Iranian officials in the first transitional government, a meeting which Vance says "surprise[d]" him.[110] However, by April, Khomeini had declared Iran an Islamic republic, and relations between Iran and the United States deteriorated as the new regime instituted fundamentalist measures and suppressed Western influences.

Around this time Carter wrote in his diary, "Zbig is a little too competitive and incisive. Cy is too easy on his subordinates. And the news media constantly aggravate the inevitable differences and competition between the two groups. I hardly know the desk officers and others in State but work very closely with the NSC people. When we have consulted closely, like in the Mideast area, at Camp David, and otherwise, we've never had any problems between the two groups."[111] However, things were clearly changing.

On the morning of Sunday, November 4, 1979, the White House situation room received an emergency call from the U.S. embassy in Tehran. The embassy had been overrun.[112] Elizabeth Anne Swift, one of the embassy staff, began to give a nonstop commentary of the situation from inside the embassy over an open line connected to a speaker on the table. From another speaker, Kathryn Koob and her staff some miles away in the American Cultural center in Iran spoke for a record day and a half until she, too, was discovered (the revolutionary authorities would later present the phone bill to her in captivity).[113] At the end of the day, sixty-six U.S. citizens were held hostage.

In the preceding months, Reza Shah Pahlavi had moved from Iran to Egypt before settling in Morocco, rather than moving straight to the United States, as he had been unequivocally invited to do. Apparently, he was still under the impression that his adherents would wrest power back from Khomeini. If this had occurred, he could have returned victorious from an Islamic country. On February 22, however, with the last vestiges of his rule gone (and Morocco increasingly agitated about his presence), the shah decided to ask Richard Parker, U.S. ambassador to Morocco, to make the necessary arrangements for his move to the United States. The Special Coordination Committee (SCC) of the NSC—chaired by Brzezinski and usually attended by Secretary of Defense Brown, CIA Director Turner, Chairman of the Joint Chiefs of Staff David Jones, Vice President Mondale, Attorney General Benjamin Civiletti, Secretary of Energy Charles Duncan, David Aaron, David Newsom, and Frank Carlucci—met on February 23, 1979, to discuss the issue.[114]

At the time, the United States was involved in delicate, highly classified negotiations with Tehran to arrange safe passage for a group of U.S. officials stuck in northern Iran. It was also worried about security threats from U.S.-based pro-Khomeini factions and possible legal action against the shah, and was trying secure the safety of Americans threatened by local "revolutionary committees" roaming Iran. Brzezinski decided that the invitation should be retracted and the shah should postpone his arrival in the United States. Moreover, Carter did not want the shah "playing tennis" in the United States while Americans ran the risk of being kidnapped.[115] As David Aaron suggested to the president, if the shah moved to the United States a "guerrilla group could retaliate against the remain-

ing Americans, possibly taking one or more Americans hostage and refusing to release them until the shah was extradited."[116] On being told of the
difficulties, the shah contacted David Rockefeller, who, together with
Kissinger, eventually arranged for the shah to move to the Bahamas for the
time being. However, they kept up the pressure for the shah to be admitted
to the United States. Kissinger gave a speech on April 9 accusing the
administration of treating a longtime U.S. ally "like a Flying Dutchman
looking for a port of call."[117]

On October 18, Secretary Vance received an unexpected report stating
that the shah was suffering from two cancers and obstructive jaundice,
conditions that the shah had kept secret even from his family. An American doctor recommended that he be admitted immediately to a large U.S.
medical center. The next day, Vance summarized the findings to Carter at
the regular Friday morning foreign policy breakfast. Carter now argued
that the United States could not refuse a longtime ally medical treatment.
The others present agreed.[118] In response, Carter prophetically wondered
out loud what advice they would give him when the Iranians took the
embassy in Tehran and held Americans hostage. Meanwhile, the embassy
in Tehran was never evacuated, because it was assumed the Iranian government of Prime Minister Mehdi Bazargan would come to the rescue, as
it had done previously on one occasion, if any attack were to occur.[119]

The attack finally came at 10:30 a.m. on November 4. A group of students assembled in front of the embassy and then rushed over the com-
pound walls. By chance, the chargé d'affaires, Bruce Laingen, had gone to
the Iranian foreign ministry that day to ask Foreign Minister Yazdi for
more protection.[120] Yazdi insisted that it was nothing more than a "student
sit-in" and that Khomeini would ask the students to leave once he was
contacted in Qom. It came as a considerable shock when the ayatollah's
son Ahmed arrived and, instead of negotiating with the students, congrat-
ulated and joined them. Prime Minister Bazargan responded by offering
his resignation to Khomeini—which was accepted by the Revolutionary
Council on November 6. The 444-day hostage ordeal began.

On November 5, Brzezinski chaired the first of the SCC meetings that
would work over the next year for the release of the hostages. The meetings would occur every morning, sometimes seven days a week, with no
agenda circulated in advance to maintain operational security. Members
who did not attend a meeting were given verbal summaries or debriefings
in the White House. At the meeting that day it was decided that an emissary would be sent—either Ramsey Clark or William Miller—to state the
chief demands of the United States, essentially the release of all the hostages,

in the hope of solving the problem quickly.[121] An offer by Yasser Arafat of the Palestine Liberation Organization (PLO) to negotiate with Khomeini was also quietly encouraged.

By the next day, the problem had become more complicated. The entire religious revolutionary leadership had thrown its support behind the students barricading the embassy. That morning at 8:00, Carter met in the Oval Office with the principals—Brzezinski, Vance, Under Secretary Newsom, Secretary of Defense Harold Brown, Chief of Staff Hamilton Jordan, press secretary Jody Powell, and Gary Sick from the NSC taking notes. Carter asked the State Department to do everything possible to get any remaining U.S. citizens out of Iran. Brzezinski suggested that a veiled public threat or a private threat to bomb Qom or Iran's oil fields should be given in case they killed hostages. Carter was not so convinced: "They have us by the balls."[122] However, Carter did ask his staff to examine the possibility of expelling students (something Walter Mondale later opposed—why would a great nation respond by "kicking out a few sad-ass students"?), freezing Iranian assets, and stopping the supply of military spare parts: "Get our people out of Iran and break relations. Fuck 'em!"[123]

At 4:30 that afternoon Carter summoned the full NSC in the Cabinet Room. He opened by asking the group to fill out policy options: What punitive options should be used if Iran began killing hostages? Should U.S. forces be sent to Iran or would this lead to them getting bogged down? After Carter was finished, Brzezinski noted that NBC had found out about the emissaries and was going to publicize the fact that evening (when the news reached Khomeini, he gave the order that no one was to meet with the emissaries). Admiral Turner gave a summary of the embassy takeover: the students had been given permission by Khomeini and had executed a skilled infiltration. Secretary Brown discussed the possibility of a rescue operation involving helicopters, but it was dismissed as too risky; helicopters could not be brought close enough to the target without alerting Iranian forces. Nevertheless, plans for an operation should be developed, Carter insisted. Brown also put additional punitive measures on the table, such as hitting kerosene refineries in Iran.[124]

By the end of the day, the administration had set out the policy priorities it would follow for the following months:

First, the United States would pursue a campaign of political, diplomatic and economic initiatives to convince the revolutionary leadership in Iran—by persuasion if possible and by pressure if necessary—that it was in their interest to release the hostages promptly and safely. . . .

Second, military contingency planning was to proceed on two tracks. A plan was to be developed for a rescue mission, in the event it was needed. At the same time, specific options were to be examined for a punitive military strike for retaliation in the event the hostages were harmed. The emphasis in planning was to be on secrecy, minimizing loss of life, avoiding a military situation where US forces would find themselves bogged down in Iran, and ensuring that US actions would be selective in their effects, i.e., to punish Iran without doing damage to US friends and interests in the rest of the world.[125]

On November 10, Carter wrote in his diary, "I asked Cy for his opinion on punitive action to be launched against Iran. His recommendations were exactly what I had already decided tentatively with our military people. We want it to be quick, incisive, surgical, no loss of American lives, not involve any other country, minimal suffering of the Iranian people themselves, to increase their reliance on imports, sure of success, and unpredictable. No one will know what I've decided—except Fritz, Zbig, Harold, David [Jones, chairman Joint Chiefs] and Cy."[126]

That same day another member of Carter's inner circle weighed in. Carter's wife Rosalynn, having returned from a visit to Cambodian refugee camps in Thailand, said that she believed that the United States should stop purchasing Iranian oil and that her husband should announce the decision as soon as possible. He discussed her proposal with members of the cabinet, and forty-eight hours later he ordered the U.S. purchases of oil from Iran to be discontinued.[127]

On November 17 the PLO initiative bore fruit. Thirteen African-American embassy officials and women were released and subsequently debriefed on November 20 in Germany.[128] The principals now learned that many of the embassy's files had been captured (prompting Carter to task Anthony Lake with a complete review of the documents) and that the conditions inside the embassy were poor: those suspected of spying were being threatened with torture and show trials. On the same day, Khomeini also threatened that "if Carter does not send the shah, it is possible that the hostages may be tried, and if they are tried, Carter knows what will happen."[129] The United States replied that Iran "would bear full responsibility for any ensuing consequences, [and that] other remedies [were available to the United States]."[130]

On November 28 a meeting that later would be one of the most contentious of the crisis was held. Until then, Vance had managed to keep the diplomatic track from being overtaken by the military track. That day Carter asked the SCC to comment on the possible mining of Iran ports to escalate military pressure on Iran. Vance was opposed, arguing that it would threaten the hostages. Brzezinski, on the other hand, suggested that it would force the Europeans to act more forcefully. Vance won the argument. As a consequence, diplomatic action continued for another two months. However, the military track began to assume greater importance. Meanwhile, the shah left the United States for Panama, the PLO initiative ended, and the Security Council was deadlocked: all the reasons that Vance was using to avoid use of force were passing.[131]

After a long and laborious effort by Hamilton Jordan, assisted by Harold Saunders, with a channel established to President Abolhassan Bani-Sadr and Foreign Minister Sadegh Ghotbzadeh, who served briefly in the early years of Ayatollah Khomeini's regime, through the French and Argentinean lawyers Christian Bourguet and Hector Villalón failed, pressure to do something more than just negotiate mounted.[132] Although the Soviet invasion of Afghanistan in December increased the interests that the United States and Iran shared, the United States continued to look impotent by continuing to negotiate.

Odom recalls:

During the crisis you've got everybody in the government working. You've got the Justice Department. You've got the Treasury Department working to freeze funds. You have a really big interagency process. Every morning at 9:00 a.m., there's an SCC on dealing with the hostages. You're dealing with the UN. You really have a big set of activities being organized at those meetings, but it's day to day. And your time horizon is a week at most. And the top presidential aides are there: Jody Powell and Hamilton Jordan, and they're all worried. One day, the vice president was at the SCC meeting. He looked around the room and lamented that there was not a single Iranian expert in the room. He, too, was worried. My private reaction was quite different: Thank God! If you include area experts in a high-level policy meeting, you'll discover that they're in love with the people from their area. They know a great many details about their area, but they are hopelessly inept at reaching sound recommendations for U.S. policy. They're the last people to ask what is the right thing to do. [He laughs.] I'm a Russian expert, I know. You don't want a Russian expert near a policymaking discussion. You'll get in trouble. You should listen to area experts before you go to the policymaking meeting. Sort out what they have to say about realities, facts, etc. You really need to listen to them. They can tell you useful things. But you don't want them telling you what to do. So, the Carter NSC staff had a good process.

And then one day, [Carter] says, I think we need a bigger view, a longer-term view of Iran and the region, not just a focus on dozens of current problems . . . and these meetings were happening five days a week. Brzezinski then announced that we would start having Persian Gulf Security Framework meetings to develop a regional strategy for the longer run, and we started holding them at least once a week, sometimes two times a week. He made me essentially the planner and staff support for this series of SCC meeting. So I set up a concept for this "framework" objective. I found a former student of mine at West Point, Christopher Shoemaker, who was a major over at the Pentagon, and brought him over to assist me in this planning endeavor on the NSC staff. We set up a four-component strategy. It had a military component, an economic component, a diplomatic component, and an intelligence component. And under each one we subdivided it into major categories of things to do. Then we further subdivided each of these things into smaller actions. This chart approach allowed us to keep a clear overall picture and to make sure that nothing was neglected. Moreover, President Carter liked charts, apparently for some of the same reasons as I did. . . . Still, several staff aides in State, Defense, and the CIA were not in agreement. They wanted to paralyze the Persian Gulf Security Framework process by initiating a major policy review study. Had that occurred, of course, it would have produced a major debate and an ideological struggle, yielding no practical recommendations. It did not occur, and I presume that it did not because the president and most of his principal advisors understood precisely the danger and ignored pleas for such a review.[133]

Once the Soviets invaded Afghanistan on December 27, the crisis grew more complex. Now, not only was Iran in turmoil, our hostages in captivity, oil markets unsteady, but the Soviet Union was making an unabashed play for a country in the region. Although the Soviets insisted they had been "invited" into the country by the local government, it was clear that this was a strategic ploy.

Carter noted at the time in his diary, "The Soviets have begun to move their forces in to overthrow the existing government. 215 flights in the last 24 hours or so. They've moved in a couple of regiments and now have maybe a total of 8,000 or 10,000 people in Afghanistan—both advisers and military. We consider this to be an extremely serious development."[134]

Via the hotline to Brezhnev he stated that the invasion "could mark a fundamental and long-lasting turning point in our relations. . . . Unless you draw back from your present course of action, this will inevitably jeopardize the course of United States–Soviet relations throughout the world."[135] He could not have known how prophetic he was. Thanks in large part to U.S. support of the anti-Soviet forces in Afghanistan—an approach devised and recommended by Brzezinski—that country became a quagmire for the Soviets, and their inability to defeat the ragtag but fierce and determined *mujahideen* fighters became a great embarrassment to the Soviet leadership and a source of real dissent in that society. Indeed, some trace the early impetus for *glasnost*, Gorbachev's policy of openness in the mid-1980s was due, among other things, to the pressure among many in Russia for the truth about the Afghanistan fiasco.

Brzezinski dismisses the notion that our support for the *mujahideen* ultimately led to the empowerment of the Taliban and Osama bin Laden, who went to Afghanistan several years later to help fight the Russians. He notes that the rise of the Taliban and of bin Laden came much later after a series of twists and turns in the fortunes of other political groups on the ground and that bin Laden, in particular, would also be motivated with regard to al Qaeda by a host of other subsequent issues, from the deterioration of the Arab-Israeli relationship that triggered the start of the Intifada to the presence of U.S. troops in Saudi Arabia in the early 1990s in the first Gulf War.[136]

After the Soviet invasion, the NSC weighed many other options, and the president ultimately enacted a number of policies that were not politically popular. These included a grain embargo, which was not embraced by farmers in the key state of Iowa, home to important party caucuses during the presidential primary season of 1980. Carter was being challenged by Senator Edward Kennedy, among others, and this was risky. But it was not his only risky political stance during this period. The boycott of the Olympics was unpopular with some groups. And, more important, Carter's decision in late 1979 not to leave the White House unnecessarily to campaign so that he could manage the hostage crisis (and not appear to be insensitive to it while pursuing his own political gains) is now cited by many as a source of his ultimate defeat in 1980. This "Rose Garden strategy," where he stayed close to home, may have been a tactical blunder, but there is no doubt that it was yet another example of political courage.

The next key meeting in the hostage crisis began at 10:45 a.m. on March 22, 1980, at Camp David. Carter met with Mondale, Vance, Brzezinski, Defense's Brown, CIA's Turner, Joint Chiefs chairman Jones, David Aaron, and Jody Powell.[137] Jones began by briefing the group on the likely success of a rescue mission. The actual attack on the embassy would be easy, it was getting there without the Iranians' knowledge (which could prompt them to move some of the hostages) and exiting Iran that would be hard. Brzezinski was highly pessimistic about the operation's remaining undiscovered along the way, given its logistical complexity. Initial preparations for a rescue mission were authorized.[138]

On April 9 Brzezinski sent a memorandum (originally drafted by Gary Sick) to Carter making the case for a military rescue of the hostages. There were essentially two choices left, the memorandum stated: an escalation of pressure on Iran that ended with the mining of harbors, or a rescue that would swipe the hostages out from underneath Khomeini and make him look weak. The memorandum ended with the following line:

> In my view, a carefully planned and boldly executed rescue operation represents the only realistic prospect that the hostages—any of them—will be freed in the foreseeable future. Our policy of restraint has won us a well-deserved understanding throughout the world, but it has run out. It is time for us to act. Now.[139]

On April 11, Carter convened a meeting of the NSC with the same participants as at Camp David, except that Vance was notably absent. He had gone on vacation a day earlier and was not informed of the meeting's results until he returned. General Jones gave an update of the preparations of the rescue mission.[140] Everyone agreed that the negotiation track was dead, apart from Warren Christopher, Vance's deputy. At this point, however, Carter's mind was already made up: the rescue operation would go ahead, as it was preferable to running the risk of uncontrollable escalation by mining Iran's harbors. By the time Vance returned and objected—saying that "our only realistic course was to keep up the pressure on Iran while we waited for Khomeini to determine that the revolution had accomplished its purpose, and that the hostages were of no further value"—the die had been cast.[141]

In the early evening of April 24, eight helicopters took off from the USS Nimitz in the Arabian Sea. While traversing the desert, one of the helicopters' warning lights went off, signaling a technical malfunction. The helicopter was abandoned on the ground, and the Delta team on board was picked up and carried on to the mission. Two hours into the operation, another helicopter, while flying through the dust clouds in the desert, decided to turn around and return to the ship (even though there were only sixty minutes to go to the desert refueling pad outside Tehran). At the same time, another helicopter developed hydraulic problems and had to be abandoned in the desert at the refueling pad. The mission was canceled—six helicopters was the minimum required for a successful assault.

To add to the failure of the mission, while the helicopters were being refueled for the way back, one of them collided with a refueling plane and both burst into flames.[142]

Carter called it the worst day of his life. He also noted with gratitude that among the few people to call with offers of support after the failure was former secretary of state and national security advisor Henry Kissinger.[143]

After the failure of the mission, the public learned that Secretary of State Cyrus Vance had resigned. Vance effectively resigned when, during a meeting with the president, Brzezinski, and Brown, they were discussing how to handle Congress and other groups regarding the rescue mission and how to handle the period after the operation in general. The president mentioned that a group opposed to the administration's policy in Iran wanted to come in and see them and that he'd like Vance to handle the meeting. Vance said he could not. Carter notes that it was the first time in his presidency that anyone had refused to obey a direct order of his. But Carter was also sympathetic to Vance, knowing how deeply upset he was by the rescue mission.[144]

Later that day, Vance submitted a resignation later and graciously agreed to stay on and stay silent until after the operation. The president did not, however, try to talk him out of his resignation. The policy gulf had grown too wide and the months of internal bickering, of leaks, of accusations and counteraccusations, had taken to great a toll. Senator Edmund Muskie, the former boss of Brzezinski's congressional liaison, Madeleine Albright, would replace Vance in early May. Among the first things on the agenda was establishing that he would be the principal spokesperson for the administration on foreign policy matters—and that he would minimize the time he spent managing the department and the issues associated with it. From that point forward, Carter and Brzezinski played an even more dominant role in the management of the administration's foreign policy simply because Vance, the main counterweight to many of their efforts, was now gone.

Iran formally and finally accepted the U.S. demands after lengthy negotiations, which concluded on January 19, 1981. Warren Christopher authorized the transfer of $7.97 billion (representing the net return of frozen assets) to the Bank of England, then on to the Algerian central bank and finally to Tehran, possibly the biggest single private transfer of funds in history. Algeria would send planes to collect the hostages. The hostages were released five minutes after the inauguration of Reagan. Later, Carter NSC staffer Gary Sick would write that he felt that some individuals associated with the Reagan campaign had communicated to the Iranians that they would benefit should the release of the hostages be delayed until after the election. Whether this is true or not, is indicative of the fact that the Iran hostage crisis was seen as one of the nails in Jimmy Carter's electoral coffin. The president, who had achieved a remarkable amount for a single four-year term, was seen as weak and ineffective because of this single chain of events—one for which it is very hard to clearly assign blame to the president. Perhaps the embrace or exile of the shah was mishandled. Perhaps a more effective rescue mission could have taken place with a different planning process. Perhaps it was all optics, and without the Rose Garden strategy and the Vance resignation and with a better effort to manage expectations, the administration could have recast events in a more tolerable way. Perhaps it was another example of how the modern media had changed the rules on a politician in midstream with Ted Koppel's *Nightline* drumbeat of "Hostage Crisis—Day 106, 107, 108 . . ." reminding people in new ways of the futility of the administration's efforts or, yet again, of the limitations on U.S. power.

In any event, by election day in 1980, the American people were eager to put the 1970s and the decade's intimations of American decline behind them. They wanted to feel good again about America. They wanted it to be "morning in America." They wanted to be the "shining city on the hill" that they felt they had been at the end of the Second World War or in their hearts or in the movies. And so they elected a movie star to be president, a man who would look the part, who would sound good, and who would make the restoration of optimism his central promise and his single greatest policy initiative.

But Reagan owed much to Jimmy Carter—and not just the Rose Garden strategy that left ample room for Reagan's effective, telegenic campaigning. Carter had overseen two watersheds in recent American history, one domestic, one international. The domestic watershed ushered in the anti-Washington era of new populism, the era of the outsider, an era in which public professions of religious faith and core values were more important than policy nuances. Reagan seized that and built upon it— although in an entirely different direction. The international watershed concerned a sweeping backlash against the declinist, secretive, realpolitik policies of the Nixon era. Carter and Brzezinski and Vance and Brown and Mondale and their team took a different approach. They saw the weakness of their principal adversary, the Soviet Union, and they sought to challenge it wherever they could, be it by developing closer relations with China or helping to turn the deserts and craggy mountains of Afghanistan into a Vietnam-like swamp through covert support for the enemies of the

Soviets. They also sought to reinject "values" into American foreign policy, seeing them not simply as an effective veneer but as the root of America's greatest success in and after the Second World War and as a source of America's strength with our allies internationally. Reagan would build on this as well—by going further in the challenge to the Soviet Union—with his "Evil Empire" rhetoric and military strategies such as the Strategic Defense Initiative (Star Wars)—and by making his perception of America's values and ideals the bludgeon of his foreign policy. In both these respects, Ronald Reagan built on Jimmy Carter's post-Vietnam, post-Watergate legacy.

However, in terms of accomplishments internationally, few presidents have ever had four years like Jimmy Carter—from the signing of the Panama Canal Treaty to the agreement on SALT II, which was important even though unratified, from the normalization of relations with China to the breakthrough at Camp David, from new military and nuclear doctrines that enhanced America's strength and flexibility to effective challenges to our principal adversary—it was a period rife with accomplishment even though it was hardly appreciated at the time and only gradually more appreciated in the years since. And the Iran hostage crisis, while bad, was no Vietnam—nor was it Iran-Contra.

8

Morning in America, Twilight at the NSC

For we must consider that we shall be as a city upon a hill, the eyes of all people are upon us.

—John Winthrop, aboard the Arabella

THE REAGAN ERA is a low point in the history of the modern NSC. The Reagan team, from the outset, tried an experiment, undertaking an effort to turn back the hands of time by downgrading the role of the president's national security advisor and his staff. The result was an undersupervised, underproductive, ingrown system that collapsed on itself and almost brought the administration down with it. The built-in weakness at the center of this system also failed to contain—and thus may have actually exacerbated—an internal feud between a secretary of state and a secretary of defense that rivaled or exceeded the Vance-Brzezinski feud in its ferocity and in the implacability of its principals. In the end, these failings produced not only an infamously "operational" NSC but policy calamities, indictments, convictions, a suicide attempt by a national security advisor and, finally, the need for dramatic changes. Fortunately, among the administration's notable second-term achievements was the deftness with which the NSC system was put back together at the very end of Reagan's tenure by a small group of highly gifted professionals, one of whom would go on to play an even more prominent role in the first years of the coming century as only the second man, after Kissinger, to serve as both national security advisor and secretary of state, Colin Powell. (Later, Condoleezza Rice would become the first woman to hold both jobs.)

Although Carter and Reagan both owed their election to the maladies of the 1960s and 1970s, they were very different men, and in fact were diametrical opposites in important ways. Carter was hands-on. Reagan was hands-off. Carter was a micromanager. Reagan didn't want to be bothered with details. Carter was interested in too many issues, drawn in too many directions. Reagan was focused on a few core concerns. Carter was an intellectual possessed of a powerful mind. Reagan was intuitive. Carter was a workaholic. Reagan liked his naps and leaving the office early. Carter was a deeply faithful man who prayed daily and struggled with the constraints his beliefs imposed upon him. Reagan talked a lot about family values but was America's first divorced president and one who was aloof and removed from his own children. Carter was an engineer. Reagan was an actor. Carter saw the world in shades of gray. Reagan saw the world in black and white—or red, white, and blue. Carter was a product of the Deep South. Reagan was as California as the Hollywood sign.

Although the stances of the two administrations on Cold War–related issues may also have seemed to be polar opposites, the reality is somewhat different. General William Odom, who stayed on during the first years of the Reagan administration and later rose to become head of the National Security Agency during roughly the same time as the Iran-Contra scandal, recognizes that many of the "cold warrior" policies attributed to Reagan were actually born during the Carter administration.[1]

.   .   .

The words members of President Ronald Reagan's inner circle use to describe him include "warm," "decent," "disciplined," and "a man of principle." They also invariably include a variation on "remote," "distant," or "disconnected," and, when referring to his later years in office, "out of touch" or "drifting away from time to time."[2]

When describing the functioning of the White House—and the NSC in particular—during the first six years of the Reagan presidency, however, there is one word that virtually all return to, friends and foes of the president alike: "dysfunctional." In the words of one, "It was almost certainly the low point of the modern NSC."[3] And this is the view of people who were part of the administration.

Criticism of Reagan seems to have gone into abeyance in recent years, and since his death he has been seen as an icon, a towering figure, one of our great presidents. It takes a truly Reaganesque lack of attention to details to embrace such a view. When it came to the management of the foreign policy apparatus of the U.S. government, Reagan's record is almost certainly the worst of any modern president. It only began to improve at the end, when the experience of the senior players and the premature fading away of the president as a factor in his own administration created an opportunity to restore some equilibrium and functionality to the White House foreign policy apparatus, the NSC, and the interagency process.

For historians, the Reagan administration is a powerful illustration of the critical importance an engaged and capable president plays in a functioning NSC, because it illustrates what happens when the president is neither engaged nor, as was the case in the final years of Reagan's term of office, capable of or inclined to make the judgments required of him. For many average Americans, of course, some of these facts of the operations of the Reagan administration have faded from memory, and the Reagan presidency is primarily seen as important because he is credited with having played a central role in ending the Cold War. (Certainly, in that respect, as in the rest of his professional life, his timing was very good, for he was in office when the economic and social entropy that drained the life out of communism finally sapped the confrontational will of our principal adversary.) Furthermore, today, his administration is also seen as the modern-day wellspring of the conservative political and policy views that make it the spiritual antecedent of the administration of George W. Bush. Bush cites Reagan as his political inspiration, and indeed, as we shall see, the similarities between many of their choices, people, and policies are striking, both in terms of their specifics and in terms of the problems they produced. Neither Reagan's ultimate willingness to embrace Gorbachev, nor his grace in doing so, nor his uncanny political sensibilities are necessarily diminished by the failings within his national security team. They exist side by side, accomplishments alongside failures, gifts alongside flaws, thus defining the true—and truly complex—Reagan legacy.

Reagan ran for president in 1980 accusing President Jimmy Carter quite unfairly of having a foreign policy that featured "vacillation, appeasement, and aimlessness."[4] During the debates, Reagan contrasted himself with Carter by underscoring the dangers of letting events get "out of control" and pledging to remain in control through the application of American strength. In short, he deftly capitalized on the appearance of Carter as a weak leader, an appearance that was created by the frustrating standoff over the hostages in Tehran, although the country's economic condition, stagflation, and energy shortages played an even greater role in his election success. Just as Carter's image of being an honest and honorable man was the antidote to the perceived problems of the Nixon era, Reagan's apparent clarity and his message of strength and hope were the antidote to the perceived weakness and bleakness of the Carter era. In virtually every election of the modern era, the people opt for the more optimistic candidate and of all these, Reagan was the apotheosis.

He also represented a conservative political tradition whose supporters had been seen as the extremist undoing of the Republican Party during the 1964 presidential campaign of Senator Barry Goldwater, those who had been regularly nudged aside by the centrist and "Rockefeller" Republicans. They were too closely tied to faith, a robust military, the NRA, and the most extreme forms of anticommunism to be mainstream. Or so many had thought. But the shift in the electorate that produced the Jimmy Carter presidency, the election of a born-again Southern governor who brought in a team that based its policies on perceived Soviet rather than American weaknesses, was actually a shift that boded well for the Reagan "revolution."

Once Reagan was in office, the usual combination of personal ambition and the desire to differentiate oneself from one's immediate predecessor were combined with a desire to differentiate the administration from previous moderate Republican administrations, notably that of Richard Nixon. At least, that was the stated intent of the "Reaganauts," the "true believers"—including longtime political intimates such as Ed Meese and Michael Deaver and leaders of conservative thought such as UN Ambassador Jeanne Kirkpatrick and even the First Lady, to name but a few. However, they had to contend with the fact that most of the experience within the party came from those who had served in earlier administrations. Hence compromises were made, and over time each of those compromises produced a battle line, a place where rift between moderate and conservative Republicans would produce tension and policy disputes. Such tensions would endure throughout the administration and cause continuing problems for the president, his team, and U.S. policy.

The first wave of problems the new administration faced had to do, once again, with the practice of reinventing the national security apparatus from the ground up in the days and weeks between the election and the inauguration. That first wave, as things turned out, would not die down for months and years thereafter because of the Reagan team's failure to set things up right at the outset.

Naturally, to differentiate themselves from Carter and Nixon, the Reagan inner circle wanted to take a step away from the strong national security advisor role that they mistakenly saw as a choice of these past presidents rather than a role that developed in response to historically growing demands on the president, the evolving nature of and relationships between cabinet agencies, and America's changing leadership position in the world. In particular, they wanted to signal that there would be no Kissinger in their administration, both because Kissinger was thought by team insiders to be a "scene-stealing, prima donna, one-man-show"[5] and because his policies, particularly that of détente, were as anathema to many of the new president's team as the "anti-American" policies of Vietnam-era protesters. They wrongly saw Brzezinski as a replay of Kissinger, and they believed that his battles with Vance, like Kissinger's with Rogers and later Schlesinger and Rumsfeld, were a symptom of a too powerful assistant to the president for national security.

At the center of the Reagan team were his "Californians," close associates from his years as governor and from his campaign who were to play the role of advisors and palace guard. Leading this group from her position in the East Wing (the residence) of the White House was the president's principal protector, Nancy Reagan, who would intercede in matters of personnel and policy throughout the president's eight years in office.

Nancy's role can be seen to echo that of Rosalynn Carter (and later the even more active role of Hillary Clinton), just as Reagan's embrace of issues like personal faith and traditional values can be seen as continuing in the direction pioneered by Carter. However, in these cases as in many others, the continuation had some twist—and not always the twist to the right that you might imagine. Whereas Carter treated Rosalynn as a full partner in his life and often discussed substantive matters with her, Nancy operated more from the shadows, a traditional wife pulling levers in a way that might seem familiar to courtiers from the era of the Medicis. A former actress who, as Nancy Davis, had starred with Reagan in the B-movie classic *Hellcats of the Navy*, Mrs. Reagan was in many respects the president's collaborator in the creation of the public persona of Ronald Reagan and such a jealous guardian of his personal life that, according to his offspring from his prior marriage to actress Jane Wyman, there was sometimes not much room for those children in Nancy's world. Some of the damage from those years was not repaired until Reagan's bout with Alzheimer's disease in his declining years. But the remoteness of the man and the attitude of his wife with regard to his own family is illustrative of an attitude that was manifested to staff during the presidency. Indeed, a former Reagan cabinet-level official told me rather ruefully that at the end of the president's tenure he disappeared without so much as a farewell or a thank-you note to most cabinet members, exiting as it were, stage left.[6] Whereas Carter turned to his family often throughout his time in office—

including to his mother Lillian, who was an emissary; his son Chip; and his daughter Amy, with whom he would discuss the issues weighing on his mind—Reagan's image as the champion of family values was really just that: an image.

With Nancy joining the president in the innermost circle of the Reagan presidency, the next closest group was the triumvirate of advisors who collectively ran Reagan's White House during the first years of the administration. They were Chief of Staff James Baker, who had been under secretary of commerce during the Ford administration and would later serve as treasury secretary under Reagan and then become secretary of state under President George H.W. Bush. Baker is a complex and extraordinarily capable figure whose value to the presidents he served is illustrated not only by his success in policy and management roles within the government, but also by his accomplishments as political campaign manager for Ford, Reagan, and the first Bush. Consequently, he was seen as a loyalist by Reagan even though he was not a right-wing ideologue like some of the president's other inside team members. Also in the troika was Baker's deputy chief of staff, Reagan imagemeister Michael Deaver, a small, polite man who was much more committed to Reagan and his image than he was to any particular political agenda. Deaver was also very close to Nancy Reagan, which gave him particular influence. The third member of the group was the president's counselor, Edwin Meese. Meese, an engaging, voluble attorney who served as attorney general in California for Governor Ronald Reagan and who would later serve as U.S. attorney general for President Reagan, was actually the man who occupied the prized West Wing corner office that had belonged to Kissinger, Scowcroft, and Brzezinski as national security advisors. Indeed, in the revised scheme of things during the first Reagan years, the national security advisor was moved back downstairs into the White House warrens around the Situation Room and, more important, was demoted from cabinet-level status and reported not directly to the president but to Meese, to whom the president's chief domestic policy advisor also reported.

The national security advisor was Richard Nixon's former campaign policy advisor Richard Allen, the man thought in 1968 to be too young and too conservative to step into the post for Nixon when he won election, thus paving the way for Kissinger. Allen had finally gotten the role he wanted, but it was significantly devalued. He seemed to welcome the changes, however, repeatedly telling reporters that the job should really be to staff the president and to leave the policy creation to the real lead dog on the president's foreign policy team, his secretary of state.

For that critical role, ironically Reagan chose a Kissinger and Nixon favorite, General Alexander Haig. Haig, who had enjoyed a meteoric rise from colonel to four-star general and White House chief of staff during the Nixon years and had recently served as Supreme Allied Commander in Europe at the helm of NATO, was seen, perhaps because of his military background and tough-guy rhetoric, as a more conservative choice than the other leading candidate for secretary of state, former Nixon treasury secretary George Shultz. Nixon called Haig the "meanest, toughest s.o.b. I ever knew, but he'll be a helluva Secretary of State."[7] And that's from a guy who knew something about mean, tough s.o.b.'s. What Nixon didn't say or perhaps even fully appreciate was that Al Haig's success was due not only to the fact that he was intelligent and loyal but also to the fact that his engine ran at a very high speed because he was so tightly wound. Very tightly wound. In fact, in the words of a former colleague, "sometimes— especially during the later months of his Reagan tenure—he could get pretty 'out there.'"[8]

Meese explains the program of the Reagan inner circle:

One of our main objectives was to restore the position of the cabinet members as the principal advisors to the president in their respective fields. We felt the national security assistant should be primarily a coordinator and recognized as it was as a staff position. We were somewhat cognizant actually of the position that Henry Kissinger had held and that disadvantaged Bill Rogers as secretary of state and we didn't want that to happen. That was why for the first year we had two "super" assistants to the president, for national security policy and domestic policy.

Our initial step was to make it clear that the assistant to the president for national security affairs was not, in effect, superior to the secretary of state and to the secretary of defense and to restore that as a staff position. It was one of the things that flowed from our experience with the governorship. The idea was to emphasize that the cabinet was primarily responsible for advising the president and that cabinet meetings were the forum for decision making. This included the cabinet as a whole and the cabinet councils. We had cabinet councils—we had eight of them in the first term and three in the second term—and one of those cabinet councils was the National Security Council.

The president liked to have issues argued out in front of him. If a consensus could be reached on which there was mutual agreement concerning a particular issue, then that recommendation would be presented to him.

But if there was disagreement among the cabinet members, they would have the opportunity to present their views directly to the president. There were a number of occasions when this would happen, such as keeping the marines in the barracks in Lebanon or putting them back on ships or whatever else it happened to be and those would be argued out. The membership of the National Security Council always included more than just statutory members. For example, I served on the National Security Council from the start. In the second term, both Jim Baker, as secretary of the treasury, and I, as attorney general, were appointed to the council by the president.[9]

Haig, of course, had watched as Kissinger launched his bureaucratic first strike on Rogers and the rest of the cabinet with his organizational memo that was presented as the first presidential directive of the Nixon administration. He had also seen how Brzezinski had orchestrated a similar preemptive maneuver with his St. Simon collaboration with Jimmy Carter. Seeing the effectiveness of these efforts and remaining consistent to his impulse, which was to be on offense whenever possible, Haig drafted a memo that would have put him and the State Department at the head of the national security decision-making process. He gave the memo to Meese. It disappeared into his inbox. He resubmitted it. Same result. He reworked it in collaboration with the secretary of defense. It passed unacknowledged again into oblivion. In fact, no such memo was produced in the early days of the Reagan administration as had occurred in the preceding administrations. It took almost a year—and a new national security advisor with a new role in the administration—before such a structure would be codified.

In the meantime, plenty happened without the benefit of an organizing memo. The troika ran the White House, and for Allen to see the president other than for his daily 9:30 a.m. intelligence briefing, or to get virtually anything of substance done, required that Baker, Deaver, and his immediate superior Meese sign off. In fact, in a real sense, given that Allen reported to Meese and Meese reported to the president, that Meese had the corner office, and that Meese and the troika controlled the president's schedule, set cabinet meetings, set NSC meetings, and so on, it would be fair to argue that the former California attorney general (with the assistance of the two other members of the troika) was playing more of the role of recent national security advisors than was the sitting national security advisor.

Meanwhile, Haig attempted to establish himself by means other than the organizing memo that kept disappearing into the oceans of paper in the West Wing. He presented himself to a preinauguration NSC meeting that included key inner circle members, such as Secretary of Defense Caspar Weinberger (a former California state budget director for Reagan) and CIA director William Casey, a former Securities and Exchange Commission chairman and Office of Strategic Services spook who was very close to the president and had perhaps too much enthusiasm for life in the shadow worlds of government intrigue. Haig said that the Reagan formula for a collegial cabinet-based government required when it came to international policy "that the Secretary of State be your vicar for the community of departments having an interest in the several dimensions of foreign policy."[10] Although Haig went on to describe for himself a policy development and policy coordination role akin to that of Brzezinski and Kissinger as national security advisors, what he really produced was the beginning of his undoing. The phrase "vicar of foreign policy" was not embraced warmly by either his colleagues or the press, who collectively saw it as high-handed and pompous because, well, it was.

In the second month of the administration Meese, all but ignoring Haig's suggested structure and Allen's very existence, created three coordinating committees, one each for defense, intelligence, and foreign policy. Each would be chaired by the agency responsible for that part of the government's activities. A month later, recognizing that there might be times when the White House would be called to play a more active coordinating role, Meese and the troika got the president to approve another committee in charge of crisis management, which was to be chaired by not the national security advisor but by the vice president, George H.W. Bush. Although Bush was not a member of the president's innermost circle and relations between Bush and Reagan were notoriously formal and even a bit chilly during the transition between the Reagan and Bush years, Bush's management of this group during several crises won him high marks from within the administration. Later, in the summer of the administration's first year, this group evolved into the National Security Planning Group, a kind of NSC-plus that was also chaired by Bush and ended up dealing with issues like the spate of terrorist attacks and other crises that confronted the administration. (A subsequent evolution of this vehicle was called the Special Situations Group, also chaired by the vice president. The group met only once, however, since "Secretary Haig immediately and forcefully complained that the SSG would remove coordinating responsibility from him.")[11] Reagan also attended these meetings and NSC sessions, and had time set aside in his schedule to attend several such gatherings each week.

Meese claims credit for the National Security Planning Group:

It was my recommendation that we ought to have a crisis management group that could be brought together in case of an ongoing emergency, like September 11, 2001. Since the president couldn't be there all the time because of his other duties, it made logical sense for the vice president to be the chairman of that other group. We had done the same thing in California during the days of disorder and campus unrest when we brought the head of the Highway Patrol, the head of the National Guard, the head of the Office of Emergency Services, and the head of the Law Enforcement Division of the Department of Justice to deal with ongoing emergencies. As a member of the governor's cabinet, I chaired this group. It was designed to handle ongoing situations so a cabinet member or his or her deputy was available on a continuing basis in a sort of "war room." Sometimes this group operated on the deputies level, such as during the *Achille Lauro* incident [a terrorist hijacking of a cruise liner in which an elderly, wheelchair-bound American was shot and tossed over the side of the boat and the escaping terrorists were captured via a midair intercept]. But on larger issues such as the Libyan air attacks, the NSC would handle the matter.[12]

To support this operation, one of the military aides to the NSC, Admiral John Poindexter, a technology specialist, helped create a high-tech crisis management center in room 208 of the Old Executive Office Building, the room that was once the office of Secretary of State Cordell Hull and was the room in which he last met with Japanese emissaries before the attack on Pearl Harbor. The room was not used very frequently, but the technologies employed in it became the basis for much of what is done today in crisis management, now handled out of the Situation Room.

Naturally, the administration also did Americans the great service that all its predecessors felt was so essential and renamed its memoranda. What were formerly PRMs were now NSSDs—National Security Study Documents—and decision memoranda were now NSDDs—National Security Decision Documents.

Beyond the inner circles were other clusters of ideologically motivated appointees mixed in with the career people that grew over the first few years of the administration. These more extreme members of the team included Oliver North, who would soon become famous as the administration's "can-do marine"; arms control specialist and neocon standard-bearer Richard Perle at Defense, known today in some circles as Dr.

Doom; many of the other so-called Vulcans (the name the foreign policy elites of the second Bush administration gave themselves), such as Paul Wolfowitz and Richard Armitage, in earlier career incarnations; and NSC staffers such as Constantine Menges, who handled Latin issues including Central America; Gaston Sigur, who handled Asia; Sven Kraemer, who handled arms control; and Kenneth DeGraffenreid, who handled intelligence programs. While these individuals were seasoned foreign policy professionals, most shared a common worldview centered on strong anticommunist, anti-Soviet credentials and a deep belief in the president.

Ambassador James Dobbins, a distinguished career foreign service officer who later rose to senior positions in the Bush, Clinton, and second Bush administrations, commented that the

> first Reagan administration and some of the second was pretty bizarre. You had a bunch of very inexperienced people who suddenly had to grapple with the sharp learning curve of coming into office. Not only that, but the longer the party has been out of office, the more difficult it is. So, if they'd been out of office eight years, it's a lot tougher than if they'd only been out of office four. Well, in this case, the Reagan wing of the Republican Party had been out of office since Calvin Coolidge. And they really didn't bring back many of the Ford, Nixon, or even Eisenhower people—except Haig, who was clearly out of place. And in terms of the White House staff, there were a lot of people who had been deeply disaffected from mainstream U.S. policy. And consequently they came up with very . . . er . . . different . . . ideas.[13]

Dobbins explained that during these early years he was a director in the political military office at the State Department.

> The Reagan administration tried to devolve the NSC's functions, even its coordination functions, back to the agencies. And so the decision was that State would run all of the arms control interagency process. In those days, I was the office director who actually ended up chairing most of those interagency meetings. We were chairing meetings that were the most divisive in the administration, because many elements of the administration were deeply opposed to any kind of arms control. And the NSC essentially came to the meetings and sided with DOD, so we spent the first year trying to find some common ground, trying to compromise, but what some really wanted was no decision. That is, they didn't want any of these negotiations to go anywhere, so they were perfectly content to get

no result from the discussion. So it was a frustrating process. It was very dysfunctional. Far too much authority was devolved—and it was devolved in a way that the agencies couldn't effectively implement it. The few decisions that were made tended to be made through or influenced through informal channels. It was Deaver and Baker and Mrs. Reagan who occasionally kept the administration from disastrous consequences. Because when someone would really go over the top or do something particularly weird, then the adults would step in and prevent the truly bizarre outcomes.[14]

Robert Kimmitt, who would serve as NSC executive secretary during the Reagan years and who spent, in total, 100 months at the NSC, says, "It just seemed like a fairly dysfunctional system in that first year, and part of it may have been that we had a lot of those ideological wrinkles that existed elsewhere in the Reagan administration between the so-called pragmatists and the true believers."[15]

The bizarre nature of these early months came on public display when in mid-March a lunatic took a few shots at the president and his entourage. Among those hit, it turned out, was Secretary of State Alexander Haig, who had been nowhere near the site of the shooting—his wound was more or less self-inflicted.

The date was March 30, 1981. The shooting took place outside the Washington Hilton. Reagan was rushed to nearby George Washington University Hospital and there his top aides, including the troika and Nancy, gathered to be near him. The vice president was in Texas. Haig, the former White House chief of staff, headed for the White House and convened a meeting in the Situation Room of available senior team members, including Allen. A mood of apprehension filled the air. On the television, they could watch as Deputy Press Secretary Larry Speakes (standing in for Press Secretary Jim Brady, who had been wounded in the attempt on the president's life) briefed the press on the president's condition. Among other things, reporters asked about the operations of the government. Who was in charge with the president in the hospital and Bush out of town? Speakes did not know. Haig, watching, leaped to his feet and made a beeline for the press room. Seconds later, he was on the air. Taut, clearly shaken, Haig responded to the queries: "As of now, I am in control here."[16]

Of course, he was not. The line of presidential succession does not pass from president to vice president to secretary of state, but makes a detour up to Capitol Hill to the Speaker of the House and the president pro tempore of the Senate. Perhaps Haig recalled the final days of Richard Nixon when, after it fell upon him to make the arrangements for the president's resignation, the conclusion was that the president's resignation letter should be addressed to the secretary of state, Henry Kissinger. But his conclusion did not sit well with Reagan's inner circle watching from the hospital.

It was the beginning of the end for Al Haig. He remained in office through the middle of 1982. But during the intervening months, he was seen as both high-handed and high-strung. However, he also was the one man on the team who actually understood foreign policy, which perhaps explains why he remained in place for fifteen months after he had his "defining moment" on national television. He was forceful in his advocacy for standing up to the Russians on fronts from Central America to Central Asia; he saw Soviet links to terrorism as further reason to combat it more aggressively; and he provided an important counterbalancing voice when it came to arms control. Indeed, in each of these areas, he can be seen as sharing a worldview with the president—even though the president himself may not have known it at the time. (Reagan's success on arms control came as a surprise to many of the "true believers," though later they saw that success as proof that his policies of confrontation, harsh rhetoric, and the Strategic Defense Initiative left the Russians no other choice but to step back from the brink.)

With Haig in decline and Allen in the basement, the foreign policy apparatus wobbled forward. The NSC had about thirty-five professional staffers in the early months with another hundred or so backing them up in support roles. The effort to downsize the operation included plans for budget cuts during the first couple fiscal years. The problem was that in the modern era, the president needs more support than that, political rhetoric or no political rhetoric. With a leadership void, the apparatus gradually started to grow, reaching record size by the dark years of Iran-Contra, perhaps the bleakest period in the history of the NSC in terms of its reputation if not in terms of the size of its payroll. Again, in government, size matters, but leadership matters even more.

Instead of that, they got process. Four policy clusters were set up in the NSC—one each for intelligence, planning, defense, and political affairs. NSC meetings took place more frequently (but to considerably less effect) than at any time since Eisenhower. Big policy papers were discussed, but little evidence of them or their impact emerged. Allen's morning briefings ultimately were cut out to streamline the president's schedule. Allen chirped that he supported the measure. His morning briefs became a morning memo. He was, however, allowed to attend the first few minutes of the

White House staff meeting. The seventy-year-old president was cheerfully disconnected from these processes, leaving the office early, padding around the residence, and trusting his team to handle big matters—and in this administration, that meant the political rather than the national security team.

Meese, the de facto national security advisor despite a striking lack of experience in foreign policy matters, helped shape the priorities. He recalls that the "international mission was basically to deal with the Soviet Union, which was the principal international problem."

The president, upon taking office, identified two major problems. One was the economic situation and one was the Cold War in its broader aspects. The answers that he gave focused on two objectives: to revitalize the economy and to rebuild our military forces. There were two other things he wanted to do—one which was less expressed—which was to revive the spirit of the American people and to restore the position of the United States in terms of world leadership which had deteriorated during the latter part of the 1970s.[17]

"In order to do that," continues Meese, who was interviewed in his offices within the headquarters building of the conservative American Enterprise Institute,

in terms of the international policy, he established what I guess [UN ambassador and one of the intellectual leaders on the Reagan team] Jeanne Kirkpatrick later called the "Reagan Doctrine." He did this by engaging the Soviet Union on a moral plane as he did in 1982 in a speech to the English Parliament and as he did '83 in the "Evil Empire" speech. Secondly, he let it be known, as he did through Haig to Soviet Ambassador Anatoly Dobrynin, that we would not stand for any further Soviet aggression, in other words, no more Afghanistans. Third, he sought to roll back previous aggressions by support of the freedom fighters in Nicaragua, support of the coup d'état in Angola, support of Solidarity in Poland, support of the freedom fighters in Afghanistan. Later on, he added the Strategic Defense Initiative (which some called "Star Wars") which had been a longtime idea of his. It was the "Five Point Program," which was perhaps less well defined early on—rebuilding the armed forces, engaging the Soviets on a moral plane, containing aggression, rolling back aggression, and developing a strategic defense initiative— that was Reagan's strategy for dealing with the Cold War.[18]

One of the early efforts to "engage on a moral plane" was a decision to try to induce America's European allies not to cooperate in the construction of a pipeline that would deliver Soviet natural gas to Western European customers. Like subsequent initiatives, the president's rhetoric was seen as inflammatory by many Europeans, who could hardly be expected to embrace a policy that would actually undercut their own interests. Tensions with some of the Europeans grew and remained high as the United States came to be seen as a narcissistic bully state that sought confrontation and viewed Europeans primarily as pawns in a great global game.

If it was hard to imagine Allen becoming any less important, then perhaps it was inevitable that the next step for him would be to actually fade away. He too helped facilitate this with a series of comic and generally trivial errors that the Washington press and the Democratic Party played up into one of those Washington scandals that blow through like a Caribbean afternoon thundershower—much intensity, briefly, followed by a return to sunshine and rapidly disappearing memories of the entire incident. The first step in his undoing was helping to set up an interview for the First Lady with three Japanese journalists. Following their traditions, the journalists gave Allen an envelope containing ten $100 bills. Allen, uncertain what to do with the money but knowing it was inappropriate to give it to Mrs. Reagan, slipped it into his office safe and forgot about it.

While Allen embraced like a good soldier the measures that reduced his influence, in so doing he effectively closed himself out of any chance to be seen as an important player. This was as important to his undoing as any hint of scandal. Indeed, the weaker the player, the smaller the scandal needed to bring him down. And as the sands of 1981 slipped through the hourglass, so too did the relevance of Richard Allen, the not-quite–national security advisor.

Haig noted that "according to the remorseless standards of judgment that apply in such cases, Allen was therefore regarded by his colleagues as irrelevant. In time, I am sorry to say, I came to regard him in that light too."[19] NSC defense cluster chief General Robert Schweitzer added, "I would feel that in that, in the forty year history, there was always a clearly defined purpose for the National Security Council, until we came to that first year of the Reagan Administration and the clearly defined purpose did not exist."[20]

Allen may have hoped that the tide against the NSC would ebb and his day would come. It did not. The cash in an envelope was discovered when his safe was reassigned to another office and an investigation was initiated. As the scandal blew up, revelations about accepting expensive wristwatches as gifts from former clients and other perceived improprieties were added to the list of black marks against the marginalized bureaucrat. His political masters in the White House saw him as a liability and began to maneuver for his replacement by a Californian, Judge William Clark, who started out the administration as Haig's deputy secretary at state.

Clark was a self-made man, a Californian who had finished neither college nor law school but who had passed the bar, become successful, hooked up with Ronald Reagan, became his acting chief of staff, and was appointed by the governor to the California Supreme Court. He was the ultimate Reagan loyalist, a pal, and his first assignment during his one year at the State Department had been to keep an eye on Haig. This was the totality of his knowledge of international affairs beyond a two-year stint in the army in Germany during the 1950s. During the confirmation hearings for his deputy secretary job at State, he stumbled on his responses to basic questions and was unable to define concepts such as "détente" or "Third World," name key world leaders, or articulate a basic position on issues such as nuclear proliferation. Suffice it to say that it helped neither the administration's early reputation nor Clark's.

But Clark was loyal and had both access to and the confidence of the president. An important feature of his role was that it was defined differently from Allen's. By a year into the administration, the leadership in the White House knew that they needed a more powerful voice as coordinator of the NSC. Interagency tensions were brewing, and somebody needed to try to find common ground and promote harmony. Clark actually got along well with Haig when they were at State together, and that was seen as a plus.

Admiral John Poindexter, who joined the NSC as a military aide in 1981 and watched the transition, observes:

> Allen wasn't close enough to the president, and so the only way that Clark would come over is if he would have direct access to the president and be the traditional national security advisor in the traditional sense. Now, going back historically, Bill Clark was President Reagan's first chief of staff when he was governor. In fact, Bill picked Ed Meese to relieve him in that job when Bill moved to the California Supreme Court. So Bill was very close to the president, and his condition for coming was direct access. During the first year of the administration we never got anywhere on NSDD [National Security Decision Document] issues, because there was so much disagreement between the triumvirate and Dick Allen and Al Haig about who was going to run foreign policy and how the national

security structure was going to operate. But as soon as Bill came over, the NSDD system started to operate because Bill would take items to the president and he essentially drove the process.[21]

As a consequence, early on in Clark's tenure NSDD-2 was finally accepted, creating a system of interagency policy groups called SIGs (Senior Interagency Groups) that handled the issue clusters described earlier.[22] As it turned out, this step toward organization itself spun out of control, and over the life of the administration almost two dozen such SIGs were created. Other NSDD efforts covered basic strategy, military policy, how to handle the Soviets, and even public diplomacy, which, given the communications focus of the administration and its commitment to waging a public relations war with the Soviets, was important. This effort was part of a long line of such efforts from the psychological warfare initiatives of the Eisenhower years to the creation of the under secretary of state for public diplomacy position during the second Bush administration. It recognized that information flows are the battle divisions of politics and that the United States, as the world's information leader, can truly be a superpower in rhetorical combat when constraints on military combat, such as cost and potential losses, have shifted the greatest strength of nuclear-era armies into the threat rather than the use of force. Consequently, the notion of nuclear deterrent is impotent without the perception that it will be used. Reagan's awareness of this fact was tied to his identity as a product of an information industry and as the "great communicator." Whereas Carter and Brzezinski effectively shifted the stance against the Soviets to a more forward-leaning position, Reagan deserves credit for communicating that shift better than his predecessors.

Clark was also restored the privilege of briefing the president daily, and Vice President Bush as well as other principals and senior NSC staffers regularly joined these meetings. Gradually Clark's influence began to grow and, with it, so did the importance of the NSC. Haig, for one, was discomfited by this trend. On returning from a trip to Israel with Clark in which the latter Clark had conducted parallel communications back to the White House, Haig protested. It was one of a long string of such complaints and ham-fisted efforts at retaining influence at State. Haig worked the press on this issue, even going so far as to suggest that there was a "guerrilla" in the White House out to get the secretary of state (perhaps teaming up with the Castro bad guys who were hunting him down).[23] His tiffs with Allen were one thing, but running up against Clark was different. Clark was wired into the inner circle and was gradually coming to be seen as the administration's foreign policy grown-up—an impressive rise for someone who didn't know the basic vocabulary of the job a year earlier. It is also a rise that reiterates the vitally important point about the role of the national security advisor—that the advisor's relationship with the president is by far the most important tool he has and his most important qualification. As a presidential staffer, his credibility and thus his power rises and falls with that relationship. As if to prove this point through a rigorous scientific experiment, the Reagan team took someone with virtually no foreign policy chops to speak of and watched him ascend to a point where he was seen as more influential than colleagues such as Haig, who had significant background at the highest levels of the foreign policy apparatus. This is not an experiment to try at home—and it boggles the mind somewhat that it took place—but it proves conclusively that there is no more important source of power in the executive branch than that afforded by a genuine connection with and the respect of the commander-in-chief.

After the Israel trip, which had been triggered by ongoing tensions in the region and escalating fighting and civilian death tolls in the Bekaa Valley and throughout southern Lebanon, Clark and Haig confronted one another. Haig had doctrine and his promised role as the leader of the foreign policy team on his side. Clark had his relationship with Reagan and made the one argument that is the most powerful weapon in the advisor's arsenal—that he represented the president's views and that they would prevail.

As Poindexter saw it, "The relationship between the White House staff and Haig was always very shaky. Al really wanted to be in charge, not just of policy—but he essentially wanted to be like a Henry Kissinger. And so Bill Clark engineered his resignation and George Shultz coming in. And at that point, things began to click."[24]

One top Reagan administration official corroborates that "Haig and Allen did not get along well as human beings. And for a while we thought that was part of the problem. But after Bill Clark came over—who got along with Haig—we determined that wasn't the problem. Haig had a hard time getting out of the mind-set of the Nixon administration, which was much more of a dog-eat-dog administration, whereas Ronald Reagan liked a collegial administration."[25] Of course, there is some irony in this statement given the rapidly engineered departures of Allen and Haig and the vituperative, bitter relationship that would almost immediately evolve between Haig's successor, George Shultz, and his counterpart in the Defense Department, Caspar Weinberger—a relationship that polls out among the 130-plus foreign policy experts with whom I spoke while preparing this book as the nastiest and most relentless of all the nasty, relentless battles that have riven every bureaucracy of the modern era. Collegial? Well, maybe that was the stance around the boss. Behind the scenes it was as acid as any administration ever.

Haig added to the tension with regular resignations, all of which had been brushed aside. But in late June 1982, when he weighed in to complain about the White House upstaging him and assuming some of his leadership prerogatives, he got a surprising response. The president accepted his resignation.[26] Haig's brief tenure as the vicar of Foggy Bottom was up.

George Shultz, who had served as secretary of labor, secretary of the treasury, and director of the Office of Management and Budget, was one of the real heavy hitters on the Republican bench. A former marine who by the time of the Reagan years was president and a director of the Bechtel Corporation, Shultz had actually been the other finalist for the State job at the inception of the Reagan administration, and Reagan had actually called him to offer him the job. The resulting conversation got off track, however, and Reagan never got around to making the offer.

Shultz was an adept and experienced bureaucrat and was widely respected within the bureaucracy for his efficiency and evenhandedness during the Nixon years. He attracted a solid team and won their loyalty. He fought for what he believed in and moderated his essentially conservative ideology when he felt it was in the national interest.

What would emerge as a central problem of the Reagan administration was that in at least two of the three areas in which the Cold War manifested itself—in the Middle East writ large, in the Caribbean basin, and in arms control talks—the secretary of state and the secretary of defense did not see eye-to-eye. In fact, worse than that, they didn't much respect each other, and they made no bones about it. On Russia both took a tough line, but whereas Shultz believed in the power of diplomacy, Weinberger was a skeptic. Shultz saw value in cultivating and maintaining the special U.S. relationship with Israel. Weinberger was inclined to be tougher on the Israelis. On arms control, Shultz supported the traditional State Department line in favor of making progress through negotiations. Weinberger, it seems, would have preferred no progress at all, concerned that arms control talks typically ended by unnecessarily weakening the United States.

One senior State Department official from the administration said:

> Oh, things were terrible. It was the worst I ever saw in several decades in the government. Clearly, they couldn't even speak civilly to one another. Shultz is a pretty tough guy and I also think he was a guy who was pretty

used to getting his way. And he was very disciplined and I think Weinberger was pretty undisciplined. If Shultz went to a meeting he expected everyone to know the subject. He expected to be able to discuss it in rational terms. And my guess is that Weinberger didn't always know the subject—wasn't always prepared to debate it—had no reasoned, rational, calm position. I think Shultz found that dispiriting, and the lack of functionality in the interagency system and discipline made things worse. But in any case, in terms of the personal relationship, you couldn't get anything done. The only person you could talk to in my experience, and get a reasonable answer, was Colin Powell.[27]

Former Secretary of Defense Harold Brown observes:

Conflicts between secretaries of state and defense tend to be partly personality conflicts and partly policy conflicts with the secretary of state usually, because that is his function, emphasizing diplomacy and the secretary of defense's responsibility is emphasizing military capability. Now both diplomacy and military capability are ways of dealing with national security. That was the rationale behind the establishment of the NSC in the first place. You would expect the secretary of state to argue against the use of force and the secretary of defense to argue for it. There is sometimes a situation in which the positions are the reverse of what you would expect. That was what often happened with Shultz and Weinberger, for example. It is usually so, by the way, that the White House people overestimate the utility of military force. I think Shultz was one of those who also overestimated the value of the use of military force.[28]

Meese indicated that this split took a toll during Lebanon, when the NSC debated whether to leave the marines on the ground or to move them to ships offshore. "George Shultz and the State Department felt that if we put them offshore that would indicate that we are not sufficiently supportive of the government in Lebanon," according to one Reagan administration official. "Cap's feeling was that they ought to be offshore, and that was the Defense Department's position. And the president decided to go with the State Department position—and unfortunately, that left the marines in a vulnerable position to terrorists."[29]

Another very senior observer, one of the State Department's most distinguished diplomats, characterized the situation this way: "It all played out in the fact that Shultz and Weinberger leaked shitty things about each in the press all the time. And so it played out in the media in a very inten- ·

sive way. It was incredibly disruptive, and I know it troubled all of them, but especially Shultz and the president—who did not like that kind of thing at all."[30]

The tensions weighed on the president in a variety of ways. Not only was there bad press to contend with, but he had to keep all his "children" happy. Shultz required a two-hour private meeting with the president each week. Weinberger was in constant touch with his old California boss. Vice President Bush got a lunch with Reagan every week. And Bill Casey, understanding the proximity-is-power equation in Washington, actually got himself an extra office in the Old Executive Office Building so he could "work the building" like the other insiders.

McFarlane commented to the *Washington Post*, "You have two very, very fundamentally opposed individuals—Cap and George—both men of good will—each believing that they are expressing what the President wants. Now this cannot be—[and] leads basically to paralysis for as long as the decision-making model is a cabinet government. . . . When it became a matter of each of those opinions going laterally to the president in a very chaotic fashion, that's dysfunctional. There was growing disorder."[31] McFarlane tried to manage this situation with what he called the Family Group Luncheon, which involved the two warring secretaries plus Casey.

These issues developed along parallel lines in 1982 and 1983. In the Middle East, the Israeli pursuit of the Palestinian Liberation Organization (PLO) into Lebanon contributed to the chaos of that country's civil war and its obvious dependence on U.S. arms shipments and other aid for support, putting the United States in a position of debating whether or not to urge the Israelis to pull back. Pressure on the PLO produced backtracking from them, and ultimately Yasser Arafat and his men withdrew to seek safe haven in Tunisia. While all this was going on, the debate in the Reagan administration about how to manage the U.S. relationship with Israel took place behind closed doors. Presidential advisor Michael Deaver threatened at one point to resign because he didn't feel he could support a policy condoning the Israeli shelling and violence against innocent civilians in Lebanon. Shultz intervened, which resulted in a call to Israeli Prime Minister Menachem Begin with a demand from Reagan that Israel's incursion into Lebanon stop. Begin acquiesced, and Reagan learned an important lesson in the real power of the president of the United States.

The civil war in Lebanon still festered, however, and the Christian militias, which were backed by the Israelis, undertook a rampage through two refugee camps in southern Lebanon that caused a global outcry. The result echoed the Eisenhower-era intervention in Lebanon, with the return of a multinational force designed to act as a buffer between combatants. U.S. marines were part of that force, and the U.S. interest in brokering a solution grew. Veteran diplomat Philip Habib ended his tenure as chief negotiator, and a team led by Deputy National Security Advisor Robert McFarlane, a former marine and a former Kissinger NSC staffer who had brought to the NSC considerable experience and a good relationship with Shultz, attempted a secret mission to Damascus to meet with the Syrians, who played a pivotal role in the Lebanese conflict. However, the Syrians and the Israelis were unyielding, and McFarlane, representing a divided interagency community, had no clear plan. Later in the year, he continued his efforts as an envoy, setting up offices in Rome and shuttling in and out of the region. Of course, this gave the NSC the type of active operational role in U.S. diplomacy that the Reagan team had initially said they would avoid. McFarlane undertook considerable risk in this capacity, as he would again during his later tenure as national security advisor. He witnessed increased hostility to U.S. forces, including unprovoked rocket and mortar attacks. Escalation followed, and the battleship *USS New Jersey* anchored off the coast of Lebanon. Later, with McFarlane doing the negotiating, the ship was used to help provide cover for Lebanese forces moving into place to help establish a cease-fire.

Also in early 1983, Central America became more prominent on the administration's radar. UN Ambassador Jeanne Kirkpatrick made a trip to the region and returned to report to the president and her ally Clark that the El Salvadoran government, which the United States had backed against communist insurgents, was faltering. In Nicaragua, the United States grew more concerned about the leftist government of Sandinista leader Daniel Ortega. Reagan became so engaged in this matter that he arranged a joint session of Congress to seek support for more aid for our allies in the region. Among conservatives on the Reagan team, this became a test of the resolve to roll back communism, standing up to it in a way that they felt Eisenhower did not when Castro made his move to power.

Just as all this was happening, James Watt, the impolitic secretary of the interior, decided to resign. Clark, who close aides say was "never comfortable" in the job of national security advisor, decided he would rather get back to his outdoorsman roots and got the president to agree to shift him to his third job in three years to replace Watt. There was an abortive effort to replace him with James Baker, who had a hankering to do more international work, but Clark and the other right-wingers literally cornered Reagan moments before the announcement was to be made and persuaded him not to do it. Baker was seen as too centrist. Certainly, he could not have been seen as less experienced than Clark or less capable than Allen. Indeed, Baker would later serve with great distinction as George H.W. Bush's secretary of state and as a critical player in the most effective national security apparatus of the modern era. Although it might be tempting to think it a pity that he did not get the NSC job back in 1983, it would not have been the same. The NSC job does not exist in a vacuum but is a partnership with the president. The problem in the Reagan era was not a lack of qualified national security advisors—the administration had six in eight years, a dubious record—but rather the failure of the president to hold up his end of the bargain by properly empowering and guiding his assistant for national security affairs.

Few would feel this absence of guidance more acutely than Robert McFarlane or his deputy, Admiral John Poindexter, who would later succeed him. Serious, capable, intelligent men, they were forced into a position of guessing at presidential motives, lashing together policy from the wreckage left behind from the Shultz-Weinberger squabbles, and trying to avoid the disastrous prescriptions of some of the loonier elements of the far right.

Within a week of McFarlane's appointment as Reagan's third national security advisor, 243 marines were killed in a terrorist attack on the U.S. marine barracks in Beirut. Reagan and his team were outraged and made impassioned and touching statements about the loss. It was time to test the resolve of this team to move past the constraints of the Vietnam era. After all, as McFarlane later said, "When President Reagan came to office, the body politic of our country was willing once more, with enough distance from Vietnam, to play a more activist role. . . . They were more willing to support congressional enactment of larger appropriations. And the president, to his credit, was able to take that political support and fiscal support and to bring down Marxism in the Soviet Union, to end the Cold War and to reduce nuclear weapons and so forth. It would not have been possible to do that 10 years beforehand."[32]

Indeed, one might argue that it was not possible to do that ever, because it didn't happen that way. First of all, claiming credit for the fall of the Soviet Union is, as was famously stated during a subsequent political debate, a little like the rooster taking credit for the dawn. Brzezinski and others had seen the handwriting on the wall years earlier. What brought down communism was the intellectual bankruptcy of the philosophy, the corruption of the Soviet government, the sclerotic Soviet leadership, and the accumulated costs of waging the Cold War for fifty years. During most of that period, Ronald Reagan was hosting television shows and doing commercials. Second, while it is true that Reagan did make considerable progress on arms reductions—largely because Soviet leader Mikhail Gorbachev recognized that the country would collapse under the costs of its military requirements rather than anything the United States did, there is precious little evidence of marshaling resources to support a robust new activism. Instead, we got anemic activism. And in the case of that particular October, hypocritical and pathetic activism. Hit hard by terrorists in Lebanon, we effectively did nothing in response. Instead, our attentions were turned elsewhere as the NSC staff was burning the midnight oil planning a response to a coup on October 12 that ousted Grenada's prime minister, Maurice Bishop, and led a week later to violence that resulted in his death and that of several of his ministers.

While McFarlane had been focused on Lebanon, the Grenada issues were being handled for him by Constantine Menges, a true believer and, until a few days earlier, a CIA employee working for Bill Casey. Menges didn't much like the new national security advisor, but he did prefer him to the even more moderate Baker. But the staffer ended up testing his boss by pushing for a meeting of the crisis group. This meeting took place, chaired by Poindexter. During the meeting Menges argued that unrest on the island could lead to a greater Soviet presence there, including nuclear weapons. Recognizing the grave threat posed by a nuclear island resort in the Caribbean, the Reagan team sprang into action. A paper was put together for the Special Situations Group. Vice President Bush chaired an NSC session. An NSDD was sought. And on the day before the Beirut attack, a meeting was held in the crisis center with Reagan and Shultz hooked in from their locations out of town (Shultz was at a golf tournament).

Thus, the simmering problem in the Caribbean provided the administration with an opportunity to show force in the wake of Beirut without the risks that a response in Lebanon itself would have entailed. Consequently, almost 6,000 troops were dispatched to Grenada, met slight resistance from a handful of Cuban troops, and took control of the island. Nineteen Americans died and 115 were wounded, and 8,612 medals were awarded for the operation. The total cost in military operations and aid was almost $200 million. America was back. The fact that there was precious little evidence of Soviet activity on the island and that the entire exercise was an absurdity more closely linked to the Marx Brothers than to Karl Marx was papered over. Reagan was hired to make America feel better about itself, and here we had a managed a neat, tidy little war with a victory and, within a few years, its own Clint Eastwood movie to memorialize it.

While the Grenada invasion was a success of the smallest order and U.S.

military initiatives elsewhere to roll back communism were of a covert variety and usually consisted of support for local forces that we used as surrogates, there was one area during Reagan's term of office that his war-like rhetoric produced more significant results—although perhaps not quite the results that Reagan's flacks and spinners would like the world to believe. That area was arms control, and one in which the president's native humanity overcame the sharp divisions among his team and pro-duced results throughout the administration's eight years. Despite his criticism of Carter, Reagan shared his predecessor's interest in eliminating nuclear weapons. As he once told Frank Carlucci, his fifth national secu-rity advisor and second defense secretary, he believed in his heart that "nuclear weapons are inherently evil."[33]

Reagan's perspective may have been informed, as Carter's was, by his philosophical outlook. He had noted in a 1980 interview with an evangel-ist that "we may be the generation that sees Armageddon." According to his biographer, the fortieth president "regarded the biblical prophecy as a useful warning. . . . Since Armageddon was coming, Reagan thought it prudent to protect people from its consequences," and Nagasaki and Hiroshima were considered evidence of humanity's possible fate.[34]

Furthermore, Reagan had been mistrustful of the methods used to reg-ulate the qualitative and quantitative growth of superpower arsenals, hav-ing criticized SALT II, which had been signed by President Carter but never ratified, as "fatally flawed" because the United States and the Soviet Union were not required to reduce the size of their weapons stocks.[35] Con-sequently, his policies on arms control were driven by a three-pronged effort—which he did not view as contradictory—to talk tough, to negoti-ate for a reduction in the size of superpower arsenals, and, in what may have been the most controversial component of the plan, to develop antimissile defenses.

Secretary of State George Shultz played a leading role in setting the administration's arms control policies and represented a pragmatic voice. Admiral Jonathan Howe, who had worked in both the Departments of State and Defense in Reagan's first term, recalled that Shultz "was a very smart man, but started with very little knowledge of arms control. He was very determined to master the subject and interested in it," and it did not take too long before he was "doing battle" at NSC meetings on the subject.[36] Shultz's position was strengthened by his warm relations with President Reagan and his wife, to whom the secretary of state had good access.[37]

He also had an ally in the Joint Chiefs of Staff, and as Howe stated, "Sec-retary Shultz certainly spent a lot of time listening to what the JCS concerns were and the issues. He went to the Pentagon with regularity. . . . The point is that Shultz knew that he wanted the chiefs' agreement. It wasn't that he just needed to have it; he wanted to have their advice and know what their concerns were. Often what we would find in those meetings was the State Department's position and the JCS position would be closely aligned."[38]

Secretary Shultz's primary adversaries were Defense Secretary Caspar Weinberger, who second-term Assistant Secretary of State for Politico-Military Affairs Allen Holmes recalled "was absolutely opposed to doing anything" with arms control, and Assistant Secretary of Defense for International Security Policy Richard Perle, who echoed Reagan's skepticism of negotiations with the Soviets but not his goal of reducing the size of superpower nuclear arsenals.[39] Perle, described as bright, skilled at bureaucratic infighting, and having Weinberger's full backing, "ended up having more impact on policy in arms control than any other official in the U.S. government," according to Strobe Talbott.[40]

Weinberger's efforts were aided by his insight into how Reagan dealt with contested policy issues; he recognized that "Reagan disliked coming down firmly on behalf of one of his principal subordinates at the expense of another."[41] For example, early in Reagan's first term, Perle crafted a "zero option" proposal in the intermediate-range missile negotiations, which advocated the removal of all Soviet SS-20s in Europe and Asia in return for the cancellation of a planned U.S. deployment of cruise missiles and Pershing IIs to Western Europe.[42] Perle and Weinberger knew it was highly unlikely that the Soviets would accept the plan, particularly as it called for the trade-off of actual missiles for missiles that had not yet been installed, but it was written to appeal to both Reagan's interest in nuclear abolition and his desire for compromise among competing agencies. The Defense proposal "provided for the illusion of a compromise," since it differentiated itself from the State Department position in two ways: the zero option as well as the definition of zero, both of which were opposed by Shultz. Weinberger and Perle were unconcerned about whether or not shorter-range nuclear weapons systems were included in the definition of zero, in contrast to the State Department, and deliberately provided Reagan with a midpoint position between Shultz's and Weinberger's. Perle recalled, "That was quite a deliberate strategy. We both made sure that the paper that went to the president divided the issue into two parts, and we let the NSC staff know that we could live with a defeat on part two."[43] Predictably, the Soviets rejected the offer, but the zero option would return to the bargaining table a few years later.

Amid the battling and stratagems between the State and Defense

Departments, the NSC acted as a "facilitator," as Howe put it. Another former NSC staffer observed that the NSC "didn't play a really driving central
role" in setting the arms control agenda.[44] As in the replacement of Haig
with Shultz, the changeover from William Clark to Robert McFarlane
resulted in the addition of a more accommodating voice on arms control
matters with the Soviets, but McFarlane did not attempt to usurp or horn
in on Shultz's role.[45] In fact, according to former Assistant Secretary of
State Holmes, "McFarlane wanted to have arms control thrown out of the
White House, out of the NSC," to the State Department, which would
mesh with Shultz's insistence that "arms control had to be embedded in
the four-part agenda with the Soviets [human rights, regional issues,
bilateral issues, and arms control]. He insisted this had to be one. You
couldn't separate out arms control. There had to be a mutually reinforcing
process and this should be done out of the State Department."[46]

The national security advisor and his staff instead focused most of their
energies on moderating the myriad interagency disputes and coordinating the activities of these two warring departments. McFarlane was also a
participant, along with Shultz, Casey, and Weinberger, in the Wednesday
breakfast meetings, which concentrated on security, foreign policy, and
arms control. Holmes, who worked with Weinberger aide General Colin
Powell to "set up the meetings, frame the decisions after they were made at
the table, and fanned them back out to the bureaucracy," recalls that these
meetings were able to address some of the outstanding matters, with
McFarlane taking issues that remained unresolved to the president.[47]

Additionally, Howe recalled how the NSC directors for arms control
"backstopped trips—they were not nonentities. And they were doing a lot
of behind-the-scenes work. They would come over to the Pentagon. They
would talk to us. They would try to pull this thing together in a helpful
way."[48] During Reagan's second term, Colonel Robert Linhard, the senior
director for defense policy and arms control on the NSC, established the
Arms Control Support Group, described by Howe as a "very unofficial,
very informal grouping of assistant secretary–level people from all the relevant places—OSD, the JCS, State, CIA. It was formed to try and forge
consensus on major arms control issues, or, at a minimum, to prepare
them in an orderly fashion for senior-level decision-making. My memory
is that developing this interagency team was critical to things actually happening elsewhere. It made some of the tough decisions that led to the INF
[Intermediate Range Nuclear Forces] treaty and some of the key START
[Strategic Arms Reduction Treaty] I decisions."[49]

While the national security advisor generally worked in the background, McFarlane did play a pivotal role in bringing what would become

a signature Reagan issue to the forefront of the Reagan administration's agenda—the Strategic Defense Initiative (SDI), more popularly known as "Star Wars." Reagan had demonstrated some interest in strategic defense before becoming president, after having visiting the North American Aerospace Defense Command (NORAD) headquarters in 1979 and learning from an air force general that the United States had no defense against Soviet missiles.[50] Weeks after the visit, one of his advisors, Martin Anderson, wrote a memorandum calling for a development of a "protective missile system," but the issue did not come up during the 1980 campaign. After the election, Anderson formed a small, informal group in the White House to discuss strategic missile defense issues. The group met with President Reagan, National Security Advisor Allen, and several others in early 1982, and although the president responded positively, he was noncommittal. The working group dissolved soon afterward, and the White House remained unengaged in antimissile defense until Congress killed the MX missile program in December 1982.[51]

McFarlane, who was then deputy to National Security Advisor Clark, responded to the defeat by reconsidering strategic defense, which he believed, if it could be accomplished, would level the playing field with the Soviets, balancing the Soviet Union's quantitative ICBM advantage with superior American technology. As McFarlane told Robert McNamara in an effort to persuade the former defense secretary about the merits of SDI, "Our leverage derives from the Soviets' fear of our technology. They are afraid that their huge investment in offensive forces will be neutralized if we go ahead with this program. That gives us real purchase."[52]

McFarlane and his deputy, John Poindexter (whom McFarlane credits for pushing him to consider the idea), collaborated with Admiral James Watkins, Chief of Naval Operations, to develop a plan.[53] While McFarlane had doubts about the feasibility of such a system, he viewed the proposed antimissile shield as a powerful bargaining chip that would force the Soviets to agree to make significant cuts in their ICBM forces. He wasn't sure if any antimissile system would ever emerge from the lab, but he believed that leveraging American technological prowess would allow the United States to exchange an untested research program for tangible reductions in actual, deployed offensive weaponry.[54]

McFarlane, accompanied by several military officers, briefed the president in February 1983 about the possibilities of a strategic defense initiative. He McFarlane made sure to emphasize that the United States could develop systems that would defeat a missile attack, reportedly saying during the presentation, "Stop! Mr. President, do you understand how important a statement that is?"[55] Reagan was enamored with the idea, which meshed with his long-standing concerns about preventing a nuclear Armageddon. Clark, recognizing the president's deep-seated interest in the proposal, recommended a rapid, dramatic announcement about a strategic defense initiative to preempt the expected opposition from Congress and the State and Defense Department bureaucracies.

With President Reagan scheduled to make a speech on the defense budget on March 23, 1983, McFarlane wrote the ending to the speech, which became known as "MX Plus." Very few people knew that the president planned to talk about strategic defense. Poindexter recalls, "We didn't tell anyone else what we were doing. The chiefs didn't know. Defense didn't know. State didn't know."[56] Weinberger and Shultz were only informed about the speech finale at the last minute, a deliberate ploy by Clark to ensure that the powerful secretaries wouldn't have time to voice their objections as well as to prevent the possibility of a leak.[57] McFarlane recalls how Perle had lobbied for a delay in the speech in order to "deliver an impassioned plea on behalf of the allies and their right to know about this sea change in U.S. nuclear policy and the importance of coordination. I found it hard to keep from laughing at Richard's advocacy in behalf of the allies. Neither before nor since had Richard Perle ever cared a whit about the allies and coordination. . . . His call was nothing but a manifestation of professional pique."[58]

With the speech completed and the element of surprise ensured, President Reagan went on national television and laid out the case for the development of a strategic defense initiative:

> What if free people could live secure in the knowledge that their security did not rest upon the threat of instant U.S. retaliation to deter a Soviet attack, that we could intercept and destroy strategic ballistic missiles before they reached our own soil or that of our allies? I know this is a formidable, technical task, one that may not be accomplished before the end of this century. . . . This could pave the way for arms control measures to eliminate the weapons themselves. We seek neither military superiority nor political advantage. Our only purpose—one all people share—is to search for ways to reduce the danger of nuclear war. My fellow Americans, tonight we're launching an effort which holds the promise of changing the course of human history.[59]

Days after his speech, President Reagan signed NSDD-85, "Eliminating the Threat from Ballistic Missiles," which called for the "development of an intensive effort to define a long-term research and development program aimed at an ultimate goal of eliminating the threat posed by nuclear ballistic missiles. These actions will be carried out in a manner consistent with our obligations under the ABM [Anti-Ballistic Missile] Treaty and recognizing the need for close consultations with our allies."[60]

As expected, the Soviets reacted very negatively to Reagan's SDI announcement, and the threat of an antimissile shield initially produced bluster rather than a willingness to return to the bargaining table. On the American side, Weinberger, Perle, and Clark continued to express their opposition to a nuclear arms reduction treaty.[61] By the summer of 1984, however, interest had been rekindled on both sides, and the Americans and Soviets agreed to meet in Geneva in March 1985 to resume negotiations, which would now include a discussion of space weapons. On the day that the delegations arrived in Geneva, the Soviet leader, Konstantin Chernenko, died and was replaced by Mikhail Gorbachev, who would become an unlikely partner in Reagan's efforts to reduce their respective nations' stockpiles of nuclear weapons.

Ambassador Rozanne Ridgway worked on the Reagan teams that had brokered the last deals with the Soviets. From her perspective, success here was a direct result of the active commitment of President Reagan and those closest to him.

> If the president decides to engage and is himself engaged, the process as it usually stands is set aside and the focus becomes how to get the job done, and other resources are pulled in to the mix.
>
> I am really describing the process in the second Reagan administration, in which President Reagan, Mrs. Reagan, and, I believe, Mrs. [Margaret] Thatcher [the British prime minister who became a good friend and advisor to the president] convinced President Reagan that it was time to engage the new leader of the Soviet Union. Once that was done, you had a different cast of characters drawing up the scenarios, doing the papers, getting things moved through outside the process, and things started to happen. Unless the decision comes from the top, nothing happens. You can't make policy from the bottom up.[62]

This is a comment worth pondering in light of the Iran-Contra problems that also dominated administration attention during the same period.

As for Thatcher's special role, Ridgway notes:

> First of all, Margaret Thatcher is the world's favorite conservative. Made

it okay to talk to Gorbachev. And for a bureaucracy which was fighting each other with labels of the kind that you see now [in 2004]—who is a patriot and who is not, who is caving in and who is not, who is sturdy and who is weak—the tough Iron Lady got up and said, This is a man we can do business with. . . . All you had to do was go out and sort of stand next to Margaret Thatcher [and] you could begin to push the bureaucracy back.

Of course, you also have to give credit to Reagan himself. Go back, for example, to the first meeting in Geneva [in 1985], with [Reagan and Gorbachev] alone in front of the fireplace. And the president started dealing with Gorbachev by saying, We are the leaders of the two greatest nations in the world. And he said I believe you are not going to get anywhere without democracy. He wasn't easy on the guy. He was just—well, he wanted to negotiate arms control and he hated nuclear weapons. A whole lot of people did not. But if you remember the first major statement in the Geneva working paper—it flowed from the president's distaste for the idea of mutual assured destruction, and I think it surprised a lot of people—in which he said nuclear war cannot be won and must never be fought. It was the very first statement in that paper. And I think there was some concern that he did not want to go down in history as a warmonger. So I think he got encouragement at home from Nancy Reagan. He got encouragement from Margaret Thatcher. He got encouragement from his own intellectual judgment.[63]

As Reagan assessed the new Soviet leader, the administration remained divided on whether to push forward on a new arms control agreement as well as whether to make concessions to the Soviet Union about SDI. On the eve of the first summit between Reagan and his new Soviet counterpart, someone within the government leaked a letter written by Secretary Weinberger on the dangers of the continued American commitment to the boundaries set by the unratified SALT II agreement, which McFarlane criticized as a "blatant attempt to undermine the president just before the summit."[64] Meanwhile, the replacement of Clark with his deputy McFarlane meant the replacement of a hard-liner with a more pragmatic voice on U.S.-Soviet relations, with Shultz and his chief arms control negotiator, Paul Nitze, advocating for a strategic arms agreement, even if it involved concessions on strategic defense, in the face of Weinberger and Perle's continued opposition.[65]

Poindexter and Linhard, the NSC arms control specialist, were forced to mediate the conflict between State and Defense and reconcile compet-

ing drafts of letters and negotiating positions on arms control before presenting anything to the Soviets.[66] President Reagan's insistence on pushing
the Soviets to make a 50 percent cut in their offensive nuclear capability
without any reduction to the American SDI program complicated the
already difficult task of trying to put together a coherent administration
position.[67]

In late July 1986, Reagan sent Gorbachev a letter detailing a "zero ballistic missiles" plan, which proposed that both sides adhere to the ABM
treaty for another seven and a half years. Gorbachev rejected this offer but
in September proposed that the two leaders have a preparatory meeting
that fall to address unresolved issues for a future Washington summit. The
United States and the Soviet Union quickly agreed to hold a meeting in
Reykjavik, Iceland, several weeks later.[68]

The American side did not presume that any groundbreaking proposals would be made in Iceland, primarily viewing the summit as an opportunity to set the agenda for the next meeting of the two superpower
leaders. However, in pre-Reykjavik meetings with his advisors, the president had expressed his continued interest in eliminating all intermediate-
range missiles from Europe, believing that he could convince Gorbachev
to agree to implement some form of the zero option that Perle had developed (but had not wanted to see implemented) in 1981. Poindexter, Perle,
and Linhard were part of the U.S. delegation in Reykjavik, and the latter
two helped in designing a counterproposal that would have resulted in a
50 percent cut in strategic nuclear arsenals, the elimination of all ballistic
missiles, and a ten-year ban on the deployment of a strategic defense system. Reagan presented the American proposal to Gorbachev, who
responded with an even more audacious plan, the elimination of all
strategic offensive nuclear weapons in ten years. The president reportedly
replied that if all nuclear weapons were to be eradicated, "we can turn it all
over to the Geneva people and they can draft the agreement and you could
come to the United States to sign it."[69]

However, no arms reduction treaty emerged because the president
would not agree to Gorbachev's insistence on a permanent ban on the
deployment of an SDI system along with the ban on nuclear weapons.
Ironically, McFarlane's plan to use a proposed strategic defense system as a
bargaining chip seemed to have borne fruit, producing significantly more
than the zero option that Reagan had embraced. Yet Reagan had always
possessed a different interpretation of the purpose of the SDI, not understanding why the Soviets would be discomfited by the notion of a U.S.
defensive shield, nor why they scoffed at his pledges to share the benefits

of the SDI research. The impasse could not be resolved, but although the Reykjavik summit ended without an agreement, the two sides did sign the INF treaty the following year, which eliminated all intermediate-range nuclear-armed ground-launched ballistic and cruise missiles while side-stepping the tricky issue of SDI. The INF Treaty was the first nuclear arms control agreement to actually reduce nuclear arms rather than establish ceilings.[70]

This particular instance of presidential leadership raises important questions because it demonstrates that even in an administration torn apart by internecine conflict, it is possible to accomplish significant policy initiatives if there is direct presidential leadership. It also indicates how important Reagan was to whatever it was that got done in the administration. Yet, when the administration was nearly undone over a complex, high-risk set of policies, trading arms for hostages in Iran and using the money from those transactions to fund the Contras in Nicaragua, it is equally interesting that the story from Reagan's protectors was that he did not know, he did not actively advocate the controversial elements of the policy, and that somehow, in an administration in which successful initiatives required the president's blessing to be hammered through the fighting bureaucracy, in this particular case, the initiative got done because the president and those close to him, such as the vice president, were not paying attention, were disengaged.

·   ·   ·

After Reagan's reelection, the anticommunist loose cannon Constantine Menges was working his magic in Central America. Having gotten wind of a Shultz plan to achieve a compromise peace with Nicaragua, Menges urged McFarlane to host an NSC meeting on the subject to ensure that the State Department did not "sell out" national interests with its plan. When McFarlane resisted, Menges reportedly threatened to freelance his position to other principal to get them interested. Whereas this threat should have had him fired, because of the perceived "juice" that the true believers had, McFarlane capitulated, and the ensuing meeting became focused on the issue of finding ways to support the Contras now that Congress had cut off funding for them. Bush and Casey supported finding a way to get third-party money. Shultz opposed it, saying, "If we go out and try to get money from third countries it is an impeachable offense."[71] This must have made McFarlane somewhat uncomfortable, for his NSC had already embarked on an initiative on that front that would, when revealed, leave the president pondering whether or not an impeachment might be in his future. Whether anyone in the room had perspective enough to recognize that the communist threat in Central America was significantly overstated and was seized upon because it offered a low-risk environment to talk tough, take action, and yet avoid confrontations with really dangerous enemies or really complex foreign policy situations is another issue. As in Grenada, fighting communists in Central America can be seen in retrospect as a kind of a therapy program for American egos wounded in Southeast Asia to win their confidence back by beating up on rag-tag resistance groups who, while dangerous to people in their path, were not appreciably worse than the right-wing regimes we were supporting and certainly never really posed a major threat to any U.S. interests. While standing up to communism was certainly a good thing that played a critical role in helping the United States to victory in the Cold War, pushing out the Sandinistas was not exactly on a par with maintaining a major military capability on our side of the Fulda Gap, with keeping our half of Berlin free, or with ensuring that Cuba did not become a Soviet missile base.

The Iran-Contra debacle stemmed from a confluence of the Reagan administration's policy initiatives in Iran and Nicaragua as well as from the perversion of the function of the NSC from a planning and coordination arm of the executive office of the president to a freelance State Department–CIA hybrid that operated under the radar at home—and not quite far enough under the radar overseas.

The Iran component of the scandal originally stemmed from concerns articulated by National Security Advisor Robert McFarlane and other administration officials about limiting Soviet influence in a post-Khomeini Iran. McFarlane wrote in a 1985 draft National Security Decision Directive that the United States needed to "increase contacts with allies and friends .. . on the evolution of the Iranian situation and possible means for influencing the direction of change" and "discreetly communicat[e] our desire for correct relations to potentially receptive Iranian leaders."[72]

Although the NSDD was never adopted,[73] an NSC consultant, Michael Ledeen, was sent to Israel in May 1985 to discuss options with Israeli officials, including Prime Minister Shimon Peres, for initiating contacts with the Khomeini regime.[74] These talks were followed by a July 1985 meeting between McFarlane and David Kimche, the director-general of the Israeli foreign ministry, in the national security advisor's basement office in the White House. Ledeen continued to act as a conduit between the NSC staff and the Israelis (and Israeli and Iranian arms dealers), noting that he "had an understanding with Mr. McFarlane that neither of us would keep any-thing in writing regarding this initiative."[75] Ledeen's ambiguous status proved useful to McFarlane when he was able to deny to Secretary of State Shultz that he had sent Ledeen to Israel on an NSC assignment.[76]

Days after President Reagan declared that Iran was part of a "confedera-tion of terrorist states ... America will never make concessions to terrorists," McFarlane met with an Israeli arms dealer to discuss an arms-for-hostages swap. President Reagan was briefed about the plan and, after additional meetings between McFarlane and Kimche, the national security advisor presented a proposal to the National Security Planning Group in August, suggesting that the United States give 100 TOW missiles to Iran in exchange for the release of all American hostages in Beirut. While Shultz and Wein-berger, often on opposing sides of issues, jointly argued against the plan, Reagan, who had become increasingly frustrated with being unable to secure the release of the seven American hostages being held in Lebanon, was loath to pass up any openings that could result in their freedom. Conse-quently, the transfer of the weaponry to Iran (via Israel) was approved in August.[77]

McFarlane oversaw the arms-for-hostages program during his remain-ing months in office and designated Lt. Col. Oliver North, a charismatic, bureaucratically savvy—and in the view of one of his colleagues in the gov-ernment, "hyperthyroid"—NSC staffer with responsibility for terrorism policy to work with the Iranian government for the release of the hostages. According to McFarlane's testimony, he expressly directed North not to violate the law but was unaware of the depth and scope of his aide's activi-ties with the Iranians and the Contras. While McFarlane wrote that he was surprised by North's actions, Elliott Abrams, assistant secretary of state for Latin America, was apparently warned by NSC staffers and even Secretary of State George Shultz to "monitor Ollie."[78] And Ronald Sable, a member of President Reagan's national security council, recalled a meeting in McFar-lane's office with the outgoing national security advisor and his replace-ment, Admiral Poindexter, when "Bud exclaimed to John, 'John, one of the things left undone that I should have taken care of is to get Ollie North out of the NSC. He is a loose cannon. That job will be left to you.'"[79] Of course, Poindexter did not take that advice and, furthermore, the Walsh Report, which was produced after years of investigation into the resulting scandal, refutes McFarlane's claim of the "compartmentation" of knowledge within the NSC, noting repeated instances, through 1986, of North and McFar-lane discussing developments in Iran and Nicaragua.[80]

Soon after McFarlane officially resigned his post in December 1985 amid a swirl of rumors about his personal life and with a nudge from White House Chief of Staff Donald Regan, with whom tensions had been growing, he met secretly with Iranian arms dealer Manucher Ghorbanifar in London to discuss an expanded Iranian proposal for the delivery of more advanced weaponry in return for the release of American hostages. After a contentious meeting, he reported back to the president, Weinberger, Casey, Regan, and Poindexter (McFarlane's replacement as national security advisor), recommending that the arms-for-hostages program be discontinued.[81] While Weinberger, Shultz, and Regan all expressed their objections to the arms transfers to the Iranians, accounts differ on President Reagan's reaction to McFarlane's counsel. The outgoing national security advisor believed that the secret dealings with the Iranians would be ended, but his advice was disregarded. Instead, Reagan approved direct U.S. arms sales to Iran in January 1986, signing a presidential finding written by Poindexter, but it was not presented to key NSC principals, including either Secretaries Shultz or Weinberger.[82]

Admiral Poindexter, a quiet, thoughtful engineer, a "remote figure even within the NSC—kept the door to his office closed and dealt with others through his deputies or by computer messages, backed the continuation of the program."[83] He subsequently provided Oliver North with considerable latitude and additional autonomy from the NSC staff to maintain and expand the Iranian operations.[84] North worked closely with Poindexter (and conferred with McFarlane) and selected individuals at the CIA to work on "Operation Recovery," a complicated, multistage plan to exchange 4,000 TOW missiles for all seven American hostages being held in Lebanon. North took full advantage of the freedom given to him to conduct the operation, utilizing clandestine networks that he had originally established to supply the Nicaraguan Contras. In fact, North, who already controlled the secret bank accounts in which these Contra funds were deposited, reportedly said that the prospect of generating funds for the Contras was an "attractive incentive" for continuing the Iranian arms sales, whether or not any hostages were released.[85]

Despite his departure from government and warnings about continuing the arms-for-hostages operation, McFarlane remained involved in the covert undertaking and in regular contact with the NSC via a secure computer link. He agreed to lead a secret May 1985 mission to Tehran, accompanying North and several CIA people to meet with top-level Iranian officials to discuss the arrangements for the arms-for-hostages deal. (While it is not unusual for former officials to continue to serve an administration in new capacities, utilizing McFarlane in such a sensitive operational capacity after his departure from his NSC post must be viewed as fairly extraordinary.) The mission proved to be a significant disappointment, given that no hostages were released, as had been expected, nor did the Americans meet with any high-ranking Iranians.[86] As they were preparing to depart from Iran, McFarlane, according to his testimony, only then learned about the diversion of arms funds to the Contras, when North said offhandedly that "it's not a total loss, at least we're using some of the Ayatollah's money in Central America."[87]

While President Reagan made repeated inquiries about the fate of the American hostages, there was little reported awareness within the administration of operational activities being directed by North, Poindexter, and the NSC. Reflecting the secrecy with which NSC staffers operated, North wrote in a February 1986 e-mail that he was withholding information about his full activities from Poindexter in order "not to compromise myself at a point in time when he needs to be absolutely certain that this can work."[88] Poindexter, who later testified before Congress that he did not notify President Reagan of the Contra diversion, was able to operate in an environment largely free of oversight from the administration's top foreign policy officials, who were often embroiled in feuding and infighting.[89] Compounding this laxness, Shultz wrote as the scandal was unfolding that "President Reagan simply did not seem to grasp what was actually going on" with the arms-for-hostages swaps. The secretary of state later told him bluntly, "Mr. President, you are not fully informed. You must not continue to say we made no deals for hostages. You have been deceived and lied to."[90]

Despite extensive efforts by North, Poindexter, and others to keep the operation hidden both inside and outside of the U.S. government, the scandal erupted, with two events in the fall of 1986 disclosing the behavior of a "wildcat" NSC staff.[91] On October 5, 1986, Nicaraguan government soldiers shot down an American cargo plane that was carrying military supplies to the contras, resulting in the capture of an American, who told his captors that he was employed by the CIA. The plane also contained documents, recovered by Sandinistas, that linked the supply operations to the United States. North quickly wound down his covert operation, destroying records of the contra disbursements as well.[92]

Several weeks later, news of the arms-for-hostages swap with the Iranians was revealed in a Lebanese newspaper.[93] The leak came from a rival faction within the Iranian government after North, disgruntled by the slow pace of hostage releases, had established a second back channel with a nephew of the Iranian speaker of the parliament in August 1986.[94] As the Reagan administration began to publicly respond to the allegations,

McFarlane e-mailed Poindexter to complain that he was "being hung out to dry" by Chief of Staff Donald Regan.[95] Despite Poindexter's efforts to tamp down the scandal,[96] a torrent of leaks led McFarlane, in a meeting with North, Poindexter, and Deputy National Security Advisor Alton Keel, to worry that knowledge about the Contra link to the Iranian arms deals would soon be revealed.[97]

As the Reagan administration's investigation expanded, North and Poindexter conducted a campaign to destroy or rewrite evidence and conjure testimony to hide their actions. More than 5,000 e-mails—via a system known as "Private Blank Check," which Poindexter, a computer expert, had set up to relay messages between North and the national security advisor—were deleted, although a White House backup copy was later discovered.[98] North threw a "shredding party" to eliminate embarrassing documents and "problem memos," and he removed more than a dozen notebooks containing classified information from NSC offices. North also witnessed Poindexter destroy what may have been the only copy signed by Reagan of a presidential covert-action finding, which retroactively authorized CIA participation in the November 1985 HAWK missile shipment to Iran.[99]

Furthermore, according to McFarlane's testimony before the Tower Commission, a chronology prepared by North "was not a full and completely accurate account of those events, but rather [an] effort to blur and leave ambiguous the President's role."[100] And, in a meeting at Ledeen's house with North and McFarlane, North apparently quizzed the former NSC consultant on what would be said about the delivery of HAWK missiles: "What concerns me is not what happened but what are you going to say happened."[101] Nonetheless, the linking of the arms dealings with the Iranians and funds diversions to the Contras was made public on November 25, 1986, when Attorney General Meese announced that Justice Department officials had discovered that some of the proceeds from the Iran arms sales had been diverted to the Contras.[102]

In December 1986, Reagan appointed Senator John Tower, former National Security Advisor Brent Scowcroft, and former Senator Edmund Muskie to a Special Review Board, also known as the Tower Commission, to review the role of the NSC staff. Reagan adopted the reforms they recommended with the signing of NSDD-266 and publicly pledged to implement "in total the Tower Report's model of how the NSC process and staff should work" and improve the NSC's "sensitivity to matters of the law."[103] Poindexter and North were fired.

Iran-Contra was a turning point for the administration and for the

National Security Council system. For the president and his team, it was a black mark that they survived but never fully recovered from. For those who worked in the system, it was a powerful message about the dangers of an operational NSC and, more important, about the dangers of an NSC operating without adult supervision. Given that the council staff lacks the congressional oversight of other executive branch agencies, it requires attentive management from the one power center to which it is accountable, the president. However, Reagan's detached chairman-of-the-board–type presidency—often touted by supporters of the president as a desirable alternative to the micromanagement of the Carter years—opened the door to the communications and oversight breakdowns that produced Iran-Contra. In particular, the president's distance from his own government and the culture he allowed to develop—one in which Poindexter, who had been in the Reagan White House since 1981, knew the president well, and felt he was being true the president's desires without feeling compelled to seek confirmation of the president's support for his actions—were to blame.

Today, almost twenty years later, there is still a sense among some former Reagan officials that they were treated unfairly, misunderstood, trying to do the right thing via the only means left to them by an obstructionist Congress. One senior Reagan administration official claims:

> It was done for a very good reason. Congress had put a limitation that no DOD or CIA funds could support the freedom fighters. The members of Congress didn't want to be blamed if the communists subverted El Salvador and we lost Central America. So they limited the use of funds from those departments but allowed them from individuals. That was the sense of one of the Boland Amendments. And therefore the only entity in the government that was left that could do anything would be the NSC, because they were not covered under the strictures about the CIA or DOD. That was how Ollie North got into this project. And then when the Iranian initiative was started, they needed somebody to do that, and again, it was such a tightly held thing that it was contained within the White House pretty much and even the CIA was hardly involved other than at the Bill Casey level, maybe one step lower. That's how Ollie North again happened to be put in charge of that. He was viewed as a kind of can-do marine who could get things done, and that's how the two happened to come together.[104]

Edwin Meese, the attorney general throughout the period, says:

John Poindexter said that he was so upset with the Congress for what he thought was selling out the freedom fighters that he allowed Ollie North to do what he did on the diversion of funds. Poindexter realized it was wrong, but he felt they might get away with it and believed that from an overall moral standpoint it was the right thing to do to help the freedom fighters. But as a result, this joined the Iranian initiative, over which there was disagreement but which the president believed was a legitimate measure, with the support of the freedom fighters, which he clearly felt was perfectly legal. When you have controversial actions, and particularly when money is involved, the political antennae go up. The diversion of funds is what caused the potential illegality, although that it was illegal was never established in any court.[105]

Poindexter says, illustrating his enduring belief that rather than doing something wrong, what he did was misunderstood and misrepresented to the American people:

The main thing that went wrong, in my opinion, was primarily my failure to work on a contingency plan, a public affairs plan once it leaked out. We should have anticipated that it would eventually leak and we didn't do that. And so, we were playing catch-up ball. With that, because of the sensitivity of what we were doing, I had directed that we minimize the amount of written material, and that may or may not have been a good decision."

Consequently, Poindexter noted the challenges in reconstructing the chronology of events, since "it started under Bud [McFarlane], and I was not fully involved in '84 . . . and by the middle of '85 I was getting more involved . . . and then in '86, of course, I had the whole thing—it was very difficult to construct a precise and accurate description about what had happened. People's recollections of events vary, and the chronology went through many drafts.

When people write about it today, invariably they say that we were doing something illegal or that we violated the Boland Amendment, which is not true. That was never charged in any of the indictments. In fact, much to our chagrin, my lawyers and I wanted the government to charge us with violation of the Boland Amendment, because we knew they were on very weak ground. So that was never charged. In fact, the Intelligence Oversight Board had ruled some time in '84—I can't remember the exact date, I think it was sometime in '84—that there wasn't anything in the Boland Amendment that prohibited the NSC staff from being involved in supplying arms to the Contras, since NSC staff was not part of the intelligence community. So in the end, the way I have always looked at it was that it was a political disagreement between the president and the Democrats in Congress, especially [Speaker] Tip O'Neill. And in my case and others, they turned it into a criminal case.[106]

Of course a central question then and now turns, as during Watergate, on "what the president knew and when he knew it." Poindexter maintains his position two decades later:

People thought that I have never told the truth about this, but indeed I have always told the truth about it—that the president didn't know about the use of the proceeds from the arms to Iran, using those to provide funds to the Contras. I decided not to tell him because I was convinced that if I had told him he would have approved and that would have put him in a very difficult situation when it did leak out.

In any event, we were never charged with anything to do with the money transfer being illegal. The charges were "lied to Congress" and I contend it wasn't lying. It was just that I didn't tell them everything I knew.[107]

As for those other than the president, one former senior State Department official said:

Shultz's claim that he didn't know what was going on always struck me as rather suspicious because about four or five months, maybe six months before this storm broke and it was revealed that we were trading weapons for hostages and Shultz replied that he was shocked. . . . Well, at about that time before it all opened up, one of the hostages was released and was brought to Frankfurt. And we went down to be there when the hostage showed up and Bob Oakley, who was the head of the terrorism office at State was there. And so we're standing on the tarmac, and one of us says something like, I wonder how this happened? And Oakley said, You don't want to know. And my colleague said, What do you mean? And Oakley replied, We got this guy because we're giving the Iranians arms. And we responded: What? And he said, Yes, that's the deal. We give them arms, they give us hostages. And so if Oakley knew this months and months before it became public, it is hard to believe that Shultz didn't know. And Oakley maintains Shultz did know what was going on.[108]

The Tower Commission's language was quite clear as it laid out its critique:

- The arms transfers to Iran and the activities of the NSC staff in support for the Contras are case studies in the perils of policy pursued outside the constraints of an orderly process.
- The "obsession with secrecy . . . deprived those responsible for the initiative of considerable expertise [available from the departments]."
- The NSC system will not work unless the President makes it work.
- [The President] . . . did not force his policy to undergo the most critical review of which the NSC participants and the process were capable. At no time did he insist upon accountability and performance review. Had the President chosen to drive the NSC system, the outcome could well have been different.

However, some of the language in the report is, shall we say, gentler or more accepting of the White House spin than a completely independent assessment might be expected to be. It remarks that the president's "intense compassion for the hostages . . . appeared to motivate his steadfast support for the initiative." It notes that "the President did not seem to be aware" of the way in which the operation was implemented. "The President's expressed concern," the report notes sympathetically, "for the safety of both the hostages and the Iranians who could have been at risk may have been conveyed in a manner so as to inhibit the full functioning of the system." And: "The President's management style is to put the principal responsibility for policy review and implementation on the shoulders of his advisors."[109] Management style? In another assessment, couldn't this be recast into the statement: "The President failed in his role as chief executive, was unaware of critical initiatives and attempted to dodge accountability for the actions of his team, and his repeated assertions that he did not know what was going on suggest that either he was negligent or he was lying."

The Tower Report did pinpoint the mistakes of the cabinet somewhat more directly and called for reforms that were soon put in place. Indeed, Brent Scowcroft's participation in the Tower Board process undoubtedly prepared him well for the role he would soon play as George H.W. Bush's national security advisor. Still, questions remain to this day about how plausible it is that the president and the vice president did not know the critical details of this high-risk policy concerning two critical areas of administration interest. Indeed, we are asked to believe that no one—not Casey, not McFarlane, not Poindexter, not Shultz, not Weinberger, not Bush, not Regan—discussed the policy with the president and yet managed to see it through despite objections to it at several key agencies. This suggests in and of itself one of the great acts of interagency coordination in U.S. government history. Perhaps we have misjudged this group.

Clearly, in the wake of Iran-Contra, change was needed at the White House. Frank Carlucci recalls, "My nomination as national security advisor came as a complete surprise to me—although I had a phone call on Sunday night from a friend of mine who said that he'd heard I was going to be named national security advisor within the next day, and I said, That's nonsense."[110]

> No one had spoken to me. At noon, I was having lunch with a friend at a restaurant, and I got a call from Don Regan asking if I could come over to the White House right away and go in the Treasury entrance so I wouldn't be observed. I met in the basement with Ronald Reagan and Don Regan—just the two of them. The president said he would like me to be national security advisor because I was the only person that George Shultz and Cap Weinberger could agree on. He didn't say anything flattering, didn't mention that I had any talent or anything like that. He just said you're the only one they could agree on. I then said, well, before you make your decision you probably want to hear some of my views. I'll tell you what I think my strengths and weaknesses are, which I did, and then I said, I think you ought to know that I disagreed with you on Iran-Contra. He attempted to justify what happened and did not do so totally to my satisfaction. Anyway, I then laid down the ground rules that I would have access to him when I wanted it and that I would have the ability to restore the NSC, which he agreed to.[111]

Carlucci accepted the post and immediately hired General Colin Powell, Weinberger's aide, as his deputy. His policy was that the two of them would be interchangeable, and they worked exceptionally closely as a unit. As for their relationship with Reagan, Carlucci recalls:

> He was a wonderful man to work for, because he was congenial and he was friendly but, as Nancy says, he was always a little distant. I mean you were never quite certain where he was except on key issues—military strength, taxes—you knew where he stood on those issues. But if you went to him with a problem, you weren't always certain where he was coming out. . . . Colin and I went back to my office and we sat down and said, Look, we're going to have to try to figure out how we make decisions in this kind of process, because we have to be faithful to what we think the president would want without getting explicit guidance from him. It's

clear that some of the people who were working for him prior to us didn't go through that kind of process. They took the lack of crisp decision making to be license to go do their thing. And that's what led to the abuse. In essence, he trusted his people too much.[112]

Carlucci continues, "He was taken advantage of. Later on I saw that if I pressed him on an issue and if I made suggestions and said this is the way I think you should go, he had wonderful instincts. I mean he would generally come out in the right place."[113]

Carlucci and Powell set about implementing an aggressive reform program, actually laying off about 60 percent of the staff at the NSC—so many, Carlucci says, that

> at one point [Vice President] George Bush came to me and said, Look, the president thinks you're firing too many people. So I wrote the president a handwritten note saying I thought this had to be done and I told him it will come out all right. And as Reagan says in his book, it did come out all right. The whole organization was dysfunctional. . . . You had Ollie North heading something called "political military affairs" . . . Well, that's the whole purpose of the NSC, so it gave, in essence, Ollie North a hunting license. And there was no general counsel . . . so I set up a general counsel's office. There was also a dual deputy system, which I don't like, since neither deputy seems to be totally accountable.[114]

Apparently, Carlucci's skills with firing became so good that he was called upon to do some heavy lifting on that front for the president.

> I saw how Don Regan had difficulty with a personality clash with Nancy. I'd had breakfast with Don Regan one morning shortly after I became national security advisor and I had picked up some reports and I said, Don, has anyone said anything to you about Howard Baker replacing you? He said no. At about 2:00 that afternoon, I got a call from Bob Tuttle, the personnel officer at the White House, saying, Frank, it's all over the TV that Howard Baker is replacing Don Regan, and I said, Well, that's very interesting, Bob, why are you calling me? He said because you're the next highest-ranking person in the White House, and I'm not sure anybody has said anything to him. And I said, Do you want me to do that? And he said, Well, somebody has to. And I said, OK, well, let me see where it stands. I called the president and I said, It's all over TV. "Uh oh." And I said, Well, Mr. President, have you said anything to Don Regan? "Uh oh."

And I said, Okay, well, listen, let me try? So I went to Don Regan's office and tossed out a *New York Times* report. I said to Don, I mentioned to you this morning they were talking about Howard Baker replacing you. I just want to tell you this is true. I guess I didn't put it in the most tactful way either, because he blew up. At that time I just went running back to my office and called the president and said, Mr. President, it didn't work, you're going to have to call him. I went running back to Don Regan's office just in time to hear the phone ring and it was one of the shortest phone calls on record. Yes, Mr. President, no, Mr. President, yes, Mr. President—click. Regan wasn't even going to take the call but I said, For Christ's sake, Don, it's the president. . . . And that's how Don Regan got fired."[115]

Regan was replaced by former Senator Howard Baker, one of the stars of the Watergate Committee hearings of the 1970s and a Republican heavyweight from Tennessee who brought his untarnished reputation to a tarnished White House much in need of it. As his deputy, he chose Ken Duberstein, a well-regarded political operative from New York City. Duberstein not only brought his network of connections with politicians and reporters to the White House, but he was also given the sensitive job of working with Nancy Reagan, who, according to Lou Cannon, "was once more openly welcomed as a political advisor."[116]

The new team functioned better than any other of the Reagan era, restoring both efficiency and reputation to the battered White House— which is not to say that it was easy. For example, Secretary of State Shultz made a run at Carlucci's authority early on, arguing in response to a new national security structure that had the national security advisor chairing a principals-level Senior Review Group that the appropriate role for the national security advisor is a staffer, not a principal of the NSC. Shultz recalled, "I told him that I had no problem with informal meetings of the National Security Council being coordinated by the national security advisor. In fact, I had created the Family Group with the idea that the meetings would be managed by the NSC advisor. But it would be a grave mistake, I said, for the NSC adviser, a non-statutory member of the National Security Council, someone not in the cabinet and not subject to confirmation by the Senate or to the accountability of appearance before congressional committees to be designated in an NSDD as the chairman of NSC meetings. Frank Carlucci is not a member of the NSC, I said, You are the staff of the NSC. You serve the principals of the NSC, especially but not exclusively the president."[117]

Carlucci brushed off the assertion, saying that he had not returned to the government to play an executive secretary role. He was a principal and, more important, he and Powell had a knack for keeping the interagency team together. Powell actually played an important role in helping to diffuse potential rivalries among the principals by creating a series of deputies-level policy review groups (PRGs) that, in fact, became a precedent for ensuing administrations—one of those few innovations any one team makes that is sufficiently good that their successors don't feel compelled to change it. Powell commented that the "Tower Report became our owner's manual. We did what it recommended. Carlucci issued an order that the NSC was not to become involved in operations. We advised presidents; we did not run wars or covert strategies."[118]

The problems with Shultz persisted as Carlucci grew more established in his role and went beyond chairing meetings to actually meeting with foreign leaders on his own (as he did on a trip to Germany in 1987). In August 1987, Shultz told the president that he was dissatisfied and that he didn't feel he could stay on. The president responded that Shultz should take a vacation and reconsider—which he did. And, as Baker later told Carlucci, Shultz complained about Carlucci to the president. Shortly thereafter, aboard Air Force One, Reagan asked Carlucci to find a way to work it out with Shultz. And so the two got together with their wives at Shultz's home in Palo Alto, California, and they spent a couple of days trying to work things out. However, by that time, it was also clear that Weinberger would be moving on and that Carlucci would replace him. So, Shultz came up with the idea that he, Carlucci, and Powell would meet each day at 7:00 a.m. in Powell's White House office. "No agenda, no substitutes, and just go over the day's events," Carlucci says, "and that proved to be a wonderful vehicle for managing foreign policy, because Colin was masterful with orchestrating the interagency process. And it certainly made the NSC more powerful."[119]

Powell and Reagan also hit it off: "President Reagan was a man of vision and big ideas and big principles. But at least from a foreign policy standpoint, he gave you wide latitude as to what you can do within these big parameters. I saw it when I worked for Weinberger and I saw it when I was at the NSC."[120]

By the time Powell was running the NSC, however, Reagan was in his late seventies and slowing down. Some in the administration felt he was fading. But even if he was, he finally had a professional team around him and they knew how to handle him. "In my days with Reagan," recalled Powell one Friday afternoon, "Reagan would leave . . . what's today, a Friday? It's now 4:30 p.m. Reagan left at 3:30. Reagan would have left an hour ago for Camp David, and I would not hear from him again until he got back on Sunday night. We didn't call him. We didn't bother him. It was Reagan's style, and the world was a little different. You can't do that any more."[121]

Duberstein recalls the late Reagan period as being one of unusual harmony on the White House staff. "One of the things we had at that time was mutuality and respect. Number two, we had people who had been around the track before. Number three, you had people who had experienced Washington before. Number four, egos were in check so that the NSC participated fully in the White House staff meetings and it wasn't separate. We organized a meeting every morning in which Carlucci, Howard, Colin, and I would sit down together prior to going to see the president."

> When I became chief of staff, I had six or seven chief assistants to the president and Colin sat in on my morning meetings before the senior staff meetings and before going to the Oval Office to sit with Reagan. After the senior staff meeting and before I first saw the president and the vice president alone, Colin and I would spend fifteen minutes together going through what I was going to bring up and what he was going to bring up when he joined us at 9:30. There were times when we agreed that I would set the stage because the president needed to have a scene setter coming from me rather than Colin hitting him just on foreign policy or national security issues. Or there were items when I would say, Let's take it off my list, you handle it, Colin. So we strategized our agendas every day. And we became a kind of family.
>
> We were kind of chief operating officers running the place on a day-to-day basis. So we would walk up and down the corridors five or ten times a day. Nothing went to the Oval Office without going through the chief of staff's office. But if you had something hot, you walk down the hallway, you pass the chief of staff's office on the way to the Oval, saying, Hey, we have to talk, here's what the situation is, and we need to let the old man know. And you'd throw on your jacket and you'd walk with Colin to the Oval Office. . . . So we're sharing an integrated version with the two of us rather than an NSC version only. We would take into account the other components, domestic and political overlays. That's how we ran the place. We made the pieces fit. Maybe it's the New York thing—Colin is from the Bronx and I'm from Brooklyn. I mean, when you're growing up on the streets of New York, you've got to put things together. You've got to build coalitions.[122]

And that they finally seemed to have learned how to do by the last years of Reagan's tenure.

In a sense, Ronald Reagan's NSC was an experiment designed to test the new model of the NSC that had been cultivated by Kissinger, Scowcroft, and Brzezinski. They tested the model the old-fashioned way, by breaking virtually every aspect of it to see what would happen. And over time, they ended up having rebuilt the system in a form that was not unlike what you might have found during the 1970s. In making mistakes, they also triggered a reexamination of the NSC structure via the Tower Commission Report that not only offered Powell and Carlucci their "owner's manual," but would also later prove to be an excellent preparation for Brent Scowcroft, the man who wrote the section on NSC reforms and would soon have the chance to implement them. Today, he is viewed as the guy who wrote the book on the NSC, and there is a reason for that: During the Reagan years, he actually did.

Of course, the costs of the experiments, failures, missteps, and political battles of the Reagan years were high. America had been bogged down in costly misadventures and there had also been a staggeringly high toll on the members of the administration themselves.

Select congressional committees held joint hearings into the Iran-Contra scandal, and in December 1986, Lawrence Walsh was named as special prosecutor to investigate wrongdoing by senior administration officials. Fourteen individuals were eventually charged with criminal offenses, including withholding information about the Contra aid from Congress, obstruction, and perjury.[123] Among those charged were former National Security Advisors McFarlane and Poindexter, Defense Secretary Caspar Weinberger, Oliver North, Richard Secord, and Elliot Abrams (who is currently on the younger Bush's NSC). While several of the officials pleaded guilty, North's and Poindexter's convictions were vacated on appeal because of immunity agreements with the Senate concerning their testimony, and outgoing President Bush pardoned Weinberger, McFarlane, and other officials who had been indicted or convicted for withholding information on or obstructing the investigation.[124]

Investigations of the Reagan administration were not limited to the Iran-Contra scandal, and a number of other ranking officials were convicted for a range of lapses. Attorney General Ed Meese was under investigation for much of his tenure in the White House and the Justice Department and resigned in 1988 after an independent prosecutor found that he "probably violated the criminal law" on four occasions but "there is no evidence that Mr. Meese acted from motivation for personal gain."[125]

The Department of Housing and Urban Development was enveloped with accusations of misconduct and cronyism, and ranking officials in the Defense Department, Commerce Department, Labor Department, Environmental Protection Agency, and Veterans Administration were also indicted and prosecuted.[126] In fact, all told, estimates of criminal prosecutions against Reagan administration officials exceed 130, by far the high for the modern era and, in all likelihood, ever.

The Reagan administration produced six national security advisors. Of the first four, the one who was probably the smartest—Poindexter—lasted the shortest time and got into the most trouble; the one who was least experienced—Clark—was probably was most successful; the one who was best known and best liked in foreign policy circles—Allen—become a complete nonentity in the job; and the one who was probably most competent—McFarlane—ended up evoking the tormented ghost of James Forrestal, one of those most responsible for creating the post in which he served, by attempting suicide in 1987 because he felt he had completely let down his commander-in-chief. But it was the last two who redeemed the process and set the stage for the shape and function of the post–Cold War NSCs even as the Cold War itself was winding to an end.

The Reagan era offers many parallels with the current administration, that of George W. Bush. In fact, the parallels border on the unsettling. For example, in 1985, during a spate of terrorist attacks in which perhaps 600 Americans were killed in a two-year span, Vice President George H.W. Bush issued a statement declaring "war on terror." That Bush was also in charge of leading that war on terror. Staffing that effort were people such as Richard Perle, Paul Wolfowitz, Douglas Feith, and others of the far right who saw the effort in ideological terms. Missile defense was a centerpiece of defense reform. We identified and overstated the capabilities of an enemy in an underdeveloped corner of the world (in the 1980s in Central America, in 2001 in the Middle East) and we waged a war against that enemy. Our "proconsul" in Honduras at the time was Ambassador John Negroponte, who became our "proconsul" in Iraq. Colin Powell played a central role and had considerable responsibility for cleaning up other people's messes. State and Defense fought bitterly. A weak NSC was eclipsed by bureaucrats who sought to gain advantage. And above all, a comparatively weak president was a comparatively ineffective manager of the interagency process that was there to serve him.

Interestingly, another parallel is that both administrations featured right-of-center, budget-busting populist politicians who won second terms handily against dry-as-dust Democratic candidates. Both presidents were popular despite the problems within their foreign policy apparatus—less so overseas, perhaps. But at home, the American people place an especially high premium on how these processes make them feel rather than how well they function in policy terms.

Ronald Reagan, despite presiding over a scandal-ridden administration and neglecting or ultimately not being up to the challenges of running the country, is one of the most popular presidents in recent American history. Whether or not it should be so is the stuff of barroom political analysis. That it is offers the crucial lesson that in the end foreign policy is about America's identity. If it enhances our sense of self or holds the promise of future enhancement, it is viewed as a success no matter how it is achieved. There is little comfort in that for wonks. However, the last years of the Reagan administration set the stage for a period in the management of U.S. foreign policy that demonstrated that one does not have to settle for image alone.

9

Across a Bright Line in History

I have but one lamp by which my feet are guided and that is the lamp of experience. I know no way of judging the future but the past.
—Patrick Henry

We stand today at a unique and extraordinary moment . . . Out of these troubled times . . . a new world order . . . can emerge: a new era—free from the threat of terror, stronger in the pursuit of justice, and more secure in the quest for peace. An era in which the nations of the world, East and West, North and South, can prosper and live in harmony. A hundred generations have searched for this elusive path to peace while a thousand wars raged across the span of human endeavor. Today that new world is struggling to be born, a world quite different from the one we've known. A world where the rule of law supplants the rule of the jungle. A world in which nations recognize the shared responsibility of freedom and justice. A world where the strong respect the rights of the weak.
—George H.W. Bush, September 11, 1990

IT IS NO WONDER that the words of President George Herbert Walker Bush on that very different September 11, on the eve of a Gulf War very different from that entered into by his son, resonated with an international perspective that was so thoughtful and measured and also so different from both his immediate predecessor and the son who would follow him to the nation's highest office. Experience matters, and few American presidents have come into office so well prepared to shape America's foreign policy. Of course, as we have seen, in the making of foreign policy, the character of presidents matters too. That is why one President Bush with a team that looks very much like that of another President Bush can have such different results. The Bush family would ultimately prove that in politics it's not nature, it's nurture—two presidents who share the same DNA but who have very different life experiences can produce radically different results.

In the recent history of U.S. foreign policy, there has been no president, nor any president's team who, when confronted with profound international change and challenges, responded with such a thoughtful and well-managed foreign policy operation as George Herbert Walker Bush. One can debate the outcome of individual policies, and, to be sure, there were missteps and misjudgments, but the elder Bush's administration, which was to be a bridge over one of the great fault lines of history, ushered in the "new world order" it described with great skill and professionalism.

That was no small feat, considering that many, if not all, of the most significant paradigms governing U.S. foreign policy for the preceding forty-five years went out the window for the team that presided over the end of the Cold War, America's emergence as the world's sole remaining superpower, and a new set of alliances to manage new threats in a new era.

Perhaps, given these changes, it is a good thing that the first Bush administration featured the last American president to have served during the Second World War, one who was steeped in the values and the debates that shaped the last great transition point in American and world history in 1945. But it was also a good thing that in the course of that president's career, which took him from Congress to running the Central Intelligence Agency, serving as U.S. emissary to China, and being an active and engaged vice president, he encountered and befriended a remarkably strong group of advisors who, with him, would form a national security team that is often described in universities today as the model of a well-functioning NSC and interagency process.

At the core of the new president's team were two men with very different but complementary skills, neither one a shrinking violet, both with very healthy egos, both extraordinarily close to the president, and both unafraid to share their unvarnished views with him. Incoming Secretary of State James Baker had run George H.W. Bush's presidential campaign and was a close associate and friend for many years, both in their shared hometown of Houston, Texas, and in Washington, D.C. Incoming National Security Advisor Brent Scowcroft had been national security advisor during the Ford years when Bush was director of the CIA. They had built a mutual respect and friendship over the years that enabled them to work successfully together during the Reagan years, with Scowcroft offering advice on strategic issues as well as serving on the Tower Commission when Bush was vice president. Scowcroft notes, "The president had been the DCI [Director of Central Intelligence] in an NSC system. He'd been vice president in an NSC system. He had watched people run it. He had good ideas about how it ought to be run. I had done it before. And we were all personal friends when it started."[1]

The comfort level among them, Scowcroft said, "enabled us to go short-hand with things like, for example, setting up a principals committee, that is, the NSC without the president, to resolve problems that didn't require him to be present. In the Reagan administration, [Secretary of State George] Shultz said he would not come to a meeting where the president was not the chair unless he was the chair. Well, you can't have a cabinet officer chairing a meeting with other cabinet officers."[2]

Baker, manager of three presidential campaigns, was clearly the more politically astute of the two. Scowcroft, with his military background and years of foreign policymaking service and study, was the more experienced international strategist. Baker was Mr. Outside, Scowcroft happier to work behind the scenes. But Scowcroft was perfectly willing to challenge his friend and knew that he was the one with greater minute-to-minute access to the president. It could have been a formula for familiar tensions. Instead, from the beginning, the two struck a bargain. "We agreed that he would be the administration's spokesperson on foreign policy but that I would speak from time to time as circumstances warranted," said Scowcroft. "And that if I was going to speak, we would try to discuss it in advance. This actually worked for the first few months. Afterwards, even if we didn't follow the deal strictly, we were always in close enough communications that there were seldom any major problems."[3]

"And," Scowcroft says with a smile that communicates volumes, "everyone did know how close I was to the president."[4]

Scowcroft quickly acknowledges that he, too, knew of Baker's close ties to the president, and that Baker could speak to him at any time on any issue. Perhaps more important, he knew that the president expected collegiality and openness from his team and would tolerate nothing less.

In *A World Transformed*, the book that Bush later wrote with Scowcroft and perhaps the most candid presidential memoir, Bush writes: "Brent and Jim did get moderately crosswise, but very rarely. Jim worried that he might be excluded from a decision that affected his department. As a former chief of staff, he knew how a strong-willed presidential advisor, if backed by the president, can easily isolate a cabinet member. It is probably accurate to say that the NSC staff and Brent were also concerned about what State might be up to. We tried very hard and I think successfully, to keep all the participants informed and eliminate personality clashes which could undermine policy-making as well as effective diplomacy."[5]

Baker, in his memoirs, says of the foreign policy team, "We not only enjoyed one another's company, we trusted one another. That's not to suggest we didn't disagree. . . . But our differences never took the form of the backbiting of the Kissinger-Rogers, Vance-Brzezinski eras or the slugfests of our national security teams during the Reagan years."[6]

A senior Bush administration official who worked for both men also saw the Baker-Scowcroft chemistry:

> They both have . . . quite different egos. Brent actually is kind of self-effacing, but he won't let anyone run over him. James Addison Baker III is not. And he doesn't preen before the cameras, but he does care a lot about how he is seen and treated by the press. Fortunately, Brent's concept of the national security advisor and indeed of the NSC was to never let us forget that the last name of the NSC is "staff." You were not the NSC but the NSC staff. That permeated his style. And, for example, I could not go up on the Hill or give a press interview without explicit permission from his office, which threw everybody. And Brent carried this forward . . . if you counted the number of times he was on television . . . you'd find a very small number. Because Brent's concept of the national security advisor is he's the inside guy, he's not the public spokesman. . . . Finally, Baker, like everybody else, had great confidence that Brent wouldn't screw him in Brent's private conversations with the president.[7]

Joining the president, Baker, and Scowcroft in the inner circle of the Bush national security team was Secretary of Defense Dick Cheney—who had been Ford's chief of staff when Bush, Scowcroft, and Baker served in that administration and who had subsequently gone on to a successful career in the congressional leadership, representing his home state of Wyoming with a cool, tough demeanor and a strongly conservative worldview. Also part of this team was Bush's chief of staff, former New Hampshire Governor John Sununu; the incoming chairman of the Joint Chiefs of Staff, Colin Powell; and several key deputies, notably Deputy National Security Advisor Robert Gates, a career CIA analyst who had risen to run the CIA's analytical operations during the Reagan years and who would later become CIA director under Bush, and Deputy Secretary of State Lawrence Eagleburger, who, like Scowcroft, until recently was a principal in the consulting firm founded by their former boss Henry Kissinger.

On the whole, the reputation that the Bush team had for effective collaboration is echoed repeatedly. This highly experienced group of professionals recognized that foreign policy creation and management is a collaborative art form—or, to use a different metaphor, a team sport. This is a fact that has been lost on many presidents who have viewed their cabinets as a series of individual slots to be filled and then could not understand why coordination became impossible, rivalries emerged, and ineffectiveness (and worse) resulted.

President Bush understood this and had fresh memories of the dysfunction of the Reagan years in his mind when he planned the team during the months after his election. Baker suggests that he knew from the beginning of the campaign that Scowcroft would be national security advisor. Baker's role was also clear. Cheney, a longtime associate of the other three and a fishing buddy of Baker's, was a natural but not first choice for secretary of defense. Indeed, some members of the Bush team have speculated that had Bush's first choice, Senator John Tower, been confirmed as defense secretary, he might not have fit in as well, nor been as easy for the president to manage given his years as an independent power source on Capitol Hill.

In addition to the Senate battle over the Tower confirmation, behind the scenes another set of battles might have suggested that all would not develop smoothly for the new administration. The transition from the Reagan to the Bush administration was not a smooth one. One senior Bush official rated it "cold to hostile." Another called it "the roughest I saw." Reaganites were quickly and coldly disabused of the notion that this was going to be a third Reagan term, as Baker reportedly told his aides that "this is not a friendly takeover."[8]

Scowcroft comments:

It was not as thorough a transition as I had with Brzezinski at the end of the Ford administration. But Colin Powell and I knew each other reasonably well. What I was interested in was what kinds of informal agreements we may have had with other countries that I might not have known about. But I didn't need a lot of detail. I told [Powell] to tell his staff that they were all fired unless I particularly asked them to stay. So I was comfortable stepping back in. I had just completed my service on the Tower Board, where we examined the NSC system and asked what went wrong with Iran-Contra and what should be done to fix it. And I talked at length with Colin Powell about how to fix it. So it's not fair to say it was a good or a bad transition.[9]

When pressed on the issue, the quiet and affable Scowcroft reflects a moment and says, "Well, yes. . . . We wanted it clearly understood that this was a new administration."[10]

As for the overall philosophy going in, Scowcroft says, "I knew that if I was not an honest broker and did not represent the views of my colleagues honestly, I wouldn't get anything done, because they would insist on seeing the president on everything. If they thought they were getting an honest shake with the president, then we could solve a lot of problems at a lower level. But the real key was the experience of the team, especially the president."[11]

To Dennis Ross, a very active member of the first Bush team as director of the Office of Policy Planning at State and who had served as Bush's campaign foreign policy advisor, it seemed that

Bush felt he was underutilized under Reagan, especially given his foreign policy expertise and that there was much more that he could have contributed. I think he was especially put off by the ideological divide between Weinberger and Shultz. It was such a constant struggle. He just felt that was dysfunctional in terms of how you conduct American foreign policy, which was obviously his main personal preoccupation. And so that was something he very much wanted to change. Moreover, though the president was personally cautious, he also felt that in many respects the Reagan administration—even with the change in Gorbachev—he felt it was too cautious, too conservative. He felt the world was changing and somehow we had to be up to it. Baker saw this as well, and we were convinced that we were on the brink of historic changes and we couldn't just wait until they emerged, we had to try to help shake them loose."[12]

Ross, a former McGovern Democrat who started as a Soviet specialist and rose through the foreign service ranks not only to the policy planning job in the Bush administration but also to renown as the chief U.S. Middle East negotiator for both the Bush and the Clinton administrations, makes an especially important observation when he notes that "every administration has a sociology":

A sociology in terms of how they are going to get along within. A sociology in terms of what the president wants in terms of the decision-making process. Both how it works but also what his relationship within that system is going to be. When Bush came in, he wanted to unlearn the lessons of the Reagan administration. He hated the leaks. He wanted the administration to work together. He wanted people who were in the key positions to be able to work together, and he wanted them to know that he expected their staffs to work together.[13]

The structure that the new administration put in place was established, per tradition, with the very first directive of the new administration, NSD-1 (yes—despite going to a more streamlined system, they, too, felt compelled to change the acronyms used for their various memoranda). There were only two subgroups to the council—the principals committee and the deputies committee. On the principals committee, which was chaired by Scowcroft, would be Baker, Cheney, Director of Central Intelligence Judge William Webster, Powell as chairman of the Joint Chiefs, and Chief of Staff Sununu. Other cabinet secretaries would be asked to join as required.

Scowcroft's deputy, Bob Gates, now president of Texas A&M University, describes the process behind the other subgroup, the deputies committee:

We had seen the subcabinet-level groups over a period of several administrations, at least I had, and Brent had seen them under Nixon and Ford, and one of the things that struck us was that they often were the number-three or number-four people in the department. Often those representatives would have trouble gaining access to their principal if a timely or quick decision or approval were needed, and the result was that the deputies or their equivalents would meet, but there were never any decisions made. The conversations would kind of go on in a circular way and people's views would be put out on the table, and something might happen, but most of the time it didn't.

So we decided to change that. The first requirement that we imposed was that everybody involved had to send their number two. That worked for the Joint Chiefs and for the DCI, but it really didn't work for Defense and with State. From State we had wanted Eagleburger, but Baker wanted Bob Kimmitt, the under secretary for political affairs . . . and, well, the corollary to the number-two goal was that we wanted somebody who could always get in touch with cabinet secretary, who could walk into his office without an appointment, who had routine communication with him all through the day, so that if we had a meeting that ended at one o'clock in the morning and I said we needed your principal's chop by four o'clock in the afternoon, we got it.

So those were the two criteria. And both Baker and Cheney made the pitch that in terms of the substantive policy issues, their number threes were in fact in more regular contact with them and knew their minds better than their deputies did, and that their deputies were more preoccupied in both cases with administering the department rather than working on substantive issues. And the result of that was that we ultimately agreed to Kimmitt and [Under Secretary of Defense Paul] Wolfowitz. And as it turned out, it worked out very well, because what the secretaries had said proved in fact to be true, that Wolfowitz and Kimmitt could get the ear of their principal at any time.[14]

In fact, during the Bush years, the deputies committee became the engine of the policy process. Formal NSC meetings were infrequent during the first two years of the administration and followed the pattern of dwindling off that takes place in all administrations, falling to only four in 1991 and three in 1992. Indeed, the principals group, while important, did not meet often either, because its structure did not consider an important factor—the interest of the president. And since a meeting was no longer simply a principals committee meeting when the president joined—and since George H.W. Bush was a very hands-on president when it came to foreign policy—another mechanism needed to evolve. As in past administrations, what filled the gap was an informal group that became exceptionally influential because of the comfort level of the key members with it and also with each other. This group, called the Gang of Eight, consisted of Bush, Scowcroft, Baker, Cheney, Sununu, Powell, Gates, and Vice President Dan Quayle. Their discussions, which were often held in the Oval Office, became especially important during the Gulf War.

This simple structure, drawn in part from the changes that had been made by Carlucci, Powell, and their colleagues in the final years of the Reagan administration, became so effective that it managed to overwhelm the impulse that had previously existed from administration to administration to toss out their predecessor's system and invent a new way, complete with new organization charts and new acronyms and usually lots and lots of new committees and subcommittees. Instead, because the next national security advisor, Anthony Lake, and those who followed him, Sandy Berger and Condoleezza Rice, all saw its merits, they have stuck with it, with slight variations, and the principals and deputies committee structure is at the center of the foreign policy formation process in the U.S. government today.

The evolution of the deputies as a linchpin in the process was supported by the uniquely high-quality nature of the deputies and senior policy staff who were part of the Bush team and by the relationships among them. At each agency, there was a core group that was exceptionally close to the principal and who worked as direct extensions of that individual with other agencies on an ongoing basis.

Baker's team was particularly tight and well defined because, as Ross put it:

> Baker doesn't have the highest trust quotient. So he trusts few people and he relies up on them. I was one of those he could rely upon very quickly. And Bob Zoellick [Baker's under secretary for economic and agricultural affairs and later U.S. trade representative under the second President Bush] was one of those people who had worked for Jim at Treasury. Margaret Tutwiler [Baker's chief spokesperson] was also obviously someone who had been with him and no one is more loyal than Margaret. And there was also [Deputy Secretary of State Lawrence] Eagleburger and [Undersecretary for Political Affairs] Bob Kimmitt, but it really didn't extend much beyond that.[15]

Cheney's close association with Wolfowitz, which later carried forward into the second Bush administration, created a similar team at Defense. Within the NSC, even with a smaller staff, there were a few who would stand out and play a much larger role on key issues than some of their colleagues. This group included, beyond Scowcroft and Gates, the two top members focusing on Russia and Eastern Europe, Bob Blackwill and Condoleezza Rice, and the Mideast specialist (who, on the streamlined staff, was also responsible for North Africa and South Asia) Richard Haass, all of whom would go on to even more significant roles in the administration of George W. Bush.

Bob Kimmitt, the under secretary who was part of Baker's inner circle, observes that the "people at the subcabinet level—Gates, Wolfowitz, myself, and others—all had grown up together bureaucratically, including during those eight years of the Reagan administration. We used to say we had long since figured out whether we liked each other and who thought what of this person's philosophy, and we really got right down to work. And we worked very, very effectively to make our bosses successful."[16] In this comment, as in several others, one must note the benefit for the members of the team (and arguably for the United States as well) provided by the remarkable period of political continuity that the United States had experienced with Republican administrations in place for twenty of the twenty-four years between 1968 and 1992. True, the Reagan top tier had included a number of more extreme voices than had been seen in other Republican administrations, but that was simply an issue of proportional representation of different factions at the highest level. Taken as an aggregate, a very similar group of politically affiliated appointees or politically acceptable career professionals had been working side by side for some time. Since top foreign policy posts are not ideally suited to on-the-job training, Judge Clark aside, particularly given the electorate's willingness to elect presidents with little or no foreign policy experience, this kind of collective seasoning is very helpful. It also points to a hidden danger in a two-party system: When one party dominates the executive for any extended period, the foreign policy skills of the other party atrophy and, even if they have a good team, they struggle to get up to speed once back in power.

Indeed, it can be argued that the reason for the success of the first Bush presidency's foreign policy team had a lot to do with the failures and struggles of the NSC throughout their professional careers. The Kissinger-Nixon obsession with secrecy, the Kissingerian *ubermensch*-centric policy processes, the Vance-Brzezinski and Shultz-Weinberger battles, the perils of "operationalism" that led to Iran-Contra, the paranoia of Nixon, the micromanagement of Carter, and the disconnectedness of Reagan all were signposts indicating what paths not to take.

The critical distinction is people, and that comes down to relationships, experience, and capabilities, beginning at the top with Bush but extending to every member of the inner circle. These interpersonal networks can afford access, speed, and efficiency that is not available even in a well-designed system if the relationships aren't there. For example, Bob Gates notes:

I don't think a deputy national security advisor—unless it was Brent with Gerald Ford—ever had a closer relationship with a president as I did. There was one time when we had a disagreement in the deputies committee about what the president wanted. So right in the middle of the meeting I said, "Well, hell, I'll just go up and ask him." So I did, I left the deputies meeting, walked up, went into the Oval Office to their little study, and I said, "Look, we're all wrapped around the axle on this issue, partly because we're not sure where you are or what you want. So, where are you?" And so I came back down and I said, "Here's what the president wants." And you only have to do that once for the word to get around that you can do that.[17]

Kimmitt drew from his experience in Nixon's NSC:

One of our ways of making things work a little bit more effectively is something I learned from the under secretaries committee back in the early Nixon years and from a couple of committees that existed in the Carter years . . . We used to try to meet as frequently after a decision was made by the president as we had before so that not everything was just about policy formation, we were also focusing on the critical issues associated with implementation.

So on a typical day during the Gulf crisis and war, I'd have a meeting of all hands in the State Department at 8:00 a.m. I'd pull in my small group at State just before the Policy Coordination Committee met at 10:00. At 11:00 a.m., we'd have a meeting of the deputies committee via video conference. At noon, I'd go over to the White House. We'd have the "deputies committee small group" meet. This group would prepare for the meeting of the Big Eight that would take place at 2:00 p.m., with Bob Gates, chair of the deputies committee, in attendance. Then the small group would often meet again after that, then the deputies committee via video, then the State Department group, and we just did an endless cycle of these meetings. I think one of the things we did especially well was getting good, clear instructions out to the field. As you well know, when the big guys meet, some issues are left open that aren't quite clear. We got these issues resolved before we sent instructions to the field rather than assuming that they would work them all out there.[18]

"We were lucky," he says, commenting on the value of having a group whose relationships and approaches to their work were tempered by decades of collective experience, "because events started hitting us fast and furious in '89, with the bubbling up of changes in Eastern Europe, then Tiananmen Square, the fall of the Wall and German reunification, the Philippines and Salvador insurrections, Panama, Liberia, the Gulf War, the coup in Moscow and the collapse of the Soviet Union. We really didn't have time for a test run. We got right into action, and it would have been a tough time for anybody. Luckily, we had a cohesive group on top and at the next levels down."[19]

Equally important, Dennis Ross claims, was the flexibility that was itself a product of experience and trust: "So much of what we did was outside the wiring that was created. There was hard wiring and there was soft wiring, and we used the soft wiring to help avoid differences before they started."[20]

Of course, there is much more to relationships than the simple practical realities of working together. These people were largely friends. Although they differed on a range of matters in terms of ideological perspective, there was no Baker-Cheney war to speak of, not only because the president would not tolerate it, but also because, in the words of Bob Gates, "they like each other, they fished together, they cussed at each other."[21]

Baker's relationship with Bush was also exceptionally close. In the words of one senior Bush administration official, "I could tell when I was in his office and [Baker] would be talking to the president and when they talked one-on-one they just talked differently than Brent did when he talked to the president. It was more of a conversation among equals—although I never heard him refer to Bush as anything other than Mr. President."[22]

The group also laughed a lot together. This might seem like a trivial observation, but in interviewing members of the senior teams for virtually every modern administration, it's a recurring theme. Successful administrations, like successful baseball teams, are loose, relaxed. NSCs and their staffs work harder than virtually any other professional group I know of, often with twelve- or fourteen-hour days, often six or seven days a week. In such an environment, humor is a critical ally.

In their joint memoir of the Bush years, the former president and his national security advisor (writing together in yet another demonstration of their special relationship) recounted more than one instance of where that sense of humor came into play. For example, Bush himself writes:

> Not that everyone always made it through NSC and cabinet meetings they attended. Often members would be racked with jet lag or had been up half the night struggling with a crisis. Despite valiant efforts to remain awake, they would sometimes fail. Brent worked the longest hours of anyone in the White House. He'd labor into the night, then go home to run, eat a light dinner, and get a few hours sleep. As a result, from time to time—well, maybe a lot—Brent would doze off in meetings. Perhaps *fall sound asleep* is a better description. He had it down to an art of style and form. He'd sleep solidly for a few seconds, then awaken as though he hadn't missed a beat of the discussion. We marveled at this ability to catnap and at what became known as the "recovery factor." This might consist of waking up and immediately writing something, anything on a pad, or a vigorous nod of approval as the speaker made what *might* have been a telling point, although Brent hadn't heard a word of the presentation.

Brent's sleep-and-recovery performance was so outstanding that in the first year of the Administration I named an award in his honor. *The Scowcroft Award for Somnolent Excellence* was presented at an annual festive dinner for the cabinet. Various cabinet members would, during the course of the season, observe the performance of contestants who they felt merited nomination for the prize, although the nominees did not need to be cabinet members themselves.

A secret, one-man "ranking committee" subjectively evaluated the contestants on soundness of sleep-and-recovery techniques, for which competitors developed all kinds of resourceful methods to take attention away from the nap itself, and from the fact that they had no clue as to what was going on around them. While the first award clearly belonged to Brent, who walked—snored—away with it, after that it became slightly more difficult to choose.

Some of the contestants earned the respect of the committee for the length of their challenges, or for the diverse nature and originality of their recoveries. Every once in a while a contender, clearly oblivious to the deep and prestigious honor of the award, would protest that he or she had not been asleep—just something caught in the eye, or the effects of a cold. The committee could not be bought off. It kept copious notes of the nominees' performances, which were then secured on a computer file.[23]

Showing a similar appreciation for the ridiculous in the job, Condoleezza Rice recounts how later during the administration,

a statue was going to be given to President Bush 41 by then-Soviet Foreign Minister Shevardnadze and it was of good conquering evil and it was St. George slaying an SS20 (intercontinental ballistic missile). And we thought that the thing—we were going to have a ceremony—and we thought that it was maybe this big (she extends her hands a few feet apart) and so it was going to be an Oval Office ceremony. This is something that Shevardnadze had personally gotten his friend to do, a personal commission, and about an hour before, I get a call and the people say, Dr. Rice, I think you better come down here. And the thing is six feet tall, it's enormous. And all of a sudden I have to arrange a new ceremony, and find, as we finished with it Brent turns to me and says, "Now find something to do with it." So, to me, it says what's it's like to be on the NSC staff. One day you're sitting meeting with Boris Yeltsin and the president, and it's kind of the height of what you thought you would be doing when you went to graduate school. And the next moment you're trying to find a place for a six-foot statue that doesn't have a home.[24]

.   .   .

Of course, most daily business was serious. History was approaching a pivotal moment, a reordering of the global power structure that required a series of dramatic reassessments of the U.S. role in the world and the challenges we would now be facing. Transitions are dangerous times. Not only does change bring upheaval, but the dangers are also amplified by the fact that all the old playbooks, the old guidelines for behavior, the old paradigms are thrown out. Leaders are forced to improvise, and the stakes are huge.

Like many other such administrations, therefore, one of the first things that the president did was request a series of policy reviews—which, naturally, had been renamed; they were National Security Review (NSR) papers, to go alongside the NSDs. Bush announced the first of these reviews along with Scowcroft's appointment two weeks after the election, on November 23, 1988. "We're going to take whatever time is necessary for a thorough review and analysis on our policy initiatives. Then [we'll] come out with our own strategic objectives and then move this country forward," said the president-elect. This was a signal that Bush would neither simply emulate the Reagan way, nor would he rush to new approaches. The reviews covered key regional concerns and important crosscutting issues such as arms control (NSR-14), which was handled by Arnold Kanter, and national security policy (NSR-12), which was spearheaded by Wolfowitz.

Scowcroft explains the rationale behind the papers:

One of the things I saw from the Nixon-Kissinger days is that there was a lot of resentment that all the policy seemed to come down from above. I thought that you ought to give everybody in Defense, in State, and so on, the sense they were participating. So you ought to have studies done. You ought to have prescriptions. . . . So whether their ideas were accepted or not, they felt like they had an honest hearing and that would give the whole process enthusiasm and help their productivity. I believed in that so deeply that when we started off the Bush administration, I started with a series of reviews of our policy in every area in the world: What's been good about it? What's been bad about the policy? And how should we change?[25]

After the briefest pause, he adds, "I've got to say, they were a real disappointment."[26] He attributes the general inability of government bureau-

cracies to do long-range planning as the source of his disappointment
with the review papers:

> When I was in the Pentagon, I was in long-range plans. We didn't do that
> very well. And again, in the administration, I set up a long-range policy
> shop, and it didn't work well. And one of my greatest frustrations in gov-
> ernment is how you do long-range planning. I don't know the answer.
> I'm still trying to figure out how you really do thoughtful work which is
> closely enough integrated with the day-to-day operation that people say,
> Yes, this gives us a kind of a road map and yet it's divorced from today's
> crisis.[27]

Of particular concern at that time to Scowcroft, Baker, and the president, however, was the uninspired nature of the review of U.S. relations
with the Soviet Union. According to those close to the process, it suffered
from the fact that many of those at the agencies writing it were simply
products of their own pasts, working to "protect their equities."[28] The
world was at a point of inflection, a watershed, and what it got was tired
bureaucratic formulations, the same old same old.

Gorbachev was the greatest puzzle facing U.S. policymakers. He clearly
intended to change the Soviet Union, but doubts remained as to whether
the Soviet Union was really changing. There was optimism among some.
Scowcroft was among the more cautious members of the team, feeling
that détente under Kissinger had become a goal in itself, rather than a factor to confront the Soviet Union.

> So the second time I brought that perspective in . . . Gorbachev . . . was
> making all these grand pronouncements and so on. But I said the bas-
> tions of the Cold War are still there. Eastern Europe hasn't changed at all.
> That's where the Cold War started. That's where it has to end. . . . And so
> our approach was that the Cold War really was not over and that we were
> still going to have to deal with the Soviet Union from a position of
> strength. But with our eyes open.[29]

Scowcroft knows that the issue is the subject of some debate among
Republican foreign policy circles. Because if what he is saying is true, the
natural conclusion is that Ronald Reagan did not, as his supporters claim,
actually bring about the end of the Cold War.

> Did Reagan's defense budget end the Cold War? I don't think so. I think

what they did is put pressure on them. But the Soviet system had its own problems. They had three aging or senile leaders in a row, Brezhnev, Chernenko, and Andropov. The system was faltering. They needed to reinvigorate it before the Reagan era. Gorbachev came in not to end the Soviet Union but to invigorate it and modernize it. And he started that by trying to increase productivity, which led to a huge boost in the economy. But in the process he started to dismantle the system which made it all work and didn't realize it. So I don't think it was direct pressure that made the Soviets realize they couldn't compete. And had it not been Gorbachev but another Brezhnev who came in, I think we still might have a Soviet Union. Of course, it would be pretty decrepit by now. But I don't think economic pressure alone ended the Cold War.[30]

Among the members of the senior Bush team with whom I spoke, there is almost universal concurrence on this subject—despite their recognition that it flies in the face of the orthodoxy of the far right.

In any event, by the time Bush had assumed office, Gorbachev's *glasnost* and *perestroika* were the new reality for Soviet leadership, and even more profound changes were afoot. Even as the policy review process was being undertaken, new developments were occurring. "Every administration," noted Richard Haass, "has key events. It's what the Kennedy School [at Harvard] would call phenomena that lead to policy windows opening. For example, the Bush administration had one, three or four weeks into it, which was February 15, 1989. That was the day of the conclusion of the Soviet military withdrawal from Afghanistan."[31] That event marked an admission of defeat on the part of the Soviets—now they, too, had lost their Vietnam—and another sign of their weakness. The change in their worldview confronted the new administration's policymakers. It came as negotiations were taking place with regard to short-range nuclear forces, and there, too, the Soviet stance had changed. Stirrings of unrest were felt again in Eastern Europe. And *glasnost* and *perestroika* were producing upheaval in the Soviet Union itself as stories of these changes, of the defeats in Afghanistan and the casualties and the errors in judgment, were actually being seen and read by the Soviet people. Frankly, it was perplexing to some in the policy hierarchy.

Dennis Ross circulated a memo by one of his staff that said that we "might well see the end of Soviet control of Eastern Europe in 1989 or thereabouts. I recall this was early on, and I recall I sent this memo around the European bureau at State and that the Europeanists all said, This is impossible. This is a nice guy who wrote this memo. But it could never happen. They were all just part of the culture—the Cold War culture—and they simply couldn't conceive that this was all going to change."[32]

But the changes were unmistakable. Especially in the nature of the dialogue between top government officials. In a meeting with Baker in March 1989, Eduard Shevardnadze, who would form a remarkably candid partnership with his U.S. counterpart, revealed the nature of that discourse when he admitted that the Soviets could produce a good ballistic missile but not a good syringe. As Ross recalled, the Soviet foreign minister asked, "How can we be called a superpower when can't produce a good syringe?"[33]

Says Ross:

> Even during the end of the Carter years, we had people doing all these demographic health studies, and by every measure you could see that this Soviet system was a system in crisis. . . . You could see that the contradictions were growing, whether by design or inadvertently. The Reagan policies may have sharpened the contradictions for a younger generation of Soviet leaders who then said, Look, you can't go on this way. If Reagan hadn't sharpened the contradictions, it would have taken more time. But it was a matter of time. Because the real shock to the Soviets is not Reagan, it was Poland. The shock to them is that here is a proletariat rising up. They know something has to change. And the leadership, at this point—they know they are the walking dead. And the Gorbachev generation knows they can't go on that way.[34]

Some of the Bush appointees to the NSC—Ross, Zoellick, Blackwill, and Rice—developed a new approach that combined the cautious desire to test Gorbachev and not to take positive changes for granted with a structure that would enable the United States to capitalize on any changes that did take place. The principal author of this approach, which really has to be seen as being of pivotal importance, was the young former ice skater who had earned her advanced degrees studying the Soviet Union at Stanford, Condoleezza Rice.

The Rice "think piece" laid out a four-point approach to dealing with Gorbachev. As Scowcroft recounts it,

> First, we should work on the domestic side to strengthen the image of America's foreign policy as driven by clear objectives. We could not meet Gorbachev head on if we did not appear confident about our purposes and agenda. Second, we needed to send a clear signal that relations with

our allies were our first priority. It would be important to underscore the credibility of NATO's nuclear deterrent through modernization. In addition, the alliance would soon require a political strategy for the upcoming conventional arms reduction talks and where we wanted them to lead. We would also have to prepare carefully for bilateral arms control, including START, which was closely watched by the world community. If we performed competently in arms control, the alliance confidence in our ability to manage the broader relationship would soar.

Third, after our review of policy, we might undertake initiatives with Eastern Europe. Since the Eastern Europeans were taking advantage of Gorbachev's invitation to exercise greater control over their own affairs, the region had become a potential weak link in the solidarity of the Soviet bloc. Our best tool would be the promise of economic assistance. Fourth, and finally, was regional stability. Recent developments in Afghanistan and southern Africa had raised hopes that U.S.-Soviet cooperation would spur agreements in other parts of the world. We had to work aggressively to promote regional stability, aware that the Soviet Union could be an important asset in some but not all places. . . .

The memo picked up on one intriguing possibility that [U.S. Ambassador to the Soviet Union Jack] Matlock, among others, had begun to suggest: that we might have leverage over Moscow because of its need for Western economic resources and know-how.[35]

The Soviet Union needed help to rebuild itself. This understanding provided the basis for the new administration's approach, which was revised as events in Eastern Europe began to unfold with unexpected but welcome rapidity.

For all the care that goes into planning foreign policy and for all the serious statements from foreign policy practitioners that make it sound as though they are dealing in the hard and fast rules and realities of a science, the processes by which any administration copes with and attempts to shape the flow of world events is much more like an art form. And if it is like any art form more than another, it is like jazz. The key players work together as a single unit, collaborating closely—the more intuitively the better, responding to new motifs and surprising changes with improvised counterthemes and working and hoping that the elements resolve themselves satisfactorily in the end.

When confronted with one monumental change after another, that is what set this group apart and enabled them to handle the rapidly shifting realities. It is easy in retrospect to assume that the collapse of the Soviet

Union, a coup in its government, revolution in Eastern Europe, "people power" revolutions around the globe that touched every government and toppled them from Warsaw to Manila, and the opportunism of Saddam Hussein, trying to capitalize on a world's distraction with such changes, would naturally have produced the world that it did or that these were all developments heading in a benign direction.

But with a lesser team, one inclined to react too quickly or to capitalize in the wrong ways or one that was not so careful to be in harmony with allies such as Thatcher and then Major in Britain, Chirac in France, and Kohl in Germany—and one that did not have the benefit of such capable allies—the outcomes could have been extraordinarily destructive.

"About four or five months into the administration, I was really struck by how pessimistic the CIA was about the prospects of Gorbachev's survival," says Gates, "and even of the survival of the Soviet regime. And so, in July, I sent a memo to President Bush and asked him for authority to set up under the deputies committee a very small, very secret task force to begin contingency planning for the collapse of the Soviet Union. And he agreed to that and it began in September of 1989, more than two years before the Soviet Union collapsed. Condi Rice was the chair, and I think the defense member of the team was Wolfowitz."[36] This small group came to play a pivotal role in helping to anticipate and prepare for some of the crucial issues to come.

As the NSC in its various forms grappled with the rapidly evolving U.S.-Soviet relationship, arms control issues were addressed largely by another small group, the "Ungroup," which was the name Kanter coined for the informal interagency arms control policy development process that he managed.[37] This interagency group, which "did not exist officially," was described by Susan Koch, NSC director for defense policy and arms control from 1991 to 1993, as much more effective on arms control matters than the "large, very unwieldy" Policy Coordinating Committee, playing a pivotal role on START II, the Conventional Forces in Europe (CFE) Treaty, the Chemical Weapons Convention (CWC), and the Open Skies Treaty.[38] Kanter noted that since President Bush was less engaged in arms control matters than in other foreign policy issues,[39] "on arms control there would be meetings of Scowcroft, Baker, Cheney, and Powell in Brent's office regularly without the president."[40] Steve Hadley, assistant secretary of defense for international security affairs (who later become deputy national security advisor and then national security advisor in the second Bush administration), ACDA director Ron Lehman, and John Gordon were also cited as important players in the arms control decision-making process and praised as a team that worked together enormously well.[41] Dennis Ross notes that "if one wanted to get things done, you worked with Steve. And it was the same way in our building. It wasn't so much the formal structure. We knew what the division of labor was in terms of who had what responsibilities."[42]

Says Kanter:

The Ungroup was interagency but it ran a gamut of bureaucratic status, which aggravated everyone. From OSD [Office of the Secretary of Defense] it was Steve Hadley, who was an assistant secretary. It wasn't Paul [Wolfowitz], who was the [higher ranking] under secretary of defense. The representative from State, Under Secretary Reg Bartholomew, was bothered to no end that he was meeting with an assistant secretary. He also didn't like that I was chairing these meetings, despite being just a special assistant to the president, while he was an under secretary. The key was figuring who could speak for their bosses and who would come with a problem-solving orientation. . . . Everyone came to the meeting and they all kind of checked their agencies' hats at the door, and it was totally a problem-solving ethos. . . . It was . . . the interagency process at its best. The people were not representing their agencies or their agency interests. It was not bureaucratic at all. And we just churned through the issues.[43]

David Gompert, who was NSC senior director for European and Soviet affairs from 1990 to 1993, also praised the Bush's arms control team, noting an

absence of ideological polarization, which I saw divide and debilitate a couple of administrations. Hawks versus doves in the latter half of the Carter administration, and unilateralists and multilateralists in the early Reagan administration. Perhaps the people who had been brought in were recruited because of their professionalism and their experience—brought in on merit and not political or ideological grounds. It was pretty much absent, or, if not absent, it was present but muted. Ideology rarely entered into debates over questions that in the past, in my experience, were always fraught with ideology. Arms control first and foremost. The only time I saw ideology creep up to the outskirts of an issue was the collapse of the Soviet Union and how rapidly we wanted to push that. Some people had been waiting for the day and others were a little bit more reserved. But I think that was mainly an idea-driven debate.[44]

Kanter drew a distinction between this process and the one they inherited, noting that "during the second Reagan administration, all matters concerning arms control became matters of high theology. And being burned at the stake was too good for people who got it wrong on these matters of faith."[45]

The arms control team devoted much of their energies to START, an initiative they inherited from the Reagan administration that a number of them would have liked to have discarded as easily as they had the ideological warfare. In particular, Bush, Cheney, and Scowcroft had notable misgivings about the late Reagan-era START process. Scowcroft had been aghast at the near-agreement at Reykjavik, writing that he felt the "Reagan Administration had disregarded the strategic aspects of arms control, placing emphasis on reductions as a goal in itself. It had, I believed, rushed to judgment about the direction the Soviet Union was heading."[46] Consequently, he convinced Bush to delay the resumption of arms control talks with the Soviets until mid-1989 and, before the 1989 Malta summit, Scowcroft once again raised concerns about "premature and illusory" progress on arms control, which he feared would be used by congressional Democrats to gut a number of military programs.[47]

American suspicions were alleviated, however, when Soviet negotiators, as Secretary of State James Baker expected, offered a number of concessions, the most important of which was a willingness to delink SDI's future from the START talks. Gorbachev's advisors had understood that Bush did not share Reagan's intense interest in the strategic defense, a sentiment held also by Scowcroft and most of the ranking members of his foreign policy team, with the exception of Vice President Dan Quayle.[48]

As the scope of Gorbachev's domestic difficulties grew, "arms control, once the centerpiece of U.S.-Soviet diplomacy, was increasingly being treated as underbrush that had to be cleared away."[49] American officials were increasingly engaged in (and astonished by) the rapid erosion of Soviet power in Eastern Europe. The reformist Soviet leader had intended to loosen control over the satellite states, granting them more political and economic autonomy. According to one of Gorbachev's aides, "Gorbachev was convinced that when these countries got their freedom, they would choose socialism with a human face. He believed they would not turn away from Moscow, nor run off to the West. He thought they would be grateful to Moscow and keep up ties of friendship with the Soviet Union."[50] However, once Hungary removed the barbed-wire barrier that prevented its citizens from entering Austria and the Polish communists offered to share power with the Solidarity movement, events took on a life of their own, dramatically highlighted by the fall of the Berlin Wall in November 1989. Robert Kimmitt recalled, "As you look back at what was going on in that spring of 1989, we were trying just to stay one step ahead."[51]

Bush and Scowcroft realized how delicate the situation was for Gorbachev, whose position they did not want to undercut, and the president took pains not to make remarks that could be seen as gloating or provocative. Before a trip to Eastern Europe in July, Bush informed several Polish journalists that "we're going in a constructive vein, not in some critical vein or not in some mode of trying to complicate things for somebody else. . . . I will not be trying to inflame change. . . . I'm not going to deliberately do anything that is going to cause a crisis."[52] Several months later, Secretary of State Baker pledged to Shevardnadze that the United States would tread carefully in Eastern Europe and would not exploit Soviet problems there, and Baker recalled that "everyone on the American side, as a matter of fact, felt it was very important that we assist Gorbachev and Shevardnadze and the reformers in the Soviet Union in any way we could to arrive at a soft landing."[53] President Bush took even more care with his words after being asked about his reaction to the fall of the Berlin Wall, scornfully noting the "foolishness" of advice from congressmen like Senator George Mitchell that he travel to Berlin to "dance" on the Wall.[54]

While President Bush and his foreign policy team avoided significant involvement in the collapse of the Soviet bloc in Eastern Europe, they did play a more proactive role in one of the main questions stemming from the withdrawal of Soviet influence—whether West and East Germany would reunify and, if so, under what conditions. While Western European leaders expressed some anxiety about the prospect of a reunified Germany, Bush saw it differently and, against the advice of Scowcroft and Baker, went on record as early as October 24, 1989—sixteen days before the fall of the wall—publicly stating, "I don't share the concern that some European countries have about a reunified Germany."[55] The president recalled in his memoirs, "I was not about to impose my own view on this highly controversial matter. I simply had a comfort level with it that others did not yet have."[56]

However, decision makers within the administration didn't share that comfort level and were divided on what steps should be taken. Initially, Scowcroft could not imagine that the Soviets would allow East Germany to leave the Warsaw Pact, let alone be permitted to join a West Germany that still maintained its membership in NATO (which had, after all, been formed to deal with the Soviet threat from the east). Noting that the "basic reality—East Germany as a Communist state within the Soviet sphere—

hasn't changed and probably won't change,"[57] Scowcroft, along with his NSC staff, was promoting an approach that would leave the decisions on the future of an undivided Germany to the Germans themselves, with the United States, the Soviet Union, and Europe uninvolved in the decision-making process. Baker, however, had opposed this approach, which he feared could result in a "train wreck."[58] Others in the State Department feared that it was "unrealistic" to preclude Moscow from playing a significant role in negotiating the economic, political, and military parameters of a reunified Germany.[59] Rather, Dennis Ross and Robert Zoellick suggested to Baker that Soviet participation was inevitable and desirable, but only under certain conditions.

After much debate, Zoellick and Ross convinced the State Department and the NSC to pursue a "two-plus-four" mechanism, in which reunification would be decided by the leaders of East and West Germany and the four victorious powers from the Second World War.[60] This formula was ultimately employed to bring about a smooth reunification of the two German states, but it caused rancor within the Bush administration

Philip Zelikow, who worked with Rice on the National Security Council (and who would later be the executive director of the 9/11 Commission and principal author of its report), added that "this 'two-plus-four' episode was a period in which there was a lot of hostility—I remember this very well. Brent was suspicious. He was suspicious of Baker personally. And at the level below Brent, that suspicion was acute and spilled over in consultations with people in Bonn, and so on. One of the interesting things about this episode, as I reflected about it much later, years later, and listened to people and recounted both sides, was that there was some real acrimony there, both personal and substantive."[61] Interestingly, though, Zelikow states that because the internal disputes never leaked into the press, the hostility dissipated and interagency coordination on Germany went on to work smoothly.[62] Such divisions are inevitable in any administration, particularly on issues that are as charged as the reunification of Germany was, given its centrality to the entire denouement of the Cold War. Successful interagency systems and the personalities of the players in such systems are capable of absorbing such tensions and then recovering, as the Bush interagency process did at that time.

Amid this seemingly unending stream of remarkable changes, American concerns mounted that the embattled Soviet leader would not be able to enforce any arms control deals reached between the two sides.[63] Furthermore, the lead arms control negotiator for the United States, Richard Burt, faced another problem—he would reach tentative deals with his

Soviet counterpart that would then be nixed by Washington, "often on personal instructions from Scowcroft." When Burt appealed to the secretary of state to intervene, Baker declined, unwilling "to tangle with the White House."[64]

Nonetheless, American and Soviet negotiators inched closer to a deal and, by June 1991, the two sides were addressing the final impasse, the issue of "downloading" warheads from existing missiles—that is, the removal (or de-MIRVing) of warheads from existing missiles.[65] Scowcroft was intransigent on this last issue, and Kanter kidded, "Desert Storm must have gone to your head, Brent. You're in the habit of achieving total victory on every issue in every negotiation," while other NSC staffers mused about abducting the national security advisor in order to gain the president's support for a resolution on the thorny downloading issue.[66]

The Ungroup was designated to resolve this matter and devised a compromise in July, but the Soviets rejected the plan. Finally, Secretary Baker intervened and persuaded Scowcroft to withdraw his objections. Kanter's Ungroup approved the final treaty language just minutes before a planned lunch between the two leaders in London. Bush and Gorbachev signed the START I treaty in Moscow at the end of July 1991, just weeks before communist hard-liners attempted to remove Gorbachev from power.[67]

They were revolutionary days, accordingly to Kanter, and wildly unpredictable: "I think it's fair to say that no one who was at that treaty signing in Moscow at the end of July had any inkling that a coup would take place in thirty days. And they would have laughed at you or had you taken away if you would have said before the year was out there would be no Soviet Union."[68]

In the remaining postcoup months of the Soviet Union, the Bush team struggled just to keep up with events, centering, of course, on the fall of Gorbachev and the concurrent rise of Boris Yeltsin.[69] In an NSC meeting on September 4, Bush's foreign policy principals debated what U.S. policy should be toward the Soviet Union, and particularly whether it should encourage a breakup of the wounded country. While there was support within the group for the independence of all of the Soviet Union's constituent republics and a significantly weakened Moscow, the administration did not declare such goals to be official U.S. policy.[70] Bush, Scowcroft, and the administration were more concerned about the fate of their diplomatic partner Gorbachev and the ascendancy of the erratic Yeltsin, described as "demagogic" by one senior administration official. As Scowcroft noted later in September, it was "not clear exactly to what end" the Russian president would use his power.[71]

Scowcroft writes that President Bush had expressed his interest, at a September 5 NSC meeting, in going beyond the START treaty to reduce the number of nuclear weapons on both sides. Defense Secretary Cheney had raised concerns about further strategic arms reductions, worrying that a START-plus treaty would be "premature" and "imprudent" and used as a means to exert pressure for large cuts in the Pentagon's budget.[72] Nonetheless, Bush was adamant, and Scowcroft noted that "we had to do this while there were leaders in power, both in the Soviet Union and in any successor states, who would work with us."[73]

At this moment, the work of the small, secret task force that Bob Gates had sought to create and that Condi Rice chaired came to be of special value. Gates remembers, "One of the key issues when the collapse came was that there were those in the administration who wanted not only the dissolution of the Soviet Union but the dissolution of Russia so they would never be a threat to us again. Defense reportedly advanced this view. But one of the principal conclusions of the small task force had been that our highest priority should the Soviet Union collapse is the maintenance of a strong central government in Moscow so as to maintain control over the nuclear weapons. We were able to use those conclusions to be able to quickly dispose of any thought of trying to make trouble in Russia."[74]

Just a few weeks after the failed *putsch*, possibly with the memory of the alarm that was felt by Powell and others about the uncertainty of who controlled the Soviet nuclear arsenal,[75] President Bush announced in September 1991, in a nationally televised address, a proposal for the world-wide withdrawal of all ground-based, short-range nuclear weapons; the removal of all nuclear-tipped cruise missiles and bombs from ships and submarines; the removal of strategic bombers from day-to-day alert status and the placement of their weapons in storage; and the removal of alert status on all long-range Minuteman II missiles.[76] Reflecting the pace of events in the final few months of the Soviet Union, NSC's Koch recalled that after the announcement of the presidential nuclear initiative,

A group of us—a standard interagency group—went to Moscow, arriving there on the 5th of October. Our task was to explain the presidential nuclear initiatives and persuade the Soviets to do something comparable. Three hours after we landed, Gorbachev went on Soviet television to announce his reply to the presidential nuclear initiatives.[77] We were extraordinarily effective—we hadn't met with anybody! Things were moving just so quickly. It was such a responsive relationship with the

Soviet government for some very specific reasons that probably will not be repeatable in history.[78]

Zelikow praised the role of the NSC in facilitating the rapid movement in arms control during this extraordinary time, stating, "Arnie [Kanter]'s group really caught some attention on that, because what they did in September of 1991 on the arms control front [and] the speed at which it was done on both the unilateral moves and the START II moves. It was done so fast that people didn't really realize the magnitude of what had been done."[79]

Gates, who for the last two years of the administration was serving as CIA director, observed, "Those arms control issues . . . tended to be the real issues, and there were generally three factions on them. One consisted of those who were most reluctant to move, naturally enough in the Defense Department—and I would add also the Joint Chiefs, who were also very cautious about how far to go. Baker wanted to go significantly further than Defense, but he was still pretty cautious. And then the radicals were the president of the United States and Brent. And Bush was always pushing people to be bolder."[80]

Several weeks after Gorbachev's agreement to match Bush's move, NATO agreed to withdraw 80 percent of its tactical nuclear weapons from Europe, and several of the Soviet successor states followed in kind over the next few months. Finally, a few weeks before Bush left office, he and Yeltsin signed the follow-up START II agreement in Moscow, which was overwhelmingly ratified by the Senate three years later.[81]

Another new element that would come to be seen as increasingly important in the ensuing post–Cold War environment began to influence the U.S.-Soviet (and soon to be Russian) relationship on arms control: the effort by American officials to stem the flow of "loose nukes" from the increasingly fractious nuclear power and to promote demilitarization. Senators Sam Nunn and Richard Lugar cosponsored the Cooperative Threat Reduction Program (generally referred to as Nunn-Lugar) in November 1991, which directed American funds and technical expertise for the safe and secure storage, transportation, and dismantling of nuclear (and chemical) weapons in the former Soviet Union.[82]

The Bush administration did not embrace the legislation, viewing the initiative as a "premature reduction of the defense budget and Congressional 'micromanagement,'"[83] but eventually backed Nunn-Lugar because they would retain discretion over how the funds were used. The effectiveness of the program was limited in the early years, however, because of resistance from Defense Secretary Cheney and other senior officials as well as a lack of centralized authority and direction within the federal government.[84] This is one of the few areas in which the Bush team's handling of the end of the Cold War and the collapse of the Soviet Union is most frequently criticized, and questions remain as to whether they acted fast enough to stabilize Russian nuclear, biological, and chemical stockpiles and to prevent the seizure of dangerous materials and weapons by independent actors.

Some attribute the poor results in this area to the simple stress of dealing with so many rapidly changing issues throughout this period, including the Gulf War. As Dennis Ross said:

> From the time of the invasion until the end of the war it was just an emotional roller coaster. You had the chairman of the Joint Chiefs saying there would be 50,000 body bags, and you didn't have the kind of support you wanted. . . . Enormous anxiety and critical energy was spent . . . by the time the war ended. . . . At the time, I was worried about the issue of nukes. I was very worried about the collapse of the Soviet Union. And I was very worried about the brain drain of Soviet scientists. I wanted us to come up with a much bigger program than we did. In the end we came up with something, but one of the things we need to consider is the simple question of how many big issues can anyone handle and for how long?[85]

The military had, at the time, a doctrine about being able to fight two and a half major wars simultaneously. But there was never such a doctrine for the very small group atop the policy pyramid. The central players run, even in easy times, from meeting to meeting and seldom have a moment to catch their breath or consider the connections between events. Particularly in the modern era, in which events transpire with great rapidity and news flows are so overwhelming—and in which threats are changing and proliferating—combating this kind of overload needs to be a new procedural and structural priority of those managing the foreign policy process. The impulse to overstreamline staffs needs to be resisted. It may look good politically, but no administration in modern history has ended up with a smaller NSC staff than it started with. The demands are too great and utterly unavoidable.

The scope of the changes experienced during the first Bush presidency was so great that its achievements cannot be minimized. Nor can its historic importance. Nor, as Condoleezza Rice recalled in 2004 as national security advisor, can we minimize the role that preceding NSCs had played in leading to this outcome.

> The last time I was here was the end of an era. And I'm quite convinced that we were harvesting decisions that had been taken fifty years before. And that the amazing thing about being here in '89 or '90 or '91 was that you would look back and you would say, Oh yeah, if we hadn't done that in '46 or '47—and I mean things like creating NATO or the decision to actually insist on a democratic Germany, when most of Europe simply wanted to split it up into, as Churchill said, as many of them as there could possibly be—you had the sense you were ending an era. And an era that had begun in times that must have seemed awfully chaotic and different, difficult, but somehow they found a way of putting in place institutions that then lasted for that fifty-year period and got to end it. I even had the sense that . . . it was like looking at the negative of an old photograph. You knew that these issues had been around for a long time.[86]

·   ·   ·

As has been noted, the timeline of the Bush era is remarkably packed with major events and secondary issues of consequence. While the collapse of communism in the Soviet Union and Eastern Europe may have dominated the headlines for much of the time from 1989 to 1991, it was far from the only newsworthy story. Two key tests also faced the administration as the dust around this "new world order" slowly settled. One, from China, concerned relations with a critical rising power. The other, from Iraq, reflected the changed rules in a world in which the U.S.-Soviet conflict no longer constrained the action of the United States—or any other country.

Indeed, the connection between those stories is part of the story of change that defines the years of the first Bush presidency, partly because the end of the Cold War coincided with the beginning of the information era. The significant adjuvant component to the end of the Soviet Union was not SDI but the newly wired world, one connected by emerging technologies and instantaneous communications. It became both increasingly difficult for closed societies to remain closed to global influences and increasingly obvious to them that they could not compete. Markets thrive on information, and managers in closed societies simply didn't have access to the information they needed to remain competitive even within their own rusting, centralized economies. To connect to the more dynamic economies of the West, *glasnost* was critical. As the societies opened, new technologies such as faxing and videocassettes along with improved television services and access to CNN and other Western news sources fueled dissent and spread news of successful initiatives to promote change.

It is largely for this reason that the velvet revolutions in Eastern Europe spread like electronic wildfire. What took years in Poland took months in Czechoslovakia, weeks in Hungary, and days in Romania—although clearly each transformation had an impact on the next. Moreover, the images of these spontaneous, peaceful, successful, people-driven revolutions spread around the globe, triggering the "people power" revolution of Corazon Aquino in the Philippines that forced the United States to rapidly drop its longtime allegiance to the corrupt administration of dictator Ferdinand Marcos. Even in China, the world's largest communist power, it looked for a while as though people power might triumph.

After the conversation with my father in Jodhpur with which this book began, I took a very unnerving flight to Bombay and from there flew to Beijing. It was early 1989, even before Bush's inauguration. When I arrived, I met with the senior officials of the Chinese newspaper that was to be my company's business partner in the publication of a small daily newspaper in Beijing later that spring. During those meetings with the executives of the paper, *China Daily*, the English-language organ of the government, we discussed planning but we did not anticipate the amazing story that would come to dominate the trip.

The Asian Development Bank meeting was held in May 1989. We toured Beijing, marveling at the long lines of customers outside the recently opened Kentucky Fried Chicken store off of Tiananmen Square. Some of the more senior members of the paper's staff were members of the Communist Party, but all of them were caught up in spontaneous demonstrations and marches that were taking place in Beijing during this year of "people power," some of them even joining the marches. The pictures I have of the events in my mind and those taken by our staff photographers show an exuberant scene, with smiles everywhere. There is a sense that this might be China's moment for a true "great leap forward."

When we left, there was no telling where it would all lead—but during the weeks we were there, it was peaceful, happy, and widely supported. Then, on the night of June 3, 1989, I watched the television in horror as the peaceful demonstrations were brutally disrupted by the Chinese government. The iconic image of the lone man standing up to the row of Chinese tanks defined the moment for the world, but the shattered dreams of the colleagues we had gotten to know in Beijing were what occupied my thoughts.

George H.W. Bush's experience of China stemmed from his experiences as a UN ambassador, CIA director, and chief of the U.S. Liaison Office in the People's Republic of China. James Baker, Bush's secretary of state, observes in his memoirs that "in the case of China policy . . . it's fair to say that very few policy initiatives were generated either by State or the National Security Council staff during my tenure. There was no real need. George Bush was so knowledgeable about China and so hands-on in managing most aspects of our policy."[87]

While U.S.-Chinese relations had been relatively trouble free after the August 1982 joint communiqué about arms sales to Taiwan, the pro-democracy unrest in the spring of 1989, leading to bloodshed in Tiananmen Square, naturally placed a considerable strain on those ties. Recognizing that "we could no longer do business as usual with the Chinese," as Baker writes, a response to Tiananmen Square had to be crafted that would acknowledge American revulsion at the killings without undermining the productive relationship that had produced economic and security benefits for both parties.[88] President Bush searched for a "measured response" that would allow the United States to remain engaged with the Chinese government and received advice from former President Nixon, who advised that "you can't let the bleeding-heart liberals destroy this relationship because of Tiananmen."[89]

After failing to get in touch with the CCP leadership by phone, President Bush wrote a letter to the Chinese leadership, which was reviewed by his national security advisor, Brent Scowcroft. Reflecting his closeness to the president, Scowcroft was given the delicate task of delivering the letter to the Chinese ambassador to the United States, which included the line, "I have thought of asking you to receive a special emissary who could speak with total candor to you representing my heartfelt convictions on these matters. If you feel such an emissary could be helpful, please let me know and we will work cooperatively to see that his mission is kept in total confidence."[90]

After Chinese leader Deng responded positively the next day, Bush quickly turned to Scowcroft, who could be more easily deployed secretly.[91] Baker agreed with the decision but asked for a State Department representative to accompany the national security advisor, recalling the deleterious consequences of allowing the NSC to "go operational."[92] Although Baker writes that he would have preferred to go on the mission himself but the need for secrecy made such a trip impossible, former Kissinger aide

Richard Solomon, who was assistant secretary for East Asian and Pacific affairs at the time, stated that "Baker dropped China like a hot potato right after Tiananmen."[93] Solomon added that Secretary of State Baker raised no objections to letting his deputy Eagleburger and Bush's NSA [National Security Advisor Brent Scowcroft] take the lead, noting, "State at that point played almost no role. Baker didn't want to get sullied by this nasty issue. He picked up on it, and he coined the phrase that 'the desk officer for China is in the White House.' He was delighted not to be involved. He let Eagleburger be the link to Scowcroft and the president."[94]

Further complicating the mission, Baker had said in testimony to Congress that he recommended the suspension of high-level contacts between the Americans and Chinese, a proposal that the secretary of state had not told the president or Scowcroft of in advance, according to Douglas Paal, a China specialist on the NSC.[95] James Lilley, who was U.S. ambassador to China at the time, also recalled the misgivings expressed by Baker's deputy about the mission, "With due respect to Larry Eagleburger, he never thought it was a good idea, right from the beginning. He said, 'This is going to have a huge domestic fallout.'"[96]

Scowcroft and Eagleburger departed from Washington early in the morning on June 30 in a modified military cargo plane whose identifying markings had been removed. After landing (with the aircraft parked in a secluded section of the Beijing airport), the Americans immediately met with Deng and several other top CCP officials. Overall, according to Scowcroft, the trip had served its purpose of conveying the "message on behalf of the President of the gravity, for the United States, of what the Chinese had done but also underscored for them . . . how important the President thought the relationship was to the national interests of the United States."[97] A second, higher-profile trip by the administration officials to Beijing to develop a "road map towards better relations" was also considered productive, although the national security advisor taking part in traditional toasts at a welcoming dinner produced widely circulated images of Scowcroft toasting the "butchers of Tiananmen Square."[98]

Criticism was pointed, and the entire sequence of events became an issue that candidate Bill Clinton later capitalized on during the 1992 presidential campaign. But, given the rapidly changing geopolitical realities confronting the United States, the collective desire of America's senior leadership not to add another crisis to their already too-full agenda can be well understood. Furthermore, as Clinton would soon learn, simply jawboning the Chinese leadership was not the most effective way to promote change in that society. China, too, was feeling the need to reinvent itself to adapt to the emerging realities of the information era and consequently would be facing pressures to change that would be far more powerful than any speech a senior U.S. official could offer. The moment to assist China with changes such as those that transformed Eastern Europe would perhaps come, but the consensus was to set aside the emotional reaction to the incident of the moment and to attempt to work the issues of change in a more muted, block-and-tackle kind of approach.

"Within the administration," observes former NSC staffer Robert Suettinger, "there wasn't really much debate."

> I mean [the president] was the China desk officer. He was described that way by a number of people. And there was always a sense you couldn't really influence policy because he was really invested in these issues. In any event, I think everybody was in agreement that this was a tragic set of events, but the relationship needed to be retained. There was no stepping back and saying, Well, those guys are real bastards and we shouldn't have a good relationship with them. [Within the White House and the administration generally] there wasn't anywhere near the level of emotional anger that there was in Congress or in the media or in the general public. Afterwards, it struck me that they just seemed to be too eager to kind of jump back into the relationship out of a sense that this was just a temporary roadblock and that everything is essentially is as it was before and that we can go back to that. The Bush people wanted to sustain the U.S.-China relationship in the face of overwhelming public approval. So it just became a question of how do we balance efforts to sustain this relationship in the face of very strong opposition from the Congress and from the media?[99]

.   .   .

While the government-led massacre in Tiananmen Square took the Bush team somewhat by surprise, the situation that was beginning to unfold in the Persian Gulf was perhaps equally unexpected. Brent Scowcroft observed that in mid-1990, "we were not preoccupied with Saddam Hussein."[100] The Bush foreign policy team was instead focused on the rapid and momentous changes taking place elsewhere. In addition, they were occupied with the usual issues of foreign affairs, from arms talks to summitry to their own "splendid little war" in Panama, during which the Bush administration essentially used the U.S. military to pick up that country's belligerent, drug-lord president, Manuel Noriega, and toss him into a prison in Florida. As a consequence, they were content to maintain the Reagan administration's policy of trying to maintain a balance between Iran and Iraq, while making "Saddam Hussein a minimally useful member of the international community."[101]

That search for a balance produced one of several great and tragic ironies of U.S. policy in the Middle East during the Reagan era. One of these was our rather indiscriminate support of the *mujahideen* who were fighting the Soviets in Afghanistan. So committed were we to pushing the Soviets out that we ended up supporting both the Taliban leaders, who later imposed one of the world's most repressive and backward regimes on that country, and Osama bin Laden, at that time a young, wealthy, not particularly well-known son of a Saudi construction mogul. Similarly, because of our desire to weaken Iran, we supported Saddam Hussein's Iraq during its war with Iran despite its horrific tactics, which included the use of poison gas.

Even when Hussein used poison gas against his own people, because of our policy we did little more than issue a press statement against the attack. One incident took place in the Kurdish town of Halbaja in March 1988. Samantha Power describes the attack in *A Problem from Hell: America and the Age of Genocide:*

> "It was different from the other bombs," one witness remembered. "There was a huge sound, a huge flame and it had very destructive ability. If you touched one part of your body that had been burned, your hand burned also. It caused things to catch fire." The planes flew low enough for the petrified Kurds to take note of the markings, which were those of the Iraqi air force. Many families tumbled into primitive air-raid shelters they had built outside their homes. When the gasses seeped through the cracks, they poured out into the streets in a panic. There they found friends and family frozen in time like a modern version of Pompeii: slumped a few yards behind a baby carriage, caught permanently holding the hand of a loved one or shielding a child from the poisoned air, or calmly collapsed behind a car steering wheel.[102]

Five thousand Kurds, including many women and children, were killed. According to Power, it was one of approximately forty such attacks by Hussein against his own people. Reagan's press secretary, Marlin Fitzwater, responded to the outcry in the press about the attacks by saying, "Everyone in the administration saw the same reports you saw last night. They were horrible, outrageous, disgusting and should serve as a reminder to all countries of why chemical warfare should be banned."[103] However, no demands were made, no actions taken. It was a pattern that would be followed after attacks in August of the same year, attacks that took place after the end of the war with Iran, could no longer use the war for cover, and were clearly just for the purposes of quashing Kurdish resistance to Hussein's government. Once again, despite a denunciation from Secretary of State Shultz, no action was taken.

In October 1989, President Bush signed NSD-26, "U.S. Policy toward the Persian Gulf," a top secret directive that stated, with regard to Iraq, "The United States should propose economic and political incentives for Iraq to moderate its behavior and to increase our influence."[104] The administration, according to Scowcroft, was also interested in facilitating the participation of American businesses in the reconstruction of Iraq after its long, ruinous war with Iran. Power, however, notes:

> The study . . . deemed Iraq a potentially helpful ally in containing Iran and nudging the Middle East peace process ahead. The "Guidelines for U.S.-Iraq Policy" swiped at proponents of sanctions on Capitol Hill and a few human rights advocates who had begun lobbying within the State Department. The guidelines noted that despite support from the Agriculture, Commerce, Defense, and State Departments for a profitable, stable U.S.-Iraq relationship, "parts of Congress and the Department would scuttle even the most benign and beneficial areas of the relationship, such as agricultural exports." The Bush administration would not shift to a policy of dual containment of both Iraq and Iran. Vocal American businesses were adamant that Iraq was a source of opportunity, not enmity. The White House did all it could to create an opening for these companies. "Had we attempted to isolate Iraq," Secretary of State James Baker wrote later, "we would have also isolated American businesses, particularly agricultural interests, from significant commercial opportunities."[105]

Because the United States had been so clear in its objective of engaging Iraq economically, Scowcroft had thought that the Iraqi dictator's tough talk about Kuwait had been bluster, not a precursor to military action.[106]

Despite all this history, or perhaps because of the mind-set we had developed over the previous several years, according to Richard Haass, the idea that Saddam Hussein would commit an as brazen as invading Iraq's oil-rich neighbor Kuwait was very hard for the policy community to gets its mind around. Even as more data on Iraq's growing belligerence toward Kuwait came to the attention of the NSC in July, Haass candidly said that the "idea that on a Sunday afternoon or something I was going to stroll into the Oval and go, by the way, Mr. President, Saddam Hussein is going to amass 100,000 plus forces and is going to walk into Kuwait and he's going to make this the 19th province of Iraq, and this is going to be major test of the post–Cold War world. It was too dramatic. . . . Maybe we thought that the era had passed when countries, if you will, [. . .] with all their military force and simply tried to erase other countries off the map. Maybe it was simply too big of a thought for us to comfortably absorb. And if that's the case, I plead guilty."[107]

Baker would later write, concerning the U.S. delay in recognizing Saddam Hussein for what he was:

> Diplomacy—as well as the American psyche—is fundamentally biased toward "improving relations." Shifting a policy away from cooperation toward confrontation is always a more difficult proposition—particularly when support for existing policy is as firmly embedded among various constituencies and bureaucratic interests as was the policy toward Iraq.[108]

Consequently, in the hours after Iraqi forces entered Kuwait, a stunned and more or less unprepared deputies committee met on the evening of August 1 to discuss the state of U.S. forces and determine which diplomatic, financial, and military measures could be implemented rapidly in order to demonstrate to its allies, as well as Saddam Hussein, that the United States was taking the Iraqi aggression seriously. Proposals to freeze Iraqi and Kuwaiti assets and offer a squadron of F-15 fighters to Saudi Arabia were discussed, while discussions of ground troops were deferred.[109]

Bush wrote that on Thursday, August 2, 1990, the first morning after the Kuwaiti invasion:

> Brent arrived just before 5:00. Visibly exhausted, he filled me in on the emerging details for the invasion and the discussions he'd had the night before. Iraq's official story was that it had moved in on the pretext that there had been a coup and that its "leaders" purporting to be the legitimate government in Kuwait, had requested their help. Our immediate options were limited. We had not yet officially been asked for help by the Kuwaitis or Saudis, but it was important to display promptly our support. I ordered our already alerted warships at the island of Diego Garcia in the Indian Ocean to head for the Persian Gulf. Our next requirement was to get air forces into the area. Brent explained that Bob Kimmitt was already

checking with the Saudis to obtain approval for sending an F-15 squadron. He handed me an Executive Order freezing the assets of Iraq and Kuwait in the United States. I signed it. At least we could take some economic measures.

After I showered, I headed for the Oval Office. At 6:30, Tom Pickering phoned to report on the UN Security Council's actions. Like Brent, he had been up all night working through the details of a resolution with the Kuwaitis and the other Council members. By morning, the Council had voted 14–0 in favor of UNSC Resolution 660 condemning Iraq's aggression, demanding that it withdraw its troops from Kuwait and demanding that the dispute be resolved by negotiations.[110]

Later that morning, the full National Security Council—including Bush, Scowcroft, Colin Powell, Norman Schwarzkopf, Dick Cheney, Paul Wolfowitz, Robert Kimmitt, DCI William Webster, and Thomas Pickering—gathered in the Cabinet Room to discuss the crisis. Webster began with an intelligence briefing, suggesting that Saddam Hussein had moved into Kuwait with more than 100,000 troops, far more than necessary, and could easily go on to defeat the Saudi's 70,000-man army. After a discussion of efforts to unite the world against the invasion, the conversation turned to U.S. interests in the region, with Treasury Secretary Nicholas Brady and Defense Secretary Cheney focused on the dangerous concentration of energy reserves in the hands of one power. Combined with Kuwait, Iraq now held 20 percent of the world oil reserves and would control 40 percent if they invaded Saudi Arabia. Add to this a million-man military, and the region faced a considerable threat, according to Cheney, a threat assessment backed by other NSC principals.[111]

Scowcroft recalled that he was not satisfied with the first meeting of the president's key foreign policy decision makers and afterward had a private meeting with the president to confer about the larger foreign policy issues that had not been addressed at the NSC meeting.[112] The national security advisor noted:

There was a discussion about what the significance of all this was and it distressed me because it was sort of, Well, it's happened now, you know, do we have to change the way we do business or whatever, but it was a sort of a resigned approach to a *fait accompli* and I thought that was not appropriate. . . . I told the president I was very distressed by the meeting, that there seemed to be no appreciation of the significance of this event to the national interests of the United States, and that if he didn't mind at the next meeting we would have . . . I would do something that I usually didn't do and make introductory comments about the significance of what had happened.[113]

Haass echoed Scowcroft's discontent with the NSC proceedings, saying, "I walked out of that meeting about as unhappy as I've ever been in government. . . . To call it unfocused would probably be uncharitable. What you had was a lot of people talking. . . . My sense was that Saddam had thrown down a gauntlet not just for the Gulf but for much bigger stakes. . . . There is a sense I had at the meeting that the people around the table didn't grasp it, they didn't get it and they were not responding commensurate with the stakes."[114]

The following day went much better, according to both Scowcroft and Haass. This time, Scowcroft opened the meeting (rather than the president, to promote a freer discussion) and made the case for a military commitment to the region—as Bush and he had discussed shortly before the meeting—arguing also that Hussein should be toppled using covert means.[115] Bush asked the secretary of defense to present military options the next day at Camp David. That afternoon, Bush and Scowcroft met with Prince Bandar, Saudi Arabia's ambassador to the United States. If the Saudis were going to ask for help, they needed assurances that the United States would not provide a halfhearted response that would leave Hussein in power and even more dangerous than before. Scowcroft called Cheney and scheduled a meeting for Bandar at the Pentagon with Powell, Wolfowitz, and Haass, where they would present the Saudi ambassador the American military plans (OPLAN 90-1002) and satellite photos showing the Iraqi disposition of forces.[116]

Haass said the Thursday and Friday NSC meetings were as different as "night and day . . . the Friday meeting mattered because it was . . . the way which the Government consensus came together after the awful first meeting and just simply, maybe by then thirty-six hours had passed, people had found their balance and had essentially gotten a sense of direction and a sense of purpose, a sense of seriousness."[117] Deputy Secretary of State Lawrence Eagleburger spoke up after Scowcroft completed his remarks, pounding the table and saying, emphatically, "Absolutely right," and a consensus quickly developed that the United States would have to respond decisively with force.[118]

Scowcroft recalled that in his discussions with the president about alternatives to the use of force to oust Iraq from Kuwait, "we both early came to the conclusion that sanctions were unlikely to be on our side. I never had any faith in sanctions and I don't think the president did either. I think he made up his mind early on that if Saddam did not withdraw of his own accord that we would force him out."[119] The meeting ended, but Bush, Quayle, Sununu, Baker, Scowcroft, Cheney, Powell, and Webster stayed behind for a restricted meeting. An intelligence report showed that the Saudis were thinking of offering large parts of their oil revenue to Iraq to stop Hussein from invading.[120]

The national security advisor was dissatisfied with the Pentagon's early briefings of military options in Kuwait at the White House and went to Cheney to let him know that he felt them to be inadequate. The image of Scowcroft, who during the second Bush administration came to be ostracized because of his concerns about the administration's Iraq policy trying to urge Cheney, a key architect of the 2003 invasion, to be more forthcoming with effective military plans for the first Gulf War presents an irony that cannot be ignored. Although Scowcroft was wary of getting involved in the military chain of command, he also proposed to talk to JCS chief Powell, but the secretary of defense offered to talk with him instead, and "Cheney subsequently developed a different kind of an option" more palatable to President Bush and Scowcroft.[121]

As the preparations for Desert Shield (designed to prevent Iraq from invading Saudi Arabia) and Desert Storm (to eject Iraq from Kuwait) unfolded over the next few days, the Policy Coordination Committee would meet at 9:00 a.m., followed by a deputies committee video conference at 11:00 a.m., which was, according participant Bob Kimmitt, the type of meeting in which "you can get about 75 percent of your work done."[122] Afterward, a subset of that committee would meet in the Situation Room, and Bob Gates, the deputy national security advisor who would chair the deputies meetings, would attend gatherings of the Big Eight.[123] Philip Zelikow, director for European and Soviet affairs on the NSC, remarked on how well the lines of communication operated, "backwards and forwards," during the Gulf War.[124]

In addition, according to Haass, parallel processes were developed to cope with the lack of advance planning within the NSC during its policy review process earlier in the administration.

The problem with too many of the policy planning notions in government at that they tend to occur at the beginning of administrations. What is important is policy planning every month you are in office. Constantly challenging what you do. During the Gulf crisis of 1990–91, every Saturday morning, Brent and I, or Brent, Bob Gates, and I, used to gather in

Brent's office. And Brent would be lying down on his couch, and he'd basically say, Okay, what do we do now? What do we do next? What aren't we thinking about? And we just institutionalized it. Every Saturday morning, the two or three of us would spend time taking a step back, saying okay, here's my list. Here's everything we're working on. What are we comfortable with? What could happen that we're not thinking of? And we just tried to do that, to stay one step ahead of events.[125]

Throughout the Gulf crisis Baker led an initiative to win support for the coalition. When the crisis began he was in Ulan Bator, Mongolia, after meetings with the Russians, and he immediately began working on the Russians as well as with the president and other top members of the team to get and retain support from key European, Asian, and Middle Eastern allies. Pickering, at the UN, handled the very painstaking work the administration undertook to ensure support for the various UN resolutions imposing sanctions and authorizing action.

While the entire administration agreed that it was critical to stop Iraq and that it was critical to have a broad international coalition in place to support us, not every player on the team had equal patience with the process of marshaling and maintaining international support. Dick Cheney "just didn't have much time for the international bureaucratic process, the diplomatic process," said one member of the team. "And in this respect, looking at his stance in the run-up to the second Gulf War, he has not changed his position when it comes to the UN or coalitions."[126]

But the work that the elder President Bush and his team did in building that international support was vital in helping to pay for first Gulf War and in sending two vital messages that the Bush team felt were central to their vision of the "new world order." The first was that Hussein's aggression "would not stand" and that in this new environment, the United States would not hesitate to enforce what we saw as the rule of law and our national interests wherever they were threatened. The second was that we would work hard in this new environment to maintain and build on established alliances, that we would not let them fall by the wayside as the main threat that they were designed to address faded away. Given the fluid nature of the times, these messages were important and helped ensure broad-based support for the president not only around the world but also on Capitol Hill.

On New Year's Day 1991, as the January 15 deadline for Iraq to withdraw from Kuwait approached, President Bush directed his NSC staff to draft a national security directive that would explain the justification for war. The following day Gates convened a deputies committee meeting to draft both the presidential directive and a letter to Saddam Hussein, which Secretary of State Baker would present to the Iraqi foreign minister at a January 9 meeting in Geneva.[127] Haass, who had helped write the letter, did not accompany Baker to Geneva but was instead working with the deputies committee to "play out" various diplomatic gambits from the Iraqis and test the coalition President Bush had crafted to ensure that Saddam Hussein wouldn't be able to "dominate a news cycle."[128]

The combat phase of the first Gulf War, which began on January 16 (Washington time), ended on February 27 after a six-week air campaign and a 100-hour ground war by U.S.-led forces. The decision to declare a cease-fire was driven by growing concerns among the president's inner circle about how images of the rout of Iraqi forces would be received by the international community. President Bush and his top aides rapidly came to a consensus to end the fighting, although it was reached largely without the input of Haass, the NSC's top official on Iraq, who was called to join the meeting after it got under way.[129] Scowcroft recalls how pictures of the "Highway of Death" (on the road leading from Kuwait to Basra in southern Iraq) and other scenes of destruction represented a "significant aspect of the decision that we did not want to look like butchers who were bent on revenge by slaughtering people."[130]

Furthermore, the administration had little interest in occupying Iraq and ousting Hussein with American forces, as then Secretary of Defense Cheney noted in a February 1992 interview:

> If we'd gone to Baghdad and got rid of Saddam Hussein, we'd have had to put a lot of forces in and run him to ground some place. . . . Then you've got to put a new government in his place and then you're faced with the question of what kind of government are you going to establish in Iraq? Is it going to be a Kurdish government or a Shia government or a Sunni government? How many forces are you going to have to leave there to keep it propped up, how many casualties are you going to take through the course of this operation?[131]

Instead, they believed that the Iraqi leader, after his overwhelming defeat on the battlefield, would be ousted by internal forces. To the surprise and consternation of the Bush administration, however, Saddam Hussein held on to power in Iraq—but many of the same decision makers would have an opportunity to deal with Iraq again, albeit in a markedly different international context.

In the choices surrounding U.S. action on Iraq, the first Bush administration chose rules and alliances, the old standards, to validate their
approach (despite resistance from the likes of Cheney). They could have
acted as the president's son, later president himself, did after the first foreign attack on U.S. soil in almost sixty years. Instead they followed in the
tradition of the vision for America and its role in the world that had been
established by Truman, Marshall, Acheson, and their colleagues in the
days after the Second World War, looking outward, investing in institutions, and building support for what the United States could do on its
own—but doesn't have to—around the world.

In the wake of the 1991 Gulf War, President Bush's popularity reached
an unprecedented high, with an approval rating exceeding 90 percent. But
the American people have a very short memory when it comes to foreign
policy. They are willing to celebrate a victory, they are willing to protest a
defeat, they are willing to mobilize in the face of a threat, but the rest of the
time, they would prefer it if their foreign policy were invisible and they
could focus on domestic issues. Unfortunately for George H.W. Bush and
his team, they peaked just a bit too early. By the following year, 1992, during the presidential campaign, the U.S. victory in Iraq had faded from the
public consciousness and Americans were more concerned with the flag-
ging economy and their president's apparent detachment from domestic
issues. Foreign policy issues grew mundane, partly because the prevailing
news, thanks to the skill of Bush's team, was positive: European unification, progress on global and regional trade accords, a new Middle East
peace initiative. The apocalyptic threat that had hung over the heads of all
humanity for two generations had seemingly disappeared, freedom and
democracy were breaking out around the world, and the United States was
more respected and, relatively speaking, more powerful than it had ever
been. The theme for the election, then, would be "it's the economy,
stupid."

And as he ran on that platform, the governor of Arkansas, a man with
very limited foreign policy experience himself, would also take shots at
some of the open issues that had been left on the international table by the
Bush team. Clinton criticized Bush's post-Tiananmen stance with China
as too soft. He condemned the Bush administration for its inaction in
Bosnia, where ethnic killing had left the streets running red with blood.
And he would express concern at violence and unrest in other parts of the
world, such as Somalia and Haiti, that had not been blessed with oil to
make them of interest to the United States.

Soon, of course, Clinton would claim his reward for a successful campaign—and assume responsibility for all these festering wounds that had been left unattended or glossed over in the last year of the Bush administration. He would also assume responsibility for crafting the "new world order" that Bush, Scowcroft, Baker, and their colleagues had ushered in. (Scowcroft coined the phrase.)

But, as Clinton took office, he and his team also had to be grateful that they would be the first post–Cold War administration, the first not to face the imminent threat of global thermonuclear war, the first to experience the freedom and responsibilities of being the sole remaining superpower, and that they would enjoy the benefits of all these developments having been ushered in without cataclysm or major mishap. Indeed, even the Gulf War, the largest conflict in which the United States had engaged since Vietnam, seemed a model of efficient warfare, superb diplomacy, and a reaffirmation of American strength in a country that just a decade before was wondering if its days of primacy were behind it. We got in, achieved the mission, and got out.

These developments were due in part to processes that had begun decades before and in part to historical happenstance, to being in the right place at the right time. But they were also due to the fact that at a pivotal moment in history, the U.S. foreign policy establishment found itself well led, well organized, and well manned.

Members of the administration have taken this message with them. Bob Gates says that the reason the political scientists at Texas A&M don't let him into their classrooms even though he is president of the university is "because I basically tell the kids to throw out their org charts and their textbooks, because I say the thing you really have to understand about Washington, D.C., is that at the top level, how things work depends on personality."[132]

Colin Powell delivers the same message another way:

Let me leave you with something I learned from Admiral Rickover, many, many years ago. I was at a ceremony when I was a young officer. And Rickover was present at the ceremony. After we promoted the person for whom the ceremony was being held, Rickover was asked to say a few words. He was legendary, and I was still a young colonel or something. And he just said, I want to remind everyone that it's not organizations that get things done. It's not fancy charts or plans. The only thing that gets everything done is people. And so the only thing that counts is the people you select for the jobs you have. And he was vicious—*vicious*—in selecting the commanders for his nuclear submarines. And the Rickover system was well known and feared. And that's why it worked so well. Because it isn't the process or the system as much as it is the people who form that process or system and who make it work—or who are responsible for its failings.[133]

10

The New, Improved, Post–Cold War, Information-Age, Indispensable Nation

History knows no resting places and no plateaus.
—Henry Kissinger, *White House Years*

A COMBINATION OF triumphalism and loss followed the end of the Cold War. Americans wanted to stop a moment and pat themselves on the back, and yet there were no ticker-tape parades, no sailors grabbing nurses for a victory kiss in Times Square. Worse, there were no immediate tangible results of the end of this war—the boys did not come back home, medals were not awarded, and the dark headlines kept filling the newspapers. The Soviet threat had been replaced by the risks of post-Soviet decay, of social chaos among nationalities that had, until that point, been held together only by force. Although Europe was no longer divided between East and West, not too far from "Trieste on the Adriatic," the place Churchill identified as the southern terminus of the Iron Curtain, there was violent unrest and perhaps much, much worse. Ironically, NATO was finally on the verge of taking military action for the first time only after the threat it was created to offset had dissipated. The insanity of mutual assured destruction seemed to have abated—and perhaps even more unsettlingly, it seemed to have worked as a doctrine—but were we actually safer, was the world actually more peaceful?

Not surprisingly, the intellectual engines of the United States were churning to produce a paper or a book or, better yet, a sound bite that would explain it all and provide a new organizing principle around which to arrange and develop America's international policies for the new era. The post–World War II era had George Kennan's "containment," the bumper-sticker version of his famed "X Article." The 1990s saw a competition afoot to coin the successor idea.

Two former members of the inner circle of the U.S. foreign policy establishment came as close as anyone to defining the parameters of the debate. One was Francis Fukuyama, a former member of the State Department policy planning staff during the early Reagan years and then its deputy director during the Bush years. The other was Samuel Huntington, Zbigniew Brzezinski's old collaborator and his former National Security Council staff coordinator of security planning. Fukuyama's book *The End of History and the Last Man*, published during the election year of 1992,[1] postulated that the politico-philosophical debate for the past several centuries over how to best organize society to both function and provide its members with necessary dignity had been resolved, it seemed, in favor of the principles of liberal philosophy. His argument was quickly oversimplified by the media. The whistle had blown, the game was over, and capitalism and democracy had won. Undoubtedly, some of the renown the book achieved was due to the fact that many people did not actually read its more subtle, nuanced, and sometimes densely academic arguments and instead wanted to buy into a kind of slightly premature, intellectually respectable millennialism: Here we are at the dawn of a new epoch, on the verge of a golden era, our way of life had triumphed and, comfortingly, would be preserved for the foreseeable future.

Huntington's *The Clash of Civilizations and the Remaking of the World Order* was published during the subsequent presidential election year, the second of the Clinton era, and was not quite as optimistic in its conclusions. Indeed, it seemed that its conclusions—if not actually formulated in reaction to Fukuyama's—were designed to respond to the post–Cold War euphoria with which *The End of History* was associated. Huntington's thesis was that with the end of the Cold War, we were entering an era not of post-historical harmony but one in which the fault lines would be cultural, not geopolitical, and that the West would find itself, again—or perhaps still—at odds with substantial portions of the globe for the foreseeable future. Huntington, too, lamented the oversimplification of his thesis by large audiences that knew the book's title but little else about it. He once wryly commented, however, that if having your thesis boiled down to a bumper sticker is what it takes to sell a lot of books, then perhaps it is worth the frustrations.

The two books have become emblematic of the debate in those imme-

diate post–Cold War years, although by no means do they offer a full picture of the range of the discussions in play at that time. What the success
of each indicates is that there was a significant hunger in the United States
(and around the world—both were global bestsellers) to make sense of
the new era.

Alongside the 1992 debates in many Washington think tanks about the
nature of the new world order, there was also debate about how America
could regain its competitive edge. Should we emulate Japan? Japanese
goods were thriving in our market, but our goods were not in theirs. It is
hard to remember now that for several years before that election, through
much of the late Reagan and Bush periods, articles were being written
about how American companies should model themselves after Japanese,
have open offices, perhaps even dress in uniforms and sing unifying company songs each morning.

At the same time, though, something else was happening that was as
momentous as the end of the Cold War. In 1989, Tim Berners Lee, a British
scientist working at the CERN nuclear research facility in Geneva, Switzerland, introduced something called the World Wide Web, enabling computer users to plug into a little-known global computer network called the
Internet (which had only 2 million U.S. users at that time) and be able to
retrieve information from throughout that network easily and swiftly.
American companies were the world leaders in the production of computers, computer software, and many of the other technologies that were
required by and would drive the information revolution. In 1992, as Bill
Clinton made his bid for the White House, the term "surfing the Web"
entered the popular vocabulary. Laptop computers were becoming popular (although my request for one at the Commerce Department in 1993
was still seen as something of an unreasonable demand and an oddity).
One of the images that helped sink President George H.W. Bush's campaign was his unfamiliarity with the optical scanner at a cash register—he
was seen to be out of touch, but perhaps worse, he was out of touch with
the force that seemed to offer the promise of saving America from relega-
tion to the second ranks of global economic leadership: technology. Bill
Clinton's vice presidential candidate, Al Gore, was famously associated
with the development of the Internet, and the two baby boomers were seen
as much more in tune than Bush with this percolating revolution that
might actually restore growth and vitality to a sluggish American economy.

Indeed, Clinton's decision to focus on the economy in the election and
the American people's decision to elect him, a man with no foreign policy
experience at all, over one of the most accomplished foreign policy presi-

dents in recent history, suggest that the one consensus that had been reached within the United States was that, at least at the outset, the difference between the Cold War and the post–Cold War periods would be defined by a shift of our focus nationally and internationally to prosperity and growth as engines of personal advancement, social harmony, justice, and peacekeeping.

This approach minimized the threats that existed and, insofar as it suggested that we could drop our guard, might be seen as somewhat premature. Indeed, the history of the Clinton era is very much a history of the tensions between the president's clear desire to put economics first domestically and internationally and the trade-offs that approach might entail or the blind spots it might create.

Whatever the merits of the approach, the new era that began with Clinton's election as president was signaled in a different way with the ringing of a telephone in a darkened hotel room in Frankfurt, Germany, just a few weeks after the election.

There, a sleepy Robert Rubin, cochairman of Wall Street's premier investment banking firm, Goldman Sachs, was awakened by Warren Christopher, the director of the president-elect's transition team. Rubin would later characterize the call as a "moment that changed his life."[2] It was also a moment that helped define the character of the Clinton era.

Rubin, a soft-spoken man who had the self-assurance of someone who had made tens of millions of dollars as a Wall Street trader and had risen to the very pinnacle of one of the world's most competitive businesses, had eyes that seemed sleepy even when he was wide awake. That night, he was invited by Christopher to meet with the president-elect to discuss a job that no one had ever held before, that of chairman of a new White House organization to be called the National Economic Council (NEC). Rubin had been a major donor and fund-raiser for Clinton and active in fund-raising for Democratic candidates for a number of years. Clearly, to some close to him, he was looking for a challenge beyond Wall Street, a world he had already conquered.

The idea of a White House economic council modeled on the NSC had been the subject of several think tank papers, study groups, and journal articles during the 1992 election year. Clinton later wrote that the NEC was conceived to "operate in much the same way the National Security Council did, bringing all the relevant agencies together to formulate and implement policy."[3] It says something about how far the NSC itself had come that in a new era in which economic issues were expected to replace security issues at the center of our national interests domestically and internationally, convening an "NSC for economics" was deemed the appropriate way to institutionalize the change in focus.

In *The Prince*, Machiavelli, whom many may consider the ultimate Washington insider despite his having died almost 250 years before the founding of the city, wrote, "It must be considered that there is nothing more difficult to carry out, nor more doubtful of success, nor more dangerous to handle, than to initiate a new order of things. For the reformer has enemies in all those who profit by the old order and only lukewarm defenders in all those who would profit by the new order."[4] The most successful reforms of this sort require the absolute commitment of a major source of power, such as the president; an exceptional champion for the reform in its early days, such as Bob Rubin was; and a little bit of luck, skill, or both.

The birth of the NEC needed to have all these things going for it, vulnerable as it was being killed off by those on the NSC or in individual departments who saw it as diminishing their power or cutting into their turf. It also needed the particular skills of Rubin and his senior staff: they would be bringing this new entity into being without the benefit of congressional approval, public debate, or the support of an experienced team in the administration—as Clinton's election marked the return of the Democrats to the White House after an absence of twelve years.

Clinton was both smart and lucky in having connected with Rubin during the campaign. He had been drawn to Rubin's intellect and accomplishment but also to his easy, unflappable manner and his humor. Rubin's low-key, self-deprecating manner would work wonders in reducing any concerns among those around him in the White House that he might be a threat. Along with the president's having unqualified respect for him and having bonded with him, events and ambition enabled Rubin to turn a job that had never existed before at the helm of an entity that had never existed before into a platform from which he launched one of the most influential cabinet careers of the past sixty years, ranking with George Marshall, Henry Kissinger, and James Baker.

In the early days of the transition, however, the idea of the NEC was amorphous at best. W. Bowman Cutter, a former executive associate director for budget of Carter's Office of Management and Budget who joined the Clinton transition team a few days after the election to work on issues related to economic agencies, recalls, "I don't think it was a highly defined idea in the president's mind. I think the president had said it was part of the economic menu that we are going to have a National Economic Council. I don't really think the president filled in the spaces below that at all."[5]

We talked about all this stuff and what it meant, and then [Jim] Johnson [then head of Fannie Mae] asked me—after Thanksgiving, I think—if I had any interest in being Rubin's deputy. And I said yes, and then Rubin and I had a couple of conversations. . . . It was in those conversations that we refined it, but basically we agreed that the NEC ought to be seen as a policy management and policy integrating organization. On the other hand, if it had followed the nebulous general consensus, it would have been a sort of in-house think tank—and that would be fun for about two months, and then it would be completely and totally irrelevant to anyone.[6]

It is clear that while much about the new council was ill defined, Rubin was working to crystallize it quickly, and he was getting the support of the president. Christopher has noted that during Rubin's trips to Little Rock he negotiated a "strong mandate for the new NEC."[7]

The path to the development of the Clinton economic team was not entirely smooth, however. As it coalesced, the team itself was taking a distinctly moderate, progrowth turn away from the Democratic Party's traditionally labor-dominated policies. Lloyd Bentsen, the incoming Treasury secretary, was known for his moderate leadership of the Senate Finance Committee, for championing the North American Free Trade Agreement (NAFTA) agreement that President Bush had gone a long way toward negotiating with the Mexicans, and for his strong presence as Michael Dukakis's running mate in 1988, where he provided the moderate, Southern balance to the ticket. Roger Altman, his deputy-to-be and a close associate of Clinton for many years, was a Wall Street investment banker. Leon Panetta, the OMB chief, had proven his centrist credentials while running the House Budget Committee for years and was seen as a real pragmatist. Ron Brown, the incoming commerce secretary, was known to be probusiness and had, as chairman of the Democratic National Committee, made an unprecedented effort to reach out to the business community during the campaign. The day after the election, Clinton had also offered the critical job of chief of staff to his friend of forty years, Thomas F. "Mack" McLarty. Although McLarty had very limited Washington experience and hence was viewed skeptically by some Clinton appointees who were more creatures of Washington, what experience he did have was on two commissions for the previous president, George H.W. Bush. Also, McLarty was himself a successful businessman and was CEO of Arkla, a Fortune 500 energy company.

This tilt to the center was discomfiting to some of the more left-leaning, traditional Democrats in the group, including, according to someone who was there in Little Rock throughout this process, two of the most influential figures in the innermost circle, Vice President Al Gore and First Lady Hillary Rodham Clinton. They were concerned that this group would be oriented too much toward "growth" and not enough toward some of the traditional concerns of the party. The discussions on the subject were apparently quite lively during the fourteen-hour days they spent hammering out who was going to be on the team.[8]

According to another source, doubts about the new NEC were bluntly expressed: Why do you need this? We already have too many agencies— aren't we supposed to be cutting back? Won't there be too much focus on production and not enough on public expenditure? Won't it complicate the process? Shouldn't the president defer more to the people he picks for the cabinet?[9]

At the same time, quiet concerns were expressed among some on the national security side that this new entity might eat into their traditional equities. The first sense that this might be the case came when Clinton chose to announce his economic team first, leaving national security selections until much later than usual. The office of the president-elect then had a well-publicized economic conference in Little Rock, convening more than 300 business leaders and economic thinkers. The summit— brainchild of Clinton campaign chairman Mickey Kantor, who would soon be nominated as U.S. trade representative—offered the president-elect a panoply of ideas on how to revive the economy, balance the budget, meet our health care obligations, and cope with a changing global economic picture. But mostly it showed him listening to the best minds in America and focusing on the issues that were most important to the American people. Almost 8 in 10 Americans looked favorably on this appetizer, this taste of things to come from an administration that was not yet in office.[10] Among other things, they saw the intellectual bent of a young president that would draw him to sharp minds and intellectual discourse, that would usher in the era of the "wonk" in Washington—and that, through the creation of the NEC and the elevation of economic issues to a central position, would create the most significant shift in both the White House's structure and the relative status of the national security apparatus in decades.

Only after this summit, and after several more cabinet appointments were made, did Clinton announce his national security team. Heading this group was Warren Christopher, who would be secretary of state. Congressman Les Aspin of Wisconsin was to serve as secretary of defense; another transition team member, former Carter NSC staffer Madeleine

Albright, would be U.S. ambassador to the United Nations (and would hold cabinet rank in this post); and R. James Woolsey was nominated as CIA director.

President Clinton recalled, "The national security advisor decision was difficult for me, because both Tony Lake and Sandy Berger had done a great job educating and advising me on foreign policy throughout the campaign."[11] In the end, Anthony Lake, Kissinger's former staffer and Vance's policy planning chief, was selected to be national security advisor. Sandy Berger, who had been Clinton's closest foreign policy advisor through the campaign, suggested that Lake, his former boss at policy planning and someone who possessed White House experience (unlike Berger and Clinton), take the role and agreed to serve as his deputy.

Richard Holbrooke, who would soon be named ambassador to Germany and would play an ever-increasing role in the Clinton administration, culminating with his service as U.S. ambassador to the UN and a member of the president's cabinet, comments, "I was a very strong supporter of Tony getting the job. I told Governor Clinton that he should get it. I also told Sandy, in an intense conversation in December of 1992, that Sandy should let Tony have the job and become his deputy, that Sandy wasn't ready for the job. I don't know whether I influenced Sandy or not . . . but I thought Tony had earned it, because of his intelligence and experience."[12] The relationship between Holbrooke and Lake went way back; they had been graduate school roommates—so close that Holbrooke made Lake the godfather of one of his children—and had both served in the foreign service as young men. Their relationship also included strong elements of rivalry, however, which would periodically produce considerable tension as the two attempted to collaborate during the Clinton administration on foreign policy operations surrounding critical issues such as Bosnia.

Lake's former boss, Henry Kissinger, reportedly said at a dinner party in 1992, right after Lake was announced for the job Kissinger once held, that although Lake was brilliant, he was temperamentally unsuited for the job and would fail in it. One of those present defended Lake, identifying his analytic skills and his in-depth understanding of the history of U.S. foreign policy formation as particular attributes in addition to his renowned intellect. That observer felt that Kissinger was speaking at least in part out of residual hard feelings linked to Lake's resignation at the time of the invasion of Cambodia during the Nixon administration. But that person, who knows the two well, also noted that the split with Kissinger was a "seminal event" in Lake's life and that once Lake became national security advisor, he was often guided at least subconsciously by a desire not to be like

Kissinger—or for that matter, Brzezinski, who had often been the bureaucratic rival of one of Lake's revered mentors, Cyrus Vance.[13]

Of the president-elect's choice for secretary of state, Clinton would later joke, "People ask me all the time, how did you ever decide to make Warren Christopher your first secretary of state? And I say, you know, I don't know—it just sort of came to me in the transition process, which Warren Christopher ran."[14] As Freudian psychotherapists would say, "There are no jokes." When planning for a high-level job in government, one excellent rule to follow is that a good place to begin is a high-level job in the transition—as did Christopher, Lake, Albright, Berger, Kantor, Robert Reich, Gene Sperling, Laura D'Andrea Tyson, Frank Raines (who later headed OMB), and Cutter (who became Rubin's deputy). Once again, proximity is everything.

Nancy Soderberg, a veteran of Senator Edward Kennedy's staff, played an active role in the campaign and in the transition and was rewarded with the number-three NSC job as staff director. She and her colleagues knew that it was critical that the relationships among them be mapped out early or they would run the risk of the kind of divisions and tensions that had afflicted the previous Democratic administration.

One of the relationships that was discussed was that of the vice president and his staff with the new NSC operation. Clinton had committed to giving Gore a strong role in the administration and expected to depend on Gore for his knowledge of the Senate and the Hill and of foreign policy. Gore, in turn, knew that he needed an active connection to the foreign policy formation process represented by the NSC. So Gore worked out a deal with the president by which his longtime foreign policy aide, Leon Fuerth, would not only serve as Gore's national security advisor but also would have the rank of a deputy national security advisor and would serve on the NSC deputies committee in his own right. Lake, Berger, Soderberg, and Fuerth discussed the details in the transition office. Fuerth recalls:

> There were very strong memories of all the dissent during the Carter administration, and they were determined to structure their arrangements and conduct themselves in a manner that would avoid ever making the same mistakes. Secondly, they recognized that there was an unusual relationship between the vice president-elect and the president-elect, and that needed somehow to be accommodated in our procedures. The net outcome of all this was that there was considerable devotion to process inside the top levels of the system. An attempt was made to create openness among the principals, and, as for me, the arrangement that had been

worked out was that I would have access to all the information that was flowing through the national security advisor's office, that I would partici-pate in all deliberations, with one proviso, that I would not take an issue to the vice president and get his fixed position on it during the time when the National Security Council was deliberating. In other words, that I would not walk into a meeting at the deputies level or the principals level and announce that the vice president had a categorical view of the issue while the others were still struggling to come up with a recommendation.[15]

Fuerth also made it clear that the vice president understood this rela-tionship and was comfortable with it.

It meant that within the principals committee and the deputies commit-tee, deliberations went on without the sense of anybody's thumb on the scale until the principals had decided. And this worked, and it worked rather well. Furthermore, another thing that was important was that we had an agreement among each other to observe a mantra, which was that if the choice was between chaos and conspiracy, choose chaos as the rea-son for something that really upsets you. By and large it was always chaos, but it put us in the frame of mind of not disintegrating into conspiracy theories about what everybody else was doing. I don't wish to present this as an arrangement that just worked smoothly from the beginning. It took a year before the patterns were laid. But the key point was that the vice president's influence with the president was such that if he walked into a meeting where the president turned to the vice president and said what do you think and the vice president then delivered an off-the-wall opinion, he could in fact derail the process. So my job was to make sure that he tracked in real time how these issues were developing, what people were thinking about them, what I thought about them—so that when the moment came, his opinion was always current and informed. As soon as he started to speak, of course, no one could predict what it was that would come out. He was not a captive of opinion elsewhere, and he had the right and the possibility of deciding differently than the emerging consensus.[16]

Those close to the process acknowledge that Gore's role was influential on foreign policy much in the way that Bush's had been with Reagan or Mondale's with Carter, and sometimes it would exceed those. Generally speaking, people felt that the system worked well, and two out of three former Clinton White House chiefs of staff with whom I spoke said they did not feel that Gore back-doored them or the process during his weekly meetings with the president. One implied that it happened occasionally and that Gore was the only person who really did do that but that his role was unique and arguably it was within his prerogative to do so.[17]

One of Lake's great contributions to the NSC process was drawn from his own history and the analysis he made in *Our Own Worst Enemy,* coauthored with I.M. Destler and Leslie Gelb, namely, the decision to retain the structure that had worked so well in the Bush administration. This was not only unprecedented, it was also something of an act of political courage, since past administrations had seen tinkering with the NSC structure as a way of imposing their identity on the process. But Lake and Berger agreed that maintaining a system built around the principals and deputies committees made sense, as did having the former chaired by the national security advisor and the latter chaired by the deputy national security advisor. Another early decision reflected in their first organizing memo, Presidential Decision Directive/NSC-2, was to elevate the position of UN ambassador to cabinet level. This was seen as an acknowledgment of the administration's commitment to multilateralism.

Lake's decision—and the president's—to maintain the Bush-Scowcroft structure essentially marked a watershed in the life of the NSC. It institutionalized the processes of the council—forty-five years after the council was created. After an incubation period during the Carlucci-Powell reconstruction of the NSC after Iran-Contra, then four years of Bush and eight years of Clinton, during which that process also worked well, the George W. Bush administration also carried it forward, giving the sense that today, after almost two decades, this is a structure that will be maintained for the foreseeable future.

However, the decision was not purely one of seeking the most efficient system or of stabilizing the processes within the organization as it went from administration to administration. It incorporated two additional, overlapping elements—recognition of a historical trend and self-interest. The historical trend was the ascendancy of the national security advisor to a position as an unchallenged equal of the other members of the national security cabinet and as an individual who, just six years after Shultz's complaints to Carlucci, was actually expected to be chairing meetings of the NSC. The self-interested element lay in Lake and Berger's desire to lock in the prerogatives and roles for themselves that had been enjoyed by Scowcroft and the strongest among their predecessors.

"Tony understood the politics of the NSC," said Berger.

He studied with Henry, the master, and one of the first things he did—

and I didn't really appreciate how important it was—was to do the PDD [Presidential Decision Directive] on organizing the foreign policy process and to get it sold during the transition. And it all was made to seem kind of basic and innocuous—and to this day, I am not sure whether Chris [Warren Christopher] understood at the time that this was really an important document in terms of how the government was going to be organized in the Clinton administration.[18]

PDD-2 was issued on the date of Clinton's inauguration, January 20, 1993. Five days later, the president signed an executive order establishing the NEC. But, as Bob Rubin explains, this institution was established, much as his own role in the government was, with a phone call.

Clinton said to me during the transition and after he had asked me to do this and I [had] said yes, that he was going to conduct all his economic policy through this process. And sometime during the transition, I don't remember when it was, I was in my office at Goldman Sachs, and he called or someone from his staff called and said he wanted to have a discussion of NAFTA. And he was going to do it by calling me and then he would arrange the meeting as a way of signaling the people this is how we plan to conduct economic policy.

It was very significant, I think, because he could easily call Sandy Berger or Tony Lake or someone else, and it easily could have unfolded in a variety of ways. But instead, he stuck to the discipline of the structure we discussed—in fact, I have to say that as a manager he really did have a good sense of discipline. And that was the beginning of it.

So [President Clinton] called me. He set up this call with Sandy and Laura [Tyson] and all these other people and then telephonically I chaired a meeting in which the president-elect conducted this discussion. That is what he said he was going to do, and he did. I had said to him at the beginning, these processes are followed or they fall apart very easily. People will start coming to you—and people tell me that you like talking to everybody that comes your way—and people come at you from all over—and maybe if they do and you start engaging with them, then you could very quickly undermine this whole idea. And he really didn't let that happen. And I have to give credit where credit is due—because Bob Reich, because of his friendship with the president, could probably have gone around the process pretty easily, but Bob didn't.[19]

Consequently, in that phone call, Clinton demonstrated the true nature of power in the inner circles of the U.S. government. It is not so much derived from statutes or congressional appropriations or executive orders as it is in a transaction between the president and the recipient of power. In fact, every top official, but especially those in the White House who do not have institutional interests and resources to back them up, is engaged in a kind of partnership, a symbiosis with the president in which the two together occupy the position in question. If the president is engaged and supportive and invests in the position and the individual with his limited and precious personal capital, then that person is empowered and able to function. If the president is not engaged or withdraws his support, then the role is diminished or made irrelevant. Sometimes individuals bring with them considerable personal stature, as did Rubin and Colin Powell, and some acquire it on the job, as did Kissinger, and this gives them somewhat more independent power—but, as we have repeatedly seen, this alone is never enough. Powell drifted away from George W. Bush and was effectively marginalized even though he had a higher popularity rating than his boss. Kissinger was diminished somewhat by the move from having two titles to just being secretary of state, because it underscored that the president wanted his role contained. And, as Rubin's successors at the NEC were to find out, if the president's commitment to an individual travels with that individual to a new post in the administration—as was the case when Rubin moved to Treasury—the relevance of the institution once associated with him can be diminished in his absence. I saw another example of this phenomenon personally when I watched as Ron Brown, purely on the basis of his very close relationship with the president, achieved a kind of authority that was unprecedented among commerce secretaries all the way back to the days of Herbert Hoover. As an official in Brown's department, I discovered—as did my counterparts at other agencies—that although Commerce had a reputation for being a powerless backwater, that reputation was trumped by the fact that the secretary could call the president directly and persuade him of the merits of his case. That Brown was the former head of the Democratic Party and was seen as a man who had helped elect the president and who had his own political base didn't hurt. When Brown died in a plane crash in 1996, despite his succession by other influential and capable men, such as Mickey Kantor and Bill Daley, in the absence of Brown's special relationship with the president and his unique political skills, the power ebbed from the department.

An effort was made early to help coordinate and balance the power of the two entities. "Before we got to the White House," recalled Rubin, "or right after we got there, Sandy and Tony got on the phone with Bo [Cutter] and me, and they said instead of having two international staffs, why don't we have one staff that will force both of us to work together, one staff working on trade and other issues where our responsibilities overlapped? And that's what we did. Sandy and Bo worked especially well together at the deputies level. Tony, as I recall, didn't have that much interest in the economic stuff for the most part."[20]

Lake actually had spent a considerable portion of his career in the years between his last term in government and the Clinton years working on issues in which development economics was very important. Berger had been a trade lawyer with the firm of Hogan and Hartson before joining the government. In this way, they also represented a change in the model for the national security advisor that was consistent with Clinton's changed view of post–Cold War priorities for the United States.

Chief of Staff Mack McLarty recalled that even before inauguration and despite assertions that Clinton had not given much thought to international matters, "President Clinton had well-formed ideas about international economics, globalization, and the whole set of emerging transnational issues. Of course, these ideas continued to evolve over his term of office, but they absolutely drove the president's commitment to the idea of the NEC."[21]

Nancy Soderberg agreed:

Clinton was always underestimated for what he knew about foreign policy. He has always had a natural instinct for it. I worked with him from June of '92 in Little Rock until he went to the White House in January. His instincts on foreign policy were impressive, and although it took him a little while to figure out how to implement them, he had a much deeper, vaster knowledge than people realized. And then, during the transition, issues kept coming up, like Haiti, like Bosnia, and like Somalia—so it became clear we were going to have to deal with them even if there was a strong desire to focus on domestic and economic issues.[22]

·   ·   ·

Meanwhile, even while the transition was taking place, the government continued to function in Washington. One example was the developing crises in Bosnia and Somalia. In the State Department, Robert Gallucci was serving as assistant secretary of state for political and military affairs. Gallucci now is dean at Georgetown University's School of Foreign Service. He recalls:

By the time we got to the election, about a thousand kids a week were dying in Somalia because aid workers wouldn't stay there and deliver food because of "the technicals" [renegade insurgents], these fourteen-year-old kids with anti-aircraft guns mounted on the back of jeeps. . . . That was the way we made the argument. We were not fools—the memo said Somalia: low risk, high payoff; Bosnia: high risk, high payoff. Bosnia had real shooters, and we did not think Somalia had real shooters. And in Somalia we could see a clear exit strategy. Anyway, Eagleburger got them to go ahead. . . . And he said we have no national security interests whatsoever in Somalia anymore and you don't know shit about Bosnia. He said, essentially, that he forgot more about Yugoslavia on a daily basis than I would ever know [Eagleburger had once been ambassador to Yugoslavia]. And I said, OK, but here are two pieces of paper, and we should do both of these things. He said to get the hell out of here and he took the paper. Two days later he called me back and he said that he couldn't get himself to argue the case for Bosnia. He argued for Somalia, and he said we are going to do Somalia. And he said, you are going to get on an airplane with Admiral [David] Jeremiah and go down to explain to the governor of Arkansas that when he gets into office he is going to find marines deployed in Somalia where we have no national security interest. . . .

[Eagleburger] was in a way my favorite person in government service. I liked his strategic approach to issues. I like his absolute clarity when he said things. I thought he cared about individual people. He cared about human beings. I think he was unhappy when he saw bad things happening he thought he couldn't do anything about. Many people in the [foreign] service were unhappy with him because he didn't fix certain things, but he was to me Kissingerian in his weighing of pros and cons, which is to say: without emotion.

Anyway, I went with Admiral Jeremiah, who was deputy chairman of the Joint Chiefs, in his airplane to Little Rock. There were Clinton, Gore, Christopher, Tony, Sandy, Soderberg, and some other people I did not recognize at the time. And when we finished, I could see that everybody wanted to ask a thousand questions. But the president-elect had, of course, the first question. His first question was not on the structure of the operation or what were the rules of engagement. He said, when will the kids stop dying? I liked that. I mean he won me, and that was the first time I met him, he won me right there.[23]

Gallucci's story illustrates the degree to which the Clinton foreign policy team was engaged in fairly serious and unanticipated issues early on.

But it also illustrates another important point about how Lake and the Clinton foreign policy team managed their development, which drew from their previous experience in government. They decided to keep a number of career staffers who had been in key positions in the Bush NSC and at State in their jobs or move them to other critical positions. Among them were people who would play a key role on critical issues for the Clinton team, such as Gallucci, who handled extraordinarily sensitive negotiations with North Korea; Richard Clarke, who became the NSC "go to" guy on critical issues ranging from multilateral affairs to the Y2K problem to, of course, terrorism; and Dennis Ross, who continued his role as quarterback of the U.S. government's Middle East efforts.

Of course, even the process of retaining those people did not go smoothly. Gallucci remembers that in the final days of the transition:

> The transition guys come in and [incoming Assistant Secretary of State for African Affairs] George Moose, whom I knew a little and respected, was working on the transition and says, we are going to need this office. And I said, I understand that. So we were expected to leave and I said, hold on a second, George, you know I'm actually a career guy and so while I will be leaving this office, you will continue to have me to kick around some more because I am prepared to declassify documents until I find something else to do. He said, OK, all right. As he left, I immediately called Tony at the NSC, I mean within five minutes, and I said, I just got fired. So if you are looking for somebody . . . And he said, well, why don't you come over and be senior director for nonproliferation. I said, yes, I accept. He said, great. So I called George and I said, George, I will be leaving actually right away because I am going to go be a senior director of the NSC. So he then calls me back five minutes after that and said, we'd like you to stay at your job here. I said, OK, that's great, George, but for how long? Until you find someone else to be the assistant secretary? And he said that was the plan. And I said, then in that case I'm going to the NSC. And then he calls back five minutes later and said, we would like you to stay permanently? And I said, will I be reconfirmed by the Senate? And he said, if necessary, yes. And I said OK. And I called Tony back and said, Tony, I'm going to stay, and he said fine.[24]

·   ·   ·

A major problem for Clinton and his team, almost from the beginning, was that they found their campaign rhetoric did not easily fit with the realities they were immediately forced to cope with. The burdens of governing descended upon the group suddenly and rather uncomfortably. Young, brash George Stephanopoulos, who was the face of the administration for many people, recalls the difficulty of those first months in office.

> It's funny, ours was a campaign that had put out comparatively few statements on foreign policy. Then we came into the White House and almost immediately we were hit with foreign policy problems. For example, you had the immediate problem with Haiti—which started even before the president was inaugurated. Haitians started to build boats and head toward the States. . . . Clinton had been seized by this when he was governor of Arkansas, but during the campaign he had criticized the policy of repatriating Haitians. It was very clear that from December 1992 on or so, unless he made a very strong statement saying that the Haitians would be returned, that he would immediately have been faced with a problem on our southern shores, which was no way to begin a presidency. So . . . he started out with a broken promise or a perceived broken promise on Haiti. Similarly, with Bosnia: very tough statements during the campaign and a lot of difficulty making good on them during the first several months of the administration. Same with China, where he had been very tough on Bush for being too close to the Chinese and then we had to pull back.[25]

Tony Lake had written about this phenomenon, and now he was put into the difficult position of having to live it. It is not just an issue of breaking campaign promises or being caught by over-promising; there is an underlying dynamic that he has given substantial thought to. Reflecting on the period and the broader issue, he observed:

> I think this is a pattern of American foreign policy throughout the Cold War and even now: the rhetoric that succeeds is the rhetoric of the shining city on the hill, morality, evil versus good, etc., whereas the realities call for pragmatism. Every president gets trapped in the difference. And some presidents are like Johnson, who, in order to sell policies that are failing in Vietnam, wrap themselves all the more in the rhetoric and sink themselves even farther as the gap between the goal—the rhetorical moral goal—and the reality of what you can do grows.[26]

He notes that this same phenomenon has afflicted virtually every modern president, whether it was Kennedy, who pressured Nixon from the right about not being tough enough on Hungary and the Suez Canal and then was trapped by his own rhetoric when it came to the Bay of Pigs, or Nixon, who tried to outflank Johnson from the left and offer peace only to get into office and struggle with the fact that peace was not nearly as easy to achieve as advertised. This rhetoric-reality gap is a stumbling block, he says, for many presidents, especially in their first years in office. Only a very few, he notes, such as Eisenhower, have had the personal stature to resist the pressures from within their parties to over-promise.[27]

"There is another piece of this," Lake adds insightfully,

and that is if you put yourself in a president's head about the domestic politics of a decision, you have to ask yourself not only what the reaction will be if he does something, but, more importantly perhaps, what the reaction will be if he does not. Let me give you just a few historical examples: Hiroshima. If Truman had not dropped the bomb on Hiroshima and later it was discovered—as it would have been—that what would have been a bloody, costly invasion or even a blockade of Japan might have been unnecessary, he would have been lynched for having the winning weapon and not having used it. Or in 1950, if Truman had not crossed the thirty-eighth parallel [in Korea], which turned into a disaster at a time when some critics were saying that he was practically a Soviet agent, their only explanation for his inaction would have been that he was soft on communism. He never could have proved that crossing into North Korea would be a mistake. Leap ahead to the Bay of Pigs. Kennedy, in the campaign, to show how tough he was, had endorsed an exile attack on Cuba. When elected, he is presented with a plan Eisenhower had developed that, politically, he has to approve. If he concluded that it wouldn't work, he was screwed, because the Cuban exiles were going to come back here and say the invasion would have succeeded. It is what Peter Widen has called the "disposal" problem. Flash forward again to Jimmy Carter in 1980 and the failed Iran rescue mission, Desert One. Cy Vance, for whom I was working, was sure it wouldn't succeed. But if Carter had canceled it, and the military planners said it would have worked, it would have confirmed a public view of Carter's "weakness," right? Now why are these examples all about Democrats? Because Republicans are somewhat inoculated from this. They are thought to be tougher. If they don't take an action—as with Eisenhower when he didn't rescue the French in 1954 in Indochina—then people trust their reasons not to have done it. But at the same time, when Republicans make war, all hell breaks loose because people instinctively think that they are predisposed to fight. . . . So, if you are a hawk, vote for the Democrats and convince them to go to war. If you are a dove, vote for the Republicans and convince them to make peace. The reason they can act politically is that they don't generally do those things.[28]

Lake's perspective on Somalia during the Clinton years is that "the cliché is that we just pulled the plug on the troops, which isn't true."

We negotiated with Congress to try to get more time and finally reached a compromise. That compromise then was portrayed as a Democrat just pulling out where Bush could have done it. But Clinton gets a bit of a pass on Haiti, Bosnia in 1995, even more on Kosovo, because he was a Democrat taking action. And if a Democrat says we need to send the troops, then people are more likely to say yes because he must have had good reasons since he was probably reluctant.[29]

Madeleine Albright says of her Democratic colleagues:

There is a desire to see all sides. I think the left is a bit less doctrinaire about things, and there probably is a difference between people who are center-left versus center-right. The far left and the far right are just as doctrinaire, and the center-right has been practically eradicated—or there are far fewer of them in the center-right before you get to the radicals. Overall, though, I think there is a quality among people who are center-left, which is a unique openness to other people's ideas—that you are more willing to listen to a lot of different angles rather than being so dead sure about something and missing the possibility of another perspective. While I recognize that these may be gross generalizations, I do think that there is more of a "democratic" view about things within the center left and that there is more of an expectation that people have a right to express their views. It may be a fault . . . but I believe it is a reflection of our recognition of the complexity of the world. The world happens to be complex. And I think there is a value in understanding the different sides. Every Democrat I've ever worked for or studied has been accused of being indecisive. Harry Truman was an exception. But from FDR to Ed Muskie, accusations of indecision have always been prevalent. However, being decisive on behalf of wrong is not a virtue. So I think that we do probably enjoy and like the intellectual decision-making process.[30]

That process was criticized as being unruly and undisciplined in the early Clinton years by some who were unaccustomed to it or uncomfort-able with it. Most notable among these was Colin Powell, who, after hav-ing attended a number of meetings with senior Clinton principals on the early challenges facing the administration, complained that the discus-sions were like college seminars. "At the very first NSC meeting," he recalled while sitting in his office during the last months of his tenure as secretary of state,

> it was a rough meeting, with the Clinton administration, maybe a few days in. And it was on Bosnia, I remember. We all showed up in the Sit Room. And in my days with Reagan and Bush, you walk in, everybody knew where you were supposed to sit and you sat there. And there was an agenda and you followed the agenda. At this meeting, Clinton was late—that told me something at the beginning. We all went into the Sit Room. Everybody grabbed whatever chair was there. And when Clinton came in—the president—there was no chair. We'd already taken the chairs around the table. We were now at the coffee house. And so we had to kind of make room for the president of the United States and the vice presi-dent of the United States. And it didn't bother anyone—I'm going oh-oh-oh—but everybody just sat around and started chatting. [If] you had come in from Mars and didn't know who was who, you would have joined that conversation [not knowing] who the president was. And that was Clinton's style—it never changed. Well . . . it changed a bit—it changed when he realized it wasn't working.[31]

Albright responded to this criticism by commenting:

> I have to describe Powell to you when he was chairman of the Joint Chiefs of Staff. Part of the problem was that we were all new, and Powell seemed like the grown-up. And this may sound crazy to you, but somebody walks in with a uniform and has a chest full of medals and is the hero of the Western world . . . there is a certain something about a winning military commander, and if you're a civilian woman, it's even worse. I do think I might have felt the same way as Powell after four years or longer in a pre-vious administration had I been there for a term prior to our new arrival, because you have to spend time unearthing the previous policies and get to the core of the issues. I think it's critical to have intelligent people dis-cuss policy, especially when you have just gone through a shift in parties and administrations. Although I wasn't in Washington for some of the first term because I was physically in New York as UN ambassador, there

is no question that we did go around in circles on Bosnia, which most certainly led to a significant amount of frustration between me and Powell. He did not want to use force, and I thought we had to.[32]

Albright, despite being just a "civilian woman," famously upbraided Powell during one of the long Bosnia debates when he spoke about the risks and resisted the use of U.S. troops and she asked sardonically, "What are you saving this superb military for if we can't use it?"[33]

Some loved the more informal meeting culture of the Clinton administration, the late nights and the pizza deliveries, the Saturday sessions in blue jeans, the casual air, the preponderance of young staffers, many from the campaign, many who had never worked in a White House before. It was like democracy in action. It was a diverse group and a smart one, and it was full of energy.

Unfortunately, the problems that it faced in rapid succession were knotty ones. Lake referred to the initial litany of foreign policy problems as their "brown blobs," according to Berger.[34] Somalia. Haiti. Bosnia. North Korea. These were the issues floating out there, threatening, demanding attention but eluding a solution.

The president stumbled and fumbled through those early months, under a variety of self-imposed problems and constraints. One was the campaign promise to cut the White House staff by 25 percent, a promise that extended to the NSC. The staff was cut from 179 to 143, of whom sixty were professional, a number they struggled to stay with during the first term as they repeated a common mistake made by new administrations: Virtually all assume that their predecessors were wasteful. Many attempt to cut the NSC. And virtually all then watch it balloon back up to the size they cut it from and usually more. Why? Because the role of the NSC has grown as the scope of issues it must keep track of for the president has grown. It is a genie that won't go back into the bottle.

The new administration also created turbulence for itself with foolish mistakes, the most notable early one being the administration's stance on gays in the military, which created a controversy over a tertiary issue that could easily have been handled later and could certainly have been handled in a different way. Instead, it produced great tension with military leaders who already were skeptical of the new president given his antiwar history and his avoidance of service in Vietnam. Furthermore, many members of his administration, including Lake, were seen to be products of the ferment and antiwar politics of the Vietnam era, and those wounds were slow to heal. Powell's dismay with the lack of discipline in meetings was one manifestation of this. The notable failures of Secretary of Defense Les Aspin as a manager at DOD were another. Despite his distinguished career on the Armed Services Committee in the House, he was not a manager, and many of those who worked most closely with him, while admiring him as a man, felt that he quickly alienated the military and civilian personnel in the Pentagon. As one put it, he "lost the building—and once you lose them, it's very, very hard to win them back."[35]

In addition to impediments, there were absurdities that neither helped the image of the administration nor the comfort level of some in it. Clinton writes in his memoirs of a retreat in late January 1993:

> On Saturday night there was a session, run by a facilitator who was a friend of Al Gore's, in which we were supposed to bond by sitting in a group, taking turns telling something about ourselves the others didn't know. Though the exercise got mixed reviews, I actually enjoyed it and managed to confess that as a child, I was overweight and often ridiculed. Lloyd Bentsen thought the whole exercise was silly and went back to his cabin; if there was something about him the rest of us didn't know, it was intentional. Bob Rubin stayed but said he didn't have anything to say—apparently such group unburdening wasn't the key to his success at Goldman Sachs. Warren Christopher did participate, probably because he was the most disciplined man on the planet and thought this baby-boomer version of Chinese water torture would somehow strengthen his already considerable character.[36]

Perhaps the greatest impediment, however, was the president's engagement in foreign affairs. While those closest to him to this day speak of his "instincts" and his "voracious appetite for knowledge" and his "brilliant ability to absorb new information," others in the administration called a spade a spade. I vividly recall a conversation with a colleague who, during the first year of the administration, stormed out of a meeting with the president and said, "You know how everyone says the problem is that this guy really isn't a foreign policy president? Well, the reality is . . . he's not. And it's hurting us." This same individual, who was very dry and professional and not inclined to innuendo, soon after expressed frustration that in those meetings the president would give my friend precious little time for his policy briefing but would offer one or another of the more attractive women in the crowd considerably more time regardless of the relative importance of the subjects being discussed.

Nancy Soderberg observed:

The difficulties were that the decisions we made were the wrong one in many cases in the first two years. We tried to do Bosnia without having to use force. We tried to do Haiti without having to use force. We were wrong about the use of force in Somalia. So it took us two years to figure out what our new approach to problems like these would be. Essentially, we had as a central question to define the role of the use of force in the post–Cold War era. When we won the Cold War, people wanted the troops to come home. They didn't understand the need to continue to engage and use force. Baker and Bush 41 felt the Europeans could solve Bosnia. We wanted to let the Europeans try and solve Bosnia for the first two years, and it took us a year and a half to figure out that they couldn't and define a much more nuanced use of force and diplomacy that worked. In hindsight, you wonder why we didn't do it faster. But when you're in there it's not obvious what the right courses are. For example, in these cases we had there was not a threat on the par of World War II or even Vietnam or Saddam Hussein being in Kuwait. And for the military, the use of force threshold was very high. We had Colin Powell saying we could only use force if we were willing to commit a couple hundred thousand troops. And I sat through meetings in the White House when Colin Powell would say we can't do anything in Bosnia with less than two hundred thousand troops. So how are you going to say, OK, overnight we're going to decide we're going to do air strikes to support diplomacy and develop an endgame when Congress didn't want to do it, the State Department didn't want to do it, the Defense Department didn't want to do it, and the American people felt . . . "you're going to do what?" It was just not clear to most policy makers in 1993 that we actually had to use force to stop the killing in Bosnia. Although Clinton called for it during the campaign, when he got in he learned . . . none of the European allies were there, nobody wanted to do it.[37]

Clinton's NSC did order military action against a familiar foe by the middle of their first year in office. The provocation was a foiled assassination plot against former President George H.W. Bush during a trip he made to Kuwait. It was very quickly demonstrated that the Iraqi intelligence service, working for Saddam Hussein, was behind the plot, which was discovered and broken up just one day before the former president's arrival in that small Gulf country. Clinton sought recommendations on how to respond to the incident and the suggestion from the Joint Chiefs was a Tomahawk cruise missile attack on Iraqi intelligence headquarters.

The argument for such a limited action was that it was proportional and would be a deterrent. Colin Powell had advised against continuing the march of American troops to Baghdad during the first Gulf War and now, again, he was recommending against a more intensive assault on Saddam and his regime.

Some in the administration were unhappy with the response. Notable among them was CIA director Jim Woolsey, whom the inner circle of the Clinton crowd very quickly came to view as a malcontent. He felt that their principal objective was to keep foreign policy out of the headlines so that they could deal with domestic economic issues, and that meant essentially doing nothing and keeping a lid on the "brown blobs." He himself felt isolated, felt that the president was not interacting with him, and he was frustrated that the president had opted to simply read his daily intelligence briefs and not have the briefer in to his office . . . so that Woolsey spent a lot of time "just cooling my heels outside the Oval Office."[38]

When the plot against Bush was discovered, Woolsey said,

> It was clear from the beginning that it was Iraqi intelligence. . . . The bomb was Iraqi-produced. It was a typical Mukhabarat bomb. The Mukhabarat does not typically go off on frolics of its own. We determined that it was Iraqi intelligence, government . . . the president wanted another look. So he sent some FBI forensic people over, and they took another couple of weeks, and they came to the same conclusion. [Then] there began some discussions—and some of these were with Tony—of what ought to be done. . . . I had some ideas, some fairly substantial targets that could have been focused on. That was known in the White House and the NSC. As the planning went on, it was not clear when and if a decision was going to be made. I was being given an award by an organization out in Montana, and I flew out to that and left my deputy in charge, Bill Studeman, former director of naval intelligence, former head of the NSA, one of the most solid and substantial and knowledgeable people about intelligence in the country. The first thing either Bill or I knew about the strike, or what had been selected for targets, was when we were called, I out in Montana at this conference, Bill, I guess, at home, that this strike was under way. So there was apparently some kind of NSC meeting at which it was discussed, and the decision was made as to what was going to be targeted or something, but you couldn't prove it by us— because neither of us was there.[39]

Now, no matter how cantankerous or difficult Jim Woolsey is or was seen to be, not having the CIA in that planning session can only be seen as carrying the idea of a "close hold" meeting a bit too far. Woolsey didn't much like the outcome, to be sure: "If there is an attempt to assassinate a former president of the United States and the response is to blow up a portion of an empty building in the middle of the night so you won't hurt anybody—I think it's hard to get much more reluctant to use force than that."[40] Clinton, in his memoirs, gives all the responsibility for the targeting to Colin Powell, which suggests that he, too, has come to conclude that perhaps the response was too anemic—but neglects the reality that he was the commander-in-chief and the man in a position to direct Powell to arrive at a different conclusion or offer a different alternative.

Apparently Woolsey was not the only one kept out of the loop. Shortly after the Baghdad Tomahawk missile attack, in the summer of 1993, Woolsey got together for one of his regular breakfasts with Secretary of Defense Les Aspin. The two were old friends from when they worked together in the Pentagon in the 1960s. As Woolsey recounts, Aspin asked him, "'Did you think when we got these jobs that we'd get together with the president sometimes and talk to him about what we were going to do?' And I said, yeah, I thought that. He said, Well, I'm not doing that, are you? And I said, No, I'm not. I thought you were. He said, No, I'm not. And I don't think Chris is. And he looked up at the ceiling and he said, I wonder who is."[41] Once again, an informal group close the president was in the driver's seat, and many of those in the administration with the most foreign policy experience were reportedly frustrated in their attempts to be heard.

During the first year of the Clinton administration, foreign policy victories were few and far between—and even foreign policy progress seemed elusive. But in two areas, some progress was being made. Both involved what were to be keys to success in the future of the administration. In both cases, the initiatives in question ended up being assigned to an individual who was given real presidential authority to champion an independent process pertaining to a fairly well-defined set of goals. And in both cases, fairly early on, the president was drawn into the issue, forged a personal relationship with the key foreign leaders involved, and then remained engaged as the issues evolved.

The two issues were among the most important and complex facing the new team. The first was managing relations with the former Soviet Union, which Clinton made a special priority. To manage the process, he created a new position, much as he had done with NEC, for a close friend of his who was an experienced Russia expert: his former Oxford housemate,

Time magazine journalist and author Strobe Talbott. The new role was shaped and given the title Ambassador at Large, and later, Special Advisor to the Secretary of State. But Talbott had another important title, and that was "friend of Bill." This designation meant, in the Clinton administration, that he had a special status that was not revealed on traditional organizational charts. He was the president's man on this issue, and the power that accrued to him was, as is typically the case, derived far more from years of history with the man in charge than from the size or location of his office in the State Department.

Talbott spoke fluent Russian and knew many members of the Russian leadership. Over time he created an interagency team consisting of a variety of senior officials who would travel with him, each of whom Talbott could point to on his missions as "our 'go to' man on Russia," in the words of his longtime friend Bill Clinton.[42] Talbott characterized the size and nature of the group that evolved—which included senior representatives from the State Department, the Treasury Department, the military, the intelligence community, and other key agencies—as the "G4 factor," meaning that this group was defined by the size of the Gulfstream IV aircraft that shuttled them around and on which they would bond as they flew from one set of meetings to the next.[43]

Later the model was cloned in other initiatives: The president or his top aides would appoint a "czar" to manage a particular issue, that person would develop a team, and the entire group would report back to the NSC or, in some cases, to the secretary of state and the president, and advance the administration's agenda with regard to those issues aggressively. There is a sense in the government that since real money and real resources are so hard to come by—particularly in the budget-balancing, cost-cutting environment that prevailed during the Clinton years—when an issue arose, the default options for the government were to appoint an emissary or convene a commission or another meeting to study the problem. Such actions were the most typical "deliverables" sought to mention in speeches, and they were relatively low cost. They could also have been emptily symbolic. But in the case of some of the important efforts, they were not.

Talbott's was one such effort. But the key to its success was the engagement of the president. That process began with a meeting in April 1993 between Russian President Boris Yeltsin and President Clinton. In his memoirs, Clinton talks about receiving encouragement from Richard Nixon to make this meeting a priority, the former president "saying I would be remembered as President more for what I did with Russia than for my economic policy."[44] Prior to the meeting Clinton and Talbott worked hard to come up with an aid package for Russia that would make a difference. On this they collaborated with Treasury Under Secretary Larry Summers and with David Lipton, a Treasury aide who himself later became under secretary and who had worked intensively on these issues while teaching at Harvard.

The constraints on them were significant. In fact, to illustrate the operating mind-set of the time, I can recall a conversation with a friend of mine who was, in the early days of the administration, hopeful of winning a job in the Treasury Department. The day came for his big interview, and he called me for some advice about how to prepare. He said he had been given a question to think about: "Name three significant things we can do for the former Soviet Union—that don't cost any money." Clearly, money would be spent—but every dollar would be measured carefully.

The aid package Clinton put together to break the ice with Yeltsin was, in the end, $2.5 billion targeted at stabilizing the economy and helping to defuse potential tensions by directing some funds to decommissioned military leaders and weapons scientists. Interestingly, this approach to Russia indicated another respect in which Clinton would follow a pattern that would later bring him success. It was politically unpopular. Three-quarters of the American people opposed giving aid to Russia. But he went ahead with it anyway—because it would seem foolish to invest half a century of effort and resources into winning the Cold War and then to watch the peace unwind simply because we were "penny wise." On issue after issue that would mark the foreign policy successes of the Clinton administration—on intervention in Bosnia and later in Kosovo, on the intervention to help stabilize the Mexican economy when it was in peril, on granting permanent normal trading status to China—Clinton defied the political calculus to make the right choice and ultimately reaped political benefits for his leadership.

Another innovation that came out of that first meeting between Clinton and Yeltsin—at which the two forged a bond they would maintain through numerous meetings during the Clinton presidency—was derived from an idea of Talbott's to create a high-level commission that would enable the two governments to work together closely on a wide range of issues by creating a permanent, high-priority dialogue between senior officials. The commission was to be chaired by Russian Prime Minister Viktor Chernomyrdin and Vice President Gore. Talbott and Leon Fuerth hammered out details of the commission, known as Gore-Chernomyrdin, with the Russians. Fuerth would later assume a central role not only in this commission but also in clones of it that were developed with other nations from South Africa to China.

The Russians quickly saw that Talbott had a unique relationship with the president and that he could deliver on promises. As a result, he was able to maintain a productive dialogue with his counterparts throughout the duration of Clinton's presidency. Talbott would carry this portfolio with him when he became deputy secretary of state in 1994, an elevation that not only further enhanced his status in dealing with the former Soviet Union but also enabled him to play a similar role in the restoration of ties between the United States and the world's largest democracy, India.

A second area where progress was made on traditional foreign policy issues was the Middle East. Initially, senior administration officials considered the Middle East "radioactive," given the enormous difficulty of making progress in that region. Dennis Ross, President Bush's Middle East negotiator, was kept on for a period that was initially intended to be just six months. During that time, the new Clinton team turned to him for assistance on a variety of fronts because of his broad background in global issues, his diverse training, and his stint at the helm of State's policy shop. He joined Warren Christopher on his promising inaugural trip, which took him to the Middle East and helped reopen lines of communication in the region and in particular initiated an emerging special relationship with Yitzhak Rabin, the former Israeli general who had been elected prime minister the preceding year. The administration soon came to see the value of keeping Ross around on a permanent basis. Indeed, it was at his farewell party that he was called away and asked to stay on as the Middle East negotiator—with a direct mandate and request to do so from the president.

Ross and Christopher worked throughout the year to develop the U.S. relationship with Israel, inviting Rabin to visit Washington and closely monitoring the secret negotiations that were taking place in Oslo between the Israelis and the Palestinians with the assistance and mediation of the Norwegian government. Those talks produced a breakthrough in September 1993, and Rabin saw U.S. support as so essential that he offered to hold the signing ceremony for the agreement produced by the Oslo talks at the White House. The ceremony would be particularly electric, as it would bring together for the first time in public Rabin and his lifelong adversary Yasser Arafat. In stage-managing the meeting between them at the signing ceremony, the United States was able to play a constructive role in advancing the dialogue between the two sides. But it was not without complications. First, Arafat had to be dissuaded from wearing a sidearm to the ceremony. Next came the question of how the two Middle Eastern leaders would greet each another and how President Clinton would respond. A handshake—one public handshake—was possible, but what if Arafat sought to kiss Rabin, as was traditional for Arabs in such situations? Rabin was not enthusiastic about that. Clinton writes in his memoirs:

> We had decided that I would shake hands with each of them first, then sort of motion them together. I was sure that if Arafat didn't kiss me, he wouldn't try kissing Rabin. As I stood in the Oval Office discussing it with Hillary, George Stephanopoulos, Tony Lake and [the NSC's senior man for the Middle East and later U.S. Ambassador to Israel] Martin Indyk, Tony said he knew a way I could shake hands with Arafat while avoiding a kiss. He described the procedure and we practiced it. I played Arafat and he played me, showing me what to do. When I shook his hand and moved in for the kiss, he put his left hand on my right arm where it was bent at the elbow and squeezed; it stopped me cold. Then we reversed roles and I did it to him. We practiced it a couple more times until I felt Rabin's cheek would remain untouched. We all laughed about it, but I knew avoiding the kiss was deadly serious for Rabin.[45]

The event itself was a great success, and, more important, it cemented Clinton's interest in and closeness to the issue. Even though the United States had not brokered the Oslo Accords, Rabin was cannily aware of the fact that U.S. support and would be essential to their success and that U.S. commitment would be linked to the degree to which the president was involved. A president yearning for a big public foreign policy win got one and at the same time established a special personal rapport with Rabin, for whom he developed great affection.

Rabin and Arafat went on to sign the Oslo II agreement in September 1995, which turned over most major Palestinian cities of the West Bank to Palestinian rule by January 1996. With President Clinton again present, Rabin had also signed a peace treaty with King Hussein of Jordan, making official the unofficial peaceful relationship between Israel and its eastern Arab neighbor. These dramatic moves by Rabin, which aimed to transform the war-torn region, had evoked strong hostility within some segments of Israeli society, particularly the agreements that established Palestinian self-governance in Israeli-occupied West Bank and Gaza and created a framework for a permanent peace accord with the Palestinians.

The November 1995 assassination of Rabin proved to be a searing but defining event for the president and produced a dogged personal commitment on his part to seek a regional peace accord—an effort he would keep up until the final weeks of his presidency.

In October 1998 President Clinton brought Israeli Prime Minister Binyamin Netanyahu and Palestinian President Yasser Arafat to a summit at Wye Mills, Maryland, which, after eight days of intense negotiations, settled some important interim issues called for by the Oslo Accords.[46] Like President Carter at Camp David, Clinton had a small, cohesive NSC–State Department contingent to assist the tense negotiations. The talks succeeded to some degree, as the Palestinians agreed to remove language from their founding charter that called for the dismantling of the Jewish state and the Israelis agreed to cede an additional 13 percent of the West Bank. However, several highly sensitive issues—Palestinian statehood, the drawing of borders, and the status of Jerusalem—remained unresolved, issues which the president would make one more intensive effort to settle.[47]

.   .   .

In Moscow, a few weeks after the signing of the 1993 Oslo Accords, hard-liners tried to depose Yeltsin. Then on October 3, a year of American frustration in Somalia turned into calamity. U.S. Army Rangers launched an assault on a building in Mogadishu in which two top lieutenants of the warlord Mohammed Aidid were thought to be. The Rangers approached in Black Hawk helicopters and took the building, capturing the men they had been sent in after. Unfortunately, street fighters associated with Aidid began to fight back fiercely and shot down two of the American helicopters. The Rangers fought to get to the wreckage and rescue one pilot who was trapped in the wreckage of one of the helicopters. The elite U.S. troops involved, vastly outnumbered, fought through the night, killing over 500 Somalis and wounding twice that many. But eighteen Americans died, more were wounded, one pilot was captured, and the body of one American pilot was dragged through the streets of the city to the cheers and taunts of crowds.

Clinton compares the fiasco to the one in Bay of Pigs, writing in his memoirs that he thought he was approving a simple action that would not be as bold or risky as a daylight raid. He asserts that is what outgoing Joint Chiefs chairman Powell had thought he was seeking approval for when he proposed the action. He implies that the failure of decision making was in the actions of U.S. ground commander Major General William Garrison, who "took full responsibility" for the decision to go forward with the raid.

Clinton blames Admiral Jonathan Howe, whom he is careful to associate with the previous administration, for making a strategic mistake. "I was responsible for an operation that I had approved in general but not in its particulars," he wrote.[48] Ultimately, after all these statements, he accepts responsibility, says he does not blame General Garrison, and says the "larger implications of it should have been made higher up."[49] Does he mean the NSC? Lake? Himself? Does he differentiate between these? Arguably, he should not.

There are two kinds of failures that took place in this situation. One was a failure of planning, a failure to understand the situation and thus to plan action that would maximize the likelihood of success. The second, however, is a failure to accept that in such circumstances unfortunate outcomes not only are possible but also happen frequently. Because it is impossible to make war risk free, we should not enter war or combat situations unless we are absolutely clear about the downside and willing to proceed in any event until our goals are achieved. This was an inexperienced president, uncertain of his goals, who failed to manage or accept responsibility for a situation for which he, as commander-in-chief, was ultimately solely responsible. Important elements of the mess in Somalia did not occur on the ground in Mogadishu. They occurred in Washington.

Woolsey offered his perspective on the October 6 NSC meeting that followed the debacle:

They had issued a call for an NSC meeting—I'm not absolutely sure it was our first NSC meeting—full meeting—on Somalia, but I'm beginning to think that it might have been. I think everything else had been principals meetings. The next day, they wanted to start with an intelligence briefing, and then we would have a full NSC meeting, and they said it was going to be too sensitive for anyone to bring any backup staff. I talked to my station chief on a secure phone and I went through all the material and what was going on in Somalia. And I got up real early in the morning and read through the overnight cables and I made up my little five-minute briefing. When we showed up in the Cabinet Room, Jeremiah, Aspin, Christopher, and I had nobody with us, but there were about ten White House staffers in the meeting, half a dozen from the domestic side, three or four from the NSC, understandable—but half a dozen from the domestic side: Dee Dee Myers, George Stephanopoulos, David Gergen, all people who were there for PR spin, public relations of one kind or another, and [Special Envoy to Somalia] Bob Oakley. Oakley was there—though we didn't know he was going to be there [Lake had invited him], and they announced at the beginning of the meeting that Oakley was going to be sent over to form a coalition government in Somalia. Now, I think, about the same time he and [Marine General Tony] Zinni were sent over to set up the release of the one Ranger who had been captured, which was important and something that they did. But the other effort was that Oakley was being sent to set up a coalition government. And the meeting skipped the intelligence briefing altogether and picked up right away with a back and forth between Dee Dee Myers and George Stephanopoulos on how we were going to get the best positive press spin out of sending Oakley to set up the coalition government. That discussion went on for fifteen or twenty minutes, with everybody, the president, the vice president, just kind of watching Dee Dee and George talk about who's going to background the *Post*, who's going to background the *Times*, who's going on the Sunday talk shows, etc. And after fifteen or twenty minutes of that, I did one of those things that I suppose really endeared me to the Clinton administration. I put up my hand. I said, Mr. President, I've got a number of people who know this country pretty well, because we were there in some numbers in the Cold War. I said, This place has been involved in clan warfare for a long time, and it's going to be involved in clan warfare for a long time in the future. Any coalition government between these guys, the chance that it would hold together is zero. And there's this long pause in which nobody says anything. It's sort of as if you're in the stands at a football game and there's a commercial time-out and the team doesn't have anything to do, so they kind of look around at the lights. It was like that. Everybody was kind of looking around. And there was a long pause. And then, finally, David Gergen, who was supposedly there for PR, but a sensible guy, chimes in and says, if what Jim says is true, none of this that we're talking about makes any sense. And then there's another commercial time-out. Long pause. Nobody looks around. Then after an embarrassingly long time, Dee Dee and George pick back up without a break with the discussion of how we're going to get the best positive spin out of sending Oakley to set up a coalition government. Nobody frowned at me. Nobody came up afterwards and said, you know Jim, you were out of line. None of that. It was just like, this is sort of an odd thing to bring up here at this NSC meeting, but Jim is odd and well, thanks for that, Jim.[50]

Although Stephanopoulos took umbrage at this description of the meeting, he said of striking the balance between communications goals and foreign policy considerations:

I think the best way to strike the balance is to factor it in. It's like anything else, factor in the political consequences, know what they are, make that part of your analysis, factor in how this is going to be communicated and how it should be communicated. Again, that shouldn't be determinate, but it's as important, especially if it's a policy that's going to require the use of military force or a policy that's going to require some commitment by the country, then you need to have a strategy for keeping the country on board. . . . I think there are lots of examples of Clinton, whether it was Bosnia or Mexico or Somalia, riding in the teeth of public opinion, but knowing that you're going to do it, and knowing the best way to at least persuade someone uncommitted, is key to having the political will to successfully proceed. So, to give you a perfect example, when we were talking about Haiti—it turns out that the American people probably believe in humanitarian intervention more than the foreign policy elite does, and one of the most powerful ways to make the case for taking action in Haiti was to actually show the victims. Now that's not a hard-headed foreign policy realist argument—but it helped build the case for something that I think there was a consensus Clinton had to do. So why would you not want that kind of information, that kind of expertise brought to the table?[51]

Soderberg added:

On Somalia, the problem was a failure to see that the situation was not going well. The reason there were no principals meetings on Somalia before that was that everybody thought it was going well. We were on track to hand over the process to the UN. There was no obvious problem, and the Pentagon got on this very proactive campaign to get Aidid because of the advice of our man on the ground there. And I think you can be fairly critical of a failure of the entire government to recognize that we needed to focus on the political process more as we handed the process over to the UN. But there was no one in the government saying that we need a meeting on this.[52]

Despite the differences in recollections or emphasis among those who participated in these decisions, the one thing that all can agree on is that the process in the early days of the Clinton administration was flawed. It revealed the inexperience of a team forced by the Somalia crisis into the costly on-the-job training our political system requires of incoming administrations from a party that has been out of office for a long period, as the Democrats had been before Clinton's election. That this was a new era and that all the old Cold War playbooks could no longer be relied upon complicated matters further.

This problem of marshaling the political will and the resources to manage the long-term processes associated with nation building haunted the Clinton administration—in Somalia, Bosnia, Haiti, and even Gaza. Later, it would haunt the Bush administration, in Afghanistan and Iraq. It is difficult to mobilize the American people in support of expense or high-risk overseas military operations, and it takes an act of great political courage for a president to go against public opinion to undertake an operation of this type. But once such an operation has been launched, if it is not quickly successful, public opposition not only becomes a huge political concern for the president, it also manifests itself in the actions of Congress. The House in particular, with its two-year election cycles and the generally weak will of the institution when it comes to international measures, is quick to force the United States to cut and run or dramatically reduce resources committed to any individual area. The kind of public diplomacy and political will–building initiatives Stephanopoulos discusses open the window a little for these activities—but not indefinitely. Combining these political realities with the post-Vietnam desire to keep our eye squarely on the exit strategy (one element of the "Powell doctrine" to ensure that we avoid future Vietnams) leads to further problems: Not only does the United States seldom undertake initiatives that are sufficiently farsighted in their planning to be successful, but also our adversaries know that the one thing that is certain after we arrive at a distant locale is that we will soon be eager to leave. This is now one of the central foreign policy conundrums of the post–Cold War era, but the U.S. government has no apparatus designed to manage difficult postconflict or nation-building exercises. The military wants to limit its responsibilities to fighting and the U.S. Agency for International Development and other aid agencies are ill equipped to stabilize crisis situations or to produce the kind of results needed to solve these problems.

Despite the early faltering on these issues in Somalia and in Haiti, a learning curve can be discerned in the Clinton years, with more successful efforts (and appropriately adjusted expectations) as time went by. "Everything taught us something else," says Fuerth. "We learned things that we applied progressively as we were drawn into military action elsewhere."[53]

Among the things learned in Somalia was that Les Aspin was not cut out for the job many had thought him to be preparing for his whole life. He was soon replaced by his quiet, studious deputy, William J. Perry, who would become one of the most significant and widely admired figures of the Clinton administration. Undersecretary of Defense John Deutch moved up to the deputy secretary position, thus giving the Clinton team a much more competent leadership arrangement at Defense, where the skill of the top people in managing relationships with both the civilian staff and the military brass is essential. Perry was a master, recalled fondly by top military leaders to this day as perhaps the best secretary of defense of the past several decades.

The "brown blobs" did not go away, however. Indeed, for a president committed to a domestic agenda, 1994 brought the Clinton administration into deeper contact with an extraordinary range of challenges that had to have some of them wondering just where the "order" was in this "new world order." In addition to the challenges of the festering Balkans, the United States assumed a role in helping negotiate a settlement to almost a century of tensions in Northern Ireland; North Korea flared into a very serious crisis; and ultimately the United States intervened in Haiti. The team was coalescing and coming to understand this new dynamic in which the absence of the Soviet adversary essentially opened the door to U.S. involvement everywhere and, in the eyes of some, made it more essential than ever. President Clinton is reported to have said, "Sometimes, I really miss the Cold War."[54]

There were a few highlights and many tense moments. Among the tensest was the confrontation with North Korea over its refusal to let inspectors from the International Atomic Energy Agency check their nuclear sites in mid-March 1994. North Korea had started a program to convert spent nuclear fuel rods into plutonium for nuclear weapons, and the United States, fearing that they might use the weapons or sell them to the highest bidder, announced a commitment to closing down the weapons program.

While the Clinton administration was dealing with North Korea, the Bosnian city of Gorazde came under siege by the Serbs. Then a plane crashed in Rwanda carrying Rwandan President Juvenal Habyarimana and President Cyprian Ntayamira of neighboring Burundi. The crash triggered a mass slaughter that left the country decimated, with one-tenth of its population of 8 million slaughtered, often by machete, in one of the most horrific genocides of recent times. Clinton calls the failure to try to stop the Rwandan disaster "one of the greatest regrets of my Presidency" and adds, "Neither I nor anyone on my foreign policy team adequately focused on sending troops to stop the slaughter. With a few thousand troops and help from our allies, even making allowances for the time it would have taken to deploy them, we could have saved lives."[55] But they did not. In the final years of a century that had seen its share of genocide, once again the United States and the international community remained immobile and impassive in the face of preventable horror. Some have attributed the inaction to the fact that the NSC and the rest of the government were overwhelmed with other crises. Others suggest that given the failure in Somalia, there was no appetite any more for such interventions. Still others, forgetting Somalia and Haiti and other priorities of the Clinton presidency, have called the failure to intervene a manifestation of a kind of racist double-standard that had us willing to intervene to stop genocide against whites in the Balkans but not against blacks in Africa.

Samantha Power dissected the U.S. inaction in her Pulitzer Prize–winning history of recent genocide, *A Problem from Hell:*

> Even after the reality of genocide in Rwanda had become irrefutable, when bodies were shown choking the Kagera River on America's nightly news, the brute fact of the slaughter failed to influence U.S. policy except in a negative way. As they had done in Bosnia, American officials again shunned the g-word. They were afraid that using it would have obliged the United States to act under the terms of the 1948 genocide convention. They also believed, rightly, that it would harm U.S. credibility to name the crime and then do nothing to stop it. A discussion paper on Rwanda, prepared by an official in the Office of Defense and dated May 1, testifies to the nature of official thinking. Regarding issues that might be brought up at the next interagency working group, it stated, "1. Genocide Investigation: Language that calls for an international investigation of human rights abuses and possible violations of the genocide convention. Be careful. Legal at State was worried about this yesterday—Genocide finding could commit [the U.S. Government] to actually 'do something.'"[56]

Power describes how request after request for intervention, more aid, radios to carry programming to counteract the broadcasts that were stirring up and directing the killers, support for other nations that were ready to intervene, support for the UN, even language that would clearly frame the problem were ignored, buried in bureaucratic paperwork, or otherwise disposed of. She observes:

> It is shocking to note that during the entire three months of the genocide, Clinton never assembled his top policy advisers to discuss the killings. Anthony Lake likewise never gathered the principals—the cabinet-level members of the foreign policy team. Rwanda was never thought to war-

rant its own top-level meeting. When the subject came up, it did so along with and subordinate to discussions of Somalia, Haiti and Bosnia. Whereas these crises involved U.S. personnel and stirred some public interest, Rwanda generated no sense of urgency and could safely be avoided by Clinton at no political cost.[57]

The situation is rife with tragic ironies. No American president has been more committed to or active in Africa than Clinton. No national security advisor had spent more of his career devoted to issues associated with Africa and its development than Lake. Clinton and Lake had established an Africa office in the NSC. They had begun their administration by carrying forward a humanitarian intervention in Somalia, and the great defining foreign policy initiative that stands above all others during their time in office was an effort begun to stop mass slaughter in Bosnia. The president took enormous political punishment for supporting initiatives that were politically unpopular in places that did not top the U.S. list of obvious national interests. Yet, in Rwanda, there was inaction, and the worst non-disease-related humanitarian catastrophe of the Clinton years went unresponded to by a team that was probably the best qualified and most inclined in U.S. history to handle it.

Another irony, of course, is that Lake clearly understood how the threat of the consequences of inaction motivated presidents to act. And yet, perhaps the greatest blot on the Clinton foreign policy record comes from its inaction in the face of this horrific tragedy. Why? When asked, one former Clinton official said, "It was many things. Among them, it was timing. We were getting beaten up for Somalia, we were under siege for conducting 'foreign policy as social work,' for being too concerned with humanitarian issues, the president's political capital was low and waning, we had become risk averse. We had just implemented PDD-25 [U.S. Policy on Reforming Multilateral Peace Operations], which was a kind of self-inflicted constraint against getting involved in too many places where we couldn't do what we set out to do. We were overworked. Maybe we were a little numb. I don't know for sure—but I do know most of the players, and I know that it haunts them to this day. It's not that they didn't care. They probably cared as much as anybody who had ever held these jobs. But they hesitated—and the world lost."[58] Process and analysis obscured moral clarity. Presidential leadership might have offered the antidote, but none was forthcoming.

In all this, there is another lesson to be learned. While it is true, as some have suggested, that the impulse of U.S. officials is all too often to ask, "What is the role for the United States?" in any international issue, one of the great countervailing biases in the bureaucratic system that manages U.S. policy is toward inaction. Policy proposals are run through a gauntlet of agency reviews that say not enough money, not enough people, not enough time, too much risk, insufficient national interest, lurking political risk—and that offer analogy after analogy of similar situations gone wrong. Indeed, the failures of Somalia did lead to the institutionalization of constraints on similar action that in turn kept the United States from acting when the clear humanitarian and moral obligation was to do so.

Clearly, if there is one area where the collaboration of all civilized peoples ought to be a given, it is in the stopping of the worst of human crimes, genocide (or mass slaughter via weapons of mass destruction or other forms of wanton killing of innocents). It is a measure of the nature of U.S. leadership, and it will be a test of that leadership, in this world in which we are the uncontested first among all nations, to see whether we can overcome our bureaucratic biases toward inaction to lead in those circumstances when the act of leadership is the sole measure of our humanity and of the moral caliber of our society. Rwanda and subsequently Congo and Darfur suggest that we have yet to rise to that challenge.

As the slaughter in Rwanda continued, the situation in North Korea worsened to become, as Tony Lake described it, the closest we came to a major war during the Clinton years.[59] The NSC had established criteria for what it called "red lines"—thresholds that, if crossed, would require military action. Notably, these included the movement of spent fuel rods out of their cooling ponds to be reprocessed. (This line was subsequently crossed with impunity during the second Bush presidency despite its tough line on weapons of mass destruction elsewhere.)

Former President Jimmy Carter contacted President Clinton and offered to go to North Korea that June, an offer Clinton accepted. Although Carter's trip produced language from the North Koreans that appeared to defuse the situation, Carter's pronouncements of his success on CNN made Lake and others watching in the White House uncomfortable. They did not trust the North Koreans, and Carter was essentially speaking for the United States in a way that was beyond the parameters that had been provided to him by the Clinton administration. This was one of a number of moments of tension that would color the Clinton-Carter relationship over the next several months and years—including later in Haiti when Carter was seen to be helping the wife of the Haitian general whose ouster he was sent to help arrange by giving her advice on how to negotiate with the United States to get the best price for the house she was being asked to leave.

The negotiating process and the North Korea strategy was formulated again by a working group led by Bob Gallucci, who was empowered to chair deputies meetings and was to work toward an agreement, which was, over time, achieved—although later it became clear that the North Koreans were not adhering to the terms of the deal, and consequently the issue remained unresolved and dangerous into the second term of the second Bush administration.

Gallucci tells a story of sitting at home one night during this period in June and receiving a call from the State Department operator. "The Secretary of State is calling for you." Gallucci says that he practically stands at attention, he is so unaccustomed to getting calls from Secretary Christopher at home. "Christopher comes on the line and says, 'Bob, I bet I know what you're doing.'" Gallucci looks around and says, "Er . . . um . . . what is it that I'm doing, sir?" Christopher says, "I bet you're watching television." Gallucci, who had been reading a book and did not have the television on, assumes that something major has just happened in Korea, that war has broken out or something. "And I say, 'Er . . . no, sir, but what would I be watching on television?' And Christopher says, 'Well, it's the most amazing thing. O.J. Simpson has gotten into this white Ford Bronco and is involved in this low-speed chase with the police.' This struck me as bizarre: the Secretary of State is watching O.J. on TV in a police chase. He saw this as a major event; I couldn't see that. He was right. At the time, I thought it was a California thing."[60] A relieved Gallucci then had a conversation with Christopher on the Korean issues he called to discuss.

Meanwhile, in South Korea, the foreign minister was holding a press conference that was being covered by *New York Times* reporter David Sanger. After the press conference, the foreign minister went up to Sanger and said, "It's really amazing, isn't it?" Sanger replied, "Yeah, it sure is . . . I've never seen an ex–American president fly in and conduct his own diplomacy like Carter did." And the Korean foreign minister said, "No. O.J. Simpson is in a white Ford Bronco involved in this slow-speed chase with police."[61]

When I tell this story to Tony Lake, he laughs and acknowledges that even as the United States was in the midst of a major crisis, the NSC staff did have one of the televisions they were watching tuned to the slow-speed chase of O.J. Simpson. Several months before that, Lake had been out to the West Coast to give a briefing to the president, who was there on a trip. After he finished the briefing, which touched on the North Korean issues, he began to walk away from the golf course clubhouse where he had been meeting with the president, and his pager sounded. The president wanted to see him again. Lake went back to the clubhouse, and the president said, "I was just talking to my golfing partner, and he has some thoughts you might be interested in on North Korea ... and by the way, I thought you'd like to meet him because I know of your interest in sports. Of course, out walks the president's golf partner, O.J. Simpson, who Lake reports gave his analysis of the significance of North Korea's million-man army and the situation on the ground. Naturally, pictures of the president playing golf with O.J. ceased to be in general circulation a couple months later.

In September 1994, the Haiti crisis reached a crescendo with Clinton again taking an unpopular stance—moving in to throw out General Raul Cedras and his regime in an effort to restore democracy and former President Jean-Bertrand Aristide to power.

"We met out at the National Defense University," says Fuerth, "which was a big enough space for this."

> What you had was a virtual board mock-up of all the command elements to bring in the military involved in the invasion of Haiti. There were massive texts to be gone through. It was very detailed ... I think, for example, at one point we were able to track how many people would be onboard vessels. We knew what had to be done by the hour in terms of generating employment for the Haitians, building roads, clearing the gutters, whatnot in order to help get them beyond total paralysis. We had, in fact, thought through everything. The only question was that we didn't know how much resistance there would be when we landed, so we sent in an overwhelming force. Later, everything that we learned in Haiti, we plowed into Bosnia and later Kosovo.[62]

There was a nail-biting negotiation that eventually, with planes full of paratroopers already in the sky heading for Haiti, resulted in the avoidance of a military confrontation. Cedras agreed to leave by October 15. The lessons of Somalia had been internalized and a battle had been avoided. Unfortunately, within a few months it became apparent that doubts about Aristide, his commitment to democracy, and his ability to rule without the support of the police or the military were well founded. But the administration was reluctant to admit this.

I saw this up close because as part of the planning for the Haiti operation I attended a sprawling meeting of officials in a townhouse conference center near the White House on behalf of the Commerce Department. At one point, one agency after another stood up and indicated what they might do to stimulate Haiti's economic revitalization. Innocently, I raised my hand and suggested that perhaps it would be best if all this was coordinated by some central figure, preferably one associated with the White House so it would have sufficient authority to get things done. Sandy Berger, who was chairing the meeting, acknowledged that made sense. A couple of days later I read in the paper that such a coordinator had been appointed. It was me.

I began to travel to the small, beset island and meeting with Aristide and other top officials fairly regularly. I also began to attend the NSC meetings on the subject and quickly found that other than the CIA's representatives and Dick Clarke, who was coordinating the post-invasion Haiti situation for the NSC, there were no others who really wanted to hear bad news about Aristide. He had become a hero to many of them and was played up in the U.S. media as if he were a kind of smaller, clerical version of Nelson Mandela. But reports soon started coming in of Aristide's people being involved in criminal activities and in attacks against their opponents.

Once again, however, the mind-set was that the objective was to get the situation stable enough for us to walk away.

It is a particular tragedy given that Haiti's 7 million citizens are hard-working and eager to build a new life for themselves. The nation on the other half of the island, the Dominican Republic, has done much better for itself and proven that it is possible to achieve growth on the island of Hispaniola, one of Columbus's first points of contact in this hemisphere. The 4 billion dollars in aid the United States promised to Aristide's Haiti could have broken a 200-year-old cycle of pain for that country—if we had been committed enough to ensure its wise use over time and if we had been willing to take a tough enough stance with Aristide. Unfortunately, very early on Aristide determined that the U.S. president had invested so much political capital in him that we needed them more than they needed us. He took advantage of that, and we allowed ourselves to be taken advantage of. It was another lesson, learned the hard way.

11

The Beginning of the End
of the End of History

If man does find the solution for world peace it will be the most revolutionary reversal of his record that we have ever known.
—General George C. Marshall

History, Stephen said, is a nightmare from which I am trying to awake.
—James Joyce, *Ulysses*

WHILE THE forty-five-year-old NSC struggled to come to grips with a post–Cold War reality that was unlike anything it had seen before (and very much unlike what it had been designed for), its clone, the brand-new, untested National Economic Council (NEC) shot out of the blocks and quickly established itself as a force to be reckoned with. In case after case, America's foreign policy interests seemed to be turning on economic considerations. This was not just because America was eager to focus again on its own growth. Nor was it because of the opportunities that were being created by simultaneous revolutions in communications and transportation that had ushered in an era of international trade and investment and popularized a term that would come to be very much associated with President Clinton and his policies—globalization. It was also because, in case after case, the new best tools in the foreign policy toolbox were economic. Economic tools were critical to stabilizing the former Soviet Union. Economic tools were the ones that could save failing states from failure or at least could help combat unrest and create opportunity and thus political support for those associated with that opportunity. Economic rivals were becoming a greater concern to the American people than military rivals. Economic goals were seen as vitally important national priorities. And America's influence over the world, consistent with our own view of our superpower status, was most likely to be extended effectively and in a way that was consistent both with our values and with the greatest likelihood of our success if we played on our strengths as an economic superpower and sought to win allies or defeat enemies by offering or withholding access to our markets, our technologies, our capital flows, our companies, our workers, and the ideas and ideologies that informed them and set them apart.

Members of Clinton's international economic policy team felt that the moment was theirs, that they were, for the first time, in the foreign policy driver's seat. For years economic issues were disdained by the makers of "high policy," seen as "low policy," "vulgar," "commercial," and unable to compete with the intricacies of arms control or the nuance of high diplomacy for the attentions of the exalted leaders in the field. Yet, as Clinton's economic policymakers would remind their colleagues, the focus on military affairs as the centerpiece of our foreign policy was a comparatively new phenomenon. From the days of George Washington until those of Woodrow Wilson, it was commonly understood that our international interests were economic interests and that the reason for keeping sea lanes open or even for acquiring or defending territories was primarily to support our commercial needs as a growing society. The preoccupations of the Cold War were ebbing, but the information age, the age of globalization, would require us to wheel out armies of technologists and fund managers, economists and business managers to build our strength, grow our influence, keep the peace, and maintain our position of leadership in the world.

Of course, having this belief was not enough. The administration would need to demonstrate results. It helped enormously that the NEC was fairly high-functioning from the start, largely because of the leadership of Bob Rubin, Bo Cutter, and Gene Sperling and the recognition from the president and the NSC that the NEC was to play a central role. On international matters, this meant that Rubin and Cutter would sit down with Lake and Berger on a regular basis.

"There was tremendous collegiality, particularly among the four of us from the beginning," reported Berger. "Bo and I got along really well. And I wasn't interested in any of the domestic economic stuff, which helped. I was happy to have Bo taking the lead on it. Although I have to say, Rubin's role was especially important. You can't just plant an institution and assume it will have all sorts of prerogatives and influence just declaring that to be so. When Rubin called a meeting, people came because he was Rubin."[1]

Of special importance in the NEC process was the deputies committee, much as it was in the NSC process. It was here that the policy heavy lifting occurred. Often the meetings would have broader attendance and as joint NSC/NEC meetings co-chaired by Cutter and Berger and attended by other representatives from State as well as from DOD and CIA. In those meetings, the real strength of the collegial approach came out because it was often impossible to tell who was chairing the meeting. "It was pretty much seamless," said one participant, "Bo and Sandy did a terrific job of keeping their own egos in check and working as a real team."[2]

Cutter and Berger, like Rubin, took the honest-broker role very seriously—which is not to say that Lake did not. It was more a matter of style. As a senior Clinton administration official who had worked with both national security advisors recalled, "As for Tony, I always describe it this way. There are professors, who, when they teach, know what answer they want to get from the students and if they don't get it, they dismiss them. And there are professors who actually want to hear what the students have to say and take that into consideration as the discussion develops. Tony was definitely the first kind of professor. Sandy was always more inclined to open up the process and hear the people."[3]

Berger said, "I think Tony had a particular style. He is a brilliant guy, and I think he was a good national security advisor, but he did not try to build a consensus among his colleagues. Basically, he knew what he thought the right answer was and he felt it was his job to get that answer to the president."[4]

Cutter saw the challenges of integrating the groups as an important first hurdle. "It was clear to me," he said, "that if you were dealing with an agency that had a forty-five-year history on the one hand and one that had nothing on the other, good coordination was a no-brainer. . . . Sandy and I met pretty regularly, formally and informally, but more informally than anybody knew. And we tried to make certain that the lines didn't get tangled. So at that level, I thought it worked pretty well."[5]

It wasn't quite so easy at the next level up among the principals, Cutter explained.

Part of it was historical biases. I think that the Department of State institutionally would just as soon never have the Treasury be part of anything. And the Department of the Treasury would abolish the Department of

State if it could do it. So I think there was a long-standing structural set of quarrels about it. And it was also often extremely hard to get, for example, Laura Tyson into meetings. And sometimes it was hard to get Secretary Brown into meetings. It seemed to me there was an overly fastidious drawing of lines that sometimes resulted in not always having the right person in meetings.[6]

The economic team had been building momentum, seeing through the tough NAFTA battle thanks to a war room that had been established and manned by future commerce secretary Bill Daley, pushing the General Agreement on Tariffs and Trade (GATT) talks forward, assembling the Russia aid package, and conducting tough negotiations with Japan to try to gain market access and reduce the U.S. trade deficit with that country.

From the beginning of the administration one of those who was most likely to identify a problem when he saw it was Larry Summers, then under secretary of the Treasury. Summers's career was meteoric thanks both to his extraordinary intelligence and to his ability to work as hard as was necessary to get a good result. Some saw him as arrogant. Indeed, the *Wall Street Journal* once wrote, "Larry Summers is to humility what Madonna is to chastity."[7] But Summers was, like Madonna, a star—although in his case, of the wonkocracy that ruled Washington in those days, which excused many of his idiosyncrasies. He always spoke his mind and was always quick on his feet. Summers was joined at Treasury by an exceptional international team that included Assistant Secretary Jeffrey Shafer (who later replaced Summers as under secretary when Summers became deputy secretary), David Lipton, a specialist in the Soviet economy (who replaced Shafer and became under secretary when Summers became secretary after Rubin's departure), and Timothy Geithner, who joined as an impossibly young-looking deputy assistant secretary and is currently the president of the Federal Reserve Bank of New York. They and their colleagues at Treasury were collectively the stars of the economic team in the administration, golden boys because of their intelligence, the mandate the president and the times had given them to take the lead on policy formation, and, not least, because of their proximity to Bob Rubin once he became Treasury Secretary.

Looking back at the first years of the economic team, one Treasury Department official recalled:

On the one hand, there was a ton of naivete about a lot of things. We were all hopelessly inexperienced. I'm not sure what we would have done that would have been so much better if we had been experienced—so I guess I'm not sure how large a price we paid for our inexperience. . . . I think we had a kind of self-importance and a sense that we were reinventing everything, with precious little awareness that sometimes it was the wheel. It must have been infuriating to the rest of the world. And we have this puzzle that people were much more willing to listen to us then, when we didn't know what we were talking about, than they were years later, when we did.[8]

Where the traditional foreign policy and the economic policy groups came into friction fairly early on was on policy toward China—again, an issue on which campaign rhetoric did not fit with acceptable choices when it came to governing. It was a test case of how these two perspectives—security and economics—interacted during the course of the Clinton years.

Since the 1992 presidential campaign, when Bill Clinton had harshly criticized President Bush for "coddling tyrants from Baghdad to Beijing" and stressed that human rights considerations would inform his policy on China,[9] the language of the new administration toward China had bordered on the confrontational. The deputy national security advisor, Sandy Berger, warned, "This is going to be an arms-length relationship at best between Washington and Beijing."[10]

Despite the strong rhetoric, China was not high on the list of the administration's priorities coming into office, which was reflected by the makeup of the NSC staff. The Asia directorate had only two professional officers covering China, Japan, Korea, and Southeast Asia.[11] Moreover, according to Robert Suettinger, director for Asian affairs for the NSC between 1994 and 1997, "There was nobody at a senior level on the National Security Council who had the gravitas or the experience to deal with Asia in a sort of comprehensive and strategic way. We paid a huge price for that. It was also true at State. There wasn't anybody at the very topmost levels of the State Department who was able to deal with this issue at the same level of expertise that had been done in previous administrations."[12] Deputy U.S. Trade Representative Charlene Barshefsky was even more dismissive of the government's expertise: "I always thought the information that I got was gleaned from newspapers and that if people had spent more time there, they would have been better informed."[13] The inattention of the administration was combined with a willingness on the part of the president to let Congress, including outspoken officials, such as Representative Nancy Pelosi and Senator George Mitchell, take the lead in setting the China agenda.[14]

These factors contributed to the Clinton administration's difficulties in crafting a strategy to link the granting of most-favored-nation (MFN) status to the Chinese government's human rights practices. The root of the problem lay in an unresolved split between the human rights activists in the State Department, Congress, and the NGO community versus economic actors such as the NEC and the Commerce Department, according to many observers, including J. Stapleton Roy, Clinton's first ambassador to China:

> The thing that plagued those first two years and then carried on was that there was a split within the administration between those who wanted to use a human rights lever and attach it to everything we did with China, and those who wanted to push trade, strategic, or other objectives without being totally saddled by the human rights thing. The administration wouldn't address that issue. And so, they drifted along with two totally conflicting viewpoints, and even when the policy went to the NSC, the human rights people in the State Department were able to stymie implementation of the policy through the human rights angle.[15]

The result was drift and incoherence. NSC Director Sandra Kristoff observes:

> The whole first two years of the Clinton administration, there was no single voice on China policy. The USTR [Office of the U.S. Trade Representative] speaks; the Defense Department speaks; the *New York Times* speaks; everybody speaks. . . . It's no longer the diplomats or even the intelligence people or the military. By then, it's the whole economic issue in the business community and the U.S. Congress and the NGOs and human rights, soon to mutate into labor and environment, that unholy alliance, if you will. Those become voices that the administration then begins to respond to in terms of trying to set China policy.[16]

In mid-1993, President Clinton signed Executive Order 12850, "Conditions for Renewal of Most Favored Nation Status for the People's Republic of China," which essentially gave the Chinese Communist Party (CCP) one year to revise its human rights policies.[17] To recommend another extension of China's MFN privileges, they would have to make "overall, significant progress" in seven specified categories. Beijing proved unresponsive to what they perceived to be an unwarranted ultimatum and, using diplomatic and economic pressure, undermined efforts by the Clinton administration to establish a strong linkage between MFN status and human rights policy in China.[18] They called the administration's bluff successfully because the policy was not well founded.

Wishing to stabilize deteriorating relations with China, Assistant Secretary of State for East Asian and Pacific Affairs Winston Lord and NSC Senior Director Kent Wiederman called for a new tactical approach of "enhanced engagement," endorsed at a principals committee meeting in July, that would remove limitations on meetings with senior Chinese officials and allow cabinet-level officials to travel to the PRC.[19] The president approved the new strategy in September, but its positive impact was limited and further checked by a disastrous trip to China in March 1994 by Secretary Christopher, who faced unwelcoming and often contentious CCP leaders, resentful of American "interference" in their domestic affairs.[20]

After the secretary of state's trip, which President Clinton described as "disappointing" and which was widely regarded within the administration as a step backward in the relationship, a new debate began within the administration about the linkage policy as the June deadline on renewing China's MFN status loomed. Lake convened a post-trip principals committee meeting to review China policy and determine the proper balance between human rights and economic considerations. With the approval of the president, the White House adopted a more pronounced role in managing China policy, with the NSC's Berger (who had been more skeptical about the linkage policy than Lake and Soderberg) regularly meeting with Bo Cutter, Robert Rubin's deputy for international economic policy on the NEC.

Cutter articulated the view of the economic agencies like the Treasury and Commerce Departments that Lord and the State Department had not properly consulted them when crafting Executive Order 12850, explaining, "We were not involved in the vetting of [the executive order] in any substantial way. And we were surprised, shocked, angered by how it came out, and thought it was going to be a fairly fast disaster" for the president.[21] Consequently, as Suettinger recounts:

> The NSC and NEC developed a small group that met about two or three times a week, usually at 6 o'clock in the evening, and would work for several hours on trying to make the policy as it had been defined work as well as possible; to give ourselves at least a maximum amount of cover for retreat from the policy. And the process was not only determined to try to put together a new policy, but to avoid spilling a lot of blood on the floor.

I mean, there were people who would have loved to have eviscerated Win Lord, but that was not what the effort was all about.[22]

In early 1994, Robert Rubin called for a delinking of trade and human rights policy, and staff changes on the NSC increased support for a policy shift from the human rights approach promoted by the State Department. At the same time, we in the Commerce Department began a detailed analysis of the consequences of losing MFN status for China. The punch line of the study was that such an action would produce rising prices on Chinese goods entering the United States and that the people who would be most negatively affected would be Americans in lower income brackets who depended on Chinese imports for their low-priced shoes, apparel, and electronics.

Two staff changes on the NSC substituted proponents of linkage with staffers who felt that the policy was not working and should be dropped. The NEC-NSC effort supplanted the interagency senior steering group headed by Lord, which, according to Suettinger, "met too infrequently and with too large a cast of characters to bring about a workable consensus."[23] Meanwhile, China effectively used American businesses to lobby against the linkage policy, frustrating (and influencing) the administration to a much greater degree than during the troubled early years of the Reagan administration.[24]

A principals meeting held in late May, with President Clinton in attendance, discussed the MFN issue. Secretary Christopher reported that the Chinese government had made "overall, significant progress" in two of seven human rights categories specified in the previous year's executive order. Christopher (and Lord) recommended targeted economic sanctions rather than a revocation of China's MFN status.[25] After several more days of consultation, President Clinton announced on May 26, 1994, that he would "delink human rights from the annual extension of most favored nation trading status for China."[26] Publicly shifting the administration's China policy from human rights–based "principled engagement" to a broader-based "comprehensive engagement," he explained:

> I believe the question, therefore, is not whether we continue to support human rights in China but how we can best support human rights in China and advance our other very significant issues and interest. I believe we can do it by engaging the Chinese. . . . We will have more contacts. We will have more trade. We will have more international cooperation. We will have more intense and constant dialogue on human rights issues.[27]

Lord claimed that the linkage policy was doomed by a combination of presidential inattention and Lake's inability to control economic actors within the administration, complaining, "We tried to get the president to give major speeches on China for four years, and he never did. His—and the NSC's—most egregious contribution was to let the economic agencies sabotage the president's own MFN policy and leave Christopher swinging in the wind."[28]

"Commercial engagement . . . effectively subordinated principled engagement" with China for the remainder of Clinton's presidency.[29] One former China hand claimed that after the collapse of the linkage policy, Winston Lord and the State Department were given a lesser role in setting policy toward China, and "China policy moved very conspicuously to the NSC" under the direction of Lake and Berger.[30]

Later in 1994, we prepared a mission to China for Secretary Brown and a group of leading U.S. businessmen. Our preparations included writing a series of speeches, including several to be given by the secretary, to frame our objectives. In one of these, I wrote a line about the importance of "economic diplomacy." My boss, Jeffrey Garten, shrewdly observed that if we included that term, all the other economic agencies and particularly Treasury would want to vet the speech, and it would be a complicated and contentious process. As a result, I changed the term to "commercial diplomacy," figuring that no one except the Commerce Department would want to be associated with anything that was overtly "commercial," which at the time still seemed like the lowest of low policy. Surprisingly, and later dismayingly, the term caught on. Whereas it was used at first to explain the objectives behind our successful trip, on which billions of dollars in new contracts were closed between U.S. businesses and the Chinese, later it became a code word for selling out interests such as human rights for commercial gain.

Nonetheless, the trip was successful on more levels than just the commercial. Secretary Brown was able to achieve something that had thus far eluded the State Department, which was the resumption of the human rights dialogue. Clearly, the Chinese were sending a signal about how they would prefer to be treated. There was no denying that a policy of multi-tiered engagement employing both carrots and sticks could be more effective. Furthermore, it was also clear that the greater integration of our two economies would result not only, as Secretary Brown put it on several occasions, "in trade in products and services but also in the exchange of ideas and ideologies." This was not just rhetoric; the concept of helping open China to the world would support the concept of engagement through China's accession to the World Trade Organization (WTO) near the end of the Clinton term.

Of course, critics responded to the trip with accusations that Clinton had sold out. The president felt the pressure. One senior official who came to me shortly after the trip, still a little shaken, recounted how the president had blown up at him and another official in the Oval Office, saying that he didn't like our China policy and that he "wished he was running against his own policy."[31] Of course, since he had successfully run against precisely the same policy two years earlier, when it was the policy of his predecessor's administration, his comfort with that approach was understandable—as was the frustration that came from his newfound understanding that what was politically comfortable for him with regard to China was not necessarily good policy or in the interests of the United States.

Among the groups who protested the policy of commercial engagement was one led by Kerry Kennedy Cuomo, head of the RFK Center for Human Rights and wife of Andrew Cuomo, who would soon be Clinton's secretary of housing and urban development. She was extremely articulate and made a very good case that the Chinese use of prison labor in the manufacture of products sold for export was wrong. None of these issues are simple, and, certainly, taking a stand to urge the Chinese to adopt more humane policies should be an imperative of any U.S. administration. That said, as she was speaking about the inhumanity of using prison labor to make products for sale to us here in the United States, I couldn't help but recall that I had recently been told that the couch she was sitting on in my office, like much of the other furniture, had been made at a nearby federal prison.

The Clinton administration was no more able to avoid the thorny issue of Taiwan than its predecessors, and relations with China once more became strained over its dealings with Taipei. Several months after the linkage policy was officially abandoned, the NSC and the State Department restarted a Taiwan policy review, begun in the early days of the administration. The final product of the interagency review did not propose any significant changes to existing U.S. policy. One adjustment, however, permitted top Taiwanese leaders to make "transit stops" in the United States under certain approved conditions, although they were still not permitted extended official or personal stays.[32] While the transit stops might be considered small potatoes in the greater scheme of global relations, they were seen as rich with symbolism about the U.S.-Taiwan relationship and thus could produce thunderous reverberations across the Pacific.

For example, such a trip proved to be contentious in March 1994, when Taiwanese President Lee Teng-hui asked to stay overnight (and play golf) in Hawaii or California on the way to an official visit to Central America. The State Department, aware of previous Chinese warnings about Lee's "vacation diplomacy," responded with a démarche opposing the request.[33] Suettinger reviewed the document, which he described as blunt and impolitic, but Lake decided not to intercede, saying (according to the NSC director's recollection), "I can't go on your feelings. Christopher has already signed off on this, and I'm not going to cross him."[34] Ambassador Roy also noted that at this time, "The NSC was not strong enough to be able to push a positive China policy, and the State Department's focus on the human rights issue meant that we were basically dead in the water with a strategy."[35] Eventually the State Department permitted the Taiwanese leader to make a refueling stop in Hawaii but not to stay overnight.[36]

Afterward, President Lee began lobbying the U.S. government to attend a reunion event at his alma mater, Cornell University, and the newly Republican-led Congress put pressure on the Clinton administration to permit the Taiwanese leader to travel to Ithaca. The NSC and the State Department, aware of the growing clamor, were meeting regularly with House and Senate staffers and, after Congress overwhelmingly passed resolutions supporting a Lee visit, Lake met with Secretaries Christopher and Perry in May 1995 to try to find a way to permit the Taiwanese president's visit without poisoning U.S.-Chinese relations.[37]

Anticipating that President Clinton would have to act soon, the NSC had prepared a recommendation proposing that the administration avoid making any move until their hand was forced by Congress, utilizing the delay both to prepare Beijing and to try to convince Taiwan to limit the scope of the trip. Suettinger further argued with Lake and Berger against Lee's visit to Cornell and searched for alternatives that would satisfy the State Department and Taiwan. In a final effort to persuade the president not to allow the trip, Suettinger wrote a memorandum describing the negative consequences to U.S.-China relations and Taiwan-China relations that would ensue. Lake asked Suettinger to rewrite the paper to stress the option of granting the visa and then managing the consequences rather than trying to fight Congress on the issue. After briefly objecting (while Berger, though in agreement with Suettinger, remained silent), the NSC director edited the memo and planned to talk with the State Department and inform the Chinese over the next week before the policy change was publicly announced.[38]

Unfortunately, the memo was leaked soon after it was approved by the president on May 17, producing a firestorm, and Lake's subsequent meeting with the Chinese ambassador to explain the approval of the "private" visit by Lee did not go well.[39] Furthermore, institutional rivalries between the State Department and the NSC, though muted, still existed and hampered efforts to explain to the CCP leadership in Beijing the shift in U.S. policy toward President's Lee travel plans. Roy explains:

> When the administration shifted its policy on Lee Teng-hui, it was a major issue. In the past, you didn't make major shifts in policy without sending somebody of importance to explain why you're doing it. I weighed in, but ran into the problem. There was no one in the State Department that could be sent. And process meant that State would block anybody else at a suitable level from going. For example, Tony Lake had never been to China at that point. He would have been the perfect envoy to have gone to explain the president's decision to permit Lee Teng-hui to come. But State would have died before they would have permitted Tony Lake to do that.[40]

As the NSC and others in the administration had expected, the visit by President Lee soured relations that had been gradually improving after the MFN debacle.

While those with responsibility for China in the State Department and the NSC worked on proposals to reverse the negative trend, the NSC also prepared a letter for President Clinton to present to CCP leader Jiang Zemin that emphasized the opportunities for cooperation between the two nations. In late 1995, Lake directed the Asia staff on the NSC to review and develop a range of contingencies to potential Chinese actions against Taiwan. The directive, amid a background of military posturing by Beijing, instructed that the planning be done quietly, "off-line and off the system."[41] Principals and deputies committee meetings were held in early 1996 to further address the problematic relationship, which led to a decision in February 1996 to initiate talks with China at the level of the national security advisor as well as to have a "strategic dialogue" with the head of Taiwan's National Security Council.[42]

In early March 1996, several days before Lake was scheduled to meet with Liu Huaqiu, the director of the State Council Foreign Affairs Office (the Chinese official considered Lake's closest counterpart), Beijing announced that they would be conducting military exercises not far from Taiwan later that month. The exercises would include missile tests near two

Taiwanese port cities and would end around the time of Taiwan's presidential election. The first missile tests took place as Liu arrived in Washington, and American indignation was conveyed to the Chinese official, who responded with criticism of American support for Lee Teng-hui's supposed plans for "Taiwanese independence."[43] The thorny issues of the missile tests, Lee's Cornell trip, and the U.S. military relationship with Taiwan continued to dominate discussions with the Chinese the following day.

A post-conference breakfast meeting held in Defense Secretary Perry's office—which included Christopher and Lord from the State Department and Lake and Berger from the NSC—considered U.S. responses to the provocative Chinese behavior, and, after some discussion, they decided to deploy two carrier battle groups to observe the Chinese military exercises, although neither would deploy into the Taiwan Strait itself. Meanwhile, a few days after the talks with Liu Huaqiu, Sandy Berger and a State Department representative met privately with the secretary-general of Taiwan's national security council to clarify U.S. plans for the region. The talks with the Taiwanese, who were supportive of the deployment of the American battle groups, went much more smoothly than those with the Chinese.[44]

In the end, the tensions receded in the Taiwan Strait, and Lake's subsequent initiative to hold talks with senior Chinese officials marked the beginning of a new and much more stable period in U.S.-China relations that endured, for the most part, throughout the second term of the Clinton administration. To the extent that problems lingered, they were characterized by ongoing disagreements with the Chinese (and the Republican Congress) about Taiwan and human rights policies as well as controversies surrounding the export of certain controlled technologies to China. In addition, during the period of the most aggressive political assaults on Clinton, a period that dominated the second term and grew more intense during the last years of the Clinton presidency, the NSC was dragged into another controversy when it became known that staffers had been involved in vetting and receiving requests from Democratic Party donors, including Johnny Chung and Charlie Trie, who were trying to use their access to the White House to facilitate business dealings in China.[45]

More important, high points in the U.S.-China relationship in the late 1990s included reciprocal state visits by Jiang Zemin and Bill Clinton. In addition, thanks to the leadership and determination of U.S. Trade Representative Charlene Barshefsky and despite considerable political pressure to forestall an agreement, the economic dimensions of the U.S.-China relationship advanced to another level with the negotiation of Chinese entrance into the WTO.

Of course, trade relations with the Chinese are exceedingly complex, and there are always contentious issues. One that came up again and again pertained to Chinese violation of U.S. intellectual property rights. Chinese counterfeiters were duplicating and stealing everything from Mickey Mouse T-shirts to videocassettes, and a great deal of pressure was applied to get them to enforce intellectual property rights agreements and arrest the counterfeiters. At the same time, even leading members of the economic team had the perspective to recognize that sometimes these economic concerns needed to be balanced against the political or security aspects of our relationship somewhat more strategically than was sometimes advocated by individual agencies. In one instance, Larry Summers, then deputy secretary of the Treasury, drove this point home with characteristic bluntness: "One of the smarter things I said in my eight years in the Clinton administration for which I got killed at the time was at a China meeting when Charlene [Barshefsky, then USTR] had gone on at some considerable length about taking a tough stand on one IPR [intellectual property rights] issue or another even as there were growing signs of fragility elsewhere in the relationship, and I allowed as how you need to keep some balance with respect to our respective interests relative to nuclear proliferation and the plagiarizing of CDs."[46] Summers got smoother over the years, but never actually became completely smooth. That, of course, is to his credit, and because he was simply one of a couple of people on the team who were in a class by themselves, he was able to get away with his directness.

Unfortunately, the 1999 NATO bombing of the Chinese embassy in Belgrade produced shock waves that rocked the relationship and produced "spontaneous" outbursts by the Chinese people protesting American violence, recklessness, or design. But the relationship was on firm enough ground that it withstood these tensions. Indeed, at the end of the Clinton presidency it was stronger than it had been at the start, despite the now-forgotten campaign rhetoric and largely because the United States was able to look at the relationship in terms of multiple, parallel lines of interest. Policymakers recognized that it is possible to take a tough stand on some issues and remain pragmatic about others and thus keep the most important strategic relationship of the post–Cold War era on an even keel.

One of the watersheds in the evolution of Clinton's international teams came late in 1994. It had been a productive year. Globalization was on the march, NAFTA was the first step, GATT the next, and it was hard to imagine what could slow it down.

358

RUNNING THE WORLD

After these accomplishments, Treasury Secretary Lloyd Bentsen decided to step down. He was one of several initial Clinton cabinet appointments who left early for one reason or another. Aspin took the fall for Somalia and was gone early. Woolsey, who was obviously not fitting in, left at the end of 1995 and was replaced by Deputy Defense Secretary John Deutch. Chief of Staff Mack McLarty, despite having won great credit from the likes of Bob Rubin for creating the atmosphere that made the NEC successful and functional, felt considerable pressure to leave his job and turn it over to someone with more inside-the-beltway experience, which he did, stepping aside for Leon Panetta. McLarty assumed the role of counselor to the president and special emissary for the Americas, which he fulfilled with great distinction. The deputy secretary of state had left and was replaced by Talbott. George Stephanopoulos had stepped down as press secretary and became an advisor to the president. There was considerable upheaval due to inexperience, tension, and in few cases, bad hires.

Bentsen's departure was another story. He was one of the most respected members of the cabinet. Summers recalled, "Bentsen, I think, had told his wife a few years before that it was going to be two years and so he didn't leave early. Maybe if he had loved it he would have kept on going longer, but my guess is that Bentsen found that he didn't much like sitting there and having to argue with [much younger] Gene and George or having to wait an hour and a quarter because President Clinton was running late or had to fool with Tony to get into a meeting. Having said that, I think he was by a wide margin the most experienced and skilled person around in dealing with the Hill."[47]

McLarty recalled that Bentsen "felt that the NSC was not giving him the same broad information and support that it was giving the State Department going into meetings. I had known Lloyd a long time and he came into my office to talk one on one, and with the force of God let me know his displeasure."[48] Rubin, too, recalled that one of Bentsen's frustrations was that he was constantly being cut out of the interagency process by Lake.[49]

So on December 22, 1994, Bentsen resigned. Two days earlier, on December 20, Mexico's new finance minister, Jaime Serra Puche, called to inform the U.S. government that unless urgent steps were taken, Mexico, our new NAFTA partner, would be forced to default on its short-term debt. A default would have shattered confidence in the Mexican economy, hammered Wall Street investors, and knocked the bottom out of the Clinton investment in NAFTA while they were at it.

Within days, the top priority of the administration and incoming Treasury Secretary Bob Rubin was to fashion a financial package that would restore faith in the Mexican market and stave off a financial crisis south of the border that would have turned Ross Perot's great sucking sound into a great screaming sound.

The issue was extraordinarily complex, and the lead naturally fell to the Treasury Department. A small group convened at Rubin's hotel room on Sixteenth Street, a few blocks from the White House and the Treasury Building. This was not the NEC. It was not the NSC. It was Rubin, Summers, Jeff Shafer (the assistant secretary of the Treasury for international affairs), and others, including Export-Import Bank president Kenneth Brody, a former Goldman Sachs partner of Rubin's. The White House gave them considerable latitude to identify and manufacture a solution. What they couldn't do was win congressional support for funding, so Rubin and his team would have to find another source—which they did, the seldom-used Exchange Stabilization Fund. They put together a package that ultimately was worth $40 billion in IMF and U.S. funds, the sum Rubin felt would give the market confidence that Mexico would be able to meet its obligations. It was a big gamble. If Mexico did not repay the debt on time or if the credit line did not stop the exodus from Mexico's market, currency, and securities, then Clinton would be severely damaged on two counts—the mistake he made with NAFTA and the mistake he made trying to save NAFTA. The result, however, was neither. Mexico ultimately paid back the money early. It was a high-wire act that ultimately established Rubin as the key player in the Clinton administration and his team at Treasury as the leading members of the administration's economic team, a reputation that they would maintain throughout the remaining six years of the administration and through another set of similar financial crises in Asia, Russia, and Latin America in 1997 and 1998. Throughout this time, they also mastered the art of saying just enough about the dollar to maintain its strength, guided the United States to a budget surplus, and presided over the biggest boom in American history, an eight-year growth streak that produced nearly 23 million new jobs.

As Rubin recounted:

Clinton was comfortable with our taking the lead on this because the issues were essentially our issues. How do we restore investor confidence? How do we assess and address the vulnerabilities of the banking system? Issues that were pretty much fiscal and market policy and ones that would clearly affect our economy and ones that Clinton himself understood pretty well. And it was centered in Treasury because, when you think about it, it was a pretty rapidly unfolding crisis and you needed to

360 RUNNING THE WORLD

be able to respond quickly, and you needed the kind of competence in the issues of the kind of people we had in Treasury. Technical is not quite the word I would use for it, but it was, in a monetary sense.[50]

David Lipton was pulled in to the Mexico situation from his work on Russia because he had handled such crises and restructurings when he worked at the International Monetary Fund.

I spent a lot of time when I was at the IMF going to countries that were in trouble. So, I said, just send me down there. So I went down there a couple times in January and February and then got pulled out of Russia work and I was fully involved in all of the negotiations with the Mexicans through to the end of the crisis. From what I could tell, this was handled almost entirely by Treasury with almost no involvement or interference from the rest of the community on the substance of the deal. Now the president wanted it that way and that's the way it was. . . . The president basically decided he was going to stake his presidency on fixing this thing and he was going to let us basically tell him how to do it.

And while Mexico has problems—when I think back to the kind of things that people were upset about back then—about drugs, about law enforcement, about immigration, about the democratization of one-party system—all of these things have turned out reasonably well in the last decade. All of this would have turned out horribly if Mexico had had a meltdown that undermined our sense of reasonable government and a relationship with the United States. So I think this was a success, and the president appreciated how much was at stake. Rubin, I know, put a fair amount of emphasis on the contagion issue—that other countries in the region might be affected by a Mexican meltdown—but to me it was always 95 percent about Mexico and what would happen to Mexico, our relationship with Mexico and support for the policies we were trying to follow in the hemisphere which were being road-tested in Mexico.[51]

While this was clearly a major foreign policy issue and the end result had the effect of stabilizing and cementing a critical relationship with a neighbor—a major regional player and one of our most important trading partners—it also exposed some weaknesses in the U.S. foreign policy-making system. One of these was the starkly inadequate intelligence provided by the CIA before and during the crisis. I overheard Larry Summers lambasting a representative from the agency about the uselessness of the product the Treasury received from the agency and pointing out to her that there was a whole industry on Wall Street with a financial incentive to track this information better and to do a better job of it, and that they were doing just that. The Treasury team's contempt for what it received in the way of intelligence to help them with this crisis was unbridled. One senior Clinton administration economic official said, referring to the CIA, "I don't think there was a debate about the value of the agency. I think there was no value from the agency."⁵²

Rubin did something very canny in a bureaucratic sense when he moved to Treasury. "I went to Leon [Panetta, the new chief of staff]," he said, "when I became secretary of the Treasury and I said, Leon, I spent the past two years going to the morning meetings at the White House [the daily staff meetings—both a small group meeting and a larger group meeting each morning—chaired by the chief of staff], and if you don't mind, I would like to keep coming, because I think we are involved in the broad range of issues you cover—which was true. The Treasury is like OMB, which also went, with regard to some of the issues. And he said, Why don't you keep coming, and I did."⁵³ With this, Rubin essentially kept a foot in both worlds and ensured that even having left the NEC, he would remain the lead voice on economic policy for the administration. Of course, successes like the Mexico intervention helped. But, like Kissinger, Rubin understood the importance of proximity to the center of the administration—in other words, to the president and his key staff. He remained the de facto chair of any economic policy discussion that took place during the administration.

Rubin's style at principals meetings was to sit quietly, watching and listening. He didn't speak until the end. He spoke softly and often using self-deprecating wit. He had heard everyone's position, given them the respect of listening to them, and then he spoke in a way that punctuated the entire discussion and, on each instance I saw him do this, determined the final outcome.

In addition to his strength, the Treasury's strong team helped them establish a unique role among the agencies. In fact, I joked with Rubin that if I had been writing this book a few years earlier, in the last years of the Clinton administration, it might have been called *How the Treasury Department Supplanted the State Department in U.S. Foreign Policy*. Another senior Treasury official speculated on the reasons for this dominance and concluded:

It was because we were, simply, smarter. And then when other people tried to get involved in our business, we would explain it to them and then hear them read their talking points and then say, yeah, that's naive and stupid for seven reasons. We actually have things pretty well under control. And then we'd go do what we wanted and so the net effect of it was to insert us into everybody else's business without much insertion of everybody else into our business. And in terms of that fact, what weight should one give to the fact that we kind of had a "fuck you" attitude and the president wasn't prepared to roll us. What fraction was it because we actually had a kind of intellectual dominance over things in our area that other people weren't able to achieve relative to us in their area?[54]

With this approach, once Rubin moved to Treasury, it became clear that while the NEC was the Clinton administration's bureaucratic innovation, the ascendancy of economic issues to greater centrality in foreign policy-making was actually the more significant shift. The NEC ebbed a bit in the absence of Rubin. But the economic agencies, led by Treasury, played a very significant role in most areas of other policy throughout the remainder of the administration.

.   .   .

While the Clinton years were marked by extraordinary economic expansion and the luxury of giving economic issues a centrality they had not had since the days of the New Deal, there was a steady drumbeat of crises that suggested that the end of the Cold War did not represent the solution to the central problem facing mankind—rather, it represented the solution to just the biggest imminent threat that had been dogging the planet. Other dogs continued to bark, to use Tony Lake's phrase, and some of them proved be noisy, unruly and harder to handle than anticipated.

There may have been a "new world order," as Brent Scowcroft had suggested, but it was clear that the "order" in question had to do with the pecking order atop the list of global powers and not the kind of global "order" that brings harmony. What is more, the United States and our allies found that we were ill equipped to face many of the threats that were emerging. Our national security apparatus, our alliances, our war-fighting doctrines, our training, and our prejudices had all prepared us for potential conflicts that now seemed less likely, and we discovered that the ones we actually had to confront were quite different in character and required new thinking, new paradigms, and new mechanisms. For example, with the threat of an invasion in Germany's Fulda Gap gone, NATO discovered that it had real problems mobilizing into effective action when the fighting in Europe broke out 700 miles to the south, in the former Yugoslavia.

Bill Clinton had run for president attacking the first Bush administration's inaction in the former Yugoslavia. Bush officials, such as Lawrence Eagleburger, who once had been ambassador to Yugoslavia and who became secretary of state late in the administration, had been criticized for being too comfortable with the regime that took over in Belgrade and too complacent about the brutality shown by the Serbs to Muslims in Bosnia. When Clinton came to office, finding a solution to this issue was a stated priority, but it quickly became apparent that a solution not only would be hard to come by but also would require a massive effort to transform NATO's vision of itself, significant public opinion battles at home, and extraordinarily complex diplomatic and military initiatives to break the stranglehold Slobodan Milosevic and his henchmen had on power in the region. Moreover, an entirely new interagency approach to managing such evolving crises would be needed, one that brought together political, military, and economic agencies together in one place so that a coordinated diplomacy could be applied, and if it failed, military force could be used, and as soon as force was no longer needed, an effort could be made to secure the peace through other means, such as the rebuilding of infrastructure in the affected country.

This process would become a hallmark of the Clinton NSC/NEC approach to emerging security threats worldwide, although as new transnational threats emerged, fueled in part by the information age and globalization, a new mix of players would be central to achieving America's next generation foreign policy goals. And as America later learned in Iraq, it would illustrate the urgent requirement that in the post–Cold War environment, in which most conflicts were likely to be "low intensity," regional affairs in which we would like to very much limit military exposure and in which the real challenge would be "winning the peace" after the fighting stopped—through restoration of civil society and the economy—that a new mix of players were central to achieving America's next generation of foreign policy goals—that marshaling and deploying soft-power assets was every bit as important as the "hard power" assets that were so important in winning the Cold War. Economic agencies, aid organizations, and others were critical. And the formula would only grow more challenging when the Clinton administration came to recognize that beyond the regional instability and conflicts caused by failed or failing states, the greater problems were associated with a new set of transnational threats that grew in importance proportionally to the progress of the information age and globalization trends that helped fuel them every bit as much as they drove international economic expansion. Foremost among these was the emerging terrorist threat posed by a new generation of technologically empowered, globally mobile nonstate actors, such as Osama bin Laden's al Qaeda organization.

· · ·

During the first months the Clinton administration's engagement with Bosnia, its policy focused on interacting with our European allies, who themselves were divided. The British and the French, to begin with, felt that the issue was theirs to lead. They were also more sympathetic to the Serbs than we were, and they were comfortable with leaving in place an embargo on the Serbs (which the Serbs seemed to be able to live with) and resisting giving aid to the Bosnians or intervening their behalf. It was, as Richard Holbrooke wrote in *To End a War*, the "greatest collective security failure of the West since the 1930s."[55] The United States did not have the political will or the inclination to take on our key allies and risk the division of the European alliance. That the position of some of those allies was based on sympathy for the Serb notion that there was no place for a Muslim state in Europe and that over a quarter million people would die and another two and a half million would be driven from their homes was not considered sufficient motivation for a break with the U.S. policy developed during the first Bush administration—despite Clinton's publicly stated frustrations with that policy.

From the outset, Lake had been an "emotional" advocate for a more proactive policy in the former Yugoslavia. When the administration entered office, he said, "the first thing we did was to spend a month or so going back over the records, trying to understand how we had gotten to where we were, holding a series of principals meetings to devise a new strategy."[56] The administration's first presidential review directive (PRD-1) called for a review of U.S. policy toward Bosnia, which Clinton had criticized during the 1992 presidential campaign.[57]

Reviews by the principals committee resulted in a draft presidential decision directive by early February 1993, leading to the first plan to address the carnage in Bosnia, known as "lift-and-strike." According to lift-and-strike, the United States would lift the arms embargo and launch air strikes against the Bosnian Serbs if they tried to take advantage of the situation before Bosnian Muslims forces were at full strength. However, the strategy never took off, partly because of the inability of Secretary of

State Warren Christopher to obtain Europe's support. As Lake ruefully recalled, "We took [lift-and-strike] to the Europeans. We didn't make the sale, and the Europeans didn't go along."[58] Closer to home, while Madeleine Albright, Vice President Gore, and Lake favored the use of air strikes, Christopher was reluctant to get involved in a seemingly unsolvable morass, and the Defense Department was leery of involvement. Colin Powell was among the opponents. As Nancy Soderberg recalls, Powell had set a very high use-of-force threshold, "saying we could only use force with a couple hundred thousand troops."[59] Ultimately, Clinton's indecisiveness and unenthusiastic support for lift-and-strike doomed the initiative.[60]

While Lake's NSC had intended to craft a strategy to proactively resolve the crisis in Bosnia, the Clinton administration usually found itself reacting to (or ignoring) events in the former Yugoslavia rather than shaping them, as evidenced by meandering principals meetings. Further hampering efforts to respond in the Balkans was that while Lake had regular access to the president (unlike other foreign policy principals), he was not close to Clinton and at times only learned of the president's shifts on Bosnia policy from other senior officials.[61] As Stephen Flanagan, an associate director and member of the policy planning staff at the Department of State, notes, "I was struck by the experience in our effort to articulate a Balkans policy. . . . It seems to me that in the first term there was an effort to delegate a lot of that to the State Department. In other words, the president really wasn't out there that much."[62]

Lake unsuccessfully tried to prevent political advisors David Gergen and Dick Morris from participating in NSC principals meetings and felt compelled to form an alliance with another political aide, George Stephanopoulos, in order to increase his leverage in the internal policy debates taking place in the Oval Office.[63] And while Lake was a skilled infighter, there was the lingering perception that "critical information did not circulate well in the Lake NSC. Lake's effort to prod the President on Bosnia by writing a confidential memo, stating that the administration's ineffectiveness in the Balkans 'was becoming a cancer on Clinton's entire foreign policy—spreading and eating away at its credibility' did not spur Clinton into action."[64] Assistant Secretary of State for European Affairs John Kornblum describes the discontent that was felt: "We went through the first year in a really— what's the right word here—depressed, almost disastrous state on the Balkans. We had essentially no policy. [The Clinton team] didn't seem able to put together a clear picture of what they wanted to do on Bosnia. And there was total either disinterest or confusion."[65]

During this period of stalemate, leaks by foreign policy principals of policy papers and memos were ongoing, including the release of Albright's memos to build support for her advocacy for air strikes against Serbian forces. As Clinton contemplated moving to a more aggressive Bosnia policy in late 1993, Christopher's chief of staff, Thomas Donilon, leaked a memo to the press that inaccurately portrayed the secretary of state as being in favor of more action in the Balkans, while misrepresenting the positions of Clinton, Lake, and Defense Secretary Les Aspin.[66] The leaks only added to the administration's inability to develop a coherent Balkans policy. Such leaks ultimately came to a head in a meeting at the Waldorf-Astoria during which Lake, Donilon, and State Department spokesperson Mike McCurry hammered out a working arrangement that they jokingly referred to as the Treaty of Guadaloupe-Hidalgo.

By the fall of 1994, Lake's frustration with the lack of a coordinated interagency response to Bosnia and the tepid support for action from Congress and NATO had grown to the point that he considered quitting his post.[67] Lake recalled his battles with the president's political advisors, who were telling Clinton that Bosnia was a no-win situation: "Every morning when I walked into the Oval Office—I was the first person [President Clinton] would see in the morning—he would be very polite, and maybe we'd tell a joke or two, and then we'd get to Topic A, and Topic A was always Bosnia. In fact, I felt sometimes as if I had a 'B' written on my forehead, and as soon as he saw it, his whole day would get cloudy as he realized he had to deal with this damn issue."[68] One colleague of Lake's observed that "to succeed in that job, you have to be able to immunize yourself against some terrible pressures. I don't think Tony was very good about letting go of Bosnia—it was probably to his credit as a human being and to his disadvantage as an NSC advisor."[69] Similarly, Richard Holbrooke describes Lake as "conflicted from day one because that is part of his character."[70]

Lake was talked out of resigning by his close friend, NSC Senior Director for European Affairs Alexander "Sandy" Vershbow, who was also one of the most vocal hawks on Bosnia in the upper ranks of the administration (and chaired the Interagency Working Group on Bosnia, which met daily to review and coordinate policy toward that volatile region).[71] Vershbow argued that whoever replaced Lake as national security advisor would not demonstrate as much commitment to this festering problem. Since Bosnia was not going to disappear, Vershbow counseled Lake to remain at his post, where he would be in a position to make a difference. Also, according to David Halberstam, Lake did not want to walk away from a high-level position a second time, failing, as he did as an aide to

Kissinger, to "bring home the policy he advocated on a transcending issue about which he felt passionately."[72]

Finally, after years of interagency deadlock and UN futility, Lake decided in the summer of 1995 that he could construct an effective Bosnia policy only by "turning away from the interagency process." He began by creating a task force to think about crafting a new policy.

This collaboration resulted in the development of the "endgame" strategy that was premised on ending the conflict by creating a single state in which the warring parties—the Croat and Muslim Bosnians and the Serbs—would be separated. The strategy rested on the establishment of a military balance of power among the ethnic factions to deter additional fighting. The Clinton administration would try to gain the support of Serbs for a resolution of the conflict by telling them that if they were unwilling to negotiate, the arms embargo would be lifted and air strikes would be conducted to support Croat and Muslim Bosnian forces. In addition, Muslim and Croat leaders were threatened with abandonment by the United States and the UN if they did not come to the negotiating table.

Meanwhile, Lake was going to exploit his proximity to the president to get his way without first waiting to forge a consensus within the foreign policy bureaucracy. In a notable change in his modus operandi, Lake moved away from his role as an honest broker and purveyor of interagency viewpoints and attempted to secure the president's support directly for his Bosnia initiative.[73] Several days after creating his endgame strategy, Lake presented his still somewhat vague proposal for the Balkans at his regular morning national security briefing, bluntly asking Clinton, "Mr. President, tell me if you don't want to do this, stop me now, because the risks are very clear."[74]

The president was receptive to the new NSC plan, although Ivo Daalder, NSC director for European affairs, noted that Lake was careful to involve the president in each step of the drafting process: "As [Lake] was developing his strategy, he would tell the president, 'Mr. President, I'm really working on this, I think we're getting somewhere.' And as soon as he had a good draft he showed it to the president. And the president said, 'I like it, I think this is a good idea.'" Lake, Daalder added, also appealed to the president for his personal involvement, saying, "Mr. President, it would be very useful if you came by and dropped in and tell them that you think we need a new policy on Bosnia, and that you like the ideas that I have. . . . I have to get the others on board [including Christopher, Perry, and the Joint Chiefs of Staff]. We have to start working with them." The massacre in Srebrenica also impelled Clinton, who raged at Berger and Soderberg several days later while putting golf balls, demanding that "this can't continue. We have to seize control of this."[75]

At a breakfast meeting in mid-July 1995 in Lake's office, the national security advisor revealed his endgame strategy to Christopher, Perry, Albright, Berger, and the chairman of the Joint Chiefs of Staff, General John Shalikashvili, telling them, "This is how I think we need to resolve the Bosnia issue. I would like to have your points of view about how you would like to do it."[76] Soon afterward, the president appeared at the meeting, telling the surprised participants, "I don't like where we are now—we have a war by CNN. Our position is unsustainable, it's killing the U.S. position of strength in the world."[77] Daalder added that the president also informed his foreign policy principals, "'You know, Tony's got some good ideas here, but I would like your ideas too about how we can resolve this issue.' But making very clear that, one, he knew where Tony Lake was coming from, and, second, that he liked those ideas; a major bureaucratic plus in the bureaucratic infighting. And from that the process moves along in order to get the State Department and the military and the Defense Department to give input to where we ought to go on Bosnia policy."[78]

With this high-level backing, Lake was able to overcome State Department and Pentagon objections, and at a principals committee meeting on August 1, he asked that each agency submit recommendations on Bosnia policy within three days, ensuring that his already-crafted approach to Bosnia would be supplemented, not replaced, by his State and Defense Department counterparts.[79] On August 7, Lake met with the president, who told him that now they had to "exhaust every alternative, roll every die, take risks" to meet with the Europeans and overcome their hesitancy on his endgame initiative. Lake would be deployed to meet secretly with the Europeans to seek their support, and President Clinton took the unusual step of personally assisting his national security advisor with his presentation to his foreign counterparts.[80] Meanwhile, John Kornblum, who was heavily involved in the Balkans negotiations, noted that Christopher, who had been uncertain about what the administration was going to do in the wake of the Srebrenica massacre, was "visibly shaken . . . when he had been presented with the Lake trip to Europe to take an initiative to get things moving towards a peace agreement in Bosnia. . . . And I can tell you that nobody in the State Department knew about this."[81]

At the conclusion of his mission, which successfully captured the backing of the major European leaders, Lake stopped in London and met with Assistant Secretary of State Richard Holbrooke, who had been given the delicate role of hammering out a peace accord with all the warring parties in Dayton. His appointment to the position was not without controversy, within both the State Department and the NSC. Holbrooke was characterized by his State Department colleagues as someone who was "domineering [and] imagines he's a seventh-floor official when he's only sixth floor. Too undisciplined to follow instructions."[82] While Holbrooke was able to develop a solid working relationship with State Department colleagues, his relations with Lake and the NSC remained strained.

Lake viewed Holbrooke as "high maintenance."[83] A senior State Department official recalled how the relationship between these two strong-willed men had deteriorated, as "they had been the deepest of friends twenty-five years earlier. By this time, they were really quite open enemies. . . . It was a continual sort of low-level warfare between the State Department and the NSC."[84] In fact, according to Holbrooke, who had long sought to lead a major international negotiation, Lake had originally proposed former Balkans special envoy Charles Redman (who had succeeded Holbrooke as U.S. ambassador to Germany) for the position.[85]

After Holbrooke threatened to leave the State Department "because I was brought back by the president to do policy" on Bosnia, he received assurances from [Christopher's chief of staff] Tom Donilon that "Christopher will make sure you're the negotiator."[86] Consequently, Lake acquiesced and Holbrooke took charge of the negotiations in Dayton, but tensions remained. Kornblum notes, "I had a good deal of conflict with Lake's European group. . . . It was not pleasant. . . . We would have these Friday meetings which were chaired always by Sandy Berger. And it was always a duel of . . . my concepts against [NSC Senior Director for European Affairs] Sandy Vershbow, who actually was a good friend of mine. But at that point, we were not good friends, because he was pushing the Tony Lake line, and so we were sort of battling it out."[87]

Kornblum also asserts that "Dick controlled the whole process after that [Lake's trip to Europe]. It was because of his strong personality but also because of his ties to people. . . . But Tony Lake moved back into the background quite clearly. The other person, of course, who was very important here, whom Dick had a good relationship with was Sandy Berger. And I think Sandy was probably the oil that kept the gears going here."[88] Similarly, David Lipton, under secretary for international affairs at the Treasury Department, says, "Holbrooke was the quarterback, and Defense and everybody was in essence working with him,"[89] although one White House participant maintains that "Tony came up with the intellectual framework for the endgame, sold it to the Europeans, and then handed it off to Dick, at which point Dick became the driving factor in it. Like we say, he's a negotiator."[90]

Holbrooke was provided with considerable autonomy. Secretary Christopher recalled that to "maximize U.S. negotiating flexibility . . . [we] felt that Holbrooke and his team had to be allowed to shape the specifics of an agreement."[91] Holbrooke, upon discovering that Lake wanted to create an NSC-led committee to oversee his negotiating efforts, responded by having Kornblum create a State Department–based informal "backstop operation" that kept Washington informed but protected the independence of Holbrooke's efforts. Holbrooke also credits Berger with protecting the negotiations from outside interference.[92]

Once the negotiating teams were in place in Dayton, Tony Lake was largely absent from the grueling day-to-day talks, although his director of European affairs, Lieutenant-General Donald Kerrick, served on Holbrooke's negotiating team. Holbrooke, who praised Kerrick's role in the peace talks,[93] maintains that the NSC was peripheral to the ultimate success in Dayton, noting the different negotiating roles that Lake and Kissinger played:

> Tony's trip had no effect on the subsequent shuttle and Dayton. The trip was consistent with his ambivalence about his relation to power. If Kissinger had been there, he would have done the whole thing, including the shuttle and Dayton. But Tony wasn't going to put himself in such a high-risk position. At the same time, he wanted to be associated with it, so he structured a safe position. He would launch the process and then take as much credit as he could if it succeeded, and say it was someone else's if it failed.[94]

While praising Holbrooke's performance in the negotiations, Lake disputes the assessment, arguing that he disengaged from the Dayton talks in order to "return to his day job" and fulfull his responsibilities as national security advisor. Holbrooke also recounts in *To End a War* how he was told by Lake at a "handoff" meeting in London that success was unlikely, but that the national security advisor would be "with me all the way." Lake added "if this fails, it's my ass more than yours."[95]

Holbrooke credits Lake for making the "critical decision as to where the negotiations would be held. And in that regard, it was a nine-to-one against an American site. Tony was the one, the only one, who bought the negotiating team theory that it should be held in the United States. A White House meeting was scheduled for October 5 to make a recommendation to the president. Tony kept our position alive. I was allowed to argue my case by phone. And we won. This was decisive. If that thing had been held in Geneva or Stockholm, we wouldn't have controlled the negotiations and we wouldn't have gotten an agreement."[96]

On November 21, 1995, after three weeks of intensive negotiations at Wright-Patterson Air Force Base, representatives of the warring parties in the former Yugoslavia finally approved the agreement that became known as the Dayton Peace Accords. The agreement provided for the continued existence of a single, though divided, state of Bosnia-Herzegovina, with 51 percent of the territory going to the Muslim-Croat Federation and 49 percent to the entity that would be known as the "Bosnian Serb Republic" (Republika Srpska). Under the agreement, the battered city of Sarajevo was to be unified under the control of the Muslim-Croat Federation.[97]

The accord stopped the fighting in Bosnia, but problems remained, particularly as the "civilian" apparatus prescribed by Dayton was slow to emerge, and pressure increased for the military to assume greater responsibility for the success of the accords. No issue may have been more contentious than whether the NATO-commanded multinational Implementation Force (IFOR) would track down and arrest indicted war criminals. For some in the administration, especially Holbrooke, the success in Dayton would not have been possible without the arrest of the Bosnian Serb leaders and indicted war criminals Radovan Karadzic and Ratko Mladic. Holbrooke argued that their continued presence and activities fueled the hopes of Bosnian Serb separatists and ended the promise of multiethnic peace.[98]

Clinton's 1996 election victory brought an end to the tensions between Lake and Holbrooke and, unintentionally, to Lake's tenure in the Clinton administration. It had been decided that after the election, Berger would replace Lake as national security advisor and that Lake in turn would replace John Deutch as CIA director. But in the face of highly partisan congressional opposition led by Alabama Senator Richard Shelby, Lake concluded that his confirmation would be difficult to obtain and withdrew from contention for the CIA post. The job went to his close friend and former NSC staffer handling intelligence issues, George Tenet. Warren Christopher also left in 1996 and was replaced by Madeleine Albright, who was in turn replaced as U.S. ambassador to the UN by Energy Secretary Bill Richardson (and later by Holbrooke). Bill Perry also was by Republican Senator William Cohen of Maine, so there was a transformation around the table in the Situation Room.

This second-term leadership team had the benefit of the first term's lessons as well as the significant benefit of Berger's tutelage under Lake and his desire to take a process that was working pretty well and upgrade it further. Berger, who had a somewhat more even-handed style than Lake, came into office with ten "commandments" for his staff that were intended both to be guidelines and to illustrate cultural changes that would come with his leadership, including an admonition that when it stops being thrilling to come to work in the White House, it is time to look for another job.

It was in mid-May 1997, after a meeting between Albright, Berger, and Cohen (known in White House parlance at the time as an "ABC meeting"), that the administration established a longer-term U.S. commitment in Bosnia. As a result of the meeting, it was agreed that the United States would push for NATO forces to assume greater responsibility for the implementation of the peace accords, including the arrest of war criminals and the return of displaced refugees. In December 1997, with the initial one-year exit plan having long passed, President Clinton announced that while the number of U.S. troops would be scaled back, withdrawal deadlines would no longer determine the length of U.S. commitment to Bosnia.

While the U.S. was struggling to stabilize the situation in Bosnia, another crisis was brewing to the southeast in another troubled part of the former Yugoslavia. The Albanian majority in the province of Kosovo, a target of Yugoslav president Slobodan Milosevic's ethnic oppression, had been disappointed by the agreement in Dayton, which, in their view, failed to recognize their long-standing and justified demand for independence. The Dayton Accords had not only recognized a Serbian governmental entity (Republika Srpska) within the new state of Bosnia-Herzegovina but also decreed that no additional changes in borders within Yugoslavia would be permitted, a precedent that worried the Albanian Kosovar community.

The Serbian minority in Kosovo also viewed the events in Bosnia and Croatia with alarm, and with both parties increasingly uneasy about their future in the territory, ethnic fighting by armed factions on both sides grew. The Albanian response to Belgrade's repression (which had begun with ethnic purges of Albanian Kosovars from government jobs in the early 1980s and escalated from there) was at first peaceful but became violent, led first by the underground National Movement for the Liberation of Kosovo and then by the Kosovo Liberation Army (KLA). The KLA's goal was to radicalize the situation in Kosovo, which they succeeded in doing by killing Serbian policemen and border guards as well as Serbian civilians in the refugee camps. Armed Serb countermeasures inevitably followed.[99]

As the civil war heated up in Kosovo and the humanitarian crisis grew, Western governments began to take notice. The new Balkans crisis was being monitored by the new set of foreign policy principals in the Clinton administration. Berger, in marked contrast to Lake, enjoyed a much closer and warmer relationship with Clinton and had a long friendship with Secretary of State Albright.[100] Furthermore, compared with Lake, who kept a low profile as the internal and public furor about Bosnia grew, Berger adopted a more visible public presence, noting on one occasion that "part of my job is to explain to the American people what our objectives are."[101] Berger was also responsible for coordinating the administration's public line on foreign policy matters, although a televised "town hall" meeting in Ohio in February 1998, given by Berger, Albright, and Cohen, represented a high-profile failure to explain the rationales of the administration's Bosnia policy.[102]

Berger notes:

I did consider Madeleine to be the foreign policy spokesperson for the administration, and she was the principal foreign policy negotiator and implementer. Policy came from both the State Department and the NSC. But I will admit that one place that I think I am a little more expansive than some others is with respect to the public role of the national security advisor. I think that communicating foreign policy has become so important to sustaining a foreign policy that you have to put all your people in the field on any particular issue. . . . I gave very few groundbreaking policy speeches. I gave speeches for the purposes of building public support. If there was to be a speech about a new direction in the Middle East or in the Balkans, that was done by the secretary of state. I think that's the right balance.[103]

During crises, Berger sometimes met daily with Albright and Cohen. However, the second Clinton foreign policy team, perhaps mirroring Clinton himself, was as divided on Balkans policy as the first team, with shifts from reluctant Christopher to hawkish Albright, hawkish Lake to a somewhat more cautious Berger, while Cohen shared Perry's lack of enthusiasm for U.S. military involvement. As a consequence of this division, and because Kosovo was overshadowed by other foreign events as well as the Lewinsky scandal and impeachment proceedings, Kosovo remained largely off the radar screen while the problems on the ground continued to flare.

Nonetheless, Kosovo couldn't be ignored forever. The United States had originally made a commitment to prevent Serbian violence in Kosovo

on Christmas Eve 1992, when the first Bush administration warned Milosevic that "in the event of conflict in Kosovo caused by Serbian action, the
U.S. will be prepared to employ military force against Serbians in Kosovo
and in Serbia proper." The warning, reiterated by the Clinton administration twice in 1993, issued "an unspecified threat, of unspecified certainty,
to prevent unspecified acts of escalation by Serbia," a vagueness that
Arnold Kanter, under secretary of state for political affairs in the first Bush
administration, said he couldn't define.[104]

The Clinton administration did not call attention to the American commitment to Kosovo in the intervening years, and the troubled province was
not on the agenda at the Dayton talks in 1995. Holbrooke defended the
decision, noting that "Bosnia was then the emergency, and it had to be
stopped. Otherwise there would have been a real risk that Bosnia would
merge with Kosovo into a huge firestorm that would destabilize the whole
region."[105]

But as the chaos grew, Kosovo forced its way back onto the agenda. Secretary Albright, speaking in March 1998 before the Contact Group on
Kosovo (consisting of the United States, Russia, the United Kingdom, Germany, France, and Italy), placed the blame for violence in Kosovo squarely
on Milosevic. She laid out the conditions that he and his government
would have to accept, including the unfettered presence of international
observers in Kosovo, "enhanced" autonomy for Kosovo within Serbia, and
a cessation of violence. Those terms and others were not met, and the war
intensified. Furthermore, her bellicose comments—meant to "lead through
rhetoric," in the words of one Albright aide—were making the Pentagon
and the White House nervous, as they did not want to promise more than
the president would be prepared to deliver in Kosovo.[106]

Sandy Vershbow, now the U.S. representative to NATO, was also
attempting to generate momentum for renewed involvement by the Clinton administration. He sent a classified cable to Washington, titled
"Kosovo: Time for Another Endgame Strategy," outlining a political settlement in Kosovo that would be made with the cooperation of the Russians.
His plan called for the creation of an international protectorate in Kosovo,
policed by a multinational military presence. It also left open the possibility that NATO might have to impose a settlement without Belgrade's consent. The architect of the original endgame strategy for Bosnia wrote,
"Sooner or later we are going to face the issue of deploying ground forces
in Kosovo. We have too much at stake in the political stability of the south
Balkans to permit the conflict to fester much longer."[107]

Although the plan generated some interest among midlevel officials in the Clinton administration, it was never adopted, in part because of fears of the troop commitments that such a plan would entail. Vershbow's cable also had the misfortune of arriving in Washington on August 7, the day of the bombings of the U.S. embassies in Tanzania and Kenya. Furthermore, his plan circulated during the planning for the cruise missile attacks against Osama bin Laden as well as Clinton's testimony before the Lewinsky grand jury.[108]

The furor resulting from the exposure of the affair between Lewinsky and the president represented the culmination of the Gingrich-led Congress's onslaught against Clinton. The largely Republican camp pounced on the president's reckless indiscretion with an intern. In the thirteen months between the beginning of the ordeal and Clinton's acquittal at his impeachment trial, the administration struggled to act as if it was doing business as usual, which included fulfilling the president's foreign policy responsibilities. Sandy Berger, who said that he rarely talked about the Lewinsky matter with the president, said in a television interview:

> We've always tried to keep foreign policy, national security policy, separated from not only whatever domestic controversy might be going on, but certainly also political cross-currents. And so it was a strange period. We tried to conduct American foreign policy based on what was in the national interest. . . . I often went home at night and called my daughter, who works for one of your competing networks, to find out what had happened that day on the scandal front. We really did try to keep a separation between that and foreign policy.[109]

And no matter the distractions facing the White House from Congress, Clinton's foreign policy team had little choice but to address the crises that were piling up on the administration's foreign policy "need-attention" lists.

The intermixing of the impeachment hearings and the conduct of foreign policy produced some uncomfortable situations for the White House. Secretary of State Albright commented on the "wag the dog" allegations that followed the retaliatory strikes against bin Laden: "Well, I think that we figured that despite the fact that there were those kinds of statements going on, we had to do what we had to do. The national security team is a very close team, and we see each other and talk to each other constantly, and kind of felt that we had a responsibility . . . to go forward. The president was always there and totally responsible and engaged. I know there may be people who criticize him for his compartmentalization, but for foreign policy, it never interfered."[110]

Similarly, John Podesta, Clinton's second-term chief of staff, was given the task of informing members of Congress that the United States was going to launch "Operation Desert Fox" just as the House impeachment vote debate was about to start.[111] The bombing operation was designed to destroy Iraq's nuclear, chemical, and biological weapons programs in response to Saddam Hussein's interference with UN Special Commission (UNSCOM) inspectors. Podesta remembered the anger and disbelief he faced when he told Congress about the imminent action:

> I knew that there was the potential for great criticism of the timing, if not the action. And I think that everybody on the national security team was really quite strong and willing to stand up and say, look, we have to do this, it's in our national interest, it's the right thing to do. Nevertheless, I envisioned what the reaction was going to be to these congressional notification calls, and it was the only time since I've been in my office where I had to sit down and take some deep breaths before I could actually pick up the telephone and call people. . . . [It] was kind of a stunned silence at the other end of the phone, and I said, "Look, this is the right thing to do, we've got to make the right call." . . . It was done with the knowledge that this impeachment inquiry was going on around us, but without really an option to let that bleed over into the decision making.[112]

The timing was awkward, Podesta acknowledged, but "the only real way to operate was like pretending the rest of it wasn't going on. I mean, you couldn't make decisions if you were trying to look at both mirrors. You just couldn't."[113]

The impeachment storm receded after February 1999, but the administration remained unenthusiastic about threatening force against the Yugoslav leader. Richard Holbrooke was sent back to the Balkans in October to see if he could broker a deal to quell the violence in Kosovo as he had done with Bosnia. After nine days of talks with Holbrooke, Milosevic agreed to accept a cease-fire in Kosovo and pledged to withdraw the bulk of his forces from the territory and permit the presence of unarmed international inspectors.[114] The deal quickly fell apart, however, with both the KLA and Serbian forces expanding their campaigns against their ethnic opponents, resulting in thousands of deaths and hundreds of thousands of displaced persons.

On the morning of January 15, 1999, the NSC principals met in the Situation Room to discuss the deteriorating situation in Kosovo. Secretary Albright lobbied forcefully for expanding U.S. and NATO involvement to stem the ethnic violence, using the threat of air strikes to enforce a peace agreement that would be monitored by NATO ground troops. Although everyone was in agreement that Milosevic was violating the October 1998 agreement to restrain his Serb forces in the restive province, she was unable to persuade her colleagues to escalate threats of military force, including an apprehensive Sandy Berger. As Clinton's national security advisor had exclaimed to a colleague several months earlier, "Are we going to bomb on Kosovo? Can I explain that to Congress? They'll kill us."[115]

Reflecting that risk aversion, the principals committee instead approved a thirteen-page classified Kosovo strategy known as "Status Quo Plus," which stated that "our fundamental strategic objectives remain unchanged: promote regional stability and protect our investment in Bosnia; prevent resumption of hostilities in Kosovo and renewed humanitarian crisis; preserve U.S. and NATO credibility."[116] The unwillingness to issue more explicit military threats to Milosevic angered Albright, who was convinced that bold action was necessary to prevent the violence in Kosovo from spiraling further out of control.[117]

The next day, Serb and Yugoslav forces killed forty-five Albanian civilians in the village of Racak. The international outrage over the killings sparked a rapid turnaround in the administration's Kosovo strategy. (It didn't hurt that William Walker, an American diplomat who was then head of the Kosovo Verification Mission of the Organization for Security and Cooperation in Europe, publicly labeled the attack a "massacre." He also apparently told Holbrooke, on a cell phone from Racak, "Dick, you can kiss your Nobel Prize good-bye."[118]) Four days after the NSC principals had rejected Albright's ambitious plan, they reconvened and approved her more aggressive approach to address Kosovo, which she later termed the "crucible of the problem" in the Balkans.[119] At the end of January 1999, NATO warned Milosevic that it was ready to use military force immediately against Yugoslav targets in order "to compel compliance with the demands of the international community and [to achieve] a political settlement" in Kosovo. Britain and France went further, indicating that they were ready to send in ground forces to enforce a peace settlement. President Clinton told his foreign policy team that "[Milosevic] may be sorely tempted to take the first round of airstrikes. I hope we don't have to bomb, but we may need to."[120]

A conference was held in Rambouillet, France, in February 1999 to negotiate a settlement for Kosovo, with the United States, Europe, Yugoslavia, and representatives of the major Albanian Kosovar groups at the table. The proposal required Yugoslavia to withdraw its forces from Kosovo, the KLA to lay down their arms, NATO peacekeeping troops on the ground to enforce the agreement, and a three-year period of autonomy— but not independence—for the local Albanians during which the local parties would settle the political future of Kosovo. Holbrooke recalls that while the Clinton administration had recently coalesced around Albright's more forceful policy against Milosevic, the team members had not been on the same page about the negotiating strategy in France:

> Madeleine and [her public affairs aide] Jamie [Rubin] announced that if the Albanians accepted our deal and the Serbs didn't, that would be a *casus belli* for military action against Milosevic and the Serbs. This was completely unorthodox, and I asked Sandy afterwards if he knew it was going to be said, and he didn't, and it just caught him off balance. By doing it, they left the U.S. government in a dilemma: either we didn't mean what we said or there would be a war, because there was no chance Milosevic was going to accept.[121]

Holbrooke credits Albright's willpower and determination for being able to outmaneuver Berger and push her plan forward at Rambouillet.[122] However, neither side was willing to accept a deal, and even after the personal intervention of the secretary of state, the talks ended after two weeks without an agreement. The threat of NATO bombing was also put on hold.[123]

The conference reconvened in Paris three weeks later and although Albright and Senator Bob Dole were able to pressure the Albanian delegation to sign the Rambouillet agreement, which would provide the Albanian Kosovar population with broader autonomy for a three-year interim period, Milosevic refused to sign.[124] President Clinton dispatched Holbrooke as a special envoy to Belgrade for one last meeting with Milosevic on March 22. Before leaving, Holbrooke "told Sandy flatly that we had less than a 10 percent chance of success."[125]

After issuing the ultimatum, decisively rejected by the Yugoslav leader, Holbrooke asked Milosevic if he understood the consequences of his refusal to sign the Rambouillet Accord. Milosevic replied, "You are going to bomb us." Holbrooke confirmed, "That's[nbs]right."[126] The NATO bombing began on March 24.

The campaign in Kosovo was led by General Wesley Clark, the talented and controversial Supreme Allied Commander Europe (SACEUR) who had the daunting job of coordinating both a fractious (and recently expanded) eighteen-member NATO alliance as well as a collection of competing agencies in Washington. Hungary, for example, had just joined NATO. "Nations see conflicts differently," notes Clark. "The second day of the war, the Hungarian ambassador came in to me and said . . . Hungary twice before in this century has joined alliances and then gone to war almost immediately. And both times Hungary lost and was dismembered. The prime minister asks that you not allow this to happen this time. . . . The United States was under no risk of dismemberment or losing; we didn't even consider it a war, in America. So there were huge gaps in perceptions that needed to be addressed effectively, and they needed to be addressed at all levels."[127]

In particular, Clark had difficulties with the Pentagon, where he "was virtually without support among the military" who had never been enthusiastic about involvement in the Balkans.[128] As the air war unfolded, the SACEUR rarely found himself able to communicate directly with Defense Secretary William Cohen—who had appointed him to the post over the Joint Chiefs' objections—a situation which represented an unwelcome change in management style from Cohen's predecessor as secretary of defense, William Perry. According to Clark, while Perry liked to have close, direct contact with his CINCs, Cohen preferred a different approach and directed his SACEUR to report through Hugh Shelton and Joe Ralston, the chairman and vice-chairman of the Joint Chiefs of Staff.

Clark, who had served as Holbrooke's top military aide in the 1995 Dayton talks, battled almost daily about target lists with Washington and also had fierce dustups with the Joint Chiefs over requests for Apache helicopters, his request to base rockets in Croatia to launch into Kosovo, and other battlefield matters.[129] Clark believed that one of the lessons learned from Vietnam and recent U.S. history had been that for peace talks to succeed, there had to be a clear incentive for the opponent to come to the negotiating table, which meant sending an unmistakable message that they had more to lose by continuing to fight than they did from talking. Consequently, Clark pushed for a robust military response in order to induce Milosevic to talk about a Kosovo settlement but the SACEUR found that at the Pentagon, some key officials at the highest levels were sluggish to respond to his concerted efforts and resentful of his pressing them.

As communication between Clark's command and the Pentagon became strained, Defense Department officials suspected that an unofficial, active line of contact existed between Clark and National Security Advisor Berger, with whom he had developed a good relationship while on the Joint Staff.[130] Pentagon officials also suspected that Clark had other outlets to lobby for his agenda for the war. As one military colleague recalled, "It was clear [Clark] was working the Hill, the White House. . . . We'd have to spend the whole day dealing with his back-channeling."[131] Finally, Joint Chiefs chairman General Hugh Shelton delivered a sharp message from Cohen to Clark, "Get your [expletive] face off the TV."[132]

Clark, however, recalls a mid-March briefing for Cohen about Macedonia that illustrates just how fundamentally he often differed with his bosses in their approach to basic issues.

> I said, well, sir . . . ten thousand troops are going to be in artillery range around this air field of the Serb border here in Macedonia. If you pull them back out of artillery range, you set off potential political repercussions to the government of Macedonia; it looks like you're going to pull out. If you leave them there, you leave them hostage to Serb counterfire. And when I . . . looked at his face and listened to him, it was clear he hadn't focused on this. These weren't U.S. troops; primarily they were other nations' troops. He was getting briefed on the U.S. situation. So, partly, it's the Joint Chiefs of Staff who as a whole don't understand the alliance and NATO. . . . And so, what you end up with, from the Joint Staff, is a very ethnocentric approach that makes it difficult for decision makers to see the larger picture.[133]

The slow and limited pace of the air campaign heightened frustrations within the Clinton administration and NATO, but a meeting in late April in Washington celebrating the fiftieth anniversary of the transatlantic alliance proved to be a turning point. With the leaders of all the member countries in attendance, President Clinton mended fences with the British and coordinated strategies about the war effort. Meanwhile, Clark, who was leading NATO forces in Yugoslavia, had not originally been invited to the celebration, and had to lobby NATO chief Javier Solana (overcoming the opposition of Secretary Cohen and General Shelton) to attend, but only on the condition that he behave "with minimum visibility".[134]

A U.S.-British compromise at the summit resulted in the decision to allow Clark to begin plans for a ground campaign, and he was given additional flexibility in his targeting options against Milosevic. By June 2, Berger wrote a memo to President Clinton laying out the available options and noted that a ground campaign, involving as many as 250,000 troops, might be required to ensure that a settlement for "Serbs out, NATO in, Albanians back" could be reached.[135] After two and a half months of bombing and sensing that a ground invasion was increasingly likely and

NATO disunity unlikely, Milosevic capitulated on June 10, acceding to a military presence within Kosovo headed by the UN but incorporating NATO troops.

General Clark may have helped to win the war in Kosovo, but he lost the battle within the Pentagon when Defense Secretary Cohen relieved him of his duties as SACEUR several months early. As David Halberstam writes, "rarely had the commanding general in a victorious cause been treated so harshly."[136] President Clinton and Sandy Berger did not realize that when they approved the Pentagon's request for a promotion of General Joseph Ralston, it would require his appointment as SACEUR, thus forcing Clark's retirement from the armed forces. Clark did not learn of the news from Cohen directly, first learning of the move from General Shelton and then from a newspaper reporter.

Berger continues:

> Clinton did not attend NSC meetings per se. The president came to NSC meetings during crises, the Haiti meeting or Kosovo or Iraq, and he and the vice president would come down for an hour to the Situation Room and meet together. But he preferred either to let Tony or me run the meetings and then bring him either a memo, which laid it out so that he could decide, or we would call a meeting in the Cabinet Room or in the Oval Office, and I would coordinate those meetings, although he'd pretty much chair those meetings himself. . . . When President Clinton approached really big decisions—decisions involving, say, the use of force—he took it very seriously, like every president does, and he would decide and then he would test that decision by challenging other people with the case against the decision. So I would often get a call at 10:00 p.m. saying, "We're about to head off a cliff: How do we deal with this or that aspect?" He had such an analytical and strong mind that he would proceed with the eleven reasons why what we were about to do was crazy, which was five more reasons than I had even thought of myself. And I would come back and rebut his arguments. He wanted to be satisfied that all the downsides had been thought through and that he had sufficient answers. For him it was like checking the bolts on the car one more time. When you check a tire and you do all the bolts, it was like going back around each bolt and tightening them each one more turn.[137]

As the years went by, the thrust of the debate about what the central organizing principles of the foreign policy should be also changed. Tony

Lake had originally proposed the idea of "enlargement" as a kind of post–Cold War flip side to containment. Enlargement would be the promotion of our core ideas about democracy and free markets to the rest of the world in an effort to consolidate the Cold War victory and ensure greater integration, prosperity, and enthusiasm for America and American ideals. Later, as globalization and the information age were understood to be core elements of the post–Cold War reality, the focus evolved to be more responsive to those realities. And then, in the later years of the Clinton administration, as a new generation of threats seemed to emerge, it became clearer and clearer that it would not be possible, as we had once hoped, to put security concerns behind us completely.

During Clinton's second term, the president and his team started to focus on a new class of "transnational threats." These threats used the connective tissues of globalization to spread, much like the benefits of market integration. Among them were the spread of diseases across borders, such as AIDS, which had already killed tens of millions in Africa and was beginning to take a toll in Asia; of organized crime, such as the trade in narcotics that linked the poppy fields of Afghanistan to the crime families of St. Petersburg to the drug cartels of Colombia to the street dealers in American cities and towns; and of terrorism, which rocked U.S. interests repeatedly from 1996—when the concern was protecting the Olympics in Atlanta from terrorists—through the attacks in the Middle East on Khobar Towers and the USS Cole and the attacks on the U.S. embassies in Kenya and Tanzania—to the millennium threat associated with the arrival of the new century. The root of all these threats was, as it had been for many years with terrorist enemies, in the Middle East.[138]

In the first days of the Clinton administration, the government was ill equipped to handle these threats. "Washington's broader counterterrorism bureaucracy, in 1993, was dispersed, plagued by interagency rivalries and fraying under budgetary pressure." The National Security Council was part of this bureaucracy.[139] But the NSC would become the focal point for the administration's evolving counterterrorism strategy, in large part as a result of the entrepreneurship displayed by one its directors, Richard Clarke, and the support he would receive from Lake and subsequently from Berger.

Terrorism was elevated to a higher (but not the highest) threat status, according to the administration's revised intelligence collection priorities. James Steinberg, director of policy planning in the State Department and later deputy national security advisor to Berger, noted that "from 1995 and 1996 on, you can see this rising curve of urgency and attention" to terrorism and other transnational threats. After Clinton signed a presidential decision directive (PDD-39) in June 1995, the "Clinton administration was the first administration to undertake a systematic anti-terrorist effort—organizationally, in terms of resources and in terms of anti-terrorist activity," according to Sandy Berger, who was then deputy national security advisor.[140]

Clarke, who joined the NSC in 1992, was among the earliest and most vocal proponents in the Clinton administration to raise the alarm about terrorism and the threat from al Qaeda. Beginning in 1995, using his post as head of the interagency Counterterrorism Strategy Group (CSG), he "bullied" government agencies while conducting brainstorming sessions "over burgers and tuna sandwiches sent over from the White House canteen."[141] Clarke, who worked in what once was Oliver North's office suite, would not hesitate to be "very abusive," sometimes sending off e-mails to highlight the incompetence of a rival agency.[142] Clarke enjoyed a good relationship with the president, his "authority deriv[ing] in large measure from the fact that Clinton shares his area of interest," and successfully lobbied him for greater authority and resources.[143] Three months before the 1998 embassy bombings, the post of national coordinator for counterterrorism was created. President Clinton named Clarke to the powerful position, giving him a seat at principals meetings with the secretaries of state and defense.[144]

Tony Lake was also "foaming at the mouth about bin Laden" as early as 1996 as a consequence of Clarke's lobbying, and Clarke also had the support of Sandy Berger, Lake's successor, as he maneuvered to obtain greater government funding throughout the president's second term.[145] Consequently, as one of his NSC colleagues noted in 2000, "It's no accident that there's a direct correlation between the number of troops that Dick Clarke has on his staff and his ability to browbeat and pummel the agencies into performing and achieving the kind of integration he has on some of the transnational issues."[146]

Despite the increase in funding and the creation of a post of national coordinator for counterterrorism on the NSC, policy disputes and turf battles between the NSC and the CIA, FBI, Justice Department, and other agencies hampered operations against bin Laden. Clarke noted, in a 1999 interview, "There is a problem convincing people that there is a threat. There is disbelief and resistance. Most people don't understand."[147] For instance, as the CSG began to mobilize in response to expected millennium attacks by al Qaeda, Clarke wrote that while CIA chief George Tenet was an ally, the CIA's deputy director for operations, James Pavitt, "thought both Tenet and I were exaggerating the whole al Qaeda threat."[148]

384 RUNNING THE WORLD

Similarly, one CSG participant noted that the Pentagon was not particularly supportive of the work of the interagency group, recollecting that "if [the Pentagon] sent anyone under the rank of general, Clarke would throw them out. 'Get the hell out of here,' he would say."[149] Says Clarke, "If an agency sent somebody of low rank, I wouldn't let them in the room. Or I wouldn't let them sit at the table or I wouldn't let them say anything. They would have to sit along the back wall and be quiet as an observer. Because if their agency couldn't send somebody of appropriate rank, then they weren't going to be represented. And I would cancel meetings, because the right people didn't show up. I would call and chew people out. And I would have Sandy Berger or Tony Lake call and chew out their bosses. You had to have high-level attendance at these things or they weren't worth doing."[150] Clarke concluded that the military was too cautious, demanding guarantees and resources, which would make it impossible for any foreign operations to be conducted against foreign terrorists. One NSC staffer said that Clarke "basically told the Pentagon they were cowards."[151] Difficulties also arose when Clarke "broke a lot of china" in pushing the CIA and the air force to deploy the Predator (unmanned reconnaissance aircraft) to locate bin Laden in Afghanistan, exclaiming on one occasion, "You're telling me it won't work. The real reason is that you don't want to do it."[152]

Nonetheless, Clarke's team did successfully coordinate administration efforts against al Qaeda before the 2000 millennium celebrations. Acting on intelligence provided by the CIA's Counterterrorism Center, Clarke sketched out a plan at one of regular Friday afternoon CSG meetings (known as the "Friday Follies") on a whiteboard in his office that became the basis of a coordinated, cross-border effort to stymie attacks on the United States.[153] Furthermore, in the fifteen months after the 1998 embassy bombings in Africa, dozens of principals meetings had been held about the al Qaeda threat. During the millennium alert in December 1999, Berger told the directors of the FBI and CIA, according to Clarke, approvingly, "We have stopped two sets of attacks planned for the millennium. You can bet your measly federal paycheck that there are more out there and we have to stop them too."[154] The CSG was in almost daily session, with Clarke directing efforts out of the White House to mobilize the FBI, CIA, FEMA, and other agencies, leading to the arrest of operatives in Washington state and Los Angeles. Ultimately, December 31 and January 1 proved to be uneventful for the administration's counterterrorism czar, who monitored New Years' Eve while dressed in a tuxedo at the Y2K Coordination Center in downtown Washington, D.C.[155]

While the NSC had successfully marshaled domestic and international law enforcement resources to counter potential terrorist violence in December 1999, they had been less persuasive in getting the military to adjust its practices. The NSC had alerted the Pentagon in 1997 to the dangers that American ships faced in ports, but warnings about Middle East ports had been disregarded, a fact that contributed to the October 2000 bombing of the USS Cole, in which seventeen sailors were killed after a small explosives-laden boat drove into the destroyer in the Aden harbor.[156] Clarke, who had been involved in the al Shifa missile strike response to the 1998 embassy bombings, had forcefully advocated military action against al Qaeda's training camps in Afghanistan in response to the USS Cole attack. However, uncertainty about al Qaeda's involvement (which was not fully established by U.S. authorities until a month after the attack),[157] the final push to craft a Middle East peace settlement, and the proximity of the upcoming presidential election resulted in an unwillingness by most of the administration's foreign policy principals to adopt any of the measures recommended by Clarke.[158] Clarke recounts the reaction of a bitterly disappointed Michael Sheehan, the State Department's counterterrorism chief: "What's it gonna take, Dick? . . . Does Al Qaeda have to attack the Pentagon to get their attention?"[159]

This episode would later be cited as a failure of the president's will, because when he explained that the reason the United States did not act was that no proof was forthcoming of al Qaeda involvement, it was pointed out that proof did in fact exist in the U.S. government at the time but he neither asked to see what we had, nor did he urgently demand further investigation. Critics have speculated that the very weak response to the embassy and USS Cole attacks encouraged terrorists and al Qaeda in particular by suggesting that they might launch assaults on the United States with relative impunity—an attitude they would certainly not have had if Clarke's advice had been followed.

Although the NSC senior director's proposals for aggressive action had been rejected by the Clinton administration, he did compose a plan to "roll back" al Qaeda, including increased covert action against al Qaeda cells, expanded support for the anti-Taliban Northern Alliance in Afghanistan to deprive the group of its sanctuary, and greater disruption of the global network of terrorist financial support.

When the new administration came into office after the 2000 election, Clarke's proposals were once again advanced, by Berger and by Clarke himself, to the incoming NSC team, led by Condoleezza Rice. However, in the changeover from the Clinton to the Bush administration, the "fight against terrorism was one of the casualties of the transition."[160] As Donald

Kerrick, the deputy national security advisor under Clinton, who remained at the NSC for the first four months of the new administration, noted, "I didn't detect that kind of focus [on fighting terrorism]. That's not being derogatory. It's just a fact. I didn't detect any activity but what Dick Clarke and the CSG were doing."[161]

.   .   .

It is ironic and worth noting that the first American deaths of the Clinton era that could be laid to hostile foreign enemies came not in Somalia or in Bosnia or in any of the "brown blobs." They came in lower Manhattan in an attack on the World Trade Center on February 26, 1993.

In some respects, then, the future was revealed to be hidden in the past. During the Clinton years, a period that could be defined in terms of our search for the elusive promise of the new world order, the elements of what would define America's post–Cold War worldview and the role we would play now that we no longer had an equal adversary were lurking in the shadows, ancient in origin, to be understood only gradually.

In one of the standard speeches we in the Commerce Department used to give during the first term of the Clinton administration about the new era in which we lived, we cited the fact—as I mentioned earlier—that for most of American history, the focus of our foreign policy had been commercial. From Washington through the early Wilson years, most Americans believed that the only reason to be involved in the daunting complexities and intrigues associated with foreigners was trade—bringing goods to our shores, selling our wares overseas, or otherwise enriching the nation. Indeed, economic ties with Europe played a central role in influencing our decisions to enter both the First and Second World Wars. Thus, we argued, the primacy of security issues during the Cold War was an aberration, and by restoring economic issues (and agencies) to central roles in foreign policymaking, we in the Clinton administration were restoring a great tradition of seeking to define the world in terms of the opportunities and convergent interests that an economic view often offers. (We were also quick to note the competitive challenges we faced, and we often cast the international challenges of our times in terms of economic rivalries with emerging economies such as China's, with frustratingly closed markets like Japan's, or even with our allies in Europe.)

We also advanced the view that in an era in which our nuclear might was no longer an effective tool in resolving most of the conflicts we were likely to face, we would have to employ new approaches using our status and resources as an economic superpower, as the first information age superpower, to induce change, encourage growth, and plant the seeds of prosperity, individual opportunity, and democracy that would bind old wounds and placate turmoil.

For a moment, it seemed that we were right and that the pocketbook issues that had always been central to American domestic politics were to become central again in our international relations in a world that was being knit ever more closely together by market forces and market-bred technologies and infrastructure.

But, as we have all discovered yet again, security always trumps economics. While the focus may first be on keeping the figurative wolf from the door, everything changes when a real wolf appears.

Looking back, it is clear that the real wolf bared its fangs early in the Clinton administration with that first, botched attack on New York City's Twin Towers. By the second term, President Clinton and his NSC, led by Sandy Berger and Dick Clarke, began to understand the shape of the new threats that would come along with the boons associated with a smaller, more interdependent planet—threats bred of cultures pressed more tightly together via information technologies and travel, threats borne across borders by new and constantly shifting global networks and virtual organizations that defied old notions of political boundaries or national allegiances, threats that enabled the few and the weak to challenge the mightiest of nations.

As a consequence of this recognition, by the end of the Clinton administration, some of the most significant national security triumphs took place in the shadows as a heightened antiterrorism awareness foiled plots against trans-Pacific jumbo jet traffic, against New York City, and, on the eve of the new millennium, against worldwide targets from the Middle East to Los Angeles Airport. A war against terrorism was already being fought, and many of the early skirmishes were being won by an America that didn't truly understand the stakes or the potential scope or impact of the new security threat.

That ignorance would last only months into the next administration. First, the truth about the character of the new threats would be brutally delivered. But perhaps just as dangerous would be the time it took after the stunning blow was struck to recall the other lessons learned—often by trial and error—during the Clinton years about the broader nature and origins of transnational threats, about the ways alliances and our leadership within them would have to change to remain relevant, about the full range of tools we would need to succeed, and about how our national security institutions would have to change to encompass not only our ability to deter and destroy but also our ability to heal and rebuild, to promote common interests and values. Indeed, it can be argued that some of these lessons have yet to be fully recalled half a decade after the first administration of the post–Cold War era ended.

12

A Thumb on the Scales: Tipping the Balance in the Battle Between the Traditionalists and the Transformationalists

Thank God we're a great country. We can stand a lot of this non-sense. But let's not test it too closely.
— General Andrew Goodpaster

R ICHARD NIXON AND Henry Kissinger made the NSC the center of foreign policy formation. Gerald Ford made Donald Rumsfeld his chief of staff, and Rumsfeld hired Dick Cheney as his assistant. Ford brought them together with his Director of Central Intelligence, George H.W. Bush, and into the mix he added Brent Scowcroft, who would later become Condoleezza Rice's mentor. Working for Scowcroft was Stephen Hadley, who in turn would be Condoleezza Rice's successor as national security advisor. Jimmy Carter brought born-again Christian professions of faith into the open during his administration and trailblazed the era of modern populism in American politics. His national security advisor, Zbigniew Brzezinski, began to combat post-Vietnam declinism and restore America to the offensive in the Cold War. Carter and Brzezinski also oversaw an era in which an unhappy American entanglement in the Middle East dominated American politics and in which American relations with Afghanistan, Iran, and neighboring states became central to our interests for the first time. Ronald Reagan ushered in the first wave of right-wing revival, entangled America in Iraq with his initial support of Saddam Hussein, underwrote the Taliban, and presided over the first time a man named Bush declared a war on terror, back in 1985. He also offered a home in government to a group of right-wing intellectuals who, calling themselves neoconservatives, began to formulate new and assertive views toward fostering change in the Middle East—and he elevated further a rising military star named General Colin Powell.

George H.W. Bush as president convened a team that included Cheney, Rice, Powell, Wolfowitz, Hadley, Armitage, Haass, and a host of others who would operate in a national security system perfected during his presidency. President Bush also offered object lessons in the presidency to another close advisor, his son, George W. Bush—and, as it turned out, he left him with a cause, to finish unfinished family business in Iraq. The philosophical differences between many of those who were closely associated with the policies of the elder Bush and those more closely associated with Reagan created a divide among Republican Party foreign policy elites, pitting what Brent Scowcroft has called the "traditionalists" of the elder Bush team against the "transformationalists" of the younger Bush (and Reagan) teams, pragmatists against neocons, internationalists against unilateralists, the people who oversaw the end of the Cold War against those who oversaw the beginning of the "war on terror."

In a way, every administration since Nixon's contributed to that of George W. Bush. But what no one could foresee was the unique historical moment that would test and ultimately reveal the character of each leader and his team—like the Cuban missile crisis for Kennedy, Vietnam for Johnson, Vietnam and Watergate for Nixon, the hostage crisis in Iran for Carter, the rise of Gorbachev and Iran-Contra for Reagan, personal peccadilloes or the challenges of a transformational era for Clinton. All presidents are tested, and in those tests political rhetoric is stripped away and the true nature of our leaders is revealed. Similarly, within the inner circles of all presidencies, those same crises result in the elevation of some, the diminution of others, and the emergence of a few who become America's voice. In the case of the second Bush administration, this process produced tension, turmoil, and an apparent reassessment of several of the core tenets of modern U.S. foreign policy. Questions that remain open are whether such a reassessment was in fact called for by the times and whether those who stepped to the forefront of American foreign policy formation made the right calls.

One thing is however, certain, looking back after the first four years of George W. Bush's leadership: Harry Truman and James Forrestal, Clark Clifford and Dean Acheson would have been very surprised at the results.

After roughly six decades, key aspects of this national security system were quite unlike what they envisioned.[1]

The post–World War II leaders had created the NSC apparatus with several principal concerns in mind. One was that the federal government never again see such concentration of power as had occurred in the hands of FDR and a small number of advisors, with the rest of the government, agencies important to our national security, left out in the cold and alienated by division, lack of information, and failure of coordination. Another goal was that the U.S. foreign policy apparatus be designed to effectively interact with the new global institutional and legal structures and alliances that they had created to help avoid ever again seeing powerful nations pursue their self-interest without regard to the views or collective interests of the global community. Finally, they wanted to make sure that the fledgling Department of Defense would be able to hold its own against the institutional powerhouse of the U.S. government, the oldest cabinet agency, the Department of State.

It hardly turned out as planned. Some differences were due to history. The Department of State had gradually faded relative to the Department of Defense and relative to the National Security Council and related structures they created. The Cold War was over, and the new tools of foreign policy included more emphasis on the economics and exigencies of fighting and winning wars and keeping the peace in small conflicts with much weaker foes. As a result, other agencies rose in influence and, of course, as in all times of conflict, Defense assumed center stage. Although history has also shown that, given human nature, leaders come to depend on small clusters of close, trusted advisors, what happened during the first term of the presidency of George W. Bush was hardly anticipated by anyone—that the dominant role in that inner circle would be played by a vice president who would himself occasionally assume the role envisioned for the national security advisor and have unprecedented influence over the president. Finally, as the rift with the traditionalists in his own party suggests, during the first term of his presidency the second Bush and his team adopted a course that eschewed international institutions, selectively sidestepped our allies, and applied American power with faint regard for the sixty years of history that had gone into shaping the global system that we, as a nation, played the central role in designing.

By 2004 it was no longer Harry Truman or Dwight Eisenhower's NSC, or George H.W. Bush's and Brent Scowcroft's, for that matter—and perhaps its transformation was appropriate, given the very different era in which it operated. As always, the character and role of Bush 43's NSC was not just a consequence of events but was also the result of internal chemistry. In particular, national security policy during the first term of the administration of George W. Bush was shaped by four intense and important personal and professional relationships—between the president and the vice president, the president and his national security advisor, the vice president and the secretary of defense, and the secretary of defense and the secretary of state—and by one pivotal moment, the morning of September 11, 2001. While other relationships among and between these four individuals and with other members of the cabinet and the circle close the president were important, these four played a disproportionate role in determining the group dynamic that would shape American policy formation in the first four years of the twenty-first century. And no administration since that of Franklin Roosevelt was more shaped by a single event: those attacks on that clear, blue September morning.

When I spoke with Condoleezza Rice late in 2004, she acknowledged that the jury was out on how history would judge the efforts of the second Bush presidency.

> I've gone back through in my own head—as we have been going through historical times that are also turbulent—and I look back and I think how it must have looked when in 1946 the communists showed considerable electoral strength in Italy and France, and when you had civil wars in Greece and Turkey, and the blockade of Berlin, and the Czech coup in '48, and in '49 the Soviet Union explodes a nuclear weapon five years ahead of schedule, and the Chinese communists win. This doesn't look so great, from ground level, at that point. And they came up with a series of solutions—NATO was an invention to rearm Germany without sending France skyward. The Marshall Plan was a response to the failed one-and-a-half year reconstruction effort in Germany, because Germans were still starving and Europe was still in disarray. And so when I look at the current period, I recognize that there isn't any such thing as a grand architectural design.[2]

Instead Rice described the most significant responses that followed the September 11 attacks as triggers for broader processes that themselves would continue to evolve:

> An ad hoc group led by Steve Hadley on homeland defense [and the] institutionalization of that in the Homeland Security Council and Homeland Security Department. I think the intel reform that you're see-

ing now is a response to a better understanding of the intelligence problems that led to 9/11. . . . I think you're seeing in the response that the
president has made on the broader Middle East initiative and on reform
in the Middle East what is probably the single most important change
strategically since containment—which is that you will not accept or do
not believe stability can be achieved in the Middle East absent democratic
reform.[3]

But Rice noted that these efforts can only really be assessed over time:
"When you look at it thirty years from now or forty years from now, people will look back and either say these were disastrous responses or really
creative responses—over the next several years, I think we are now going
to have to make those responses work."[4]

Rice is one of those who will play a central role in determining their
success. For the first four years of the Bush administration as national
security advisor, and then, in the second term, in the role of secretary of
state, Rice was almost certainly President Bush's closest and most loyal
senior foreign policy advisor—even if she was not—at least during the
first term—always the most influential. On a typical day as national security advisor, she saw him seven or eight times, and many days she was by
his side between four and six hours. She worked out in the gym with him.
She spent so much time with him at Camp David that she had her own
cabin there. She joined the Bush family for Sunday dinner on a regular
basis. Once, when they slipped off to Iraq for a Thanksgiving surprise for
the troops, Bush commented that their being whisked away in an
unmarked car with baseball caps pulled down low over their eyes made
them "look . . . like a normal couple."[5] Journalists, the public, and inside-
the-beltway White House watchers are fascinated with the closeness of
Rice and Bush, the extraordinary rapport between the two. Both love
sports. (Rice and the president have often joked about her ambition to
become NFL commissioner after her time in government is done; the
president once was a part-owner of the Texas Rangers baseball team.)
Both are born-again Christians. They share a sense of humor and, more
important, a worldview. Both learned their trade watching the first Bush
presidency in action.

Rice clearly admires the president greatly. When she speaks of the president, there is no hint of the ambivalence that often develops over time
when high-level government officials work closely together in intense and
demanding circumstances. She is passionately loyal, commenting on him
with equal parts admiration and fondness. She is even willing to make a

comparison with his father's very successful tenure at the helm of U.S. foreign policy when she says that "this president is more strategic than any other president I have dealt with."[6]

By "strategic," she is referring to Bush's habit of sizing up a sweeping problem without much preamble: "We'll be sitting there working on a puzzle and all of a sudden he'll say, you know, I was just thinking—the China situation. Sometimes he has one-on-ones with his cabinet secretaries and it'll be something they bring up. But it will very often be that they'll bring up something very specific—there's a UN Security Council resolution coming to the floor. The problem really is, how do you get leadership for the Palestinians. Not, should we veto the resolution, but how do you get leadership? So, that's something I think is not very well understood about the president. And unless you sit with him in the Oval Office, you can't see it."[7]

Rice has clicked with Bush since they met at a spring 1998 gathering, organized by former secretary of state George Shultz, for the Texas governor and several academics at Stanford University. She became his top foreign policy advisor during the 2000 campaign.[8] By then she was better known than in her earlier years with his father's administration—when once, approaching the presidential aircraft, she was accosted and stopped by Secret Service agents who did not recognize her and had a hard time believing that a young black woman would have risen to a position of such prominence in the U.S. government. Being African American has, according to those who know her well, had a measurable impact on her foreign policy views—particularly in the area of her emphasis on the importance of democracy and basic freedoms. That focus, in turn, gave her a sense of sympathy and direction in her studies that began with special attention to the countries of Eastern Europe and the former Soviet bloc, countries where political emancipation was America's objective. She studied initially with Josef Korbel—who happens to have been Madeleine Albright's father, once again revealing the exceptionally tight-knit nature of the foreign policy community. Community may even be too broad a word. It is really more like a club. Rice dedicated her first book to Korbel as well as to her parents, who were also an extremely important influence in her life.

Of the sixteen national security advisors who preceded Rice, many of the most influential have come from one of two groups: social outsiders who relied on exceptional intelligence and ambition to fight their way to the center of power, and traditional, eastern blue-bloods who inherited entrée into the inner circles of American power. Some of the better national security advisors, in terms of intellect, education, and capabilities, were from the blue-blood group, such as McGeorge Bundy and Anthony Lake. But many of the most influential have been from the other group, perhaps because it has taken more for them to prove themselves academically, then professionally, then within the very competitive world of the policy and political communities. Kissinger and Brzezinski were immigrants. Rice and Powell were African Americans in white America. Berger, like Walt Rostow, was a Jew who made his way up through a society that has a complex and not always healthy relationship with the Jewish community. Carlucci, too, came from an immigrant background. Virtually all of these individuals attended first-tier universities as the first rung on the ladder up, but it was not an easy path for any of them.

Rice's academic background and her experience in the first term of the Bush administration inform her views today toward the spread of democracy as an imperative. Her view and that espoused by the administration more broadly (often articulated by leading neocons such as Deputy Defense Secretary Paul Wolfowitz, one of the intellectual powerhouses of the administration's inner circle, who was subsequently named World Bank President) is that America's role in this new era is to lead the spread of democracy and freedom worldwide—both because it is right and because it advances our national interests by producing a safer, more stable world that is likely to be more sympathetic to American views. The strategy does not so much follow in the empire-building tradition of former great powers, but rather builds on a prominent tradition in the American past, that of missionaries, proselytizing quasi-sacred elements of our way of life. (Of course, by quasi-sacred, I mean sacred without actually being religious in nature, although we commonly refer to our freedoms and our system in the language of religion.)

This notion of missionary America is rendered somewhat more powerful when coupled with the style of George W. Bush's administration. The embrace of protestant fundamentalist values has become central not only in a political sense—as the religious Right was the most solid base for the president, with Christian fundamentalists voting 4 to 1 for him during the 2004 election—but also in a philosophical sense.

Says Rice:

> You need not only a set of initiatives . . . you need an anchor . . . much like containment was anchored in the notion that if you maintained the values, and Germany became democratic, and you worked for those values, that you would eventually have stability because you'd have democratic development. In the Middle East today, that's also the key. It's not a "real-

ist" view of the Middle East—it is one that says the democratic values and the stability or the security are indivisible.

Now this doesn't mean that you think Saudi Arabia is going to be a Jeffersonian democracy in the next ten years. As a matter of fact, the United States was not a Jeffersonian democracy for quite a long time in its history. What it does mean is that you use the presidency to make clear that without a fundamental shift in the political values in the Middle East, you're never going to get to stability. . . . Sometimes I talk to my French colleagues, and they essentially believe that the Arab world will never be democratic. And I say to them, you know that the status quo is not sustainable in the Middle East and they say, yes. It seems to me that there are two poles: one is the kind of extremist Osama bin Laden pole, and the other is the development of more pluralistic, ultimately democratic society. Why would you not opt to work on that one even if you think that the chances are slim? So I think this question of how values play in American foreign policy is extremely important.[9]

George W. Bush—like Jimmy Carter, Ronald Reagan, and Bill Clinton— has felt that the public display of his religious views is a political asset, to say nothing of a manifestation of his deeply held beliefs. Oddly, despite frequent assertions to the contrary by America's unique cadre of politico-religious leaders, this is a clear break from the largely deist founders of the republic, who, while speaking of God, often did so in the Enlightenment-era sense of a greater power, or "nature." For Bush, the born-again approach reflects a way of doing business. Carter and Clinton were religious in the more analytical, sometimes even tortured, Augustinian tradition. For people like them, religion is a pillar and a guidepost in a constant struggle with life's complexities and countervailing trends. But for Bush, who struggled early in life to find his way, religion seems to be a simplifying force, dividing the choices into right and wrong, black and white, with shades of gray being seen almost as the work of darker forces—temptation away from clarity. This sense of moral absolutes has clearly informed the administration's foreign policy and largely defines the core tension within the foreign policy establishment between the "traditionalists" and the "transformationalists."[10] Traditionalism is shorthand for traditional internationalists, people who see foreign policy as a way to manage our relations within a diverse global community, moving in the direction of our ideals, but recognizing the limitations on us and the need to balance the optimal with the practically possible. Transformationalists might decry such views as moral relativism or as implying a willingness to subjugate our national interests to the wishes of the larger community of nations; in any event, their view is that we need to make the world more like us.

George Bush's campaign stump speech rhetoric—"by serving the ideal of liberty, we serve the deepest ideals of our country—freedom is not America's gift to the world; freedom is the Almighty God's gift to every man and woman in this world"—was not only a crowd-pleasing line finely tuned to the ears of his supporters but also a line that defined the work of America in the world as God's work.[11] These views are held by a religiously diverse group within the administration; their zeal is not a phenomenon limited to Christian fundamentalism. The conviction among them is that it is our moral duty and our strategic need to change the world to fit our vision of it. Ironically—and ominously—that same belief is shared, to very different ends, by the jihadists and extremists that the president has identified as our enemies in the world.

Those who know the president well suggest that his much-admired decisiveness as a leader can be attributed in large part to a higher power. "You have to look at the president and religion," one Bush family friend noted. "That may be an important motivating factor. I don't know exactly what it means to be a born-again Christian, but, if it means that Jesus has entered your soul, then does it mean that you are infallible? I don't know the answer to that. But it may impart a certitude to the president that affects the way he reacts to his team and everything else."[12]

However, as Brent Scowcroft commented, the problem with absolutist beliefs is "that they can get you into traps in which the ends justify the means. It can be dangerous to believe that one's motives are so noble that therefore anything we do becomes OK because we are doing it for a good cause. . . . For example, we advocate the export of democracy, and yet we find ourselves embracing a number of leaders who are anything but democratic in order to advance other policies or even the spread of democracy elsewhere. You cannot argue for absolutes and then practice pragmatism without opening yourself up to criticism."[13] It's a neat paradox—the less moral ambiguity you have in your worldview, the more you can justify in your life.

"My sense," added Scowcroft, a man who cowrote his memoirs of the first Bush administration with George H.W. Bush but who has since had a falling out with the second Bush administration over his criticism of its Iraq policies, "is that good policy development doesn't work that way. Because my approach to almost every question is: . . . If it doesn't work, what happens? To view it with informed skepticism. To me that is the heart of good policy formation. It's not just coming up with ideas. It is testing the ideas against the things that can happen in the real world and usually do."[14]

Former Nixon, Ford, and Carter cabinet member James Schlesinger compares Bush with Carter:

> Because both of them have a deep-seated notion of what is right, and even though Carter was immensely studious, and this President Bush is not immensely studious, ultimately that conviction that they know what the Lord's will is tended to dominate policy. Now they are poles apart in their substantive views, but in terms of this conviction that a moral judgment should dominate decision, I think they are not dissimilar. . . . Now I am not sure that either Carter in his own way despite his studiousness and despite the fact that he would go through memoranda at great length . . . that some of the larger picture might not escape him. And the larger picture may escape this president in that he, too, seems inclined to make moral judgments and to impose those judgments on the policy.[15]

There is an intellectual as well as a religious basis to the views that have largely driven the policies of this first administration of the twenty-first century. They derive largely from the work of a group of philosophers that includes Leo Strauss, a professor at the University of Chicago who saw liberalism and moral relativism as among the causes of the social weakness that led to the downfall of Weimar Germany and the onset of the Nazism from which he escaped. Paul Wolfowitz, who emerged as one of the dominant intellectual forces within the Bush team, was a student of Strauss.

James Mann, in *Rise of the Vulcans*, a superb profile of the like-minded members of Bush's war cabinet, wrote:

> Strauss's influence is surprising because his voluminous, often esoteric writings say virtually nothing specific about issues of policy, foreign or domestic. Like [Harold] Bloom, he wrote mainly about the importance of understanding the classics, especially Plato and Aristotle, along with European philosophers from Locke and Rousseau to Nietzsche and Heidegger. One core idea in Strauss's work was a denunciation of the spirit of moral tolerance that, he argued, had come to dominate intellectual life in Europe and the United States. He described what he called "the crisis of liberalism— . . . a crisis due to the fact that liberalism has abandoned its absolutist bias and is trying to become entirely relativistic." The problem with relativism and with liberalism, Strauss argued, was that they can degenerate into the "easygoing belief that all points of view are equal

(hence, none really worth passionate argument, deep analysis, or stalwart defense) and then into the strident belief that anyone who argues for the superiority of a distinctive moral insight, way of life, or human type is somehow elitist or anti-democratic—and hence immoral." Strauss spoke of the need for an elite group of advisors, as in Plato's *Republic*, who could impress upon a political leader and upon the masses the need for virtue and for strong moral judgments about good and evil.[16]

Strauss called, metaphorically, for a morally motivated NSC.

Another University of Chicago philosophy professor, Robert Pippin, has pointed out a second feature of Strauss's influence: "Strauss believed that good statesmen have powers of judgment and must rely on an inner circle. The person who whispers in the ear of the King is more important than the King. If you have that talent, what you do or say in public cannot be held accountable in the same way."[17]

In his book, Mann tracks the development and rise of six members of the first-term Bush team—Cheney, Rumsfeld, Powell, Armitage, Wolfowitz, and Rice—but he also notes the intellectual community from which they were drawn and the membership of other Bush team members such as Cheney's chief of staff, I. Lewis "Scooter" Libby, Under Secretary of Defense Doug Feith, Feith staffer and another former Strauss protégé Abram Shulsky, Under Secretary of State for Arms Control John Bolton (later nominated to become UN ambassador), and Defense Advisory Board member Richard Perle. Just as Reagan had his true believers—and many of these individuals were members of that first group—so too is there an intellectual core at the center of the Bush group. If they have one unifying characteristic, it is their adherence to transformational beliefs.

While I was interviewing people for this book, I often found, even in talking to Republican insiders, that the term "neocon" was being used to describe an even smaller subset of this group—people such as Wolfowitz, Libby, Feith, Perle, Shulsky, and Elliott Abrams. This group was often described as having an "Israeli bias" or being driven by "Israeli interests." This is one of those classic examples of coded speech in Washington and American life, when what the critics or those characterizing the group are trying to say is that these people are Jews and are driven by their Jewish biases. But the suggestion that they represent a Jewish cabal is flawed on several other levels, not the least of which is that they all worked for and were secondary in influence to Bush administration principals who were not Jewish.

Further, whatever their sympathies, many of the most important policies driven by this group and the neocons writ large did not have what could fairly be characterized as an Israeli bias. Richard Haass, who worked with this group as head of policy planning in the Bush State Department, and who is also Jewish, notes:

> The biggest discretionary foreign policy initiative of this administration was Iraq. The Israelis were not pushing Iraq, however. Most Israelis I spoke with, even the hard-liners, raised their eyebrows about it and thought Iran was a much bigger threat. They were worried the United States was getting distracted by Iraq. But, that said, I do think that many of the senior people in this administration had views that were pretty close to those of the Likud or [former Israeli prime minister Binyamin] Netanyahu or [current Israeli prime minister] Ariel Sharon. The Bush policy resembles that of Netanyahu and now [Minister for Jerusalem Affairs Natan] Sharansky in believing that we can't have any meaningful agreements in the Middle East until nearly everybody's a democrat.[18]

On the defining foreign policy choice of this administration, this group opted to go in a direction inconsistent with Israel's priorities. To suggest that the neocons somehow place allegiance to another country above their own smacks of the "John Kennedy will report to the Vatican" slurs of the 1960 election campaign and is vehemently condemned by the members of this group with whom I have spoken.

What has happened is that the interests of the Christian Right and the neocons have come into alignment with regard to taking a strong stand in support of Israel. However, it is worth noting that the Christian Right seeks to preserve Israel in order to fulfill Biblical prophecies that, in the end, don't turn out very well for the Jews. And the neocons tend to support the right-wing view on Israel for a variety of reasons, but the one at the top of their list has at least as much to do with the secular religion of democracy—Israel being the only democracy yet to take root in the Middle East—and with U.S. strategic interests than with traditional religious orientation. The conflation of these views into a strong stance for Israel has led to misinterpretation.

The neocons have been empowered not by their religious orientation but by the fact that the president of the United States shares their view that absolutes matter and governs on the basis of his deeply held beliefs—a fact that is admired by a great cross-section of his supporters in the U.S. electorate.

It is particularly revealing about the character of the country that the collective national response to the confusion and division of the Vietnam era seems to have been a strong impulse toward moral absolutism. On the one hand, it is quite understandable, given the discomfort the nation felt with its own moral ambiguities at the time of Vietnam and Watergate and in particular with how inconsistent those ambiguities were with our World War II–forged self-image of the United States as the global champion of undistilled good. The simple positives of Jimmy Carter's "government as good as its people" and Ronald Reagan's "city on the hill" fighting off an "evil empire" were an antidote to doubts and confusion and the greater fogs of that particular war and era. However, it is also ironic that the group that challenged the policies in Vietnam and the actions associated with Watergate were liberals, who at the time were seen to be standing for certain absolute goods in the face of the corrupting views of Kissingerian "realism," pragmatism gone too far. Somehow, those same liberals who had taken a stand for moral absolutes were branded moral relativists. The American people have chosen Republican administrations for twenty out of thirty-two years since 1976, with the intervening Democratic governments being "centrist" or "conservative" Democrats. Among the Republican presidents, the two who have dominated the political development of the dominant party were Reagan and George W. Bush, men who embraced absolutism and offered moral crusades—one against "an evil empire," the other against "an axis of evil" and "evil-doers."

America in the late 1970s was a bit of a lost soul, seeking comfort from simple truths in the way that a wayward drinker might find his path back to health by embracing a twelve-step program or rediscovering religion. The president himself went through just such a personal transformation when, at about age forty, he found his personal bearings. Thereafter, he has found his life oriented by a few simple principles of faith. As president, he has introduced a similarly faith-based approach to U.S. foreign policy that offers America as the instrument of God's will advancing His gifts of freedom and democracy to the less fortunate of the world. What Condoleezza Rice characterizes as the president's strategic vision is the application of these views to global circumstances.

As Colin Powell commented, "Each president is different. Bush 43 is like 41 in that he is ready to act, but [for 41] it was a more deliberate process whereas 43 is guided more by a powerful inertial navigation system than by intellect. He knows what he wants to do, and what he wants to hear is how to get it done."[19] This has empowered those close to him with the ability to translate his perception of good and evil into action—and it has also empowered those near him who are pure, undistilled Washington pragmatists to use the latitude offered by a president who is focused on the broad brush strokes to accumulate great power in the management of the day-to-day shaping and implementation of the policies used to support the president's larger objectives. It has also created problems when policies based on deeply held beliefs foundered. As Scowcroft noted pithily, "If you believe you are pursuing absolute good, then it is a sin to depart from it."[20]

.   .   .

As with most past administrations, when the Bush team came into office, they laid out their national security structure. National Security Presidential Directive 1 (NSPD-1), which is what they called presidential decision memoranda, continued many of the traditions established during the late Reagan, the first Bush, and the Clinton years, including centering operations on principals and deputies meetings to be chaired by the national security advisor, Rice, and her deputy, Stephen Hadley. Hadley, who attended Cornell and got his law degree from Yale, had worked on the NSC staff during the Ford years and later worked very closely with Scowcroft and the other members of the Tower Commission as its general counsel. In the first Bush administration he served as assistant secretary of defense and senior aide to Dick Cheney. In addition, Hadley had practiced law and in the 1990s was a principal of Scowcroft's company, the Scowcroft Group.

NSPD-1 reaffirmed the Clinton administration's commitment to international economics by stating that "national security also depends on America's opportunity to prosper in the world economy."[21] The Bush administration also chose to maintain the National Economic Council. Bush appointed Lawrence Lindsey to run it and then, when Lindsey ran afoul of the administration by correctly asserting that the cost of the Iraq war would be quite high, replaced him in 2002 with Bob Rubin's former partner as co-chairman of Goldman Sachs, Stephen Friedman. Despite maintaining a fairly active commitment to international trade through the skill and leadership of Ambassador Robert Zoellick, Jim Baker's former close advisor and the man who later went on to serve as Condoleezza Rice's deputy secretary of state, the administration otherwise let the NEC fall from the public eye and from influence. Other economic agencies during the first four years of the second Bush administration focused their efforts primarily on winning and then defending tax cuts—and then on cleaning up the fiscal mess those cuts and a sluggish economy caused in terms of burgeoning federal budget deficits and poor job growth. On the international front, the administration's stance was quite laissez-faire in terms of letting some foreign countries, such as Argentina, make their own way out of financial calamities. More important, the Bush team chose a path of letting the dollar slide lower, which would trigger tensions with our trading partners, many of whom happened to be European allies who were also unhappy with our policies in the Middle East. On the whole, however, if one of the defining trends of the Clinton years was the ascension of economic issues to foreign policy centrality, then the Bush team, despite giving the Treasury secretary a seat on the NSC, reversed that trend with its dominant focus being on security issues. Indeed, even on those aspects of security issues where economic expertise was critical, we will see that the Department of Defense, given the lead, underplayed, ignored, or simply did not seek the advice it might need from the economic side of the administration. And by the beginning of the second term of the Bush administration, the once powerful NEC had become all but invisible.

The Bush NSC also very quickly tried to distinguish itself from that of the Clinton administration in word and in deed. "ABC" was an acronym heard in and around the White House: Anything But Clinton or Any way But Clinton's way. Said one senior official from within the Bush administration:

> The part I noticed right away was that they had a great disdain for Clinton and his policies and by association anybody who had worked for Clinton. So they were ready to throw them out—the presumption was that Clinton policy should go, all Clinton policy, unless proven otherwise. It was sort of guilty until proven innocent. And that's pretty unusual. . . . The assumption typically is "continuity of policy" unless there is reason to change it. But with this crowd, it was the reverse. . . . So in that sense, they were very ideological or partisan or however you would like to describe it.[22]

The official cited as an example of this the March 6, 2001, statement by Secretary of State Colin Powell that expressed an inclination to continue Clinton's policies with regard to North Korea, which generated an almost instantaneous rebuke from the White House and forced Powell to withdraw his position. An interesting sidebar as to how ideological stances influenced this position comes from Charles L. "Jack" Pritchard, who was the NSC senior director handling North Korean issues. He was asked to sit in the Oval Office with Bush when the president was on the telephone for the first time with South Korean President Kim Dae Jung. Kim began to speak about his "sunshine policy" of more openness to the North, a policy consistent with some of the inroads the Clinton team had been trying to make, and which Bush either distrusted or had been briefed on by someone other than Pritchard to disparage. Bush then held the phone away from his head, covered the mouthpiece while Kim was singing the praises of this policy, and mouthed "who does this guy think he is?" suggesting that Kim did not understand the dynamic of the peninsula or the true nature of the North Koreans (a charter member of the axis of evil) as well as Bush did.[23] Kim, of course, is a winner of the Nobel Peace Prize for his efforts to rebuild trust between the two Koreas.

The official also cited the "ABC" approach as one that led to the discounting of the terrorism warnings of Sandy Berger and his team during the transition and then unease and skepticism about counterterrorism czar Richard Clarke, the career civil servant who worked for both administrations in the lead counterterrorism capacity.

Clarke himself confirmed the bias, and when asked when he knew that the Bush administration was really different from the Clinton administration, he said, wryly, "Well, I remember in Condi's first big meeting with the senior staff her telling us that the president was 'not a big reader.' I thought that was pretty comic. She also made clear that this president wanted the departments to take the lead and that in their view the NSC staff under Berger had gotten too big, too bloated, and too powerful."[24]

In fact, Rice began by cutting the NSC staff by about a third, only to discover later, as her predecessors had, that the demands of the job would force her to regrow it. Four years later she had a staff 50 percent larger than the one she started with.[25] She also used the press early—and ironically—to send the message that she would, in the words of a *Washington Post* article, "be seen and heard far less than her predecessor."[26] To support this approach, she also eliminated the communications and legislative affairs functions at the NSC. Again, with the demands of the job and the evolution of her role, these changes were also undone, and one of Rice's subsequent innovations was to appoint the first deputy national security advisor for communications, a job that went to Jim Wilkinson, previously the spokesperson for Operation Iraqi Freedom commander General Tommy Frank. Rice also added a number of deputy posts in addition to the principal deputy post held by Hadley. During the first term, these included making her former mentor Robert Blackwill the deputy national security advisor for strategic planning and making top economic advisor

Gary Edson and later Faryar Shirzad deputy national security advisor for economic affairs.

"I really wanted to have an NSC that functioned a lot like Brent's NSC," Rice recalled, "low-key, very much more of a coordinating function, much less operational, smaller. The first thing I tried to do was cut it, but the accretion of issues was something you just couldn't solve.... [The] transnational threats [that] became the dominant factor in American foreign policy, if you think about it, they're not only transnational, they're transfunctional, and that means they cross all kinds of jurisdictional boundaries in the government and it's therefore not surprising that the integration comes here. And that probably, to me, was the biggest change from when I was here before. Because when I was here before, the Office of Transnational Affairs was four or five people, and Africa was part of it, International Organizations was part of it, and it was really quite a small directorate. Now it's the biggest staff I've got."[27] Despite this growth of transnational issues, and in what some foreign policy scholars interpreted as an early warning sign of the antimultilateral biases of the administration, the Bush team removed the cabinet-level status of the UN ambassador's post.

Rice tried to instill a supportive culture into her NSC team.

I spend a lot of time when I meet with every new director before I hire them and then when they are hired, and these guys will tell you that I always say, 'Your first responsibility is to staff the president.' If that means the president got a paper and he wanted it in twelve-point type and it is in ten-point type, it's your job to go fix that. . . . Your first responsibility is to staff the president. And I consider it my first responsibility to be staff and counsel to the president, because he doesn't have anywhere else to go for that. The second most important responsibility is to make sure that when he wants to move an agenda in a particular direction that you can get this huge ship of state turned around and moved in the direction he wants to go. So we've actually been the engine on things like the AIDS initiative, like the early decision to pursue peace talks in Sudan, like the initiation of the six-party talks on North Korea—because those were things that the president cared a lot about and didn't particularly like the direction things were going. The third most important function is to coordinate the rest of the government. . . . [That's] important, it's a critical function. . . . I'm not saying that you can let any of them slide. But staffing the president and pushing his high-priority items, he has nobody else to do that but the NSC.[28]

For this view and set of priorities she has won praise for her loyalty and attention to the president's needs and also some degree of criticism. "There are two models for being national security advisor," observed Scowcroft, "staffing the president or running the institution. The trick is doing them both."[29] Others within the administration who still work at the NSC or within NSC member agencies put it another way—that she was so preoccupied with being the president's "body man," at his side every minute, whispering in his ear, being his "alter ego on foreign policy matters," "tutoring him on areas he does not understand or is not up to speed on," that she has let the NSC become weak and, worse, the NSC processes become weak.[30] "I am not saying she is not seeking to play the role of honest broker," said one. "She is earnest and dedicated and very smart. But she can't be in two places at once, and [Rice's then-deputy] Steve Hadley hasn't stepped in to fill the void. The guys in this administration are old hands, experienced players, and you can't leave them to their own devices, or they will eat your lunch."[31]

Rice acknowledged the challenges when she said, "I mean, I'm by far the baby in this group," but asserted that the group runs well, "more as a council than as their specific agencies."[32]

Antony Blinken, a former NSC staffer and senior staff director for the Senate Foreign Relations Committee, suggested that given Rice's access, the NSC staff should also have had much more influence than it actually did. "I will give you a very specific example," he said. "There was a memo—to Condi's credit, produced by the NSC staff—that, based on extrapolations from previous peacekeeping missions and looking at the peacekeeper to population ratios, concluded that we would probably need in the vicinity of 500,000 troops to secure the peace in Iraq. In the Clinton administration, something like that, generated by the most dominant actor on the foreign policy side in the administration—especially as it was in the second term—would have carried a tremendous amount of weight in the judgments that were made. Even with the Pentagon. But clearly, this didn't."[33]

This view was amplified in mid-2004 when another assessment of the workings of the system was offered by the 9/11 Commission. One senior individual closely involved with the 9/11 Commission told me:

> We concluded as a group that the National Security Council was dysfunctional. That even in the best of times it would have to struggle with challenges of the sort we face now. . . . The way in which you address Islamic fundamentalist threats of the sort that we have now cuts across almost the entire government, and there's no quarterback. Everywhere you look there was a sort of balkanization.

If you look at the report, there are a number of instances that should just jump off the page: The fact that both Rice and Hadley said that they had no role in ensuring a domestic response to the terrorist threat in the summer of 2001. That's an extraordinary statement, because no else does, and when you ask who did, their answer is the CSG [Counterterrorism Strategy Group]. And when you say, but excuse me, the CSG reported to you, they say no, not on domestic matters. Well to whom did it report? [White House Chief of Staff Andrew] Card? That's absurd. How could you leave such an orphan in the summer of 2001?[34]

After the September 11 attacks, NSC meetings became more frequent, but the president preferred to rely primarily on an inner circle—his "war cabinet," which was led by Cheney, Powell, Rumsfeld, and Tenet.

To say that the process was harmonious—despite the best efforts of Rice and the long professional histories that many on the team shared—would be stretching the truth. Said one member of the deputies committee, "It had the potential for being a very good process. But it bumped along, and we discovered a couple of challenges. First of all, it was whether the NSC, and particularly the national security advisor, was going to impose discipline and make the process fair. And I think here, a lot of times, the Pentagon had their thumb on the scale. And secondly, although the structure was all there, we have in this administration a very, very powerful vice president, which changes the dynamic of the whole interagency process."[35]

Richard Haass contrasted it with the previous Bush administration, in which he served:

In this administration, the process didn't work nearly as well, for several reasons. One is the principals disagreed on lots of issues. There was much less consensus. Secondly, it was tilted. I thought if in Bush One there was a bias toward moderation, in this administration there is a bias much more toward one side of the field. There are maybe four fundamental differences that contributed to this. One is that JCS had a lot less of a voice in this administration. The Pentagon in previous administrations really had two voices. Not in this administration. It was just Rumsfeld. Second of all, the vice president's office has become the equivalent of a separate institution or bureaucracy. When I was in the White House in 41, the vice president's office had one or at most two people doing foreign policy. They were basically only there to advise the vice president. In this administration, the vice president has his own mini-NSC staff.

And at every meeting, they had a voice and a vote. The vice president ended up getting, from what I could tell, three bites at the apple. He had his staff at every meeting. He would then come to principals meetings. And then he'd have his one-on-ones with the president. And given the views that came out of the vice president's office, it introduced a certain bias to the system. The NSC tended to position itself somewhat in that direction. As a result, I felt that at just about every meeting, the State Department began behind two and one half to one. That was my basic calculation of this administration. CIA had no policy voice whatsoever. The Joint Chiefs had no policy voice whatsoever. You had the vice president's office, Defense, and the NSC tilting in the direction of what OVP [Office of the Vice President] and Defense favored? I thought there was not enough quality control in terms of countering that leaning. Too many assumptions got accepted or built in.[36]

The NSC is "the half" in Haass's definition given what he saw as the tilt of the NSC staff. "I do not think they did enough to balance or counter that. Too many assumptions got accepted or built in. To use a football analogy, in this administration they were playing between the forty-yard line and the ten-yard line on the right side of the field. Now, if you're the State Department, it forces you, if you want a voice, to operate between the thirty-five and forty-yard line on that side of the field."[37]

State, although diminished in this calculus, was not without influence. Colin Powell entered office with a higher approval rating than the president and a massive national following. He maintained that throughout his time in office.

Within the State Department both career officials and appointees were exceptionally supportive of Powell, who was greeted with a standing ovation from State Department employees when he entered the building for his first day of work. Experienced at managing bureaucracies, Powell quickly addressed the needs of his team, from putting the Internet on every desk in the building to bringing with him a sense of gravitas and political weight that State staff thought would make them a more relevant player.

But gradually it became clear that Powell, his deputy and close friend Richard Armitage, Haass, and the other senior officials at the State Department were on the opposite side of the "traditionalist" vs. "transformationalist" divide from the rest of the administration on many issues. After the awkward slap on the wrist he received on North Korea, Powell became a somewhat lonely voice for working issues through the international system. Nonetheless, Powell remained, at least publicly, the good soldier even as frustrations built beneath the surface (and manifested themselves from time to time in meetings or in off-the-record comments to friends).

The system, said Powell, is

> a manifestation of the personality of the president, the kind of system he wanted to have. The personalities of his cabinet officers and the perspectives each of us brought to it were how he wanted to manage it. And that includes a vice president who has been an important national security figure, as he was a former secretary of defense coming in with a president who did not have strong national security credentials. . . . He determined, with the president's permission, that he would play a different role than previous vice presidents. . . . Vice President Cheney's role was kind of fundamentally shaped by 9/11 when this new enemy was upon us, and he went at it with a vengeance because it was a new enemy upon us. And there are these virtual networks because the administration came in with the Vulcan team. And Condi was the president's national security advisor during his campaign period. And so she formed a relationship with him that was unique and intensely personal. But the national security advisor always has had a unique relationship with the president. You're the one who sees him in the morning. You're the one who sees him all day long and at night. Now I see the president a lot. I would guess that if there are foreign visitors around, I [would] always go over before—and we'll have some private time together. I [would] see him ten to twelve times a week. So there [was] no lack of communication or shortage of opportunity to exchange. But on the weekend when the call is actually made about some crisis or other, it's the national security advisor, just as I would do for Reagan.[38]

Some would attribute Powell's diminished influence to the secular trend that has led to the reduction of influence on the part of the State Department since the days of Kissinger. Marc Grossman, a career Foreign Service officer who served as Powell's under secretary of state for political affairs, the number three job at State, discussed this trend with Powell and observed:

> First of all, I think it's a question of decision cycles. Decision cycles sped up so much that the way we do business at the State Department is now too slow. And the fact that there is a trend toward diminishing influence at the Department of State is 5 percent, 10 percent somebody else's fault.

But it's 90 percent the State Department's responsibility. One of the things we had tried to do [during the first term of the second Bush presidency] is tell everybody here that if we don't change the way we do business, then we're going to go out of business. There will still be a building here and people will still come to work, but it will be like any other irrelevant bureaucracy. And we don't want to do that. . . . Our whole struggle here for the past four years has been to try to change that culture, and say to people, this isn't about observing, reporting, and sending it back for other people to act and decide on.[39]

"After 9/11," said Grossman shifting his focus to another set of challenges State faces, "you had a militarization of foreign policy which I think is natural and maybe not even wrong."

Second, you have just an unbelievable disparity, especially when you sit here and live it every day with money and people. Doug Feith [under secretary of defense for policy during the first term and Grossman's DOD counterpart], has got, I don't know, quadruple the number of people that I can bring to any problem on any given day. And so they are faster and in some cases smarter and can move all over these problems. And third, to go back to State's issues, this institution is still not turning over fast enough to compete in today's world. The main challenge here is to the department. And I would submit to you that the great gift, the great thing that Colin Powell has done for the State Department over the past four years is he has allowed people to think about their jobs in new ways. And one of the things we set out to do was hire twelve hundred new people. And we hope that they'll be our subversives throughout their careers and not think about their jobs in the same way. And so far we've found that to be true. But we have to keep at that.[40]

One former senior State Department official said, "I think the State Department is today as well led and managed, and certainly as well funded as it has ever been, but it appears less relevant to the policy process than it has in decades. It is hard to pinpoint many major State Department–led initiatives in recent years."[41]

The critique that Powell has not fought more vigorously for his views against Rumsfeld and Cheney became a popular one during the Iraq war. Those close to him cite his loyalty as a soldier. Yet he is well known to be comfortable with speaking to the media off the record and letting them know his views, and he also has, on several occasions, won significant victories, most conspicuously in persuading the president to stick to working with the United Nations in the run-up to the Iraq war when others on the team—notably Cheney and Rumsfeld—were arguing to go it alone and do so sooner.

One top State Department official who worked very closely with Powell throughout his tenure as secretary of state said:

> A lot of people look at Colin Powell and they see the Colin Powell G.I. Joe doll, action figure. And they want to dress him up in their own clothes. And so people against the war think Colin Powell is against the war. People that would have quit think Colin Powell should have quit. He's the projection of everyone from the center right to the far left of the ideological spectrum. There's a lot of people who identify with him. They think, I'm smart and he's smart. I'm honorable and he's honorable.
>
> I remember when he first started traveling and he did a roundtable at the World Economic Forum in Davos before the war. And he actually was forced to get pretty explicit with the Europeans and say, I'm not the man you think I am. I'm not fighting your case in the American government. I think differently than you. I think we have to deal with Iraq. I think the president will decide if we have to do that militarily or not. But you guys have to understand, I am not the European spokesman inside the administration.[42]

The senior official recalls remarks that Powell made at the Marshall Foundation to explain his admiration for one of his predecessors, General George Marshall.

> "I admire Marshall," he said, "because of his commitment to service." . . . [Powell] knows and believes in every fiber of his being and has exemplified throughout his life the idea that the president is elected by the people to make decisions. . . . He told the story about the time Harry Truman decided to recognize Israel and Marshall came back from the meeting and somebody said to him, Shouldn't you resign, the president went against you. Just like Colin Powell. He said no. I gave him my best advice. I gave him my best analysis. And he made the decision. That's his job.[43]

He concluded with one more point:

> That probably tells more about Powell than it does about Marshall. He is there to give the president his best advice—the president is elected to

decide. But there's a third thing . . . that the press doesn't understand. There is obviously a lot of attention given to anyplace where there [are] battles going on. So Iraq and Afghanistan are hogs of space and there's serious things going on there that need to be reported. But we think and hope that in the final analysis it will be clear that diplomacy, including multilateral diplomacy, played a major factor in the war on terror. In the long run, we're going to get at terrorism by choking off the money, arresting people, sharing intelligence, stopping people at borders. Those are all the things we're doing diplomatically. There are places like Pakistan, Saudi Arabia, Yemen, Sudan, Libya, and probably others that were safe havens or supporters of terrorists. And we've drained those swamps. They're no longer places that are hospitable to terrorists.[44]

While that last comment would probably come as a surprise to members of the intelligence community who are risking their lives trying to identify continuing Saudi sources of support for terrorism and Islamist radicalism, the point that Powell's team hope is recorded by history is that diplomacy may not have made the headlines, but there was more of it than many Americans or others may have thought.

Perhaps, however, it just felt like more to Powell, who had to fight an uphill struggle against colleagues in the administration who either were pitted against him or, as in the case of the president and Rice, would only selectively agree with him. In any event, what Powell and his senior staffers saw as an imbalance, the president saw as a source of tension he could do without, and that is what led to the move at the end of Bush's first term to replace the outspoken and obviously frustrated Powell with the loyal-to-a-fault, practically-a-family-member Condoleezza Rice.

At the heart of Powell's frustration was an old struggle between State and Defense. But this time Defense was supported by the heft of the proactive vice president and former defense secretary. Dick Cheney often reportedly has joked, "When I look at Don Rumsfeld, I see a fine Secretary of Defense. When Rumsfeld looks at me, he sees a former assistant to Don Rumsfeld."[45] Cheney is an acknowledged power center in his own right. But to this day says one very close friend of both of them, "sometimes when you see them together at a party, you're not sure who is working for whom."[46]

I have been told that Henry Kissinger described Rumsfeld as the "most ruthless man" he had met while in government. It is a view that is disputed by virtually no one and, Washington being what it is, in many cases it is said with considerable admiration. Virtually all who know him acknowledge that he is exceptionally intelligent, hardworking, and skillful. But his unique relationship with the vice president and the exceptional network that binds their offices and the rest of the administration has set the center of gravity of this administration wherever these two men are standing together.

Next to them in importance in that network is Paul Wolfowitz, the deputy secretary of defense during Bush's first term, and "Scooter" Libby, the chief of staff and national security advisor to the vice president. Wolfowitz, the former dean of the Johns Hopkins University School of Advanced International Studies, is a very thoughtful man who, while possessed of strong feelings and the aforementioned allergy to moral relativism, is by no means a reflexive ideologue. Sometimes he and Rumsfeld split on issues, and Rumsfeld has been known to dismiss his deputy's views at administration meetings, although generally they are seen to form an effective team.

Just as Libby's boss is the most powerful vice president in history, so is Libby the most powerful vice presidential chief of staff in history. This is because he serves both as the vice president's senior staff officer and as his national security advisor, giving him a substantial independent voice at interagency meetings. Indeed, as an assistant to the president, he carries the same technical title as does the national security advisor.

Beneath them during the first term, however, was an interconnecting network of individuals with very close ties to the vice president's office. The vice president's men include Under Secretary of Defense Doug Feith, who ran the mini–State Department within the Defense Department, and aides to him such as William Luti, who ran the special Middle East office that was empowered to make the case against Saddam Hussein. Luti would regularly tell meetings of his staff that he was preparing materials for "Scooter" or that he had to "get back to Scooter" as a way of motivating them—even though their chain of command ran another way.[47] Rumsfeld had made it clear from his very first day on the job that the national command authority ran from the president to him with no stops in between. But he seems to have been tolerant of the vice president's office's involvement in his department's affairs. Feith was been cited regularly as a source of tension with other departments. Extremely conservative and not a very skillful bureaucrat, he alienated perhaps more people within the administration than any other figure. John Bolton, the under secretary of state handling arms issues during President Bush's first term, was Cheney's man in the State Department, which was considered from the beginning to be essentially too moderate to be trustworthy. Stephen Hadley, although himself a former colleague of Brent Scowcroft, the dean of the traditionalists, was identified by many as another member of this group because he had served closely with Cheney in the Defense Department.

As an example of how these alliances resulted in a "thumb on the scale," one senior official told of "fairly regular" instances in which, after a deputies meeting, notes would be adjusted on the basis of comments that appeared to come from the Department of Defense.[48] In one instance, a call was made to the White House from a senior Defense Department official on his way back to the Pentagon saying that he would like to amend certain of the conclusions that had collectively been reached by the group. Hadley obliged, and another official, outraged, later reportedly confronted him about this, asserting "This is not Stalinist Russia, you can't simply rewrite history."[49]

A former senior official in the first Bush administration put it this way: "People on the NSC staff believe that the secretary of defense has four points of entry into the White House. He can go to Condi for the easy stuff; he can go to [White House Chief of Staff] Andy [Card] for the stuff that's a little tougher; to Cheney, if it's really difficult; and then, for the ace in the hole, direct contact with the president if necessary. You just can't run a system like that and expect it to work."[50]

Said another very senior official within the administration, referring to Rumsfeld's inclination to ignore process and go his own way when it suited him, "I have never seen more high-level insubordination in the U.S. government in almost thirty years than I have seen in this administration."[51] As an example, he told a story of a White House meeting in which a number of important issues were decided about Iraq. From that meeting, the administrator of the U.S. Coalition Authority in Iraq, L. Paul "Jerry" Bremer, flew to Baghdad and proceeded to announce a variety of positions that had not been agreed to in the White House meeting. Secretary Powell was infuriated, and the view within the State Department was that Bremer had simply cleared it with his boss: Donald Rumsfeld.[52]

Bremer is intelligent, highly capable, independent-minded and very conservative. Rumsfeld saw him as ideal—a former Foreign Service officer who would be open to the kind of working relationship and approaches Rumsfeld wished to advance.[53] In the end, even in the White House, many saw him as either a captive of the DOD perspective or, in the words of one White House official who grumbled about policy freelancing by the Coalition Provisional Authority, he became a "kind of viceroy" who was very hard to control.

Rumsfeld, despite his bravura performances with the press, during which he displayed great intelligence, command, and wit, did not do himself any favors with the bureaucracy with his operating style. Very quickly he alienated the military brass through a combination of pushing radical transformational ideas (including at least briefly considering firing all the one-star generals in the army to make way for a new generation of higher-quality leadership), acting "abusive toward employees," and being "frequently dismissive of senior military officers' advice."[54] He would "go nuclear" on four-star officers frequently, and, accustomed to a degree of deference, they did not like it one bit. Says former Defense Secretary William Perry, "When I was secretary, my primary goal was working effectively and creatively with our military. That relationship is today as bad as I have ever seen it. And that creates dysfunctionality not only within the Defense Department but which affects the whole operation of the national security apparatus."[55]

The tensions between how the State Department and the Defense Department operated were revealed and well illustrated during the administration's first small crisis, which involved the collision on April 1, 2001, between a U.S. Navy EP-3 turboprop electronic eavesdropping aircraft and a Chinese F-8 fighter jet. After the American plane was forced to land on Hainan Island, the rhetoric between the United States and China grew increasingly heated. China demanded an apology for the incident, which had resulted in the death of the Chinese fighter pilot, and the United States urgently sought the release of the EP-3's twenty-four American crewmen. The State Department took the lead in the negotiations for the crew through Ambassador Joseph Prueher, a Clinton appointee, in Beijing. Because he was a Clinton appointee, one element of this process actually included drafting an official letter reassuring the Chinese that he was empowered to speak for the current U.S. administration.[56]

Rice played the honest broker on this issue, stepping back from the NSC's traditionally more involved role with China issues. Defense also stayed out of the center of the negotiations while the issue was the crew, leaving the matter to Prueher. A crisis team was convened, led by Rice, which included Hadley, Libby, Wolfowitz, Powell, and Armitage. Prueher, a retired navy four-star admiral and former commander-in-chief of the U.S. Pacific Command, was exceptionally well suited to the task, had built high levels of confidence among the Chinese, and within eleven days had negotiated the release of the airmen.[57]

At that point, Prueher reportedly went back to Powell and said he was now prepared to lead the effort to get the plane back (its sensitive electronics had been scuttled as the plane was making its dramatic emergency

landing, in which the pilot managed to regain control of the heavily damaged aircraft and bring it in safely against considerable odds). But the secretary of state told him that it had been decided that Defense would take
the lead on that portion of the negotiations, since it was DOD property
that they were dealing with. Powell encouraged Prueher to offer his services to the Pentagon.

Prueher then did so, offering in a letter to work on behalf of the Defense
Department and acknowledging that they were in charge. The response he
got back said, Thanks, but we'll handle it from here.[58] Defense then sent
over a junior-level official who presented himself to the confused Chinese.
The Chinese went to Prueher and explained that they thought he was their
interlocutor, but he demurred and advised them to negotiate with the
Defense official. That official then proceeded to lay out a set of harsh
demands for the Chinese in peremptory language to which the Chinese
took great offense. Again they went to Prueher, who again said reluctantly
that he could not help. So the Chinese, angered by the lack of diplomatic
skills on the part of the Defense representative, chopped the plane into little pieces and mailed it back in crates. Prueher believes he could have gotten the entire plane flown out in days with just a little sensitivity to certain
Chinese considerations.[59]

This incident encapsulates the foolishness of turf wars: The U.S.
ambassador to China, a career military official who had risen to the top of
the world's largest military command, the very command from which the
plane in question had come, who was not only ambassador but who knew
many of the Chinese from military-to-military meetings and exchanges,
and who reported to a secretary of state who was one of the country's
most noted military officers, was removed in favor of a junior official from
a rival department. Rumsfeld and Wolfowitz would not trust Prueher and
Powell, the two men who had so successfully won the release of the air
crew. Instead, they turned the exercise into both a turf battle and a case
study in failed diplomacy.

What is perhaps more disturbing is that after this incident, it appears
that Wolfowitz, the administration's leading China hawk, gained the
bureaucratic upper hand in the evolution of future policies toward China
and Taiwan. It was Wolfowitz who, when advised by a senior military team
to be cautious with regard to giving in too far to Taiwanese demands, rep-
rimanded the admiral who was offering the advice by saying, "This is not
the Clinton administration's China policy, admiral. Taiwan is a democratic country and we will support them."[60] This sort of drift in U.S. policy—away from the one-China policy that had been theology for thirty

years, most of which had been led by Republican administrations—was later further amplified in a statement by President Bush that the United States would do "whatever it took to help Taiwan defend herself" against possible Chinese military attack and then allowing longer stays to Taiwanese leaders transiting through the United States than had been offered in the past.[61]

The rhetoric reversed itself in May 2003 when Douglas Paal, the de facto U.S. ambassador to Taiwan (and a former NSC staffer in the Reagan and first Bush administrations), led an effort to have President Bush declare that the United States "opposed" rather than would "not support" Taiwan's independence. This was due to concerns that political shifts in Taiwan might lead them to an act of provocation that could be extremely dangerous.

Furthermore, James Moriarty, a Taiwan specialist on the NSC, purportedly wanted the United States to announce that they would not unequivocally defend Taiwan in the event of a military attack by Beijing in response to any provocation by Taipei that moved the island decisively toward independence. Conservatives, led by officials in the Defense and State Departments, decried the proposed policy reversal, which would add new restrictions to U.S. arms sales to Taiwan, as violating the 1979 Taiwan Relations Act and representing a dramatic shift away from the "whatever it took" comments that had so heartened them.[62]

Moriarty traveled to Taipei in November 2003 to personally deliver a warning to President Chen Shui-Bian about holding a referendum on the topic of the island's independence, but the Taiwanese leader was unmoved and planned to go ahead with the controversial vote. Consequently, Taiwan received an even higher-level reproach when President Bush, standing next to Chinese Premier Wen Jiabao, declared that the United States did not support Chen's referendum. According to one observer, President Chen had—not surprisingly—ignored previous warnings from the Bush administration because they had sent mixed signals about the referendum from the seemingly rather confused U.S. government. The underlying tensions that led to that confusion continued into 2004, when the China hawks in the Pentagon reportedly expressed unhappiness about the appointment of CIA analyst Dennis Wilder to be the NSC's top China specialist. Wilder was seen as too liberal and a purveyor of the "China is not a threat" line that is anathema to the hawks.

Because the rise of China is perhaps the most important foreign policy development since the end of the Cold War, such divisions have compromised the ability of the United States to manage minor crises or to deliver clear diplomatic messages. The fact that an alternative policy is being pursued in the Department of Defense, which was never intended to play a lead role in the formation of such policies, is even more revealing about the nature of policy formation in Bush's foreign policy inner circle. It is an ominous development.

The Defense Department's heavy-handed and ideological approach produced reactions from other agencies that were often impolitic. Indeed, the acrimony between Defense and other agencies has become legendary. According to one individual who served on the Bush NSC staff, they were "just out of control, an endless nightmare."[63] "OSD [Office of the Secretary of Defense] was nuts," said a career official who also served in the Bush NSC:

> We would say they were out of their fucking minds both from a policy perspective and from a process perspective. In effect [Rumsfeld] said, I don't give a shit what the NSC staff says, I am going to do whatever I feel is in my right to do as the chain of command to the president. So you had an OSD staff given the direction by the secretary of defense not to work through the process and not to play ball. Then you had a secretary of defense who was also a policy entrepreneur who liked to dabble. He was like his own venture capitalist. He liked to dabble in different areas and throw things here and throw things there . . . on issues that were totally out of his way . . . on the Middle East peace process . . . on how to deal with Syria. We would characterize Rumsfeld as Secretary Strangelove when I was still working at the NSC. And one of the problems was that he didn't realize that when you are out of office for eight years the world has changed. The approach has changed [but] he had not.[64]

A similar comment was made by a senior minister from a foreign government who met with Rumsfeld and immediately after confided to a group of friends, "He was not of this century."

One career Foreign Service officer who worked closely with the Defense Department during the first term of the Bush administration said:

> My analysis of Rumsfeld is that back in the Ford days, he was too smart, too successful, too young, and now he is too old; that his early success and clear competence and intelligence led to a sense of self-confidence, not to say arrogance. So my assessment of Rumsfeld was that he was too self-confident, that he wasn't mastering his briefs, but he thought he knew everything. . . . He thought he understood the world [but] the world wasn't

the way it was twenty years ago. And Rumsfeld would never come to meetings prepared. He'd come not having read any of his briefing papers and so would extemporize, which was frustrating for everyone else.[65]

Rumsfeld's willful unpredictability affected every meeting in which Defense participated, whether he (or his deputy, Wolfowitz) was there or not. If less senior people from Defense attended, this former senior official remembers, they "would come to meetings in one of two postures. Either they would say that they couldn't decide because they didn't know what the secretary wanted or they would decide and then come back later and say they had changed their minds. So in either case it was worthless. Either you didn't decide anything or if you did it was always countermanded. There was no process. There was no internal process within DOD, and Rumsfeld clearly felt absolutely no compunction undercutting his subordinates and making them look like absolute fools."[66]

Numerous other top officials, many still at high levels within the administration, reported such problems, which continued throughout the first four years of the Bush administration. One such official who had also served at a high level on the elder Bush's team speculated that the president may have been frustrated by the reports of Rumsfeld as a rogue cabinet member and may even have been angry with him fairly frequently but that he was "just flat-out afraid to fire him,"[67] perhaps concerned about the consequences of an articulate and angry Rumsfeld offering the American people his take on what went right and what went wrong within councils of the administration while it waged its expanding "war on terror."

Articulating a view common among many former senior military officials with whom I spoke, General Wesley Clark commented that the structure of this administration, the reporting lines, seemed out of whack. "It's a function of the distribution of power and the personalities of the people that are there. The chain of command runs—one retired officer told me, who's very close to the Republican Party power structure—from Rumsfeld to Cheney to Bush: that Rumsfeld says to Cheney, Cheney then says to Bush what he should do."[68]

This assertion is dismissed as urban legend by those close to the president—but even they will acknowledge the unprecedented power of the Rumsfeld-Cheney team. Rumsfeld is almost certainly the most influential defense secretary since McNamara, and no American vice president has ever had anything approaching the power of Dick Cheney.

Other than the president himself, Vice President Dick Cheney is ultimately seen by many as the engine that really drives the group dynamic, and that Cheney and Rumsfeld, working in conjunction, drove Bush's inner circle in the directions they wanted to go. A useful illustration comes from General Jay Garner, briefly in charge of Iraqi reconstruction, recounted his frustration at being blocked from hiring two "superbly well-qualified" State Department Iraq experts for his team by Rumsfeld, who somewhat disingenuously asserted that the decision was being made "above his pay grade." Later, Garner found out through back channels that Rumsfeld had collaborated with the vice president's office in making the decision. This example resonates because it illustrates a key pitfall that plagued the first term of the Bush administration. The two senior experts who were kept from Garner's team had considerable experience and views that could have prevented many of the missteps that took place in the early days of the reconstruction process. But for reasons of turf, the desire to control the process, the potential value of their expertise was for a time marginalized and the benefits of a process that drew equally and in a balanced way from all corners of the U.S. government were lost. Similar cases in which intelligence or expertise existed within the bureaucracy but did not ultimately influence final decisions were also the result of an imbalanced policy process that enabled the agendas of a very small number of like-minded people to dominate the U.S. government and to ignore useful and at times potentially vital views elsewhere within the government.

Cheney's power was accrued in several ways. He had served as a White House chief of staff at thirty-seven years of age and had become an institution in the Republican Party. When he was in Congress, even though he represented sparsely populated Wyoming, he successfully worked his way up in the leadership. One of his friends even suggested to me that had Senator John Tower actually been confirmed to be George H.W. Bush's secretary of defense, Cheney very likely would have become Speaker of the House within a few years. Next, because he became secretary of defense in the first Bush presidency and managed the Gulf War with great competence, he was seen as a great asset and a useful advisor by candidate George W. Bush.

In fact, it has been suggested that the reason the Bush administration did not issue NSPD-1 until almost a month after assuming office was that an internal discussion was going on about the vice president's desire to chair key meetings or subgroups of the National Security Council. The most compelling evidence in support of this claim, beyond some of the rumors, is the role that the vice president actually established for himself and for his staff.[69] It grew so disproportionately beyond what any previous vice president had achieved that it is commonly asserted that the vice president is a co-president or prime minister.

Those at the center of the Bush administration, as we have seen, try to play it down or "put it into perspective." But what Cheney has carved out, even as they describe it, is highly unusual. Powell said, "Oh, he is a senior policymaker. And policy advisor to the principals meetings. Unless he is out of town, he's there, whereas in the former administrations I've worked in, he might be there, he might not be there. And [Cheney's chief of staff] "Scooter" [Libby] is there with his much larger staff, so it makes a difference."[70]

Rice says:

> The vice president has actually been terrific, in that he has been able to sit as a principal without a bureaucratic domain to defend, so he's always just a really wonderfully wise voice in the principals councils. The vice president's staff actually sits in on the deputies meetings . . . his groups of deputies sit in with Steve [Hadley]'s deputies, so they've very well integrated into our process and they play that role. . . . And the vice president and the president have a lot of interactions, they do have lunches and so forth and I know the vice president will tell the president what he thinks and very often he will have told me, I think "x" and I've told the president that. So, I can't overemphasize how valuable it is to have somebody of his stature go without a bureaucratic perch to worry about.[71]

Others see it differently, including many officials within the administration who note that the value of a principals committee meeting is to allow the president's advisors to have a free and open discussion about the advice they wish to give the president. Unfortunately, they assert, when Vice President Cheney is at the table, he is not like the others, not simply, as Rice characterizes it, just a wise old principal without a portfolio. He is seen as an 800-pound gorilla whose views carry much more weight than the others', and which skews discussions and quashes open dissent—inadvertently or otherwise.

Furthermore, there are assertions that his staff has grown to become, as described earlier by Richard Haass, a "mini-NSC."[72] Estimates of the number of staffers, consultants, and individuals seconded from other agencies to his office to work on foreign policy issues have ranged from fifteen to thirty-five—figures that are difficult to confirm because the Office of the Vice President is not covered under the provisions of the Freedom of Information Act and therefore does not need to disclose details of its operations.

Nonetheless, the perception inside and outside the government is that something extraordinary has happened. In November 2003, a *Newsweek* article asserted, "On the road to war, Cheney in effect created a parallel government that became a real power center."[73] Cheney, responding to such stories with characteristically ultra-dry humor, said, "Am I the evil genius in the corner nobody ever sees come out of his hole? It's a nice way to operate actually."[74]

Realistically, however, the Darth Vader myth of Dick Cheney must be separated from the facts, which are not as startling or as extreme as some of the wild rumors about a malevolent Rasputin controlling the mind of a slightly dim and malleable president. However, they do paint a portrait of a vice president who, if he has not actually assumed the role of the presidency, has become much like a prime minister and who has certainly usurped many of the prerogatives that have traditionally accrued to national security advisors. NSPD-1 notwithstanding, the driving force behind national security policy formation in Bush administration did not sit in the corner office that has been occupied by assistants to the president for national security policy for most of the years since Kissinger first claimed it. Instead, he sat a little ways down the hall, in the West Wing office of the vice president.

One reason Cheney could not justifiably be described as a prime minister is that he was not elected on his own merits. The vice president is selected to complement the ticket that is inevitably chosen or rejected on the basis of the presidential candidate. As it happened, of course, Cheney chaired the president's vice presidential search efforts, in which, in the end, Cheney was selected. He also was very influential in a number of other key appointments, including those of his old mentor Rumsfeld, his longtime associate Paul O'Neill as secretary of the Treasury, Paul Wolfowitz, Stephen Hadley, and Robert Joseph, NSC senior director for Proliferation, Strategy, Counterproliferation, and Homeland Defense.

According to the Federal Yellow Book, in winter 2005, Cheney's office listed only forty-four employees (forty-nine if you count Mrs. Cheney and her staff). However, the overall staff is generally believed to consist of fifty to sixty people, including schedulers, speechwriters, secretaries, specialists on domestic issues, and regional and military experts who perform international advisory services for the vice president. The discrepancy is largely due to the fact that while the Yellow Book lists only four national security staffers, it is generally acknowledged that Cheney's national security team consists of thirteen to fifteen people and that this group has at times been supplemented through secondments and the hiring of consultants. One NSC expert estimated the staff at well over thirty-five.[75] This is a considerable difference from past vice presidents, whatever the figure you use.

Although Vice President Al Gore's staff overall was perhaps larger than Cheney's, he had only Leon Fuerth and two other aides working on national security matters.

If Cheney actually has almost fifteen staffers working on national security issues, as most observers believe he does, then he is working with a national security staff larger than the team of professionals on John Kennedy's NSC. According to Leslie Gelb, former president of the Council on Foreign Relations, Cheney's staff is "unprecedented in size, scope, and power. They cover almost every issue and region."[76]

Since Cheney's national security staff is ideologically cohesive and smaller than the eighty-person NSC—and since Cheney and Libby run a tight ship with unquestioned authority—it can operate efficiently and present cogent, persuasive option papers to the vice president, which he can then relay directly to the president. In a former NSC staffer's words, "With several of his political allies, including Deputy National Security Advisor Stephen Hadley and Middle East director Elliott Abrams [who serves on the NSC], Libby is able to 'run circles around Condi.'"[77]

Cheney's chief of staff, "Scooter" Libby, who was Wolfowitz's deputy under secretary of defense for policy during the first Bush 43 administration and had been a student of his at Yale, has, in addition to his titles with the vice president, the title of assistant to the president, putting him on the president's staff and giving him a disproportionately influential role compared with any of his predecessors.

Cheney's wider influence across the administration includes various networks, such as the neoconservative Project for the New American Century. Eleven of the twenty-five signatories, including Cheney, Wolfowitz, and Libby, worked in the U.S. government during the first Bush administration.[78] Libby and his top foreign policy aide during the first years of the Bush administration, Eric Edelman, drafted the Defense Planning Guidance of 1992–93, which argued that the United States should prevent any potential competitor to American power from emerging. William Luti went from the vice president's foreign policy team to become deputy under secretary of defense for Near Eastern and South Asian affairs.

Cheney spends considerably more time with the president than his predecessors. While Gore had a weekly lunch with Clinton, Cheney not only has a weekly lunch but also on most days when they are in Washington, he spends "many hours a day" with the president. He attends national security briefings with the president daily, economic and domestic policy meetings, and principals meetings as they come up. After important meetings, the vice president often stays behind to speak with Bush alone.[79]

Visiting foreign leaders very often hold private meetings with Cheney in addition to sessions with Powell or other cabinet members. Seventeen presidents or prime ministers met with Cheney in the first half of 2002 alone. In 2004, Cheney met with Pakistani President Pervez Musharraf, Japanese Prime Minister Junichiro Koizumi, and Chinese President Hu Jintao, among others. Many past vice presidents would primarily get their opportunity to be in the presence of other heads of state when attending their funerals.

Cheney was appointed the head of administration task forces on energy policy and protection against the threat of biological and other weapons of mass destruction (WMD) terrorism in the United States. Cheney's energy task force had a significant national security agenda. According to a top-secret NSC document dated February 3, 2001, the NSC staff was directed to cooperate fully with the task force as it examined "melding the review of operational policies toward rogue states . . . and actions regarding the capture of new and existing oil and gas fields."[80]

Cheney became one of the principal supporters of Ahmad Chalabi, the leader of the Iraqi National Congress (INC) and one-time Pentagon ally, despite intelligence community concerns about him. Cheney helped provide funding for the INC in 2001, and during the first few months of the Bush administration, in almost weekly senior staff discussions of Iraq policy, he pushed for additional support for the INC to help it topple Saddam Hussein.

Cheney has been meeting regularly with Federal Reserve Chairman Alan Greenspan since he took office. By early spring of 2004, the two long-time friends had met seventeen times since the administration entered office (compared with Greenspan's eleven meetings with Rice, six meetings with Card, and one meeting with Powell). In 1996, for example, Greenspan had three appointments with White House officials other than the president. From 2001 to 2003, he averaged forty-four a year.[81]

On September 11, 2001, from the bunker beneath the White House, Cheney regularly spoke with the president, providing him valued guidance at length before the president made any public statements or decisions. (This is not to say that his role in this respect was in the least inappropriate. Quite the contrary. Rather, it is merely to underscore his centrality and special role.) Cheney also apparently ordered aircraft scrambled to intercept an incoming aircraft although the vice president has no authority to make such orders within the context of the national command authority if the president is alive and accessible.[82]

Cheney's active consumption of Iraq intelligence and his trips to the

CIA in the run-up to the invasion of Iraq were cited by some in the CIA as White House political pressure to produce evidence justifying an invasion of Iraq.

Cheney sent his own representatives to a meeting of seventy Iraqi army defectors in London in July 2002. The Pentagon and the State Department also sent representatives.

Members of the Defense Department's policy office—who were closely affiliated with the vice president's office through Feith, Luti, and others—prepared the analysis that contradicted the CIA view that no links between Iraq and al Qaeda could be proved and briefed Cheney and Bush on the evidence of those ties in August 2002. It was their view that prevailed in the administration's public utterances. Elements of Powell's compelling February 2003 UN testimony were first drafted by Libby and others in the Office of the Vice President.

The last thing George Bush did before making the final decision on March 19, 2003, to try to assassinate Saddam Hussein by bombing Dora Farm was to meet privately with Cheney. At approximately 7:00 p.m. that evening, Bush asked everyone in the Oval Office at the time—including Powell, Card, advisor Karen Hughes, and a CIA official—to leave so he could speak with the vice president. He then issued the order at 7:12 p.m.[83]

When the war in Iraq began, Bush ordered cabinet officials not to give any preferential treatment to the INC. Soon after, in April 2003, the Pentagon flew Chalabi and 600 of his armed followers into southern Iraq "with the approval of the vice president."[84]

Libby was one of the targets of the investigation of the White House source who exposed Valerie Plame as a CIA operative in an attempt to get back at her husband, Ambassador Joseph Wilson, for uncovering false reports about yellowcake uranium allegedly being sold by Niger to Saddam Hussein.

A contrasting view of the vice president's role was offered by those who have worked closely with him. Eric Edelman was the vice president's top foreign policy advisor after "Scooter" Libby, and later became U.S. ambassador to Turkey. A career Foreign Service officer who had worked on the staff of Strobe Talbott at the State Department, Edelman offered this perspective of the vice president's intent:

> It was clear from the outset that the vice president felt that the great strength he brought to the president was having long experience in national security, which President Bush—who is a very, very smart guy, perhaps deceptively, so since he is sometimes not the most articulate guy

in the world when speaking off the cuff—clearly lacks. . . . We were given very direct instruction—not from "Scooter" but from the vice president—that he did not want us involved operationally in foreign policy. And, as a result, he wanted to disestablish all the commissions that Gore set up.

What the vice president made clear was that, first of all, he regarded his primary responsibility as advising the president. . . . He had a couple of advantages, of course. One was that everyone knew that he did not harbor any presidential ambitions. . . . He also made it clear to us that he did not want us talking to anybody about what his advice to the president was. He was going to give private advice, and he was not going to talk about it in the press.[85]

At the idea that the vice president is an intimidating force in meetings—or that he might have intimidated analysts at the CIA into changing their positions—Edelman bridled, "I was in some of the meetings where they were in with the intelligence community and . . . I don't think people who were in the room felt they were being pressured. Unless people can't stand having . . . their presumptions and assertions challenged by people saying, 'What's the basis for this?' Because he was and is a very acute and careful student of intelligence. He asked a lot of questions . . . He's a quiet man . . . I would not say he is intimidating but intellectually formidable."[86]

Edelman, an extremely effective and thoughtful career Foreign Service officer, of course presents a view from the perspective of the Cheney team, and while his account balances some of the wild accusations, his observations don't undercut the universal conclusion that Cheney is, of all the members of the president's team, the first among equals and, with Donald Rumsfeld, he represents the power center of the Bush administration. This is true not because the president is, as some have asserted, an empty vessel. He is clearly not, and those who have worked with him, including visiting foreign dignitaries, present a starkly different picture of him as engaged, intelligent, and highly competent. Rather, Cheney and the president share deep-seated conservative convictions. The president trusts his vice president to act as he would and to do so with the benefit of great intelligence and experience. Rumsfeld is seen as a power center who has been given a long leash by virtue of his relationship with Cheney—he is in some respects the prime facilitator, the prime driver of action within the administration.

As for the vice president's philosophies, some observers are puzzled by his emergence in his current role, especially those who saw him as a professional but non-ideological cabinet secretary during the administration of George H.W. Bush. "You know, the big mystery to me is Dick Cheney," said one senior Republican who has known him since the Ford years. "He instinctively started from the conservative base, but if you made a compelling rational argument, he was not an ideologue. My sense is that now, for whatever reason, he has become an ideologue—and I don't know whether it is because he is an extraordinarily powerful vice president, more powerful than any in our history, and nobody talks to him and says, 'Dick, you're full of shit'—or whether he's only now able to let his true feelings come out, or whether there was some kind of shift."[87]

Others who worked with Cheney in the past saw hints then of some of the views he has espoused during the first term of his vice presidency. He has never had much patience for multilateral processes. He has always been vigorously supportive of maintaining a strong presidency and presidential prerogatives and has long been committed to fighting against the erosion of presidential authority by Congress and other contenders.

In this value-driven administration, then, several sets of values were brought to the table. The president contributed his sense of good and evil, of the divinely inspired values that America represents and advances, as well as his filial obligation to unfinished business in Iraq, a feeling shared by Cheney, Wolfowitz, and others among the neocon network in the administration. Wolfowitz and the other neocons came with Straussian absolutism—and applied it to their ideas about the weakness of European liberalism and the need to extend American values worldwide. Those ideas fit well with Condoleezza Rice's Cold War–era views about extending American-style freedoms to people who had been deprived of them. If Rumsfeld brought any particular ideological component to this mix, it was the idea that the modern military should be transformed fundamentally. The final contribution was Cheney's strong belief that America and American presidents must be able to act on their own, in their own interests, unencumbered by alliances, multilateral procedures, or Congress nipping at their heels.

Some within the Republican establishment acknowledge that September 11 was a catalytic event, not only revealing the core views or character traits within the members of the group but also changing the dynamics and interrelationships of the group as a whole and in turn producing a shift in the philosophical foundations of U.S. foreign policy and behavior. "The traditionalists," notes Brent Scowcroft in discussing this pivotal moment,

> believe in operating within the traditions of twentieth-century U.S. foreign policy—that one proceeds in foreign policy in conjunction with, or

reaching out to our friends, allies, and international organizations. The transformationalists argue that 9/11 showed that the world environment was deteriorating rapidly and we had to be bold. Friends and allies would only hold us back. We know what has to be done and we have the power to do it. What has to be done is to transform the Middle East into a collection of democracies. That will bring peace and stability, and when that has been done, we will be applauded by the world.[88]

·   ·   ·

During a series of transitional NSC briefings in January 2001 covering issues including Russia, China, and nuclear proliferation, Sandy Berger told Condoleezza Rice that the Bush administration "will spend more time . . . on terrorism generally, and al Qaeda specifically, than any other subject."[89] Richard Clarke, whom Rice asked to stay on, later presented his comprehensive new anti–al Qaeda strategy to Rice and provided a three-page memorandum of his plans and priorities to Stephen Hadley, after requesting a high-level review of the subject. However, Clarke's counterterrorism plan was placed on the slow track as the Bush foreign policy team "had to learn about [al Qaeda] and figure out where it fit into their broader foreign policy."[90]

Afghanistan and its Taliban leadership attracted even less attention from Bush's foreign policy team before September 11, much as the preceding Clinton and Bush administrations had shown limited interest in the war-torn country after the Soviet withdrawal. It is reported that the first President Bush said early in 1991, on learning that American arms were still arriving in Afghanistan, "Is that thing still going on?"[91] Thanks to a warning that likely came from Pakistani intelligence sources, Clinton's decision to fire seventy-seven Tomahawk missiles at a suspected encampment of Osama bin Laden gave new meaning to the term "pound sand." By 2001, the desolate country represented a minor part of the portfolio of Zalmay Khalilzad, who was then NSC senior director for the Gulf and Southwest Asia—even though it was home to bin Laden and the Taliban and was the world's leading exporter of opium.[92]

Meanwhile, Rice shifted the focus of the NSC staff to the priorities given to her by the president and shaped largely by the vice president and the secretary of defense—including national missile defense, to be handled on the NSC by Cheney ally Robert Joseph.[93] The Office of Transnational Threats (Clarke's division) was retained after some debate, albeit in a diminished role, as Clarke's special position of national coordinator for counterterrorism was downgraded. Clarke would no longer be a member of the principals committee, and the Counterterrorism Strategy Group (CSG) would report to deputy instead principal secretaries.[94] In practice, transnational threats were not acknowledged as the dominant challenge for this administration, despite Rice's assertions to the contrary noted earlier in the chapter. During this early process, one Rumsfeld ally stated about Rice's ability to manage the foreign policy process, "She's going to be crushed. It's as simple as that."[95]

As the Bush administration fashioned its foreign policy team—which included a number of noted Iraq hawks as well as some key decision makers from the first Gulf War—the new national security advisor displayed no sense of urgency toward counterterrorism policy, Clarke frustratingly recalls. The first deputies meeting did not take place until late April 2001. That meeting included heated exchanges between Clarke and Deputy Defense Secretary Wolfowitz, who didn't "understand why we are beginning by talking about this one man bin Laden," a viewpoint that was rebuffed not only by Clarke but by Deputy Secretary of State Richard Armitage as well. Wolfowitz also asked why they weren't talking more about "Iraqi terrorism" against the United States, a concern for which deputy CIA director John McLaughlin said no evidence existed.[96]

While Clarke's counterterrorism plans slowly wound their way through the bureaucracy, he convened the CSG in July 2001 to discuss the al Qaeda threat in response to a growing volume of intelligence indicating a heightened but still vague threat. Without more specific information, a public warning could not be issued, although Clarke asked the Federal Aviation Administration (FAA) to send another security warning to the airlines and airports. The FBI also sent an alert to 18,000 police departments, and counterterrorism response staffs canceled their summer vacations.[97]

Despite "urgent" requests for principals meetings, no NSC meetings were held on the subject of terrorism in the pre–September 11 period when President Bush or Vice President Cheney attended. Meanwhile, two principals meetings and four deputies meetings were convened about Iraq between February and July 2001, where a range of nonmilitary and military options were discussed.[98] An e-mail Clarke sent to Rice and the NSC staff in the spring of 2001, in which he reminded them of the al Qaeda threat and the need to act before there were "hundreds of dead in the streets of America," did not speed up the process of reviewing Clarke's proposals for action against the terrorist organization.[99]

Nor did the vice president conduct a government-wide review of managing the consequences of a terrorist attack in the United States, as had been announced by the president in May 2001.[100] The lack of interest displayed by the Bush Treasury Department toward cutting terrorist financing also reflected the lower priority of terrorism issues during this period. Clarke's plan, largely unchanged from the version given to Rice in January 2001, was approved by the principals committee on September 4, 2001, and had finally and poignantly just reached President Bush's desk when the September 11 attacks took place.[101]

As Clarke reports in his book *Against All Enemies*, he had returned to the White House minutes after the first plane hit the World Trade Center, and Rice quickly designated him as the crisis manager for the administration.[102] Officials at the NSC were as stunned as the rest of the government, as one official said on the day of the attack, "We don't know anything here. We're watching CNN too."[103] Clarke and his several NSC colleagues, who were among the only people remaining in the White House complex that day, were at the center of efforts to coordinate the government's response.[104] As with the attack on the *USS Cole*, Clarke immediately suspected that al Qaeda was responsible for the hijackings. Unlike in October 2000, however, the Bush administration rapidly began to consider plans to respond with what would be termed the "war on terror," initially along the lines of what Clarke had been advocating.[105]

Hours after the September 11 attacks, the first in a series of NSC meetings was held to fashion an immediate response to the crisis, with the president deciding by the end of that evening to "punish whoever harbors terrorists, not just the perpetrators."[106] The NSC principals met every day (and sometimes more often, with the president joining via secure video teleconference) in the days that followed September 11 to develop a response to a threat and a country that had not been of primary interest to the foreign policy team.[107] During this period, Cheney was a major and constant player, sitting on the president's right at NSC meetings he attended and meeting with him privately afterward, quarterbacking key elements of the policy development process even when he was at an "undisclosed location." Rice said that she envisioned her role in this turbulent period as one of "coordinator." She was not considered at the time to be a strong independent voice and on some occasions would not offer her views unless they were explicitly sought.

Within a day of the terrorist attacks, NSC principals were formulating plans for an attack on bin Laden's terrorist camps in Afghanistan. And once Afghanistan became the focus of the administration's post-attack strategy, the NSC's Khalilzad, a protégé of Wolfowitz who had worked in the Reagan and first Bush administrations, played a central role in shaping the Bush administration's post-Taliban political strategy.[108] Khalilzad, Rice, and Clarke also played a role in toughening the language about the Taliban in the president's September 2001 address to Congress.[109] Meanwhile, President Bush, perhaps acknowledging that his administration needed to get up to speed on Afghanistan, noted in late September 2001 that "we need to plan as if things won't go well." According to Rice, at an NSC meeting he also posed a question about the post-Taliban political transition that hadn't been considered by his foreign policy team.[110]

Yet even in the earliest stages of the planning for the campaign against the Taliban, NSC principals were arguing about whether to expand the soon-to-be-launched "war on terror" to Iraq, with Deputy Secretary of Defense Wolfowitz the most vocal proponent of this course in the administration.[111] In fact, there was a split between supporters of Richard Perle, who were known as the "string of Perles" because Perle had advocated Saddam Hussein's removal in the 1990s, and supporters of Brent Scowcroft, who represented a more cautious, moderate line of action. Rice and Hadley were viewed—in May 2002—as honest brokers between the two factions.[112]

Secretary Powell and others prevailed—in the short term—in an NSC meeting on September 17, 2001, as President Bush declared, "I believe Iraq was involved, but I'm not going to strike them now. I don't have the evidence at this point."[113] Rice said that the president informed her on September 16 that "Iraq is to the side" in setting priorities for the "war on terror," and Bush maintained in an interview several days later that "obviously, there were some who discussed Iraq. That's out of the question at this point."[114] After an NSC meeting at Camp David, Powell, Tenet, Card, and Cheney supported the president's decision (Rumsfeld abstained) to leave Iraq out of the initial round of military strikes.[115]

Nonetheless, according to critics such as Clarke and Seymour Hersh, the attention of the Bush foreign policy team shifted away from Afghanistan and toward Saddam Hussein even before the Taliban had been ousted.[116] Clarke recounts his surprise when just one day after the terrorist attacks, the president, wandering in the White House Situation Room, directed the staff of the National Security Council to investigate whether any links between al Qaeda and Saddam Hussein could be found. President Bush said, "Look, I know you have a lot to do and all . . . but I want you, as soon as you can, to go back over everything, everything. See if Saddam did this. See if he's linked in any way . . . I want to know any shred."[117] The NSC director responded that "we will look—again" and reports that his follow-up memo, in which he reported that no evidence was found tying Iraq to the terrorist attacks, was "immediately bounced back" from Stephen Hadley.[118] Other administration officials with whom I spoke discount whether this meeting took place, and many contest other details of the Clarke account. What is beyond dispute, however, is that somehow—and, according to Bob Woodward, without any direct conversation on the subject with either Powell or Rumsfeld—the president made the decision to seriously consider going after Iraq within days or weeks of the attacks on the World Trade Center and the Pentagon.

Consequently, in November 2001, even as combat operations were still unfolding against al Qaeda in Afghanistan, President Bush directed the secretary of defense to generate war plans for Iraq. In fact, according to one military planner, the Pentagon's Central Command had been ordered to draw up scenarios for an assault on Iraq (which originally focused on securing Iraqi oil fields) on September 13, almost the same time it was tasked with the Afghanistan operation.[119]

While the ouster of the Taliban and the creation of a new regime in Afghanistan bumped Iraq from center stage in the fall of 2001, Saddam Hussein became the focus of the Bush administration and the NSC by the following year. The NSC senior director for defense policy and arms control, Franklin Miller, headed a little-reported interagency task force, the Executive Steering Group, which was established by the White House in the summer of 2002, months before the outbreak of hostilities, to coordinate Iraq war planning efforts. This NSC-chaired deputy under secretary–level assemblage addressed strategic planning and policy recommendations for deputies committee meetings. The NSC participated in two other interagency groups—the Iraq Political-Military Cell and the Humanitarian/Reconstruction Group—that prepared plans for the political and economic rebuilding of post-Hussein Iraq.[120]

The NSC also took part in efforts to coordinate the administration's public message about its Iraq policy. Participants in the White House Iraq Group, whose purpose was to "educate the public" about the threat from Saddam Hussein, included Rice, Hadley, Libby, political guru Karl Rove, and Cheney aide Mary Matalin plus several high-ranking communications officials. A "strategic communications" task force under the White House Iraq Group planned speeches and white papers, with particular emphasis on Iraq's potential short-term nuclear threat.[121] Separately, Bush directed Rice and Card to improve the case for war for "Joe Public" after an unconvincing White House briefing by the CIA deputy director.[122]

Rice and the NSC became enmeshed in another, increasingly controversial component of prewar planning, the vetting of intelligence and the synchronization of dissenting interpretations of data on Iraq's weapons programs.[123] Rice and several NSC staffers were embroiled in controversy about prewar claims articulated by Cheney and other members of the Bush administration about the state of Iraq's nuclear program.[124] A separate Pentagon-based intelligence unit, the Policy Counterterrorism Evaluation Group, privately briefed senior White House officials on alleged ties between Iraq and al Qaeda without the knowledge of the CIA. Another Pentagon-based unit, the Office of Special Plans, was "established by Rumsfeld, Douglas Feith, and other hawks expressly to bypass the CIA and other intelligence agencies."[125]

According to CIA director Tenet, NSC officials had proposed the inclusion of questionable information about Iraqi nuclear intentions in speeches given by the Bush administration.[126] Rice reportedly did not fully read an October 2002 National Intelligence Estimate that included the same disputed data on Iraqi nuclear assessments and contained a State Department dissent about Saddam Hussein's pursuit of uranium from African sources.[127] Robert Joseph had rejected a plea from a CIA official to remove claims from Bush's 2003 State of the Union address about Iraqi efforts to purchase uranium from Niger; Hadley also took responsibility for the error.[128] A former Clinton NSC staffer, Ambassador Joseph Wilson, was asked by the CIA to evaluate the Niger yellowcake uranium evidence. He later went public with his negative assessment of the intelligence, resulting in the retaliatory exposure of his wife's CIA position by one or more White House officials (who, at the time of writing, remain unidentified).[129]

After the invasion of Iraq in March 2003 and rapid battlefield success, controversy within the Bush administration resumed over the often contentious (and sometimes hasty) process of postwar Iraq planning, a process that was largely controlled by Donald Rumsfeld and the Pentagon. An early sign of that strife was the airlift by the Pentagon of Chalabi and his armed fighters into Iraq without informing the NSC and the State Department.[130]

However, in October 2003, reflecting growing frustration with the Defense Department–led reconstruction efforts in post-Hussein Iraq, President Bush established the Iraq Stabilization Group (ISG), explaining that "it's common for the National Security Council to coordinate efforts—interagency efforts." An unnamed senior administration official noted that the move "puts accountability right into the White House,"[131] while Condoleezza Rice described the shift as reflecting a "recognition by everyone that we are in a different phase" now that the administration's request for $87 billion in reconstruction and military aid was being considered by Congress.[132] Headed by Rice, the ISG was designed to ensure that a larger number of agencies—including the State and Treasury Departments and the CIA—would be more regularly involved in a policy process that had been dominated by the Pentagon. The ISG consisted of four interagency coordinating committees, each headed by an NSC staffer, addressing the Iraqi economy (chaired by Gary Edson), counterterrorism (Frances Townsend), political institutions (Robert Blackwill), and communications (Anna Perez).[133]

The news of the new stabilization group was released in a public manner meant to embarrass Secretary Rumsfeld, who told reporters that he had been unaware of the changes in advance.[134] While the formation of the ISG was generally viewed as a bureaucratic stratagem designed to diminish the authority of the Pentagon and Secretary Rumsfeld on Iraq policy, one analysis described the NSC-led group as a political ploy by President Bush, filled with "political lightweights. The new Iraq Stabilization Group is, in effect, headed by a team of minor technicians with the exception of Rice."[135] There has indeed been almost no mention of the Iraq Stabilization Group since its establishment.[136] It disappeared into a puff of smoke while the Department of Defense has continued to play a central role in the "stabilization" of Iraq.

Although the NSC may not have been at the hub of the administration's Iraq's postwar planning, at least one NSC official may have played a role in the Abu Ghraib prison abuse scandal. Lieutenant Colonel Steven Jordan, the prison's top officer overseeing interrogations, testified that he was under intense "pressure" from the White House, Pentagon, and CIA last fall to get better information from detainees.[137] One sign of that pressure, according to Jordan, was the visit of NSC counterterrorism director Frances Townsend (who subsequently moved from the NSC to the Homeland Security Council) to the prison on a November 2003 trip, where she spent two hours but says "she did not discuss interrogation techniques or the need to obtain more information from detainees, and neither witnessed nor heard about abuse of detainees."[138] The NSC's exact role in shaping interrogations policy is not clear. Townsend said that her visit (which she described as brief) focused on developing measures to improve the interagency handling and sharing of data on the causes of the anti-U.S. insurgency violence, which had been spiking that month.[139] (It is one of the great ironies of the Bush administration that the person who built the notorious legal firewalls that separated the intelligence and enforcement sides of the FBI during the Clinton years and thus made it difficult for them to do their job in combating terror was later promoted to be the head of the White House's Homeland Security Council. That individual, Fran Townsend, had something going for her in addition to her own tough-as-nails reputation as a prosecutor—her husband had been a fraternity brother of the president's at Yale.)

The development of the Homeland Security Council and the Department of Homeland Security are cited by President Bush as being among the greatest achievements of his administration, as major innovations in the structure of the U.S. national security establishment, the greatest since 1947. As noted at the outset of this book, the text of the 1947 act specifically calls for the National Security Council to "advise the President with respect to the integration of domestic, foreign and military policies relating to the national security so as to enable the military services and the other departments and agencies of the government to cooperate more effectively in matters of national security." In other words, the National Security Council was originally conceived of as a mechanism to handle both domestic and foreign concerns—even if the sort of terrorist threat encountered in 2001 was hardly what the authors of that legislation envisioned. The fact that both a new council and a new cabinet department had to be organized to respond to that threat demonstrates on one level a failure of the implementers of the legislation to fulfill its mandate. Furthermore, previous administrations had mobilized far more actively to respond to terror threats and foil them—as with the millennium plot or the al Qaeda plot in 1995 to down as many as a dozen 747s crossing the Pacific—without the benefit of such a department. The Department of Homeland Security has occupied itself largely with the bureaucratic imperatives of merging vast, formerly separate bureaucracies into a single whole. Ironically, among those bureaucracies are not the two—the CIA and the FBI—whose disconnectedness was seen as the single greatest contributor to our lack of preparedness to identify or reduce the threat of terrorism before September 11.

In the same vein, the 9/11 Commission's recommendation to create a national intelligence director to coordinate and integrate the fifteen agencies of the U.S. government that conduct intelligence operations—a recommendation that later became the basis for the Intelligence Reform bill that Congress passed in early 2005—has been cited to me by individuals close to the commission as something that would have been unnecessary had the national security advisor and the National Security Council played the role they had been intended to play. Again, as noted in the National Security Act of 1947, the Central Intelligence Agency and the position of director of central intelligence were created "for the purpose of

coordinating the intelligence activities of the several Government departments and agencies in the interest of national security," and the purpose of
the CIA, "under the direction of the National Security Council," was,
among others, "to advise the National Security Council in matters concerning such intelligence activities of the Government departments and
agencies as related to national security." The idea of a single individual,
directly connected to the White House national security apparatus (and
with a status identical to that of the chairman of the Joint Chiefs of Staff),
was also developed and written into law fifty-four years before the September 11 attacks, suggesting that the objectives behind those words were
not being realized.

Armitage, who was deputy secretary of state during Bush's first term,
reportedly described Rice's NSC as "dysfunctional. . . . The NSC is not performing its traditional role, as adjudicator between agencies" during the
preparations for Iraq and other crises.[140] Criticizing her management of
the NSC as undisciplined and uncoordinated, Armitage, Powell, and others felt that the president was not being well prepared for the foreign policy upheaval that has taken place during his tenure in office. Members of
the 9/11 Commission privately used similar language.

.   .   .

The attacks on the World Trade Center and the Pentagon produced
immediate and striking changes within the White House. Cheney snapped
into action and immediately went from being a very influential conservative vice president to being the hub of the ideologically driven policy-for-
mation process his colleagues have described. His closest ally in the cabinet,
Rumsfeld, in mid-2001 deemed by conventional wisdom to be the most
likely cabinet member to depart the administration early, was redeemed
that day and the primacy of his department for the foreseeable future was
ensured. While he was reportedly driven less by ideology than some of his
colleagues, his self-interest resulted in his becoming inextricably tied to
"transformationalist" objectives and initiatives. The importance of Rice to
a president for whom national security was now the central issue grew
geometrically, and she was drawn inexorably to his side and away from
process and the institution she might otherwise have managed quite like
Scowcroft had. The role of the State Department ebbed further as the
nation and its dominant leaders had little patience for the compromise
and delays of diplomacy and as foreign policy itself became "militarized."
The neocons saw the opportunity to assert their case that diplomatic bal-

ancing acts in the Middle East had created danger for the United States and that the time had come for stronger measures, whatever the cost—a view for which those emerging as centers of power within the inner circle had great sympathy. As for the man at the center, the president, the only one, as Truman put it, "a vote," Scowcroft said late in 2004, "It's possible that the transformation came with 9/11, and the current President, who is a very religious person, thought that there was something unique if not divine about a catastrophe like 9/11 happening when he was president. That somehow that was meant to be and his mission is to deal with the war on terrorism."[141] The lightning bolt had struck and the transformation of the transformationalists had begun.

Will the ascendancy of these foreign policy revolutionaries during the first term of the Bush administration be followed by the realization of their vision? A key factor in answering that question will be whether they will retain their influence in the years ahead, especially as the shock of 9/11 slips further into memory.

With Powell's departure and the history of the first term of the Bush administration, many felt that power had consolidated around the neo-cons as the second term began. However, some moderating forces came into play. First is the old Washington rule, now familiar to the reader, that where you stand depends on where you sit. Condoleezza Rice is almost certainly being changed by the State Department more than she is changing it. She immediately surrounded herself with a team of experienced "traditionalists," such as former U.S. Trade Representative and James Baker protégé Ambassador Robert Zoellick and career diplomat and former ambassador to NATO Nicholas Burns. Her hiring them not only signaled that she wanted to make the department work, but also, because they are steeped, as she is, in the history of our trans-Atlantic alliances, it signaled a desire to rebuild or restore relationships that were damaged because of the conduct of our invasion of Iraq. They are "realists," of the old school.

In addition, pressure to wind down the U.S. involvement in Iraq—ideally through fortifying progress toward democracy, progress elsewhere in the Middle East, and efforts to work more closely with allies to resolve festering issues such as nuclear programs in Iran and North Korea could result in the restoration of old-fashioned diplomacy to the center of U.S. foreign policy. This would lessen the influence of a Department of Defense already wounded by its missteps, from perceived authorship of misleading analyses that justified the invasion of Iraq to the bungled process of rebuilding Iraq after the invasion to the prison abuses at Abu Ghraib. As a consequence, at least in the early days of the second term of the Bush administration, it seemed as though there was a new impulse toward a somewhat greater emphasis on "traditional" values and a United States that was more easily embraced by the world at large.

That said, the medium- to longer-term consequences of first-term policies will play a central role in determining the future viability of the neocon arguments. Above all else, the progress of democracy in the Middle East will be decisive. Should the transformationalists have an opportunity to argue unilateral interventionism was effective in the pursuit of American national interests, they will certainly retain enough adherents at the highest levels of the Bush administration and the Republican Party foreign policy establishment to produce a shift away from what has been the traditional center in American politics.

The nominations of Paul Wolfowitz to head the World Bank and of John Bolton, a neocon ally of Vice President Cheney, to be the U.S. Ambassador to a UN of which he has been harshly critical were cited by some as a sign of a desire to institutionalize the anti-multilateral tendencies of the avatars of the right in the Bush Administration. This too, however, may be an oversimplification given the reality that having men like Wolfowitz and Bolton, given their access and influence, at the highest levels, actually increases the likelihood that issues associated with these institutions will be more front-of-mind overall among Bush team members. This is not to underplay that seeking to send a UN-basher to the UN (Bolton was not confirmed by the Senate as of this writing) sends a message about the skepticism with which the institution is viewed by the Bush team nor is it to overlook that the appointment was cited by some observers as an example of transformationalist muscle-flexing after Rice quashed an earlier attempt to make the irascible Bolton her deputy. Rather it is to note that the appointments were more complex in their implications than the caricature-driven analyses that often made their way into the media, especially those segments of the media with a political agenda.

Indeed, to "Kremlinologists" studying the inner workings of the Bush team, subtle and often confusing hints about their intentions and the future balance between the different camps and players within the administration were common during the first months of the second term. Bolton got the job but his appointment was announced by Rice. This emphasized her primacy but also diminished the UN ambassador's role in a way that was consistent with the anti-multilateral intent of the neocons. Similarly, even as Administration critics bemoaned the nominations of two transformationalists to important new posts, it was possible to see the selections as a weakening of the neocon camp because two leading exponents of neocon views were turfed out to positions of secondary influence. Adding to this perception is the fact, at least during the first months of George W. Bush's second administration, that it seems clear that Rice is strengthened by being partnered with a National Security Advisor who is her former deputy and that rivalry between the two seems unlikely to present itself in the ways that it has in the past. The two have a very solid working relationship and Hadley seems very much inclined to be a dependable, thoughtful, mostly-behind-the-scenes national security advisor in the mold of his former colleague Brent Scowcroft. Some who know Hadley well have puzzled over this apparent contradiction in his personality, his ties to the more unilateralist members of the arms control community and his simultaneous associations with many moderates as well as Scowcroft. However, perhaps it is precisely both Hadley's and Rice's recurring roles as bridge-builders during the first term that offer the clearest hint that the Administration is heading toward more synthesis between the two perspectives, a desire to advance key elements of the transformationalist worldview in a way that is more palatable to the other nations of the international community.

The decision by the President to let incoming Director of National Intelligence John Negroponte assume responsibility for Bush's daily intelligence briefings was also seen as an important development by several current and former top national security officials—perhaps as important as his new titular position atop the intelligence community "org chart." Indeed, one former national security advisor compared Negroponte's new role with the way Brzezinski gained immeasurable bureaucratic influence by assuming direct control of those briefings himself.

In the end, of course, a disproportionate amount of influence as to these outcomes within the administration will come down to Vice President Cheney and, above all, as it always does, to the president himself. The NSC, as we have seen, is built differently from those parts of the U.S. government for which the Constitution provided for institutional structures to be more important than the influence of any one person. If a president chooses to use it as a system to present him with various views and to test those views before implementing any one of them, it tends to work rather well. If he chooses it as a mechanism that is more focused on implementation than debate—or more focused on debate than effective implementation, as sometimes happens—then it does not. If he chooses to ignore formal structures and depend on informal ones, as do most presidents, the relevance of formal ones fades.

Furthermore, the chemistry of the group and the personalities of the individuals within it play a far greater role in determining the NSC's true function than does any preconceived aspect of the structure. Indeed, the structure of the actual "committee in charge of running the world"—that is, the ad hoc group the president relies on, rather than the formal NSC itself—is based on a constantly changing series of transactions between the president and its members in which he offers or withdraws access, trust, influence, and power. Statutes and history are far less important than the personal transactions that continuously remake this powerful entity. Thus, success and shifting public opinion will have a major role in determining how the nucleus of the U.S. national security apparatus—those closest to the president with the greatest influence on his views—will shift and evolve during George W. Bush's second term.

Philosophies are, of course, centrally important in this process, for they shape the character of the group. Tugs-of-war over ideology are a long-standing tradition within the NSC and, indeed, are part of its raison d'être. The struggle in the Bush administration shares much with those of the past, particularly those that have divided the Republican Party throughout the modern era from Dwight D. Eisenhower onward. Indeed, the tension between those who view the United States as the leading member of the global community and those who see the United States as an independent actor that ought to be driven by narrowly defined national interests has dominated much of the foreign policy debate since the end of the Second World War.

Of course, beyond the practical issues associated with running an effective NSC process—formal and informal—are broader questions as to whether the philosophical arguments advanced by transformationalists as an alternative to traditional approaches are in fact good ones.

As the neocons see it, the attacks of September 11, 2001, not only transformed the Bush team and validated their views but also ushered in a new era in U.S. foreign policy, providing us with a new organizing principle to replace that of the Cold War. Others, myself included, feel that the horrible tragedy of that day just awakened America to harsh and disturbing realities that the rest of the world had been living with for years. Indeed, if you look at world events since September 11 and eliminate those triggered by U.S. action—the invasion of Afghanistan, the invasion of Iraq, and other initiatives associated with the "war on terror"—essentially nothing has changed. The economies of the world still churn. China and the emerging powers still rise while Europe and Japan still struggle with their demographic burdens. Globalization and the information age still march forward. AIDS still ravages the populations of Africa and threatens those of the rest of the world. The equivalent of twelve World Trade Centers full of children die every day for lack of clean water, food, or easily available medications. Three billion people continue to live on less than a dollar a day, and most of them have never heard a dial tone.

What has changed clearly, though, is America's self-image. We recognize our vulnerability. We also recognize our power and must struggle with strong impulses to direct it wherever threats may lie. In the name of the changes that took place, we undertook a war that was vastly easier to win than the peace will be to keep. The Middle East remains the great challenge for the next generation of U.S. foreign policymakers. At the heart of this effort must be a recognition that our interest in the region is oil, and that what we seek is stability. Whether stability is brought about by the spread of democracy or by other, interim means, we must recognize that it is the decay of Middle Eastern civilization that is the threat to us; the terrorists bred by that decay are only a symptom of the bigger problem. They must be crushed, but we must also eliminate the forces that create new armies of terrorists each year.

We must also address the rise of a class of new powers—China, India, Brazil, and the other economic giants of tomorrow, each with their own domestic and regional aspirations, each posing great complications. And we must cope with the fact that to remain vital, alliances and multilateral institutions must evolve and adapt to new circumstances.

Above all, we must recognize that the authors of the National Security Act of 1947 and the other foreign policy giants of that era were correct— there was no going back for America. Our role in the world could not be abdicated or abridged. We cannot and "opt out" of the international community or the institutions, customs, or practices that bind it together. All these issues will involve us in one way or another. And that, in turn, calls for a functioning, efficient national security structure to serve not only the elected presidents of the United States but also the people who elected them.

13

U.S. Foreign Policy in the Age of Ambiguity

Character determines fate.

—Heraclitus

The world in all but doth two nations bear—
The good, the bad; and these mixed everywhere.

—Andrew Marvell

JUST BEFORE VISITING Jodhpur on the trip I described at the outset of this book, my father and I spent several days in Jaisalmer, an ancient city on the edge of the Thar desert, not far from the border with Pakistan. Jaisalmer was known as the "Golden City" because it was built of yellow sandstone that glowed brilliantly in the sun. It was among the last of the Indian states to have succumbed to the British in the nineteenth century.

Jaisalmer, a walled, twelfth-century fortress town atop a modest hill, was a charming place of narrow streets, grand Rajput mansions, and small shops specializing in everything from scooter parts to local cuisine. The most striking aspect—other than the rich aroma that is unique to ancient desert cities that still rely to some degree on open sewers—was the juxtaposition of evidence of the city's eight centuries of existence with that of the modern world, ochre *havelis* (mansions) with intricately carved stone work and tiny one-room stores with proprietors crouched in front of televisions, kitchen appliance distributors offering Japanese-made toaster ovens and fabulous Jain temples with gilded gates, familiar global brand names and the exotic bustle of the Manak Chowk, the main marketplace.

This remote corner of India was, in 1989, still in the process of connecting with the modern world. We were evidence of this contact. But the humbling reality was that this place had actually been slowly globalizing for centuries as one of India's portals on the Silk Road. Here, Rajput princes would support their lavish lifestyles by levying heavy tariffs on caravans passing through, some journeying westward to the Middle East, others traveling east across India and perhaps on to China.

We like to think of the challenges of our era as being unique, but globalization has been going on since the first two tribal settlements were connected by a path through the woods, since migrants from Africa peopled Europe or migrants from Asia walked across the land bridge to the Americas. In fact, integration by choice, by necessity, or by force has been the one constant of international relations. It was fueled by the rise of empires and by the creation of transportation and communications technologies. Our era is different in that the velocity and scope of integration have increased and the dimensions of functioning communities have effectively exploded to global scale as a result of the ability to communicate and conduct commerce or project force over virtually any distance, instantly.

Clashes of civilizations in this environment are the by-product of resistance to integration—because all civilizations are built to preserve the equities of their establishments, equities associated with the dominion of elites over the nation, state, or tribe they lead. And all such elites have used nationalistic and cultural tools to build unity within their groups and to differentiate them from others. These reflex actions work like antibodies within the local body politic, adhering to, clustering around, and trying to kill what is alien—until they can no longer do so and the national immune system breaks down and the former entity is transformed one way or another. Sometimes this is done by force, sometimes very gradually over time. But every culture, every national identity is dynamic, plastic, and ever-evolving and all are gradually drawn more closely together, more similar, more interwoven.

Even in a remote corner of India, even in the very last days of the Cold War era, even before the acknowledged onset of the "era of globalization," this was a strikingly evident trend much more important than any momentary issue of international policy.

Integration is the fundamental force of international affairs. Backlash and division are dangerous, but relatively speaking, they are weaker forces. Since the end of the Cold War, we have been engaged in a tug-of-war over which of these forces would define and drive our foreign policy. The economically, multilaterally oriented Clinton administration chose integration as the organizing principle—although sometimes it was called engagement. The post-9/11 Bush administration chose a "with us or against us" vision of a divided world as its defining idea. Naturally, such statements oversimplify—our impulse to label things always produces oversimplifications. However, the tension between these two views has defined U.S. foreign policy on many levels. The 2004 presidential campaign revealed this in its debates about Bush's unilateralism and the charge that Democratic challenger John Kerry would "seek permission slips" from our allies, from right-wing Republicans' desire to use homeland security as a pretext for reducing immigration (a particularly powerful integrative force), and Democrats' arguments that we should revitalize our international institutions.

Wherever one stands on these issues, it is important to acknowledge that there are historical trends and forces greater than the will of even the greatest of nations and that these have to do with those aspects of historical development that are driven by the collective human nature of the global community—such as the drives toward improvement, toward equity, toward dignity, toward better lives, to survive, to eliminate risks—to weave together ever more tightly and broadly the fabric of the global community.

These impulses more than, say, containment—the crown jewel of U.S. postwar foreign policy—drove us to the successful conclusion of the Cold War. Containment was a strategy to help us to hold back an identified foe so we that could foster the kind of global development and integration and growth that would strengthen our hand, weaken theirs, and ultimately make it impossible for their closed societies to effectively compete in our more open global civilization. It contributed to the ultimate outcome, but it worked because of how it helped channel the impulse toward integration and the greater exchange of ideas, information, goods, services, and people—the accelerating forces of globalization, which our system could harness and theirs could not.

Not far from where the camel caravans were the lifeblood of a centuries-earlier version of this integrative impulse, on a warm January evening in 1989, my father and I sat in a small café in Jaisalmer. The menu was a marvel, many pages long, printed in very small type. Every sort of dish you could imagine was listed. Of course, when I walked through the kitchen to the rest room, I noticed there was really only one big black pot full of bubbling brown liquid that was ladled onto every plate—sometimes with rice, sometimes in a bowl, sometimes over vegetables that were themselves a not entirely encouraging shade of brown. Not too far over-head—close enough to rattle our dinner plates—flew pairs of Indian Air Force MiG-21s and 23s—Russian planes, with Israeli avionics, flown by Indian pilots, patrolling the Pakistani border, itself armed by the Chinese and the Americans. Just another late afternoon on the Silk Road on the eve of the twenty-first century.

Over dinner, my father reflected on the story of General Charles Napier, a career British soldier who during the summer of 1842 was offered by the Court of Directors of the East India Company their Bombay presidency. Napier did not think much of this company, whose grandiloquently named board he denounced as a "shopocracy" that was exploiting India in the worst possible way:

> The English were the aggressors in India and, although our sovereign can do no wrong, his ministers can and no one can lay a heavier charge upon Napoleon than rests upon the English ministers who conquered India and Australia and who protected those who commit atrocities. . . . Our object in conquering India, the object of all our cruelties was money—a thousand million sterling are said to have been squeezed out of India in the last ninety years. Every shilling of this has been picked out of blood, wiped and put in the murderers' pockets; but wipe and wipe the money as you will, the "damned spot" will not "out."[1]

Despite his misgivings, not only did Napier take the job, he participated in some of the most brutal elements of the conquest of India. In fact, no matter how caustic his critique of English aggression on the subcontinent, there can be no more scathing indictment of the undertaking than his own surpassing hypocrisy. He was both the best critic and the best example of the problem.

During the Battle of Mlani, with only 2,800 troops (only five hundred of whom were British), Napier defeated 22,000 Sindhis, killing or wounding 6,000. Five weeks later, fighting in 110 degree heat, he sent 5,000 men against 26,000 at Dubba, battling Shir Muhammad, the Lion of Mirpur, and winning another great victory to put down Sindhi resistance with seeming finality.[2]

According to legend, at the conclusion of his victory, Napier couriered a message to his commanders that said only: "Peccavi,"[3] the Latin for "I have sinned"—or rather, in terms of his real meaning, "I have Sindh." This is one of the great puns in history as well as the kind of military dispatch

admired for both its brevity and its élan. Later, the British satirical magazine *Punch* published a cartoon of Napier walking amid the dead at the
battle; the caption was Napier's one-word dispatch, this time intended not
as a pun but as an accusation.[4] Already it was clear that imperial Britain's
self-appointed global mission was a morally flawed venture.

Napier's example resonates today on many levels. Once again we are
deeply engaged in the region. Again, a small, militarily superior force has
achieved a conquest, or liberated a people, or overthrown an upstart—
depending on your point of view—at the cost of many lives from the
regional population. We are fighting in many of the same places as did our
British cousins of a few generations ago, bedeviled by similar problems,
self-justified because we are advancing our ideals, which we brand as universal, and playing much the same role in the world that they did (even
without an actual empire of our own). We are, as they were, drawn to
these conflicts because of our economic interests. But clearly the world
has changed, and not just in that modern technologies of destruction and
two centuries of bloodshed have together removed all pretense of jaunti-
ness from modern warfare—though we still cling to the notion of its
nobility. The stakes of modern warfare are higher. The vulnerability of
great powers to lesser powers is much greater. Hopefully, we have ban-
ished the nineteenth-century European notion of superior and lesser civilizations and peoples from the rationales or analyses we prepare for our
own conflict management schemes.

Perhaps most important, the world in which we find ourselves at the
beginning of the twenty-first century is as different from that of Napier
and his dressed-up barbarism as it is from that of the American triumph
over Nazi evil in the Second World War or the superpower rivalry of the
half century or so that followed it. Neither great powers nor lesser ones,
neither enemies nor friends, neither war nor peace are quite what they
used to be. Indeed, they are much farther from what they used to be than
we seem to comprehend. For this reason, despite the great and changing
complexity of the world, perhaps our greatest challenges lie within—in
accepting and adjusting to what makes this new world different, which is
prerequisite for adapting our institutions, our systems, and our strategies
to the requirements of this emerging era.

To understand how the NSC and the American foreign policy establishment must develop in the future, we need to try to better understand
the global dynamics we face. How will the larger historical forces pushing
us toward greater integration and deeper degrees of globalization affect
that world? How will the backlash against those forces, the consequences

of the displacements and disequilibria caused by those forces, the reaction of various nations' global antibodies to those forces and their consequences change the world scene at any given moment? We are entering a period of transition in which we can see trends and understand the greater integrative forces at work. But transitional periods are extremely dangerous because they are volatile; it is hard to separate short-term from long-term concerns, and therefore it is hard to prioritize. A deep human bias projects past experience onto new situations—for example, to assume that because an adversary or an ally or a battlefield is the same or similar, old rules might apply. So we end up fighting the previous war.

The post-9/11 era confronts us with a particular set of questions. How is this era different from the one for which our plans, policies, philosophies, and people were prepared? What should drive our policies in the future? Do we focus on the forces of integration, on globalization, and on the growing importance of economics and address transnational threats as a subset of these drivers, as did the Clinton administration? Or do we focus on the near-term threats—what a navy friend of mine calls the "wolves closest to the sled"—and the underlying dynamics fueling those tensions and divisions, as the Bush administration has both been forced and chosen to do since the September 11 attacks? Above all, what philosophical framework for dealing with our role as the sole superpower in the era of these changing global dynamics should we develop?

Some members of the current administration's leadership are less introspective about these issues than they should be. One gets the sense that for them introspection is akin to indecision, that it is seen as a sign of weakness. But the problems of the future organization of our national security establishment, the philosophies that guide it, and the nature of the people put in place to enact those philosophies won't simply go away because we don't face them. Nor will they disappear simply because we shuffle around boxes on an organizational chart and create a Department of Homeland Security or a more centralized intelligence community structure—precisely because without a new understanding of the world, new philosophies, new attitudes and thinking at the top, and the bureaucratic cultural changes that are required, it doesn't matter what system you have: it will fail.

Friends, Enemies, and the Difficulty in Telling Them Apart

RECENTLY I CONDUCTED an informal survey at the Carnegie Endowment for International Peace to gather expert insights into America's international priorities over the short term, using several categories: nonproliferation, global military power, terrorism, science and technology, space, global health, resource issues, global warming and the environment, international economic development, international labor issues, and democracy and human rights.

We contacted almost 180 well-known experts, scholars in seventeen different categories of international affairs studies. We also sought contributions from clusters of regional security experts who focused on Southeast Asia, South Asia, Africa, the Western Hemisphere, the Middle East, the former Soviet Union and Central Asia, and Europe.[5] While such a sample is by no means definitive, it does represent a significant enough cross-section of top-level U.S. foreign policy specialists to give useful insights into the thoughts of that community and to suggest the nature and the degree of some of the changes that may be afoot. In other words, it wasn't a scientific study, but it could be a useful one.

The study was prompted by a Goldman Sachs analysis late in 2003 that identified a group of economic powers to watch in the new century, christening them the "BRICs": Brazil, Russia, India, China.[6] The study estimated that if growth in these markets were to continue along trajectories consistent with Goldman's projections, by midcentury these would be four of the six largest economies in the world—joining the United States and Japan. European countries were treated individually and not collectively as the European Union (EU), which would have produced different results. The vagaries of methodology aside, it is clear that these countries are on the rise and that the international institutions have yet to fully adjust to the new reality of their presence. For example, the G8 is supposed to be a principal platform for economic coordination, yet it is attended by Italy and Canada and not by China or India. In fact, it was only in late 2004 that a Chinese minister was invited to attend for the first time as a guest. The UN Security Council is another such institution designed around post–World War II realities and long overdue for reform. The absence of major regional powers such as India, Brazil, Nigeria, and South Africa from this body just doesn't make sense given the likelihood that they will play influential roles in resolving the kind of regional and international security threats most likely to arise in the years ahead.

Within the U.S. government itself, there are hierarchical differences in the way those dealing with different regions of the world are treated and in the way spending and staffing priorities are oriented toward "high-status" countries. Clearly, the former Soviet Union, our European allies, and Japan once topped this list. The country status biases have are translated into practice and policy in a variety of ways. For instance, during the Clinton years, a very capable diplomat, Ambassador James Dobbins, was made senior director of inter-American affairs at the National Security Council despite having very little experience in Latin America other than helping to lead efforts in Haiti, a country that is an anomaly in the region. Dobbins had done great work in Europe, had been assistant secretary of state for European affairs, and is exceptionally talented. The notion that a Latin American specialist of similar accomplishments would be given a top job in formulating U.S. policy toward Europe, however, is hard to imagine. Another prominent former NSC staffer recounted to me a job interview process for a top Africa assignment that consisted of little more than a very brief conversation during a car ride with a key official, in which little more than the names of three African capitals were asked before the job was awarded. Although the story was a bit tongue in cheek given the solid qualifications of the interviewee, it is revealing, even as an anecdote of a mindset. One can hardly imagine people telling the same "joke" about getting a similar job dealing with containing the Soviet threat or terrorism.

The results of our small survey identified the top twenty-five countries or international entities that those polled felt would be most important to the United States during the next five years as an ally, an adversary, or a critical player with regard to the participants' areas of expertise:

1. China
2. Russia
3. Iran
4. Japan
5. United Kingdom
6. India
7. Pakistan
8. EU
9. Saudi Arabia
10. France
11. Canada
12. Iraq
13. North Korea
14. Australia

15. Brazil
16. Israel
17. Germany
18. Venezuela
19. South Korea
20. Sudan
21. Mexico
22. South Africa
23. Nigeria
24. Egypt
25. Indonesia

The list is both familiar and different. Of course, had it been made before the end of the Cold War, the Soviet Union would have topped it, the Warsaw Pact nations would have been near the top of the list, the EU would not have existed, and NATO would have been the institution highest on the list (NATO finished thirty-first in this study, behind the European Space Agency, Turkey, Afghanistan, Syria, and Colombia). Cuba would have been higher perhaps. (It was thirty-second.) Headlines and momentary issues distort such poll data. Iraq may have ranked higher immediately before the U.S. invasion, and Iran may have been placed higher than it should have been because of news coverage of the Iranian nuclear program simultaneous with the study. But it is worth noting other aspects of the list that probably are indicative of broader trends: seventeen of the top twenty-five countries could be classified as emerging; China, Russia, India, and Brazil are in the top fifteen, joined by a number of other less-developed economies that are themselves hot spots or potential hot spots, including Iran, Pakistan, Saudi Arabia, Iraq, and North Korea. Japan and the United Kingdom clearly have special prominence among our traditional allies. The EU finished ahead of any individual nation of continental Europe. Brazil is the only country from our hemisphere in the top fifteen. Israel didn't make it into the top fifteen, and Mexico lagged behind Canada substantially and probably finished well behind where it should have, given its importance as a trading partner and a neighbor. Certain entities were conspicuous by their absence: the UN finished essentially off the chart in sixty-seventh place, well behind al Qaeda, Hezbollah, and the United Arab Emirates.

When asked to undertake the same kind of ranking over a twenty-year period, the experts we contacted offered opinions that resulted in the following list:

1. China
2. Russia
3. India
4. Japan
5. Pakistan
6. Saudi Arabia
7. Iran
8. EU
9. Brazil
10. United Kingdom
11. Iraq
12. Egypt
13. Canada
14. France
15. Nigeria
16. South Africa
17. Germany
18. Israel
19. Mexico
20. Turkey
21. Indonesia
22. Australia
23. NATO
24. North Korea
25. Venezuela

What is interesting about this list are the countries or entities that move up—India, Pakistan, Saudi Arabia, Brazil, Iraq, Indonesia, and NATO—and the countries that move down—Iran, the United Kingdom, Canada, France, Israel, Australia, North Korea, and Venezuela. All those that moved up except NATO are from the emerging world (there was a sense from the group that NATO would grow more important as the EU coalesced and its new mission crystallized). Among those that moved down, a number were traditional first-world allies. Iran moved down only a few slots but was still in the top ten. North Korea obviously fell fairly substantially, as many experts felt it would no longer exist as a separate Korea in twenty years.

Unmistakably, the priority identified by the Carnegie study is a special class of nations in the emerging world or faltering-state hot spots. In both the five-year and the twenty-year projections, just under a third of the top twenty-five were Islamic countries and a similar number (nine in the five-year scenario, seven in the twenty-year) could be classified as Asia/Pacific (though the number grows if you include the United States, Canada, and Mexico as Pacific nations). Only five European countries—including Russia—are in the near term list, and six—including Russia and Turkey—in the longer term list.

But the story becomes even more interesting when you look at how the experts ranked our most likely allies and adversaries over the five-year and twenty-year horizons. Indeed, the result of this exercise was unexpected and is deeply revealing about the nature of the new world we are facing.

The countries and entities cited as most likely to be important allies, friends, or otherwise important to the support of U.S. initiatives over the next five and the next twenty years were:

Likely Allies— Next Five Years	Likely Allies— Next Twenty Years
1. China	1. China
2. United Kingdom	2. India
3. Japan	3. Russia
4. Russia	4. Japan
5. India	5. United Kingdom
6. EU	6. EU
7. Pakistan	7. Brazil
8. Australia	8. Canada
9. Saudi Arabia	9. France
10. France	10. Germany
11. Germany	11. Iraq
12. Israel	12. Israel
13. Mexico	13. Iran
14. South Korea	14. Mexico
15. Brazil	15. Saudi Arabia
16. South Africa	16. Egypt
17. Egypt	17. Pakistan
18. Iraq	18. South Africa
19. NATO	19. Turkey
20. Turkey	20. Nigeria
21. Colombia	21. Australia
22. Nigeria	22. NATO
23. Iran	23. Kenya
24. Poland (tie)	24. Poland
25. Indonesia (tie)	25. South Korea

Although this data is best viewed as an impressionistic picture of the situation, some very clear pictures emerge. Clearly, that Russia is, even today, number four on the near-term ally list is quite a change from the Cold War era and suggests a triumph of post–Cold War Russia policy on some levels and, given events in post-Soviet Russia, considerable optimism on others. But China's position atop both lists is striking, as is the position of other emerging or less-developed powers such as Russia, India, Pakistan, Saudi Arabia, Mexico, South Korea, Brazil, South Africa, Egypt, Iraq, Turkey, Colombia, Nigeria, Iran, and Poland on the five-year list. On the twenty-year list, the importance of this group is in some respects even more pronounced among the leaders, with China, Russia, and India topping the list; Brazil joining them in the top ten; and Iraq, Iran, Mexico, Saudi Arabia, Egypt, Pakistan, Turkey, Nigeria, Kenya, Poland, and South Korea also appearing the top twenty-five. Also interesting is that both lists are quite balanced between these new powers and more traditional allies, with five traditional allies in the top ten for the next five years (United Kingdom, Japan, EU, Canada, and Australia) and six in the top ten for the twenty-year outlook (Japan, United Kingdom, EU, Canada, France, and Germany). This clearly suggests that we will need greater balance between the way we treat these two groups, but also that our traditional alliances will remain important even in the face of global change. The fact that India moves ahead of the United Kingdom on the twenty-year list is an irony that would not be lost on Napier or the Court of Directors of the East India Company—not enjoyed perhaps, but not lost either.

However, it is when we come to the list of likely potential adversaries, rivals, or challengers to our interests that the results of this study become most interesting. They are:

Likely Adversaries—
Next Five Years
1. China
2. Iran
3. Russia
4. North Korea
5. Pakistan
6. Saudi Arabia
7. Iraq
8. Sudan
9. India

Likely Adversaries—
Next Twenty Years
1. China
2. Russia
3. Pakistan
4. Saudi Arabia
5. Iran
6. India
7. Japan
8. EU
9. Indonesia

Likely Adversaries—
Next Five Years, *cont.*

10. Syria
11. Venezuela
12. Brazil
13. Cuba
14. EU
15. France
16. Belarus
17. Indonesia
18. Japan
19. Afghanistan
20. Al Qaeda
21. Burma
22. European Space Agency
23. Israel
24. Nigeria
25. Colombian Rebels

Likely Adversaries—
Next Twenty Years, *cont.*

10. North Korea
11. Syria
12. Brazil
13. Egypt
14. Nigeria
15. Iraq
16. Al Qaeda
17. Belarus
18. European Space Agency
19. South Africa
20. Venezuela
21. Afghanistan
22. Algeria
23. Argentina
24. Hamas
25. Hezbollah

Clearly, the definition of adversary, rival, or challenger is important to understanding this data. Since respondents came from different disciplines, some defined "adversary" in terms of security threats, others in terms of threats to initiatives the United States would seek to advance internationally, and others in terms of economic rivalries. The challenges we might face in the coming years could be in all these areas. Some of the results here—such as the identification of the EU and the European Space Agency—are better expressed as competitive rivalries, some—such as the China, Russia, and potential rogue states—are security threats, and some—such as the terrorist groups listed—are more useful as an indicator that such groups would be factors instead of as prognostications about the specific groups mentioned.

Most striking of all is the similarity between the lists of adversaries and the lists of potential allies over the same period. China tops all four lists. But of the potential adversaries or rivals on the five-year list, fifteen of the top twenty-five are also listed on the likely allies or supporters list. To look at the same group another way, seven of the top ten members of the groups cited most often as potential allies during the next five years were also on the potential adversary list—and this was true for ten of the top twenty and thirteen of the top twenty-five. The pattern is the same in the twenty-year prediction.

In short, we are entering an age of "friendemies," in which the line between ally and adversary is blurred, in which those on whom we will have to depend are also in some circumstances those with whom we are managing tensions, in which drawing lines around countries and seeking to contain their expansion is impossible, and in which foreign policy will involve using all the tools available to build ties where possible and use them to counterbalance, to lever, to resist the forces leading to conflict or pushing nations apart.

We are entering an age of ambiguity in which those who see the world in black and white are as good as blind because they will be unable to see the many layers and substories that will be woven together to form the fabric of international affairs.

Unfortunately, as we have seen, every individual in a responsible position in the U.S. foreign policy establishment has come of age amid the binary realities of the Cold War world. Therefore, it should not be completely surprising that we find ourselves with leaders and policies that attempt to impose Manichean, with-us-or-against-us ordering principles on today's realities. But in the eyes of a broad cross-section of the leading experts who study America's role in the world, starkly different pictures of our present and future realities emerge—pictures in which old ideas of good guys and bad guys or even of traditional allies or adversaries no longer apply. In this new, rapidly changing era, not only are a new set of countries likely to be central to our interests, but also we will have to learn to better manage friendships with those who are our rivals.

Perhaps coping with such ambiguities and nuances come more easily to other, more mature societies. We like things to be simple. The media, through which our politicians derive their power and manage public interests, like it simple. We package it and frame it simple. In this impulse, we are like young adults for whom all is straightforward and extreme and we are now called upon to enter the kind of maturity that comes naturally to people as they age and take on broader responsibilities. We have to recognize that learning to deal with nuance is a sign of greater intellectual sophistication, not vacillation. This is by no means a defense of opportunist political weathervanes who undercut the value of reasoned, substantiated nuance by conflating it with their own flip-flopping—but it is certainly an indictment of ideologues who would force America into the policy handcuffs of dogma and alienate the world with their simplistic worldviews.

In this different world of the near future, neglected regions must win more support, attract better people, become higher priorities, and become the subject of new institutional relationships that provide the communications and understanding on which we build and manage our international affairs. We can ill afford the lack of basic foreign-language skills or intelligence assets. A recent Defense Science Board study found that in the entire Department of Defense, we have only five qualified speakers of Pashto—the most important language in Afghanistan, a country in which we have been waging a war since 2001.[7] Despite the critical importance of Pakistan (as suggested not only by the Carnegie survey but by a casual read of any daily newspaper)—a nuclear power of 150 million people, many of whom are very sympathetic to Osama bin Laden and Islamist extremists even as the country itself is a vital U.S. ally in combating terrorism—we have only seventy-two speakers of Urdu, the primary language spoken there. In fact, there are only some 1,600 qualified speakers of Mandarin Chinese in the Department of Defense and only 2,800 qualified speakers of Arabic among the millions who work for that sprawling bureaucracy.[8] This limitation on our basic understanding is even worse in other government agencies.

It is also clear that in a world in which friends and rivals will often be one and the same, we will need to manage the full range of diplomatic tools at our disposal much more effectively. The president and the National Security Council will need to be able to advance economic issues and strike new trade deals even as they battle over questions of proliferation and of regional primacy, to handle human rights one way and UN diplomacy another, to build military-to-military communications even as they fight hard for tough treaty language regarding weapons of mass destruction. This is not new—we have been trying to do it for years, notably with China. But it requires that we do not define our allies or our adversaries in absolutist terms. The world cannot be divided into the wholly evil and the wholly good. It never could. It is more dangerous than ever to do so now. We need a high-functioning NSC with as broad a membership as possible to provide the fullest array of tools to the president. It must incorporate and work closely with the NEC and with the international community. It must be more careful to be an honest broker, because institutional biases are much more damaging when they frame our efforts to maintain and manage multidimensional international relationships.

Adapting the System
to the New Environment

W E ARE AT A WATERSHED not unlike the one we faced at the end of the Second World War, but it is defined by the emergence of an entirely new climate, a transformed geopolitical ecosystem, rather than by the emergence of a new enemy. After the Second World War, the goal was to balance the well-established State Department and the new Defense Department, diplomacy and security. Today, with an ascendant Defense Department dominating a declining State Department, it will fall on the NSC and future presidents to strike a new balance, not just one between these agencies but one that encompasses diplomatic, security, intelligence, political, developmental, trade, law enforcement, homeland security, global health, global environment, science and technology, international, bilateral, regional, public and private, permanent, and ad hoc factors. Given the internal complexity of relationships in this new era, and their multitiered, counterbalanced nature, challenges will arise not only for policymakers but also for political actors, because it will be harder for the public to understand where we stand, harder to communicate these issues to a base of disconnected voters through a set of media filters that seek simplicity and maximum drama. Consequently, it will be more difficult to develop, maintain, and sell strategies or build political will to support such strategies.

Among the greatest constraints on the effective realization of policy are those associated with the evolution of the U.S. Congress, which plays critical funding, oversight, and political roles in the foreign policy process. Over time, the way congressional elections work has been retooled, in manifold ways, to dramatically favor incumbents. Turnover in the U.S. Congress is lower than that found in the Supreme Soviet of the USSR. In the 2004 elections it was estimated that perhaps twenty-five House seats were actually up for grabs.[9] Given the incumbent advantage, congressional representatives know they are likely to win in the general elections, so they tend to worry more about primary elections. Primaries have an even lower turnout than general elections and are dominated by the most activist members of local parties. This effect, in combination with district gerrymandering by state majority parties, gives the extreme right and the extreme left disproportionate influence in the political process.[10]

The majority of Americans are in the center, but their views go unheard because of the perverse nature of the system. For example, 75 percent of the American people have indicated that they are comfortable with the UN and with the United States working within the UN structure, but you will seldom see a Washington politician stand up and make a positive statement about the UN because the vocal extremes oppose the organization as part of their skepticism about ceding sovereignty elsewhere, their resistance to directing aid dollars overseas, and their concerns about international engagement generally.

This tilt in the congressional system influences the other players in Washington in turn—lobbyists, columnists, and so on—to create what John Hamre, president of the Center for Strategic and International Studies and former deputy secretary of defense, has characterized as a "Washington microclimate that bears little resemblance to the rest of the country."[11] Issues driven by, funded by, and oriented to the extreme wings of the parties, and debates tailored to their needs and tastes, have led to a poisonous partisanship that has infected Washington during the past several years and to an irresponsible separation between the will of the majority of America and the will of the representatives of the American people. This has enduringly distorted and undermined the deliberative processes that are essential to effective policymaking.

Beyond Process:
The Biases within the System

UNDERSTANDING THE mechanisms of the foreign policy processes within the U.S. government is comparatively easy. Indeed, for the most part they have served us rather well. But they contain certain biases and tendencies. In particular, advisory systems are liable to fall into the trap of seeking consensus among advisors. Such an approach virtually guarantees that the proposal with the broadest approach will win—and in some cases, perhaps in many cases, it will win over what is the best proposal. "Honest broker" systems provide presidents with good choices and objective analyses of their pros and cons to help presidents make informed decisions. Unpopular choices must not be eliminated, as they may often have merits that outweigh their unpopularity.

If government adopted a true business model, it would never tolerate such an approach. Businesses are not and cannot be consensus driven; they are results driven, driven by performance absolutes. It is absurd that we should expect or hold the performance of an organization on which the future of our society depends to lower levels of management quality than we would expect from, say, a pencil factory. The National Security Council is a system to advise the president of the relative merits of different approaches. All too often, however, the United States has been shortchanged because of the mistaken notion that if the majority of advisors think something is the right course, it is. We need to avoid the bias toward consensus, because it leads directly to mistakes.

There is also a bias toward reaction built into the system. Despite the best efforts of many national security advisors, efforts to establish strategic planning sections within the NSC have typically faltered. The problem is associated with the tyranny of the news cycle and of modern media in general. Everything becomes a story thanks to global coverage by television news networks and the Internet. There is a dedicated news-gathering force that is organized around the idea of seeking the reaction of the president and the White House to all such events. The fact that the events are visible makes them political; reactions and non-reactions alike have political consequences.

Also, some stories take on a life of their own. Because they become stories, everything associated with them becomes newsworthy—and these, too, take on not just media consequences, but political and policy consequences. The most common U.S. diplomatic reaction, initiative, or tool is the presentation of ideas or thoughts through the media. What the State Department once did through cables and démarches and emissaries, today is conducted by the White House media team and the NSC through the media. This has consumed an enormous amount of staff resources. Moreover, new information technologies have overwhelmed NSC staffers with massive amounts of intelligence from both closed and open sources and bombarded them, according to one estimate, with perhaps 500 e-mails a day.[12] The result is that the general state of mind within this critical institution is one of constant, frenzied reaction. Planning seems not only a luxury, but almost a dereliction of duty given the pressures of the moment. This would be dangerous under any circumstances but is worse in the absence of basic marching orders of the sort that existed during the Cold War. In an era for which there are few precedents or guidelines, the result is, as we have seen, adopting old models to new circumstances for which they may be ill suited or, alternatively, reactively backing into a pattern of behavior that has not been thought out in advance. Leaders must make a commitment to breaking this cycle. Otherwise, we will work without the benefit of vision and the ability to differentiate between tactical threats (such as terrorism) and strategic ones (such as the potential for the rise of real rivals to the United States), as we have done during the past several years.

Sandy Berger articulated this distinction with a reference to Iraq: "I've always said containment is aesthetically displeasing but strategically sufficient. You wake up in the morning and Saddam Hussein is still there and it would be far preferable if he weren't. As for 'getting Saddam,' most Americans would recognize that option would be emotionally gratifying but the costs of it would be greater than our national interest."[13] He said this in 1998. The notion of strategic sufficiency is an important one. One of the paramount lessons of the past sixty years—sixty years as the world's preeminent power—has to do not so much with the problems caused by the extent of our power but with the limitations on our power. We have enough power to get into many situations, to win many battles. But we do not, we find, have enough power or resources or political will to then effectively get out of those situations with our objectives achieved, to keep the peace, to rebuild, to change the world.

Hence the need for strategic planning. Winning the "combat phase" in Iraq was comparatively easy. But winning the peace is geometrically more difficult—especially when we act effectively unilaterally. It should have received the majority of our attention before we set out on the venture. The impulse among American voters is for swift, dramatic, emotionally satisfying solutions to the issues of the day. But most issues require long, time-consuming, complex, expensive commitments. It makes it more urgent that we do what is sufficient to achieve our strategic goals but try not to do more because we recognize our limitations of capacity and will.

Winning the wrong war—the quick, easy one—is an expression of a clichéd characteristic of all bureaucratic systems, from which U.S. policy is not immune: inertia. Doing nothing in the face of complex challenges is a frequent reflex; doing the wrong, facile thing is merely a better-dressed version of inertia. The status quo is the usual victor in most foreign policy debates, and often this leads to persistent involvement in the same old issues and frequent ignoring of new phenomena. This is exactly what led to the decision to refight the 1991 Gulf War twelve years later, by which time the decision made little sense.

Our system has evolved the way it has because for almost all of U.S. history, back to the days of the founders' admonitions against foreign entanglements, the bias among America's leaders has been the view that we are not part of the world at large, that overseas events are indeed "foreign," and that we are better off remaining apart.

Being on but not of this world meant that we would be free to attend to the business of building our own homes and communities without the peril of "infection" by the problems of others. To this day, that remains the attitude of most Americans. They fear and distrust the rest of the world, both for its unfamiliarity and because of the aspects of it with which they are familiar—from terrorism to anti-Americanism, from recent wars to job losses, from daily headlines to ineffable "senses" of global reality that get handed down from generation to generation. Indeed, we have given birth to a culture of exceptionalism, of thinking that our very "apartness" from the world is part of what makes us good. Exceptionalism has led us to think that other parts of the world do not matter much.

The history of U.S. foreign policy during the twentieth century is the history of our struggle to come to grips with the realities of a planet on which—by virtue of our size, the breadth of our interests, and the techno-logically driven, changing nature of the global community—we had a role to play beyond our borders that we could no longer ignore. From Wilson through Clinton and into the first term of the first presidency of the new millennium, that of George W. Bush, we struggled like an adolescent with the growing recognition that we would have to venture out from the com-forts of our home and rise to the challenges of the community of which we were part whether we liked it or not. Still, we approach every alliance or overseas engagement with a focus on its limitations, on constraining our obligations, on limiting its duration, on figuring out our exit strat-egy—we act much like a fox, not because of our cleverness but because of our tendency to want to essentially dart out of our burrow to capture our prey and then as quickly as possible return to the comforts of our confin-ing but secure home.

Even in the era of globalization, in which it is now clear to every Amer-ican that previously remote events such as the social turmoil on the other side of the world can have immediate and deadly consequences on our shores, we view our forays overseas with skepticism. Even as we are acknowledged to be the world's most powerful force, its greatest economy, even as we depend on that economy for our growth and see fit to project our will on the rest of the planet as it suits us, we do so with the sense that once our goals are accomplished we will return home, leave the distant lands, disengage.

In the twenty-first century, a system with a tendency toward inertia or isolationist minimalism in our concern for the rest of the world is an out-dated liability. Other branches of our government and of the American private sector know it. No financial markets trader can consider whether to opt out of the global markets. No manufacturer in any sector can sim-ply ignore the supply chains or interlinked markets that stretch around the globe and determine every aspect of his business, from the cost of labor to the greatest concentrations of potential consumers. While every chief executive or investor faces fundamental decisions about asset allocations, none could afford a system in which the bias is against action or toward isolation from the forces that will affect their destiny.

The stasis of Cold War containment is a defunct strategy now. We are part of the wide, fluid world, and we need a global perspective to embrace it. After a century that produced both repeated genocides and the growing threat of weapons of mass destruction, we have yet to effectively mobilize the global community to respond collectively—and effectively—to those problems. That, it seems, must be the first order of business. If we cannot do that, then we have failed as leaders in the global community and the community itself has failed to meet the minimum standards of civilization or foresight.

Does Philosophy Matter Anymore?

NOT LONG AGO, the mayor of Beijing appeared at a meeting at Yale University and spoke to a group of students and faculty. It was 2004, an election year, and in the course of his remarks the mayor half-facetiously said, "I think we in the rest of the world should get maybe 20 percent of the vote in your presidential election. After all, many of the decisions that your government makes have a major impact on us—wherever we may live in the world."[14]

He has a point. We live in a society in which our public institutions derive their legitimacy from the consent of those they govern. The provenance of the idea, from the ancient Greeks through Hobbes to John Locke and his *Second Treatise on Government* to the Declaration of Independence, is the story of man's struggle to perfect the means by which he brings order to society, thereby establishing peace and opening the door to more rewarding lives for the people of that society.

Later this fundamental idea was expanded to include developing concepts of social equity, the notion that by "the governed" we meant all citizens within a society, whether they are men or women, rich or poor, and regardless of ethnic origin, cultural heritage, or system of beliefs. We didn't come by this easily. Many of these concepts, although acknowledged as the philosophic underpinnings of our way of life, were accepted into law only in recent decades and to this day are not fully practiced in virtually any society on earth.

So, despite our desire to canonize the principles we adhere to for organizing our society, to carve them in stone or to ascribe them to God or, as did Hobbes and Locke, to nature, the reality is that we are still very early on in the development of a functioning global social order—and some nations are further behind than others.

Indeed, we are at a juncture where some of our most basic ideas about governments are worthy of reexamination—whether it is comfortable or not—as the mayor of Beijing recognized. That is because the basic terms that are the building blocks of our concept of social order are changing. The concept of the nation state is built around the idea of boundaries, but the idea of boundaries is becoming less and less meaningful.

In no respect is this truer than with regard to decisions taken by the United States. We are able to project our will globally. We do this in countless ways. Should we decide that a country is a threat, we can remove its leadership via military action. We can choose to promote a change in its system of government and thereby its laws, or we can use force to attempt to change it. We can assert our veto authority in international financial institutions to determine whether projects are funded or not. We can use our dominant position in capital markets to set rules that will guide capital to one set of investment opportunities or another. We can use our power as the world's first information-age superpower to project our ideas and cultural concepts on other societies and to promote them in ways that make it difficult for alternatives to compete. While our powers are neither absolute nor universal, they are certainly as great as or greater than the power many other governments have to resist us or to compel their citizens to use different approaches.

In a more basic sense, certain fundamental notions of government are growing less easy to understand or to define rules for. Governments have taxed citizens in order to pay for government services. But if transactions take place in cyberspace, who is to levy taxes? Who has jurisdiction? Vast areas of business are beyond regulation because there are no adequate global regulatory mechanisms. Significant threats to the international system, such as disease and environmental pollution, are difficult to contain because we do not have government mechanisms that correspond to the transnational concerns involved. Yet in each of these instances, America's power to influence outcomes is greater than that of virtually all other nations.

Also, in facing these new challenges, Einstein's analysis from 1946 still holds: "Our defense is not in armaments, nor in science, nor in going underground. Our defense is in law and order."[15] Our past, and the past of every other nation, tells us that law and war were opposites, two means to resolve differences, one guided by commonly agreed-upon standards of justice, the other resolved by the calculus of power.

In 1946, emerging from a global conflict, we made the stunning choice to help the international community uphold law. Standards of justice required submitting ourselves to the will of a community in which our power advantage, however appreciable, was considerably less than it would have been at that moment had we chosen to resolve issues by force. We made the calculus then that virtually all civilizations have made since the beginning of history, namely, that peace and stability were preferable to submitting to the will of the strongest—and we recalled that power always ebbs and flows, that the accumulation of power motivates others to contain, undermine, or surpass that power and thus that power advantages are always negated over time.

We built a set of institutions, our national security apparatus, to help balance our ability to work within that system and our ability to protect ourselves against those who did not. They were conceived as institutions not to expand our dominion over the world but to ensure our safety and prerogatives within the global community of nations we were creating. They were also designed to enable us to respond to the potential threat we saw growing in the Soviet Union and to demonstrate our ability to manage the kind of conflict with the Soviets that we thought would never come but that we knew weakness might invite.

Over the course of the past sixty or so years, those institutions have faced countless challenges, shifted their shape, grappled with the ebb and flow of American power, and reflected in their actions and inaction this nation's changing sense of itself and its role in the world. For most of that period, they reflected, and indeed were often defined in terms of, the ideals established by the post–World War II generation, who were in fact the equivalent of America's founding fathers in terms of codifying our international role in the world. Much as the drafters of the U.S. Constitution saw the flaws of the Articles of Confederation as they grappled with the new problems of self-government and democracy, so too did this new generation of accidental internationalists see the flaws of Wilsonian efforts to shape the rules of the global community and America's position in that community and attempt to remedy them with enduring structures founded in basic philosophies.

But a break with those traditions occurred during the first years of the twenty-first century. The United States appeared to revert to the old, discredited idea that because we had power we could impose it if we saw doing so to be in our national interest—regardless of the views of the community we were a part of and regardless of our preferences or even our acknowledgment of its existence. It was argued that we did so in response to a threat that was so great that it warranted our unilateral action. But such a threat did not exist. It was, as it turned out, either misperceived or manufactured to justify our actions. My own personal belief, based on the fact that President Bush's team came into office already discussing the removal of Saddam Hussein, long before they were seriously considering the risks posed by terrorism, is that they chose to see what they wanted to see in the evidence of that threat and that they manipulated public perceptions of that threat to justify their actions.

The precedents involved in the invasion of Iraq are significant and troubling. "Preemption" is not the issue. Throughout American history, we have reserved the right to strike first to eliminate imminent threats to our people. Even the Clinton administration, home to many who would later be among the most vigorous critics of the Bush administration's foreign policy, publicly reserved the right to preempt the threat of nuclear weapons in North Korea in 1994. Even "unilateralism" might have its place: it's possible to be a minority of one and still be right. Our global system is imperfect and underdeveloped, and there will be times when the United States must reserve the right to pursue defensible aims because the system is incapable of ensuring just outcomes.

But in Iraq, where the justification for our actions was a threat that did not in fact exist, our leaders either failed to fulfill their responsibility to accurately assess the threat—which is a very high responsibility in such a case—or they chose to deceive the public, themselves, or both. The alternative choices are negligence and malfeasance. But if the costs included violations of international laws, the infliction of great destruction, death, and injury, and an apparent repudiation of our most basic philosophies about the nature of the international community, neither of these is a misdemeanor. From the perspective of students of the NSC, the mechanism by which the decision was made, it was a failure on many levels—a failure of intelligence, of analysis, and of the moral responsibilities of leadership.

Also, we did not work within the international system that we have attempted to build. George Washington once said that it was his wish that the fledgling country he briefly guided would show a decent respect for the opinions of the global community. We were either so convinced of our rectitude or so dismissive of the views of the global community that we did not. If we were going to use the threat of weapons of mass destruction in Iraq as a justification for actions that were anathema to our allies and to our own principles as we have repeatedly espoused them, it was our responsibility to the system to know with a very high degree of certainty that the threat existed.

America has made errors of judgment in the past, to be sure—with great frequency. That is certainly one of the lessons of this history of the NSC. Indeed, such errors provide a strong argument that we need to expect that we will make mistakes, that this is a system run by human beings who are capable of errors of judgment or defects of character— and that therefore, much as the founders did, we need to build into the system checks and balances to attenuate the effects of such mistakes. But in 2003, the response to the revelation that a mistake occurred was to dismiss it and claim that the end justified the means: we were rid of a bad man.

Bad men walk our streets, kill our children, steal our money, threaten the fabric of our communities. Yet we have agreed that it is in our collective interest as a society not simply to eliminate them vigilante-style because of our strong belief that they are bad. Our disregard for this principle is perhaps made more understandable by the fact that in the same administration that violated the philosophies of social justice that we would apply to ourselves in its actions against Iraq, there has been a pattern of decisions showing a willingness to bend or negate the law as circumstances dictate. The violation of civil liberties of prisoners in U.S. custody, the legal opinion of the White House counsel that the Geneva Accords were "obsolete" and "quaint" (despite the constitutional stipulation that treaties were an even higher form of law than domestic statutes), and the abridgment of civil liberties as a consequence of the passage and implementation of the Patriot Act (a law that has been used in the majority of instances in cases that did not involve the terrorist threat that was used to justify it) are examples of the corrosive belief that the ends justify the means. At the heart of this view is a corrosive double-standard. We seem to accept two codes of behavior—one for our domestic society and one for global society. To make matters worse, we seem to have adopted a system of beliefs that makes more such mistakes very likely in the future.

Part of the reason for this situation is that we have accepted an organizing principle for U.S. international policy that is based on a tremendous error in judgment. Terrorism truly is a threat. The possibility of terrorist use of weapons of mass destruction is perhaps the most serious near-term physical threat we face. But it is not a strategic threat. It poses a threat quantum levels of scale beneath that of the Cold War. There are greater dangers. As Zbigniew Brzezinski said, terrorism is a tactic, not an enemy.[16] Terrorists are a symptom of the failure of the societies from which they come to offer them opportunities or the lives they seek within those societies. They are a sign that the stability threshold of those societies—the moment when citizens feel they benefit more from working within the system than they would from opposing it—has yet to be passed. To eliminate terrorists, we need to present a better alternative. Democracy and reform are, indeed, parts of that alternative. Failing to recognize that to advance such goals by abrogating the principles on which they are founded is a fatal flaw.

The real strategic threats come from those who would offer an alternative to our leadership that would damage American interests and undercut our ability to grow, lead, prosper, or maintain the peace in the future. The origins of such strategic threats are less likely to be found among terrorists than among those who offer a solution to perceived injustices that is an alternative to the one we are seen to advance. During the 1990s, when America was so closely identified with globalization and the spread of markets and information-age culture, some NGOs and political leaders overseas organized opposition to our "cultural imperialism" and the social inequities that exist within many capitalist—and democratic—societies. Today they have the additional argument that America imposes its will on the world, that we have a double standard, that we do not require facts and resort to lies to undercut the international order, and that we act not in the interest of justice but in the interest of cultural considerations such as religious beliefs that we long ago agreed should not be confused or conflated with our beliefs about governing or our justifications for public-sector action.

In short, through a series of bad judgments or through mishandled execution of our plans, we have undercut the moral authority of American global leadership. While positive progress toward democracy in Iraq, Afghanistan, and elsewhere may go a long way to help offset that erosion, damage has been done that will take years to repair. Further, we have done all this while failing to take any steps forward in grappling with the changing set of responsibilities that we have to the ever more integrated global community in which we play such a unique role. Indeed, we have undercut the institutions and legal underpinnings of that community while complaining of their weakness and yet doing nothing to repair or strengthen them.

In so doing, we have opened the door to a greater danger while pursuing a lesser one. We have called into question the legitimacy of our claim to leadership, and the reasons we have done so are rooted in a breakdown at the center of the decision-making processes that were developed to help ensure an opposite result. Paul Wolfowitz and his associates have written papers in the past about understanding, identifying, and eliminating threats to future U.S. supremacy in the world. They seem to have made the mistake of assuming that such threats would come in the form of the rise of rivals with measurable advantages economically or militarily, that is, traditional sources of power. What they have failed to acknowledge is that although we have, despite great current advantages, some vulnerability in those areas to challenges from rising powers, our greatest vulnerability by far is linked to the legitimacy of our leadership. No nation is in a better position to undercut our legitimacy, and thus our ability to lead, than we are. Worse, it could pass to a different system or set of values that seems to the global majority to promise more justice, more equity, more security than do American values. Such an alternative could galvanize the majority of the world's population—who are today effectively disenfranchised from reaping the benefits of the world we have been leading—into a new bipolarity or into other forms of fractiousness that threaten our true national values.

In this context, it is useful to consider that somewhere out in the world today may be "the next Marx."[17] He or she won't be a communist, and almost certainly not a German expatriate working away in the British Library. Instead, he or she might be today protesting in the streets of Buenos Aires or studying in a classroom at Fudan University in Shanghai. He or she may even believe in some of the principles of capitalism and democracy—or not. He or she will offer a perspective that acknowledges that we have by no means reached the "end of history," that the fundamental debates of political philosophy of the past several hundred years have not been resolved, that the question of providing *thymos* (dignity) has not been answered to everyone's satisfaction by Western liberal values—and that there is a better way. This person will argue that our system has exacerbated rather than resolved basic problems of inequity in the world. A cornerstone of his or her argument will be that American legitimacy does not, in fact, derive from the consent of those who feel like they are, at least in part, governed by us, be they the mayor of Beijing or a Baghdad shopkeeper whose shop and family were destroyed by the voluntary and insupportable act of a handful of people in Washington, D.C.

The law of the marketplace of ideas ensures that such competition will come. Our choice is whether we understand the dynamic that might create a demand for an alternative to the "American" brand that encompasses both our stated ideals and our practice in creating our markets, our democracy, and our view of what the global community should be like and respond to it constructively or whether we wait and are surprised when millions around the world start buying into "a better way."

.   .   .

It is thus vitally important that we take a step back from the exigencies of governing and begin to come to grips with the philosophical underpinnings of our actions. The Cold War provided us with a good vs. evil duality that served to justify our actions and help us understand our role in the world. It is a new world now—more integrated, more interdependent, more diverse in terms of both those who are truly global actors and those who touch our lives or whom we touch. It requires a rethinking of our role in it, much as the U.S. actions that followed the Second World War required such a philosophical framework. Unfortunately—or perhaps fortunately—those philosophical underpinnings were arrived at the hard way, through global devastation and the lessons of Munich, of fascism, of totalitarianism in other forms, of letting ambition and power supplant reason in human affairs.

For the most part, the character of the people I met with or studied who were entrusted with the highest positions of responsibility in the U.S. national security establishment was remarkable. We have been very lucky. The world has been very lucky. Many of them do not simply study international affairs as a profession but are consumed by it. The best of them view the world as a puzzle that they are constantly working at, constantly trying to decipher. For them, the facts change with every morning's newspaper, and they are always trying to think many moves ahead, like good chess players. They are constantly questioning their assumptions and debating them with others they view as peers. Others have taken a received worldview and tried to force the puzzle pieces into the spaces their worldview allots for them. But even among these decidedly lesser professionals, I met or read about very few who did not believe in their hearts that they were trying to do what was best for the American people. Some were nasty, some were narcissistic, many had sharp elbows and a taste for infighting—you don't get to the top in Washington without wanting it very, very badly—but the vast majority were dedicated, hard-working, and every bit as capable as their counterparts from around the world.

We are inclined to say that these are the worst of times and that the threats we face are unequaled. They are not. Our enemies in the Second World War, the threat of global thermonuclear war, these were great threats—and they are gone. For all the problems we face, the world is better off today than ever in its history; in most parts of the world, people are safer, healthier, live longer, are better educated, and have more opportunities than ever before. In other words, despite disaster and despite the litany of mistakes made by the world's most powerful committee since its formation, we're better off. How did we get that way? By staying alert to the problems of the day and by addressing them in a way that was consistent with the best nature of the American people and our friends and allies around the world. Certainly, the study of the history of such problems and solutions should help us in that direction.

In the end, though, it is important and healthy to accept that the sometimes glorious record of the United States in foreign policy is also a checkered one. We have, at times, been misguided, insensitive, and arrogant, and we have great quantities of blood on our hands. Yet, as we have seen, few if any evil men and women have sat on this committee that finds itself with a disproportionate role in influencing the course of world affairs, this "committee in charge of running the world." Most have sought to do the best they could. Most have been moral. Most have valued American ideals. Yet the vast majority have, from time to time, erred—sometimes egregiously—for different reasons, in differing circumstances. In fact, error is one of the few constants in the history of the NSC. We do well enough, but viewing the errors, we certainly must acknowledge that we can do better.

The key is to recognize this fact and to create and manage the systems of our government as our forefathers intended, seeing them in the context of human fallibility. (George Washington chose to subordinate himself to the law out of a recognition of the need to place laws above men—we can create them but we destroy them if we attempt to transcend them.) We must then recognize that one of the qualities to be valued most in our leaders is constant questioning and constant reevaluation. Rigidity, certainty, and lack of questioning from advisors are as deadly to leaders as indecision or corruption. That is also why we need checks and balances in the system—within and beyond the executive branch. The ultimate check is an educated American public—an American public that better understands and accepts its role as influential citizens of an international community. We, the American people, are where the buck really stops. Even the president and "the committee" report to us. Ultimately we are responsible to the world and to history for their actions.

A Guide to Abbreviations and Acronyms

ACRONYMS ARE mother's milk to the bureaucracy. They simultaneously exclude those who don't understand them, make opaque that which should be clear, and offer a convenient shorthand for those who need more time to write memos about bureaucratic bottlenecks—like the addiction to acronyms. One vignette describes the phenomenon best for me: At some point the U.S. Navy became aware that there were so many acronyms floating around that they compiled them in a single Dictionary of Naval Abbreviations which, of course, soon became known as the DICNAVAB.

ABM	Anti–ballistic missile
ACDA	Arms Control and Disarmament Agency
ARVN	Army of the Republic of Vietnam
CCP	Chinese Communist Party
CFE	Conventional Forces in Europe
CIA	Central Intelligence Agency
CINC	Commander-in-chief
CSG	Counterterrorism Strategy Group
CWC	Chemical Weapons Convention
DCI	Director of Central Intelligence
DEFCON	Defense Condition
DOD	Department of Defense
EU	European Union
FAA	Federal Aviation Administration
FBI	Federal Bureau of Investigation
FEMA	Federal Emergency Management Agency
GATT	General Agreement on Tariffs and Trade
ICBM	Intercontinental ballistic missile

IFOR	Implementation Force
INC	Iraqi National Congress
INF	Intermediate-range nuclear forces
ISG	Iraq Stabilization Group
JCS	Joint Chiefs of Staff
KLA	Kosovo Liberation Army
MBFR	Mutual and Balanced Force Reductions
MEMCON	Memorandum of Conversation
MFN	Most favored nation
NAFTA	North American Free Trade Agreement
NATO	North Atlantic Treaty Organization
NEC	National Economic Council
NGO	Nongovernmental organization
NSA	National security advisor; National Security Agency
NSAM	National Security Action Memorandum
NSC	National Security Council
NSD	National Security Directive
NSDD	National Security Decision Directive
NSDM	National Security Decision Memorandum
NSPD	National Security Presidential Directive
NSR	National Security Review
NSRB	National Security Resources Board
NSSD	National Security Study Directive
NSSM	National Security Study Memorandum
NUWEP	Nuclear Weapons Employment Plan
OCB	Operations Coordinating Board
OEOB	Old Executive Office Building
OMB	Office of Management and Budget
OSA	Office of System Analysis
OSCE	Organization for Security and Cooperation in Europe
OSD	Office of the Secretary of Defense
OSS	Office of Strategic Services
OVP	Office of the Vice President
PLO	Palestinian Liberation Organization
PB	Planning Board
PD	Presidential Directive
PDD	Presidential Decision Directive
PFIAB	President's Foreign Intelligence Advisory Board
PRC	Policy Review Committee
PRD	Presidential Review Directives

PRG	Policy Review Groups
PRM	Presidential Review Memorandum
PSB	Psychological Strategy Board
SACEUR	Supreme Allied Commander Europe
SALT	Strategic Arms Limitation Talks
SCC	Special Coordination Committee
SDI	Strategic Defense Initiative
SEC	Securities and Exchange Commission
SIG	Senior Interdepartmental Group (Johnson); Senior Inter-agency Group (Reagan)
START	Strategic Arms Reduction Treaty
UN	United Nations
UNSCOM	United Nations Special Commission
USIA	United States Information Agency
USTR	United States Trade Representative
WMD	Weapons of mass destruction
WSAG	Washington Special Action Group
WTO	World Trade Organization

Acknowledgments

YOU LOOK AT WHAT you hold in your hands now and see a book. I see a reminder of the people who made it possible. What they have contributed to the book is immeasurable, and what they have offered to me in terms of time, energy, wisdom, and support is irreplaceable. Working with them and getting to know all of them better or for the first time was the great privilege and the pleasure of the process that resulted in the book itself.

To begin with I want to thank Peter Osnos, my publisher at PublicAffairs, and Clive Priddle, my editor, for their faith in me, their patience, their guidance, and their abundant and welcome good humor. In addition, Esmond Harmsworth, my agent, was the one who approached me about doing a book such as this in the first place, and he has never failed to provide insightful counsel throughout the roughly eighteen months between its conception and its publication.

The Carnegie Endowment for International Peace offered me an exceptional environment in which to work throughout the process. Jessica Tuchman Mathews, herself a distinguished former NSC staffer among her many accomplishments, could not have been kinder or smarter. The work she has done with Paul Balaran and George Perkovich in making Carnegie into the world's first truly global think tank has been extraordinary; it is my great good fortune to be associated with them.

One of the best aspects of my arrangement with Carnegie has been that it has enabled me to hire and work with a group of extraordinary research assistants. Geoff Taubman, despite being a Philadelphia Eagles fan, was a wonderful collaborator and contributed immeasurably to many of the most challenging aspects of putting this book together. In addition, he is a first-rate researcher and possesses not only impeccable judgment but also the straightforwardness to let me know when that judgment calls for a different approach or a judicious cut (or many). Heather Boynton also played a vital role in the process, managing it before her departure from the swampland of the Potomac to the sunny shores of Florida and continuing to contribute extensively thereafter. With great intelligence and creativity, she played a central role in everything from developing the structure of the book to actively participating in the interview process.

The interviews were virtually all set up by my hugely valued and terrific assistant, Leslie Fromm, without whom I literally could have accomplished nothing during the time I was working on this book. She managed to keep everything running on track while assisting me with all the other diverse and demanding work I was doing—and she managed to infect everyone she encountered (including me) with her seemingly limitless enthusiasm.

Also assisting in the process during its early research stages at Carnegie were Heinrich Merz, undoubtedly the best U.S. national security researcher Andorra has ever produced, and the very talented and hardworking Katie Holt. Also of great help at Carnegie, offering advice and support, were Carmen McDougall and Cara Santos Pianesi.

I would not have been at Carnegie, nor would I have been able to get through this entire book-writing process intact, without having access to the intelligence and (occasionally off-color) humor provided by Moises Naim, editor and publisher of *Foreign Policy*. He is in a small category of those special, irreplaceable friends who have provided me with many of my best ideas and have had the grace not to acknowledge this fact when they have had plenty of opportunity to do so. Also in this group are my old dear pal Mark Holechek; my college roommate turned publishing advisor and therapist, Andrew Greenspan; my former business partner and brother from the planet Hendon, Richard Burns; and my former colleagues from the Clinton administration, including Jeff Garten, Sue Esserman, Bo Cutter, Bob LaRussa, Rob Stein, Ev Ehrlich, and Susan Levine. Especially useful advice on this project has also come from several of my friends who are journalists and authors, including Tom Friedman, David Sanger, Jane Bussey, Paul Blustein, Sidney Blumenthal, and John Judis.

The world of the National Security Council and the inner circles of the U.S. government foreign policy apparatus is complex and ever-changing, and navigating it required the services of special guides. I am certain I would not even have attempted the book had it not been for the considerable time I spent working with Henry Kissinger at Kissinger Associates or Tony Lake at Intellibridge Corporation. Both are extraordinary men and great teachers from whom I am still learning. In addition, in the course of my time in Washington I have been fortunate enough to get to know a number of people who were especially helpful in the process of formulating the book and determining what to focus on and how. They include Brent Scowcroft, Sandy Berger, Richard Holbrooke, Senator Bob Graham, Bob Hormats, Leon Fuerth, Jim Steinberg, Ivo Daalder, Rick Inderfurth, Don Baer, Nick Rey, and Tara Sonenshine.

This book required the contribution of literally hundreds of people, most of whom made themselves available in interviews. While I can't acknowledge for reasons of confidentiality many of those who were so generous with their time, a partial list of those who made themselves available to me in interviews includes: Morton Abramowitz, Madeleine Albright, Charlene Barshefsky, Sandy Berger, Dennis Blair, Antony Blinken, James Bodner, Stephen Bosworth, Richard Boucher, Lael Brainard, Harold Brown, Zbigniew Brzezinski, William Burns, Richard Bush, Kurt Campbell, Frank Carlucci, Heng Chee Chan, Wesley Clark, Richard Clarke, Roger Cressey, Bowman Cutter, Ivo Daalder, James Dobbins, Thomas Donilon, Kenneth Duberstein, Eric Edelman, Stuart Eizenstat, Susan Esserman, Gerald Ford, Thomas Friedman, Leon Fuerth, Robert Gallucci, John Gannon, Jay Garner, Robert Gates, Timothy Geithner, Robert Gelbard, Marc Ginsberg, Andrew Goodpaster, Jamie Gorelick, Slade Gorton, Bob Graham, Marc Grossman, Richard Haass, John Hamre, Richard Holbrooke, Jonathan Howe, Karl Inderfurth, George Joulwan, Arnold Kanter, James Kelly, Robert Kimmitt, Henry Kissinger, Jonathan Kornblum, Paul Kurtz, Karen Kwiatkowski, Anthony Lake, Charles Larson, David Lipton, Winston Lord, Thomas Maertens, Jessica Tuchman Mathews, Michael McCurry, Thomas F. McLarty, Edward Meese, Franklin Miller, Walter Mondale, Joseph Nye, William Odom, Leon Panetta, William Perry, Thomas Pickering, John Podesta, John Poindexter, Daniel Poneman, Colin Powell, Jack Pritchard, Joseph Prueher, Charles Redman, Otto Reich, Condoleezza Rice, Susan Rice, Rozanne Ridgway, Dennis Ross, Stanley Roth, Stapleton Roy, Robert Rubin, Miriam Sapiro, Harold Saunders, James Schlesinger, Jill Schuker, Brent Scowcroft, Jeffrey Shafer, John Shattuck, Wendy Sherman, Gary Sick, Steve Simon, Walt Slocombe, Gayle Smith, Nancy Soderberg, Steve Solarz, Tara Sonenshine, James Steinberg, George Stephanopoulos, Jessica Stern, Robert Suettinger, Lawrence Summers, John Sununu, Strobe Talbott, Paul Thompson, Arturo Valenzuela, William Wechsler, James Wilkinson, and James Woolsey. Collectively they provided over 2,000 pages of transcripts and vastly more fascinating insights, great stories, and valuable lessons than could ever be contained within the pages of one book. I am immensely grateful for all of it and tried to reflect as much of it as possible on every page, in every line of the book or, at the very least, between them.

Above all, of course, my greatest inspiration came from my wonderful family. My mother is herself an editor and writer who, using all available tools of nature and nurture and great personal example, ensured that my fingers would end up, as they are, working their way across this keyboard. She also provided her eagle-eyed editorial skills in a most helpful way. My father is a scientist and teacher with a well-developed allergy to conventional wisdom that I hope I have inherited and whose appetite for constantly seeking to view the world around him in new ways not only sustained us through the trip through India that frames the story of this book but has benefited all his children throughout our lives. Perhaps that is part of the reason my brother Paul and my sister Marissa were both of such great support throughout this process, as they are always.

When I worked well into the wee hours of the night on this project or was frustrated with my inability to form an intelligent sentence or simply could not decipher one more national security acronym, my wife, Adrean, was an ever-present angel of mercy, offering encouragement, breathtaking patience, and invariably sound advice. (She also performed valuable service as a cat wrangler, keeping our two unnaturally large and hairy felines, Leo and Señor Vivo, away from me when their continued presence would have jeopardized the overly indulged and slothful existence they enjoy in our household.) Of course, it is not widely known that teenage daughters can likewise be such a calming and comforting influence, but mine were that and much, much more. They—Joanna and Laura—have been the lights of my life since they first entered it, and the only thing that would surprise me more than finding I could love them even more would be if they actually were to read this book.

What you may find that is good or worthwhile in this book is due to the collective contributions of all those I have listed here and those whom I have been unable to mention. For everything else, I am entirely responsible.

Notes

CHAPTER 1: The Committee in Charge of Running the World

1. Bijal Triveda, "Survey Reveals Geographic Illiteracy," *National Geographic Society*, 20 November 2002. Available online at http://news.nationalgeographic.com/news/2002/11/1120_021120_GeoRoperSurvey.html.
2. "The National Security Act of 1947." Available online at http://www.iwar.org.uk/sigint/resources/national-security-act/1947-act.htm.
3. "The National Security Act of 1947."
4. Office of the Historian: U.S. Department of State, "History of the National Security Council," August 1997. Available online at http://www.whitehouse.gov/nsc/history.html#truman.
5. Madeleine Albright, interview with the author, 10 September 2004.
6. This despite the fact that, as former U.S. National Security Advisor Anthony Lake put it to me, "If something that the government does can either be the product of a conspiracy or an accident, bet on the accident. It's just far too hard to get elements of the government working together well enough to conduct and execute—and keep secret—a conspiracy."
7. Oliver North with Joe Musser, *Mission Compromised* (New York: Broadman and Holman Publishing, 2002), 6.
8. North, 31–32.
9. North, 3.
10. I.M. Destler, Leslie Gelb, and Anthony Lake, *Our Own Worst Enemy: The Unmaking of U.S. Foreign Policy* (New York: Simon and Schuster, 1984), 166.
11. Destler, Gelb, and Lake, 167.
12. Steve Earle, "Condi, Condi," *The Revolution Starts . . . Now*, 2004. Later, as secretary of state, Dr. Rice passed another pop cultural milestone by inspiring the creation of an "action" heroine doll, produced by Herobuilders.com, featuring Rice in a blue pants suit, a light blue blouse, and a pearl necklace.

CHAPTER 2: Washington's Choice

1. James Rees, "The Importance of George Washington in a Changing World," *Scottish Rite Journal* (February 1998). Available online at http://srjarchives.tripod.com/1998-02/Rees.htm.
2. Gordon Wood, "President George Washington, Republican Monarch," February

2004, 4. Available online at http://web.princeton.edu/sites/jmadison/events/confer-ences/leadership/Washington%20Gordon%20Wood.pdf.

3. "The Farewell Address, 19 September 1796," *The Papers of George Washington*. Available online at http://gwpapers.virginia.edu/farewell/transcript.html.

4. Patrick Garrity, "Warnings of a Parting Friend: US Foreign Policy Envisioned by George Washington in His Farewell Address," *The National Interest* (Fall 1996), 20.

5. Garrity, 20.

6. Garrity, 26.

CHAPTER 3: Greatness Thrust Upon Them

1. Robert Dallek, *Franklin D. Roosevelt and American Foreign Policy, 1932–1945* (New York: Oxford University Press, 1979), 29.

2. Michael Beschloss, *The Conquerors: Roosevelt, Truman, and the Destruction of Hitler's Germany, 1941–1945* (New York: Simon and Schuster, 2002), 200.

3. Beschloss, 200.

4. Beschloss, 217.

5. Stephen Ambrose, "When the Americans Came Back to Europe," *International Herald Tribune*, 28 May 1997, 5.

6. Walter Isaacson and Evan Thomas, *The Wise Men: Six Friends and the World They Made* (New York: Simon and Schuster, 1986), 424.

7. "Address to the United Nations Conference in San Francisco," 25 April 1945. Available online at http://www.trumanlibrary.org/publicpapers/viewpapers.php?pid=17.

8. Mark Hatfield, *Vice Presidents of the United States, 1789–1993* (Washington, DC: U.S. Government Printing Office, 1997). Available online at http://www.senate.gov/art andhistory/history/resources/pdf/john_garner.pdf.

9. David McCullough, *Truman* (New York: Simon and Schuster, 1992), 342.

10. Dean Acheson, *Present at the Creation: My Years in the State Department* (New York: W.W. Norton, 1969), 196.

11. Stephen Schlesinger, *Act of Creation: The Founding of the United Nations* (Boulder: Westview Press, 2003), 16.

12. McCullough, 287.

13. McCullough, 287.

14. McCullough, 287.

15. Dennis Ross, interview with the author, 16 July 2004.

16. Clark Clifford with Richard Holbrooke, *Counsel to the President: A Memoir* (New York: Random House, 1991), 145.

17. Clifford, 146.

18. "President Harry S. Truman's Address Before a Joint Session of Congress, March 12, 1947." Available online at http://www.yale.edu/lawweb/avalon/trudoc.htm.

19. "The Marshall Plan Speech," 5 June 1947. Available online at http://www.cnn.com/SPECIALS/cold.war/episodes/03/documents/marshall.plan/.

20. Harry S. Truman, *Memoirs by Harry S. Truman*, Vol. 1: *Year of Decisions* (Garden City, NY: Doubleday, 1955), 70–71.

21. McCullough, 375–376.

22. Truman, *Memoirs*, Vol. 1, 102.

23. Isaacson and Thomas, 289.

24. Isaacson and Thomas, 306.

25. George Kennan, *Memoirs: 1925–1950* (New York: Little, Brown and Co., 1967), 294.

26. Acheson, 196.

27. Clifford worked with his assistant and close associate, George Elsey, on the report.

28. Arthur Krock, *Memoirs: Sixty Years on the Firing Line* (New York: Funk & Wagnalls, 1968), Appendix A; "Oral History Interview with Clark M. Clifford," Truman Presidential Museum and Library, 13 April 1971.

29. Krock, Appendix A.

30. "Oral History Interview with Clark M. Clifford," Truman Presidential Museum and Library, 16 March 1972.

31. Not least of which is that Kennan's telegram was followed up by his famous "X Article" in *Foreign Affairs* magazine, in which he outlined the policy of containing Soviet expansionism that became the foundation for U.S. Cold War policy.

32. Deborah Welch Larson, *Origins of Containment* (Princeton, NJ: Princeton University Press, 1985), 282.

33. Isaacson and Thomas, 371.

34. Steven Ambrose and Douglas Brinkley, *Rise to Globalism: American Foreign Policy since 1938* (New York: Penguin Books, 1997), 71.

35. Ernest May, "The Development of Political-Military Consultation in the United States," in Karl F. Inderfurth and Loch K. Johnson, eds., *Fateful Decisions: Inside the National Security Council* (New York: Oxford University Press, 2004), 9–10.

36. May, 10

37. May, 10.

38. Harry S. Truman, *Memoirs by Harry S. Truman*, Vol. 2, *Years of Trial and Hope* (Garden City, NY: Doubleday, 1956), 46.

39. Clifford, 146.

40. Robert Kimmitt, interview with the author, 16 August 2004.

41. Ferdinand Eberstadt, "Postwar Organization for National Security," in Karl F. Inderfurth and Loch K. Johnson, eds., *Fateful Decisions: Inside the National Security Council* (New York: Oxford University Press, 2004), 18.

42. Eberstadt, 20.

43. Truman, *Memoirs*, Vol. 2, 48, 49.

44. Clifford, 150.

45. Clifford, 151.

46. Clifford, 172.

47. Michael J. Hogan, *A Cross of Iron: Harry S. Truman and the Origins of the National Security State, 1945–1954* (New York: Cambridge University Press, 2000), 56.

48. Hogan, 57.

49. Jeffrey Dorward, *Eberstadt and Forrestal: A National Security Partnership, 1909–1949* (College Station, TX: Texas A&M Press, 1991), 147.

50. Walter Millis, ed., *The Forrestal Diaries* (New York: Viking Press, 1951), 294.

51. Condoleezza Rice, interview with the author, 4 August 2004.

52. Clifford, 160.

53. John Prados, *Keeper of the Keys* (New York: Morrow, 1991), 34.

CHAPTER 4: Gulliver Embarks

1. Jonathan Swift, *Gulliver's Travels* (New York: Signet Books, 1999), 136.

2. Anthony Lake, interview with the author, 30 June 2004.

3. Richard Nixon, *The Memoirs of Richard Nixon* (New York: Simon and Schuster, 1990), 88.
4. Nixon, 88.
5. Walter Mead, "Once Were Warriors," *Wall Street Journal*, 21 January 2004. Available online at http://www.cfr.org/pub6698/walter_russell_mead/once_were_warriors.php; Nixon, 112.
6. Fred Greenstein and Richard Immerman, "Effective National Security Advising: Recovering the Eisenhower Legacy," in Karl F. Inderfurth and Loch K. Johnson, eds., *Fateful Decisions: Inside the National Security Council* (New York: Oxford University Press, 2004), 48.
7. William Odom, interview with the author, 7 May 2004.
8. William Doyle, *Inside the Oval Office: The White House Tapes from FDR to Clinton* (New York: Kodansha America, 1999), 82.
9. Doyle, 82.
10. Greenstein and Immerman, 49.
11. James Schlesinger, interview with the author, 24 September 2004.
12. Andrew Goodpaster, interview with the author, 3 August, 2004.
13. Andrew Goodpaster, interview with the author, 3 August 2004.
14. Andrew Goodpaster, interview with the author, 3 August 2004.
15. Andrew Goodpaster, interview with the author, 3 August 2004.
16. Andrew Goodpaster, interview with the author, 3 August 2004.
17. Andrew Goodpaster, interview with the author, 3 August 2004.
18. Andrew Goodpaster, interview with the author, 3 August 2004.
19. Robert Bowie and Richard Immerman, *Waging Peace: How Eisenhower Shaped an Enduring Cold War Strategy* (New York: Oxford Press, 1998), 47, 125.
20. Andrew Goodpaster, interview with the author, 3 August 2004.
21. Andrew Goodpaster, interview with the author, 3 August 2004.
22. Andrew Goodpaster, interview with the author, 3 August 2004.
23. James Schlesinger, interview with the author, 24 September 2004.
24. James Schlesinger, interview with the author, 24 September 2004.
25. Andrew Goodpaster, interview with the author, 3 August 2004.
26. Andrew Goodpaster, interview with the author, 3 August 2004.
27. Andrew Goodpaster, interview with the author, 3 August 2004.
28. Nixon, 198.
29. James Schlesinger, interview with the author, 24 September 2004.
30. Andrew Goodpaster, interview with the author, 3 August 2004.
31. Andrew Goodpaster, interview with the author, 3 August 2004.
32. James Schlesinger, interview with the author, 24 September 2004.
33. Andrew Goodpaster, interview with the author, 3 August 2004.
34. Andrew Goodpaster, interview with the author, 3 August 2004.
35. Nixon, 151.
36. Nixon, 153.
37. Nixon, 154.
38. Greenstein and Immerman, 48.

CHAPTER 5: Bound in Lilliput

1. John Kennedy, *The Strategy of Peace* (New York: Harper, 1960), 133.
2. Kennedy, 137, 139.

3. Well described in I.M. Destler, Leslie Gelb, and Anthony Lake, *Our Own Worst Enemy: The Unmaking of U.S. Foreign Policy* (New York: Simon and Schuster, 1984).

4. Richard Reeves, *President Kennedy: Profile of Power* (New York: Simon and Schuster, 1993), 36, 110.

5. "Bay of Pigs, 40 Years After: Chronology," see entry for 16 October 1960. Available online at http://www2.gwu.edu/~nsarchiv/bayofpigs/chron.html.

6. "Bay of Pigs, 40 Years After: Chronology," see entry for 21 October 1960.

7. William Odom, interview with the author, 7 May 2004.

8. Robert Holden and Eric Zolov, *Latin America and the United States: A Documentary History* (New York: Oxford University Press, 2000), 221.

9. Trumbull Higgins, *The Perfect Failure: Kennedy, Eisenhower, and the CIA at the Bay of Pigs* (New York: W.W. Norton, 1987), 60.

10. John Prados, *Keeper of the Keys* (New York: Morrow, 1991), 100–102; Ivo Daalder and I.M. Destler, "A New NSC for a New Administration," *Brookings Institution*, Policy Brief 68, November 2000. Available online at http://www.brookings.edu/comm/policybriefs/pb68.htm.

11. Stanley Falk, "The NSC under Truman and Eisenhower," in Karl F. Inderfurth and Loch K. Johnson, eds., *Fateful Decisions: Inside the National Security Council* (New York: Oxford University Press, 2004), 44.

12. McGeorge Bundy, "Letter to Jackson Subcommittee," in Karl F. Inderfurth and Loch K. Johnson, eds., *Fateful Decisions: Inside the National Security Council* (New York: Oxford University Press, 2004), 83–84; Office of the Historian: U.S. Department of State, "History of the National Security Council," August 1997. Available online at http://www.whitehouse.gov/nsc/history.html#kennedy.

13. Andrew Goodpaster, interview with the author, 3 August 2004.

14. William Odom, interview with the author, 7 May 2004.

15. "Memorandum from the President's Special Assistant for National Security Affairs (Bundy) to President Kennedy (18 February 1961)," *Foreign Relations of the United States, 1961–1963*, Vol. 10: Cuba, 1961–1962. Available online at http://www.state.gov/www/about_state/history/frusX/46_60.html.

16. Piero Gleijeses, "Ships in the Night: The CIA, the White House, and the Bay of Pigs," *Journal of Latin American Studies* 25 (1995), 22.

17. "Memorandum of Meeting with President Kennedy (8 February 1961)," *Foreign Relations of the United States, 1961–1963*, Vol. 10: Cuba, 1961–1962. Available online at http://www.state.gov/www/about_state/history/frusX/31_45.html.

18. "Memorandum from the President's Special Assistant for National Security Affairs (Bundy) to President Kennedy (18 February 1961)."

19. "Memorandum of Meeting with President Kennedy (8 February 1961)."

20. For one of Mann's critiques, see "Memorandum From the Assistant Secretary of State for Inter-American Affairs (Mann) to Secretary of State Rusk (15 February 1961)," *Foreign Relations of the United States, 1961–1963*, Vol. 10: Cuba, 1961–1963. Available online at http://www.state.gov/www/about_state/history/frusX/31_45.html.

21. Gleijeses, 25.

22. Gleijeses, 26.

23. The CIA may have led him to believe that the internal politics of several Latin American countries would be affected.

24. Higgins, 120.

25. Arthur Schlesinger, *A Thousand Days: John F. Kennedy in the White House* (Boston: Houghton Mifflin, 1965), 251.

26. Higgins, 111; Schlesinger, 252.

27. Higgins, ch. 8.
28. Lawrence Freedman, *Kennedy's Wars: Berlin, Cuba, Laos, and Vietnam* (New York: Oxford Press: 2002), 144.
29. Freedman, 145.
30. Michael Beschloss, *The Crisis Years: Kennedy v. Khrushchev, 1960–1963* (New York: Edward Burlingame Books, 1991), 144–45.
31. Michael Bohn, *Nerve Center: Inside the White House Situation Room* (Dulles, VA: Brassey's, 2003), 23.
32. "The Cuban Missile Crisis, 1962: Chronology of Events," The National Security Archive, George Washington University. Available online at http://www2.gwu.edu/~nsarchiv/nsa/cuba_mis_cri/chron.htm.
33. Sheldon Stern, *Averting "The Final Failure": John F. Kennedy and the Secret Cuban Missile Crisis Meetings* (Stanford: Stanford University Press, 2003), 61, 64.
34. Robert Kennedy, *Thirteen Days* (New York: W.W. Norton, 1999), 25.
35. "Off the Record Meeting on Cuba (16 October 1962)," *Foreign Relations of the United States, 1961–1963,* Vol. 11: Cuban Missile Crisis and Aftermath. Available online at http://www.state.gov/www/about_state/history/frusXI/01_25.html.
36. "Off the Record Meeting on Cuba (16 October 1962)."
37. "Off the Record Meeting on Cuba (16 October 1962)."
38. "The Cuban Missile Crisis, 1962: Chronology of Events," *The National Security Archive.* Available online at http://www2.gwu.edu/~nsarchiv/nsa/cuba_mis_cri/chron.htm.
39. Stern, 84–85.
40. Timothy Naftali and Philip Zelikow, eds., *The Presidential Recordings: John F. Kennedy: The Great Crises,* Vol. 2: September–October 21, 1962 (New York: W.W. Norton, 2001), 526.
41. Naftali and Zelikow, 540.
42. Naftali and Zelikow, 546.
43. Naftali and Zelikow, 576.
44. William Newmann, *Managing National Security Policy: The President and the Process* (Pittsburgh: University of Pittsburgh Press, 2003).
45. Andrew F. Krepinevich, *The Army and Vietnam* (Baltimore: Johns Hopkins University Press, 1986), 62.
46. Freedman, 331.
47. Prados, 128.
48. James Schlesinger, interview with the author, 24 September 2004.
49. Harold Saunders, interview with the author, 23 July 2004.
50. Clark Clifford with Richard Holbrooke, *Counsel to the President: A Memoir* (New York: Random House, 1991), 459.
51. James Schlesinger, interview with the author, 24 September 2004.
52. "Editorial Note (28 August 1964)," *Foreign Relations of the United States, 1964–68,* Vol. 1: Vietnam, 1964. Available online at http://www.state.gov/www/about_state/history/vol_i/255_308.html.
53. "Summary Notes of the 538th Meeting of the National Security Council, Washington, August 4, 1964, 6:15–6:40 p.m.," *Foreign Relations of the United States, 1964–68,* Vol. 1: Vietnam, 1964. Available online at http://www.state.gov/www/about_state/history/vol_i/255_308.html.
54. John Mueller, *War, Presidents, and Public Opinion* (New York: John Wiley and Sons, 1973), 201.
55. Brian VanDeMark, *Into the Quagmire: Lyndon Johnson and the Escalation of the Vietnam War* (New York: Oxford University Press, 1995), 76.

56. "Letter from Clark M. Clifford to President Johnson (17 May 1965)," *Foreign Relations of the United States, 1964–68*, Vol. 2: Vietnam, January-June 1965. Available online at http://www.state.gov/wwwbout_state/history/vol_ii/301_310.html.

57. Excerpt from Clark Clifford, *Counsel to the President*, in Nathaniel May, *Oval Office: Stories of Presidents in Crisis from Washington to Bush* (New York: Thunder's Mouth Press, 2002), 137.

58. May, 137–38.

59. May, 138.

60. May, 139.

61. "Summary Notes of the 553d Meeting of the National Security Council (27 July 1965)," *Foreign Relations of the United States, 1964–68*, Vol. 3: Vietnam, June-December 1965. Available online at http://www.state.gov/www/about_state/history/vol_iii/090.html.

CHAPTER 6: America in Decline, the NSC Ascendant

1. Christopher Matthews, *Kennedy and Nixon: The Rivalry That Shaped Postwar America* (New York: Touchstone, 1997), 137.

2. Richard Reeves, *President Nixon: Alone in the White House* (New York: Touchstone, 2001), 181.

3. Thomas Pynchon, *V* (New York: Perennial Classics, 1999), 468.

4. Walter Isaacson, *Kissinger: A Biography* (New York: Simon and Schuster, 1992), 83.

5. Andrew Goodpaster, interview with the author, 3 August 2004.

6. Andrew Goodpaster, interview with the author, 3 August 2004.

7. Harold Saunders, interview with the author, 23 July 2004.

8. James Schlesinger, interview with the author, 24 September 2004.

9. Andrew Goodpaster, interview with the author, 3 August 2004.

10. Andrew Goodpaster, interview with the author, 3 August 2004.

11. Henry Kissinger, interview with the author, 27 May 2004.

12. The eight major interagency policy groups were the Senior Review Group, the Under Secretaries Committee, the Intelligence Committee, the Verification Panel, the Defense Program Review Committee, the Washington Special Action Group, the "40" Committee, and the International Energy Review Group.

13. Senior official, interview with the author.

14. Henry Kissinger, interview with the author, 27 May 2004.

15. Henry Kissinger, interview with the author, 27 May 2004.

16. Henry Kissinger, interview with the author, 27 May 2004.

17. Henry Kissinger, interview with the author, 27 May 2004.

18. Henry Kissinger, interview with the author, 27 May 2004.

19. Henry Kissinger, interview with the author, 27 May 2004.

20. Richard Clarke, interview with the author, 11 May 2004.

21. Richard Clarke, interview with the author, 11 May 2004.

22. Richard Clarke, interview with the author, 11 May 2004.

23. Jonathan Howe, interview with the author, 9 July 2004.

24. Henry Kissinger, interview with the author, 27 May 2004.

25. James Schlesinger, interview with the author, 24 September 2004.

26. Terry Terriff, *The Nixon Administration and the Making of U.S. Nuclear Strategy* (Ithaca, NY: Cornell University Press, 1995), 51.

27. Lawrence Freedman, *The Evolution of Nuclear Strategy* (London: International Insti-

tute for Strategic Studies, 1981), 246. The level of destruction defined by the Pentagon as "assured destruction" consisted of killing 20–33 percent of the Soviet population and destroying 50–75 percent of Soviet industrial capacity.

28. Henry Kissinger, *White House Years* (Boston: Little, Brown and Company, 1979), 216. He also poses a series of questions about the utility of assured destruction in an era of strategic equivalence between the United States and the Soviet Union.

29. "Oral History Roundtables: The Nixon Administration National Security Council," The Brookings Institution and the Center for International and Security Studies at Maryland, 8 December 1998, 19–20. Available online at http://www.cissm.umd.edu/documents/nixon.pdf.

30. Fred Kaplan, *Wizards of Armageddon* (New York: Simon and Schuster, 1983), 367.

31. Terriff, 53.

32. Kaplan, 367.

33. Kaplan, 366.

34. David H. Dunn, *The Politics of Threat: Minuteman Vulnerability in American National Security Policy* (New York: St. Martin's Press, 1997), 52–53.

35. Dunn, 52.

36. Kaplan, 366.

37. Terriff, 53.

38. Kissinger, *White House Years*, 216.

39. Kissinger, *White House Years*, 217.

40. Terriff, 61; Freedman, 376. Kissinger also described the unsatisfactory response he received, over eight years, in response to a specific 1969 presidential directive inquiring into the rationale of naval programs, describing the reply as "always short of being insubordinate but also short of being useful." See Kissinger, *White House Years*, 217.

41. Richard Nixon, *U.S. Foreign Policy for the 1970s: A New Strategy for Peace* (Washington, DC: Government Printing Office, 1972), 92.

42. Terriff, 67–68.

43. Kissinger, *White House Years*, 217.

44. "Paper Prepared in the National Security Council Staff, 23 January 1970," *Foreign Relations of the United States, 1969–1976*, Vol. 1: *Foundations of Foreign Policy, 1969–1972*. Available online at http://www.state.gov/r/pa/ho/frus/nixon/i/20703.htm.

45. Terriff, 64.

46. Terriff, 68.

47. Kaplan, 368.

48. Freedman, 376; Terriff, 87.

49. Dunn, 53.

50. David Kunsman and Douglas Lawson, "A Primer on U.S. Strategic Nuclear Policy," *Sandia Report* (January 2001), 123. Available online at http://www.nti.org/e_research/official_docs/labs/prim_us_nuc_pol.pdf.

51. Kaplan, 370.

52. Kaplan, 371.

53. Kaplan, 372.

54. Terriff, 187; Freedman, 377–78.

55. Kaplan, 373; Terriff, 188–89; Freedman, 378.

56. Winston Lord, interview with the author, 15 July 2004.

57. Morton Abramowitz, interview with the author, 29 June 2004.

58. Richard Nixon, *The Memoirs of Richard Nixon* (New York: Simon and Schuster, 1990), 545.

59. Raymond Garthoff, *Détente and Confrontation: American-Soviet Relations from Nixon to Reagan*, rev. ed. (Washington, DC: Brookings Institution Press, 1994), 242; Kissinger, *White House Years*, 164–65.

60. "Oral History Roundtables: China Policy and the National Security Council," The Brookings Institution and the Center for International and Security Studies at Maryland, 4 November 1999, 7. Available online at http://www.cissm.umd.edu/documents/china.pdf.

61. Garthoff, *Détente and Confrontation*, 243–44.

62. John Prados, *Keeper of the Keys* (New York: Morrow, 1991), 321.

63. Garthoff, *Détente and Confrontation*, 245; Kissinger, *White House Years*, 191.

64. "Oral History Roundtables: China Policy and the National Security Council," 10.

65. "Oral History Roundtables: China Policy and the National Security Council," 4.

66. "Oral History Roundtables: The Nixon Administration National Security Council," 6. See also Garthoff, *Détente and Confrontation*, 243.

67. "Oral History Roundtables: The Nixon Administration National Security Council," 16.

68. Prados, 321; Garthoff, *Détente and Confrontation*, 245. Two more NSSMs on China, dealing with trade and Sino-Soviet relations, were also produced by the NSC later that year.

69. "Oral History Roundtables: China Policy and the National Security Council," 6; Nixon, 546. Lord makes similar points about how the "NSSMs helped provide intellectual fodder." "Oral History Roundtables: The Nixon Administration National Security Council," 18.

70. Prados, 321.

71. James Schlesinger, interview with the author, 24 September 2004.

72. Nixon, 550.

73. "Oral History Roundtables: China Policy and the National Security Council," 9.

74. "Oral History Roundtables: The Nixon Administration National Security Council," 8.

75. Winston Lord, interview with the author, 15 July 2004.

76. "Oral History Roundtables: China Policy and the National Security Council," 10.

77. For instance, see Kissinger, *White House Years*, 688, 690, 691, 709–10.

78. Henry Kissinger, *Years of Upheaval* (New York: Little, Brown and Company, 1982), 65.

79. Winston Lord, interview with the author, 15 July 2004.

80. Graham Allison, *Essence of Decision: Explaining the Cuban Missile Crisis* (New York: Pearson Education, 1999), 316.

81. "Oral History Roundtables: China Policy and the National Security Council," 12.

82. Nixon, 549; Kissinger, *White House Years*, 713.

83. "Oral History Roundtables: The Nixon Administration National Security Council," 46–47.

84. "Oral History Roundtables: The Nixon Administration National Security Council," 26.

85. Kissinger describes the evolution and dynamics of these back channels in *White House Years*, chapter 18. Also see Garthoff, *Détente and Confrontation*, 246–48.

86. Prados, 322; Nixon, 550. According to Kissinger's account (*White House Years*, 716), "Rogers's name did not come up; nor could it have, given Nixon's determination that he, not the State Department should be seen—justly—as the originator of China policy."

87. Kissinger, *White House Years*, 717.
88. Prados, 322. Kissinger devoted somewhat less energy to his ping-pong game, which he practiced with Winston Lord and had an opportunity to play while in China.
89. Kissinger, *White House Years*, 721–22, 728–29, 732.
90. Prados, 322.
91. Kissinger, *White House Years*, 738–40.
92. "Oral History Roundtables: The Nixon Administration National Security Council," 42.
93. "Oral History Roundtables: The Nixon Administration National Security Council," 42.
94. "Interview: Winston Lord," *CNN Cold War*, 1988. Available online at http://edition. cnn.com/SPECIALS/cold.war/episodes/15/interviews/lord/.
95. Kissinger, *White House Years*, 756; Nixon, 553.
96. Nixon, 576; Garthoff, 266–67.
97. "Oral History Roundtables: The Nixon Administration National Security Council," 27.
98. "Nixon's China Game," *The American Experience*. Available online at http://www. pbs.org/wgbh/amex/china/index.html. Also "Oral History Roundtables: The Nixon Administration National Security Council," 44.
99. Richard Holbrooke, interview with the author, 15 July 2004.
100. Winston Lord, interview with the author, 15 July 2004.
101. Henry Kissinger, "The Vietnam Negotiations," *Foreign Affairs*, 47:2 (January 1969), 214.
102. Reeves, 70.
103. Kissinger, *White House Years*, 277–79.
104. Iwan Morgan, *Nixon* (New York: Oxford University Press, 2002), 115.
105. Winston Lord, interview with the author, 15 July 2004.
106. Prados, 297–98.
107. In fact, I saw the letter hanging there on the day I walked through his home in 2001 just before buying it and converting that study into my own.
108. Henry Kissinger, interview with the author, 27 May 2004.
109. William Odom, interview with the author, 7 May 2004.
110. Senior official, interview with the author.
111. Walter Isaacson, *Kissinger: A Biography* (New York: Simon and Schuster, 1992), 507; Prados, 349–50.
112. William Burr, ed., "The October War and U.S. Policy," *The National Security Archive*. Available online at http://www.gwu.edu/~nsarchiv/NSAEBB/NSAEBB98/index. htm. Also Kissinger, *White House Years*, 450–51.
113. William Quandt, *Decade of Decisions* (Berkeley: University of California Press, 1977), 166–67.
114. Quandt, *Decade of Decisions*, 171–72; Isaacson, 513; Prados, 343.
115. Kissinger, *White House Years*, 485- 86; Quandt, *Decade of Decisions*, 173–76.
116. "Memcon between Kissinger and Ambassador Huang Zhen, PRC Liaison Office," 6 October 1973, in Burr, "The October War and U.S. Policy," Document 17. Available online at http://www.gwu.edu/~nsarch/NSAEBB/NSAEBB98/octwar-17.pdf.
117. Isaacson, 516.
118. Kissinger, *White House Years*, 491; Isaacson, 518.
119. Isaacson, 518–21; Kissinger, *White House Years*, 494–95.
120. Quandt, 179; Kissinger, *White House Years*, 486; Isaacson, 519.

121. Between October 14 and the October 25 cease-fire, more than 11,000 tons of equipment and forty F-4 Phantoms and twelve C-130 transports were airlifted to Israel. See Quandt, 185n46; Isaacson, 522.

122. Isaacson, 514.

123. Prados, 347.

124. Burr, "The October War and U.S. Policy."

125. Quandt, 183.

126. Quandt, 190; Isaacson, 523–24.

127. Kissinger, *White House Years*, 547–48.

128. Garthoff, *Détente and Confrontation*, 417; Quandt, 191–92; Kissinger, *White House Years*, 547.

129. Isaacson, 526.

130. Isaacson, 528; Quandt, 194; Kissinger, *White House Years*, 559–67.

131. Kissinger, *White House Years*, 580–81; Isaacson, 530.

132. Quandt, 196; Prados, 348.

133. Gerald Ford was not at the meeting either, since he had been named but not confirmed as vice president.

134. Kissinger, *White House Years*, 585. Kissinger writes in his memoirs that Haig was implying President Nixon was too emotionally distraught to participate, which was reflected in his telephone conversation earlier that evening with the president. However, Garthoff writes, in a footnote (425n78), that two participants of the late night meeting had been informed by Kissinger that President Nixon had been drinking heavily.

135. Isaacson, 531.

136. Quandt, 197; Garthoff, 427; Isaacson, 532; Prados, 348.

137. Quandt, 198–99.

138. Garthoff, 428.

139. Henry Kissinger, interview with the author, 27 May 2004.

140. James Dobbins, interview with the author, 2 July 2004.

141. James Dobbins, interview with the author, 2 July 2004.

142. Jonathan Howe, interview with the author, 9 July 2004.

143. Gerald Ford, interview with the author, 13 May 2004.

144. Winston Lord, interview with the author, 15 July 2004.

145. Robert Gates, interview with the author, 4 June 2004.

146. Brent Scowcroft, interview with the author, 25 August 2004.

CHAPTER 7: A Superpower in Search of Itself

1. "Oswald Spengler: Decline of the West, 1922," *Modern History Sourcebook*. Available online at http://www.fordham.edu/halsall/mod/spengler-decline.html.

2. Neil McInnes, "The Great Doomsayer," *National Interest* 48 (Summer 1997), 69.

3. Reply by Paul Kennedy to Joseph Nye, "What to Do about Decline," *New York Review of Books* 36:10 (15 March 1989). Available online at http://www.nybooks.com/articles/3996.

4. Jimmy Carter, *Keeping Faith* (New York: Bantam Books, 1984), 215; Raymond Garthoff, *Détente and Confrontation: American-Soviet Relations from Nixon to Reagan,* rev. ed. (Washington, DC: Brookings Institution Press, 1994), 54.

5. Zbigniew Brzezinski, interview with the author, 21 May 2004.

6. Zbigniew Brzezinski, *Power and Principle: Memoirs of the National Security Advisor, 1977–1981* (New York: Farrar, Straus and Giroux, 1983), 6.

7. "The Second 1976 Presidential Debate," 6 October 1976. Available online at http://www.pbs.org/newshour/debatingourdestiny/76debates/2_a.html.

8. Brzezinski, 10.

9. Brzezinski, 11.

10. Brzezinski, 11.

11. Brzezinski, 4.

12. Brzezinski, 59.

13. Zbigniew Brzezinski, interview with the author, 21 May 2004.

14. Carter, *Keeping Faith*, 39.

15. Walter Mondale, interview with the author, 19 May 2004.

16. Walter Mondale, interview with the author, 19 May 2004.

17. Zbigniew Brzezinski, interview with the author, 21 May 2004.

18. Brzezinski, 21.

19. Carter, *Keeping Faith*, 401.

20. Brzezinski, 31.

21. Brzezinski, 32.

22. Zbigniew Brzezinski, interview with the author, 21 May 2004.

23. Walter Mondale, interview with the author, 19 May 2004.

24. Walter Mondale, interview with the author, 19 May 2004.

25. Jessica Tuchman Mathews, interview with the author, 17 August 2004.

26. Madeleine Albright, interview with the author, 10 September 2004.

27. Harold Brown, interview with the author, 21 July 2004.

28. Carter, *Keeping Faith*, 159.

29. Carter, *Keeping Faith*, 159.

30. Carter, *Keeping Faith*, 160–61.

31. Carter, *Keeping Faith*, 167.

32. Senior official, interview with the author.

33. Carter, *Keeping Faith*, 171.

34. Carter, *Keeping Faith*, 173.

35. Harold Brown, interview with the author, 21 July 2004.

36. Carter, *Keeping Faith*, 867. The JCS was aghast at the idea and it was soon dropped.

37. Brzezinski, 455. William Odom, Brzezinski's military assistant on the NSC, echoed the national security advisor's views, recalling that the "force structure that we had built to contain or deter the Soviets in the '50s and '60s was heavily dependent on nuclear weapons. Now the Soviets equaled us or perhaps were going to exceed us in strategic nuclear capabilities. How credible would our nuclear deterrent remain?" See "Interview with Zbigniew Brzezinski with Madeleine Albright, Leslie G. Denend, and William Odom," (Miller Center for Public Affairs, University of Virginia), 18 February 1982, 32. Available online at http://millercenter.virginia.edu/scripps/diglibrary/oral-history/carter/transcripts/brzezinski.pdf.

38. William Odom praises Huntington's "intellectual power" in the development of PRM-10, which gave the NSC an "analytic advantage" versus other agencies. See "Interview with Zbigniew Brzezinski with Madeleine Albright, Leslie G. Denend, and William Odom," 42. Also see Desmond Ball, "Development of the SIOP, 1960–1983," in Desmond Ball and Jeffrey Richelson, eds., *Strategic Nuclear Targeting* (Ithaca, NY: Cornell University Press, 1989), 75. A separate section of the PRM-10 study reviewing the U.S. force posture was conducted by the Department of Defense. See Garthoff, 868.

39. "Interview with Zbigniew Brzezinski with Madeleine Albright, Leslie G. Denend, and William Odom," 31.

40. John Prados, *Keeper of the Keys* (New York: Morrow, 1991), 407–408; Garthoff, 868.

41. Ball, "Development of the SIOP," 76; Desmond Ball, "Counterforce Targeting: How New? How Viable?" *Arms Control Today* 2:2, February 1981, 2; Garthoff, 868.

42. Ball, "Development of the SIOP," 76; The National Security Archive, "Presidential Directives on National Security from Truman to Clinton." Available online at http://nsarchive.chadwyck.com/pdessayx.htm.

43. Brzezinski, 456.

44. "Interview with Zbigniew Brzezinski with Madeleine Albright, Leslie G. Denend, and William Odom," 35.

45. Zbigniew Brzezinski, interview with the author, 21 May 2004.

46. Brzezinski, 456–57. Fritz Ermath, Victor Utgoff, and Gen. Jasper Welch worked with Odom, and Brzezinski praises these individuals as possessing "considerable expertise and capacity for doctrinal innovation." Prados, 411.

47. Fred Kaplan, *Wizards of Armageddon* (New York: Simon and Schuster, 1983), 383.

48. Brzezinski, 457; Kaplan, 384.

49. Ball, "Development of the SIOP, 1960–1983," 77; Brzezinski, 458.

50. Prados, 411; Ball, "Counterforce Targeting," 6; Brzezinski, 458.

51. Colin Gray, *Strategic Studies and Public Policy: The American Experience* (Lexington: University Press of Kentucky, 1982), 157.

52. Stephen Cimbala, "War-Fighting Deterrence and Alliance Cohesiveness," *Air University Review*, Sept.-Oct. 1984. Available online at http://www.airpower.maxwell.af.mil/airchronicles/aureview/1984/sep-oct/cimbala.html.

53. "Secretaries of Defense: Harold Brown." Available online at http://www.defenselink.mil/specials/secdef_histories/.

54. Garthoff, 870 n117.

55. Prados, 390. Donovan happens to have been the journalist who first recommended Carter to Brzezinski for inclusion among the ranks of the Trilateral Commission.

56. Senior Carter administration official, interview with the author.

57. Senior Carter administration official, interview with the author.

58. Senior Carter administration official, interview with the author.

59. As the disparity between pay for top Washington jobs and that for top private-sector jobs has grown dramatically in the two decades since, it is no wonder that the quality of young people drawn into the government's service has declined precipitously. We ought to look more closely at the example of countries like Singapore, in which top government ministers make salaries comparable to private sector top executives, thus ensuring that their public issues are addressed by the best and the brightest available.

60. Prados, 405.

61. Brzezinski, 350.

62. Carter, *Keeping Faith*, 171.

63. Harold Brown, interview with the author, 21 July 2004.

64. Harold Brown, interview with the author, 21 July 2004.

65. Cyrus R. Vance, *Hard Choices: Critical Years in America's Foreign Policy* (New York: Simon and Schuster, 1983), 78–79; Brzezinski, 222.

66. Patrick Tyler, "The (Ab)normalization of U.S.-Chinese Relations," *Foreign Affairs* 78:5 (September/October 1999), 96–97.

67. "Oral History Roundtables: China Policy and the National Security Council," The Brookings Institution and the Center for International and Security Studies at Mary-

492 NOTES TO PAGES 189–194

land, 4 November 1999, 11–12. Available online at http://www.cissm.umd.edu/documents/china.pdf.
68. Richard Solomon said, "My sense is that there were better relations among the pros ... than there were higher up the line." William Glysteen, who worked on China issues for Holbrooke, also notes that NSC-State Department collaboration at lower levels functioned well, at least "at the early stage," but the collegiality eroded due to the problems between Brzezinski and Vance. See "Oral History Roundtables: China Policy and the National Security Council," the Brookings Institution and the Center for International and Security Studies at Maryland, 4 November 1999, 13–15, 18.
69. Tyler, "The (Ab)normalization of U.S.-Chinese Relations," 97, 99.
70. Carter, 191–92; Tyler, "The (Ab)normalization of U.S.-Chinese Relations," 100–101; James Mann, *About Face: A History of America's Curious Relationship with China, From Nixon to Clinton* (New York: Knopf, 1999), 82–84.
71. Vance, 82–83; Tyler, "The (Ab)normalization of U.S.-Chinese Relations," 101–102.
72. "Oral History Roundtables: The Nixon Administration National Security Council," The Brookings Institution and the Center for International and Security Studies at Maryland, 8 December 1998, 57. Available at http://www.cissm.umd.edu/documents/nixon.pdf; Richard Evans, *Deng Xiaoping and the Making of Modern China* (New York: Penguin Books, 1997), 227.
73. "Oral History Roundtables: China Policy and the National Security Council," 12; Tyler, "The (Ab)normalization of U.S.-Chinese Relations," 104; Prados, 422; Brzezinski, 204–205.
74. Tyler, "The (Ab)normalization of U.S.-Chinese Relations," 104.
75. Prados, 422; Brzezinski, 205, 206; Tyler, "The (Ab)normalization of U.S.-Chinese Relations," 105.
76. Tyler, "The (Ab)normalization of U.S.-Chinese Relations," 106–107; Mann, 87. Brzezinski (213) has a more benign description of Holbrooke's exclusion.
77. Brzezinski, 217.
78. Brzezinski, 206; Carter, *Keeping Faith*, 195–96.
79. Brzezinski, 214.
80. Tyler, "The (Ab)normalization of U.S.-Chinese Relations," 108–110.
81. Carter, *Keeping Faith*, 197; Garthoff, *Détente and Confrontation*, 775–76; Tyler, "The (Ab)normalization of U.S.-Chinese Relations," 112.
82. Brzezinski, 230; Tyler, "The (Ab)normalization of U.S.-Chinese Relations," 113–14, 116.
83. Mann, 91-92; Tyler, "The (Ab)normalization of U.S.-Chinese Relations," 116–17.
84. Initially Brzezinski retorted that the assistant secretary of state would find out about the normalization agreement when President Carter spoke to the nation.
85. Richard Holbrooke, interview with the author, 15 July 2004.
86. Tyler, "The (Ab)normalization of U.S.-Chinese Relations," 118; Carter, *Keeping Faith*, 198.
87. Brzezinski, 231.
88. Tyler, "The (Ab)normalization of U.S.-Chinese Relations," 119–20; Brzezinski, 231–32.
89. Carter administration official, interview with the author.
90. Richard Holbrooke, interview with the author, 15 July 2004.
91. Carter did not take Holbrooke's criticism of Brzezinski well and "never initiated another conversation with Holbrooke. Their relationship was over." See Tyler, "The (Ab)normalization of U.S.-Chinese Relations," 95, 97–98.

92. Carter, *Keeping Faith*, 52.
93. Carter, *Keeping Faith*, 53.
94. Carter, *Keeping Faith*, 53.
95. Jimmy Carter, "Being There," *Foreign Affairs* 78:6 (November/December 1999), 164–65.
96. Jia-Rui Chong, "Carter Shares Personal Recollections, Advice on U.S. Policy with China," *Stanford Report*, 8 May 2002. Available online at http://news-service.stanford. edu/news/2002/may8/carter-58.html.
97. Chong, "Carter Shares Personal Recollections, Advice on U.S. Policy with China."
98. Carter, "Being There."
99. Carter, *Keeping Faith*, 282.
100. Erwin Hargrove, *Jimmy Carter as President: Leadership and the Politics of the Public Good* (Baton Rouge: Louisiana State University Press, 1988), 128; Carter, *Keeping Faith*, 402; "Interview with Jimmy Carter," Miller Center of Public Affairs, University of Virginia, 29 November 1982, 17; Brzezinski, 238, 242; Vance, *Hard Choices*, 203–05, 218–19; Quandt, *Camp David*, 194–96, 207, 210.
101. Brzezinski, 273, 288; "Zbigniew Brzezinski, Exit Interview," Jimmy Carter Library, 20 February 1981, 10. Available online at http://www.jimmycarterlibrary.org/library/exit Int/exitBrzski.pdf.
102. Harold Saunders, interview with the author, 23 July 2004.
103. William Odom, interview with the author, 7 May 2004.
104. Carter, *Keeping Faith*, 443, 446, 449; "Interview with Jimmy Carter," Miller Center of Public Affairs, University of Virginia, 29 November 1982, 17; Brzezinski, 354–55, 363–64, 366–67, 368, 375–76, 381; Gary Sick, *All Fall Down* (New York: Random House, 1985), 69–70; Hamilton Jordan, *Crisis: The Last Year of the Carter Presidency* (New York: Putnam, 1982), 102; Prados, 436–37, 438; James A. Bill, *The Eagle and the Lion: the Tragedy of American-Iranian Relations* (New Haven: Yale University Press, 1988), 248–49, 251–52.
105. Stansfield Turner, *Terrorism and Democracy* (Boston: Houghton Mifflin, 1991), 31, 79; Bill, 251–52.
106. Sick, 61, 67, 71, 90, 98–99; Brzezinski, 359–60, 369–70; William H. Sullivan, *Mission to Iran* (New York: Norton, 1981), 171–72; Prados, 440; Bill, 249; Barry Rubin, *Paved with Good Intentions* (New York: Oxford University Press, 1980), 251.
107. Vance, 328; Brzezinski, 360–70; George Ball, *The Past Has Another Pattern* (New York: W.W. Norton, 1982), 458, 462.
108. Brzezinski, 367; Sullivan, 194; Sick, 87–88; "Zbigniew Brzezinski, Exit Interview," 18.
109. Michael Ledeen and William Lewis, *Debacle: The American Failure in Iran* (New York: Alfred A. Knopf, 1981), 170–71, 180; Carter, *Keeping Faith*, 440, 449–50.
110. Vance, 373; Brzezinski, 475–76.
111. Carter, *Keeping Faith*, 450.
112. Brzezinski, 477.
113. Sick, 196.
114. Sick, 177; Brzezinski, 482.
115. Carter, *Keeping Faith*, 453.
116. Rose McDermott, *Risk Taking in International Politics* (Ann Arbor, MI: University of Michigan Press, 1998), 91.
117. Lyn Boyd, "A King's Exile: The Shah of Iran and Moral Considerations in U.S. Foreign Policy," *Institute for the Study of Diplomacy*, 2000, 6.
118. Sick, 181–84; Jordan, *Crisis*, 41–42; Carter, *Keeping Faith*, 455.

119. Prados, 442; Sick, 190–91.
120. Sick, 195.
121. Sick, 209.
122. Daniel Yergin, *The Prize: The Epic Quest for Oil, Money, and Power* (New York: Simon and Schuster, 1991), 291.
123. Sick, 246, 249.
124. Brzezinski, 478; Sick, 214.
125. Sick, 216.
126. Carter, *Keeping Faith*, 461.
127. Carter, *Keeping Faith*, 461.
128. Sick, 264.
129. David Farber, *Taken Hostage: The Iran Hostage Crisis and America's First Encounter with Radical Islam* (Princeton, NJ: Princeton University Press, 2004), 161.
130. Sick, 273.
131. Brzezinski, 483–84.
132. Carter, *Keeping Faith*, 484–85.
133. William Odom, interview with the author, 7 May 2004.
134. Carter, *Keeping Faith*, 471.
135. Carter, *Keeping Faith*, 472.
136. Zbigniew Brzezinski, interview with the author, 21 May 2004.
137. Brzezinski, 487.
138. Sick, 284–85.
139. Sick, 290.
140. Carter, *Keeping Faith*, 507; McDermott, 58.
141. Vance, *Hard Choices*, 410; Carter, *Keeping Faith*, 507.
142. Brzezinski, 498–500.
143. Carter, *Keeping Faith*, 518.
144. Carter, *Keeping Faith*, 513.

CHAPTER 8: Morning in America, Twilight at the NSC

1. William Odom, interview with the author, 7 May 2004.
2. Former Reagan officials, interviews with the author.
3. Former Reagan officials, interviews with the author.
4. Ronald Reagan, "State of the Union Speech," 13 March 1980, in Kiron Skinner, Annelise Anderson, and Martin Anderson, eds., *Reagan, In His Own Hand: The Writings of Ronald Reagan That Reveal His Revolutionary Vision for America* (New York: Free Press, 2001), 472.
5. For accounts of the views of Reagan insiders toward Kissinger, see Walter Isaacson, *Kissinger: A Biography* (New York: Simon and Schuster, 1992), 719; Frances FitzGerald, *Way Out There in the Blue* (New York: Simon and Schuster, 2000), 98; Deborah Strober and Gerald Strober, *The Reagan Presidency: An Oral History of the Era* (Dulles, VA: Brassey's Inc., 2003), 24.
6. Senior Reagan administration official, interview with the author.
7. Lou Cannon, *President Reagan: The Role of a Lifetime* (New York: Simon and Schuster, 1991), 78.
8. Former colleague of Alexander Haig, interview with the author.
9. Edwin Meese, interview with the author, 13 July 2004.

10. John Prados, *Keeper of the Keys* (New York: Morrow, 1991), 450.

11. Office of the Historian: U.S. Department of State, "History of the National Security Council," August 1997. Available online at http://www.whitehouse.gov/nsc/history.html#reagan.

12. Edwin Meese, interview with the author, 13 July 2004.

13. James Dobbins, interview with the author, 2 July 2004.

14. James Dobbins, interview with the author, 2 July 2004.

15. Robert Kimmitt, interview with the author, 16 August 2004.

16. Alexander Haig, *Caveat: Realism, Reagan, and Foreign Policy* (New York: Macmillan, 1984), 160.

17. Edwin Meese, interview with the author, 13 July 2004.

18. Edwin Meese, interview with the author, 13 July 2004.

19. Haig, 85.

20. Prados, 457.

21. John Poindexter, interview with the author, 13 July 2004.

22. NSDD-1 covered a defense policy review.

23. Don Oberdorfer and Martin Schram, "Haig Believes a Reagan Aide Is Campaigning against Him," *Washington Post*, 4 November 1981.

24. John Poindexter, interview with the author, 13 July 2004.

25. Former senior Reagan administration official, interview with the author.

26. Officially, Haig resigned over disagreements about the Soviet gas pipeline to Western Europe. Haig, 311–14.

27. Former senior Reagan administration official, interview with the author.

28. Harold Brown, interview with the author, 21 July 2004.

29. Former senior Reagan administration official, interview with the author.

30. Senior State Department official, interview with the author.

31. Phil McCombs, "McFarlane and the Web of Rumor: The Ex-Security Adviser, His Frustrations in Office, and the Recurrent Tales of Trouble at Home," *Washington Post*, 18 April 1986.

32. "A Forum on the Role of the National Security Advisor," Woodrow Wilson International Center for Scholars and James A. Baker III Institute for Public Policy of Rice University, 12 April 2001. Available online at http://www.rice.edu/webcast/speeches/text/20010412secadv.pdf.

33. Cannon, 291.

34. Cannon, 289–90; Marjorie Hyer, "Armageddon: Group of Church Leaders Asks Candidates to Repudiate Nuclear Doomsday Theory," *Washington Post*, 24 October 1984.

35. Coit Blacker, *Reluctant Warriors: The United States, the Soviet Union, and Arms Control* (New York: W.H. Freeman, 1987), 99–100.

36. "Oral History Roundtables: Arms Control Policy and the National Security Council," the Brookings Institution and the Center for International and Security Studies at Maryland, 23 March 2000, 35. Available online at http://www.cissm.umd.edu/documents/armscontrol.pdf.

37. Allen Holmes, assistant secretary of state for politico-military affairs during Reagan's second term, noted that "1984 had been a critical year where Shultz won his battles in the White House. He had direct access to the president, but he didn't want to overuse that." See "Oral History Roundtables: Arms Control Policy and the National Security Council," 38, 40, 42.

38. "Oral History Roundtables: Arms Control Policy and the National Security Council," 35–36. Shultz's discussions with the JCS did not go uncontested. Holmes recalled

that Shultz "had battles with Cap over his insistence that he, as the secretary of state, was a charter member of the National Security Council and had as much right to have direct and continuous contact with the chiefs as Cap did. And Cap said, 'Okay, but I'll always be there.'" The meetings were also held in the "Tank," a secure meeting center in the Pentagon. See "Oral History Roundtables: Arms Control Policy and the National Security Council," 40, 42.

39. "Oral History Roundtables: Arms Control Policy and the National Security Council," 38; FitzGerald, 182–86.

40. Strobe Talbott, *Deadly Gambit* (New York: Vintage, 1985), 17; Michael Krepon, *Arms Control in the Reagan Administration* (New York: University Press of America, 1989), 255–59. Among Perle's assistants was Douglas Feith, who would play a prominent role in the Iraq planning of the George W. Bush administration.

41. Cannon, 303.

42. Talbott, 169–70; Blacker, 146.

43. Cannon, 303–04.

44. "Oral History Roundtables: Arms Control Policy and the National Security Council," 37.

45. Blacker, 158.

46. "Oral History Roundtables: Arms Control Policy and the National Security Council," 39.

47. "Oral History Roundtable: Arms Control Policy and the National Security Council," 40.

48. "Oral History Roundtables: Arms Control Policy and the National Security Council," 37.

49. "Oral History Roundtables: Arms Control Policy and the National Security Council," 37–38.

50. More than a decade before his NORAD visit, Governor Reagan attended a briefing by Edward Teller, who was discussing missile defense technologies. George P. Shultz, *Turmoil and Triumph: My Years as Secretary of State* (New York: Scriber, 1993), 261.

51. FitzGerald, 192; Shultz, 262–63.

52. Strobe Talbott, *The Master of the Game* (New York: Alfred A. Knopf, 1988), 203, 205; FitzGerald, 195.

53. Robert McFarlane, with Zofia Smardz, *Special Trust* (New York: Cadell and Davies, 1994), 227.

54. FitzGerald, 198; Talbott, *The Master of the Game*, 204.

55. McFarlane, 229; Frederick Hartmann, *Naval Renaissance* (Annapolis, MD: Naval Institute Press, 1990), 256.

56. Hartmann, 117; McFarlane, 230.

57. Talbott, *Master of the Game*, 193; FitzGerald, 205–206. Even the White House press secretary, Larry Speakes, hadn't been warned about the announcement of this initiative.

58. McFarlane, 232–33.

59. "Address to the Nation on National Security by President Ronald Reagan, March 23, 1983." Available online at http://www.fas.org/spp/starwars/offdocs/rrspch.htm.

60. "Eliminating the Threat from Ballistic Missiles," 25 March 1983. Available online at http://www.fas.org/spp/starwars/offdocs/nsdd085.htm.

61. FitzGerald, 256–57.

62. Rozanne Ridgway, interview with the author, 8 July 2004.

63. Rozanne Ridgway, interview with the author, 8 July 2004.

64. Weinberger denied being the source of the leak. Perle speculated that the defense secretary's opponents released the letter to discredit him. Cannon, 750; McFarlane, 317.
65. Poindexter, McFarlane's replacement, did not play a major role in the administration's arms control debates.
66. FitzGerald, 338–39.
67. The pro-SDI faction in the administration gained an unexpected ally when the State Department's legal advisor, Abraham Sofaer, presented a memorandum at a meeting of the Senior Arms Control Group in October 1985, providing an interpretation of the ABM treaty that would allow the testing of a missile defense system as well as laboratory research. See FitzGerald, 292–301.
68. Talbott, 304–308; Shultz, 753–54.
69. Don Oberdorfer, *The Turn: From the Cold War to a New Era* (New York: Touchstone, 1991), 203; FitzGerald, 362–63.
70. Federation of American Scientists, "Intermediate-Range Nuclear Forces." Available online at http://www.fas.org/nuke/control/inf/.
71. Lawrence Walsh, *Final Report of the Independent Counsel for Iran/Contra Matters*, 4 August 1993, Part I. Available online at http://www.fas.org/irp/offdocs/walsh/.
72. Peter Kornbluh and Malcolm Byrne, *The Iran-Contra Scandal: The Declassified History* (New York: New Press, 1993), 220–28, 232–33; *The Tower Commission Report: The Full Text of the President's Special Review Board* (New York: Times Books, 1987), 20–21; McFarlane, 18–20; Shultz, 793–94; Theodore Draper, *A Very Thin Line: The Iran-Contra Affairs* (New York: Hill and Wang, 1991), 148–51.
73. The draft NSDD was not well received in the Defense and State Departments, with Defense Secretary Weinberger describing plans to engage in dialogue with Khomeini's government as "almost too absurd to comment on." Kornbluh and Byrne, 228.
74. Lawrence E. Walsh, *Firewall: The Iran-Contra Conspiracy and Cover-Up* (New York: Norton, 1997), 37; McFarlane, 17–19. An account by McFarlane of the meetings with Kimche is described in a July 1985 cable to Secretary of State Shultz. Kornbluh and Byrne, 255–60.
75. Ledeen was removed from the Iran arms operation by Poindexter, who said he wanted someone with more technical expertise, and Oliver North informed him that the arms deals "had been shut down." Nonetheless, Ledeen remained in contact with Manucher Ghorbanifar into the following year. Also Walsh, *Final Report of the Independent Counsel for Iran/Contra Matters*, Part IV, chapter 1.
76. Walsh, *Final Report of the Independent Counsel for Iran/Contra Matters*, Part IV, chapter 1.
77. *The Tower Commission Report*, 26–27; Shultz, 783–85.
78. Walsh, *Final Report of the Independent Counsel for Iran/Contra Matters*, Part VII, chapter 25. Instead, Abrams included North on the Restricted Interagency Group, a more select body for setting Central American policy for the Reagan administration.
79. Ronald Sable, interview with the author, 4 March 2005.
80. McFarlane, 78; Walsh, *Final Report of the Independent Counsel for Iran/Contra Matters*, 5–7.
81. On the other hand, North, in a memo to McFarlane and Poindexter, had a more upbeat assessment of the meeting and argued for more operational control over the arms transfers by the U.S. government. Kornbluh and Byrne, 279–82.
82. McFarlane, 46–52; *The Tower Commission Report*, 35–37, 38; Shultz, 812; Kornbluh and Byrne, 232, 315.

83. Cannon, 625; Prados, 506–07.

84. In early 1986, he also was given more office space and staff by Poindexter. Draper, 40; Prados, 523.

85. Congress had placed increasing restrictions on aid to the contras, banning all assistance after the passage of the Boland Amendment in 1984. Despite the congressional action, President Reagan had directed McFarlane to keep the contras "body and soul together," which was accomplished in part by soliciting contributions from third countries and private sources. See Walsh, *Firewall: The Iran-Contra Conspiracy and Cover-Up*, 19; Draper, 33; Kornbluh and Byrne, 198.

86. McFarlane, chapter 4.

87. North, in a memo to Poindexter, proposes diverting to the Contras $12 million of the proceeds from the sale to Iran. Kornbluh and Byrne, 319–23; Walsh, *Final Report of the Independent Counsel for Iran/Contra Matters*, 26; McFarlane, 66.

88. "Note from Oliver North, Subject: Exchanges," 27 February 1986, from "Iran Contra: White House E-mail," *CNN Cold War*, Episode 18. Available online at http://www.cnn.com/SPECIALS/cold.war/episodes/18/archive/. North also sarcastically noted that while "I only had to deal with our enemies, [Poindexter] has to deal with the cabinet."

89. Prados, 482, 483; Cannon, 596–97.

90. Shultz, 814, 828.

91. Shultz, 822.

92. Walsh, *Final Report of the Independent Counsel for Iran/Contra Matters*, Part I.

93. *The Tower Commission Report*, 51; Draper, 457–59.

94. *The Tower Commission Report*, 48; Draper, 399–402.

95. "Robert McFarlane, Subject: Current Events," 7 November 1986, from "Iran Contra: White House E-mail."

96. In a cable to Shultz in November 1985 Poindexter wrote, "I . . . remain convinced that we must remain absolutely close-mouthed" and recommended that they tell the media that "we are not going to comment on news reports and speculation" (Kornbluh and Byrne, 312–14). Shultz's response, "to save the Reagan presidency," was to "get policy on Iran and on antiterrorism back on track, into my hands and away from the NSC staff."

97. Walsh, *Final Report of the Independent Counsel for Iran/Contra Matters*, Part IV, chapter 1; Shultz, 818; Donald T. Regan, *For the Record: From Wall Street to Washington* (New York: St. Martin's Press, 1989), 26, 28, 30; Kornbluh, 313.

98. Walsh, *Final Report of the Independent Counsel for Iran/Contra Matters*, Part IV, chapter 2, 3; "Iran-Contra: White House E-mail."

99. Walsh, *Final Report of the Independent Counsel for Iran/Contra Matters*, Part IV, chapter 2; Draper, 506–507.

100. Walsh, *Final Report of the Independent Counsel for Iran/Contra Matters*, Part IV, chapter 1.

101. Walsh, *Final Report of the Independent Counsel for Iran/Contra Matters*, Part IV, chapter 1.

102. Draper, 505–23; Cannon, 691–704.

103. "Iran Contra," *The Reagan Information Page*, 4 March 1987. Available online at http://www.presidentreagan.info/speeches/iran_contra.cfm.

104. Former senior Reagan administration official, interview with the author.

105. Edwin Meese, interview with the author, 13 July 2004.

106. John Poindexter, interview with the author, 13 July 2004.

107. John Poindexter, interview with the author, 13 July 2004.
108. Former senior Reagan administration official, interview with the author.
109. *The Tower Commission Report*, 79.
110. Frank Carlucci, interview with the author, 19 May 2004.
111. Frank Carlucci, interview with the author, 19 May 2004.
112. Frank Carlucci, interview with the author, 19 May 2004.
113. Frank Carlucci, interview with the author, 19 May 2004.
114. Frank Carlucci, interview with the author, 19 May 2004.
115. Frank Carlucci, interview with the author, 19 May 2004.
116. Cannon, 733.
117. Shultz, *Turmoil and Triumph*, 903.
118. Colin Powell, interview with the author, 23 July 2004.
119. Frank Carlucci, interview with the author, 19 May 2004.
120. Colin Powell, interview with the author, 23 July 2004.
121. Colin Powell, interview with the author, 23 July 2004.
122. Kenneth Duberstein, interview with the author, 18 May 2004.
123. Eleven individuals were convicted, but two convictions were overturned on appeal. Two individuals were pardoned before trial, and one case was dismissed when the Bush administration declined to declassify information necessary for trial.
124. Lawrence Walsh, *Final Report of the Independent Counsel for Iran/Contra Matters*, "Summary of Prosecutions."
125. George Lardner Jr., "McKay Reports Four 'Probable' Meese Offenses," *Washington Post*, 19 July 1988.
126. Cannon, 794–802.

CHAPTER 9: Across a Bright Line in History

1. Brent Scowcroft, interview with the author, 25 August 2004.
2. Brent Scowcroft, interview with the author, 25 August 2004.
3. Brent Scowcroft, interview with the author, 25 August 2004.
4. Brent Scowcroft, interview with the author, 25 August 2004.
5. George Bush and Brent Scowcroft, *A World Transformed* (New York: Alfred A. Knopf, 1998), 36.
6. James A. Baker III, *The Politics of Diplomacy* (New York: G.P. Putnam's Sons, 1995), 21–22.
7. Senior Bush administration official, interview with the author.
8. Michael Beschloss and Strobe Talbott, *At the Highest Levels* (Boston: Little, Brown and Company, 1993), 26.
9. Brent Scowcroft, interview with the author, 25 August 2004.
10. Brent Scowcroft, interview with the author, 25 August 2004.
11. Brent Scowcroft, interview with the author, 25 August 2004.
12. Dennis Ross, interview with the author, 9 June 2004.
13. Dennis Ross, interview with the author, 9 June 2004.
14. Robert Gates, interview with the author, 4 June 2004.
15. Dennis Ross, interview with the author, 9 June 2004.
16. Robert Kimmitt, interview with the author, 16 August 2004.
17. Robert Gates, interview with the author, 4 June 2004.
18. Robert Kimmitt, interview with the author, 16 August 2004.

19. Robert Kimmitt, interview with the author, 16 August 2004.
20. Dennis Ross, interview with the author, 9 June 2004.
21. Robert Gates, interview with the author, 4 June 2004.
22. Senior Bush administration official, interview with the author.
23. Bush and Scowcroft, 33–34.
24. Condoleezza Rice, interview with the author, 4 August 2004.
25. Brent Scowcroft, interview with the author, 25 August 2004.
26. Brent Scowcroft, interview with the author, 25 August 2004.
27. Brent Scowcroft, interview with the author, 25 August 2004.
28. Beschloss, 24–25; Robert Gates, *From the Shadows: The Ultimate Insider's Story of Five Presidents and How They Won the Cold War* (New York: Touchstone, 1996), 460.
29. Brent Scowcroft, interview with the author, 25 August 2004.
30. Brent Scowcroft, interview with the author, 25 August 2004.
31. Richard Haass, interview with the author, 15 July 2004.
32. Dennis Ross, interview with the author, 9 June 2004.
33. Dennis Ross, interview with the author, 9 June 2004.
34. Dennis Ross, interview with the author, 9 June 2004.
35. Bush and Scowcroft, 40–41.
36. Robert Gates, interview with the author, 4 June 2004.
37. Kanter notes, in an interview with the author, 25 August 2004, "The name is also a familiar example of my failure of imagination. It was partly due to the fact that this group existed was, certainly in the beginning, very sensitive. And so the question was what do we put on our calendars, right? What do we call this? I don't know we can't call it this group or that group but we needed something to call it so I said, to my assistant, Let's just call it the Ungroup." The group would meet regularly in the White House Situation Room.
38. "Oral History Roundtables: Arms Control Policy and the National Security Council," the Brookings Institution and the Center for International and Security Studies at Maryland, 23 March 2000, 46. Available online at http://www.cissm.umd.edu/documents/armscontrol.pdf.
39. Dennis Ross recalled that "the president really didn't have an interest in knowing the details of the arms control agreement." See "Oral History Roundtables: The Bush Administration National Security Council," the Brookings Institution and the Center for International and Security Studies at Maryland, 29 April 1999, 8. Available online at http://www.cissm.umd.edu/documents/bush.pdf.
40. "Oral History Roundtables: The Bush Administration National Security Council," 8.
41. "Oral History Roundtables: Arms Control Policy and the National Security Council," 46–47.
42. "Oral History Roundtables: The Bush Administration National Security Council," 10.
43. Arnold Kanter, interview with the author, 25 August 2004.
44. "Oral History Roundtables: The Bush Administration National Security Council," 9.
45. Arnold Kanter, interview with the author, 25 August 2004.
46. Bush and Scowcroft, 12.
47. Beschloss and Talbott, 115–17, 127; Bush and Scowcroft, 12, 15–16, 46–47.
48. Baker, 117, 119.
49. Beschloss and Talbott, 181, 205.
50. "The Wall Comes Down," *CNN Cold War*. Available online at http://www.cnn.com/SPECIALS/cold.war/episodes/23/script.html.
51. "Oral History Roundtables: The Bush Administration National Security Council," 21.

52. Beschloss and Talbott, 85.
53. "The Wall Comes Down."
54. Bush and Scowcroft, 149.
55. Josef Joffe, "Putting Germany Back Together: The Fabulous Bush and Baker Boys," *Foreign Affairs* (January/February 1996). Available online at http://www.foreignaffairs.org/19960101fareviewessay4180/josef-joffe/putting-germany-back-together-the-fabulous-bush-and-baker-boys.html.
56. Bush and Scowcroft, 188.
57. Beschloss and Talbott, 136.
58. Baker, 197–98; Bush and Scowcroft, 188.
59. Michael Boll, "Superpower Diplomacy and German Unification: The Insiders' Views," *Parameters* (Winter 1996–97), 109–21. Available online at http://carlisle-www.army.mil/usawc/Parameters/96winter/boll.htm.
60. Baker, 198–99; Beschloss and Talbott, 184; Bush and Scowcroft, 188.
61. "Oral History Roundtables: The Bush Administration National Security Council," 14–15.
62. "Oral History Roundtables: The Bush Administration National Security Council," 15.
63. Baker, 252.
64. Burt resigned in the spring of 1991. See Beschloss and Talbott, 373.
65. The Reagan administration had first proposed a downloading provision in 1987 to enable the United States to meet START ceilings by converting the Minuteman III from a three-warhead to a single-warhead ICBM. Scowcroft saw the issue as one of overriding strategic importance and wanted to ensure that Soviet leaders in the future could not reload their missiles with warheads that had been removed under the terms of START.
66. Beschloss and Talbott, 403.
67. Beschloss and Talbott, 406.
68. Arnold Kanter, interview with the author, 25 August 2004.
69. Bush and Scowcroft, 141–43, 541–45; Beschloss and Talbott, 347, 360.
70. Baker, 523–26; Bush and Scowcroft, 543.
71. Beschloss and Talbott, 444. Eventually, the U.S. ambassador to the Soviet Union, Robert Strauss, complained to the State Department about the "Yeltsin bashing" coming from the White House.
72. NSC staffers began referring to Cheney as the "defensive secretary." See Beschloss and Talbott, 445.
73. Bush and Scowcroft, 544.
74. Robert Gates, interview with the author, 4 June 2004.
75. Beschloss and Talbott, 423–24.
76. Ann Devroy and R. Jeffrey Smith, "President Orders Sweeping Reductions in Strategic and Tactical Nuclear Arms," *Washington Post*, 28 September 1991; "Tactical Nuclear Arms Control: History," *Briefing Book on Tactical Nuclear Weapons* [available online at http://www.armscontrolcenter.org/prolifproject/tnw/chap4.pdf]; Baker, 658.
77. Gorbachev unilaterally announced that the Soviet Union would destroy all nuclear artillery ammunition, mines, and nuclear warheads of tactical nuclear missiles; remove all nuclear weapons from ships and multipurpose submarines; remove strategic bombers from standby alert and place their nuclear weapons in depot storage; remove 503 ICBMs from alert status; reduce Soviet armed forces by 700,000; and suspend nuclear tests for one year. See Fred Hiatt, "Gorbachev Pledges Wide-Ranging Nuclear Cuts," *Washington Post*, 6 October 1991.

78. "Oral History Roundtables: Arms Control Policy and the National Security Council,"
    48.
79. "Oral History Roundtables: The Bush Administration National Security Council," 27.
80. Robert Gates, interview with the author, 4 June 2004.
81. Baker, 659–60. The United States ratified the original START II agreement in January
    1996, but never ratified a 1997 protocol extending the treaty's implementation dead-
    line or the concurrently negotiated ABM Treaty succession, demarcation, and confi-
    dence-building agreements. On May 4, 2000, Russian President Vladimir Putin
    signed the resolution of ratification for START II, its extension protocol, and the
    1997 ABM-related agreements. However, Russia announced on June 14, 2002, a day
    after the United States withdrew from the Anti-Ballistic Missile (ABM) Treaty, that it
    would no longer be bound by its START II commitments. See Arms Control Associa-
    tion, "START II and Its Extension Protocol at a Glance," January 2003. Available
    online at http://www.armscontrol.org/factsheets/start2.asp.
82. Jason Ellis, "Nunn-Lugar's Mid-Life Crisis," *Survival* 39:1 (Spring 1997), 84; Amy
    Woolf, "Nunn-Lugar Cooperative Threat Reduction Programs: Issues for Congress,"
    Congressional Research Service, 23 March 2001. The latter is available online at http://
    www.fas.org/spp/starwars/crs/97–1027.pdf.
83. Ellis, 96.
84. Further hampering the utility of Nunn-Lugar was the expected confusion in the
    post-Soviet states as the bureaucracies in Russia and newly independent Belarus,
    Ukraine, and Kazakhstan tried to determine how to employ the funds. Ellis, 96.
85. Dennis Ross, interview with the author, 9 June 2004.
86. Condoleezza Rice, interview with the author, 4 August 2004.
87. Baker, *The Politics of Diplomacy*, 100.
88. Baker, 104–05; Bush and Scowcroft, 89, 97.
89. "Oral History Roundtables: The Nixon Administration National Security Council,"
    the Brookings Institution and the Center for International and Security Studies at
    Maryland, 8 December 1998, 22. Available online at http://www.cissm.umd.edu/doc-
    uments/nixon.pdf; Bush and Scowcroft, 98.
90. Bush and Scowcroft, 102.
91. Bush and Scowcroft, 104–05; Baker, 109–10; Patrick Tyler, *A Great Wall* (New York:
    PublicAffairs, 1999), 365.
92. Baker, 109.
93. Oral History Roundtables: The Nixon Administration National Security Council,"
    52; Mann, 209.
94. "Oral History Roundtables: China Policy and the National Security Council," the
    Brookings Institution and the Center for International and Security Studies at Mary-
    land, 4 November 1999, 22. Available online at http://www.cissm.umd.edu/documents
    /china.pdf.
95. Mann, 205–206.
96. "Oral History Roundtables: China Policy and the National Security Council," 21;
    Tyler, *A Great Wall*, 359.
97. Bush and Scowcroft, 105–10. Lilley shared Scowcroft's positive assessment, claiming
    that the "Chinese remembered the terrible savaging Bush took for them. And when it
    came time to collect the fee for that, he could do it. In my view, that was not a big pol-
    icy mistake, but all I'm saying is that we preserved the strategic relationship with
    China." See "Oral History Roundtables: China Policy and the National Security
    Council," 21.

98. Bush and Scowcroft, 174; Mann, 220–21.

99. Robert Suettinger, interview with the author, 28 April 2004.

100. "The Gulf War, Oral History: Brent Scowcroft," *Frontline*, 9 January 1996. Available online at http://www.pbs.org/wgbh/pages/frontline/gulf/oral/haass/1.html.

101. "The Gulf War, Oral History: Brent Scowcroft."

102. Samantha Power, *"A Problem from Hell": America and the Age of Genocide* (New York: Basic Books, 2002), 188.

103. David Ottoway, "U.S. Decries Iraqi Use Of Chemical Weapons," *Washington Post,* 24 March 1988.

104. William Arkin, "The Gulf War: Secret History," archived at *The Memory Hole,* http://www.thememoryhole.org/war/gulf-secret.htm.

105. Power, 233.

106. "The Gulf War, Oral History: Brent Scowcroft"; Bob Woodward, *The Commanders* (New York: Simon and Schuster, 1991), 223.

107. "The Gulf War, Oral History: Richard Haass," *Frontline*, 9 January 1996. Available online at http://www.pbs.org/wgbh/pages/frontline/gulf/oral/haass/1.html.

108. Baker, 273.

109. Lawrence Freedman and Efraim Karsh, *The Gulf Conflict, 1990–1991* (Princeton, NJ: Princeton University Press, 1993), 86; Woodward, *Commanders,* 223–24; "The Gulf War, Oral History: Brent Scowcroft."

110. Bush and Scowcroft, 314.

111. Freedman and Karsh, 74; Woodward, *Commanders,* 224–26.

112. Woodward, *Commanders,* 230–31, 235.

113. "The Gulf War, Oral History: Brent Scowcroft."

114. "The Gulf War, Oral History: Richard Haass."

115. Freedman and Karsh, 76; Woodward, *Commanders,* 237–38.

116. Woodward, *Commanders,* 242–44.

117. "The Gulf War, Oral History: Richard Haass."

118. "The Gulf War, Oral History: Brent Scowcroft."

119. "The Gulf War, Oral History: Brent Scowcroft."

120. Woodward, *Commanders,* 253.

121. "The Gulf War, Oral History: Brent Scowcroft."

122. Robert Kimmitt, interview with the author, 16 August 2004.

123. "Oral History Roundtables: The Bush Administration National Security Council," 32. See also Freedman and Karsh, 208.

124. "Oral History Roundtables: The Bush Administration National Security Council," 33.

125. Richard Haass, interview with the author, 15 July 2004.

126. Senior Bush administration official, interview with the author.

127. Interestingly, Baker's initial plan to travel to Baghdad to meet with the Iraqi leader (which ultimately never happened) was not revealed to Haass until after it had been agreed to by President Bush. Haass said it was "not my happiest day bureaucratically" and complained to Deputy National Security Advisor Gates, to whom he felt comfortable voicing his concerns about policy matters. "The Gulf War, Oral History: Richard Haass"; Woodward, *Commanders,* 335–37, 345, 353–54.

128. Iraqi Foreign Minister Tariq Aziz read the letter, but he did not accept the communication or deliver it to Saddam Hussein. "The Gulf War, Oral History: Richard Haass"; Woodward, *Commanders,* 362.

129. Haass recounts that Gates called him to attend the pivotal February 27 meeting at

the Oval Office about a half hour after it had begun and that "when I walked into the conversation, it was like walking into a movie halfway through. I was surprised that's what they all had decided." See "The Gulf War, Oral History: Richard Haass" and Freedman and Karsh, 405.

130. "The Gulf War, Oral History: Brent Scowcroft."
131. Freedman and Karsh, 413.
132. Robert Gates, interview with the author, 4 June 2004.
133. Colin Powell, interview with the author, 23 July 2004.

CHAPTER 10: The New, Improved Indispensable Nation

1. Fukuyama's 1992 book was based on his celebrated 1989 article in *The National Interest*, "The End of History?"
2. Warren Christopher, *Chances of a Lifetime* (New York: Scribner, 2001), 170. Rubin would characterize the invitation to join the administration as an "extraordinarily interesting [opportunity] to see what the world looked like from inside a White House . . . there was never any question about doing it." See "The Clinton Years: Interview with Robert Rubin," *Frontline*, 16 January 2001. Available online at http://www.pbs.org/wgbh/pages/frontline/shows/clinton/interviews/rubin.html.
3. Bill Clinton, *My Life* (New York: Alfred A. Knopf, 2004), 452.
4. Niccolo Machiavelli, *The Prince* (New York: Penguin, 1985), 51.
5. W. Bowman Cutter, interview with the author, 15 July 2004.
6. W. Bowman Cutter, interview with the author, 15 July 2004.
7. Christopher, 170.
8. Former senior White House official, interview with the author. Also see Bob Woodward, *The Agenda: Inside the Clinton White House* (New York: Simon and Schuster, 1994), 59.
9. Former senior White House official, interview with the author.
10. Clinton, 453; Dan Balz, "From Promise to Performance: Can Clinton Bring Discipline to Policy?" *Washington Post*, 17 January 1993.
11. Clinton, 457–458.
12. Richard Holbrooke, interview with the author, 15 July 2004.
13. Senior official, interview with the author.
14. "Remarks by the President at Portrait Unveiling of Secretary Warren Christopher," 30 March 1999. Available online at http://clinton4.nara.gov/WH/New/html/19990330-1371.html.
15. Leon Fuerth, interview with the author, 7 May 2004.
16. Leon Fuerth, interview with the author, 7 May 2004.
17. Thomas McLarty, interview with the author, 28 May 2004; Leon Panetta, interview with the author, 8 June 2004; John Podesta, interview with the author, 12 July 2004.
18. Samuel Berger, interview with the author, 28 May 2004.
19. Robert Rubin, interview with the author, 25 May 2004.
20. Robert Rubin, interview with the author, 25 May 2004.
21. Thomas McLarty, interview with the author, 28 May 2004.
22. Nancy Soderberg, interview with the author, 15 July 2004.
23. Robert Galluci, interview with the author, 26 May 2004.
24. Robert Gallucci, interview with the author, 26 May 2004.
25. George Stephanopoulos, interview with the author, 26 August 2004.

26. Anthony Lake, interview with the author, 30 June 2004.
27. Anthony Lake, interview with the author, 30 June 2004.
28. Anthony Lake, interview with the author, 30 June 2004.
29. Anthony Lake, interview with the author, 30 June 2004.
30. Madeleine Albright, interview with the author, 10 September 2004.
31. Colin Powell, interview with the author, 23 July 2004.
32. Madeleine Albright, interview with the author, 10 September 2004.
33. Madeleine Albright, *Madam Secretary: A Memoir* (New York: Hyperion, 2003), 182.
34. Samuel Berger, interview with the author, 28 May 2004.
35. Senior Clinton administration official, interview with the author.
36. Clinton, 489.
37. Nancy Soderberg, interview with the author, 15 July 2004.
38. R. James Woolsey, interview with the author, 6 July 2004.
39. R. James Woolsey, interview with the author, 6 July 2004.
40. R. James Woolsey, interview with the author, 6 July 2004.
41. R. James Woolsey, interview with the author, 6 July 2004.
42. Clinton, 504.
43. Strobe Talbott, interview with the author, 18 May 2004.
44. Clinton, 505.
45. Clinton, 543.
46. The 1996 replacement by the Israeli voters of Shimon Peres, one of the architects of Oslo, with Binyamin Netanyahu, a stauch opponent of the 1993 framework, did not curtail the efforts of Clinton and Secretary of State Albright to push the two sides to keep negotiating towards a permanent peace settlement. Secretary Albright relayed three separate messages (described by some as "ultimatums"), one public and two private, to force a recalcitrant Netanyahu to participate in the peace process. See Barton Gellman, "Ultimatums Were a U.S. Tool in Middle East Talks," *Washington Post*, 4 November 1998.
47. "Shattered Dreams of Peace: The Road from Oslo," *Frontline*, 17 June 2002. Available online at http://www.pbs.org/wgbh/pages/frontline/shows/oslo.
48. Clinton, 552.
49. Clinton, 553.
50. R. James Woolsey, interview with the author, 6 July 2004.
51. George Stephanopoulos, interview with the author, 26 August 2004.
52. Nancy Soderberg, interview with the author, 15 July 2004.
53. Leon Fuerth, interview with the author, 7 May 2004.
54. Ann Devroy and R. Jeffrey Smith, "Clinton Reexamines a Foreign Policy Under Siege," *Washington Post*, 17 October 1993.
55. Clinton, 593.
56. Power, 359.
57. Power, 366.
58. Former Clinton administration official, interview with the author.
59. Anthony Lake, interview with the author, 30 June 2004.
60. Robert Gallucci, interview with the author, 26 May 2004.
61. Conversation with the author.
62. Leon Fuerth, interview with the author, 7 May 2004.

CHAPTER 11: The Beginning of the End of the End of History

1. Samuel Berger, interview with the author, 28 May 2004.
2. Senior Clinton administration official, interview with the author.
3. Senior Clinton administration official, interview with the author.
4. Samuel Berger, interview with the author, 28 May 2004.
5. W. Bowman Cutter, interview with the author, 15 July 2004.
6. W. Bowman Cutter, interview with the author, 15 July 2004.
7. Clay Chandler, "For Treasury's Self-Assured Summers, a Senate Test Looms," *Washington Post*, 21 July 1995.
8. Clinton Treasury Department official, interview with the author.
9. Lake, a foreign policy advisor to Bill Clinton during the campaign, had helped to craft that phrase. Patrick Tyler, *A Great Wall* (New York: PublicAffairs, 1999), 29, 386; David Lampton, *Same Bed, Different Dreams: Managing U.S.-China Relations, 1989–2000* (Berkeley: University of California Press, 2001), 32–33.
10. "Oral History Roundtables: China Policy and the National Security Council," the Brookings Institution and the Center for International and Security Studies at Maryland, 4 November 1999, 28. Available online at http://www.cissm.umd.edu/documents/china.pdf.
11. Suettinger, 159.
12. "Oral History Roundtables: China Policy and the National Security Council," 31.
13. Charlene Barshefsky, interview with the author, 30 July 2004.
14. James Mann, *About Face: A History of America's Curious Relationship with China, from Nixon to Clinton* (New York: Knopf, 1999), 279–82; Tyler, *A Great Wall*, 393–94; Lampton, 34.
15. "Oral History Roundtables: China Policy and the National Security Council," 29.
16. "Oral History Roundtables: China Policy and the National Security Council," 28.
17. For a complete text of the executive order, see *Federal Register*, 58:103, 1 June 1993. Available online at http://www.archives.gov/federal_register/executive_orders/pdf/12850.pdf.
18. Lampton, 40–41.
19. Suettinger, 178; Lampton, 42.
20. Warren Christopher recounts his difficult 1994 trip in his memoirs, *Chances of a Lifetime* (New York: Scribner, 2001), 236–39, and "My Trip to Beijing Was Necessary," *Washington Post*, 22 March 1994. Also see Daniel Williams, "Chinese Rebuff Christopher on Human Rights," *Washington Post*, 13 March 1994; Jim Hoagland, "Battered in Beijing," *Washington Post*, 15 March 1994.
21. Robert Suettinger, *Beyond Tiananmen: The Politics of U.S.-China Relations, 1989–2000* (Washington, DC: Brookings Institution Press, 2003), 191–92. Lord has a harsher view of the role of these agencies, stating, "Whatever you thought of modest conditions on MFN with China, . . . any chance we had of moving the Chinese on human rights enough so that we could continue MFN without reversing our policy was lost by the economic agencies undercutting the policy and the President's not disciplining them." See "Oral History Roundtables: The Nixon Administration National Security Council," the Brookings Institution and the Center for International and Security Studies at Maryland, 8 December 1998, 57. Available online at http://www.cissm.umd.edu/documents/nixon.pdf.
22. "Oral History Roundtables: China Policy and the National Security Council," 31.

23. Suettinger, 192–93; "Oral History Roundtables: China Policy and the National Security Council," 36.

24. Michael Weisskopf, "Backbone of the New China Lobby: U.S. Firms," *Washington Post*, 14 June 1993; Jim Mann, "Executives Press Clinton to Smooth U.S.-China Ties," *Los Angeles Times*, 19 November 1993.

25. Christopher, 241–42; Hobart Rowen, "Administration in Disarray on China Trade Policy," *Washington Post*, 20 March 1994; Daniel Williams, "Christopher Cites Progress on Human Rights in China," *Washington Post*, 24 May 1994.

26. "Press Conference of the President," 26 May 1994. Available online at http://clinton6. nara.gov/1994/05/1994–05–26-president-in-press-conference-on-china-mfn-status. html.

27. "Press Conference of the President"; see also Lampton, 45; Myers, 46.

28. "Oral History Roundtables: China Policy and the National Security Council," 40.

29. Myers, 54.

30. "Oral History Roundtables: China Policy and the National Security Council," 29.

31. Former Clinton administration official, interview with the author.

32. Tyler, 414–15.

33. Jim Mann, "How Taipei Outwitted U.S. Policy When Washington Denied It Recognition," *Los Angeles Times*, 8 June 1995.

34. "Oral History Roundtables: China Policy and the National Security Council," 35. Ambassador Roy also objected to the State Department policy, saying that, "My position was the opposite. I wanted to hold the line on cabinet visits because it was quite logical. In addition, I didn't think we could block a Lee Teng-hui visit. I thought it was foolish for us to put ourselves in a position of trying to hold the line on a [later] visit by Lee Teng-hui to his old alma mater. I saw that as a loser. . . . I did something I've never done before. I weighed in from Beijing and said, 'I thought we could be more permissive in the handling of the Lee Teng-hui stopover.' And normally when you're sitting in Beijing you keep your fingers out of the Taiwan issue. But I was so upset by the domestic consequences of the way it was being handled that I actually sent in a cable and said, 'Hey, I think you guys can relax a bit on this.'" See "Oral History Roundtables: China Policy and the National Security Council," 38.

35. "Oral History Roundtables: China Policy and the National Security Council," 39.

36. "Oral History Roundtables: China Policy and the National Security Council," 34–35.

37. Christopher, 243–44.

38. "Oral History Roundtables: China Policy and the National Security Council," 41–42.

39. Steven Greenhouse, "Aides to Clinton Say He Will Defy Beijing and Issue Visa to Taiwan's President," *New York Times*, 22 May 1995.

40. "Oral History Roundtables: China Policy and the National Security Council," 41. One senior State Department official referred to this as the "Christopher Doctrine," defined as "I'm not going to China but no one else is either." See Barton Gellman, "U.S. and China Nearly Came to Blows in '96," *Washington Post*, 21 June 1998.

41. Suettinger, 247.

42. R. Jeffrey Smith and Ann Devroy, "U.S. Seeks Closer Ties with China," *Washington Post*, 21 February 1996; Barton Gellman, "Reappraisal Led to New China Policy," *Washington Post*, 22 June 1998.

43. "The Clinton Years: Interview, Tony Lake," *Frontline*, 16 January 2001. Available online at http://www.pbs.org/wgbh/pages/frontline/shows/clinton/interviews/lake. html. See also Gellman, "U.S. and China Nearly Came to Blows in '96."

44. "The Clinton Years: Interview, Tony Lake"; "The Clinton Years: Interview, Sandy

Berger," *Frontline*, 16 January 2001. Available online at http://www.pbs.org/wgbh/pages/frontline/shows/clinton/interviews/berger.html. John O'Neil, "U.S. Sending More Ships to Taiwan Area in Warning to China," *New York Times*, 11 March 1996; Patrick Tyler, "China Warns U.S. to Stay Out of Taiwan Feud," *New York Times*, 12 March 1996.

45. Mann, 349–51; Nancy Gibbs et al., "Cash-and-Carry Diplomacy," *Time*, 24 February 1997, 22; Suettinger, 234–35. Lake recounted the role of the NSC in checking the background of donors with foreign origins, noting that it was a new and unique responsibility for his group: "I'm not aware that any national security adviser before or since got deeply into the questions of who enters the White House or who doesn't. Not only am I not aware of it, I've worked previously in the NSC. I'm convinced that was never the case. The way the process works is that [the donors] are going to be invited. If they have foreign connections, it goes through the staff secretariat right to our staff people, who would not do an independent investigation of these people, but instead would go to the agencies and say, 'Hey, have you got anything on these people?' If they had anything, then they would convey it back. So they did their job wonderfully, our staff people. And I can't criticize any of them. They did, in effect, blow a whistle. But, since we didn't have this larger context, it was never the kind of issue in which somebody was saying, 'Hey, wait a minute. They're going to make a big mistake here.' The issue comes up to me, and I would have to weigh in with the chief of staff or anybody else. I can't remember any of these cases ever working their way up that way because we were doing our job." He also described the congressional reaction to the affair as "hysterical." See "The Clinton Years: Interview, Tony Lake."

46. Lawrence Summers, interview with the author, 7 July 2004.

47. Lawrence Summers, interview with the author, 7 July 2004.

48. Thomas McLarty, interview with the author, 28 May 2004.

49. Robert Rubin, interview with the author, 25 May 2004.

50. Robert Rubin, interview with the author, 25 May 2004.

51. David Lipton, interview with the author, 6 May 2004.

52. Senior Clinton Treasury Department official, interview with the author.

53. Robert Rubin, interview with the author, 25 May 2004.

54. Senior Clinton Treasury Department official, interview with the author.

55. Richard Holbrooke, *To End a War* (New York: Random House, 1998), 21.

56. "The Clinton Years: Interview, Tony Lake."

57. Ivo Daalder, *Getting to Dayton* (Washington, DC: Brookings Institution Press, 1999), 8.

58. "The Clinton Years: Interview, Tony Lake."

59. Nancy Soderberg, interview with the author, 15 July 2004.

60. Bob Woodward, *The Choice* (New York: Simon and Schuster, 1996), 254; Daalder, 17.

61. Elizabeth Drew, *On the Edge: The Clinton Presidency* (New York: Simon and Schuster, 1994), 160–61, 273–74; Douglas Jehl with Elaine Sciolino, "Conflict in the Balkans: The President," *New York Times*, 24 April 1994; Ruth Marcus, "Anthony Lake's Secretive Mission," *Washington Post*, 20 December 1993; "The Clinton Years: Interview, Tony Lake."

62. "Oral History Roundtables: The Clinton Administration National Security Council," the Brookings Institution and the Center for International and Security Studies at Maryland, 27 September 2000, 31. Available online at http://www.cissm.umd.edu/documents/clinton.pdf.

63. Drew, 152, 283; George Stephanopoulos, *All Too Human* (Boston: Little, Brown and

Co., 1999), 380–83; Woodward, 204; "The Clinton Years: Interview, Tony Lake." Thomas Lippman and Ann Devroy, "Clinton's Policy Evolution: June Decision Led to Diplomatic Gambles," *Washington Post*, 11 September 1995.

64. Woodward, 253.

65. John Kornblum, interview with the author, 24 May 2004.

66. Drew, 152, 280; Daalder, 54.

67. Drew, 143–44, 285; Ruth Marcus and John Harris, "Behind U.S. Policy Shift on Bosnia: Strains in NATO," *Washington Post*, 5 December 1994.

68. It did not help that Lake's briefings on Bosnia and other foreign policy issues often took place early in the day and the president was not considered to be a morning person. "The Clinton Years: Interview, Tony Lake"; Anthony Lake, *Six Nightmares* (Boston: Little, Brown and Co., 2001), 143–44; David Halberstam, *War in a Time of Peace: Bush, Clinton, and the Generals* (New York: Scribner, 2002), 290.

69. Halberstam, 286.

70. Richard Holbrooke, interview with the author, 15 July 2004.

71. Daalder, 86.

72. Halberstam, 286.

73. Daalder, 85; Warren Christopher, *In the Stream of History* (Stanford: Stanford University Press, 1998), 349; Woodward, 259; Lippman and Devroy, "Clinton's Policy Evolution: June Decision Led to Diplomatic Gambles."

74. Woodward, 258; "Give War a Chance: Interview, Ivo Daalder," *Frontline*, 11 May 1999. Available online at http://www.pbs.org/wgbh/pages/frontline/shows/military/etc/daalder.html.

75. "Give War a Chance: Interview, Ivo Daalder."

76. "Give War a Chance: Interview, Ivo Daalder."

77. Woodward, 261.

78. "Give War a Chance: Interview, Ivo Daalder."

79. Lake, 146.

80. Woodward, 265–66; Lake, 147–49; Daalder, 106–11.

81. John Kornblum, interview with the author, 24 May 2004.

82. Roger Cohen, "Taming the Bullies of Bosnia," *New York Times Magazine*, 17 December 1995, 58.

83. Cohen, "Taming the Bullies of Bosnia."

84. Senior State Department official, interview with the author.

85. Cohen, "Taming the Bullies of Bosnia."

86. Richard Holbrooke, interview with the author, 15 July 2004.

87. John Kornblum, interview with the author, 24 May 2004.

88. John Kornblum, interview with the author, 24 May 2004.

89. David Lipton, interview with the author, 6 May 2004.

90. Senior Clinton administration official, interview with the author.

91. Christopher, *In the Stream of History*, 349.

92. Holbrooke, 170–71.

93. Holbrooke, 251–60.

94. Richard Holbrooke, interview with the author, 15 July 2004.

95. Holbrooke, 74.

96. Richard Holbrooke, interview with the author, 15 July 2004.

97. The agreement created a new constitution, a new parliament, and a constitutional court; provided for democratic elections; and established a central bank as well as transportation, utilities, and postal bodies. Other provisions guaranteed refugees the

right to return home safely and to receive compensation for lost property, established commissions to protect human rights and national monuments, and created a UN International Police Task Force to monitor and train local law enforcement organizations. A foreign official was charged with overseeing economic reconstruction, aid, and the "civilian" aspects of the ambitious settlement.

98. Jim Mokhiber and Rick Young, "Nation Building in Bosnia," *Frontline*, 11 May 1999. Available online at http://www.pbs.org/wgbh/pages/frontline/shows/military/etc/peace.html.

99. "A Short History of Kosovo." Available online at http://lamar.colostate.edu/~grjan/kosovohistory.html.

100. John Harris, "As Clinton Adviser, Berger Combines Stagecraft with Statecraft," *Washington Post*, 7 July 1997; Frank Ahrens, "The Reluctant Warrior," *Washington Post*, 24 February 1998; John Harris, "Berger's Caution Has Shaped Role of U.S. in War," *Washington Post*, 16 May 1999; Steven Erlanger, "Grading the Secretary: Albright, a Bold Voice Abroad, Finds Her Role Limited at Home," *New York Times*, 1 September 1998.

101. Ahrens, "The Reluctant Warrior." Marcus, "Anthony Lake's Secretive Mission"; Harris, "As Clinton Adviser, Berger Combines Stagecraft with Statecraft."

102. Harris, "Berger's Caution Has Shaped Role of U.S. in War"; "Oral History Roundtables: The Clinton Administration National Security Council," 37.

103. Samuel Berger, interview with the author, 28 May 2004.

104. Barton Gellman, "The Path to Crisis: How the United States and Its Allies Went to War," *Washington Post*, 18 April 1999; "War in Europe: Interview, Richard Holbrooke," *Frontline*, 22 February 2000. Available online at http://www.pbs.org/wgbh/pages/frontline/shows/kosovo/interviews/holbrooke.html.

105. Elaine Sciolino and Ethan Bronner, "Crisis in the Balkans: The Road to War; How a President, Distracted by Scandal, Entered Balkan War," *New York Times*, 18 April 1999.

106. Gellman, "The Path to Crisis."

107. Sciolino and Bronner, "Crisis in the Balkans: The Road to War."

108. Sciolino and Bronner, "Crisis in the Balkans: The Road to War."

109. "The Clinton Years: Interview, Sandy Berger."

110. "The Clinton Years: Interview, Madeleine Albright," *Frontline*, 16 January 2001. Available online at http://www.pbs.org/wgbh/pages/frontline/shows/clinton/interviews/albright.html.

111. "Operation Desert Fox," *GlobalSecurity.org*. Available online at http://www.globalsecurity.org/military/ops/desert_fox.htm.

112. "The Clinton Years: Interview, John Podesta," *Frontline*, 16 January 2001. Available online at http://www.pbs.org/wgbh/pages/frontline/shows/clinton/interviews/podesta2.html.

113. John Podesta, interview with the author, 12 July 2004.

114. Gellman, "The Path to Crisis"; Sciolino and Bronner, "Crisis in the Balkans: The Road to War."

115. Harris, "Berger's Caution Has Shaped Role of U.S. in War."

116. Barton Gellman, "Slaughter in Racak Changed Kosovo Policy," *Washington Post*, 18 April 1999.

117. Gellman, "The Path to Crisis."

118. Alexandra Niksic, "International Observer Blames Serb Troops for Racak Massacre," *Agence France-Press*, 11 April 2002. Available online at http://www.unmikonline.org/press/2002/wire/apr/imm120402PM.htm.

119. Gellman, "The Path to Crisis"; Sciolino and Bronner, "Crisis in the Balkans: The Road to War."

120. Gellman, "The Path to Crisis."

121. Richard Holbrooke, interview with the author, 15 July 2004.

122. Richard Holbrooke, interview with the author, 15 July 2004.

123. Ivo Daalder and Michael O'Hanlon, *Winning Ugly: NATO's War to Save Kosovo* (Washington, DC: Brookings Institution Press, 2000), 81–82.

124. Daalder and O'Hanlon, 83–84.

125. Richard Holbrooke, interview with the author, 15 July 2004.

126. Sciolino and Bronner, "Crisis in the Balkans: The Road to War."

127. Wesley Clark, interview with the author, 8 July 2004.

128. Halberstam, 465.

129. Steven Lee Myers and Eric Schmitt, "Crisis in the Balkans: The Leadership," *New York Times*, 30 May 1999.

130. Myers and Schmitt, "Crisis in the Balkans: The Leadership."

131. Lois Romano, "A Hero to Some: To Others Headstrong," *Washington Post*, 19 October 2003.

132. Romano, "A Hero to Some: To Others Headstrong."

133. Wesley Clark, interview with the author, 8 July 2004.

134. Halberstam, 469.

135. Halberstam, 476.

136. Halberstam, 478–79; Romano, "A Hero to Some: To Others Headstrong."

137. Samuel Berger, interview with the author, 28 May 2004.

138. "Oral History Roundtables: The Clinton Administration National Security Council," 19.

139. Steve Coll, *Ghost Wars* (New York: Penguin Books, 2004), 253.

140. Barton Gellman, "Struggles Inside the Government Defined Campaign," *Washington Post*, 20 December 2001.

141. Gellman, "Struggles Inside the Government Defined Campaign"; Roberto Suro and Dana Priest, "Plan to Overhaul Anti-Terrorism Strategy Would Boost NSC's Role," *Washington Post*, 24 March 1998; Tim Weiner, "The Man Who Protects America from Terrorism," *New York Times*, 1 February 1999; Ellie Laipson, "While America Slept: Understanding Terrorism and Counterterrorism," *Foreign Affairs* (January/February 2003); Daniel Benjamin and Steven Simon, *The Sacred Age of Terror* (New York: Random House, 2002), 230–31.

142. Michael Dobbs, "An Obscure Chief in U.S. War on Terror," *Washington Post*, 2 April 2000; "Clinton's Secret War," *The Guardian*, 20 January 2002.

143. Dobbs, "An Obscure Chief in U.S. War on Terror"; Benjamin and Simon, 232; Lake, *Six Nightmares*, 56–57. Estimates from the OMB showed an increase on aggregate spending on terrorism from $5.7 billion in fiscal year 1996 to $11.1 billion in 2001, according to Gelman, "An Obscure Chief in U.S. War on Terror."

144. Gellman, "An Obscure Chief in U.S. War on Terror"; Michael Elliott, "Could 9/11 Have Been Prevented?"; Weiner, "The Man Who Protects America from Terrorism"; Benjamin and Simon, 233; Suro and Priest, "Plan to Overhaul Anti-terrorism Strategy Would Boost NSC's Role."

145. Benjamin and Simon, 230, 243.

146. "Oral History Roundtables: The Clinton Administration National Security Council," 51.

147. Elizabeth Becker and Tim Weiner, "Homeland Security: New Office to Become a

White House Agency," *New York Times*, 28 September 2001. Also see Steve Coll, "Policy Disputes over Hunt Paralyzed Clinton's Aides," *Washington Post*, 22 February 2004; Benjamin and Simon, 263, 270, 292, 295, 296, 303–304; David Johnston and Thom Shanker, "Threats and Responses: Terrorist Bombing," *New York Times*, 1 October 2002.

148. Richard Clarke, *Against All Enemies* (New York: Free Press, 2004); "Clinton's Secret War."

149. "Clinton's Secret War."

150. Richard Clarke, interview with the author, 11 May 2004.

151. Benjamin and Simon, 295; "Clinton's Secret War."

152. "Clinton's Secret War"; Barton Gellman, "Broad Effort Launched after '98 Attacks," *Washington Post*, 19 December 2001.

153. Dobbs, "An Obscure Chief in U.S. War on Terror"; Clarke, 205.

154. Richard Clarke, interview with the author, 11 May 2004.

155. Clarke, 211–13; Lawrence Wright, "The Counter-Terrorist," *New Yorker*, 14 January 2002, 50; Benjamin and Simon, 311–12.

156. Benjamin and Simon, 323–23; Clarke, 223.

157. "Overview of the Enemy," *National Commission on Terrorist Attacks upon the United States*, Staff Statement 15, 16 June 2004, 8. Available online at http://www.9-11commission.gov/staff_statements/staff_statement_15.pdf.

158. "The Man Who Knew: Interview, Richard A. Clarke," *Frontline*, 3 October 2002. Available online at http://www.pbs.org/wgbh/pages/frontline/shows/knew/. See also Benjamin and Simon, 323–24; James Risen, "Question of Evidence: To Bomb Sudan Plan or Not: A Year Later, Debates Rankle," *New York Times*, 27 October 1998; Barton Gellman, "A Strategy's Cautious Evolution," *Washington Post*, 20 January 2002. "Clinton's Loss," *National Review Online*, 11 September 2003. Available online at http://www.nationalreview.com/interrogatory/interrogatory091103b.asp.

159. Clarke, 224.

160. Elliott, "Could 9/11 Have Been Prevented?"; Benjamin and Simon, 327–28.

161. Gellman, "A Strategy's Cautious Evolution."

CHAPTER 12: A Thumb on the Scales

1. Of course, they might well be surprised that after the halting start their system got off to, it is not only thriving but also forms the institutional heart of the most powerful government in history, that their words and ideas continue to shape the behavior of the committee in charge of running the world.

2. Condoleezza Rice, interview with the author, 4 August 2004.

3. Condoleezza Rice, interview with the author, 4 August 2004.

4. Condoleezza Rice, interview with the author, 4 August 2004.

5. Elisabeth Bumiller, "President Steals Away to Baghdad in a Surprise Visit to American GI's," *International Herald Tribune*, 1 December 2003.

6. Condoleezza Rice, interview with the author, 4 August 2004.

7. Condoleezza Rice, interview with the author, 4 August 2004.

8. James Mann, *Rise of the Vulcans* (New York: Viking, 2004), 249–53.

9. Condoleezza Rice, interview with the author, 4 August 2004.

10. Brent Scowcroft, interview with the author, 25 August 2004.

11. "President's Remarks at Traverse City, Michigan Rally," 16 August 2004. Available online at http://www.whitehouse.gov/news/releases/2004/08/20040816-4.html.

12. Bush family friend, interview with the author.

13. Brent Scowcroft, interview with the author, 25 August 2004.

14. Brent Scowcroft, interview with the author, 25 August 2004.

15. James Schlesinger, interview with the author, 24 September 2004.

16. Mann, 26, citing Leo Strauss, *The Rebirth of Classical Political Rationalism: An Introduction to the Thought of Leo Strauss* (Chicago: University of Chicago Press, 1989), xxv.

17. Seymour Hersh, "Selective Intelligence," *The New Yorker*, 12 May 2003. Available online at http://www.newyorker.com/fact/content/?030512fa_fact.

18. Richard Haass, interview with the author, 15 July 2004.

19. Colin Powell, interview with the author, 23 July 2004.

20. Brent Scowcroft, interview with the author, 25 August 2004.

21. National Security Presidential Directive 1, "Organization of the National Security Council System," 13 February 2001. Available online at http://www.fas.org/irp/off-docs/nspd/nspd-1.htm.

22. Senior Bush administration official, interview with the author.

23. Jack Pritchard, interview with the author, 2 June 2004.

24. Richard Clarke, interview with the author, 11 May 2004.

25. Condoleezza Rice, interview with the author, 4 August 2004.

26. Karen DeYoung and Steven Mufson, "A Leaner and Less Visible NSC: Reorganization Will Emphasize Defense, Global Economics," *Washington Post*, 10 February 2001.

27. Condoleezza Rice, interview with the author, 4 August 2004.

28. Condoleezza Rice, interview with the author, 4 August 2004.

29. Brent Scowcroft, interview with the author, 25 August 2004.

30. Bush administration officials, interviews with the author.

31. Bush administration official, interview with the author.

32. Condoleezza Rice, interview with the author, 4 August 2004.

33. Antony Blinken, interview with the author, 4 June 2004.

34. Anonymous source, interview with the author.

35. Senior Bush administration official, interview with the author.

36. Richard Haass, interview with the author, 15 July 2004.

37. Richard Haass, interview with the author, 15 July 2004.

38. Colin Powell, interview with the author, 23 July 2004.

39. Mark Grossman, interview with the author, 24 August 2004.

40. Mark Grossman, interview with the author, 24 August 2004.

41. Former senior State Department official, interview with the author.

42. Senior State Department official, interview with the author.

43. Senior State Department official, interview with the author.

44. Senior State Department official, interview with the author.

45. Senior official, interview with the author.

46. Official, interview with the author.

47. Franklin Foer and Spencer Ackerman, "The Radical," *The New Republic*, 1 December 2003.

48. Senior official, interview with the author.

49. Senior official, interview with the author.

50. Former George H.W. Bush administration official, interview with the author.

51. Senior official, interview with the author.

52. Senior official, interview with the author.
53. I should add that I used to be partners with Jerry Bremer when I was at Kissinger Associates and I know him very well. For that reason, when he was appointed administrator in Iraq, I immediately concluded that the stories saying that he was given the job as a concession to State Department interests were inaccurate.
54. Dave Moniz, "Rumsfeld's Abrasive Style Sparks Conflict with Military Command," *USA Today*, 10 December 2002.
55. William Perry, interview with the author, 18 August 2004.
56. Joseph Prueher, interview with the author, 20 May 2004.
57. Joseph Prueher, interview with the author, 20 May 2004.
58. Joseph Prueher, interview with the author, 20 May 2004.
59. Joseph Prueher, interview with the author, 20 May 2004.
60. Former Senior Defense Department official, interview with the author.
61. Steven Mufson, "U.S. Taiwan Policy Hits New Level of Ambiguity," *Washington Post*, 27 April 2001.
62. Claudia Rosett, "NSC Pushing Shift of Policy on Taiwan," *New York Sun*, 3 December 2003; William Kristol and Gary Schmitt, "A Dangerous New Policy toward Taiwan," *Weekly Standard*, 2 December 2003. The Taiwan Relations Act, passed in the wake of the full normalization of relations with China (and subsequent downgrading of relations with Taipei) in 1979, says that American arms sales to Taiwan will be determined by the president and Congress "based solely on their perception of the needs of Taiwan" and not the demands of China.
63. Bush administration official, interview with the author.
64. Bush administration official, interview with the author.
65. Former senior Bush administration official, interview with the author.
66. Former senior Bush administration official, interview with the author.
67. Senior Bush administration official, interview with the author.
68. Wesley Clark, interview with the author, 8 July 2004.
69. Jane Perlez, "Directive Says Rice, Bush Aide, Won't Be Upstaged by Cheney," *New York Times*, 16 February 2001; John Prados, "The Pros from Dover," *Bulletin of the Atomic Scientists* 60:1 (January/February 2004), 44–51.
70. Colin Powell, interview with the author, 23 July 2004.
71. Condoleezza Rice, interview with the author, 4 August 2004.
72. Richard Haass, interview with the author, 15 July 2004.
73. Mark Hosenball, Michael Isikoff, and Evan Thomas, "Cheney's Long Path to War," *Newsweek*, 17 November 2003, 34–40.
74. "Dick Cheney: GOP's Most Dogged Warrior," *MSNBC*, 1 September 2004. Available online at http://www.msnbc.msn.com/id/5762300/.
75. Former senior NSC official, interview with the author.
76. Susan Page and Barbara Slavin, "Cheney Rewrites Roles in Foreign Policy," *USA Today*, 29 July 2002.
77. Jim Lobe, "Does Cheney Hold the Reins?" *Inter Press Service*, 22 October 2003.
78. The eleven signatories who worked in the administration of George H.W. Bush are: William Bennett, Richard Cheney, Eliot Cohen, Paula Dobriansky, Francis Fukuyama, Zalmay Khalilzad, I. Lewis Libby, Dan Quayle, Peter Rodman, Henry Rowen, and Paul Wolfowitz.
79. James Carney and John Dickerson, "'Big Time' Punches In," *Time*, 12 February 2001, 56; Nicholas Lemann, "The Quiet Man: Dick Cheney's Discreet Rise to Unprecedented Power," *New Yorker*, 7 May 2001; Nancy Gibbs, "Double-Edged Sword," *Time.com*, 23

December 2002. Available online at http://archives.cnn.com/2002/ALLPOLITICS/
12/23/timep.partners.tm/.

80. Jane Mayer, "Contract Sport," *New Yorker*, 16–23 February 2004. Available online at
http://www.newyorker.com/fact/content/?040216fa_fact.

81. Nell Henderson, "A More Frequent Visitor," *Washington Post*, 27 May 2004.

82. Dana Milbank, "Cheney Authorized Shooting Down Planes," *Washington Post*, 18
June 2004.

83. Bob Woodward, *Plan of Attack* (New York: Simon and Schuster, 2004), 391–92.

84. Glenn Kessler and Peter Slevin, "Rice Fails to Repair Rifts, Officials Say," *Washington
Post*, 12 October 2003.

85. Eric Edelman, interview with the author, 7 June 2004.

86. Eric Edelman, interview with the author, 7 June 2004.

87. Senior Republican official, interview with the author.

88. Brent Scowcroft, interview with the author, 25 August 2004.

89. Daniel Benjamin and Steven Simon, *The Age of Sacred Terror: Radical Islam's War
Against America* (New York: Random House, 2002), 328; Elliott, "Could 9/11 Have
Been Prevented?"; Gellman, "A Strategy's Cautious Evolution."

90. Benjamin and Simon, 334; Gellman, "A Strategy's Cautious Evolution."

91. Steve Coll, *Ghost Wars* (New York: Penguin Press, 2004), 228.

92. Elisabeth Bumiller, "Afghan Adviser: The Country's in His Blood," *New York Times*,
28 October 2001.

93. Scowcroft also says that "there is no question she can do it." See Barbara Slavin,
"Rice Called a Good Fit for Foreign Policy Post," *USA Today*, 18 December 2000.
During the 2000 campaign, Bush appeared be unaware about the Taliban in
response to an interviewer's question, only recognizing the name of Afghanistan's
ruling regime after being provided with a hint. See James Traub, "The Bush Years:
W's World," *New York Times Magazine*, 14 January 2001, 28.

94. Steven Mufson, "Overhaul of National Security Apparatus Urged: Commission
Cites U.S. Vulnerability," *Washington Post*, 1 February 2001; DeYoung and Mufson,
"A Leaner and Less Visible NSC: Reorganization Will Emphasize Defense, Global
Economics"; Richard Clarke, *Against All Enemies: Inside America's War on Terror*
(New York: Free Press, 2004), 230. Additionally, the counterterrorism czar would no
longer have power to review budgets with the assistant director of OMB nor have
two NSC senior directors working on terrorism issues.

95. Lawrence Kaplan, "Containment," *The New Republic*, 5 February 2001.

96. Clarke, 231–34; Elliott, "Could 9/11 Have Been Prevented?"

97. Lawrence Wright, "The Counter-Terrorist"; *New Yorker*, 14 January 2002. Benjamin
and Simon, 340–42; Julian Borger, "Interview: Richard Clarke," *Guardian* (London), 23 March 2004. Clarke, 235–36.

98. Woodward, *Plan of Attack*, 1, 13, 15, 21–22.

99. "Bush Administration's First Memo on al-Qaeda Declassified," National Security Archive, 10 February 2005. Available online at http://www.gwu.edu/~nsarchiv/NSAEBB
/NSAEBB147/.

100. Gellman, "A Strategy's Cautious Evolution"; Ted Bridlis, "Top Security Advisers Met
Just Twice on Terrorism before Sept. 11 Attacks," *Detroit News*, 29 June 2002.

101. Bob Woodward, *Bush at War* (New York: Simon and Schuster, 2002), 36, 62; Ben-
jamin and Simon, 339; Elliott, "Could 9/11 Have Been Prevented?"; Benjamin and
Simon, 343–46. There is no mention of plans from Richard Clarke or Clinton-era
NSC director for transnational threats William Wechsler to target terrorist financ-

516   NOTES TO PAGES 430–432

ing in Ron Suskind's collaborative book about O'Neill, *The Price of Loyalty* (New York: Simon and Schuster, 2004). The only pre–September 11 discussion of terrorist financing is a brief note on pp. 180–81, without any specific mention of al Qaeda.

102. Clarke, 2.

103. Steven Mufson, "Attacks Were an Act of War—But Who's the Enemy?" *Washington Post*, 11 September 2001.

104. Clarke recounts that day in chapter 1 of *Against All Enemies*.

105. Borger, "Interview: Richard Clarke."

106. Woodward, *Bush at War*, 27–33.

107. Mike Allen and Alan Sipress, "Attacks Refocus White House on How to Fight Terrorism," *Washington Post*, 26 September 2001. CIA Director George Tenet and White House Chief of Staff Andrew Card attended most of these NSC meetings, and the treasury and transportation secretaries would sometimes appear as well.

108. Bumiller, "Afghan Adviser: The Country's in His Blood"; David E. Sanger and Patrick E. Tyler, "Foreign Policy Team: Wartime Forges a United Front for Bush Aides," *New York Times*, 23 December 2001; Kaplan, "Containment"; Jacob Weisberg, "Bush's Favorite Afghan," *Slate*, 5 October 2001; "Bush Names Afghan-Born Adviser as His Special Envoy to Afghanistan," *Associated Press*, 31 December 2001.

109. Bumiller, "Afghan Adviser: The Country's in His Blood."

110. Woodward, *Bush at War*, 136, 195.

111. Jane Perlez, "Capitol Hawks Seek Tougher Line on Iraq," *New York Times*, 5 March 2001; Jane Perlez, "Allies Bomb Iraqi Air Defenses in Biggest Attack in 6 Months," *New York Times*, 11 August 2001.

112. Jane Perlez, "Bush Team's Counsel Is Divided on Foreign Policy," *New York Times*, 27 March 2001; Dana Milbank, "Who's Pulling the Foreign Policy Strings?" *Washington Post*, 14 May 2002; James Gerstenzang, "Bush Answers GOP Foes of a War on Iraq," *Los Angeles Times*, 17 August 2002.

113. Doyle McManus, "National Security Council: From the Start, Bush Plan Was to Use the Big Stick," *Los Angeles Times*, 9 October 2001; Robin Wright and Doyle McManus, "Military Options: Bush Camp Split on Anti-terror Policy," *Los Angeles Times*, 21 September 2001; Allen and Sipress, "Attacks Refocus White House on How to Fight Terrorism."

114. Woodward, *Bush at War*, 137.

115. Bob Woodward and Dan Balz, "At Camp David, Advise and Dissent," *Washington Post*, 31 January 2002; Woodward, *Bush at War*, 84–85.

116. Seymour Hersh, "The Other War," *New Yorker*, 12 April 2004; Clarke, 241–42; Allen and Sipress, "Attacks Refocus White House on How to Fight Terrorism"; McManus, "National Security Council: From the Start, Bush Plan Was to Use the Big Stick."

117. Clarke, 32. In October, keeping to a timetable he had agreed on with Rice in June, Clarke left his counterterrorism post to focus on cyber-terrorism and left the administration in 2003. While Clarke's relationship with President Bush was said to be warm, the White House was not terribly upset to see him leave in 2003, as "Clarke's bulldozing style did not fit as well with the quiet consensus that the White House looks for now." Clarke also did not enjoy good relations with Chief of Staff Andrew Card and several other top Bush aides. See Barton Gellman, "Anti-terror Pioneer Turns in the Badge," *Washington Post*, 13 March 2003.

118. Borger, "Interview: Richard Clarke."

119. Kenneth Walsh, "In the Eye of the Storm," *U.S. News and World Report*, 5 April 2004.

James Fallows, "Blind into Baghdad," *Atlantic Monthly* (January/February 2004); Woodward, *Plan of Attack*, 1.

120. Barton Gellman and Walter Pincus, "Depiction of Threat Outgrew Supporting Evidence," *Washington Post*, 10 August 2003; Woodward, *Plan of Attack*, 172.

121. Keven Whitelaw, Thomas Omestad, and Mark Mazzetti, "After the Fall," *U.S. News and World Report*, 2 December 2002, 133:21, 18; Woodward, *Plan of Attack*, 321–322. Also, "Pre-war Planning for Post-war Iraq," undated. Available online at http://defenselink.mil/policy/isa/nesa/postwar_iraq.html.

122. Bob Woodward, "With CIA Push, Movement to War Accelerated," *Washington Post*, 19 April 2004.

123. James Risen, David E. Sanger, and Thom Shanker, "Weapons Intelligence: In Sketchy Data, Trying to Gauge Iraq Threat," *New York Times*, 20 July 2003; Kessler and Slevin, "Rice Fails to Repair Rifts, Officials Say."

124. Dana Priest and Karen DeYoung, "CIA Questioned Documents Linking Iraq, Uranium Ore," *Washington Post*, 22 March 2003; David Sanger, "The Speech: A Shifting Spotlight on Uranium Sales," *New York Times*, 15 July 2003; David Sanger with Judith Miller, "Intelligence: National Security Aide Says He's to Blame for Speech Error," *New York Times*, 22 July 2003.

125. Greg Miller, "Spy Unit Skirted CIA on Iraq," *Los Angeles Times*, 10 March 2004; Dana Priest, "Pentagon Shadow Loses Some Mystique," *Washington Post*, 13 March 2004.

126. In the case of an October 2002 speech, Hadley did agree to delete a reference about Niger. Priest and DeYoung, "CIA Questioned Documents Linking Iraq, Uranium Ore"; Sanger, "The Speech: A Shifting Spotlight on Uranium Sales."

127. Dana Milbank and Dana Priest, "Warning in Iraq Report Unread: Bush, Rice Did Not See State's Objections," *Washington Post*, 19 July 2003; Risen, Sanger, and Shanker, "Weapons Intelligence"; Dana Milbank and Mike Allen, "Iraq Flap Shakes Rice's Image," *Washington Post*, 27 July 2003.

128. Maura Reynolds, "White House Admits CIA Warned It before Speech," *Los Angeles Times*, 23 July 2003; Sanger and Miller, "Intelligence: National Security Aide Says He's to Blame for Speech Error"; Sanger, "The Speech: A Shifting Spotlight on Uranium Sales."

129. Richard Leiby and Walter Pincus, "Retired Envoy: Nuclear Report Ignored," *Washington Post*, 6 July 2003; Douglas Jehl, "Weapons Intelligence: Iraq Arms Critic Reacts to Report on Wife," *New York Times*, 8 August 2003.

130. Kessler and Slevin, "Rice Fails to Repair Rifts, Officials Say."

131. "The Iraq Wars," *News Hour with Jim Lehrer*, 9 October 2003; David Sanger, "White House to Overhaul Iraq and Afghan Missions," *New York Times*, 6 October 2003.

132. Sanger, "White House to Overhaul Iraq and Afghan Missions."

133. "Who's Who," *Washington Monthly*, 1 November 2003, 11:35, 12; Sanger, "White House to Overhaul Iraq and Afghan Missions"; Doyle McManus and Sonni Efron, "In Iraq Debate, Bremer Comes Out a Winner," *Los Angeles Times*, 23 November 2003; "Change without Substance," *Stratfor*, 10 October 2003.

134. In a testy exchange with reporters, the defense secretary said, "I happened not to know that Rice was going to write a memo. I said I don't know. Isn't that clear?" See "The Iraq Wars"; Maureen Dowd, "Is Condi Gaslighting Rummy?" *New York Times*, 9 October 2003.

135. "Change without Substance."

136. Pamela Hess, "U.S. Must Embrace 'Nation Building,'" *UPI*, 18 March 2004; Dana Mil-

bank, "Stabilization Is Its Middle Name," *Washington Post*, 18 May 2004. Similarly, according to James Fallows's ("Blind into Baghdad") critique of the Bush administration's postwar planning, "The other conspicuously absent figure was Condoleezza Rice, even after she was supposedly put in charge of coordinating administration policy on Iraq, last October."

137. Blake Diamond and John Diamond, "Pressure at Iraqi Prison Detailed," *USA Today*, 17 June 2004; R. Jeffrey Smith, "Bush Adviser Toured Abu Ghraib"; *Washington Post*, 19 June 2004.

138. Diamond and Diamond, "Pressure at Iraqi Prison Detailed."

139. Smith, "Bush Adviser Toured Abu Ghraib"; Diamond and Diamond, "Pressure at Iraqi Prison Detailed." Townsend reported that she spent about fifteen minutes in the detention areas at Abu Ghraib.

140. Seymour Hersh, "The Debate Within," *New Yorker*, 11 March 2002; "Taming the Octopus," *Economist*, 25 September 2003; Kessler and Slevin, "Rice Fails to Repair Rifts"; Woodward, *Plan of Attack*, 414–15.

141. Andrew Rice, "Brent Scowcroft Calls Iraq War 'Overreaction'", *New York Observer*, 4 September 2004.

CHAPTER 13: U.S. Foreign Policy in the Age of Ambiguity

1. Edward Rice, "General Charles Napier and the Conquest of Sind," *The Victorian Web*. Available online at http://www.victorianweb.org/history/empire/napier.html.

2. Rice, "General Charles Napier and the Conquest of Sind."

3. Rice, "General Charles Napier and the Conquest of Sind."

4. Rice, "General Charles Napier and the Conquest of Sind." I would like to note here that while Kissinger was probably the wittiest national security advisor, the champion punster of the twenty who have served thus far is undoubtedly Anthony Lake, who regularly made his staff cringe with wordplay that was both brilliant and ghastly at the same time.

5. The experts themselves were former high-ranking government officials, well-respected academic experts, residents of leading think tanks, former military officers, and senior experts working in the private sector. We discussed with each which countries or entities (including supranational entities like the EU and nonstate actors like al Qaeda) would be most important to the United States in the near term and in the medium to long term as allies or as adversaries. Participants were free to name as many countries or entities as they wished. Specifically, they were asked to identify those countries most likely to be U.S. allies or potential collaborators during the next five years and those most likely to be U.S. adversaries or rivals during the next twenty years. The objective was to focus on potential affinities and potential tensions and to identify which countries would simply be most important to the United States during this new era.

6. Dominic Wilson and Roopa Purushothaman, *Dreaming with BRICs: The Path to 2050*, Global Economics Paper No. 99, 1 October 2003. Available online at http://www.gs.com/insight/research/reports/99.pdf.

7. Defense Science Board, *Transition to and from Hostilities*, December 2004, 143. Available online at http://www.acq.osd.mil/dsb/reports/2004-12-DSB_SS_Report_Final.pdf.

8. *Transition to and from Hostilities*, 143.

9. Carl Weiser, "In Most Congressional Districts, It's No Contest," *USA Today*, 10 October 2004. Available online at http://www.usatoday.com/news/politicselections/nation/ushouse/2004-10-10-no-contest_x.htm.
10. John Hamre, interview with the author, 9 July 2004.
11. John Hamre, interview with the author, 9 July 2004.
12. Antony Blinken, interview with the author, 4 June 2004.
13. Frank Ahrens, "The Reluctant Warrior," *Washington Post*, 24 February 1998.
14. Anecdote related by Yale School of Management Dean Jeffrey Garten.
15. Quoted in Linus Pauling, "Nobel Prize Acceptance Speech," 11 December 1963. Available online at http://www.illuminingtalks.org/academic/linus_pauling/nobel_prize_acceptance_speech.
16. Zbigniew Brzezinski, *The Choice: Global Domination and Global Leadership* (New York: Basic Books, 2004), 28.
17. David Rothkopf, "Whatever Capitalism's Fate, Somebody's Already Working on an Alternative," *Washington Post*, 20 January 2002.

Bibliography

BOOKS

Acheson, Dean. *Present at the Creation: My Years in the State Department*. New York: W.W. Norton and Co., 1969.

Albright, Madeleine. *Madam Secretary: A Memoir*. New York: Hyperion, 2003.

Allison, Graham. *Essence of Decision: Explaining the Cuban Missile Crisis*. New York: Pearson Education, 1999.

Allison, Graham, and Gregory Treverton. *Rethinking America's Security: Beyond Cold War to New World Order*. New York: W.W. Norton and Co., 1992.

Ambrose, Stephen. *Eisenhower: Soldier and President*. New York: Touchstone, 1991.

Ambrose, Stephen, and Douglas Brinkley. *Rise to Globalism: American Foreign Policy since 1938*. New York: Penguin Books, 1997.

Baker, James A., III. *The Politics of Diplomacy*. New York: G.P. Putnam's Sons, 1995.

Ball, Desmond, and Jeffrey Richelson, eds. *Strategic Nuclear Targeting*. Ithaca, NY: Cornell University Press, 1989.

Ball, George. *The Past Has Another Pattern*. New York: W.W. Norton and Co., 1982.

Benjamin, Daniel, and Steven Simon. *The Age of Sacred Terror: Radical Islam's War Against America*. New York: Random House, 2002.

Berman, Larry. *Lyndon Johnson's War: The Road to Stalemate in Vietnam*. New York: W.W. Norton and Co., 1989.

Berman, Larry. *No Peace, No Honor*. New York: Touchstone, 2001.

Beschloss, Michael. *The Conquerors: Roosevelt, Truman, and the Destruction of Hitler's Germany, 1941–1945*. New York: Simon & Schuster, 2002.

Beschloss, Michael. *The Crisis Years: Kennedy v. Khrushchev, 1960–1963*. New York: Edward Burlingame Books, 1991.

Beschloss, Michael, and Strobe Talbott. *At the Highest Levels*. Boston: Little, Brown and Co., 1993.

Best, Richard, Jr. *The National Security Council: An Organizational Assessment*. Huntington, NY: Nova Science Publishers, 2001.

Bill, James A. *The Eagle and the Lion: the Tragedy of American-Iranian Relations*. New Haven, CT: Yale University Press, 1988.

Bird, Kai. *The Color of Truth*. New York: Touchstone, 1998.

Blacker, Coit. *Reluctant Warriors: The United States, the Soviet Union, and Arms Control*. New York: W.H. Freeman and Co., 1987.

Blustein, Paul. *The Chastening: Inside the Crisis That Rocked the Global Financial System and Humbled the IMF*. New York: PublicAffairs, 2003.

Bobbitt, Philip. *The Shield of Achilles: War, Peace, and the Course of History*. New York: Knopf, 2002.

Bohlen, Charles. *Witness to History, 1929–1969*. New York: W.W. Norton and Co., 1973.

Bohn, Michael. *Nerve Center: Inside the White House Situation Room*. Dulles, VA: Brassey's, 2003.

Bowden, Mark. *Black Hawk Down*. New York: Signet, 1999.

Bowie, Robert, and Richard Immerman. *Waging Peace: How Eisenhower Shaped an Enduring Cold War Strategy*. New York: Oxford Press, 1998.

Brugioni, Dino. *Eyeball to Eyeball*. New York: Random House, 1990.

Brzezinski, Zbigniew. *Between Two Ages: America's Role in the Technetronic Era*. New York: Viking, 1976.

Brzezinski, Zbigniew. *The Choice: Global Domination and Global Leadership*. New York: Basic Books, 2004.

Brzezinski, Zbigniew. *The Grand Chessboard: American Primacy and Its Geostrategic Imperatives*. New York: Basic Books, 1997.

Brzezinski, Zbigniew. *Power and Principle: Memoirs of the National Security Advisor, 1977–1981*. New York: Farrar, Straus and Giroux, 1983.

Brzezinski, Zbigniew, and Brent Scowcroft. *Differentiated Containment: U.S. Policy toward Iran and Iraq*. New York: Council on Foreign Relations Press, 1997.

Bundy, McGeorge. *Danger and Survival*. New York: Random House, 1988.

Bundy, McGeorge, William Crowe, and Sidney Drell. *Reducing Nuclear Danger*. New York: Council on Foreign Relations Press, 1993.

Burr, William. *The Kissinger Transcripts: The Top Secret Talks with Beijing and Moscow*. New York: The New Press, 1999.

Bush, George, and Brent Scowcroft. *A World Transformed*. New York: Alfred A. Knopf, 1998.

Cannon, Lou. *President Reagan: The Role of a Lifetime*. New York: Simon & Schuster, 1991.

Carlucci, Frank, Robert Hunter, and Zalmay Khalilzad. *Taking Charge: A Bipartisan Report to the President-Elect on Foreign Policy and National Security*. Santa Monica, CA: RAND, 2001.

Caro, Robert. *Master of the Senate: The Years of Lyndon Johnson*. New York: Alfred A. Knopf, 2002.

Caro, Robert. *Means of Ascent: The Years of Lyndon Johnson*. New York: Alfred A. Knopf, 1990.

Caro, Robert. *The Path to Power: The Years of Lyndon Johnson*. New York: Alfred A. Knopf, 1982.

Carter, Jimmy. *The Blood of Abraham*. Fayetteville, AK: University of Arkansas Press, 1993.

Carter, Jimmy. *Keeping Faith*. New York: Bantam Books, 1984.

Christopher, Warren. *Chances of a Lifetime*. New York: Scribner, 2001.

Christopher, Warren. *In the Stream of History*. Stanford, CA: Stanford University Press, 1998.

Christopher, Warren, et al. *American Hostages in Iran: The Conduct of a Crisis*. New Haven, CT: Yale University Press, 1985.

Clark, Wesley. *Waging Modern War: Bosnia, Kosovo, and the Future of Combat*. New York: PublicAffairs, 2001.

Clarke, Richard. *Against All Enemies*. New York: Free Press, 2004.

Clifford, Clark, with Richard Holbrooke. *Counsel to the President: A Memoir*. New York: Random House, 1991.

Clinton, Bill. *My Life*. New York: Alfred A. Knopf, 2004.

Coll, Steve. *Ghost Wars*. New York: Penguin Press, 2004.

Crabb, Cecil, and Kevin Mulcahy. *American National Security: A Presidential Perspective*. Pacific Grove, CA: Brooks/Cole Publishing Company, 1990.

Daalder, Ivo. *Getting to Dayton*. Washington, DC: Brookings Institution Press, 1999.

Daalder, Ivo, and James Lindsey. *American Unbound: The Bush Revolution in Foreign Policy*. Washington, DC: Brookings Institution Press, 2000.

Daalder, Ivo, and Michael O'Hanlon. *Winning Ugly: NATO's War to Save Kosovo*. Washington, DC: Brookings Institution Press, 2003.

Dallek, Robert. *Franklin D. Roosevelt and American Foreign Policy, 1932–1945*. New York: Oxford University Press, 1979.

Destler, I.M., Leslie Gelb, and Anthony Lake. *Our Own Worst Enemy: The Unmaking of U.S. Foreign Policy*. New York: Simon & Schuster, 1984.

Dobrynin, Anatoly. *In Confidence: Moscow's Ambassador to American's Six Cold War Presidents (1962–1986)*. New York: Crown, 1995.

Dorward, Jeffrey. *Eberstadt and Forrestal: A National Security Partnership, 1909–1949*. College Station, TX: Texas A&M Press, 1991.

Doyle, William. *Inside the Oval Office: The White House Tapes from FDR to Clinton*. New York: Kodansha America, 1999.

Draper, Theodore. *A Very Thin Line: The Iran-Contra Affairs*. New York: Hill and Wang, 1991.

Drew, Elizabeth. *On the Edge: The Clinton Presidency*. New York: Simon & Schuster, 1994.

Dunn, David H. *The Politics of Threat: Minuteman Vulnerability in American National Security Policy*. New York: St. Martin's Press, 1997.

Ellis, Joseph. *Founding Brothers: The Revolutionary Generation*. New York: Vintage, 2002.

Evans, Richard. *Deng Xiaoping and the Making of Modern China*. New York: Penguin Books, 1997.

Farber, David. *Taken Hostage: The Iran Hostage Crisis and America's First Encounter with Radical Islam*. Princeton, NJ: Princeton University Press, 2004.

Felix, Antonia. *The Condoleezza Rice Story*. New York: Newmarket Press, 2002.

Fitzgerald, Frances. *Way Out There in the Blue*. New York: Simon & Schuster, 2000.

Ford, Gerald. *A Time to Heal*. New York: Harper & Row Publishers, 1979.

Freedman, Lawrence. *The Evolution of Nuclear Strategy*. London: International Institute for Strategic Studies, 1981.

Freedman, Lawrence. *Kennedy's Wars: Berlin, Cuba, Laos, and Vietnam*. New York: Oxford University Press, 2002.

Freedman, Lawrence, and Efraim Karsh. *The Gulf Conflict, 1990–1991*. Princeton, NJ: Princeton University Press, 1993.

Friedman, Alan. *Spider's Web: The Secret History of How the White House Illegally Armed Iraq*. New York: Bantam Books, 1993.

Friedman, Thomas L. *The Lexus and the Olive Tree*. New York: Farrar, Straus and Giroux, 1999.

Garthoff, Raymond. *Détente and Confrontation: American-Soviet Relations from Nixon to Reagan,* revised edition. Washington, DC: Brookings Institution Press, 1994.

Gates, Robert. *From the Shadows: The Ultimate Insider's Story of Five Presidents and How They Won the Cold War*. New York: Touchstone, 1996.

Gertz, Bill. *Betrayal*. Washington, DC: Regnery Publishing, 1999.

Gorbachev, Mikhail. *Memoirs*. New York: Doubleday, 1995.

Gray, Colin. *Strategic Studies and Public Policy: The American Experience*. Lexington: University Press of Kentucky, 1982.

Haig, Alexander. *Caveat: Realism, Reagan, and Foreign Policy*. New York: Macmillan, 1984.

Halberstam, David. *The Best and the Brightest*. New York: Ballantine Books, 1993.

Halberstam, David. *War in a Time of Peace: Bush, Clinton, and the Generals*. New York: Scribner, 2002.

Haldeman, H.R. *The Haldeman Diaries*. New York: G.P. Putnam's Sons, 1994.

Hargrove, Erwin. *Jimmy Carter as President: Leadership and the Politics of the Public Good*. Baton Rouge, LA: Louisiana State University Press, 1988.

Hartmann, Frederick. *Naval Renaissance*. Annapolis, MD: Naval Institute Press, 1990.

Hartmann, Frederick, and Robert Wendzel. *Defending America's Security*. Washington, DC: Pergamon-Brassey's International Defense Publishers, 1988.

Higgins, Trumbull. *The Perfect Failure: Kennedy, Eisenhower, and the CIA at the Bay of Pigs*. New York: W.W. Norton and Co., 1987.

Hirsch, John, and Robert Oakley. *Somalia and Operation Restore Hope: Reflections on Peacemaking and Peacekeeping*. Washington, DC: United States Institute of Peace Press, 1995.

Hitchens, Christopher. *The Trial of Henry Kissinger*. New York: Verso, 2001.

Hogan, Michael J. *A Cross of Iron: Harry S. Truman and the Origins of the National Security State, 1945–1954*. New York: Cambridge University Press, 2000.

Holbrooke, Richard. *To End a War*. New York: Random House, 1998.

Holden, Robert, and Eric Zolov. *Latin America and the United States: A Documentary History*. New York: Oxford University Press, 2000.

Holdridge, John. *Crossing the Divide*. Lanham, MD: Rowman and Littlefield, 1997.

Hyland, William. *Mortal Rivals*. New York: Random House, 1987.

Inderfurth, Karl F., and Loch K. Johnson, eds. *Fateful Decisions: Inside the National Security Council*. New York: Oxford University Press, 2004.

Isaacson, Walter. *Kissinger: A Biography*. New York: Simon & Schuster, 1992.

Isaacson, Walter, and Evan Thomas. *The Wise Men: Six Friends and the World They Made*. New York: Simon & Schuster, 1986.

Johnson, Chalmers. *Blowback: The Costs and Consequences of American Empire*. New York: Metropolitan Books, 2000.

Johnson, Chalmers. *The Sorrows of Empire: Militarism, Secrecy, and the End of the Republic*. New York: Metropolitan Books, 2004.

Jordan, Hamilton. *Crisis: The Last Year of the Carter Presidency*. New York: Putnam, 1982.

Kaplan, Fred. *Wizards of Armageddon*. New York: Simon & Schuster, 1983.

Kaplan, Robert. *Warrior Politics: Why Leadership Demands a Pagan Ethos*. New York: Vintage, 2003.

Kapuscinski, Ryszard. *The Emperor*. New York: Vintage, 1989.

Kennan, George. *Memoirs: 1925–1950*. New York: Little, Brown and Co., 1967.

Kennedy, John. *The Strategy of Peace*. New York: Harper, 1960.

Kennedy, Robert. *Thirteen Days*. New York: W.W. Norton and Co., 1999.

Khadduri, Majid, and Edmund Ghareeb. *War in the Gulf, 1990–1991*. New York: Oxford University Press, 1997.

Kissinger, Henry. *Crisis: The Anatomy of Two Major Foreign Policy Crises*. New York: Simon & Schuster, 2003.

Kissinger, Henry. *Diplomacy*. New York: Simon & Schuster, 1994.

Kissinger, Henry. *White House Years*. Boston: Little, Brown and Co., 1979.

Kissinger, Henry. *Years of Renewal*. New York: Little, Brown and Co., 1998.

Kissinger, Henry. *Years of Upheaval*. New York: Little, Brown and Co., 1982.

Kornbluh, Peter, and Malcolm Byrne, *The Iran-Contra Scandal: The Declassified History*. New York: New Press, 1993.

Krepinevich, Andrew F. *The Army and Vietnam*. Baltimore: Johns Hopkins University Press, 1986.

Krepon, Michael. *Arms Control in the Reagan Administration*. Lanham, MD: University Press of America, 1989.

Krock, Arthur. *Memoirs: Sixty Years on the Firing Line*. New York: Funk & Wagnalls, 1968.

Lake, Anthony. *Six Nightmares*. Boston: Little, Brown and Co., 2001.

Lampton, David. *Same Bed, Different Dreams: Managing U.S.-China Relations, 1989–2000*. Berkeley: University of California Press, 2001.

Larson, Deborah Welch. *Origins of Containment*. Princeton, NJ: Princeton University Press, 1985.

Ledeen, Michael. *Perilous Statecraft*. New York: Scribner, 1988.

Ledeen, Michael, and William Lewis. *Debacle: The American Failure in Iran*. New York: Alfred A. Knopf, 1981.

Leffler, Melvyn. *A Preponderance of Power: National Security, the Truman Administration, and the Cold War*. Stanford, CA: Stanford University Press, 1992.

Lord, Carnes. *The Presidency and the Management of National Security*. New York: Free Press, 1988.

Machiavelli, Niccolo. *The Prince*. New York: Penguin, 1985.

Mann, James. *About Face*. New York: Knopf, 1999.

Mann, James. *Rise of the Vulcans*. New York: Viking, 2004.

Marton, Kati. *Hidden Power: Presidential Marriages That Shaped Our History*. New York: Anchor Books, 2002.

Matthews, Christopher. *Kennedy and Nixon: The Rivalry That Shaped Postwar America*. New York: Touchstone, 1997.

May, Ernest, and Philip Zelikow. *The Kennedy Tapes: Inside the White House during the Cuban Missile Crisis*. Cambridge, MA: Belknap Press, 1998.

May, Nathaniel. *Oval Office: Stories of President in Crisis from Washington to Bush*. New York: Thunder's Mouth Press, 2002.

McCullough, David. *Truman*. New York: Simon & Schuster, 1992.

McDermott, Rose. *Risk Taking in International Politics*. Ann Arbor: University of Michigan Press, 1998.

McFarlane, Robert, with Zofia Smardz. *Special Trust*. New York: Cadell & Davies, 1994.

Meese, Edwin, III. *With Reagan: The Inside Story*. Washington, DC: Regnery Publishing, 1992.

Menges, Constantine. *Inside the National Security Council*. New York: Simon & Schuster, 1988.

Millis, Walter, ed. *The Forrestal Diaries*. New York: Viking, 1951.

Moise, Edwin. *The Tonkin Gulf and the Escalation of the Vietnam War*. Chapel Hill: University of North Carolina Press, 1996.

Morgan, Iwan. *Nixon*. New York: Oxford University Press, 2002.

Mueller, John. *War, Presidents, and Public Opinion*. New York: John Wiley and Sons, 1973.

Naftali, Timothy, and Philip Zelikow, eds. *The Presidential Recordings: John F. Kennedy: The Great Crises*, Vol. 2. New York: W.W. Norton, 2001.

Newmann, William. *Managing National Security Policy: The President and the Process*. Pittsburgh: University of Pittsburgh Press, 2003.

The 9/11 Report: The National Commission on Terrorist Attacks Upon the United States. New York: St. Martin's Paperbacks, 2004.

Nitze, Paul, with Steven Rearden and Ann Smith. *From Hiroshima to Glasnost: At the Center of Decision*. New York: Grove Press, 1989.

Nixon, Richard. *The Memoirs of Richard Nixon*. New York: Simon & Schuster, 1990.

Nixon, Richard. *U.S. Foreign Policy for the 1970s: A New Strategy for Peace*. Washington, DC: Government Printing Office, 1970.

North, Oliver. *Under Fire: An American Story*. New York: HarperCollins, 1991.

Nye, Joseph. *Soft Power: The Means to Success in World Politics*. New York: PublicAffairs, 2004.

Oberdorfer, Don. *The Turn: From the Cold War to a New Era*. New York: Touchstone, 1991.

Oberdorfer, Don. *The Two Koreas: A Contemporary History*. New York: Basic Books, 1997.

Odom, William, and Robert Dujarric. *America's Inadvertent Empire*. New Haven, CT: Yale University Press, 2004.

Oren, Michael. *Six Days of War: June 1967 and the Making of the Modern Middle East*. New York: Presidio Press, 2003.

Patterson, Bradley H., Jr. *The White House Staff: Inside the West Wing and Beyond*. Washington, DC: Brookings Institution Press, 2002.

Phillips, Kevin. *American Dynasty: Aristocracy, Fortune, and the Politics of Deceit in the House of Bush*. New York: Viking, 2004.

Posner, Gerald. *Why America Slept: The Failure to Prevent 9/11*. New York: Random House, 2003.

Powell, Colin, with Joseph Persico. *My American Journey*. New York: Ballantine Books, 1996.

Power, Samantha. *A Problem from Hell: America and the Age of Genocide*. New York: Basic Books, 2002.

Prados, John. *Keeper of the Keys*. New York: Morrow, 1991.

Quandt, William. *Camp David: Peacemaking and Politics*. Washington, DC: Brookings Institution Press, 1986.

Quandt, William. *Decade of Decisions*. Berkeley: University of California Press, 1977.

Reagan, Ronald. *An American Life*. New York: Pocket Books, 1990.

Reeves, Richard. *President Kennedy: Profile of Power*. New York: Simon & Schuster, 1993.

Reeves, Richard. *President Nixon: Alone in the White House*. New York: Touchstone, 2001.

Regan, Donald T. *For the Record: From Wall Street to Washington*. New York: St. Martin's Press, 1989.

Rostow, W.W. *The U.S. in the World Arena*. New York: Clarion, 1960.

Rubin, Barry. *Paved with Good Intentions*. New York: Oxford University Press, 1980.

Rubin, Robert, and Jacob Weisberg. *In an Uncertain World: Tough Choices from Wall Street to Washington*. New York: Random House, 2003.

Schlesinger, Arthur. *A Thousand Days: John F. Kennedy in the White House*. Boston: Houghton Mifflin, 1965.

Schlesinger, Stephen. *Act of Creation: The Founding of the United Nations*. Boulder, CO: Westview Press, 2003.

Schwarzkopf, H. Norman. *It Doesn't Take a Hero*. New York: Bantam Books, 1993.

Secord, Richard, with Jay Wurts. *Honored and Betrayed*. New York: John Wiley and Sons, 1992.

Shoemaker, Christopher. *The NSC Staff: Counseling the Council*. Boulder, CO: Westview Press, 1991.

Shultz, George P. *Turmoil and Triumph: My Years as Secretary of State*. New York: Scribner, 1993.

Sick, Gary. *All Fall Down*. New York: Random House, 1985.

Sick, Gary. *October Surprise*. New York: Times Books, 1991.

Sifry, Micah, and Christopher Cerf. *The Iraq War Reader*. New York: Touchstone, 2003.

Skinner, Kiron, Annelise Anderson, and Martin Anderson, eds. *Reagan, In His Own Hand: The Writings of Ronald Reagan That Reveal His Revolutionary Vision for America*. New York: Free Press, 2001.

Soros, George. *The Bubble of American Supremacy*. New York: PublicAffairs, 2004.

Stein, Kenneth. *Heroic Diplomacy*. New York: Routledge, 1999.

Stephanopoulos, George. *All Too Human*. Boston, MA: Little, Brown and Co., 1999.

Stern, Jessica. *Terror in the Name of God: Why Religious Militants Kill*. New York: Ecco, 2003.

Stern, Sheldon. *Averting "The Final Failure": John F. Kennedy and the Secret Cuban Missile Crisis Meetings*. Stanford, CA: Stanford University Press, 2003.

Strauss, Leo. *The Rebirth of Classical Political Rationalism: An Introduction to the Thought of Leo Strauss*. Chicago: University of Chicago Press, 1989.

Strober, Deborah, and Gerald Strober. *The Reagan Presidency: An Oral History of the Era*. Dulles, VA: Brassey's, 2003.

Suettinger, Robert. *Beyond Tiananmen: The Politics of U.S.-China Relations, 1989–2000*. Washington, DC: Brookings Institution Press, 2003.

Sullivan, William H. *Mission to Iran*. New York: W.W. Norton and Co., 1981.

Suskind, Ron. *The Price of Loyalty*. New York: Simon & Schuster, 2004.

Swift, Jonathan. *Gulliver's Travels*. New York: Signet Books, 1999.

Szulc, Tad. *The Illusion of Peace*. New York: Viking, 1978.

Talbott, Strobe. *Deadly Gambit*. New York: Vintage, 1985.

Talbott, Strobe. *The Master of the Game*. New York: Alfred A. Knopf, 1988.

Terriff, Terry. *The Nixon Administration and the Making of U.S. Nuclear Strategy*. Ithaca, NY: Cornell University Press, 1995.

Thomas, Evan. *The Very Best Men*. New York: Touchstone, 1995.

Thornton, Richard. *The Nixon-Kissinger Years: The Reshaping of American Foreign Policy*. St. Paul, MN: Paragon House Publishers, 2001.

The Tower Commission Report: The Full Text of the President's Special Review Board. New York: Times Books, 1987.

Truman, Harry S. *Memoirs by Harry S. Truman*, Vol. 1: *Year of Decisions*. Garden City, NY: Doubleday and Co., 1955.

Truman, Harry S. *Memoirs by Harry S. Truman*, Vol. 2: *Years of Trial and Hope*. Garden City, NY: Doubleday and Co., 1956.

Turner, Stansfield. *Terrorism and Democracy*. Boston: Houghton Mifflin, 1991.

Tyler, Patrick. *A Great Wall*. New York: PublicAffairs, 1999.

Vance, Cyrus R. *Hard Choices: Critical Years in America's Foreign Policy*. New York: Simon & Schuster, 1983.

VanDeMark, Brian. *Into the Quagmire: Lyndon Johnson and the Escalation of the Vietnam War*. New York: Oxford University Press, 1995.

Walsh, Lawrence. *Final Report of the Independent Counsel for Iran/Contra Matters*, 4 August 1993.

Walsh, Lawrence. *Firewall: The Iran-Contra Conspiracy and Cover-Up*. New York: W.W. Norton and Co., 1997.

Weinberger, Caspar. *Fighting for Peace*. New York: Warner Books, 1990.

Weinberger, Caspar, with Gretchen Roberts. *In the Arena*. Washington, DC: Regnery Publishing, 2001.

Wilson, Joseph. *The Politics of Truth*. New York: Carroll & Graf, 2004.

Wit, Joel, Daniel Poneman, and Robert Gallucci. *Going Critical: The First North Korea Nuclear Crisis*. Washington, DC: Brookings Institution Press, 2004.

Woodward, Bob. *The Agenda: Inside the Clinton White House*. New York: Rockefeller, 1994.
Woodward, Bob. *Bush at War*. New York: Simon & Schuster, 2002.
Woodward, Bob. *The Choice*. New York: Simon & Schuster, 1996.
Woodward, Bob. *The Commanders*. New York: Simon & Schuster, 1991.
Woodward, Bob. *Plan of Attack*. New York: Simon & Schuster, 2004.
Yeltsin, Boris. *Midnight Diaries*. New York: PublicAffairs, 2002.
Yergin, Daniel. *The Prize: The Epic Quest for Oil, Money, and Power*. New York: Simon & Schuster, 1991.
Zegart, Amy. *Flawed by Design: The Evolution of the CIA, JCS, and NSC*. Stanford, CA: Stanford University Press, 2000.
Zelikow, Philip, and Condoleezza Rice. *Germany Unified and Europe Transformed: A Study in Statecraft*. Cambridge, MA: Harvard University Press, 1995.

ARTICLES, JOURNALS, AND REPORTS

Ahrens, Frank. "The Reluctant Warrior." *Washington Post*, 24 February 1998.
Allen, Mike, and Alan Sipress. "Attacks Refocus White House on How to Fight Terrorism." *Washington Post*, 26 September 2001.
Ambrose, Stephen. "When the Americans Came Back to Europe." *International Herald Tribune*, 28 May 1997.
Balz, Dan. "From Promise to Performance: Can Clinton Bring Discipline to Policy?" *Washington Post*, 17 January 1993.
Becker, Elizabeth, and Tim Weiner. "Homeland Security: New Office to Become a White House Agency." *New York Times*, 28 September 2001.
Boll, Michael. "Superpower Diplomacy and German Unification: The Insiders' Views." *Parameters*, Winter 1996–97.
Borger, Julian. "Interview: Richard Clarke." *The Guardian*, 23 March 2004.
Boyd, Lyn. "A King's Exile: The Shah of Iran and Moral Considerations in U.S. Foreign Policy." *Institute for the Study of Diplomacy*, 2000.
Bridlis, Ted. "Top Security Advisers Met Just Twice on Terrorism before Sept. 11 Attacks." *Detroit News*, 29 June 2002.
Brzezinski, Zbigniew, and Anthony Lake. "For a New World, a New NATO." *New York Times*, 30 June 1997.
Bumiller, Elisabeth. "Afghan Adviser: The Country's in His Blood." *New York Times*, 28 October 2001.
Bumiller, Elisabeth. "President Steals Away to Baghdad in a Surprise Visit to American GI's." *International Herald Tribune*, 1 December 2003.
"Bush Names Afghan-Born Adviser as His Special Envoy to Afghanistan." *Associated Press*, 31 December 2001.
Carney, James, and John Dickerson. "'Big Time Punches In.'" *Time*, 12 February 2001.
Carter, Jimmy. "Being There." *Foreign Affairs* 78:6, November/December 1999.
Chace, James. "After Hiroshima: Sharing the Atom Bomb." *Foreign Affairs* 75:1, January/February 1996.
Chandler, Clay. "For Treasury's Self-Assured Summers, a Senate Test Looms." *Washington Post*, 21 July 1995.
Chong, Jia-Rui. "Carter Shares Personal Recollections, Advice on U.S. Policy with China." *Stanford Report*, 8 May 2002.

Christopher, Warren. "My Trip to Beijing Was Necessary." *Washington Post*, 22 March 1994.

Cimbala, Stephen. "War-Fighting Deterrence and Alliance Cohesiveness." *Air University Review*, September-October 1984.

"Clinton's Secret War." *The Guardian*, 20 January 2002.

Cohen, Roger. "Taming the Bullies of Bosnia." *New York Times Magazine*, 17 December 1995.

Coll, Steve. "Policy Disputes over Hunt Paralyzed Clinton's Aides." *Washington Post*, 22 February 2004.

Daalder, Ivo, and I.M. Destler. "A New NSC for a New Administration." Brookings Institution, Policy Brief No. 68, November 2000.

Defense Science Board, *Transition to and from Hostilities*, December 2004.

Devroy, Ann, and R. Jeffrey Smith. "Clinton Reexamines a Foreign Policy Under Siege." *Washington Post*, 17 October 1993.

Devroy Ann, and R. Jeffrey Smith. "President Orders Sweeping Reductions in Strategic and Tactical Nuclear Arms." *Washington Post*, 28 September 1991.

DeYoung, Karen, and Steven Mufson. "A Leaner and Less Visible NSC: Reorganization Will Emphasize Defense, Global Economics." *Washington Post*, 10 February 2001.

Diamond, Blake, and John Diamond, "Pressure at Iraqi Prison Detailed." *USA Today*, 17 June 2004.

"Dick Cheney: GOP's Most Dogged Warrior." *MSNBC*, 1 September 2004.

Dobbs, Michael. "An Obscure Chief in U.S. War on Terror." *Washington Post*, 2 April 2000.

Dowd, Maureen. "Is Condi Gaslighting Rummy?" *New York Times*, 9 October 2003.

Ellis, Jason. "Nunn-Lugar's Mid-Life Crisis." *Survival* 39:1, Spring 1997.

Erlanger, Steven. "Grading the Secretary: Albright, a Bold Voice Abroad, Finds Her Role Limited at Home." *New York Times*, 1 September 1998.

Fallows, James. "Blind into Baghdad." *Atlantic Monthly*, January/February 2004.

Foer, Franklin, and Spencer Ackerman. "The Radical." *The New Republic*, 1 December 2003.

Garrity, Patrick. "Warnings of a Parting Friend: U.S. Foreign Policy Envisioned by George Washington in His Farewell Address." *The National Interest*, Fall 1996.

Gellman, Barton. "Anti-Terror Pioneer Turns in the Badge." *Washington Post*, 13 March 2003.

Gellman, Barton. "Broad Effort Launched after '98 Attacks." *Washington Post*, 19 December 2001.

Gellman, Barton. "The Path to Crisis: How the United States and Its Allies Went to War." *Washington Post*, 18 April 1999.

Gellman, Barton. "Reappraisal Led to New China Policy." *Washington Post*, 22 June 1998.

Gellman, Barton. "Slaughter in Racak Changed Kosovo Policy." *Washington Post*, 18 April 1999.

Gellman, Barton. "A Strategy's Cautious Evolution." *Washington Post*, 20 January 2002.

Gellman, Barton. "Struggles Inside the Government Defined Campaign." *Washington Post*, 20 December 2001.

Gellman, Barton. "Ultimatums Were a U.S. Tool in Middle East Talks." *Washington Post*, 4 November 1998.

Gellman, Barton. "U.S. and China Nearly Came to Blows in '96." *Washington Post*, 21 June 1998.

Gellman, Barton, and Walter Pincus. "Depiction of Threat Outgrew Supporting Evidence." *Washington Post*, 10 August 2003.

Gerstenzang, James. "Bush Answers GOP Foes of a War on Iraq." *Los Angeles Times*, 17 August 2002.

Gibbs, Nancy, et al. "Cash-and-Carry Diplomacy." *Time*, 24 February 1997.

Gibbs, Nancy. "Double-Edged Sword." *Time*, 23 December 2002.

Gleijeses, Piero. "Ships in the Night: The CIA, the White House, and the Bay of Pigs." *Journal of Latin American Studies* 25, 1995.

Greenhouse, Steven. "Aides to Clinton Say He Will Defy Beijing and Issue Visa to Taiwan's President." *New York Times*, 22 May 1995.

Harris, John. "As Clinton Adviser, Berger Combines Stagecraft with Statecraft." *Washington Post*, 7 July 1997.

Harris, John. "Berger's Caution Has Shaped Role on U.S. in War." *Washington Post*, 16 May 1999.

Henderson, Nell. "A More Frequent Visitor." *Washington Post*, 27 May 2004.

Hersh, Seymour. "The Debate Within." *New Yorker*, 11 March 2002.

Hersh, Seymour. "The Other War." *New Yorker*, 12 April 2004.

Hersh, Seymour. "Selective Intelligence." *The New Yorker*, 12 May 2003.

Hess, Pamela. "U.S. Must Embrace 'Nation Building.'" *UPI*, 18 March 2004.

Hiatt, Fred. "Gorbachev Pledges Wide-Ranging Nuclear Cuts." *Washington Post*, 6 October 1991.

Hoagland, Jim. "Battered in Beijing." *Washington Post*, 15 March 1994.

Hosenball, Mark, Michael Isikoff, and Evan Thomas. "Cheney's Long Path to War." *Newsweek*, 17 November 2003.

Hyer, Marjorie. "Armageddon: Group of Church Leaders Asks Candidates to Repudiate Nuclear Doomsday Theory." *Washington Post*, 24 October 1984.

Jehl, Douglas. "Weapons Intelligence: Iraq Arms Critic Reacts to Report on Wife." *New York Times*, 8 August 2003.

Jehl, Douglas, with Elaine Sciolino. "Conflict in the Balkans: The President." *New York Times*, 24 April 1994.

Joffe, Josef. "Putting Germany Back Together: The Fabulous Bush and Baker Boys." *Foreign Affairs*, January/February 1996.

Johnston, David, and Thom Shanker. "Threats and Responses: Terrorist Bombing." *New York Times*, 1 October 2002.

Kennedy, Paul. "What to Do about Decline (reply to Joseph Nye)." *New York Review of Books* 36:10, 15 March 1989.

Kessler, Glenn, and Peter Slevin. "Rice Fails to Repair Rifts, Officials Say." *Washington Post*, 12 October 2003.

Kissinger, Henry. "The Vietnam Negotiations." *Foreign Affairs* 47:2, January 1969.

Kristol, William, and Gary Schmitt. "A Dangerous New Policy toward Taiwan." *Weekly Standard*, 2 December 2003.

Kunsman, David, and Douglas Lawson. "A Primer on U.S. Strategic Nuclear Policy." *Sandia Report*, January 2001.

Laipson, Ellie. "While America Slept: Understanding Terrorism and Counterterrorism." *Foreign Affairs*, January/February 2003.

Lardner, George, Jr. "McKay Reports Four 'Probable' Meese Offenses." *Washington Post*, 19 July 1988.

Leiby, Richard, and Walter Pincus. "Retired Envoy: Nuclear Report Ignored." *Washington Post*, 6 July 2003.

Lemann, Nicholas. "The Quiet Man: Dick Cheney's Discreet Rise to Unprecedented Power." *New Yorker*, 7 May 2001.

Lippman, Thomas, and Ann Devroy. "Clinton's Policy Evolution: June Decision Led to Diplomatic Gambles." *Washington Post*, 11 September 1995.

Lobe, Jim. "Does Cheney Hold the Reins?" *Inter Press Service*, 22 October 2003.

Mann, Jim. "Executives Press Clinton to Smooth U.S.-China Ties." *Los Angeles Times*, 19 November 1993.

Mann, Jim. "How Taipei Outwitted U.S. Policy When Washington Denied it Recognition." *Los Angeles Times*, 8 June 1995.

Marcus, Ruth. "Anthony Lake's Secretive Mission." *Washington Post*, 20 December 1993.

Marcus, Ruth, and John Harris, "Behind U.S. Policy Shift on Bosnia: Strains in NATO." *Washington Post*, 5 December 1994.

Mayer, Jane. "Contract Sport." *New Yorker*, 16–23 February 2004.

McCombs, Phil. "McFarlane and the Web of Rumor: The Ex-Security Adviser, His Frustrations in Office, and the Recurrent Tales of Trouble at Home." *Washington Post*, 18 April 1986.

McInnes, Neil. "The Great Doomsayer." *National Interest* 48, Summer 1997.

McManus, Doyle. "National Security Council: From the Start, Bush Plan Was to Use the Big Stick." *Los Angeles Times*, 9 October 2001.

McManus, Doyle, and Sonni Efron, "In Iraq Debate, Bremer Comes Out a Winner." *Los Angeles Times*, 23 November 2003.

Mead, Walter. "Once Were Warriors." *Wall Street Journal*, 21 January 2004.

Milbank, Dana. "Cheney Authorized Shooting Down Planes." *Washington Post*, 18 June 2004.

Milbank, Dana. "Stabilization Is Its Middle Name." *Washington Post*, 18 May 2004.

Milbank, Dana. "Who's Pulling the Foreign Policy Strings?" *Washington Post*, 14 May 2002.

Milbank, Dana, and Dana Priest. "Warning in Iraq Report Unread: Bush, Rice Did Not See State's Objections." *Washington Post*, 19 July 2003.

Milbank, Dana, and Mike Allen. "Iraq Flap Shakes Rice's Image." *Washington Post*, 27 July 2003.

Miller, Greg. "Spy Unit Skirted CIA on Iraq." *Los Angeles Times*, 10 March 2004.

Moniz, Dave. "Rumfeld's Abrasive Style Sparks Conflict with Military Command." *USA Today*, 10 December 2002.

Mufson, Steven. "Attacks Were an Act of War—But Who's the Enemy?" *Washington Post*, 11 September 2001.

Mufson, Steven. "Overhaul of National Security Apparatus Urged: Commission Cites U.S. Vulnerability." *Washington Post*, 1 February 2001.

Mufson, Steven. "U.S. Taiwan Policy Hits New Level of Ambiguity." *Washington Post*, 27 April 2001.

Myers, Steven Lee, and Eric Schmitt. "Crisis in the Balkans: The Leadership." *New York Times*, 30 May 1999.

Niksic, Alexandra. "International Observer Names Serb Troops for Racak Massacre." *Agence France-Press*, 11 April 2002.

Oberdorfer, Don, and Martin Scharm. "Haig Believes a Reagan Aide Is Campaigning against Him." *Washington Post*, 4 November 1981.

O'Neil, John. "U.S. Sending More Ships to Taiwan Area in Warning to China." *New York Times*, 11 March 1996.

Ottoway, David. "U.S. Decries Iraqi Use Of Chemical Weapons." *Washington Post*, 24 March 1988.

Page, Susan, and Barbara Slavin. "Cheney Rewrites Roles in Foreign Policy." *USA Today*, 29 July 2002.

Perlez, Jane. "Allies Bomb Iraqi Air Defenses in Biggest Attack in 6 Months." *New York Times*, 11 August 2001.

Perlez, Jane. "Bush Team's Counsel Is Divided on Foreign Policy." *New York Times*, 27 March 2001.

Perlez, Jane. "Capitol Hawks Seek Tougher Line on Iraq." *New York Times*, 5 March 2001.

Perlez, Jane. "Directive Says Rice, Bush Aide, Won't Be Upstaged by Cheney." *New York Times*, 16 February 2001.

Prados, John. "The Pros from Dover." *Bulletin of the Atomic Scientists* 60:1, January/February 2004.

Priest, Dana. "Pentagon Shadow Loses Some Mystique." *Washington Post*, 13 March 2004.

Priest, Dana, and Karen DeYoung. "CIA Questioned Documents Linking Iraq, Uranium Ore." *Washington Post*, 22 March 2003.

Rees, James. "The Importance of George Washington in a Changing World." *Scottish Rite Journal*, February 1998.

Reynolds, Maura. "White House Admits CIA Warned It Before Speech." *Los Angeles Times*, 23 July 2003.

Rice, Andrew. "Brent Scowcroft Calls Iraq War 'Overreaction'," *New York Observer*, 4 September 2004.

Rice, Condoleezza. "Campaign 2000: Promoting the National Interest." *Foreign Affairs*, January/February 2000.

Risen, James. "Question of Evidence: To Bomb Sudan Plant or Not: A Year Later, Debates Rankle." *New York Times*, 27 October 1998.

Risen, James, David E. Sanger, and Thom Shanker, "Weapons Intelligence: In Sketchy Data, Trying to Gauge Iraq Threat." *New York Times*, 20 July 2003.

Romano, Lois. "A Hero to Some: To Others Headstrong." *Washington Post*, 19 October 2003.

Rosett, Claudia. "NSC Pushing Shift of Policy on Taiwan." *New York Sun*, 3 December 2003.

Rothkopf, David. "Whatever Capitalism's Fate, Somebody's Already Working on an Alternative." *Washington Post*, 20 January 2002.

Rowen, Hobart. "Administration in Disarray on China Trade Policy." *Washington Post*, 20 March 1994.

Sanger, David. "The Speech: A Shifting Spotlight on Uranium Sales." *New York Times*, 15 July 2003.

Sanger, David. "White House to Overhaul Iraq and Afghan Missions." *New York Times*, 6 October 2003.

Sanger, David, with Judith Miller. "Intelligence: National Security Aide Says He's to Blame for Speech Error." *New York Times*, 22 July 2003.

Sciolino, Elaine, and Ethan Bronner. "Crisis in the Balkans: The Road to War; How a President, Distracted by Scandal, Entered Balkan War." *New York Times*, 18 April 1999.

Slavin, Barbara. "Rice Called a Good Fit for Foreign Policy Post." *USA Today*, 18 December 2000.

Smith, R. Jeffrey. "Bush Adviser Toured Abu Ghraib." *Washington Post*, 19 June 2004.

Smith, R. Jeffrey, and Ann Devroy. "U.S. Seeks Closer Ties with China." *Washington Post*, 21 February 1996.

Suro, Roberto, and Dana Priest. "Plan to Overhaul Anti-terrorism Strategy Would Boost NSC's Role." *Washington Post*, 24 March 1998.

"Taming the Octopus." *Economist*, 25 September 2003.

Traub, James. "The Bush Years: W's World." *New York Times Magazine*, 14 January 2001.

Triveda, Bijal. "Survey Reveals Geographic Illiteracy." *National Geographic Society*, 20 November 2002.

Tyler, Patrick. "China Warns U.S. to Stay Out of Taiwan Feud." *New York Times*, 12 March 1996.

Tyler, Patrick. "The (Ab)normalization of U.S.-Chinese Relations." *Foreign Affairs* 78:5, September/October 1999.

Weiner, Tim. "The Man Who Protects America from Terrorism." *New York Times*, 1 February 1999.

Weisberg, Jacob. "Bush's Favorite Afghan." *Slate*, 5 October 2001.

Weiser, Carl. "In Most Congressional Districts, It's No Contest." *USA Today*, 10 October 2004.

Weisskopf, Michael. "Backbone of the New China Lobby: U.S. Firms." *Washington Post*, 14 June 1993.

Whitelaw, Kevin, Thomas Omestad, and Mark Mazzetti. "After the Fall." *U.S. News and World Report*, 2 December 2002.

"Who's Who." *Washington Monthly*, 1 November 2003.

Williams, Daniel. "Chinese Rebuff Christopher on Human Rights." *Washington Post*, 13 March 1994.

Williams, Daniel. "Christopher Cites Progress on Human Rights in China." *Washington Post*, 24 May 1994.

Wilson, Dominic, and Roopa Purushothaman. "Dreaming with BRICs: The Path to 2050." *Goldman Sachs*. Global Economics Paper No. 99, 1 October 2003.

Woodward, Bob. "With CIA Push, Movement to War Accelerated." *Washington Post*, 19 April 2004.

Woodward, Bob, and Dan Balz. "At Camp David, Advise and Dissent." *Washington Post*, 31 January 2002.

Woolf, Amy. "Nunn-Lugar Cooperative Threat Reduction Programs: Issues for Congress." *Congressional Research Service*, 23 March 2001.

Wright, Lawrence. "The Counter-Terrorist." *New Yorker*, 14 January 2002.

Wright, Robin, and Doyle McManus. "Military Options: Bush Camp Split on Anti-terror Policy." *Los Angeles Times*, 21 September 2001.

ORAL HISTORIES

"The Clinton Years: Interviews." *Frontline*, 16 January 2001.

"A Forum on the Role of the National Security Advisor." Woodrow Wilson International Center for Scholars and the James A. Baker III Institute For Public Policy of Rice University, 12 April 2001.

"Give War a Chance." *Frontline*, 11 May 1999.

"The Gulf War: An Oral History." *Frontline*, 9 January 1996.

"Interview with Jimmy Carter." Miller Center of Public Affairs, University of Virginia, 29 November 1982.

"Interview with Zbigniew Brzezinski with Madeleine Albright, Leslie G. Denend, and William Odom." Miller Center of Public Affairs, University of Virginia, 18 February 1982.

"The Man Who Knew." *Frontline*, 3 October 2002.

"Oral History Interview with Clark M. Clifford." Truman Presidential Museum and Library, 13 April 1971.

"Oral History Roundtable: Arms Control Policy and the National Security Advisor." The Brookings Institution and the Center for International and Security Studies at Maryland, 23 March 2000.

"Oral History Roundtable: The Bush Administration National Security Council." The Brookings Institution and the Center for International and Security Studies at Maryland, 29 April 1999.

"Oral History Roundtables: China Policy and the National Security Council." The Brookings Institution and the Center for International and Security Studies at Maryland, 4 November 1999.

"Oral History Roundtables: The Clinton Administration National Security Council." The Brookings Institution and the Center for International and Security Studies at Maryland, 27 September 2000.

"Oral History Roundtables: The Nixon Administration National Security Council." The Brookings Institution and the Center for International and Security Studies at Maryland, 8 December 1998.

"War in Europe." *Frontline*, 22 February 2000.

"Zbigniew Brzezinski, Exit Interview." Jimmy Carter Library, 20 February 1981.

Index

PUBLICAFFAIRS is a publishing house founded in 1997. It is a tribute to the standards, values, and flair of three persons who have served as mentors to countless reporters, writers, editors, and book people of all kinds, including me.

I. F. STONE, proprietor of *I. F. Stone's Weekly,* combined a commitment to the First Amendment with entrepreneurial zeal and reporting skill and became one of the great independent journalists in American history. At the age of eighty, Izzy published *The Trial of Socrates,* which was a national bestseller. He wrote the book after he taught himself ancient Greek.

BENJAMIN C. BRADLEE was for nearly thirty years the charismatic editorial leader of *The Washington Post*. It was Ben who gave the *Post* the range and courage to pursue such historic issues as Watergate. He supported his reporters with a tenacity that made them fearless, and it is no accident that so many became authors of influential, best-selling books.

ROBERT L. BERNSTEIN, the chief executive of Random House for more than a quarter century, guided one of the nation's premier publishing houses. Bob was personally responsible for many books of political dissent and argument that challenged tyranny around the globe. He is also the founder and was the longtime chair of Human Rights Watch, one of the most respected human rights organizations in the world.

.   .   .

For fifty years, the banner of Public Affairs Press was carried by its owner Morris B. Schnapper, who published Gandhi, Nasser, Toynbee, Truman, and about 1,500 other authors. In 1983 Schnapper was described by *The Washington Post* as "a redoubtable gadfly." His legacy will endure in the books to come.

Peter Osnos, *Publisher*